W9-BBB-841

CONFLICT AND
COOPERATION
AMONG NATIONS

DATE DUE

DATE DUE			
OCT 18 '65			
MAR 1 3 '67			
OCT 15 '68			
FEB 17 '69			
MAR 4 '69			
APR 2 '70			
APR 16 '70			
APR 20 '70			
MAY 5 '71			
AP 21 '78			
GAYLORD			PRINTED IN U.S.A.

JX
1395
D78

21639

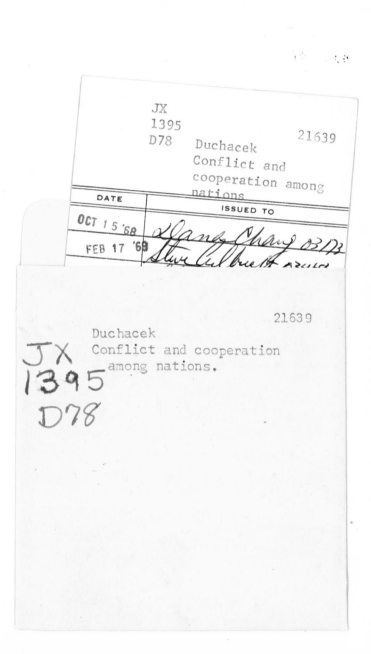

JX
1395
D78   Duchacek   21639
       Conflict and
       cooperation among
       nations

DATE	ISSUED TO
OCT 15 '68	Yang Chang 0373
FEB 17 '69	Steve Culbreth 0749

21639

Duchacek
Conflict and cooperation
among nations.

JX
1395
D78

UNITED STATES COLLECTIVE DEFENSE ARRANGEMENTS

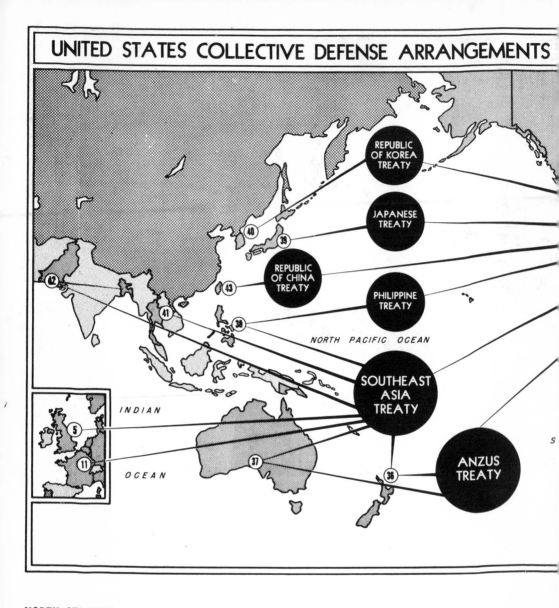

NORTH ATLANTIC TREATY (15 NATIONS)

Provisions of collective self-defense apply to territories of any of the Parties in Europe and North America; Algerian departments of France; armed forces of any party, stationed in Europe; and islands, vessels, and aircraft in the Atlantic north of the Tropic of Cancer. Signed April 4, 1949.

1 UNITED STATES	9 LUXEMBOURG
2 CANADA	10 PORTUGAL
3 ICELAND	11 FRANCE
4 NORWAY	12 ITALY
5 UNITED KINGDOM	13 GREECE
6 NETHERLANDS	14 TURKEY
7 DENMARK	15 FEDERAL REPUBLIC
8 BELGIUM	OF GERMANY

O.A.S. OR RIO TREATY (21 NATIONS)

The treaty area comprises the whole Western Hemisphere, including portions of North and South Polar Regions, Canada (which is not a member), Greenland, Alaska, Aleutian Islands, and Galápagos Islands. It does not include Hawaii. Signed September 2, 1947.

1 UNITED STATES	22 EL SALVADOR	29 PERU
16 MEXICO	23 NICARAGUA	30 BRAZIL
17 CUBA	24 COSTA RICA	31 BOLIVIA
18 HAITI	25 PANAMA	32 PARAGUAY
19 DOMINICAN	26 COLOMBIA	33 CHILE
REPUBLIC	27 VENEZUELA	34 ARGENTINA
20 HONDURAS	28 ECUADOR	35 URUGUAY
21 GUATEMALA		

ANZUS TREATY (3 NATIONS)

The treaty region comprises the metropolitan territory of any of the Parties, the island territories under their jurisdiction in the Pacific, and their armed forces, public vessels, or aircraft in the Pacific. Signed September 1, 1951.

1 UNITED STATES
36 NEW ZEALAND
37 AUSTRALIA

SOUTH KOREA TREATY (BILATERAL)

The treaty applies to the territories of both Parties in the Pacific. Signed October 1, 1953.

1 UNITED STATES
40 REPUBLIC OF KOREA

THE SOVIET POWER BLOC

Africa

& FRANCE
S.E. ASIA
TIVE DEFENSE
REATY

NORTH ATLANTIC TREATY

RIO PACT

Map Lab No. 203 W.T.

ORGANIZATION OF AMERICAN STATES (PACT OF RIO), 1947

Twenty-one American republics (Canada is not a member) agree to regard an armed attack or threat directed against the Western Hemisphere or any American State as an attack or threat directed against all. Concrete measures are to be adopted following a two-thirds vote by an assembly of foreign ministers, called "Organ of Consultation." Military sanctions may be recommended by the same majority but are never obligatory. The Treaty provides for concrete measures in case of attack or threat coming either from without or from within the area.

NORTH ATLANTIC TREATY, 1949

Fifteen nations pledge to take such action individually or collectively as they deem necessary in case of external armed attack on any of them, regarded as an armed attack on all. Member nations are to consult in NATO Council in case of other than armed attack or threat against their territorial integrity or political independence. Armed forces are assigned to NATO command prior to the outbreak of hostilities. Unlike Rio Treaty, NATO contains no provisions concerning conflicts between member nations; it is directed solely against attack or threat coming from without.

U.S.—PHILIPPINES TREATY, 1951

The two nations agree to act "to meet the common danger in accordance with their constitutional processes." (This formula appears also in ANZUS, Korea, SEATO, Taiwan, and Japanese treaties.) Armed attacks on the territory of either nation or other forms of threat to the territorial integrity, political independence, or security of either nation are specified as dangers calling for action or consultation.

TRI-PARTITE TREATY—U.S., AUSTRALIA, NEW ZEALAND (ANZUS), 1951

The treaty assures Australia and New Zealand that the United States, "in accordance with its constitutional processes," would assist these two nations in case of a renewal of Japanese imperialism. This, rather than defense against the Communist danger, was the main motive for the conclusion of the Treaty.

U.S.—KOREA TREATY, 1953

At Korea's request the United States accepts the right to station armed forces in and about Korea. Mutual-help provisions include the Philippine treaty formula.

SOUTHEAST ASIA PACT (SEATO), 1954

Eight nations agree to resist armed attack and to prevent subversive activities directed from without against their territorial integrity and political stability. They proclaim a Pacific Charter. The United States has added an interpretative statement according to which the treaty obligations apply only to Communist aggression.

CHINESE SECURITY TREATY, 1954

The Chinese Government on Taiwan (Formosa) grants and the United States accepts the right to station armed forces in Taiwan. The mutual-obligations formula of the Philippine treaty has been adopted. Agreement to prevent "Communist subversive activities directed from without" against the Chinese and American territories in the Western Pacific has been made part of the treaty.

CENTRAL TREATY ORGANIZATION (CENTO), 1955

United Kingdom, Turkey, Iran, and Pakistan pledge to consult on measures of self-defense in case of danger against peace and security in the Middle East. The United States, although not formally a signatory member, is a member of its joint planning and its economic, antisubversion, and military committees. There are no others. Formerly called the Baghdad Pact Organization, it became CENTO in October 1959 after Iraq (whose capital is Baghdad) withdrew in March 1959, from the Pact. This followed Premier Kassim's 1958 revolt against King Faisal.

U.S.—JAPANESE SECURITY TREATY, 1960

The pact declares that the signatories have a "common concern in the maintenance of international peace and security in the Far East." Each party declares its readiness "to act to meet the common danger in accordance with its constitutional provisions and processes." The United States land, air, and naval forces are granted the use of facilities and areas in Japan for the purpose of contributing to the security of Japan. The Treaty of 1960 brought Japan into alliance with the United States as an equal. It replaced the first U.S.-Japanese Security Treaty signed September 8, 1951, which had placed Japan in the inferior position of a protected country (e.g. U.S. forces in Japan could also be used for the purpose of "putting down large-scale riots").

341
D

CONFLICT AND COOPERATION AMONG NATIONS

by IVO D. DUCHACEK, *City College, New York*

with the collaboration of

Kenneth W. Thompson

HOLT, RINEHART AND WINSTON, INC.
NEW YORK

WINGATE COLLEGE LIBRARY
WINGATE, N. C.

Copyright © 1960 by Holt, Rinehart and Winston, Inc.
Library of Congress Catalog Card No. 60–7974

August, 1961

21940–0110

The copyrighted selections in this volume are reprinted by special permission of their respective copyright holders and may not be reprinted without similar permission from them.

Printed in the United States of America

To

Harold Kline of Lost Lake

21639

Preface

This book integrates two types of materials which are usually found in two separate volumes: *textbook* with *selected readings* on international relations. The essential value of such combination lies in the constant interplay of the textbook with the reading selections which amplify or challenge some of the preceding concepts or themes. Thus the study of factors which condition cooperation, domination, or conflict among nations becomes more meaningful than if comparable contents were treated separately.

Each of the six major parts into which the volume has been divided opens with twenty to fifty pages of text. It is concluded by a brief summary which sets the stage for subsequent topical groups each containing one to seven selections by different authors. An explanatory comment introduces not only each of the twenty-eight topics, but also each of seventy-five selected readings.

Excellence, originality, and variety of viewpoints have determined the selection of the readings. Analyses and studies written by prominent scholars are contrasted with statements made by policymakers over widely different ages—from David Hume to Dag Hammarskjöld, from Thucydides to Churchill, from Clausewitz to Khrushchev, and from Ernest Renan to Ho Chi Minh. Theories are tested against practice, political foresight against erroneous judgments, and rationally conceived plans against improvisation or emotional reactions. Identical problems are viewed from different, often opposing, angles.

My experience in teaching undergraduate and graduate courses at Yale and the City College of New York, as well as my previous active participation in the making of foreign policy, have led me to the conclusion that such constant confrontation of hypotheses with actual policy decisions may help the student better to comprehend the complex subject of international politics and make his own value judgments.

In view of the global dimension of the conflict between free nations and the Sino-Soviet bloc, the book departs from the usual preoccupation with Europe and includes samples of significant voices of modern Asia. While the different forms of international contacts, the mechanism of the United Nations, and treaty-making procedures are described and analyzed, the focus constantly remains on reasons and forces which cause and condition the use or misuse of different institutional frameworks. The book heeds John Stuart Mill's admonishment of a century ago: "In politics as in mechanics the power which is to keep the engine going must be sought for *outside* the machinery; and if it is not forthcoming, or is insufficient to surmount the obstacles which may reasonably be expected, the contrivance will fail." [1]

The textbook-plus-readings formula represents a response to the need for a new and stimulating approach to the study and teaching of international relations. Additional assignments may be easily added to the comprehensive framework, following the instructor's particular field of interest or new developments on the world scene. The new formula should be especially suited for large classes which sometimes pose problems as to library assignments.

In writing a book of a modest length dealing with such a vast subject as international politics, many aspects of international relations had to be passed by or mentioned only briefly. Easily accessible documents, maps, charts, and bibliographies were omitted.

No author can properly thank everyone for the assistance extended to him while preparing a book of such scope. I can mention only those whose assistance, inspiration, and constructive criticism have been outstanding.

In preparing this book I have had the advantage of having constant counsel, cooperation, and encouragement of Dr. Kenneth W. Thompson. He not only saw and commented on the very first outline and then many others which were to follow; he also went over the first draft of the book and finally over the entire manuscript when it was completed. His suggestions of both a substantive and editorial nature based on his great erudition and broad experience were extremely valuable. In addition, he has contributed the Introduction and Conclusion to the book, an analysis of major problems of nuclear weapons, and three other selections which had originally appeared in scholarly magazines. He has in a real sense collaborated on this book.

I am also greatly indebted to Professor Arnold Wolfers, Director of the Washington Center of Foreign Policy Research (affiliated with Johns Hopkins University). His detailed suggestions concerning the structure and the concept of the book and the selection of articles represent but a portion of his influence on its final form. Since 1949 most of my teaching and research projects in the field of international relations have greatly profited from his learned guidance and friendly advice. In addition to his own three contributions to the book, Professor Wolfers was able to provide me with additional studies while they were being prepared for publication by other members of the Washington Center: Hans J. Morgenthau, Paul H. Nitze, and Charles Burton Marshall.

Comments and constructive criticism offered by Professor Vernon Van Dyke, Chairman of the Department of Political Science at State University of Iowa, have also proved valuable; in addition, he made available to me the results of three faculty seminars "For the Improvement of Teaching in International Relations," held successively at Iowa City and Emory University in 1955, 1956, and 1957. Papers presented by Edward S. Claflin of Bowling Green State University, Arno J. Meyer of Brandeis University, and J. David Singer of Vassar College have proved particularly useful.

[1] John Stuart Mill, *Considerations on Representative Government* (New York, Harper and Brothers, 1862), p. 21.

Portions of the book which deal with Communism and Soviet policies in East Central Europe are based on material collected and analyzed with the assistance of a grant-in-aid for research from the American Philosophical Society in Philadelphia.

Advice and suggestions given by my colleagues at the City College, in particular by Hillman M. Bishop and Samuel Hendel, are gratefully acknowledged.

Finally—although I should have perhaps started with this expression of gratitude—my thanks are addressed to my wife Helena. Her initiative, constructive editorial criticism, extreme patience in typing and indexing, and above all her encouraging determination made it possible for us to complete the book in a relatively short time. It could not have been done without her.

For whatever merit this book possesses, all the above are entitled to much of the credit. Errors of omission and commission and other weaknesses must of course remain my own responsibility.

I. D. D.

January, 1960

Contents

CONFLICT AND
COOPERATION
AMONG NATIONS

International Relations in
Historical Perspective

Modern man is often profoundly skeptical that history has anything to teach us about the present crisis. We are told that statesmen of the past lived in an era that knew nothing of hydrogen bombs, intercontinental ballistic missiles and outer space. In an era so radically different if not unique is there any point to seek lessons from the past? In a day and age of novel world institutions what place is there for the balance of power, conventional sources of strength or tactical and strategic calculations? In a world which must learn to live by reason or accept mutual annihilation what have the last four centuries with all their passion and ambition that so frequently overwhelmed sanity and reason to teach us? Moreover, what purpose is served by consulting the past brimming over with costly errors, tragic failures and for most civilizations ultimate destruction?

Some Introductory Remarks on History as a Means of
Viewing the Present and Future

In the face of an uncertainty of lessons of the past and the baffling character of the present, any honest mind approaching the problems of world politics is tormented by a sense of inadequacies and limitations. It is true that we know more about the world in which we live than we did a century or two ago. Statistics are better, and knowledge of the past is more complete. We have better birth rates, death rates and emigration rates. Through the public press and democratic institutions men have a greater stake in their government; the elemental factors responsible for the growth and prosperity of nations are better understood and controlled. Yet although knowledge is greater, the factors that must be assessed have increased in number and complexity to a bewildering degree. In place of the isolated rivalries of the past, we are facing struggles that involve directly or indirectly the whole habitable globe. Our problems have become so vast, their solution so painful and doubtful and the weight of contingencies so overwhelming that even for the

1

wisest statesman foreign policy is at least three-fourths guesswork. Moreover, for all our statistics, historical and economic knowledge and responsible governments, we have had little success in foreseeing future events, let alone coping with present ones.

Failures in political prophecy are, of course, nothing new. History records countless examples of decisive political developments which caught even the most experienced observers by complete surprise. In the eighteenth century neither Benjamin Franklin nor Frederick the Great appear to have anticipated the approaching French revolution, yet both were constant observers of the course of French affairs. Nor did someone as active in revolutionary politics as Madame Roland make a single allusion before 1789 to the impending downfall of the French monarchy in her voluminous correspondence. Napoleon was confident that "Europe will be either Cossack or Republican," and Pitt prophesied that the end of the Papacy was in sight.

Political prophecies concerning foreign states are especially fraught with difficulties and have most often fallen short of the mark. The knowledge that people possess of the social and political conditions of another country is almost always so imperfect, superficial, and parochial that popular generalizations tend to go widely astray. In 1760 Rousseau predicted that in twenty years England would be ruined and have lost her liberty. And the statesmen of Europe joined Rousseau in proclaiming England a decadent and second-class power, a sort of insular Poland, selfish, faction-torn, without nerve and consistency, and destined probably to fall under Russia's domination. This illusion was shared by Joseph II of Austria, Frederick II of Prussia and Catherine II of Russia. Their erroneous estimates provided the basis for momentous policies which affected the future of the world. In much the same way the Kaiser and Hitler underestimated both Britain and America and chose courses that changed the history of the West and of the rest of the world as well.

If these experiences carry any lesson for the present, it is that future events may be decisively shaped by the estimates we make of Britain or Russia or India or China. We and the Russians must expect as often as not to be wrong about each other's intentions as they were with our intervention in Korea and we with the communist Chinese action in North Korea.

Fortunately we also find in history examples of leaders who pierced the veil of the future, who foresaw the course of history more clearly than their contemporaries. We find philosophers and statesmen who were attuned to the larger forces and impending issues that now are seen as the major determinants of the future. Burke saw with a clarity greater than his contemporaries the potential strength of the American Colonies, the rise of the peoples of India and the irrepressible dynamism of the French Revolution. His world view was faulty in many respects but, because he saw the truth of a few essential principles, his writings cast a golden shaft of light into the dark corners of the future.

Polybius predicted the rise of the Roman Empire and its unifying role throughout the Mediterranean world and foresaw the signs and causes of its eventual decline. De Tocqueville anticipated the race problem in America, the coming of the "War Among the States," and he forecast the appearance of those recurrent and perennial problems of democracy such as the tyranny of public opinion, the decrying of personal excellence and superior virtue and the intolerances of patriotism. At the same time he had the wisdom to confess the shortcomings of "all the ingenious and erroneous systems with the aid of which men had tried to explain a present which was not yet clearly seen and to predict a future which was not seen at all." And to give the devil his due, Karl Marx predicted that the seizure of Alsace-Lorraine by Prussia in 1871— which Bismarck also viewed with misgivings—would throw France into the arms of Russia and force Germany to confront the combined strength of the Slavs and the Latins.

More recently, in March, 1936, Mr. Winston Churchill warned Britain and a world not yet prepared to heed his words: "For four hundred years the foreign policy of England has been to oppose the strongest, most aggressive, most dominating Power on the continent and particularly to prevent the low countries falling into the hands of such a power." And he asked: " . . . which is today the power which is strongest, and which seeks in a dangerous and oppressive sense to dominate. Today, for this year, probably for part of 1937, the French Army is the strongest in Europe." But no one feared France. He concluded: "Therefore, it seems to me that all the old conditions present themselves again, and that our national salvation depends upon our gathering once again all the forces of Europe to contain, to restrain, and if necessary to frustrate, German domination." However, in the same debate before the House of Commons Neville Chamberlain saw little in the "necessarily excessive" figures on German rearmament, and for the moment his appraisal won acceptance.

As we reflect on these prophecies, the question arises, why were some philosophers and statesmen, like Burke, Churchill and de Tocqueville, more prescient and far-sighted than others? What accounts for their greater wisdom? What part is the outgrowth of reason, and how much is the result of the instinctive and acquired knowledge that civilization accords its keenest observers? Perhaps the most compelling of possible answers is one offered by Mr. Churchill, who has many times pointed to the importance of an organizing theory: "Those who are possessed of a definite body of doctrine and of deeply rooted convictions upon it will be in a much better position to deal with the shifts and surprises of daily affairs." Accordingly, political prediction, insofar as it rests at all upon an intellectual process, is little more than historical generalization which varies according to the knowledge and acumen of the prophet. In one sense the "right" political prediction is no more than the outcome of a powerful and creative mind playing on a situation. Despite modern ingenuity in contriving devices to replace superior human judgment, no substitute has been found for practical wisdom nor a Univac to replace unique moral and intellectual endowments. It may not be stretching a point to say that Rembrandt and Picasso are to the minor painters what Thucydides and Churchill are to the minor philosophers and statesmen.

On the other hand, it is fair to ask whether these heroic figures are unique in every respect or whether they embrace certain common approaches, concerns and qualities. This much can be asserted. In political theory in general, at least in western civilization, and in the theory of international politics in particular, it seems clear that the lasting contributions have come from men who resisted the fateful divorce of theory from practice. From Machiavelli to Clausewitz, from Admiral Mahan to Hugh Gibson and George F. Kennan, we note a fruitful relationship between man's struggles with the intractable facts of political behavior and their evaluation of these facts. It would appear that political prognosis thrives on political practice, however this practice may be experienced and however the hazards and perils of a too-passionate involvement of commitment are met. Perhaps a parallel can be drawn with the medical sciences where research and practice are intimately related, and where the experimenter is never far removed from the patient's bedside. Medical scientists take for granted the link between human problems and research. The case then for political science—conceived as a pure science of human behavior or as the worship of apparently irrelevant abstractions unrelated to life's problems and of towering objectivity in social affairs—is probably based on a false conception of the nature of science itself.

There are a few qualities that those whose predictions were true held in common. First of all, great students of international politics have brought to their task a lively sense of history. We do well to remind ourselves of this, however obvious it may seem, for modern man, in his impatience to confront and solve present-day problems, is by instinct suspicious if not contemptuous of this approach. How often one hears that history never repeats itself, or that no one ever learns anything from history! How frequently do the words "let the dead past bury itself" or "change is the first law of the universe" resound in both scholarly and public discourse! This conviction may stem partly from an incurable faith in progress and in the upward march of mankind. Most of us shared the vague expectation that the First World War and more recently the Second were to usher in a new era, replace old ideals with new ones, establish the human family on a more amicable basis and eliminate once and for all the poisonous emotions infecting past international relations. Few if any observers saw these tragic events as a fatal retrogression from which we could recover only by long and painful struggles. More basically, however, the rejection of history involves the substitution of spurious and simple-minded interpretations for the onerous demands of a patient search for meaning among the complexities of the past.

It is said that Sir Nevile Henderson, Britain's Ambassador in Berlin from 1937 to 1939, felt that his reading of *Mein Kampf* on board ship when he was returning home from Latin America fully prepared him for observing developments in Germany. He apparently believed that the underlying appeal of German militarism, the legacy of Bismarck and Frederick the Great and Germany's historic objectives were of little immediate importance, an illusion that is traced in his *Failure of a Mission*. It is instructive to contrast his views with the cogent analysis, informed by history, of Sir Eyre Crowe of the Foreign Office, which offered a rational basis for policies that might have prevented a second war. More recently an American Secretary of State declared that the only prerequisite for understanding Soviet foreign policy is a reading of the Communist Manifesto—as if this could explain Soviet tactics toward Yugoslavia, Sino-Russian rivalries or Soviet ties with anti-revolutionary dictatorships in the Middle East.

Great social groupings, classes and nations tend to react in similar ways to similar situations. History in terms of these recurrent patterns provides the ground on which more intricate and individual patterns of social conduct can be worked out. Mr. Churchill's firm grasp of world politics was rooted in history. His conception of the Grand Alliance was based on the lessons of the coalition that resisted Louis XIV. His historical masterpiece, *Marlborough: His Life and Times,* was written during the decade of the "Gathering Storm," about which he warned not *ex post facto* but as the first signs of dark clouds were appearing on the horizon. As Marlborough was the linchpin of the first Grand Alliance that thwarted the French attempt to dominate Europe, so Churchill played a parallel role in marshalling resistance to Germany's expansion.

One lesson of history is expressed in the saying that you may drive out history with a pitchfork but it always comes back. In England, Cromwell and the Army sought to make a drastic break with the past by scrapping the time-honored monarchial form of government. With the death of Cromwell traditional forms came sweeping back and the monarchy was restored. Sorel, in his great work *L'Europe et la Révolution Française,* traces the continuity of French policy during the Revolutionary and Napoleonic periods with that of the Ancien Regime. Today in the Soviet Union the absence of political freedom, the ever-present secret police and the unquestioning acceptance of an authoritarian regime are reminders of Tsarist Russia. The sharp break between past and future foreseen by some liberal historians can hardly be supported by the record. Listen to these words: "It is probable . . . that the resumed march of Russia towards her age-long objectives, toward an Atlantic port, in the Baltic and the Balkans, towards a Mediterranean outlet, in the Middle and Far East, will occupy important pages in what is to come of twentieth century history." They were written by a British historian in 1944. Precisely a decade before the Polish and Hungarian revolutions of 1956, George F. Kennan predicted uprisings in the Soviet empire in about 10 years. The grounds for his prediction were a knowledge of Russian history and of the anatomy of totalitarian regimes.

The second quality worth mentioning is the assumption by most great historians and statesmen that an understanding of political phenomena, whether international or domestic, is inseparable from a clear picture of human nature. This view, it must be said, runs counter to much of present-day thought. Social scientists are disposed to argue that man is a bundle of contradictory impulses and his behavior must be tested and analyzed experimentally before we can say anything at all. Political institutions and procedures preoccupy the scholar as more manageable units of study. Yet the question with which Reinhold Niebuhr began the Gifford Lectures in the spring of 1939 returns to haunt us: "Man has always been his most vexing problem. How shall he think of himself?" This is the starting point for all serious philosophers, whatever the answer they give. Alexander Hamilton, in seeking the cause of conflict among states, concluded: "To presume a want of motives for such contests would be to forget that men are ambitious, vindictive and rapacious." Other philosophers, who assume that men are by nature cooperative and virtuous, view the international system as cast from another mold. Even writers who claim to be entirely free from presuppositions about man carry a heavier baggage of assumptions than they know; and the gravest problems arise from theories of the world founded upon a conception of man that is concealed, and for this reason, never examined.

A third condition of the theories of the prophetic political philosophers derives from their attitude toward human progress. One view is the Enlightenment conception, that man's history is essentially an upward spiral, with each generation becoming wiser, better and more prosperous than the last. Another view is espoused by millennial Christians and liberals or Marxist secularists alike; it is an article of faith for them all that man is corrupted and depraved but that he awaits one decisive event which will bring "a new heaven and a new earth." In the past men have been selfish, grasping and evil; with one blinding act they will be transfigured from mortal men to members of a classless society—progress indeed!

But more prevalent by far is the theory of progress that sees man transforming himself through newer, more rational institutions. In *Essays on the Social Gospel,* Adolph Harnack declares: "Retrogression is no longer possible for us; and shame upon those who desire it." This is less obviously pernicious than other determinist creeds. Yet it is equally mischievous because it suggests that progress is waiting at the other end of a charter, a constitution or a court judgment. The United Nations was presented by some of its American champions as an organization that would do away with alliances, balance of power and bitter rivalries among states—in other words, this novel institution would overnight create a new form of international behavior. The world would be done with blocs, security guarantees and regional arrangements except as they might spring from the new international organization. How prophetic were these disciples of progress? Newspaper dispatches and headlines give the answer: NATO, SEATO, the Eisenhower Doctrine, the Baghdad Pact, the Warsaw Pact, and the bilateral security arrangements between the United States and more than forty countries.

One must hasten to add that a rejection of these extravagant views of progress does not imply a denial of progress as such. It is progress as perfectibility that is questioned. History is the record of significant human advances, but of advances marred by retreat and retrogression. Moreover, more often than not progress is the half-step, the partial advance which is accepted when the ultimate goal is beyond reach. This truth is one that wise men perceive, and in perceiving it make their contribution to progress.

Finally, the enduring philosophies of international politics possess a viable, workable concept of politics. It is politics that presents the statesman with his severest test on the international scene; it is politics that demands meaningful analysis and generalization. Yet it is politics, on the international no less than on the national scene, that suffers the calumnies, contempt and abuse. Many of our leaders want not so much to understand politics as to eliminate it. An American President proclaims that politics is one thing he doesn't care much about, and others contrast the high principles of the statesman with the low tactics of the politician. Professor Carl Becker pointed out that "the term politics has taken on a certain unsavory meaning, as when we say 'playing politics' or 'it's only politics.' In international relations playing politics, otherwise known as 'the diplomatic game,' has recently become a little more unsavory or even sinister, by being described as 'power politics.'"

If politics is anything, however, it is compromise, the adjustment of divergent interests and the reconciliation of rival moral claims. Politics calls for the highest moral stamina if men are to stand on uncertain terrain where to act may be to act unjustly, where there are few if any absolutes and where success, unhappily, is the most common criterion. Henry Ward Beecher observed that not that which men do worthily but that which they do successfully is what history makes haste to record. Success in politics, just as success in business, is contingent on an understanding of its principles or "laws." This understanding has been achieved by men whose predictions ring true; lack of understanding is the cause of the failure of those whose words are foolishness today. Two principles particularly deserve our attention: the concept of power and nationalism.

Power in Politics

The continuing influence of power in world politics appears inescapable. The pattern of relations among states is fundamentally one of inequality. The differences in influence and power of individuals *within* any society are modest indeed compared to the differences, say, between the United States and Ecuador. Equality of opportunity under law is a basic moral principle in the West. Since, however, no effective system of world law exists and since war as the final arbiter lurks always in the background, the great powers play overwhelmingly the most important role. They do this even when like the U.S. they accept world leadership hesitatingly and with nostalgia for a less responsible past. In the absence of world law and world government, the policies of those nations who by persuasion and force can influence and rally to their side other powers determines the course of international history. On the national scene, this state of affairs prevails when a civil war is raging or when locally the forces of law and order decay. In a sense, the condition that Hobbes described as *bellum omnium contra omnes* (the war of each against all) is the more or less permanent condition of contemporary international society. The problem that students of international relations stubbornly disregarded throughout most of the inter-war period is the enormous gap in practice between the legal rights and status of sovereign states and their actual role and influence.

The nature of international politics is related, furthermore, to the stabilizing element through which order is achieved. Some system of political dynamics operates in every society to preserve its identity. In domestic societies this purpose is generally served by regulated political competition among parties and pressure groups. Among nations where a number of mutually independent states strive for influence and power, one ordering force is in the balance of power. The agony and pathos of contemporary world politics is commonly attributed to the balance of power. Some have discovered in it the true cause of war. Many asserted after World War II that the great game of the balance of power had been forever exposed and discredited. Yet today serious students of international politics set forth another less absolute view. They maintain that it was the early abandonment rather than the blind pursuit of a balancing policy which hastened and made inevitable both World Wars. Before World War I, the fruits of three Bismarckian Wars led to so great an accumulation of power in German hands that war alone could re-establish the balance. Even England, whose foreign policy has become a by-word for prudence and political wisdom, remained passive and indifferent to threats to the equilibrium of the "Europe System." Only in 1900 did it stir and, responding to the challenge of a new German navy, emerged from its coma of "splendid isolation." There followed overtures to Japan and to France. The Entente which resulted was no longer an effort to reestablish an equilibrium of power but rather an attempt belatedly to bolster the military strength of the allies for the impending conflict. When Lord Grey sought to reassert the principles of the Concert and the balance of power this was merely a frantic and hopeless gesture. So powerful was Germany by this time that no counterpoise could be found to equalize the scales of the balance now overweighted by the elements of German national power. What caused the failure in this instance was not the balance of power but the policy of indifference and isolationism which had taken its place.

What is the idea of the balance of power? What are its underlying assumptions? Its traditional definition is in terms of the maintenance of such an approximate equilibrium between nations or groups as to prevent any member or combination of members from attaining the power that would enable them to impose their will upon the rest. The "great unconscious tradition" of British foreign policy has been to forestall the domination of all Europe by any single power. The principle is broader and more far-reaching than international politics. Some social scientists maintain there is a general social principle underlying the relations of independent units, which provides that stability can be achieved through a tendency of the separate units to establish and reestablish some kind of equilibrium. This equilibrium is uncertain, precarious, and temporary, for life can never be kept in balance or equilibrium but is subject to unceasing change and variation. A rough stability is achieved from time to time, however, through forces which combine to reestablish the lost equilibrium.

This social "law" has sometimes been formulated in the broadest if not universal terms as in the following general statement by Julian Huxley:

> If one species happens to vary in the direction of greater independence, the inter-related equilibrium is upset and cannot be restored until a number of competing species have either given way to the increased pressure and become extinct, or else have answered pressure with pressure and kept

the first species in its place, by themselves too discovering means of adding to their independence.[1]

In our national government, a similar process is in evidence. Ours is a government of limited powers and systems of checks and balances. Underlying our system are political beliefs which perhaps are best contained in the aphorism: If men were gods, government would not be necessary; if men were devils, government would be impossible. Since they are somewhere between these extremes, governments of limited powers are the best means of attaining relative justice. The legislature has acted traditionally as a brake on the executive; the judiciary, in turn, restrains the legislature. Interest groups have throughout history worked through one or the other branch to press their ambitions. During the Civil War period, the Northern interests found an ally in the Supreme Court. In a more recent period, the executive-legislature became the voice of labor and the judiciary spoke in behalf of the business community.

Finally, the balance of power has been most conspicuous and overt from the first century of the modern era in international relations. From 1075-1475 A.D. among the little North Italian city-states, a system of pressures and balances operated to preserve the independence of individual states and prevent their domination by any would-be conqueror. In the sixteenth and seventeenth centuries there were regional systems of the balance of power, as in Northern Europe against Sweden; in the eighteenth and nineteenth centuries the system became Continental in extent. Then the objective of England as "balancer" was to maintain the equilibrium of Europe. At last in our own day there are only two major weights in the balance, the United States and the Soviet Union. But the fundamental process of the balance of power, whatever its changing forms, has been an enduring feature of the pattern of world politics. Its recurrence should suggest that its roots are more than superficially embedded in the preferences of a handful of diplomats or leaders.

It is appropriate to note that the balance of power bears marked resemblances to the contemporary system called collective security. Both systems seek to apply sanctions, one through the action of a "balancer" or a combination of power, the other theoretically by the whole family of nations. These differences in techniques are less significant in practice. Balancing is achieved by a combination or collectivity of nations; the much vaunted collective security system of the League and the United Nations has in practice become a process of collective self-help by fewer than all nations. Decisions as to troops and assistance remain with sovereign states despite constitutional provisions in the Charter.

If the techniques of the two systems are not qualitatively different, however, the same can hardly be said with regard to timing. The rule by which action is taken is different in each case. The commandment to be upheld for the balance of power is: "Thou shalt not grow too formidable"; for collective security it might read: "Thou shalt not make war." The most fundamental

---

[1] Julian S. Huxley, *The Individual in the Animal Kingdom* (London: Cambridge University Press, 1912), pp. 115-116.

difference is the attempt by the traditional system to meet the challenge at an earlier stage before conditions have been created that only war can change. Moreover, the objective of the older system is to prevent only those struggles that involve unpleasant consequences for the whole family of nations, and to localize the others. It is not my purpose to become an advocate for one system or the other. But the relative successfulness of the older system should teach us some measure of humility regarding our political inventions or at least make us less disdainful of past political practices.

Nationalism

Nationalism is at present the most powerful determinant of international behavior. It is a man-made phenomenon and yet it has achieved enduring characteristics. In some respects it is not novel, for there have been primitive societies in which men worshipped the political community as today modern societies glorify the nation. There were few signs of nationalism anywhere in Europe during the Middle Ages. The way was prepared for it, however, by the quickening of national consciousness inspired by the Crusades. Frenchmen, Castilians, Portuguese, and Catalans were brought into contact with people who spoke their language or dialect. These contacts served to inspire a feeling of pride in their own nationality and a consciousness of rivalry with others. Loyalty to an area or locality and the growth of a spirit of community among a people through the spread and effects of a language or dialect were among the seeds from which nationalism was to grow. The fundamental nature of modern nationalism is the demand of such a group for a state or an independent political organization of its own. The achievement of this stage in modern nationalism awaited the popular revolutions in the late eighteenth and nineteenth centuries.

There were, however, traces and signs of a precocious nationalism somewhat earlier than this. The development of contemporary nationalism was foreshadowed in the North Italian city-states of the fifteenth and sixteenth centuries. Their origin corresponded with the breakup of the seamless web of universal Christendom. In Florence, Milan, and Venice this new crop of Central and North Italian city-states revived the pagan religion of "tribalism." These tiny city-states constituted in microcosm the modern nation-state. The same rules for the art of politics which Machiavelli perceived and described for the city-states have become the accepted principles for the practice, if not the theory, of politics among nations. These miniature city-states served as laboratories for proving and testing techniques of diplomacy and power politics.

In the seventeenth and eighteenth centuries a new form of nationalism, half-hearted in character, appeared. If one identifies this at all with contemporary nationalism it must be distinguished as a much weaker and more diluted form. It is in the nature of this form of nationalism that its followers were partly starved of any plausible object of worship. In the dynastic nationalism of this period the idol had to be the vested interest of the dynasty. This hardly compares as a wellspring of emotion and loyalty with the incarnation of a sovereign people.

This is one side of the coin of dynastic nationalism. The other is the fact that dynastic regimes were drawn together by the firm bonds of common membership in an "aristocratic international." There was more community between two princes or rulers than there was between a prince and his own subjects. Frederick the Great of Prussia spoke the French language more fluently than German, which he confessed he always spoke as a coachman. Since rulers and ruled were essentially indifferent to the symbols of nationalism, it should not be surprising that this era did not produce strong nationalist sentiments among their subjects and citizens.

The late eighteenth and nineteenth centuries heralded the birth of a new epoch. In a series of revolutionary convulsions, which racked the world from 1775 to 1918, nations were substituted for dynastic states. The uninspiring figures of monarchs such as Louis XIV and George III were replaced by the effulgent images of "France," "England," and "America." These incarnations of national communities were to acquire the same splendor as Ancient Rome or Athens. They furnished an object of worship which no "Prince" could supply.

A series of events mark this change. Fanaticism and ruthlessness toward foes and former friends is foreshadowed in the harsh treatment of the Loyalists by the Americans in 1783. The same emotional pattern is continued throughout Europe beginning with the French revolutionary *levée en masse,* the German *Befreiungskrieg,* the Belgian Revolution of 1830, the burning of Moscow, and the Italian *Risorgimento.* International politics since these days has become increasingly infected with the virus of unqualified national loyalty and mutual hostility until the old forms of moderation and accommodation have disappeared. A signpost of this development is the contrast between the last moderate peace treaty of 1866 (we might say that the Japanese Peace Treaty of 1951 is an exception only because of the demands that both sides acquire allies in the "Cold War") and the Peace Treaty of 1871 between France and Germany. The latter treaty was the direct consequence of a German nationalism which, under the fostering hand of Bismarck, had become so strong by 1871 that it became his master rather than his servant. Because of this pressure and against his better judgment, Bismarck was compelled to inflict a rankling wound on the French national consciousness by tearing away Alsace-Lorraine from the French body-politic.

Nationalism today has become a political religion. In the days of Giuseppe Mazzini, intellectual spokesman for Italian unity in the nineteenth century, and Thomas Masaryk, first President of the Republic of Czechoslovakia, nationalism was characterized by its humanitarianism and moderation. The aim of ethnic and national groups was to establish their own independent state. But correlative to this idea was the widely acknowledged view that other groups in turn had the right to set out to achieve this same goal and purpose. Thus Mazzini wrote in the "Pact of Fraternity of Young Europe": "Every people has its special mission, which will cooperate towards the fulfillment of the general mission of humanity. This mission constitutes its nationality. Nationality is sacred." [2]

Humanitarian nationalism of this easy-going variety has been supplanted by the new universalism of present day nationalism. Three conditions have led to the almost unlimited concentration of power in the hands of the state. They are technological, psychological, and politico-religious factors. The most astounding changes of modern history, indeed all of history, are those surrounding the Industrial Revolution. Within the past half-century, and even the past decade, the globe has been shrunken by changes in transportation and communication. It is possible to circle the globe in less time than was required to travel from Philadelphia to Washington in 1790. Whereas the range of weapons was only a few hundred yards in the sixteenth century, in the twentieth century bombers have attained an operational range of 7,000 miles. The social-psychological development which accentuates national fervor is the increase in unfulfilled ambitions in modern society. The tasks of present day industry are specialized and fragmentary and the laborer who spends his days performing minor tasks in assembly-line production must realize his thirst for influence and prestige elsewhere. By projecting his unfulfilled aims and aspirations into the world actions of the great nation of which he is a citizen, he experiences a vicarious fulfillment of his needs and desires, which contemporary society would otherwise have thwarted. The claims he makes upon his nation in world affairs are therefore less moderate than those the eighteenth century diplomats would require. Finally, the role of nationalism has been secured by the disappearance of supernational forces which might compete successfully for the minds of men. Religion as a universal force had at one time an equal claim on men's loyalties. The doctrine of the "Two Swords" was the philosophy which ascribed equal influence in their own spheres to church and state. Today the emotional fervor which once characterized loyalty to the spiritual order has been united with the patriotism of the past. Compounded together, religious fervor and patriotism have become the most powerful and dynamic force of our day.

Together these changes in technology, psychology, and religion, have created the Leviathan. They have strengthened the state and made it nearly invulnerable to popular revolutions. Not only does it possess a monopoly over the means of violence but its power has become so overwhelming that over wide regions or areas popular rebellions can be stamped out with great effectiveness. Control within the Soviet Empire, for example, is easier to maintain than in any earlier empire. Dissension can be crushed by massive air squadrons carrying atomic bombs almost instantaneously to the scene of the trouble, whereas at the beginning of the nineteenth century revolts in the provinces of Spain or Italy against Napoleon required full-fledged military campaigns. Nationalism has absorbed the dynamics of industrialism in the sense that production in every country is geared to preserving the products and resources of the state for the eventuality of war. Nationalism, moreover, has played a more decisive role in determining the ultimate loyalties of workers than socialism. For example, the French laborers fought German workers in the World

[2] *Life and Writings of Joseph Mazzini, III* (Smith, Elder and Co., 1905).

Wars despite visions of a workers international. Finally, in the case of Titoist Yugoslavia and perhaps in Poland and Hungary, loyalty to the nation out-lasted allegiance to Moscow-dominated world Communism. It should be clear that plans for rapid change through new international institutions must recognize the power of contemporary nationalism or suffer failure, with disillusionment and despair. We are merely deceived if we conceive of present-day nationalism as brittle, fragile, and transitory.

The prevailing philosophy of international relations in Western society has looked for approaches to peace in plans and blueprints for the future. The idealistic outlook has achieved its great force and influence by pointing the way toward new and better forms of international relations unfettered by past institutions and practices. These programs have been formulated in deep sincerity and high moral dignity and have captured the hopes of millions, for whom traditional foreign policy has become corrupting and outmoded.

However, it should be recognized that only in the field of international relations has there been such bold and unqualified contempt for the lessons of the past. Historical method has moved through successive stages, law has broadened with the accumulation of precedents and contemporary economic theory finds wisdom as well as folly in Ricardo and Adam Smith. In contrast, the Wilsonian tradition in rejecting institutions and experience from past international policies set the stage for unparalleled disillusionment when claims made in behalf of novel institutions proved unrealized and unrealizable. The twentieth century has been a century of unparalleled conflict. This is our supreme tragedy for if Mr. Winston S. Churchill is right, both World Wars could have been prevented. One ray of hope in an otherwise gloomy picture is the fact that our peril has caused sensitive minds to reexamine the scroll of past centuries and compare our era of total war and "Fighting Faiths" with the underlying beliefs and practices of other epochs and centuries. No one can imagine that twentieth century man can recover or recreate the past. The only relevant question is whether or not he can learn from it something about the perennial nature of world politics, rivalry among states and the means of preserving a greater measure of international peace and order.

WINGATE COLLEGE LIBRARY
WINGATE, N. C.

Part 1

THE NATURE OF
INTERNATIONAL SOCIETY

FORCES THAT CAUSE and condition tensions and violent conflicts among nations, or effect their cooperation and harmony, are the principal subject of the study of international relations.

The way in which individuals, clans, tribes, cities, factions, political parties, pressure groups, churches, states, empires, or ideological blocs have been acting since the beginning of history has often been violent and unsatisfactory. People fear that now, with the advent of the hydrogen bomb, missiles, and rockets to the moon, failure to settle a major international dispute peacefully might result in the self-annihilation of mankind.

Many view the situation with pessimism; in their expectation of the inevitable they concentrate only on their own family survival shelter. Others, on the contrary, are optimistic. They feel certain (or almost certain) that the very destructiveness of modern weapons will prevent use of those weapons. They hope that for the first time in human history world unity is within reach. Mutual terror is expected to impose unity on humanity.

Neither utter pessimism nor easy optimism is warranted. A systematic study of international politics will reveal that men and nations do often act egoistically, irrationally, and destructively. Some harsh facts of life cannot be daydreamed out of existence. We should not be too optimistic.

On the other hand, we may observe that men and nations have also proved their capacity to be generous, use reason, act intelligently, sometimes even with foresight. We should not be too pessimistic.

This mixture of emotion and reason, egoism and altruism, foolishness and wisdom, narrow-mindedness and enlightenment, the tendency to destroy and the zeal to construct—all this is *human*. And international politics deals with *men* organized in groups called nations.

The fundamental precondition for understanding international relations is study of the world as it is and not as it should be. Too many reforms and plans for a better world have been conceived intuitively without analysis of

15

what was to be reformed. International politics is not a subject on which anyone can form an intelligent opinion without taking the trouble (as one also
has to do in medicine, chemistry, physics, or engineering) to inquire into
relevant facts.[1]

The term "relevant facts" should be understood as including both material and *spiritual* factors. Material factors such as weapons, manpower, industrial establishment, and raw materials, should not be overlooked. Yet their
movement and direction are determined by aims conceived in human minds.
Political concept and critique, traditions and hopes for the future, reasoning
and irrational human impulses are all triggers of action. A noble ideal,
but also a wrong idea, may have serious material consequences for nations
and humanity.

In the study of international politics we endeavor to untie an intricate
knot of material and spiritual factors, including irrational motivation. Each
factor acts upon the other. Their interaction is so complex and constant that
different elements may be both cause and effect. Arms and alliances are both
the result *and* the cause of fear. They also may be the result or cause of
ambition.

As a complete untangling of the intertwined whole is impossible, this
book has followed the example of Alexander the Great, who, unable to untie
the intricate Gordian knot, arbitrarily cut it.

The subject of international politics has been cut into several arbitrary
sections. They necessarily overlap; they should not be viewed as watertight
compartments. None of them could have been isolated from the others even
though, perhaps, their order could have been reversed. Ideally, all these problems, treated in different sections, should be studied and understood simultaneously and not in succession. Yet, the only practical possibility, given the
complexity of the matter, is to proceed from one problem to another, bearing
in mind the interaction of factors.

Mankind and Its National Components

The foundation of international society may be viewed as a mosaic composed of almost three billion human beings.

The number of individual units in the international mosaic is expected
to increase in the foreseeable future in what is generally called a population
explosion. The population branch of the United Nations estimates that world
population, which in 1959 totalled 2,700,000,000, may reach a total of
6,300,000,000 in the year 2000. This estimate was made on the basis of such
factors as birth and death rates but its projection into the future may be subject to some changes. A great atomic war, for instance, would certainly alter
the preceding calculation.

Almost two-thirds of the human race lives and *thinks* under conditions

---

[1] This is a paraphrase of a warning with regard to the related subject of international
law, contained in James L. Brierly's book *The Outlook for International Law* (Oxford:
Clarendon Press, 1944), p. 2. James L. Brierly was a prominent English scholar and
authority on the subject of law of nations.

of extreme poverty, illiteracy, and ill-health. Too much energy is absorbed by a strenuous struggle for food and against the rigors of an intemperate climate.

Yet over one-third of mankind lives and *thinks* under conditions of relative prosperity, literacy, hygiene, and temperate climate.

There are also contrasts of a spiritual nature. Western societies, for instance, based on Judean-Christian ethics, have traditionally put great emphasis on the worth of every individual—that is on his human dignity and personality. In other parts of the world, not necessarily the underdeveloped ones, the stress has been traditionally laid on collective goals.

While men everywhere are similar because they are all members of the human race and will necessarily share in its ultimate destiny, due to these different conditions they are bound to develop different, sometimes conflicting ambitions, fears, and sets of values, and different goals and methods to achieve them. Such generalities as "pursuit of happiness," "prosperity," "justice," and even "life" itself mean different things to different groups because of the contrast in traditions and material conditions under which they may realize their goals.

In matters of *international politics* the most important influence on outlook and aims proves to be the *national* environment. In their relations with other national groups, men do not think primarily as members of one human race; nor even as members of underdeveloped regions of the world in contrast to the well-developed ones; nor as heirs to Judean-Christian ethics and traditions as opposed to other beliefs and systems. In politics men primarily think and act as citizens or subjects of their respective territorial states.

A common past and present, their glory or tragedy, as well as a common program for the future make men conscious of being part of a unit, which (with its collective will) is different from the rest of humanity. The abstraction—a nation and its state—thus becomes an almost tangible reality. By contrast, the concept of mankind and its interests appears hazy, distant, unreal.

A Frenchman, however violently he may disagree on other matters with his compatriots, is deeply affected by the glory or tragedy of his national history; so is an Asian or African whose recent history was that of national humiliation (examples of the intensity of this feeling may be found in Topic 3); and so is a Russian who has survived a brutal invasion and now enjoys the triumph of the first sputnik or the first rocket to the moon.

However, nationalism has not eliminated the differences among men within a national community or eliminated all feelings of similarity and affinity transcending national boundaries. Obviously, not all members of a national community think alike. There are party, religious, professional, and individual differences. Neither do all members of a national community differ in their thinking and conclusions from other individuals and groups in other nations. A Hindu may dream of a shiny new Cadillac as some Americans do. An American may try to escape his time and place for a Hindu-like contemplation. Socialists, Catholics, and Protestants have established international groupings with the aim of basing their individual and national actions on common international concepts (see p. 35). A French Communist may feel more akin to some foreign Communist than to General de Gaulle. Maurice Thorez, then the leader of French Communism, declared in 1948 that it was the duty of French Communists to greet the Soviet armies as liberators from capitalistic oppression if they invaded France.

Yet, as a rule, we observe that loyalty to other-than-national concepts proves weaker than the identification of the people with each other and with their national goals. In World War I and World War II the European Social-ists supported their respective national states notwithstanding their doctrine of proletarian internationalism, which had seemed so strong before the na-tional crisis had broken out.

Some may express the wish that men everywhere felt and acted as mem-bers of one indivisible human race first, and as citizens or subjects of their respective national states second. So far, however, this has remained only a wish.

In principle, humanity is one and indivisible. In fact, for centuries it has been living half-free and half-slave, half-hungry and half-overfed, half-literate and half-illiterate, and above all, for the past three hundred years it has lived divided into national states.

In theory, the interests of humanity and those of its national components complement each other. One should serve the other. In practice, these inter-ests have often been in conflict, both suffering as a consequence.

Many observers warn that these divisions are unnatural today. The divisions do not fit our era of interdependence and may even be suicidal in a time of atomic weapons. If nationalism and territorial states are, as some suggest, passing phenomena like many other human institutions, then the time for them to pass away is now.

Keeping always in mind that the world must be observed as it is and not as it should be, we have to note that there are no practical indications of change on the part of national communities. Three billion members of the human race constitute the foundation layer of the world mosaic. Simultane-ously they insist on constituting its second layer, the layer of national states.

Nations and Their Unity

The total number of national units is not expected to rise dramatically. It may even decrease somewhat if some nation-states combine into higher and larger units—a practice attempted by some West European, Arab, and Afri-can nations.

In 1959 eighty-two states were members of the United Nations. One state, recognized as such by all, is not a member and does not intend to be-come one: neutral Switzerland. (Switzerland's case is discussed on p. 381.) Some other states have not been admitted to the world organization because of their division by the conflict between the Communist and non-Communist blocs of nations. Such states are Germany, Korea, and Viet-nam, all of which are divided into Communist and non-Communist parts; and the People's Re-public of Mongolia, which is not recognized as a state by Western democ-racies.

In the 1940's Asia added most of the new names to the roster of national states; in the late 1950's and 1960's it was Africa's turn to present new candidates for independent nationhood: Somalia, Nigeria, Rhodesia, Nyasaland, Mali Federation.

Only about a dozen new names are expected to be added to the United Nations' list before the year 2000, at which time the world population will be doubled. Architects who are in charge of additional facilities and seating accommodations at the United Nations' headquarters in New York base their current plans for new construction on a realistic estimate of ninety-five to one hundred member states, at the most, within the coming decades.

The name of the world organization, the United Nations, can be misleading if it is interpreted too literally. It is primarily the term "nations" that refers to the actual facts. Their "unity" is only a goal, a grand design, a program for the future.

Yet, in spite of the name, the charter of the United Nations is quite modest and realistic. (It was drafted by three Great Powers—America, Russia, and England—and accepted by the rest of the world, with some modifications, in San Francisco in 1945.) It does not propose to absorb nations into one world state or world federation. It proclaims that "the organization is based on the principle of *sovereign equality* of its members." It recognizes the fact that all nations *claim* to be equal to each other as well as sovereign, i.e., supreme within their territory.

In another article (art. 27), the charter recognizes also another fact of the international life: although nations claim to be equal and sovereign, they are not. Some nations, to paraphrase George Orwell, are "more sovereign and more equal than others." These are the five permanent members of the Security Council who are endowed with the veto power: America, Russia, England, France, and China. Moreover, countries like India, Japan, and Canada exert a disproportionate influence in the Assembly. (The problems of legal equality, sovereignty, and veto power are analyzed in Part VI.) The charter recognizes these two mutually exclusive facts. It does not reconcile them because it cannot.

Another clash of claims is implied in the articles which describe the purposes of the world organization: that of the interests of the national components with the interest of the whole. Realistically, the charter offers the states a common framework and some machinery to assist them in handling some of their common problems, provided that member-states agree that these problems are common and that they could and should be solved by common efforts.

The charter defines the purposes of the United Nations as follows: "To maintain international peace, . . . to develop friendly relations among *nations,* . . . to achieve international cooperation in solving international problems of economic, social, cultural, and humanitarian character, . . . to be a center for *harmonizing* the actions of *nations* in the attainment of these common ends." [2]

The individual personality and responsibility of each member-state is

[2] *The U.N. Charter,* chap. i, art. 1. (Italics added.)

further stressed by another statement of the United Nations charter: "Nothing in the present Charter shall authorize the United Nations to intervene in matters which are *essentially within the domestic jurisdiction* of any state. . . . " [3] As the charter does not specify what matters are considered to be essentially within the domestic jurisdiction of any state, it is left (in most cases) to the sovereign decisions of sovereign states to determine whether to participate in, or abstain from, the common effort to solve problems and crises affecting humanity. (The possible exception to this rule—the binding character of a substantive decision of the U.N. Security Council on nations which do not have the status of a great power—will be discussed in Part VI.)

The U.N. charter, as well as experience and observation, confirm the fact that the fate of the world is not determined by mankind acting as a whole, but by nations—that is, the territorial states and their representatives.

Territorial States

With the exception of dependent peoples who are administered by national states, every single square mile of the inhabitable surface of our globe has been placed under direct jurisdiction of one of the territorial states.

When, a few years ago, an American citizen, Garry Davis, proclaimed himself to be a citizen of the world and renounced his American citizenship, he had to negotiate with the French police since his unilateral change of status had occurred in France, a territorial state. In our world one may be a citizen of a state, or a stateless guest of a territorial state, but one cannot be outside the confines of one territorial state or another. The above-mentioned would-be citizen of the world has resumed his American citizenship since.

The territorial states into which our globe has been divided represent the largest manageable units of centralized organization.

The modern territorial state is the product of the seventeenth century. But the efforts to establish peace and order through a coercive system within a given territory are as old as humanity. They reflect the fact that men, not being angels, sometimes have to be prevented by force or threat of force from committing evil acts.

The attempt of a cave family to keep its cave clean and warm, as well as secure against dangers from without, was probably the first attempt to establish a miniature "territorial state." As this proved less self-contained and defensible than originally assumed, other territorial organizations followed: a combination of caves, a village, a city, a league of cities, an empire, a modern territorial state, and its extension into regional or ideological groupings.

The modern territorial state with its centralized legislation, law enforcement, judicial system, and tax collection is largely the creation of the absolute monarchy which proved victorious against two competing sources of territorial authority: the universalistic authority of the Holy Roman Empire, and the local authorities exercised until then by practically sovereign feudal princes, dukes, and barons. The centralized royal power asserted its authority to give and enforce law within a territory which was larger than the territories

[3] *Ibid.,* art. 2, par. 7. (Italics added.)

dominated by feudal lords, yet not too large to necessitate a risky dilution of the royal power.

This concentration of power in one center within a manageable territorial unit emerged most clearly in Western Europe, especially following the Thirty Years' War marked by intense religious conflicts. It was ended by the Peace of Westphalia of 1648, which gave the rulers not only the right to give, adjudicate, and enforce law, and collect taxes centrally, but also to determine the dominant religion of their subjects. The modern government's controls or supervision of mass communication media had their beginnings here.

Similar developments occurred in other parts of the world. It was, however, first in Western Europe that this evolution was fully consummated. It has maintained itself ever since. In spite of the present-day criticism of the obvious shortcomings of the territorial nation-state in our era, nations and leaders fail to conceive a real alternative. We will see that the combination of small states into a bigger one really is not a departure from the territorial pattern. In the 1960's the Westphalian formula of 1648 still finds numerous imitators in completely different environments and climates.

Why is it so? Three factors explain the successful performance of the territorial nation-state. All of them are absent on the international scene, a fact which explains frequent interruptions of international peace and order by violence, while quiet is maintained on the internal, national scale. These factors are:

1. *Government.* Peace and order are results of the existence and action of a central authority which has the monopoly of violent means of law enforcement; some or full control of education and mass communication media; and influence or full control over the economy and social welfare.

2. *Nationalism.* If people identify themselves with their territorial government as well as with each other, if they are aware of their collective separateness from the rest of the world, and of the beneficial effects of their unity —such a state of mind may discourage them from disturbing peace and order in their community.

3. *Moral and political consensus.* In this context, this means the people's general acceptance of the rules of peaceful procedures. When people are convinced that their government is generally responsive to their pressures for change and that it is willing and capable of redressing their most serious grievances, the use of violence becomes unnecessary to further any important claim. Violence and legitimate counter-violence are then limited to individual cases of criminal behavior.

Government

Government, the first major cause of internal peace and order, includes its traditional ingredients: (1) the executive, (2) the legislative, and (3) the judicial.

The *executive branch* administers the law and holds a monopoly on coercive and violent means of law enforcement—executioners, prisons, police establishments, etc. Citizens and private groups, as a rule, are not allowed to possess private armies or use weapons, except under severely restricted conditions—self-defense, etc.

The very existence of such monopoly of violence normally discourages any attempts to oppose and change the legal order by violence. If the government maintains an effective control over the violent means of enforcement, it may crush any such violent attempt.

In democracies the executive branch of the government influences, and in dictatorships it completely controls, the mass communication media and general education. Continuous training in peaceful procedures, a persuasive argument, or a constant flow of propaganda may discourage people from pressing their claims and even considering violence. The governmental means of enforcement may remain in the background.

Finally, modern governments—their executive branch in combination with the legislative—influence national economy through different controls over income (taxation power), currency, tariffs, prices, credit, social security, etc. On the basis of moral and political consensus, the power of the government over men's livelihood has been increased. When people claimed "freedom *of* speech," their aim was to reduce the influence of government to a minimum. When today they claim "freedom *from* want," they ask the government to play a more active role in the economy.

A modern authoritarian government usually controls national economy in every detail.

The combination of these different controls is often able to insure domestic peace and tranquility.

In a dictatorship the intensity of these controls—police, propaganda, and government's total control over the economy—is the major means of the maintenance of peace and order. People either do not dare to use violence or they do not even consider it, their will having been paralyzed by the government's capacity to impose its own will.

In a democracy the absence of violence can be partly attributed to government controls, especially its monopoly of law enforcement; partly to the ability of the people to influence the government policies (moral and political consensus).

The *legislative branch* of the government translates the wishes of the decisive forces into a body of enforceable rules, called the legal system. These decisive forces are: in a democracy—the majority; in a dictatorship—the dictatorial clique.

The legal order—the fruit of legislative labors—helps to maintain domestic peace and order not only because the executive branch of the government is willing and ready to enforce it, but also by its sheer existence. The law notifies the people as to its rights and duties. If these rules are clear and understandable, and generally in tune with the aspirations of an important portion of the people, they do not have to be constantly enforced. Their existence helps to reduce the number of disputes and violations.

The *judicial branch* of government interprets the law. If, in their disputes, both the plaintiff and the defendant accept the validity of the legal rules as binding for both, the court system is an effective tool for maintaining domestic peace. It succeeds in transforming the primitive forms of settling disputes (by fist or duel) into a legal battle, usually conducted by attorneys on behalf of the parties to the dispute. The issue is then determined by an impartial judge, whose award is accepted as binding and is submitted to peacefully.

Nationalism

Nationalism may be defined as "a state of mind in which the supreme loyalty of the individuals is felt to be due to the nation-state. . . . It recognizes the nation-state as the ideal form of political organization and the nationality as the source of all creative energy and economic well-being." This is Hans Kohn's definition, which this foremost expert on nationalism further qualifies and refines in his many books on this subject. (Samples are reproduced in Topic 1.)

Admittedly, the terms "nationalism," "nationality," "national language," "national minorities," "multinational state," "minority state," "patriotism" and its intolerant forms "jingoism" and "chauvinism" cannot be defined with absolute precision. In the United States, for instance, the term "state" is reserved for the component parts of the federation which is called "nation." On the other hand, after World War II, following the expulsion of the German minority, Czechoslovakia referred to itself as a "state composed of two nations, the Czechs and the Slovaks."

The rise of the territorial state logically coincides with the emergence of modern nationalism. One causes and conditions the other. The territorial state helped nationalism to crystallize, while, at the same time, groups which had developed a national consciousness tended to lay claim for a territorial nation-state of their own.

Within the territorial states, all kinds of activities, undertaken in common, helped to foster a feeling of unity among the people: living, learning, working and remembering together; solving problems, suffering and hoping for a better future in common; and, above all, fighting as a unit against external dangers. These activities did not eliminate economic, social, or religious differences but placed them in an inferior position in the hierarchy of values. In the case of an external danger, no value could be higher than the loyalty to the national whole.

Hand in hand with this growth of firm bonds among individuals and groups that constitute a national community went also a greater or lesser degree of identification with (or at least loyalty to) the monarch and the territory. Later, with democracy emerged also loyalty to political institutions, programs, procedures and aims of the national entity itself.

This feeling of loyalty to the abstract entity, the nation, may be so strong that people may temporarily forgive their government wrong-doing or lack of response to their wishes. The slogan "My country, right or wrong" clearly tends to postpone the estimate of one's government's performance to a more suitable time or subordinate it to the need of unity *vis-a-vis* another nation. One also recalls the rallying cry Mussolini used to marshal support for his policies when he proclaimed that "sixty million Italians cannot be wrong."

In the name of national glory, governments and their implacable domestic enemies may sometimes forget hostility and together bask in the sun
of foreign acclaim. During the Brussels Exposition in 1958, for instance,
many Eastern European enemies of communism could hardly conceal their
pleasure when their national exhibits gained world-wide acclaim. These exhibits were organized and financed by the Communist governments of these
countries with the obvious aim of propagandizing communism. The governments interpreted their success as victory for communism. The anti-
Communists of these countries, on the other hand, interpreted that success as
recognition of permanent qualities of their nations: "Communist or non-
Communist—my country."

When in the late nineteenth and then in the twentieth century the territorial state became also an agency for planned economic and social development, additional impulses for increased identification with the state were
added to the Westphalian ones. This is particularly true of many new Asian
and African territorial states.

In spite of their revolt against Western Europe, the birthplace of the
territorial state but also of colonialism,[4] the political leaders of the formerly
colonized areas imitate the Western European concept of the state in almost
every detail. This includes even symbols calling for emotional response, such
as the national flag, anthem, coat of arms, etc. To the leaders and their masses
the territorial state represents the best available form of effective administration in a larger community, a useful instrument for creating homogeneity
where it does not yet fully exist and a suitable vehicle for centralized economic
and social planning, rapid industrialization, national education, modernization
of agriculture, and defense against any possible return of foreign domination.

(Professor E. H. Carr analyzes the nature of loyalty and attachment of
the masses to their "socialized nation" in Topic 1.)

In the name of their new national states and their independence, the
national leaders ask for (and receive) adequate support for their often over-
ambitious plans. "Independence is not a cure-all," wrote a young African
nationalist. "It is, nevertheless, the psychological spur which is indispensable
for arousing enthusiasm for building a modern state."[5]

Such is the strength of nationalism that the formerly exploited masses
appear willing to accept a hard life for many years to come, if the result is
greater power of their new state. "Our main measuring rod is that of national
strength and power," writes an Indian socialist.[6] (Professor Carr expresses
some doubts as to the permanence of such enthusiasm if—after independence
has been won—standards of individual freedom and prosperity do not rise,
but sink. See p. 61 on nationalization of socialism.)

Nationalism may be, as some suggest, a passing phenomenon. Others

[4] Colonialism: expansion of a territorial state and imposition of its interests and administration on other nations.
[5] Secretary General of the Istiqlal Party of Morocco, Ahmed Balafrej, in his article
"Morocco Plans for Independence," Foreign Affairs, Vol. XXXIV, No. 3 (April, 1956),
p. 489.
[6] M. R. Masani, "The Mind of Asia," Foreign Affairs, Vol. XXXIII, No. 4 (July,
1955), p. 549. M. R. Masani is the founder of the All-India Congress Socialist Party.

believe that "whether we like it or not, some form of nationalism is likely to continue indefinitely."[7] Whatever the future, nationalism and the quest for statehood represent dynamic political forces today, as they have for the past 250 years, and remain decisive factors in international politics.

Nationalism is often asserted against other important values such as good government, prosperity, humanism, and peace. We find a great variety of opinions on nationalism. These opinions may be roughly divided into two broad categories: the force of nationalism is a blessing or a curse.

Nationalism—a Curse

According to the first school of thought, nationalism and the territorial nation-state represent the sources of most evils afflicting mankind. War is one of them. Nationalism divides humanity into mutually intolerant units. As a result people think as Americans, Russians, Chinese, Egyptians, or Peruvians first, and as human beings second—if at all.

"Nationalism is a proud and boastful habit of mind about one's own nation," writes an American historian, "accompanied by a supercilious or hostile attitude toward the other nations; it admits that individual citizens of one's country may do wrong but it insists that one's nationality or national state is always right. Nationalism is either ignorant and prejudiced or inhuman and jaundiced; in both cases it is a form of mania, a kind of extended and exaggerated egotism . . . it is far from ennobling; in a word it is a patriotic snobbery."[8]

"Despite the universality of the general concept of nationalism, its cult is based on a tribal idea. . . . The good at which it aims is a good for one's own nation only, not for all mankind. . . . Nationalism as a religion represents a reaction against historic Christianity, against the universal mission of Christ; it re-enshrines the earlier tribal mission of a chosen people. The ancient reflective Roman imagined that one chosen people—the Hebrew nation—was one too many for general comfort and safety; the thoughtful modern Christian may be pardoned for being a bit pessimistic about a world devoid of a Roman empire and replete with dozens upon dozens of chosen peoples. Nationalism as a religion inculcates neither charity nor justice; it is proud, not humble; and it signally fails to universalize human aims. . . . Nationalism's kingdom is frankly of this world, and its attainment involves tribal selfishness and vainglory, a particularly ignorant and tyrannical intolerance,—and war."[9]

In his indictment of nationalism, Carlton J. H. Hayes describes seven outstanding evils:

"First is the spirit of exclusiveness and narrowness. The national state, through education in national school, national army, and national journalism, through the social pressure of national patriotism, inculcates in its citizens the fancy that they are a world by themselves, sufficient unto themselves; it

[7] Carlton J. H. Hayes, *Essays on Nationalism* (New York: Macmillan Co., 1926), p. 275. By permission of The Macmillan Company.
[8] *Ibid.*
[9] *Ibid.*, pp. 124-125.

teaches them that they are a chosen people, a peculiar people, and that they should prize far more what is theirs as a nationality than what is theirs as human beings.

"Secondly, nationalism places a premium on uniformity. It prescribes national models of art, national standards of thought, and national norms of conduct, and to these it expects all the inhabitants of each national state to conform. Individual differences, class differences, religious differences, are alike deemed unfortunate; and the individual of genius is suspect, especially if his genius displays itself in criticism of national uniformity. . . .

"Thirdly, nationalism increases the docility of the masses. As a result of their national upbringing and their life-long nationalist education, they are seldom inclined to question the providential character of their nationality, of their state, of their government, or of the economic circumstances in which they live. . . . In the name of national rights, national interests, and national honor, they will forego their own individual rights. . . They are ready in the name of liberty, of freedom of their nationality to abridge the liberty of fellow citizens and to take away the freedom of other nationalities. . . .

"Fourthly, nationalism in its present form focuses popular attention upon war and preparedness for war. . . . Military heroes outrank in national pantheons the heroes of science and art and learning."[10]

(As the fifth, sixth, and seventh outstanding evils of nationalism, Professor Hayes mentions jingoism, imperialism, and intolerance.)

"If in these respects nationalism is not mitigated, it will be an unqualified curse to future generations."[11]

Sovereignty—an Illusion

Nations and their states claim or pretend to be legally supreme within their national territory. No other state, bloc of states, or even the United Nations as an organization of all of them, has the right to exercise executive or legislative functions within the territory of a sovereign state. In 1957, following the Anglo-French-Israeli intervention in the Suez area, the presence of the United Nations military contingent in the Gaza strip depended on the consent of the sovereign states of Israel and Egypt. In 1959 a fact-finding mission of the U.N. Security Council could proceed to Laos only at the invitation of the Laotian government.

This claim to legal supreme authority within one's territory is called sovereignty. Legal questions apart, the man in the street usually supports the idea of national sovereignty, as it suggests to him his national community's freedom of action, that is, its independence from the will and interests of other nations. People do not normally expect that other nations (or such abstract entities as humanity or a continent) would attend to their specific needs with the same care and understanding as does *their own* state and government. This is why a nation usually prefers an inferior government of its own to an effective one by foreigners. The former Indian Ambassador to the United

[10] *Ibid.*, pp. 257-260.
[11] *Ibid.*, p. 260.

States, G. L. Mehta, quoted with approval a former British Prime Minister's statement: "Good government is no substitute for self-government." (See Topic 3.)

The concept of sovereignty is often at variance with economic and political realities. Many of the so-called sovereign nation-states are heavily dependent on outside economic support and balance of power among major nations to preserve their make-believe independence. The Kingdom of Libya (formerly three Italian colonies—Tripolitania, Cyrenaica, Fezzan) has been fully dependent on United States and British financial support ever since it became a nation-state under the auspices of the United Nations. Another example is Somalia, also a former Italian colony in East Africa. Before Somalia achieved the status of an independent state in 1960, it estimated need for yearly support of four million dollars to balance its budget, as well as the prolonged presence of some Italian experts to avoid collapse of its administration and services.

Critics of nationalism and territorial states point out that claims of independence and sovereignty represent an anachronism in our era of growing interdependence. In an age marked by the spread of literacy, mass communication media, mass production, and methods of mass destruction, no state can claim to be isolated from the others. Radioactive fallout pays no heed to national boundaries. Universalism, not nationalism, should mark the evolution of relations among modern men. (This viewpoint is presented by J. H. Herz in Topic 5.)

Nationalism—a Blessing

The opposite school of thought not only considers nationalism inevitable but actually a source of considerable good. Throughout the ages, nationalism acted to preserve variety in arts, music, and all other esthetic manifestations of man's civilization. Nationalism is especially important in our age of mass production and mass entertainment, with their dangers of conformity and monotony.

While certain evils, perpetrated in the name of nationalism, cannot be denied, many writers argue that these have always been the result either of distortions of nationalism or of its mesalliance with inhumanity, expansionism, egotism, totalitarianism, and other undesirable manifestations of the human mind. Many of these evils had existed long before modern nationalism entered the global scene. The defenders of nationalism argue that as long as it is not abused or exaggerated, nationalism benefits mankind.

Different adjectives usually accompanying the word "nationalism" (humanitarian, Jacobin, liberal, traditional, integral, expansionist, intolerant, etc.) suggest that nationalism is many things depending on circumstances. Topic 1 contains descriptions of different types of nationalism (C. Hayes, pp. 41-60) as well as analysis of welfare-state nationalism (E. H. Carr, pp. 60-64).

When we consider the disadvantages and evils of nationalism and the national state, we have a tendency to condemn them. But let us ponder the alternatives. The French philosopher Ernest Renan warned that discarding nationalism might be a premature step and the result might be worse than the present state.

"Nations are not eternal," Renan said in his famous speech "What Is a Nation?" "They . . . will be replaced by a confederation. But such is not the law of the age in which we live. Nowadays, it is a good, and even necessary, thing that nations should exist. Their existence is the guarantee of liberty, which would be lost if the world had but one law and one master."

These thoughts were expressed in 1882. Seventy-five years later they were echoed by the American poet, Robert Frost, who turned down the idea of "one world." Receiving the Holland Society's gold medal for "outstanding contribution to the field of fine letters," Robert Frost described himself as an "obstinate nationalist" and said: "You must belong to the land that belongs to you—that's what makes nations."

Finally, many observers who recognize the inadequacy of the territorial state and the dangers of nationalism in the international sphere recognize also the constructive and cohesive force of modern nationalism and the modern state. Through the machinery of the territorial states great portions of the earth were pacified. Homogeneous, and therefore manageable, communities have been created. The primitive tendency to solve disputes by violence rather than by compromise has sharply declined within the states. Individuals now tend to take their disputes to the courts; and group conflicts are often peacefully decided through the intermediary of some central arbiter, be it a majority vote in a legislative assembly or a decision of a dictator. There is a direct relation between homogeneity of the community, its political and moral consensus as to the peaceful procedures and effective government, and the final result: peace, order, and welfare. One conditions the other.

Moral and Political Consensus

The term "moral and political consensus" is used to describe the basis of peaceful change within a democratic nation. It includes a great number of implicit and explicit agreements among the people of a nation-state; their identification with each other, with the state, and with their government; their fundamental agreement as to the structure and aims of their society; and—as no society is static and free of conflicts and tensions—their agreement as to the peaceful procedures and techniques in response to the demands for change.

An important aspect of moral and political consensus is the absence of violent methods in promoting one's own interest. However, the lack of violence on the part of the people in a dictatorial state does not indicate the presence of common consensus. There, people abstain from violence because overwhelming power is concentrated in the hands of the government.

Yet, even a totalitarian government endeavors to create a *substitute* for political and moral consensus. It tries to manipulate and shape the public opinion by a constant flow of propaganda; it investigates the feelings of its people in order to find out where the totalitarian boot pinches most. This is done through state agencies which are in close contact with the people on the local level, such as the party cells, mass organizations, and the informing elements of the secret police.

How Domestic Peace May Be Broken

If government, nationalism, and political and moral consensus constitute the main ingredients of peace and order within a territorial state, the absence of either or all of them may cause peace and order to be disturbed.

Government may prove incapable of monopolizing the means of violence and preventing the use of means of violence by others. This may be the result of government's corruption, internal dissension, or the effect of serious economic or international crisis.

Nationalism, the feeling of unity, may give place to nationalist disunity. A state, created in the name of national self-determination, may be shaken by the same principle from within. (Alfred A. Cobban discusses the limits and excesses of national self-determination in Topic 2.) This may happen if a state is composed of mutually intolerant racial, ethnic, or religious groups.

And, the political and moral consensus may disappear when the obstinacy of one group prevents the satisfaction of other groups by the methods of peaceful change; or when one social, economic, or ideological group places its special interests above the real or imagined interests of the whole. If, in addition, a government proves incapable of preventing violence, a previously homogeneous and orderly society becomes a battlefield. A civil war ensues. The American War between the States is a meaningful illustration of the fact that the existence of one government *minus* common consensus may lead to a war *within* a nation.

Civil war may break out even when the government is strong enough to quell a violent attempt to change the political, legal, or economic order, and when the majority of the nation stands behind its government. This happens when a relatively weak minor group within a nation gets military or other assistance from beyond the national borders. Such was the case in the Spanish Civil War. Ethnic or ideological minorities (German minorities in Eastern Europe before World War II; Chinese minorities in South East Asia at present; Communist parties operating in non-Communist countries) may have their numerical, political, or military insignificance multiplied by the support offered by a Great Power, attuned to their causes.

Stalin on Revolution

A specialist in the arts of revolution and civil war, Joseph Stalin, has often stressed the need of *outside* support for a proletarian revolution, in addition to his other classic conditions for a successful revolution. Stalin, often quoting Lenin,[12] defined these conditions as follows:

1. "When the revolutionary mood of the masses . . . brims over . . . "* "When the lower classes do not want the old way."†

[12] Translated by "Historicus" from the following works by J. Stalin: * *Sochineniia,* V, 73; † *Voprosy Leninizma* (11th ed.; 1945), p. 25; ‡ *Voprosy* (11th ed.; 1945), p. 104.

2. "When uncertainty and confusion, disintegration and dissolution in the adversary's camp have reached the highest point. . . . "† "When the upper classes cannot carry on in the old way."†

3. "When the so-called neutral elements, all that mass of many millions of city and village petty bourgeoisie begin definitely to turn away from the adversary—and seek alliance with the proletariat" . . .* "Revolution is impossible without a nationwide crisis, affecting both the exploited and the exploiters."†

4. "The development of world revolution will be the more rapid and thorough, the more effective the aid rendered by the first Socialist country to the workers . . . of all other countries. . . . This [first Socialist] country is transformed into a base for the further unfolding of world revolution, into a lever for the further disintegration of imperialism."‡

If we apply Stalin's own analysis to the causes of peace or revolution in Communist totalitarian states, we may assume that the first three conditions, to some extent, developed within Poland and Hungary in 1956.

1. The revolutionary mood of the workers began to brim over.

2. As a result of Stalin's death, followed by Khrushchev's relaxations, the Communist upper classes could not carry on in the old way. Uncertainty, confusion, and dissolution in the Communist camp reached a high point.

3. Neutral, opportunist elements began to turn away from the Communists, including some rank and file of the Party itself.

Despair and the assumption that the Communist power had been weakened or corrupted by the strength of nationalism had a greater influence on the thinking of Hungarian revolutionary leaders and masses than the facts of the international situation. Had they been cautiously examined, it would have become apparent that the fourth of Stalin's conditions for a successful revolution—outside support for the revolutionaries—was absent.

The weakness of the minority group in power was overcome by Moscow's readiness and willingness to use Soviet armored divisions to restore Communist government. "Together with the Hungarian people," noted a Communist commentary broadcast by Radio Prague, "we feel a profound gratitude toward the Soviet Army, which as always and now again came to help in time." [13]

The Hungarian revolution confirms the analysis (which will be discussed in more detail in Part III) that wars, international or civil, may start on the basis of an erroneous estimate of the situation.

Peace and Order through World Government?

None of the three factors which usually insure peace, order, and promotion of welfare within a state exists on the international scene. There is no government with central authority to create, interpret, and enforce the law. (Part VI will discuss the nature and the limitations of the Law of Nations.) There is no global "nationalism," that is, no state of mind in which "the supreme loyalty of the individual is felt to be due to mankind." As we have

[13] *Radio Prague,* November 4, 1956.

seen, in matters of politics loyalty to one's nation proves to be superior to loyalty to such abstract and distant concepts as humanity or the human race. And there is no moral and political consensus. There is no agreement as to the desirability of one government and its nature and aims.

We observe that even such an international doctrine as communism, with its final concept of One Communist World under One Communist Government, has not succeeded in solving some dramatic clashes between the interests of individual Communist states (Yugoslavia) and the interests of the Communist whole, as promoted and interpreted by its leader, the Soviet Union. (The clash between nationalism and proletarian internationalism is described in Topic 4.)

However, many established nation-states of today were preceded by similar situations, in which there had not been either government, or national homogeneity, or even a desire to constitute a nation under one government. In spite of this, heterogeneous and often quite antagonistic groups finally combined into territorial states and have enjoyed a reasonable degree of peace, order, and welfare ever since.

How did it happen? In some cases unity was imposed from above, by conquest and dictatorial rule. Theoretically, this is also possible on a world scale if one nation or group of nations were to impose its ideology and form of government on the whole globe (by atomic blackmail, for instance).

In other cases, moral and political consensus antedated the state. The state was the result of a pre-existing community. In many cases either a common enemy or geographic isolation has compensated for the lack of original homogeneity which, otherwise, would have probably prevented the creation of one common state.

The United States and Switzerland, two federations which were capable of combining diversity with homogeneity, are often referred to as models to be copied eventually by the world.

"Whoever invented the motto 'E pluribus unum,'" writes John Gunther, "has given the best three-word description of the United States ever written. The triumph of America is a triumph of a coalescing federal system. Complex as the nation is, almost to the point of insufferability, it interlocks. Homogeneity and diversity—these are the stupendous rival magnets." [14]

Common struggle against a common enemy certainly neutralized the centrifugal forces which were represented by the different interests and orientations of the original thirteen colonies. Geographic isolation was an additional factor. The combination of geography and a common enemy created a community from which the concept of one nation with one government could emerge, and survive the serious challenge of the 1860's.

The case of Switzerland combines similar elements. In spite of Switzerland's four different languages (German, French, Italian and Romansch) and different religions (Catholic and Protestant), the isolation from the rest of Europe by the then forbidding Alps and the outside pressures of Hapsburg enmity combined to make the idea of unity prevail over differences.

[14] John Gunther, *Inside USA* (New York: Harper & Bros., 1947), p. 911.

Fear as a Unifying Force

The science fiction theme, an invasion from another planet, would certainly bring all mutually exclusive enemy forces into sudden union. But it seems unlikely that a common enemy will emerge from without, one who would force humanity to do what it is reluctant to do voluntarily.

Could the nightmare of hydrogen destruction be such a creator of homogeneity among heterogeneous elements? Some believe so. They argue that presently our world must unite or perish. Others express their doubts as to the beneficial effects of a danger which threatens us not from the outside but from within our planet.

"Undoubtedly, fear may be a creative force," writes the Protestant theologian Reinhold Niebuhr.[15] "The scared man can run faster from the pursuing bull than he ever thought possible. But the creative power of fear does not increase in proportion to its intensity. Fear, finally, becomes paralyzing. Furthermore, the fear of mutual destruction easily degenerates into a fear of a particular foe. Even now it may be regretfully recorded that the fear of Russia in the West and of the West in Russia seems more potent than the common fear of destruction."

Fear and opposition to a powerful enemy threatening the security of several nations in one region may result in *regional* nationalism. Local nationalisms may merge into a higher concept.

The pressure of West European colonialism in Asia, while it lasted, made certain racial, ethnic, and cultural groups aware of their common destiny as Asians. "The sons of Asians who thrilled in response to the victory of Japan over Tsarist Russia," writes an Indian Socialist, "respond similarly to the military and diplomatic successes of Communist China over the Americans in Korea and the French in Indochina."[16]

A similar combination of past resentments and new fears has induced some Arab leaders to work and strive for a Pan-Arab Union; North African leaders for Maghreb (literally "the West"—a North African Union of Morocco, Algeria, and Tunisia); and other African leaders for an African Community of Nations (south of Sahara).[17]

The emergence of a serious threat to all the nations of Western Europe, emanating from the Soviet Union, assisted these nations in overcoming their old antagonisms (particularly the French-German one) and combining into "Little Europe." (Common Market; Euratom; and Coal and Steel Community, composed of France, Germany, Italy, Belgium, Netherlands and Luxemburg, the last three referring to themselves as Benelux.)

In addition to a common fear of possible Soviet expansion westward, there are other reasons which explain the relative success of West European integration. Among them is the hope of some West Europeans that a multinational federation may achieve a degree of power which would make it inde-

[15] Reinhold Niebuhr, "The Myth of World Government," *The Nation*, Vol. CLXII (March 16, 1946).
[16] M. R. Masani, *op. cit.*, p. 549.
[17] The *New York Times* reported on negotiations held (with this aim in mind) between the Prime Ministers of Liberia, Ghana, and Guinea on July 20, 1959.

pendent of both the United States and the Soviet Union. François Mauriac, a famous French novelist, expressed this idea by saying that West Europeans should fear more what America and Russia have in common than what divides these two materialistic giants.

In the light of the preceding examples we may conclude that danger from the outside proves the most potent unifying force. It induces nations to submerge their antagonisms and form larger, regional, supranational systems. But when today some states are willing to combine into larger federal or confederal units, their aim is not to create a stepping stone toward world unity. In reality, they want a larger territorial state. They hope that such a larger multi-national unit may prove more prosperous, more powerful, and therefore more independent in the face of pressures by big powers. E. H. Carr, evaluating this tendency (see also p. 438), points out that "a division of the world into a small number of large multinational units . . . would be simply the old nationalism writ large."

Civil War on a World Scale

Some observers hopefully expect that the trend toward larger territorial units is ultimately bound to lead, step by step, to one world government. We cannot *a priori* exclude it.

Yet, we should recall that the existence of a government *per se* has not proved a guarantee of peace, order, and welfare. The central authority, established either by consent or conquest, may be weakened as a consequence of corruption or intramural struggle for power. Or the original consensus may collapse. In both cases civil war will ensue.

In the second half of the last century, two relatively successful federations were almost torn apart by civil strife. This was the war between the Confederacy and the Union in America; and extreme tension between Catholics and Protestants in Switzerland.

Therefore, we should not exclude the possibility of a world civil war which might follow the establishment of one world government. Professor Quincy Wright shows in his book, *A Study of War*,[18] that of 278 wars fought between 1480 and 1941, 78—that is 28 percent of the total—were civil wars. And civil wars may be as cruel and inhuman as the international ones. Kenneth W. Thompson notes that losses in civil wars before the twentieth century often exceeded those suffered in international wars.

During World War II, approximately fifteen and a half million men and women were killed. On August 6, 1945, when the first atomic bomb exploded over Hiroshima, 50,000 people were killed outright, and later the fatalities rose close to 100,000.

On the other hand, in the territorial state of Nazi Germany, about six million people were exterminated in an operation which cannot even be described as civil war but only as the police action of a sovereign state against its own citizens.

[18] Quincy Wright, *A Study of War* (Chicago: University of Chicago Press, 1942), part I, p. 651.

In the 1930's, during the forcible collectivization drive in the Soviet Union, about five million people perished.

The parallel between fifteen million killed during an international war, and eleven million dead within two nations in a period of international peace demonstrates our point. It shows that extreme violence, inhuman treatment of prisoners, and other uncivilized behavior is not limited to conflicts among nations but may occur within what could be considered a well integrated community.

Governments—Main Actors on the International Scene

As the preceding analysis has shown, the territorial state is the largest community which may be viewed as an active unit. "The modern nation," says Reinhold Niebuhr,[19] "is the human group of strongest social cohesion, of most undisputed central authority, and of most clearly defined membership."

This remains so in spite of many warnings to the effect that nationalism and nation-states are not in tune with the realities and rhythms of the present age.

In the study of international relations we are still primarily (but not exclusively) concerned with the thoughts, decisions, and actions of those who qualify as spokesmen of their national communities. Governments acting on behalf of their nations, whether responsive or not to their will, are the main actors on the international scene.

Their thoughts, decisions, and actions are the result of many factors: their own intellectual capabilities, experience, knowledge, and skills; the quality of the political group which supports them and is led by them; the public at large, which may manifest its opinions and preferences through public debate, free press, or pressure on legislators. Finally, decisions and actions of a government are also the result of friendly or unfriendly pressures exercised by other governments, rival, allied, or neutral.

Besides these obvious influences on governmental policies, three additional sources of pressure deserve special note:

1. *Nonsovereign entities,* such as national minorities, colonies, protectorates, trust territories, or temporarily occupied territories. Some such units may have recently lost sovereign status and may try to regain it. Others have a developed national consciousness and strive for independent statehood. They may appear on the international scene as important elements, especially if their actions and claims are sponsored by powerful nations. Occupied and divided Germany after the war, and French Algeria are examples.

2. *Political and pressure groups* which do not participate in government but either support or oppose it in a parliamentary or revolutionary fashion. Such groups often engage in international activities independently of national foreign policies. They establish their own contacts and form their own international groupings: federations of Socialist, Christian Democratic, or Com-

[19] Reinhold Niebuhr, *Moral Man and Immoral Society* (New York: Charles Scribner's Sons, 1932), p. 83.

munist parties (Internationals); federations of trade unions, cooperatives, business associations, chambers of commerce, women's clubs, youth groups, professional associations, etc. Churches are usually international in both their outlook and contacts.

These international groupings of nongovernmental bodies do not represent, in reality, a marked departure from the national divisions of our society. They usually agree on a common program or plan of action to be implemented by pressures on their respective *national* governments.

It should be further added that profound differences and extreme tensions may often exist between different concepts of internationalism as proclaimed by these "Internationals." The violence of feelings which frequently exists among nations is sometimes surpassed by the enmity which divides, for example, the Marxist internationalists from their liberal or Christian opponents, the Catholics from the Protestants, the Socialist International from the Comintern, etc.

This enmity between different kinds of internationalism certainly has a limiting effect on hopes that nongovernmental international groupings may sneak up on nationalism, eventually replace it, and become a basis for a world community.

On the contrary, we often see that international groups are used and misused by national governments to further their particular national aims. One international federation of trade unions (WFTU—World Federation of Trade Unions) is oriented to support Soviet political aims, while another one (ICFTU—International Confederation of Free Trade Unions) serves the opposite policies. The Communist International, founded by Lenin after World War I, proved to be an agency of the Soviet state. Under the guise of proletarian internationalism, it was to promote the interests of the world base of Communism, that of the U.S.S.R.

The United Nations charter attempts to associate the nongovernmental international groupings with its work. Article 71 states:

> The Economic and Social Council may make suitable arrangements for consultation with nongovernmental organizations which are concerned with matters within its competence. Such arrangements may be made with international organizations and, where appropriate, with national organizations after consultation with the Member of the United Nations concerned.

Such arrangements were made with several nongovernmental organizations such as the International Chamber of Commerce, International Federation of Agricultural Producers, World Veteran Association, International Organization of Employers, International Parliamentary Union, International Cooperative Alliance, International Federation of Christian Trade Unions, and many others including the two other differently oriented trade union federations. On the whole, it may be said that "the hopes at San Francisco that nongovernmental organizations might become a kind of Second Estate of the U.N. have been largely quenched by the experience of the last nine years." [20]

[20] Robert E. Asher, Walter M. Kotschnig, and William A. Brown, Jr., *The United Nations and Economic and Social Cooperation* (Washington, D. C.: Brookings Institution, 1957), p. 516.

Although many of the international groupings have more members and greater financial resources than many nation-states, nationalism and the resulting loyalty to one's government keep the national governments in the leading roles both within the United Nations and on the international scene in general.

3. *Influential individuals* whose views, information, and opinion on international politics have influence on their environment. Anyone—a student, a teacher, or a civic leader—discussing international politics participates to some extent in the creation of pressures on national government, and thus becomes an indirect participant in international politics.

This is even more so in the case of very influential individuals, whose opinions and views are read or listened to with some respect. By their writings, speeches, crusades, and programs, philosophers, scientists, scholars, journalists, radio commentators, professors, preachers, and reformers may influence leaders or inspire movements or activities in support of their causes. (These may be disarmament, world government, stopping atomic tests, recognition of Communist China, etc.) In this way they indirectly influence the policies of national governments.

Many individual crusaders adopt a nonnational attitude and claim to speak on behalf of humanity rather than its national components. They are at a disadvantage against those who, advancing their causes, rely on the nationalistic feelings of their audience. There are three main factors which limit the success of the nonnational appeal:

1. As opposed to spokesmen on behalf of humanity, the spokesmen on behalf of nations are usually equipped with an impressive array of economic means, military power, and mass communication media including the existing educational system. The methods of competition favor the nationalist crusaders.

2. The words of national spokesmen are supported by a great majority of citizens or subjects, who identify their individual interests with the interests of their immediate environment rather than with such a distant and abstract concept as humanity.

3. The opposition to a national concept in the name of a nonnational one (humanity, for example) may represent an unwitting support of a rival national interest. Humanity may not be served by it at all. If nation A seriously considers unilateral atomic disarmament in order to serve humanity, it may greatly facilitate atomic blackmail on the part of nation B.

The sincerity and effect of such individual or group crusades for the sake of humanity should not be underestimated, especially in our age. But one should avoid confusing the true and rare interpreters of human brotherhood with those leaders or groups who proclaim that the interest of humanity is best served by the promotion of their national standards and ideologies. The formula usually is: "What's good for Americans (or Russians) is good for the rest of the world." This may be the case. But often it is not.

Summary

Three main features characterize the world in the second half of the twentieth century:

1. Mankind remains divided into roughly ninety-five to one hundred closed compartments of *different* sizes, ways of life, and aspirations. They are called territorial states, and are considered as units of strongest social cohesion, the most undisputed central authority, and the most clearly defined membership.

Authorized spokesmen of these states are governments. In international politics we are primarily concerned with their decisions and actions. Yet, we recognize that their decision-making process is the sum of manifold pressures emanating from other states as well as nongovernmental sources.

2. Nationalism remains the most dynamic force in the world today. It is partly the result and partly the cause of the present division of the world into territorial states. Religious, economic, and ideological interests, and even fears transcending national boundaries, have so far proved weaker than the emotional identification of individuals with the past, the present, and the future of their national communities.

3. The third feature stands in contradiction to the preceding two: it is a growing awareness of the economic, cultural, and physical interdependence of mankind in our age of advanced technology, mass production and communication, and hydrogen weapons.

Yet, none of the existing international or supranational groupings have been conceived as a stepping stone to a world state. They are either regional or ideological and usually aim at increasing their power against other regions or ideological alliances.

TOPIC I

Is Nationalism Constructive
or Destructive?

"There is no agreement as to precisely what nationalism is or as to whether it is good or bad, transitory or eternal," wrote Carlton J. H. Hayes, one of the foremost American authorities on nationalism, in 1926.

The disagreement continues on the following pages. Yet there seems to be one common conclusion: whether good or bad, transitory or eternal, nationalism is still the most potent force extant today. Nationalism splits mankind into nations. Paradoxically, this is the one powerful creed which humanity has in common.

►WHAT IS A NATION?

ERNEST RENAN

Geography, race, religion, language, and economic interests determine the
consciousness of nationality in some but not all cases. Rather than any of
these factors, it is the common heritage and determination to continue living
together which make a nation. This is the thesis of the classic lecture which
the famous French historian Ernest Renan (1823-1892) delivered at the
Sorbonne University in Paris on March 11, 1882. The conclusion is repro-
duced below.

A nation is a soul, a spiritual principle. Two things, which are really
only one, go to make up this soul or spiritual principle. One of these things
lies in the past, the other in the present. The one is the possession in common
of a rich heritage of memories; and the other is actual agreement, the desire
to live together, and the will to continue to make the most of the joint inheritance. . . . To share the glories of the past, and a common will in the
present; to have done great deeds together, and to desire to do more—these
are the essential conditions of a people's being. . . . The Spartan song "We
are what ye were, and we shall be what ye are," is, in its simplicity, the
abridged version of every national anthem.

In the past, a heritage of glory and of grief to be shared; in the future,
one common plan to be realized; to have suffered, rejoiced and hoped together; these are things of greater value than identity of custom-houses and
frontiers in accordance with strategic notions. These are things which are
understood, in spite of differences in race and language. I said just now "to
have suffered together," for indeed common suffering unites more strongly
than common rejoicing. Among national memories, sorrows have greater
value than victories; for they impose duties and demand common effort. Thus
we see that a nation is a great solid unit, formed by the realization of sacrifices in the past, as well as of those one is prepared to make in the future.
A nation implies a past; while, as regards the present, it is all contained in
one tangible fact, viz., the agreement and clearly expressed desire to continue
a life in common. The existence of a nation is (if you will forgive me the
metaphor) a daily plebiscite, just as that of the individual is a continual
affirmation of life. . . .

We have excluded from politics the abstract principles of metaphysics
and theology; and what remains? There remains man, with his desires and
his needs. But you will tell me that the consequences of a system that puts
these ancient fabrics at the mercy of the wishes of usually unenlightened
minds, will be the secession and ultimate disintegration of nations. . . .
Human wishes change indeed: but what in this world does not? Nations are
not eternal. They have had beginnings and will have ends; and will probably

Translation from *Modern Political Doctrines,* edited by Sir Alfred Zimmern (Oxford:
The Clarendon Press, 1939).

be replaced by a confederation of Europe. But such is not the law of the age in which we live. Nowadays it is a good, and even a necessary, thing that nations should exist. Their existence is the guarantee of liberty, which would be lost, if the world had but one law and one master.

►HEBREW AND GREEK ROOTS OF MODERN NATIONALISM

HANS KOHN

Modern nationalism is characterized by the demand that each nationality should establish its own territorial state and that the state should include the whole nationality. The three significant traits of modern nationalism and the clashes between nationalist exclusiveness and international universalism are examined by Hans Kohn, Professor of History at the City College of New York. He has written several books on nationalism, among them The Idea of Nationalism, The Twentieth Century, *and* Nationalism and Liberty.

The twentieth century is the first period in history, in which the whole of mankind has accepted one and the same political attitude, that of nationalism. . . .

Nationalism has become the determining political and cultural force among all the races and civilizations on earth. Though thus establishing a common world-wide element, nationalism is a deeply divisive force, if it is not tempered by the liberal spirit of tolerance and compromise or the humanitarian universalism of a non-political religion. Its stress upon national sovereignty and cultural distinctiveness hardly helps to promote cooperation among peoples at the very time when for technological and economic reasons they grow more and more interdependent.

Nationalism is a state of mind, in which the supreme loyalty of the individual is felt to be due the nation-state. A deep attachment to one's native soil, to local traditions and to established territorial authority has existed in varying strength throughout history. But it was not until the end of the eighteenth century that nationalism in the modern sense of the word became a generally recognized sentiment increasingly molding all public and private life. Only very recently has it been demanded that each nationality should form a state, its own state, and that the state should include the whole nationality. Formerly, man's loyalty was due not to the nation-state, but to differing other forms of social authority, political organization and ideological cohesion such as the tribe or clan, the city-state or the feudal lord, the dynastic state, the church or religious group. Throughout many centuries the political ideal was not the nation-state but the, at least, theoretically world-wide empire

The selection is from *Nationalism, Its Meaning and History* (Princeton, N. J.: D. Van Nostrand Co., Inc., copyright 1955).

comprising various nationalities and ethnic groups on the basis of a common civilization and for the assurance of a common peace.

Nationalities are the products of the living forces of history, and therefore fluctuating and never rigid. They are groups of the utmost complexity and defy exact definition. Most of them possess certain objective factors distinguishing them from other nationalities like common descent, language, territory, political entity, customs and traditions, or religion. But it is clear that none of these factors is essential to the existence or definition of nationality. . . . Although objective factors are of great importance for the formation of nationalities, the most essential element is a living and active corporate will. It is this will which we call nationalism, a state of mind inspiring the large majority of a people and claiming to inspire all its members. It asserts that the nation-state is the ideal and the only legitimate form of political organization and that the nationality is the source of all cultural creative energy and of economic well-being.

The Modernity of Nationalism

Even before the age of nationalism, we find individuals who profess sentiments akin to nationalism. But these sentiments are confined to individuals. The masses never feel their own life—culturally, politically, or economically—to depend upon the fate of the national body. Danger from the outside may arouse a passing feeling of national cohesion, as it happened in Greece during the Persian Wars or in France in the Hundred Years War. But as a rule, wars before the French Revolution did not arouse deep national emotions. In the Peloponnesian War Greeks bitterly fought Greeks. In religious and dynastic wars of early modern times, Germans fought against Germans, and Italians against Italians, without any realization of the "fratricidal" nature of the act. Even as late as the eighteenth century, soldiers and civilians in Europe entered the service of "foreign" rulers and served them often with a loyalty and faithfulness which proved the absence of any national sentiment.

Nor was nationality regarded as a source of cultural life until very recently. Education and learning, the formation of man's mind and character, were throughout most of history not determined by any national limits. Religion was regarded in many ages as the fountainhead of all cultural and spiritual life. During and after the Renaissance, education in Europe everywhere was rooted in the common tradition of classical civilization. The ideals of knighthood in Medieval Europe or the model of the French court in the seventeenth and eighteenth centuries spread beyond all national boundaries. Only in nineteenth century Europe and America and in twentieth century Asia and Africa have the people identified themselves with the nation, civilization with national civilization, their life and survival with the life and survival of the nationality. From this time on nationalism has dominated the impulses and attitudes of the masses, and at the same time served as the justification for the authority of the state and the legitimation of its use of force, both against its own citizens and against other states.

Ancient Hebrews and Greeks

In spite of its modernity some fundamental traits of nationalism were developed long ago. The roots of nationalism spring from the same soil as Western civilization, from the ancient Hebrews and the ancient Greeks. Both peoples had a clearly defined consciousness of being different from all other peoples: the Hebrews from the Gentiles, the Greeks from the Barbarians. The bearer of group consciousness was with them not king or priesthood but the people as a whole, every Hebrew or every Greek. With the other peoples of antiquity, only rulers and empires left their traces on history. With the Hebrews and the Greeks it was the national character and the spiritual creative energy of the people which endured. It is because their cultural continuity proved stronger than racial, political, or geographic continuity, that they live on today. The idea of the nation-state was unknown to them but they had the strong consciousness of a cultural mission.

Three essential traits of modern nationalism originated with the Hebrews: the idea of the chosen people, the emphasis on a common stock of memory of the past and of hopes for the future, and finally national messianism. At the beginning of Hebrew history stands the Covenant concluded between God and His people. From the time of the prophets on, the Hebrews envisaged the whole of history as a unified process, as a continuity from one source to one goal, with a special distinctive role for the Hebrews at its center. In the kingdom of God the drama of universal history was to find its atoning conclusion and the idea of the Covenant its fulfillment. Messianism became a philosophy of history justifying the ways of God to suffering man. Not only oppressed nationalities took refuge in the hope of a messianic mission; at other times it became a symbol of national pride and an often dangerous call to greatness and overreaching power; it expressed also the struggle of heretical sects and oppressed classes for the realization of their dreams and aspirations, and as the secular idea of historical progress it still retains today some of its religious fervor.

►FIVE TYPES OF NATIONALISM

CARLTON J. H. HAYES

Nationalism may be consonant with humanitarian aims or it may be their negation. Nationalism is either beneficial or evil, according to the circumstances and historical eras.

Carlton J. H. Hayes is Professor Emeritus of History at Columbia University and author of several authoritative books on nationalism.

1. Humanitarian Nationalism

In the eighteenth century, rather suddenly, emerged a philosophy of nationalism. It emerged in the midst of dynastic and colonial wars and of the

From *The Historical Evolution of Modern Nationalism,* copyright, 1931, by Carlton J. H. Hayes. Used with permission of The Macmillan Company.

popular unrest occasioned by them. It emerged also in the midst of the curious intellectual developments that were equally characteristic of that century. It promised a way of escape from the crazy evils of the time to a logical millennium of the near future, and faith in just such a millennium was a marked trait of eighteenth-century thought.

The eighteenth century was *par excellence* the century of "serious thinkers." It was the century when every person who thought at all thought himself an intellectual and termed himself "enlightened." "Enlightenment" was conceived of, indeed, as the goal of all human effort. Monarchs, the despots of the age, were "enlightened." Philosophers were "enlightened." Professors, preachers, and priests, even business men and gentlemen farmers, were "enlightened."

Eighteenth-century "enlightenment" was a fourfold concept. First, it involved the substitution of the natural for the supernatural, of science for theology, and the assumption that the whole universe of matter and mind is guided and controlled by ineluctable *natural law*. Secondly, it exalted and almost deified human *reason,* which could and should be utilized by the individual to discover the laws of nature and to enable him to conform his life to them. Thirdly, assuming that man would use his reason and obey the natural law, it promised the *progress* and perfectibility of the human race. Fourthly, it included a tender regard for the natural rights of the individual and a predilection for the social blessings of an enlightened *humanitarianism.* . . .

In the name of humanity and with the zeal of humanitarians, the "enlightened" set in motion a multitude of reform movements. There was a movement to reform the laws. There was a movement to reform the prisons. There were movements against slavery, against serfdom, and against intolerance. All the reforms, it was argued, were demanded by reason and rendered feasible by progress.

It was in this intellectual milieu of the eighteenth century that the first systematic doctrines of nationalism were expounded, and though they differed from each other in certain details, as their several authors were differently circumstanced, they all were infused with the spirit of the Enlightenment. They were based on natural law. They were evolved by more or less pure reason. They were presented as inevitable and therefore desirable steps in human progress. In object they were strictly humanitarian. They were urged, in truth, with motives so obviously humanitarian—with so kindly an eye to the well-being of the whole human race, with so touching a regard for the rights of other nationalities, and with so resentful an attitude toward jingoism and intolerance—that they may justly be described as variant specimens of a single humanitarian nationalism. . . .

National self-determination was a natural corollary alike to the doctrine of nationalism and to that of democracy. Both involved the recognition of the right of individuals in any region to determine not only under what government they would live but also to what state they would belong. If the people in a particular region, hitherto not a part of France, wished to be French, their wishes should be respected, regardless of what Grotius or any other exponent of the earlier internationalism had said. The wishes of the people of such a region could easily be ascertained by letting them vote, or, as the French revolutionaries styled it, by holding a plebiscite. Thus, when the inhabitants of the papal districts of Avignon and Venaissin voted by majority vote in July, 1791 that they wished to join France and become members of the French nationality, the French Government, despite the protests of the pope, acceded to their wishes and incorporated them in the Fatherland, contending that it was thereby safeguarding the natural rights of human beings against the artificial "rights" of a despot. Similar plebiscites were held in Savoy in 1792 and at Nice in 1793, with results somewhat disadvantageous to their former suzerain, a lay despot, but highly favorable to France and the principle of national self-determination.

Foreign peoples did not have to join France. But in the interests of humanity they should exercise the right of national self-determination. They should destroy tyrants and freely choose to live under a government of their own making which would guarantee them the blessings of liberty, equality, and fraternity. Only thereby could international peace and universal brotherhood be secured. . . .

Eventually, in April 1792, France went to war with Austria. But in the minds of the French revolutionaries it was a new kind of war. It was a war to make the world safe for democracy and nationalism. It was a war, not between dynasts or between peoples, but between despots and nationalities. It was a war, not for material gain, but for the welfare of humanity. Accompanying the formal declaration of hostilities was this remarkable proclamation: "The National Assembly proclaims that . . . the war which it is forced to prosecute is not a war of nation against nation, but the just defense of a free people against the unjust aggression of a king; . . . that it adopts in advance all foreigners who, abjuring the cause of its enemies, shall range themselves under its banners and consecrate their efforts to the defense of liberty, and it will promote by all means in its power their settlement in France. . . ."

In December of the same year, with the tide of battle turning in favor of France and with the revolutionaries thoroughly committed to the democracy and nationalism of Jean Jacques Rousseau and ready to decapitate their own late despot—Louis XVI, now "Citizen Capet"—the National Convention of the Republic stated the case in a more threatening manner; but from the French viewpoint it was still an humanitarian case. "The French nation declares that it will treat as enemies every people who, refusing liberty and equality or renouncing them, may wish to maintain, recall, or treat with the prince and the privileged classes; on the other hand, it engages not to subscribe to any treaty and not to lay down its arms until the sovereignty and independence of the people whose territory the troops of the Republic shall have entered shall be established, and until the people shall have adopted the principles of equality and founded a free and democratic government." Apparently other nationalities were to be free to exercise the right of self-determination, if they exercised it in accordance with French models, but not otherwise. To the French, the dictate still appeared to be at the behest of humanity and in its interests. But to many foreigners at the beginning of 1793 it seemed to be less in the cause of humanity than in that of fanatical French nationalism. . . .

Humanitarian nationalism was undergoing a seasonal alteration. As the eighteenth century neared its end, new robes of thought became fashionable, and among the outmoded clothing was the gossamer cloak of humanitarianism. This cloak nationalism laid temporarily aside. But nationalism, thus nakedly exposed, was not a single thing; it was aristocratic and democratic and neither. Each thing which it was, proceeded promptly to don a new dress. Democratic nationalism became "Jacobin"; aristocratic nationalism became "traditional"; nationalism which was neither democratic nor aristocratic became "liberal." Each of the new entities claimed to be the chief if not the sole heir to humanitarian nationalism, and each on occasion admired and boasted of the beautiful old cloak that had been laid aside. . . .

To the successors and in a sense the carriers of humanitarian nationalism we may now turn our attention. First and foremost, at the close of the eighteenth century, is the complex of doctrines and practices which may conveniently be labelled Jacobin nationalism.

2. Jacobin Nationalism

"Jacobin" was originally the name of a Parisian monastery. When, during the French Revolution, one of the clubs which members of the National Constituent Assembly formed for social purposes, the Breton Club,[1] appropriated the hall of the monastery for its own meetings and headquarters, "Jacobin" became the popular designation of the Club itself. This Club speedily gained great and wide influence. It admitted members who were not members of the National Assembly; it held formal meetings and discussions to which the general public was admitted; it established some twelve hundred branches throughout the country and conducted a regular correspondence with them. Its power increased, until it became actually greater than that of the National Assembly. When the National Assembly finally adjourned in September, 1791, the election of the Legislative Assembly was accomplished mainly under the guidance of the Jacobin Club. Many of the stirring events which followed in swift succession were determined by the voice of Jacobins, whose deliberations were regarded by the Parisian masses with more interest than those of the Legislative Assembly. The Club reached the zenith of its power when the National Convention met in September 1792 and proclaimed France a Republic. The agitation for the death of the ex-king, the storm which destroyed the Girondist Party, the excitement of the lowest classes against the bourgeoisie, and the inauguration of the Reign of Terror over all France, were largely the work of the Jacobins. . . .

Jacobin nationalism, as it developed in the midst of foreign war and domestic rebellion, acquired four characteristics. In the first place, it became

[1] This was the original name of the Club. Subsequently, its official name was changed to "The Society of Friends of the Constitution."

suspicious and quite intolerant of internal dissent. It labored to root out and destroy any faction which appeared to be lacking in supreme loyalty not only to France in general but also to the particular France of Jacobin dreams— France, one and indivisible, democratic and republican, egalitarian and secular. It perceived a dangerous enemy in every person or tendency that might realize for France any other kind of dream. It fought regionalism and "federalism" and every tendency toward provincial autonomy and away from the disciplined centralization of the state. It clamored against royalists and feudalists, guilds and classes, kings and aristocrats, priests and monks, against anyone who might mislead the "people" and restore "privilege." Its pro-gramme was nicely summarized by Barère:[2] "Liberty and equality—these are our rights; unity and indivisibility—these are our maxims; the constitution and the laws—these are our blessings; the destruction of La Vendée, the punishment of traitors, the extirpation of royalism—these are our needs; the prompt reunion and use of all our forces against common enemies—these are our sacred duties." With the Jacobins, the needs and duties bulked larger than the rights. Their nationalism created and throve in an atmosphere of suspicion; and for lapses, real or fancied, from a rigorous orthodoxy they invented and utilized the guillotine. The Terror was their work, and in their excess of suspicion and intolerance they slew not only "reactionaries" but groups of their own kind—Girondists, Dantonists, Hébertists, Robespierrists.

Secondly, Jacobin nationalism, to attain its ends, relied eventually on force and militarism. Against domestic dissenters, compulsion and violence were employed. Against foreign foes, all the resources of a new military spirit and machine were set in motion. . . .

Thirdly, Jacobin nationalism became fanatically religious. Into the pure reason of the "Enlightenment" it infused the thrilling emotion of a novel and romantic religious experience. The symbols and ceremonies which it evolved —the national flag, the national anthem, the national holidays, the national shrines, the liberty caps, the altars to *la Patrie,* the graven tablets of the national law, the republican baptisms and funerals, the solemn parades and eulogies, the inscriptions of *Mort pour la Patrie*—were touching manifesta-tions of the new religion of nationalism which the Jacobins substituted for the older Catholic faith. . . .

Fourthly, Jacobin nationalism was characterized by missionary zeal. Little of the earlier humanitarian nationalism had been zealously or fiercely missionary. But the nationalism of the Jacobins was different. It was more religious than rational, and what religion does not require proselytes? It was political as well as cultural, and it appropriately produced political instru-ments. It was democratic and republican, and, as has been said, highly intol-erant; and its apostles quite naturally felt the need and the urge to employ every conceivable means to secure popular conformity. Abroad, its missionary zeal was evidenced by its armies and its wars. At home, it was displayed in

[2] Bertrand Barère (1755-1841), President of the National Convention when the sentence was passed upon Louis XVI. He declared then that "the tree of liberty could not grow unless it were watered with the blood of kings."

the creation and functioning of numerous novel agencies of nationalist propaganda. It is these agencies which peculiarly distinguish Jacobin from humanitarian nationalism. . . .

A new type of army was created by the Jacobins and utilized for nationalist ends. For several centuries previously, the usual European army had comprised professional soldiers, led by aristocratic commanders and loyal to a monarch. Such had been the nature of the French army on the eve of the Revolution. . . . Later, under Jacobin influence and in face of foreign war, the revolutionaries set forth a new ideal and established a new practice. The ideal, in Barère's words, was that "in France the soldier is a citizen, and the citizen a soldier." It was the new modern ideal of "the nation in arms."

In July 1792, under the inspiring leadership of Carnot, the country was proclaimed "in danger"; all citizens capable of bearing arms were put "in a state of permanent activity"; every citizen, under pain of imprisonment, had to declare to republican officials his arms and ammunition; and the government might requisition any material or supplies for "national defense." In August 1793 was introduced a systematic and unsparing conscription—the most remarkable event that is recorded in the history of armies,—and within a few months the French Republic had a national army of 1,200,000 men, five times as many as Louis XIV, at the height of his power, had been able to enlist in his royal army. In 1798 conscription, hitherto regarded as an emergency-measure, was formally adopted as a permanent national policy. It was enacted that every able-bodied young Frenchman was liable to conscripted military service for five years. It was a notable triumph for Jacobin nationalism. It took the French peasants who, only a few years earlier, used to hide in caves or forests like escaped slaves, and made soldiers of them. These same peasant-soldiers, as the event proved, were not to lay down their arms until they had conquered Europe.

The new conscript armies of France were nationalist. They could not have been formed, the rank and file would not have submitted to them, if nationalist sentiment had not been widespread in the land, and especially if there had not been a popular fear of what the triumph of the enemy might mean to the country and its citizens. The enthusiasm with which volunteers and conscripts rallied to the national colors is well attested and indicates clearly the driving force of nationalist emotion in the masses. But this emotion was intensified and molded by the Jacobins, who perceived in the new militarism not only the indispensable means of removing the foreign menace but also a most effective agency for propagating their own nationalist principles within France. The Jacobins did not stop with the creation of a citizen army and with equipping and sending it for battle against the enemy. They identified civil with military patriotism; they labored for an intimate union between the army and the republic, between the army and the nation. By inducting recruits into military service with solemn rites and patriotic orations, they fired them with initial zeal. By mingling conscripts from widely separated regions in common service under the national tricolor and marching them to the stirring strains of the national *Marseillaise,* they impressed upon them the unity and indivisibility and the spiritual mission of the national state. . . .

The armies of the French Republic were infused with Jacobin nationalism, and they also became its special missionaries, both abroad and at home. At home they put down insurrection and suppressed dissent. Abroad they caused kings to tremble and aristocrats to despair. . . .

The "nation in arms" was one Jacobin concept of great significance for nationalist propaganda. The "nation in public schools" was another. Previous to the French Revolution, it had long and generally been held that children belonged to their parents and that it was for parents to determine what schooling, if any, their children should have. . . . For centuries, in almost every country of Europe, education had been private and voluntary; it had been conducted by the church rather than by the state; it had been a privilege for some rather than a right of all; it had been directed toward the classics and Christian piety rather than toward the vernaculars and national patriotism. . . .

The Jacobins talked much about the need for the new education, and they actually suppressed the old by dissolving the religious teaching orders and closing the church schools. They envisaged a system in which all French children would be obliged to attend state-supported and state-controlled schools, where they would be thoroughly grounded in the national language and revolutionary doctrines, in devotion to the republic and the fatherland. . . .

"The principles that ought to guide parents [Bertrand Barère declared in 1793] are that children belong to the general family, to the republic, before they belong to particular families. . . . The spirit of private families must disappear when the great family calls. The republic leaves to parents the guidance of your first years, but as soon as your intelligence forms itself the republic proudly claims the rights it holds over you. You are born for the republic and not for the pride or the despotism of families."

The revolutionaries were clear as to the value and need of the new education for nationalist propaganda, but circumstances prevented them from devoting to it the attention and funds which they devoted to the new militarism. It remained for Napoleon—a Jacobin himself, in his own fashion—to take the first important steps toward the actual establishment of a complete system of national schools. Since his time, the almost universal adoption of the institutions of the new education and their utilization for patriotic purposes have been an outstanding productive legacy of Jacobin nationalism.

If the original Jacobins were sluggish in translating all their theories of education into action, they were prompt to recognize the significance of language as the basis of nationality and to try to compel all inhabitants of France to use the French language. They contended that successful rule by "the people" and united action by the nation were dependent, not only on a certain uniformity of habits and customs, but even more on an identity of ideas and ideals which could be effected by speeches, the printing press, and other instruments of education, provided that these employed one and the same language. Confronted with the historic fact that France was not a linguistic unit—that, in addition to widely variant dialects in different parts of the country, "foreign" languages were spoken in the west by Bretons, in the south by Provençals, Basques, and Corsicans, in the north by Flemings, and in the northeast by Alsatian Germans—they resolved to stamp out the dialects and the foreign languages and to force every French citizen to know and employ the French language. Otherwise, they argued, it was idle to carry on national propaganda among people who could not read even the Declaration of the Rights of Man and who constituted a danger to the republic because they could not appreciate the necessity for acting with it. The French Jacobins were the first, but by no means the last, who have sought systematically to destroy linguistic minorities in a country and to exalt and expand a dominant nationality by forcing its language upon all the citizens of a state. . . .

The rise of Jacobin nationalism synchronized with the rise of a new type of journalism—the sheet of news and editorial comment which was written in popular and sensational style, printed rapidly, sold cheaply, and read widely. Many of the Jacobin leaders were founders and editors of just such sheets, and the Jacobins in general believed ardently that if "the people" were to be democratic and patriotic, they must be provided with daily information and opinion and incitement. In theory, the Jacobins asserted the absolute freedom of the press; every citizen had the "natural right" to publish or read whatever he would, and logically this might cover a journalism that was pacifist and even anti-patriotic. In fact, however, the Jacobins were quick to paralyze the hands, by cutting off the heads, of such journalists as "misled" the people; and the new journalism became a most effective agency for the propagation of Jacobin nationalism.

It was likewise in respect of a new type of voluntary association which now appeared—the semi-private, semi-public propagandist society. Here, too, the Jacobins paid much lip-service to the freedom of association as a "natural right" of all men, but they actually forbade associations of workingmen and persecuted associations of clergymen, while fostering and lauding associations of patriots. The revolutionary clubs—the Jacobin, the Cordelier, and others— were the earliest examples of a kind of propagandist organization which is nowadays commonplace, the organization of private citizens in order to influence the opinion and activity of the government and the general public and employing as means to its end a national headquarters, branch societies, and more or less professional speakers, pamphleteers, and lobbyists. Such organizations exist today for very many different purposes, but their original prototype was militantly patriotic; it was at once a product and a propagator of Jacobin nationalism.

The new militarism, the new schooling, the new journalism, the new patriotic societies: these were intended, or at any rate served, to quicken the consciousness of common nationality among Frenchmen and to inspire them with supreme devotion to a nationalism which was democratic and republican, secular and egalitarian. But perhaps the agency by which the Jacobins set chief store was that of nationalist ritual. . . .

Under Jacobin auspices, the citizens were enabled almost constantly to see the "glorious tricolor," to hear the *Marseillaise,* that "religious invocation," to smell and taste the gunpowder which was fired at solemn celebrations of national victory, and to touch the relics of civilian or military heroes. National fêtes were frequently celebrated at Paris and in the provinces. Altars and temples were dedicated to *la Patrie.* Sculpture, painting, and all the other arts were pressed into the service of nationalist propaganda. . . .

"How are you to know a Republican?" asked Barère. You will know him when he speaks of *"la Patrie* with a religious sentiment" and of "the majesty of the people with religious devotion." The Jacobin faith in the mystic power of words and formulas, ritual and symbols, was at bottom religious, and its exercise contributed immeasurably to the promotion and intensification of nationalism.

The Jacobins rendered their nationalism much more exclusive and paramount than had been that nationalism which earlier Humanitarians had extolled. Perhaps it was because the Jacobins were essentially religious. Perhaps it was because they were fiercely democratic. Perhaps it was because they had to deal practically with conditions of war and terror which had not been foreseen in the theorizing of their "enlightened" predecessors. The fact remains, whatever its explanation may be, that to the Jacobins "the people" has become "the nation," a mystical entity, an absolute sovereign, a Moloch not only of classes but of individuals. . . .

It conscripts youth for war or for schools and abrogates the historic rights of the father and the family. It can seize everything and destroy anything, for above it there is no law. The will of the nation is God. It feels itself immense and irresistible. It has a horror of divisions, schisms, minorities. It labors for unity, uniformity, concentration. It proudly proclaims personal liberty and boldly abridges particular liberties which appear to be at variance with national interests. Its vaunted liberty, in last analysis, is not for the individual but for the national state. The nation may do whatever it will; the individual may do only what the national state determines. Above all, the individual owes supreme loyalty and the devoutest worship to *la Patrie,* the *Great Mother.* . . .

None can seriously question the idealism of the revolutionary Jacobins. Nor should one belittle their very real and very great achievements, which have profoundly influenced our modern world and have made it in many respects a better and more comfortable place for human habitation and development. One should recognize, too, that the "excesses" of the Jacobins—the Terror, the intolerance, the bloodshed—were the outgrowth not exclusively of their own fanaticism but of the fanaticism of their opponents at home and abroad. They themselves performed their labors in the midst of a fiery furnace of foreign war and domestic revolt. Their labors would doubtless have been somewhat different, and the nationalism associated with their name would have been of another hue, if no foreign monarchs and no French aristocrats had taken arms against them. It is one of the ironies of history that the most "excessive" Jacobins, both Robespierre and Marat, opposed vigorously the declaration of war by France in 1792 against Austria. They held that war was "the last refuge of scoundrels" and that it would increase the misery of the French people. Robespierre prophesied that it would produce in France a dictator who would destroy liberty.

The tragedy of the Jacobins was that they were idealists, fanatically so, in a wicked world. They instituted or confirmed a host of reforms which they knew to be good, not only for themselves, but for everyone, but which large sections of the world promptly reacted against as being very bad. In the circumstances Jacobin Frenchmen fought and killed, altruistically and enthusiastically. But the more they fought, the more nationalist they grew. Embarking upon the Great War of 1792 in order to make the world safe for liberty, equality, and the right of national self-determination, it was not long before they were waging it primarily for the greater glory of France. Gradually under the influence of war, especially of unprecedented military victories, their attitude toward other peoples underwent a change. Increasingly they tended to dislike and to hate not only tyrannical monarchs and reactionary governments but peoples who failed to rise against their rulers and make common cause with the French Revolution. This led the Jacobins to vindictiveness against foreigners, to pride in and ambition for their own nation, to conquest, and eventually to a new imperialism. It was all gradual and almost imperceptible. Yet by 1797 the French Republic of Jacobin nationalists had incorporated Belgium (with the sanction of a partisan plebiscite) and the German Rhineland (without even the pretense of a plebiscite) and had surrounded itself with a string of vassal states in Holland, Switzerland, and Italy.

The evolution of Jacobin nationalism rendered possible and perhaps inevitable the evolution of the new Jacobin militarism. This militarism became associated with imperialism and afforded the opportunity for the rise of a military dictator. Napoleon Bonaparte fulfilled the prophecy of Maximilien Robespierre. Bonaparte proudly boasted that he was "the son and heir of the Revolution," and, though an Italian by birth and mother-tongue, his heirloom from the Revolution was French nationalism. . . .

Bonaparte based his influence at home and his real strength abroad on Jacobin nationalism. . . . All the agencies of nationalist propaganda which the Jacobins had invented, Bonaparte employed to the full. He was strong for nationalist ritual. His legions flew the revolutionary national flag and his bands played the revolutionary national anthem. He built national monuments, celebrated national fêtes, and made the patriotic gesture appropriate to national triumph or national bereavement. No revolutionary Jacobin surpassed Napoleon Bonaparte in effectiveness of patriotic oratory.

Bonaparte took from the Jacobins, also, the idea of "the nation in arms" and made it the cornerstone of his brilliant military career. He took from them, too, the idea of "the nation in public schools" and largely realized it. The importance of the cheap popular press he understood even better than they. He forced it to be unswervingly nationalist and he consciously employed it to stimulate national morale. No French newspaper even mentioned the defeat at Trafalgar so long as Bonaparte was in power, and he hired our old friend Barère to indite journalistic philippics against the English. . . .

It has been argued by recent apologists, who deem Jacobinism fundamentally pacific rather than bellicose, that nationalism under Napoleon was
but a caricature of the original Jacobin nationalism. They may be right. They
should bear in mind, however, that every caricature is derived from an
original.

3. Traditional Nationalism

Not every thoughtful person in the eighteenth century sympathized with
the dominant intellectual tendencies of the "Enlightenment." Here and there
in Europe, even before the French Revolution, voices were raised or pens
employed in criticism of the "rationalism" of the age and in depreciation of
the contemporary faith in natural law, natural rights, and the perfectibility of
mankind.

These pens became more caustic, these voices became louder, as the
French Revolution developed. It was proclaimed with growing bitterness that
the terrors of the Revolution and the ensuing horrors of the Revolutionary
and Napoleonic Wars were the inevitable products of the false philosophy of
the "Enlightenment" and that the only hope for the true happiness of mankind lay in a return to the thought and institutions of an earlier day. Against
the Jacobins, particularly, these "reactionaries" declaimed. It was the Jacobins,
they said, . . . who in the name of reason had behaved most unreasonably,
who in their attempt to demonstrate the perfectibility of man had amply
proved his depravity. . . .

The reactionary critics of Jacobinism were humanitarians themselves.
With no faith in the inevitably natural "progress" of the human race, they yet
believed that man was capable of considerable quiet happiness in his fallen
state if only he would learn the lessons of the past and appreciate his own
limitations. They ardently believed, moreover, that man in his fallen state had
received the gift of tears, and that tears should be shed for human wrong and
injustice and suffering. They shed many tears, at least metaphorically, over
the sins and frailties of human nature and especially over the cruel slaughter
of human beings by Jacobin guillotine in the Place de la Révolution or by
Jacobin muskets on the field of battle. . . . Of course, the reactionaries shed
more tears over the aristocratic victims of Jacobin deviltry than over the fate
of the masses, but they were sure that the quiet happiness of humanity could
be assured less by the masses than by the classes. Aristocrats were the best
people. If the best people were guillotined or shot, what hope remained for
humanity at large?

Such criticism was expressed by French foes of the Revolution, and likewise by its foes in Germany and England. In England, perhaps, it received its
classical form. Wherever it was expressed, it was accoutered with one very
important weapon from the arsenal of Jacobinism; it assumed a kind of
nationalism.

England preceded all countries on the Continent in the development of
an acute popular consciousness of common nationality. Long before the
French Revolution, at a time when Frenchmen had thought of themselves

primarily as Burgundians or Gascons or Provençals, Englishmen had been Englishmen and had rallied with real national patriotism to the secularizations of Henry VIII and the exploits of Elizabeth. . . . It was natural, therefore, that any Englishman who would enter the lists against Jacobinism should be arrayed in trappings of nationalism.

In the case of Frenchmen, Germans, and other Continentals, it was not quite so natural. Indeed, it might be supposed that a Frenchman who detested the Revolution would detest all its works, including certainly its most characteristic work, which was its nationalism. But nationalism was altogether too profound and too widespread a phenomenon in France during the Revolution to be ignored or overcome by French counter-revolutionaries. These soon recognized that they could not wean their compatriots from Jacobinism if they themselves withheld the milk of French patriotism. . . .

Certain intellectuals who most vigorously opposed the French Revolution and Napoleon proceeded to champion nationalism and to dress it up in distinctive clothes. The clothing was not "reason" or "revolution" but history and tradition. This type of nationalism, like Jacobin nationalism, claimed to be humanitarian, but as the Jacobins departed in one direction from the humanitarian nationalism so their opponents departed from it in another direction. The latter made a significant place in their system for aristocracy and an even more significant place for tradition. Indeed, their system may most appropriately be termed traditional nationalism. . . .

The rise of traditional nationalism was almost if not quite as significant in modern history as the rise of Jacobin nationalism. . . .

The disciples of traditionalism were numerous and socially irreproachable. They included many Tory and Old-Whig Englishmen, many French émigrés, many aristocrats and clergymen, many conservative intellectuals, and many sincerely religious Christians among the various nationalities of Europe. Such eminent gentlemen feared and detested the French Revolution and almost everything that Jacobinism was supposed to stand for: popular sovereignty, individualism, liberty and equality, destruction of privilege, etc. In only one respect did they stoop to imitate the French Jacobins, and that was in their quickening of national consciousness and their exalting of nationality. They learned to combat Jacobinism by representing themselves, in contradistinction to the Jacobins, as the best and most rightful standard-bearers of national patriotism. Their own traditional patriotism, they insisted, was true patriotism, whilst that of the Jacobins was false patriotism.

There were real doctrinal differences between Jacobin and traditional nationalisms. The one based national patriotism on natural rights; the other based it on historic rights. The one was democratic; the other was aristocratic. The one was revolutionary; the other was evolutionary, if not reactionary. The one stressed the absolute sovereignty of the national state and strove to develop about it a paramount popular religion of nationalism. The other, while preaching national patriotism, tended to regard sovereignty as plural and sought to reconcile loyalty to the national state with continuing loyalty to class and locality, and, perhaps chiefly, with continuing loyalty to traditional Christianity. . . .

Such was the theory. But in practice traditional nationalism proved to be as bellicose and violent as the Jacobin variety. It has already been suggested that if Jacobinism had not been opposed by reactionaries in France and in Europe it might not have involved domestic terror and foreign war and might not have produced an excess of nationalism. Similarly, it may here be suggested that if traditionalism had not been confronted with menacing Jacobins in France and with their disciples in other countries it would not have felt the necessity of overcoming them by brute force and in all probability would not have evolved a fierce counter-nationalism. As it was, the Jacobins seemed to be resolved to conquer all Europe for their cause, whilst the traditionalists certainly did their utmost to repulse the Jacobins and to subjugate France. Traditional nationalism was a powerful motive force in back of the revolts within France, particularly in La Vendée, in back of growing popular resistance on the Continent, as exemplified in the nationalist awakenings in Germany, Holland, Portugal, Spain, and even Russia, and in back of the ceaseless military and naval efforts of the British. If Napoleon Bonaparte and his marshals were products of Jacobin nationalism, then traditional nationalism flowered in Pitt and Castlereagh, Nelson and Wellington, the Archduke Charles and the Tsar Alexander. The battle of Waterloo was the climax to a bloody tragedy which for twenty-three years had been enacted on the European stage between the forces of Jacobinism and those of traditionalism. . . .

4. Liberal Nationalism

Midway between Jacobin and traditional nationalism was liberal nationalism. Like the others, this type originated in the eighteenth century. It originated in England, that country of perpetual compromise and of acute national self-consciousness, and in the mind of Jeremy Bentham [1748-1832], that grave prodigy and professional reformer. . . .

Bentham has been so much discussed as utilitarian and liberal that his contributions to nationalism have been grossly underrated or entirely overlooked. Yet liberalism from the outset involved a kind of nationalism, and Bentham was himself a patriot—after a fashion. . . .

He was also, in the best eighteenth-century manner, a good deal of a cosmopolite, and he felt no inner conflict between the two loyalties. He could proclaim that he belonged to no party and to no country, and on occasion could address himself to "My fellow citizens of France! My fellow citizens of England! My fellow citizens of the civilized world! My fellow citizens of future ages!" . . .

Bentham believed that nationality is the proper basis for state and government. In an address to the French nation, he vehemently urged them to emancipate their colonies on the ground that the colonists were not Frenchmen and should therefore not be subjected to French rule. A like plea he made in behalf of the English colonies. The same principle he invoked to justify his indignation at the partition of Poland. Never would he seek to impose the domination of any particular country upon other peoples; rather, he would help them to find happiness through the establishment of national states of their own on liberal principles. Nor did he think that England had a mission to perform toward backward peoples. The purpose in his nationalism, as in all his projects, was to assure the greatest happiness to the greatest number of persons and peoples, and this did not admit of a militant or imperialist spirit or of any aggressive course of action. In his nationalism he was pacifist and anti-imperialist, a "Little Englander," and a stout upholder of the right of national self-determination for all peoples, large and small alike.

Bentham coined the word "international." He used it first in 1789 in his *Introduction to the Principles of Morals and Legislation;* and subsequently in his *Principles of International Law* he made fully apparent the significance which the new word possessed for him. It bespoke a relationship between national states and peoples which should supplant cosmopolitanism and yet mitigate nationalism. The old cosmopolite had attempted to be a "citizen of the world" by spurning nationality and decrying patriotism. The new internationalist should be a good nationalist in order to bring about a better world order. But being a good nationalist meant doing to other nations what you would have them do to you. It meant that while love of country and national zeal were commendable sentiments, national partiality and prejudice were to be eschewed. It meant also that while the political map of the world should be redrawn on national lines, the emerging national states should compete and coöperate in works good for all humanity.

To Bentham, what was peculiarly bad in existing international relations was war. He was certain that the dynastic and colonial wars which had been waged between European states for two or three centuries had wrought vast evil for a great number of individuals and nations, and he was fearful lest even vaster evil might result from the more intensive and passionate wars of his own day. Consequently he devoted the greater part of his *Principles of International Law* to an exposition of the causes and cure of war. The causes of war, he explained, were: national pride; commercial rivalry; disputes over boundaries; attempts at conquest; disputes over royal succession; quarrels over new discoveries; violations of territory; and religious hatreds. The principal means which he urged of preventing war were: the use of reason; the establishment of free trade; the perfecting of international law; the confederation of nations for mutual defense; international arbitration; and the limitation of armaments. Here was the foundation for a new internationalism, grounded in liberal nationalism. . . .

The principles and purposes of liberal nationalism were expounded during the first two thirds of the nineteenth century by a host of theorists and agitators. . . .

There were many differences in detail among these sundry apostles as to the scope and implications of liberal nationalism. In general, however, they all assumed that each nationality should be a political unit under an independent constitutional government which would put an end to despotism, aristocracy, and ecclesiastical influence, and assure to every citizen the broadest practicable exercise of personal liberty, political, economic, religious, and educational. They all assumed, moreover, that each liberal national state in serving its true interests and those of its own citizens would be serving the true interests of humanity at large and that "true interests" could best be served by national policies of free-trade, anti-militarism, anti-imperialism, and international cooperation and peace. A few of the apostles of liberal nationalism were devout democrats, but most of them agreed with John Austin's contention that government should be of property-owners inasmuch as the rest of the people do not know their own interests. On the question of intervention in the affairs of a foreign country, they were likewise divided. Some held that such intervention was never permissible, whilst the majority maintained that it might be undertaken to free a people from despotism or alien oppression. All nineteenth-century liberals, however, were sufficiently under the influence of romanticism to feel the liveliest sympathy with the nationalist aspirations and struggles of every "oppressed" or "enslaved" people and to shed tears over their plight and subscribe to funds for their relief, if not actually to bear arms in their behalf.

Nineteenth-century liberal nationalism, indeed, drew heavily on romanticism. It was romanticism which not only magnified the sympathy of the general run of liberals, the world over, for the "underdog," for the sufferings of the downtrodden masses and for the misery of enslaved peoples, but also stimulated a vast deal of research by liberal scholars with a view to demonstrating why a particular nationality was great in the past and should be united and free in the future. Liberal professors and literary men under the influence of the romantic movement took a most active part in restoring the purity of national languages, in resuscitating folk-songs and folk-customs, in reviving national traditions, and in arousing popular enthusiasm for national heroes of the past. Incidentally, it should be remarked that they extolled and utilized for their own propaganda certain agencies which the French revolutionaries and Jacobin nationalists had devised, such as national schools, national journals, national societies, and national ceremonies and symbols. It was romantic liberals who composed novel anthems and designed new tricolors for a profusion of would-be nations.

Liberal nationalists were high-minded, optimistic, and devoted to the cause of peace. But optimism and high-mindedness even greater than theirs could not have convinced Metternich and other reactionaries who were in actual control of most of the European states during the first two thirds of the nineteenth century that liberal nationalism was right-headed or essentially pacific. Most of the European states were not national states. The Empires of Russia, Austria, and Turkey comprised numerous nationalities. Neither Germany nor Italy possessed national unity or was much more than a "geographical expression." Belgium was composed of Dutchmen and Frenchmen. Norway was yoked with Sweden, Hungary with Austria, and Ireland with England. Throughout eastern and central Europe, moreover, the existing non-national or super-national states were not liberal states. They lacked written constitutions, representative governments, and guaranties of personal liberties. They supported aristocracies of landed nobility and official clergy. They protected class privileges. They pursued policies of tariff protectionism and dynastic militarism. In the circumstances it gradually became only too obvious that in order to reconstruct Europe on liberal and national foundations it would be necessary for peace-loving liberal nationalists to resort to violence and war. They would have to incite peoples to rise in rebellion against reactionary governments. They would have to arouse peoples to fight for national unity and freedom.

Here, then, was the tragedy of liberal nationalism, not unlike that of the earlier Jacobin nationalism. Its logic and its fine intentions were not sufficient of themselves to insure its triumph. It needs must grasp the sword and slay its adversaries.

The sword, therefore, it repeatedly grasped, and its adversaries it slaughtered in vast numbers. Revolt followed revolt, and war followed war. Under liberal auspices occurred the terrible rebellions of "enslaved" Greeks and Yugoslavs against the Ottoman Empire and of "oppressed" Latin Americans against Spain; the riots of 1820 in Italy and Spain; the widespread insurrections of 1830 in France, Belgium, Germany, and Italy; the even more widespread and deadly insurrections of 1848 in France, Germany, Italy, Austria, Switzerland, and Ireland; the Polish uprisings of 1831 and 1863; the Crimean War of 1854-1856; the wars of Italian unification in 1848-1849, 1859-1860, 1866, and 1870; the wars of German unification in 1848-1849, 1864, 1866, and 1870-1871; and the mighty struggle of 1861-1865 in the United States for the preservation of a national union and the emancipation of an enslaved race.

By 1871 some progress toward the goal of liberal nationalism could be recorded. France and England and a considerable number of other countries were under liberal governments. Germans and Italians possessed national states, and likewise, with full independence or a large degree of autonomy, Greeks and Yugoslavs and Rumanians and Latin Americans. And, most portentous event of all, these partial successes of liberal nationalism were so many fertile seeds which were to reach fruition in the later and greatest nationalist war of 1914-1918. . . .

Yet liberal nationalism in achieving its goal suffered a transformation. Its liberalism waned as its nationalism waxed. Latterly, too, it has had to vie with a newer and more drastic type of nationalism—that which we may term "integral"—and to integral nationalism, liberal nationalism in its evolution has contributed, quite certainly if quite unwittingly. To the doctrine of integral nationalism, we may now attend.

5. Integral Nationalism

. . . Liberal nationalism, arising in the nineteenth century through the fusion of the teachings of Jeremy Bentham with the democratic dogma of Jacobinism and with the historical tendency of romanticism, has not perished in the World War of 1914-1918. It is still with us, very much with us. It nowadays arouses the "oppressed" nationalities of Asia and Africa, as formerly it aroused the "oppressed" nationalities of Europe. It still looks forward hopefully and optimistically to a world of independent national states, liberal and democratic, cooperating in a universal league of nations. Woodrow Wilson, whom some persons have the temerity to describe as the "last of the liberals," is dead, but his soul goes marching on. . . .

In the twentieth century . . . particularly in Europe and America, has come clearly to light yet another and novel brand of nationalism, a brand which rather arbitrarily may be designated as "integral nationalism." The designation is what Charles Maurras [employed before World War II] to describe the nationalist doctrine of his small and hysterical political party in France— the "Action Française"—but it may conveniently be used, without undue imagination or ambiguity, to indicate certain significant elements in Italian Fascism and even Russian Bolshevism and, curiously enough, in the attitude and behavior of millions of nationalists throughout the world who do not indulge in much theorizing and who are certainly unaware that they are integral nationalists.

Integral nationalism may be defined, in the words of Maurras himself, as "the exclusive pursuit of national policies, the absolute maintenance of national integrity, and the steady increase of national power—for a nation declines when it loses military might." It has to do, it will be noted, not with "oppressed" or "subject" nationalities, but rather with nationalities which have already gained their political unity and independence. . . .

Integral nationalism is hostile to the internationalism preached by humanitarians and liberals. It makes the nation, not a means to humanity, not a stepping-stone to a new world order, but an end in itself. It puts national interests alike above those of the individual and above those of humanity. It refuses coöperation with other nations except as such coöperation may serve its own interests real or fancied. It is jingoistic, distrusts other nations, labors to exalt one nation at the expense of others, and relies on physical force. It is militarist and tends to be imperialist. In the face of it, a league of nations or any international sense of peace and security is threatened with sterility and destruction. Besides, in domestic affairs, integral nationalism is highly illiberal and tyrannical. It would oblige all citizens to conform to a common standard of manners and morals and to share the same unreasoning enthusiasm for it. It would subordinate all personal liberties to its own purpose, and if the common people should murmur it would abridge democracy and gag it. All these things it would do "in the national interest." . . .

A cardinal principle of the new integral nationalism which most sharply distinguishes it from all earlier philosophies of nationalism is its admitted and boasted reliance on brute force. . . .

Such a summary of the teachings of integral nationalism is not derived from the study of a few theorists but, rather, from the observation of hard cold facts in the contemporary world. . . . One may note the development of the Bolshevists in Russia, who, beginning as economic and social reformers, with loud protestations against militarism, imperialism, and nationalism, soon discovered, like the French revolutionaries before them, that the world is not equally prepared for their messianic altruism, and have ended by exalting a peculiarly integral nationalism in the Union of Socialist Soviet Republics— living to themselves alone, serving their own interests, brandishing a sword, destroying democracy and liberty, and worshipping at the shrines of their dictators that are now their national heroes. The extreme nationalism of the Russian Bolshevists is likely to be remembered when the details of their economic experiments shall have been forgotten. . . .

Whence has come this integral nationalism? It seems so different in character and purpose from the nationalisms that were humanitarian or liberal or even traditionalist. Yet it is, in the twentieth century, so widespread. The answer is that, while we have become acutely conscious of it only recently, it has been in process of fashioning since the middle of the nineteenth century. . . .

The philosophy of integral nationalism [can be traced to groups of intellectuals in Germany, Italy, and France] during the nineteenth and first years of the twentieth century. But integral nationalism could hardly be the living force that it is among the masses in contemporary Europe and even in contemporary America, giving them attitudes and moving them to action, were it not for certain historical factors which, apart from theories, have prepared the way for popular acceptance of a more intensive and forceful nationalism. Of course, the "masses" do not know that they are "integral nationalists," and many of them would probably profess admiration for "liberal" principles and detestation of "integral" principles, if these should be frankly and fully explained to them. Yet the fact remains . . . that the "masses" in most national states today acquiesce in, and on occasion applaud, public policies which partake of the nature of integral nationalism. Even in countries where personal liberties are still guaranteed, where a republican constitution still exists, and where democratic government still functions, the "masses" tend increasingly to evince a chauvinism, an intolerance, and a fanaticism strangely out of keeping with the individualism and internationalism which an older generation of patriots associated with liberal democratic nationalism.

Three factors may be mentioned as specially operating to convert large numbers of Europeans and Americans from the liberal nationalism which was so popular and altruistic at the middle of the nineteenth century into the integral nationalism which is now so widespread and menacing. One has been the militarist spirit engendered by the wars which were undertaken by liberal nationalists in order to free and unify "oppressed" nationalities. Liberal nationalists, it should be recalled, made pacifism an important part of their creed. They desired neither war nor undue preparedness for war. Their pacifist desires, however, they had to reconcile with their paramount desire to redraw the political map along lines of nationality, and they soon discovered that the only way in which they could accomplish this desire, in the existing world of reality, was to incite armed revolts against tyrants and military uprisings against foreign oppressors. Such revolts and uprisings often led to international complications and wars; and liberal nationalists would have been less than human if they had not viewed these struggles as glorious and the military leaders of them as heroic.

Giuseppe Mazzini [1805-1872], for example, was a pacifist at heart, but to realize his dream of a free and united Italy he felt constrained to wage popular insurrections within his country and a series of wars against Austria;

and the insurrections, once successful, and the wars, once won, took on a halo in Italian hearts and were naturally glorified by Italian historians and all Italian patriots, liberals included. It was much the same elsewhere. German liberals failed to unify their country without bloodshed in 1848; but when Bismarck succeeded by means of copious bloodletting in three wars from 1864 to 1871, all German nationalists, liberals included, thenceforth looked upon the German army as not only the creator but also the bulwark of German unity and freedom.

In other words, liberal nationalists themselves unwittingly fashioned a martial monster which helped mightily to transform liberal into integral nationalism. For, once "oppressed" nationalities had won their independence by force of arms and accorded enthusiastic praise to their generals and soldiers, they came more and more to feel that only force of arms could maintain their independence and insure their rightful place and prestige in the world. In this way, newly free and erstwhile peace-loving nations armed themselves as they had never been armed when they were unfree, disunited, and less liberal; they now entered into military rivalry with one another on an unprecedented scale; and the World War of 1914-1918 was a result. And the World War itself, in part a consummation of liberal nationalism, has notoriously been, in many places and among many persons, the powerful spark which has ignited the powder-train of integral nationalism.

A second important factor in the transformation has been the feeling of superiority engendered by success. Many a would-be nation, inspired by liberal nationalism, began its struggles for freedom and unity in the nineteenth century with humility and noble resolves; and for its plight and self-sacrificing efforts it won the sympathy and sometimes the active support of foreign nations. But when it actually secured unity and freedom, its success seemed to turn the heads of its people. They grew proud of themselves and self-satisfied. . . . Having reached the goal of liberal nationalism and being flushed with victory, they treated that goal as a starting-point for a continuing race toward integral nationalism. . . .

A third factor in the transition from liberal to integral nationalism has been the actual operation of certain propagandist instruments which Jacobin and liberal nationalists had devised and employed within unified national states. Those nationalists had established systems of public schools, directed and controlled by the state and compulsorily attended, the original purpose of which was to make the rising generation literate and to train it for liberty and self-government as well as for particular vocations. As such school-systems expanded and developed and required more funds for their support, they naturally became both more highly centralized and more responsive to mass-prejudices. Soon they were being used for the direct inculcation of nationalism. The majority of their pupils learned enough to be gullible but not enough to be critical. Thus as nationalism became less liberal and more integral, the schools tended at once to reflect and to hasten the process. . . . Or, let the critical student of popular education contrast the programme of studies in the contemporary public schools of France with the programme set forth by Condorcet during the Revolution, or the practical programmes of present-day schools in Italy and Russia with the theories advanced in the middle of the last century by Italians and Russians of liberal persuasion.

The freedom of the press and the freedom of association, like free public schools, were advocated by Jacobins and liberals as means of propagating their principles among the masses. But the new freedom was especially utilized by journalists to establish cheap newspapers which, aiming at the widest and greatest possible circulation, catered increasingly to sensationalism and jingoistic[3] nationalism. Thereby these newspapers contributed to the production of integral nationalists. Similarly the new freedom was attended by the founding of many patriotic societies by liberal revolutionaries or veterans of liberal wars, but these very societies in a second or third generation tended to minimize their liberal origins and to emphasize their extreme nationalism. . . .

Now, in the twentieth century, integral nationalism is essentially religious, fanatically religious. Earlier forms of nationalism, notably the Jacobin and the liberal, were religious, too. But if those earlier forms represented a kind of "New Testament" religion of love and service, with the promise of an apocalypse to the faithful, integral nationalism represents a kind of "Old Testament" religion with jealous and angry gods that insist upon an eye for an eye and a tooth for a tooth.

▶"SOCIALIZATION" OF NATIONALISM

EDWARD HALLETT CARR

In the following article E. H. Carr, an English authority on international politics and their history, examines the effect of democracy and socialism on nationalism and finds that both have dangerously increased its potency. Edward Hallett Carr is a Fellow at Trinity College at the University of Oxford. In 1959 he was at the Center of Behavioral Sciences at Palo Alto, California.

The success of [the] 19th-century compromise between a closely-knit world economic system and unqualified recognition of the political diversity and independence of nations was rendered possible by two subtle and valuable pieces of make-believe which were largely unconscious and contained sufficient elements of reality to make them plausible. These two salutary illusions were, first, that the world economic system was truly international, and second, that the economic and political systems were entirely separate and operated independently of each other. . . .

[3] Probably derived from the phrase "by jingo," which was a part of a bellicose and patriotic song current at the time of English-Russian tension over the Eastern Mediterranean in 1878. The phrase in its context: "We don't want to fight, but by jingo if we do, We've got the ships, we've got the men, We've got the money, too."

This selection is from *Nationalism and After* (London: Macmillan & Co. Ltd., 1945, and New York: St. Martin's Press).

After World War I, however, nationalism began to operate in a new political and economic environment. The phenomenon cannot be understood without examination of the three main underlying causes which provoked it: the bringing of new social strata within the effective membership of the nation, the visible reunion of economic with political power, and the increase in the number of nations.

The rise of new social strata to full membership of the nation marked the last three decades of the 19th century throughout western and central Europe. Its landmarks were the development of industry and industrial skills; the rapid expansion in numbers and importance of urban populations; the growth of workers' organizations and of the political consciousness of the workers; the introduction of universal compulsory education; and the extension of the franchise. . . . The "democratization" of the nation in the earlier part of the century had resulted in the establishing of popular control over the functions of maintaining law and order. . . . The "socialization" of the nation which set in towards the end of the century brought about a far more radical change. . . . Henceforth the political power of the masses was directed to improving their own social and economic lot. The primary aim of national policy was no longer merely to maintain order and conduct what was narrowly defined as public business, but to minister to the welfare of members of the nation and to enable them to earn their living. The democratization of the nation in the second period had meant the assertion of the political claims of the dominant middle class. The socialization of the nation for the first time brings the economic claims of the masses into the forefront of the picture. The defence of wages and employment becomes a concern of national policy and must be asserted, if necessary, against the national policies of other countries; and this in turn gives the worker an intimate practical interest in the policy and power of his nation. The socialization of the nation has as its natural corollary the nationalization of socialism.

The 20th-century alliance between nationalism and socialism . . . in its modern form . . . dates from Bismarck, who, schooled by Lassalle, showed the German workers how much they had to gain from a vigorous and ruthless nationalism. . . . In the same period the word "jingoism" was coined in Great Britain to describe something that had not hitherto existed—the nationalism of the masses. . . . National policy was henceforth founded on the support of the masses; and the counterpart was the loyalty of the masses to a nation which had become the instrument of their collective interests and ambitions.[1]

. . . In the 19th century, when the nation belonged to the middle class and the worker had no fatherland, socialism had been international. The crisis

---

[1] In a work originally published in 1907 the Austrian Social Democrat, Otto Bauer, argued that socialism meant "an increasing differentiation of nations, a sharper emphasis on their peculiarities, a sharper division between their characters," and attacked those who believed that socialism would "diminish or even remove the differences between nations" (Otto Bauer, *Die Nationalitätenfrage und die Sozialdemokratie,* 2nd ed. pp. 105-6). Writers on international relations in English-speaking countries had less insight; for the most part they were content to congratulate themselves on the increasing "popular" interest in international affairs and believed that this would promote international concord.

of 1914 showed in a flash that, except in backward Russia, this attitude was everywhere obsolete. The mass of workers knew instinctively on which side their bread was buttered; and Lenin was a lone voice proclaiming the defeat of his own country as a socialist aim and crying treason against the "social-chauvinists." [2] International socialism ignominiously collapsed. Lenin's desperate rear-guard action to revive it made sense only in Russia, and there only so long as revolutionary conditions persisted. Once the "workers' state" was effectively established, "socialism in one country" was the logical corollary. The subsequent history of Russia and the tragi-comedy of the Communist International are an eloquent tribute to the solidarity of the alliance between nationalism and socialism.

The second underlying cause of the modern inflation of nationalism—its extension from the political to the economic sphere through the reassertion of political power over economic policy—has been everywhere recognized. But it has commonly been attributed to the perversity of politicians or to the nefarious influence of big business, and its far more significant connexion with the socialization of the nation overlooked. The democratic nationalism of the 19th century had proved manageable and compatible with some kind of international order precisely because its aspirations were predominantly political and could be satisfied within the framework of the 19th-century *laissez-faire* . . . state. The social nationalism (or national socialism) of the 20th century, by shifting the ground from political to economic aspirations, brought about the abdication of the *laissez-faire* state in favor of the "social service" state. . . . Henceforth the functions of the nation-state were as much economic as political. . . . Nationalism had invaded and conquered the economic domain from which the 19th century had so cunningly excluded it. The single world economy was replaced by a multiplicity of national economies, each concerned with the well-being of its own members. . . .

The re-establishment of national political authority over the economic system, which was a necessary corollary of the socialization of the nation, was no doubt one of the factors contributing to the situation which produced the two world wars. But it received from them so powerful an impetus that its relation to them is as much one of effect as of cause. The immediate and revolutionary consequence of the outbreak of war in 1914 was the assumption by every belligerent government of the right to create and control its own national money and the deposition of sterling from its role as the universal currency. . . . It soon became clear that the terms of peace, whichever side emerged victorious, would constitute an attack on the standard of living of the defeated nation. . . . War among socialized nations inevitably became an instrument for securing economic advantages for the victor and inflicting economic disabilities on the defeated. Modern wars are fought to a finish and the loser has no rights.

. . . As custodians of the living standards, employment and amenities of

---

[2] Derived from the name of Nicholas Chauvin of Rochefort. His demonstrative patriotism and attachment to Napoleon at the time of the Empire came to be ridiculed by his comrades. *Chauvinism* is now applied to a vainglorious, bellicose, or intolerant form of patriotism.

their whole populations, modern nations are, in virtue of their nature and function, probably less capable than any other groups in modern times of reaching agreement with one another.

The contrast between the comparatively law-abiding habits of members of a national community and the law-breaking proclivities of nation members of the international community has long been a truism; and recent rapid decline in the observance of international law is common ground among all observers. The decline, like the decline in international agreement, is easily explicable in terms of the preceding analysis. The international law of the 17th and 18th centuries rested on the good faith of sovereigns. What was at stake was the personal execution of personal promises and obligations; and the sense of solidarity among monarchs was sufficient to leave them with a certain desire to keep their word to one another. In the 19th century solidarity between middle-class governments, buttressed on respect for the rights of property, and reinforced by fear of offending the international financial authorities in London by any irregularity in the discharge of obligations, still sufficed to keep the observance of international law and agreements on a tolerably high level. Paradoxically enough, it was Bismarck who first diagnosed the symptoms of decline and ascribed it to the unreliability of democracies. The diagnosis was too narrow. The decline was due not to any particular form of government or constitution, but to the socialized nation of which Bismarck was one of the first promoters. . . .

. . . The first obligation of the modern national government, which no other obligation will be allowed to override, is to its own people. It would be absurd to lament this state of affairs as proof of increased human wickedness; it might equally well be regarded as proof of a sharpened social conscience. But whatever view we take of it, it would be folly to neglect the overwhelming evidence that modern national governments cannot and will not observe international treaties or rules of international law when these become burdensome or dangerous to the welfare or security of their own nation. Any so-called international order built on contingent obligations assumed by national governments is an affair of lath and plaster and will crumble into dust as soon as pressure is placed upon it. In peace, as in war, the international law of the age of sovereigns is incompatible with the socialized nation. . . .

The third cause of the inflation of nationalism—the startling increase in the number of nations during our third period—is one of which sufficient account is rarely taken. Here too the year 1870 marks a significant turning-point. Down to that time the influence of nationalism had been to diminish the number of sovereign and independent political units in Europe. In 1871 after the unification of Germany and Italy had been completed there were fourteen; in 1914 there were twenty; in 1924 the number had risen to twenty-six. It would be an understatement to say that the virtual doubling in fifty years of the number of independent European states aggravated in degree the problem of European order. . . . National self-determination became a standing invitation to secession. The movement which dismembered Austria-Hungary and created Yugoslavia and Czechoslovakia was bound to be succeeded by movements for the dismemberment of Yugoslavia and Czechoslovakia. Given the premises of nationalism the process was natural and legitimate, and no end could be set to it. After 1914 it spread rapidly to the Arab world, to India, to the Far East. . . .

The whole machinery of economic nationalism was set in motion to develop their industries and bring them some fraction of the power and prestige which went with industrial development. Such procedures inevitably curtailed international trade and multiplied competition for narrowing markets. The results were disastrous: yet nobody was to blame for them. They arose simply from the multiplication of the number of sovereign and independent nations, each claiming its share in the profits and prerogatives of industrial production. . . .

The extension of the geographical limits of nationalism has meant not only a multiplication of the number of nations, but a planting of nationalism in new and unfamiliar soils. In western Europe nationalism had grown in soils fertilized by the traditions of Christendom, of natural law and of secular individualism. In German lands the natural law and individualist traditions had struck only light roots; in Russia and other countries dominated by the Orthodox Church they had been ignored or rejected. Beyond Europe nationalism was now spreading to countries where every Christian or European tradition was alien, and where the illogical inhibitions which had for so long helped to restrain European nationalism were unknown. . . .

The second world war thus marks the climax and the catastrophe of the third period of modern international relations, and leaves us on the threshold of a new period whose character will probably shape the destinies of mankind for a century to come. A first view suggests beyond doubt that nationalism has never been stronger than at this moment; and this view would lead to almost unqualified pessimism about the future of international relations. Yet closer analysis may reveal certain trends, not necessarily more reassuring, but at any rate sufficiently different to suggest that, whatever may be in store in the next few years, nations and international relations are in process of undergoing another subtle, not yet clearly definable, change. . . .

►THE NATION-STATES OF THE WORLD

The following list reflects the situation as of 1960.

Asia (25)

Afghanistan	Laos
Burma	Lebanon
Cambodia	Malaya
Ceylon	Mongolia[3]
China[4]	Nepal
India	Pakistan
Indonesia	Philippines
Iran	Saudi Arabia
Iraq	Thailand
Israel	Turkey
Japan	Vietnam[1]
Jordan	Yemen
Korea[1]	

Americas (22)

Argentina	Guatemala
Bolivia	Haiti
Brazil	Honduras
Canada	Mexico
Chile	Nicaragua
Colombia	Panama
Costa Rica	Paraguay
Cuba	Peru
Dominican	United States
Republic	Uruguay
Ecuador	Venezuela
El Salvador	

Africa (14)

Cameroons	Nigeria
Ethiopia	Somalia
Ghana	Sudan
Guinea	Tunisia
Liberia	Union of South
Libya	Africa
Mali Federation[6]	United Arab
Morocco	Republic[2]

Australasia (2)

Australia
New Zealand

Europe (26)

Albania	Luxembourg
Austria	Netherlands
Belgium	Norway
Bulgaria	Poland
Czechoslovakia	Portugal
Denmark	Rumania
Finland	Spain
France	Sweden
Germany[1]	Switzerland
Greece	Union of Soviet
Hungary	Socialist
Iceland	Republics[5]
Ireland	United Kingdom
Italy	Yugoslavia

[1] Divided into two separate sovereign regimes. Not members of the United Nations.
[2] Formed in 1958 by Egypt and Syria.
[3] Not member of the United Nations.
[4] Divided into Communist China on the mainland, and Nationalist China on Taiwan. The latter remains the member of the United Nations with the status of a great power.
[5] Soviet Ukraine and Soviet Byelorussia, two of the fifteen Union Republics composing the Union of the Soviet Socialist Republics, are members of the United Nations and have the right to vote, in addition to the Soviet Union, which has the voting status of a great power. According to the Soviet Constitution, all Union Republics have the right to have independent diplomatic relations. This right has never been implemented, not even in relation to other Communist countries. And only two of the fifteen were given the right to join the United Nations.
[6] Formed in 1959 by former French colonies, French Sudan and Senegal. Other former French territories in Africa now aiming at greater autonomy or independence are: Central African Republic; Chad; Congo Republic; Dahomey; French Somaliland; Gabon; Ivory Coast; Malagasy Republic (formery Madagascar); Mauritania; Niger; and Voltaic Republic. Algeria, which the French Constitution considers a part of metropolitan France, belongs to a special category.

TOPIC 2

The Principle of National
Self-Determination

Following the French revolution of 1789, two important changes marked the subsequent development of nationalism:

1. Masses began to identify themselves with their states, although these had originally been created by absolute monarchs. The people passed from the role of subject to that of sovereign. The effect of nationalism was integration.

2. But within empires or states nationalism also caused disintegration. Some communities developed or regained consciousness of being different and separate from other groups within the state. Within empires such groups are usually referred to as *dependent* or *colonial* peoples. Within states groups which claim protection of their collective personality against the domination by other groups are usually called *minorities*. The struggle of both for statehood or self-government is based on the principle of national self-determination.

The problem is: when a group develops a consciousness of separate political entity, should its claim for independent statehood be considered an *absolute* right, that is, a right which must be complied with irrespective of circumstances? Or is the demand for national self-determination to be considered only a *relative* right, or rather, a principle which may or may not be implemented according to such circumstances as the national group's numerical size, economic viability, or strategic location? The following selections attempt to give an answer to this question.

►SELF-DETERMINATION AS THE BASIS FOR PEACE

WOODROW WILSON

According to Woodrow Wilson, national self-determination is an "imperative principle." Its disregard is said to be the cause of war. Its recognition should be the basis of peace.

This excerpt from Wilson's Fourteen Points indicates that in practice his "imperative principle" was meant as applying only to minorities in Europe and the Middle East. Colonial peoples in Africa and Asia were not considered to be an identical problem at that time.

Statement of February 11, 1918.

"Self-Determination" . . . is an imperative principle of action, which statesmen will henceforth ignore at their peril. We cannot have general peace for the asking, or by the mere arrangements of a peace conference. It cannot be pieced together out of individual understandings between powerful states. All the parties to this war must join in the settlement of every issue anywhere involved in it; because what we are seeking is a peace that we can all unite to guarantee and maintain, and every item of it must be submitted to the common judgment whether it be right and fair, an act of justice, rather than a bargain between sovereigns. . . .

This war had its roots in the disregard of the rights of small nations and of nationalities which lacked the union and the force to make good their claim to determine their own allegiances and their own form of political life. Covenants must now be entered into which will render such things impossible for the future; and those covenants must be backed by the united force of all the nations that love justice and are willing to maintain it at any cost.

The Fourteen Points (Points VII-XIII)[1]

VII. Belgium, the whole world will agree, must be evacuated and restored, without any attempt to limit the sovereignty which she enjoys in common with all other free nations. No other single act will serve to restore confidence among the nations in the laws which they have themselves set and determined for the government of their relations with one another. Without this healing act the whole structure and validity of international law is forever impaired.

VIII. All French territory should be freed and the invaded portions restored, and the wrong done to France by Prussia in 1871 in the matter of Alsace-Lorraine, which has unsettled the peace of the world for nearly fifty years, should be righted, in order that peace may once more be made secure in the interest of all.

IX. A readjustment of the frontiers of Italy should be effected along clearly recognizable lines of nationality.

X. The peoples of Austria-Hungary, whose place among the nations we wish to see safeguarded and assured, should be accorded the freest opportunity of autonomous development.

XI. Rumania, Serbia, and Montenegro should be evacuated; occupied territories restored; Serbia accorded free and secure access to the sea; and the relations of the several Balkan states to one another determined by friendly counsel along historically established lines of allegiance and nationality; and international guarantees of the political and economic independence and territorial integrity of the several Balkan states should be entered into.

XII. The Turkish portions of the present Ottoman Empire should be assured a secure sovereignty, but the other nationalities which are now under Turkish rule should be assured an undoubted security of life and an absolutely unmolested opportunity of autonomous development, and the Dardanelles

---

[1] The Fourteen Points were presented to the United States Congress on January 11, 1918.

should be permanently opened as a free passage to the ships and commerce of all nations under international guarantees.

XIII. An independent Polish state should be erected which should include the territories inhabited by indisputably Polish populations, which should be assured a free and secure access to the sea, and whose political and economic independence and territorial integrity should be guaranteed by international covenant.

►NATIONAL SELF-DETERMINATION

ALFRED COBBAN

Wilson's "imperative principle" underwent further changes under the weight of realities which confronted the Peace Conference of 1919. The conference was to implement the principle of national self-determination in practice. As this could not be done completely, the very right of self-determination, which was to eliminate the problem of national minorities, created new ones. This is described by an English authority on nationalism, Alfred Cobban, in his now classic book on national self-determination. Excerpts are reproduced below.

National Self-Determination as a Theory

The right of national independence, which came to be called, during the first World War, the principle of self-determination, is, in general terms, the belief that each nation has a right to constitute an independent state and determine its own government. . . .

. . . Democracy, in the modern sense of the word, was born in the second half of the eighteenth century. Such democratic tendencies as are to be found before this time take the form of assertions of a right of representing the people in the government, of checking the government by the political action of the people, or of directing it in the interests of the people. But with the French Revolution democracy became something more than this. It was not merely the representation of individuals, much less of classes or corporations, in a parliament exercising a constitutional control over the government: the people itself became the supreme authority, the single active principle in the state. It passed from the role of subject to that of sovereign.

The post-medieval form of the theory of the Divine Right of Kings, which had been the chief political gospel of the early modern period, received a mortal blow from the French Revolution. It was replaced by the Divine Right of the People. Under the influence of the new national and democratic ideas, the people ceased to be an atomic dust of individuals: it took shape and form, became a *whole,* was called the *Nation,* endowed with sovereignty,

The selection is from *National Self-Determination* (London: Oxford University Press, under the auspices of the Royal Institute of International Affairs).

and identified with the state. The revolutionary theory that a people had the right to form its own constitution and choose its own government for itself easily passed into the claim that it had a right to decide whether to attach itself to one state or another, or constitute an independent state by itself. The effect of revolutionary ideology was to transfer the initiative in state-making from the government to the people. Nation-states had formerly been built up, in the course of centuries, from above, by the influence of government: henceforth they were to be made much more rapidly from below by the will of the people. The logical consequence of the democratization of the idea of the state by the revolutionaries was the theory of national self-determination. . . .

The Application of Self-Determination at the Peace Conference in 1919

When the Peace Conference opened in 1919, its leading principle, or so the world thought, was to be self-determination for all nations. . . . To the tribes of man, sickened by four years of carnage, the product of a generation of imperialism and centuries of power politics, it appeared as the light of salvation, beaconing humanity onwards to a happier future. A sceptical observer might have reflected that circumstances rather than design had placed it in the forefront of Allied policy. The Fourteen Points and the Four Principles had proclaimed it to the world, but it is to be remembered that Wilson had in a sense forced these on his Allies. He issued the Fourteen Points when he did because of the failure of the American Mission to secure from an Inter-Allied Conference the manifesto on war aims he desired. By his announcement he hoped to counteract the effect of the revelation of the secret treaties by the Bolsheviks, keep Russia in the war, and launch an effective propaganda offensive against Germany. Once the President's principles had been given publicity, his allies could not stand out against them. . . . In their reply to the German proposals for an armistice, the Allied Governments declared their willingness to make peace on the terms laid down in President Wilson's address of 8 January 1918 and his subsequent speeches. . . . It is true that there were demands in the Fourteen Points which were hardly reconcilable in practice with self-determination, and that the Americans and British—apart from a loose sentence by Mr. Lloyd George—did not contemplate its application to colonial populations. . . . The important fact is that world opinion certainly thought that the victorious Allies were committed to the principle of self-determination in its most absolute form, and expected it to be clearly and unequivocally put into practice.

The Italian View. The statesmen who assembled in Paris had fewer illusions. They had used the appeal to self-determination as an instrument of war, not necessarily hypocritically; but not many were anxious to apply it where it conflicted with the interests of their own states in drawing up the terms of peace. Their true sentiments can be gathered from their private rather than their public utterances. In the pre-Armistice negotiations, for example, the Italian statesman Sonnino had been anxious to introduce a reservation to Point IX, making it clear that Italy expected to receive the frontier which she regarded as necessary for her security, regardless of ethnic considerations or the wishes of the populations concerned. . . .

The French View. The French attitude was much more complicated. The project the French Government had prepared for the Conference proposed, indeed, to remove one serious obstacle to the policy of self-determination by cancelling all inter-Allied treaties; and advocated the 'right of peoples to decide their own destinies by free and secret vote.' But . . . the dominating figure in the French delegation was Clemenceau, who had little tolerance for Wilsonian ideals. In the course of the discussions he frankly declared, according to Mr. Lloyd George, 'that he did not believe in the principle of self-determination, which allowed a man to clutch at your throat the first time it was convenient to him, and he would not consent to any limitation of time being placed upon the enforced separation of the Rhenish Republic from the rest of Germany.'

The British View. The British delegation was less reserved in its attitude towards self-determination, but it had its doubts also. Balfour, on the principle that strong frontiers made for peace, had earlier expressed to Wilson the view that strategic necessity should in some cases be allowed to override the principle of nationality. In general, however, the British delegation was prepared, at least until it discovered some of the ethnological difficulties, to support a consistent and thorough-going application of the principle of self-determination. As Mr. Lloyd George ingenuously put it, 'There were many questions regarding which the great powers were perfectly impartial. For instance, they were quite impartial regarding the Roumanian claims on Hungary.' In such a case he proposed a reference to the experts. The real difficulty from the British point of view arose from the existence of a large subject empire. Mr. Harold Nicolson explains that, 'The most ardent British advocate of the principle of self-determination found himself, sooner or later, in a false position. However fervid might be our indignation regarding Italian claims to Dalmatia and the Dodecanese it could be cooled by a reference, not to Cyprus only, but to Ireland, Egypt and India. We had accepted a system for others which, when it came to practice, we should refuse to apply to ourselves.' . . .

The American View: the Principles of President Wilson. Even the American delegation was not united on the question of self-determination. Wilson's Secretary of State, Robert Lansing, at a later date revealed his violent hostility to the chief plank in his leader's programme. He described the phrase as 'loaded with dynamite,' and said, 'it will raise hopes which can never be realized. It will, I fear, cost thousands of lives. In the end it is bound to be discredited, to be called the dream of an idealist who failed to realize the danger until too late to check those who attempt to put the principle in force. What a calamity that the phrase was ever uttered! What misery it will cause!' Both Canada and the United States, Lansing points out, only continued to exist because of their denial of the principle. If self-determination had been accepted, the Southern States would have been allowed to secede and French Canada would have formed an independent state. What effect, he asks, will it have on the subject peoples of the world—the Irish, Indians, Egyptians, Boers, Mohammedans of Syria and Palestine, and even of French North Africa? Considerations of national safety, historic rights, and economic interests, which would be overridden by it should, he held, all have preference over the principle of self-determination.

Even the President himself possibly did not realize fully the significance of the truly explosive principle which he had done so much to set in action. . . .

The Problem of Minorities

. . . We shall be looking at the question in the wrong perspective if we imagine the Allies sitting down with a blank map of Europe, a list of principles, and a free hand in drawing up the new frontiers. In many cases the claims had already been staked out and occupied, and only military action on a large scale could have ousted the new possessors.

Another difficulty was that the great powers in making their decisions, although in a few instances they sent commissions of inquiry to ascertain as far as possible the actual sentiments and composition of the populations concerned, inevitably took in most cases one or another group of national leaders as representative of the wishes of each nationality. The assumption that the point of view of the nationalist leaders was identical with that of the whole nationality was in some cases a grave injustice. . . .

Three other major obstacles emerged to the practical application of the principle of self-determination. In the first place, as we have said, the Allies had no intention of applying self-determination at the expense of their own empires. Secondly, it proved impossible, in altering frontiers or setting up new states, to avoid creating new minorities. These two weaknesses in the settlement were only fully appreciated in the years that followed the Peace Conference. Thirdly, and this was a point of immediate importance, there was the difficulty of discovering a generally valid definition of the conditions a nation should satisfy before it could legitimately claim a right of self-determination. . . .

The Serbs asserted that when President Wilson spoke of the self-determination of nations 'his thoughts never went as far as the small communities.'

Mr. Lloyd George made a bitter comment on the tendencies manifested by the newly liberated nations at Versailles. 'It fills me with despair,' he said, 'the way in which I have seen small nations, before they have hardly leapt into the light of freedom, beginning to oppress other races than their own. They are more imperialistic than either England or France, certainly than the United States. . . .

The danger of leaving large minorities at the mercy of small states with such an intense national feeling had not been unforeseen, and the Peace Conference endeavored to guard against it by means of the minority treaties. In one way or another, every one of the lesser states in Central and Eastern Europe compulsorily or voluntarily undertook to guarantee certain rights to its minorities. Great hopes were placed on this widespread acceptance of what was generally, though mistakenly, believed to be the innovation of minority guarantees, but from the beginning it suffered from certain fatal defects.

On the one hand, few of the new states accepted the minority guarantees willingly. The experience of the minority treaties showed that it was unwise to expect small states to live up to rules which the great states refused to contemplate for themselves. Most of them regarded the compulsory signature of minority treaties as a mark of inferiority of status, which they bitterly resented. . . . What the minorities were guaranteed were civil rights and liberties as citizens of a national state. This was far from all they wanted. Neither side was satisfied by the treaties and guarantees, and in place of a gradually improving minority situation, there was one which, in most cases, fairly steadily deteriorated.

There was one possible agency through which this deterioration might conceivably have been prevented. The minorities had been put, to a limited extent, under the wardship of the League of Nations. How would the League interpret its responsibilities? A hostile critic might suggest that its policy was directed more to protecting the states against their minorities than the minorities against oppression by the state. The right of self-determination sank into the background. A League Commission pointed out in 1920 that there was no mention of it in the League Covenant. The grant or refusal of the right, it declared, is, exclusively, an attribute of the sovereignty of every state which is definitely constituted.

This may be juridically a sound view, but one cannot but ask what has become of the principle of self-determination only one year after the Treaty of Versailles. The Committee of Jurists had no doubts on that point. 'Positive International Law,' it said, 'does not recognize the right of national groups, as such, to separate themselves from the state of which they form part by the simple expression of a wish, any more than it recognizes the right of other states to claim such a separation.' It admitted that in an international crisis, when ordinary rules are not operating, self-determination may play its part, but in ordinary times it is only one factor among many.

The minorities were therefore left to the protection of the minority treaties. The literature of the minorities question is extensive and this is not the place to re-tell its history. Excessive delays and inadequacy of treatment were the rule, impartiality the exception. 'The acceptance of a settlement,' it has been said, 'has been more often proof that it offends no important interest than that it secures justice.' The League took effective action only when it was pushed into it by the championship of a state powerful enough to have intervened in defense of the minority had there been no League or minority treaties at all. In the annual League debate on minorities of 1930 the British delegates frankly adopted the view that where German minorities were concerned it was for the German Government to look after their interests.

►DEFINITION AND CLASSIFICATION OF MINORITIES

THE U.N. GENERAL SECRETARIAT

The United Nations undertook the study of the problem of minorities soon after its inception. The problem was considered as belonging to the field of interest of the Human Rights Commission. A special Sub-commission on Prevention of Discrimination and Protection of Minorities was created. In 1950 the Secretary General submitted a memorandum to that Sub-commission, defining and classifying different types of minorities," in order to facilitate discussion of this item." The memorandum, a portion of which is here reproduced, "attempts to present, in organized fashion, the principal elements which must be taken into consideration in any attempt to define or classify minorities. Essentially it represents a compilation, a summary, and an organization of the findings of the social and political sciences with respect to minorities."

Two points should be noted: (a) a minority does not necessarily mean a group which is inferior in numbers. The status of a group as a minority is determined by its political inferiority, and awareness of it; (b) the democratic device of deciding issues by a majority vote cannot apply to situations in which one nationality is dominated by another. In such cases there is no moral or political consensus. On the contrary, the minority desires to dissolve the existing bond while the majority tries to preserve it.

The antagonism between the Greek majority and Turkish minority on Cyprus could not be solved by the democratic device of vote.

The Concept of "Minority"

4. As a provisional orientation, it will be recalled that in modern times the term "minority" has been applied to more or less distinct groups, living within a State, which are dominated by other groups.

5. A fundamental distinction ·may be drawn between (*a*) minorities whose members desire equality with dominant groups in the sense of non-discrimination alone, and (*b*) those whose members desire equality with dominant groups in the sense of non-discrimination *plus* the recognition of certain special rights and the rendering of certain positive services.

6. The minorities in category (*a*), on the whole, do not wish to preserve the particular characteristics which distinguish them from the dominant group, but prefer to be assimilated fully or in part by the dominant group. They are therefore primarily concerned that no discrimination of any kind shall be made between various groups, particularly in respect of any of the rights and freedoms set forth in the Universal Declaration of Human Rights (see article 2 of the Declaration).

7. The minorities in category (*b*) are equally concerned with the principle of non-discrimination. They feel, however, that even full realization of this principle would not place their group in a position of real equality—but only of formal equality—with respect to the dominant group.

8. The "positive services" and "special rights" which such minorities feel they must have if their equality within the State is to be real, vary greatly, but usually include one or more of the following:

(a) Provision of adequate primary and secondary education for the minority in its own language and its cultural traditions;

(b) Provision for maintenance of the culture of the minority through the establishment and operation of schools, libraries, museums, media of information, and other cultural and educational institutions;

(c) Provision of adequate facilities to the minority for the use of its language, either orally or in writing, in the legislature, before the courts, and in administration, and the granting of the right to use that language in private intercourse;

(d) Provision for respect of the family law and personal status of the minority and their religious practices and interests; and

(e) Provision of a certain degree of autonomy.

9. The rendering of "positive services" may take either of two forms:

(a) Provisions effected at the expense of the minority; or

(b) Provisions effected out of public funds and facilities.

The Nation and the State

15. There are many possible arrangements between nation and State, as will be shown below. Sometimes a nation has its own State, sometimes it is divided among two or more States, and sometimes it is included under the jurisdiction of a multi-national State. Although nation and State are different concepts, many contemporary nations have resulted from the integrative action of the State.

Relationship between Nation and State

29. There are "national States" in which the State frame is largely co-extensive with the nation. There are also States in which several nationalities have been integrated, and in which the State may act as a factor, (a) for promoting common solidarity among all the individuals and groups within the nation, and (b) for developing an entirely new and more comprehensive nation.

30. In modern times, most nations have their own State, and most States represent the juridical organization of a single nation. This is true even in the case of States formed by groups having widely varying cultural traditions. But there are also other arrangements between nation and State which must be taken into account, as in the case of a State which includes two or more nations, a nation which is included in one State but reflects the culture of another, a nation divided between two or more States, etc.

32. A "national" State is one formed either by a previously-existing nation alone, or by successful merging of several previously-existing nations into a single one. A "multi-national" State, on the other hand, is formed by

two or more nations, existing as different communities, each of which is aware of—and desires to retain—its own distinguishing characteristics.

33. "Multi-national" States may be divided into two principal categories: (*a*) those in which the State reflects the culture of the predominant nation, whilst the other nations are considered as minorities; and (*b*) those which do not reflect the culture of a predominant nation, but are neutral in so far as the various nations submitted to their jurisdiction are concerned. In the case of States in the latter category, it is impossible to speak of either a national majority or a national minority except from the purely numerical standpoint; one may only speak of different national groups. In the case of multi-national States in which the various nations integrated therein are loyal to the State, a more comprehensive national community often results and co-exists.

. . . Taking the desires of various minority groups as a criterion, the following types can be distinguished:

(*a*) A minority which wishes at most only to preserve certain of its distinguishing characteristics and has little or no interest, because of a feeling of active solidarity with the predominant group, in becoming autonomous;

(*b*) A minority which not only desires preservation and further development of its distinguishing characteristics but also desires to attain either political or administrative autonomy, or full independence or annexation to another State. . . .

41. Modern nationalism has affected minorities in different—even opposite ways. On the one hand, in certain countries it has aided the assimilation of minorities by the predominant group, resulting in a real homogeneity. On the other hand, in other countries it has aroused a consciousness of differences and in some cases has even stirred up the antagonism of the minority. Where the differences were relatively less marked, nationalism has had a unifying effect (e.g., France, Italy and Germany); where they were relatively great (e.g., Austria-Hungary), nationalism has caused the development of minority consciousness. . . .

57. Opinions differ regarding the best solution of the problem created by the existence of minorities. This variety of opinion stems from the widely varying characteristics of different States and from varying conceptions of the goal to be aimed at: assimilation on the one hand, or the preservation of the distinguishing characteristics of particular groups on the other. . . .

58. It would seem that minorities entitled to special positive services and special rights are restricted to groups of citizens held together by ties of common descent, language, culture, or religious faith, etc., who feel that they differ in these respects from the rest of the population, and who desire to preserve their special characteristics and to develop them further.

►NON-SELF-GOVERNING TERRITORIES

CHARTER OF THE UNITED NATIONS

The following three chapters of the U.N. charter deal with dependent peoples. Chapter XI is concerned with the well-being of peoples in colonies, protectorates, dependencies, territories (as Hawaii and Alaska used to be and Guam, the Virgin Islands, or Samoa still are). Such non-self-governing territories are considered to be "owned" by the administering states and therefore within their domestic jurisdiction.

Signatories to the charter accepted as a "sacred trust" promotion of self-government (full independence is not mentioned) in such territories, but carefully avoided establishing any U.N. machinery which would effectively control their administration of colonies. Article 73 (e) obligates administering nations to transmit to the Secretary General only technical data on other than political conditions in such territories.

Chapters XII and XIII are concerned with trust territories which are administered by individual states but not owned by them. Here the goal of independence and self-government is mentioned (art. 76, b). Although the charter envisaged a broad and varied application of the provisions of Chapters XII and XIII to an increasing number of dependent territories, in practice their use has remained limited. Thus only former German colonies in Africa and in the Pacific, which after World War I were administered by the victorious Allies (England, France, Japan, Belgium, New Zealand, Australia) as mandates, have become trust territories after World War II. The United States, for example, administers the former Japanese mandate (originally a German colony—the Marshall, Marianas, and Caroline Islands in the Pacific) as a strategic trust territory (arts. 82, 83). Only one former colony, Somalia, was administered by Italy as a trust until 1960 when it became a state.

Each trust territory is administered by a single nation only. Although often proposed, no collective administration by the United Nations has ever been established (art. 81).

Chapters XII and XIII establish quite an effective control by the United Nations: (1) inhabitants are given the right of petition; (2) administering powers submit—on the basis of a detailed questionnaire—annual reports on conditions in their trust territory (art. 88); (3) these reports are examined by a special United Nations body, the Trusteeship Council (chap. xiii); and (4) every two years special United Nations missions visit and report on trust territories (art. 87). Examples of such reports and problems encountered (especially the lack of homogeneity and exaggerated forms of local patriotism in pygmy-size territories) are reproduced on pages 82-83.

CHAPTER XI.   DECLARATION REGARDING NON-SELF-GOVERNING TERRITORIES

Article 73. Members of the United Nations which have or assume responsibilities for the administration of territories whose peoples have not yet attained a full measure of self-government recognize the principle that the interests of the inhabitants of these territories are paramount, and accept as a sacred trust the obligation to promote to the utmost, within the system of international peace and security established by the present Charter, the well-being of the inhabitants of these territories, and, to this end:

a. to ensure, with due respect for the culture of the peoples concerned, their political, economic, social, and educational advancement, their just treatment, and their protection against abuses;

b. to develop self-government, to take due account of the political aspirations of the peoples, and to assist them in the progressive development of their free political institutions, according to the particular circumstances of each territory and its peoples and their varying stages of advancement;

c. to further international peace and security;

d. to promote constructive measures of development, to encourage research, and to cooperate with one another and, when and where appropriate, with specialized international bodies with a view to the practical achievement of the social, economic, and scientific purposes set forth in this Article; and

e. to transmit regularly to the Secretary-General for information purposes, subject to such limitation as security and constitutional considerations may require, statistical and other information of a technical nature relating to economic, social, and educational conditions in the territories for which they are respectively responsible other than those territories to which Chapters XII and XIII apply.

Article 74. Members of the United Nations also agree that their policy in respect of the territories to which this Chapter applies, no less than in respect of their metropolitan areas, must be based on the general principle of good-neighborliness, due account being taken of the interests and well-being of the rest of the world, in social, economic, and commercial matters.

CHAPTER XII. INTERNATIONAL TRUSTEESHIP SYSTEM

Article 75. The United Nations shall establish under its authority an international trusteeship system for the administration and supervision of such territorites as may be placed thereunder by subsequent individual agreements. These territories are hereinafter referred to as trust territories.

Article 76. The basic objectives of the trusteeship system, in accordance with the Purposes of the United Nations laid down in Article 1 of the present Charter, shall be:

a. to further international peace and security;

b. to promote the political, economic, social, and educational advancement of the inhabitants of the trust territories, and their progressive development towards self-government or independence as may be appropriate to the particular circumstances of each territory and its peoples and the freely expressed wishes of the peoples concerned, and as may be provided by the terms of each trusteeship agreement;

c. to encourage respect for human rights and for fundamental freedoms for all without distinction as to race, sex, language, or religion, and to encourage recognition of the interdependence of the peoples of the world; and

d. to ensure equal treatment in social, economic, and commercial matters for all Members of the United Nations and their nationals, and also equal treatment for the latter in the administration of justice, without prejudice to the attainment of the foregoing objectives and subject to the provisions of Article 80.

Article 77.   1. The trusteeship system shall apply to such territories in the following categories as may be placed thereunder by means of trusteeship agreements:

a. territories now held under mandate;

b. territories which may be detached from enemy states as a result of the Second World War; and

c. territories voluntarily placed under the system by states responsible for their administration.

2. It will be a matter for subsequent agreement as to which territories in the foregoing categories will be brought under the trusteeship system and upon what terms.

Article 78.   The trusteeship system shall not apply to territories which have become Members of the United Nations, relationship among which shall be based on respect for the principle of sovereign equality.

Article 79.   The terms of trusteeship for each territory to be placed under the trusteeship system, including any alteration or amendment, shall be agreed upon by the states directly concerned, including the mandatory power in the case of territories held under mandate by a Member of the United Nations, and shall be approved as provided for in Articles 83 and 85.

Article 80.   1. Except as may be agreed upon in individual trusteeship agreements, made under Articles 77, 79, and 81, placing each territory under the trusteeship system, and until such agreements have been concluded, nothing in this Chapter shall be construed in or of itself to alter in any manner the rights whatsoever of any states or any peoples or the terms of existing international instruments to which Members of the United Nations may respectively be parties.

2. Paragraph 1 of this Article shall not be interpreted as giving grounds for delay or postponement of the negotiation and conclusion of agreements for placing mandated and other territories under the trusteeship system as provided for in Article 77.

Article 81.   The trusteeship agreement shall in each case include the terms under which the trust territory will be administered and designate the authority which will exercise the administration of the trust territory. Such authority, hereinafter called the administering authority, may be one or more states or the Organization itself.

Article 82.   There may be designated, in any trusteeship agreement, a strategic area or areas which may include part or all of the trust territory to which the agreement applies, without prejudice to any special agreement or agreements made under Article 43.

Article 83.   1. All functions of the United Nations relating to strategic areas, including the approval of the terms of the trusteeship agreements and of their alteration or amendment, shall be exercised by the Security Council.

2. The basic objectives set forth in Article 76 shall be applicable to the people of each strategic area.

3. The Security Council shall, subject to the provisions of the trustee-

ship agreements and without prejudice to security considerations, avail itself of the assistance of the Trusteeship Council to perform those functions of the United Nations under the trusteeship system relating to political, economic, social, and educational matters in the strategic areas.

Article 84. It shall be the duty of the administering authority to ensure that the trust territory shall play its part in the maintenance of international peace and security. To this end the administering authority may make use of volunteer forces, facilities, and assistance from the trust territory in carrying out the obligations towards the Security Council undertaken in this regard by the administering authority, as well as for local defense and the maintenance of law and order within the trust territory.

Article 85. 1. The functions of the United Nations with regard to trusteeship agreements for all areas not designated as strategic, including the approval of the terms of the trusteeship agreements and of their alteration or amendment, shall be exercised by the General Assembly.

2. The Trusteeship Council, operating under the authority of the General Assembly, shall assist the General Assembly in carrying out these functions.

CHAPTER XIII.   THE TRUSTEESHIP COUNCIL

COMPOSITION. *Article 86.* 1. The Trusteeship Council shall consist of the following Members of the United Nations:

a. those Members administering trust territories;

b. such of those Members mentioned by name in Article 23 as are not administering trust territories; and

c. as many other Members elected for three-year terms by the General Assembly as may be necessary to ensure that the total number of members of the Trusteeship Council is equally divided between those Members of the United Nations which administer trust territories and those which do not.

2. Each member of the Trusteeship Council shall designate one specially qualified person to represent it therein.

FUNCTIONS AND POWERS. *Article 87.* The General Assembly and, under its authority, the Trusteeship Council, in carrying out their functions, may:

a. consider reports submitted by the administering authority;

b. accept petitions and examine them in consultation with the administering authority;

c. provide for periodic visits to the respective trust territories at times agreed upon with the administering authority; and

d. take these and other actions in conformity with the terms of the trusteeship agreements.

Article 88. The Trusteeship Council shall formulate a questionnaire on the political, economic, social, and educational advancement of the inhabitants of each trust territory, and the administering authority for each trust territory within the competence of the General Assembly shall make an annual report to the General Assembly upon the basis of such questionnaire.

VOTING. *Article 89.* 1. Each member of the Trusteeship Council shall have one vote.

2. Decisions of the Trusteeship Council shall be made by a majority of the members present and voting.

PROCEDURE. *Article 90.* 1. The Trusteeship Council shall adopt its own rules of procedure, including the method of selecting its President.

2. The Trusteeship Council shall meet as required in accordance with its rules, which shall include provision for the convening of meetings on the request of a majority of its members.

Article 91. The Trusteeship Council shall, when appropriate, avail itself of the assistance of the Economic and Social Council and of the specialized agencies in regard to matters with which they are respectively concerned.

►REPORTS ON THE PROGRESS TOWARDS SELF-GOVERNMENT OR INDEPENDENCE IN TRUST TERRITORIES

Following are excerpts from reports on trust territories which were prepared by relatively unbiased United Nations missions. They inspected conditions in trust territories in Africa and in the Pacific. The administering nations are committed (art. 76 b of the U.N. charter), "to promote . . . their [i.e. the inhabitants of the trust territories] progressive development toward self-government or independence as may be appropriate to the particular circumstances." The United Nations charter then clearly recognizes the relative nature of the right to independent statehood.

Trust Territory of New Guinea. *The island of New Guinea is divided into three sections. Western New Guinea is a Dutch colony, which the republic of Indonesia claims as part of its national territory under the name of Irian. Another part is called Papua. It is an Australian colony. Only Chapter XI of the U.N. charter applies to both of these. And the third part, a former German colony, is administered by Australia as a trust territory. It is therefore subject to regular inspection by the U.N. mission. The report on the administration of the trust territory submitted to the United Nations General Assembly of 1956 described the problems relevant to the territory, as follows:*

Geographical characteristics often play an important part in shaping a country's history and nowhere is this more evident than in New Guinea. Europeans who first entered the area in the sixteenth century were discouraged by its rough topography and its swamps and left New Guinea well alone. Moreover, these factors have also influenced the type and course of administration. New Guinea's isolation came to an end in the last quarter of the nineteenth century. . . . The need of European industries for coconut oil provided for the first time a market for one of New Guinea's natural products.

United Nations Visiting Mission to Trust Territories in the Pacific, 1953, *Report on the Trust Territory of the Pacific Islands,* Trusteeship Council, Official Records, T/1077, Supplement No. 3.

In the 1870's the largest trading firm in the Pacific, Godeffroy's, of Hamburg, began trading for copra in the New Guinea Islands. In 1884 Germany formally took possession of what is now the Trust Territory of New Guinea. The administration of the new Territory, then known as German New Guinea, was placed in the hands of a chartered company, the German New Guinea Company, but by 1899 it felt that the burden of administration was too heavy and the Imperial Government assumed control. In 1914 the Territory was occupied by Australian troops and administration was carried out by a military administration until 1921.

In 1920 the League of Nations, in pursuance of Article 22 of the Covenant, conferred upon His Britannic Majesty, for and on behalf of the Government of the Commonwealth of Australia, a Mandate for the Government of the Territory of New Guinea. . . .

The Territory continued to be administered under Mandate until the Japanese invasion brought about the suspension of civil administration and large areas of the Territory were devastated. . . .

With the surrender of the Japanese in 1945 civil administration of the Territory was progressively restored between October, 1945, and June, 1946.

The Trusteeship Agreement for the Territory was approved by the General Assembly of the United Nations on the 13th December, 1946.

The *Papua and New Guinea Act* 1949-1954 approved the placing of New Guinea under the International Trusteeship System and provided for the government of the Territory in an administrative union with the Territory of Papua with the title of the Territory of Papua and New Guinea. . . .

The United Nations Visiting Mission to the Trust Territories in the Pacific, 1956, visited the Territory in 1956. The members of the Mission were—

Sir John Macpherson, G.C.M.G. (United Kingdom), Chairman;
Mr. Daniel Massonet (Belgium);
Mr. José Rolz Bennett (Guatemala);
Mr. M. E. Chacko (India).

The Mission arrived at Rabaul on 15th March, 1956. Arrangements were made for the members to see the conditions and activities in the Territory and to meet all sections of the community.

Some of its observations follow:

The Trust Territory of New Guinea . . . covers some 93,000 square miles and includes that part of the Island of New Guinea north of the Papuan and east of the Dutch New Guinea borders, the islands of the Bismarck Archipelago, of which New Britain, New Ireland and Manus are the largest, and the two northernmost islands of the Solomon Group, namely Buka and Bougainville.

New Guinea Mainland.—The central core of this zone is a massive cordillera which extends from one end of the island to the other, a distance of 1,500 miles. This cordillera is one of the great mountain systems of the world, reaching in several places a height of 15,000 feet. . . .

The total indigenous population of the Territory is estimated at 1,273,837, while the non-indigenous population numbers 13,455. . . .

The indigenous inhabitants of the Territory comprise a great diversity of physical types and a large number of linguistic groups. . . .

Linguistically the picture is varied and so great is the diversity that members of villages only a few miles apart are sometimes unable to understand one another without the aid of an interpreter or recourse to a *lingua franca*. In coastal areas language groups exceeding 5,000 are unusual and a great many are well below that figure. . . . However, it has been possible to recognize three main linguistic groups—Papuo-Melanesian speakers, Papuan speakers and Melanesian pidgin speakers. . . .

Melanesian-pidgin has become the *lingua franca* for the whole of the Trust Territory. The vocabulary includes a large number of words of English derivation, some Melanesian terms from Blanche Bay, New Britain, and a few German, Malay and Polynesian terms. In some cases this medium is used in formal education, but the policy is to eventually make all the people literate in English. The value of its use as a *lingua franca* until the people become literate in English is obvious, and it has also played an important part in breaking down the isolation of the language groups. . . .

The people's sense of community fellowship rarely extends beyond the village or collection of neighboring hamlets. Within the larger groupings made up of those speaking the same language there is usually no strong or widespread feeling for common interests and aims, though there is a consciousness of difference from other groups speaking a different language. . . .

Though these and other modifications of old ways of life may be noted, the Territory remains an area of very great diversity linguistically and socially. Furthermore, it remains one in which concentration of loyalty on village or hamlet groups tends to obscure any conception on the people's part of a community of interest on a Territory-wide scale.

U.S. Trust Territory of the Pacific Islands

Following Japan's defeat in World War II, the Marshall, Marianas, and Caroline Islands became a trust territory, administered by the United States. This territory is an agglomeration of 2,141 individual islands. This makes the implementation of the right of national self-determination or autonomy a stupendous task. The U.N. visiting mission frankly admits the difficulty in its report, submitted to the United Nations General Assembly in 1953.

Three things are of fundamental importance in any consideration of the Trust Territory of the Pacific Islands. These are the vast oceanic zone over which the very small land areas are scattered, the Territory's negligible resources and the diversity of its population. Geography, resources and population are of paramount importance in any Trust Territory, but none is faced with the particular combination of difficulties which are caused by such factors in the Pacific Islands.

The Territory consists of 96 distinct island units or 2,141 individual islands with a combined area of 687 square miles. These consist of three groups: the Marshalls, the Carolines, and the Marianas with the exception of

Guam. They extend from latitude 1° to 20° north and from longitude 130° to 170° east.

A map of the Territory shows a great expanse of ocean studded with small islands. In most cases even the dot locating an island is a gross exaggeration of its size since frequently its land area is actually only a fraction of a square mile. . . .

To administer such a widely scattered Territory, the Administering Authority must maintain six separate administrative centers and furnish them with sea and air communications. . . .

Even with valuable and well developed resources the Territory would still find communications a major problem. The fact that the Pacific Islands on the contrary have meagre and poorly developed resources magnifies the difficulty. Geography and resources are complementary aspects of the general economic situation of the Territory, and the paucity of natural resources, in the Mission's opinion, is a basic obstacle to the immediate development of a self-sufficient economy and the maintenance of an adequate communication system in the Territory. . . .

With the exception of the people on the islands of Nukuoro and Kapingamarangi, who are Polynesians, the rest of the indigenous people are classified as Micronesians. Aside from this convenient classification, scarcely any other unity exists. The people in the Mariana Islands, Yap, Palau, Truk, Ponape, Kusaie, Nukuoro, Kapingamarangi and the Marshall Islands each speak their own separate and distinct languages. They have their own customs and patterns of living. . . .

A characteristic of the islanders is the placing of local interests ahead of wider ones. Natural loyalties are to the family or clan, then to the home village. Rarely do these extend beyond the individual island. District unity is still only a sophisticated concept accepted by the more advanced Micronesians, and such a thing as national unity is desired by only a few. . . . In these circumstances the development of local government must begin from the family or clan level and progress from these to the village, island, district and Territory as a whole. An attempt to force this process of advancement would inaugurate a social revolution which would have unforeseeable repercussions throughout the whole structure of the indigenous societies. . . .

There exists great insularity among the majority of the inhabitants and . . . in some instances there is to be found a degree of cultural hostility between the members of different island groups. An instance of this . . . is to be found in a petition . . . which the Mission received in the Marshall Islands and which protests against the activities of a Ponapean trading company. A passage in this petition may be cited as follows: "We understand and appreciate the American ideal of 'One People' but we are a separate country from Ponape with our own separate customs and culture and language and have no more desire to be classed with or merged with the Ponapeans than France has desire to merge with Germany or China with Japan. We feel that it is unfair to us as a people to be lumped together with other groups of Micronesian peoples as one people. We are proud of our race and our heritage and fear any attempt to merge us culturally or otherwise with other peoples with the resultant loss of our own culture and individuality.". . .

Like its predecessor, the Mission on several occasions received requests from indigenous inhabitants for a closer relationship with and even incorporation into the United States of America. In each case the Mission explained that under the terms of the Trusteeship Agreement the Micronesians would have an opportunity to voice their wishes concerning their future status at an appropriate time.

TOPIC 3

Nationalism in Asia and Africa

While closely related to nationalism in Western Europe, nationalism in Asia and Africa has some specific features:

1. The nationalist leaders of Asia and Africa have asserted their national aspirations *against* the West. This may imply certain racial overtones: it is a struggle against *white* supremacy waged by possibly united *colored* races. In such a framework, imperialism is usually defined as a domination by Europeans of non-European colored masses. The term "imperialism" would not be used by Asians and Africans with regard to the Soviet forms of expansion in Eastern Europe.

"It is understandable," writes the founder of the All India Congress Socialist Party,[1] "that deprived now of British or Dutch rule on which to blame all our misfortunes, we should look outside our country for a whipping boy to take the place of our old masters. Memories of past political subjection combine with resentment at continuing claims to white supremacy to make the United States, the current symbol of white supremacy, the obvious target of our righteous anger. By a queer twist, the Great Russian, who is also a white man, is excluded from this hated category! For one thing, Russia has been presented to us as a great Eurasian Power, and the unfortunate use of the terms 'East' and 'West' by the statesmen and columnists of England and America only helps to confirm this."

In their struggle against Western encroachment, some Asians advocate complete isolation from the Western way of life and forms of thinking. Others, on the contrary, advocate the imitation of the West, its dynamism and its philosophies. These include communism, which came to Asia from the West along with democracy, liberalism, socialism, fascism, and other West European creeds.

2. In Asia and Africa the idea of nationalism electrified the masses which live in extreme misery and backwardness. Under such circumstances national independence has become a symbol, not only of freedom from foreign domi-

[1] M. R. Masani, "The Mind of Asia," *Foreign Affairs*, Vol. XXXIII, No. 4, p. 556.

nation but also of freedom from want. Impatience and search for a quick solution of economic and social problems is more typical than concern for a liberal concept of national freedom combined with individual liberties within the new nation. National strength has become the most important criterion.

3. The new states are confronted with greater handicaps in terms of administrative and technical personnel than were the minorities in more advanced areas of Europe. British and French rulers in Asia and Africa were separated from their subjects by a much more significant cultural gap than that existing in the liberation movements of the Slavs (against Germans and Austrians) or the Irish (against the British).

Finally, there is one discouraging similarity between the nationalisms of Asia and Europe. The common struggle against the common enemy—the West—eliminated or minimized the antagonisms between ethnic or religious groups in Asia and Africa. This was, for instance, the case of Moslem-Hindu enmity in India. Following the attainment of independence from the West, several inter-Asian or inter-African rivalries long dormant made a quick appearance. India split into three units: India proper, and Moslem Pakistan (speaking Urdu and Punjabi) in the West, and Moslem Pakistan (speaking Bengali) in the East. Mutual intolerance, suspicion of each other's ultimate objectives, disloyalty of minority groups, demands for secession (the perhaps unavoidable result of national self-determination), and other undesirable aspects of European nationalism tend to repeat themselves in Asia and Africa.

Harsh treatment of Chinese minorities in Southeast Asia in general, and in Indonesia in particular, as well as those minorities' disloyalty to the host countries, remind us of similar tensions which used to prevail in East Central Europe with regard to German, Hungarian, or Slavic minorities.

In addition, tension between communism and democracy has separated one Asian nation from another and has created the Communist, the pro-Western, and the uncommitted groupings. It also cuts *across* otherwise homogeneous nations. The divisions of China, Viet-nam, and Korea are only the most obvious and physical expressions of the deep divisions which fragment the whole of Asia and Africa.

►ASIAN NATIONALISM VIS-À-VIS OTHER ASIAN NATIONS

GAGANVIHARI L. MEHTA

An Indian nationalist discusses the dynamism of Asian nationalism, its relation to the impact of West European thought and system on Asia, and the need to accompany political emancipation with the economic one. The author is former Ambassador of India to the United States. He is a frequent contributor to Indian journals.

The selection appeared as an article in *The Annals of the American Academy of Political and Social Science,* July, 1958, p. 89.

Nationalism in Asia, as we know it today, is undoubtedly the most significant development of this century. Although its roots are embedded in ancient cultural heritage, it emerged and grew in Asia after it had appeared in Europe. . . .

The development of Asian nationalism like its origins has been different from that of European nationalism. Historically, the development of Asia has been in terms of regional rather than national groupings such as China and East Asia; India and South East Asia; West Asia comprising the Arab lands; and Central Asia. The great religions of Asia—and I may add parenthetically that all the spiritual religions have had their origin in Asia and the East—Hinduism, Buddhism and Islam spread over the continent at different times and in different phases and complexions. These religions have in many ways been a primary impulse for the regional groupings and cultural inheritance of Asia. Similarity of culture is often as important as a common racial origin. Within each of these religions there have been a variety of ethnic, cultural, economic and political associations. But the concept in each case may be compared to that of Christendom in post-Roman Europe rather than to that of separate nation states. Within these regional groups there have, no doubt, been different competing states, princedoms, tribal groups, and so forth. Regional rivalries and contests for local supremacy have divided them, but these have taken the form of a struggle for domination within the group rather than of country against country as in Europe.

European Impact in Asia

. . . It was the coming of Europeans into Asia that produced a tremendous impact. Europeans first came to Asia as traders and it has been said that they acquired their empires in Asia unintentionally and as though by accident. India, said the historian Seeley, was conquered by the British in a fit of absent-mindedness. Unfortunately, however, peoples of these lands did not have the necessary presence of mind to counter the absent-mindedness that was so positive. The fact is that Europeans were pushful, aggressive traders prepared to use force and to hold territories to the extent necessary for commercial exploitation. It was rather the Asians who lost their freedom—political or economic or both—through inadvertence. Inspired by local rivalries rather than national feeling, many a ruler sought the help of one European power or another against his rival, only to find that he himself had become subject to his foreign friends. . . .

. . . This is not to deny that what is loosely called "colonialism" did bring some benefits to these peoples and lands. Apart from the spread of literacy, better health standards, communications and rudiments of industries —which, incidentally, would have been possible through contacts with the West without alien domination—Eastern countries owe to the West concepts of law and forms or representative government and administrative system. Even Marxists do not deny that such alien capitalism could be a step forward from indigenous feudalism. No impartial person can deny many concrete advantages which foreign rule has brought to Asian countries. Moreover, what an eminent Irishman, Sir Horace Plunkett, said about his own country is equally pertinent for Asian countries which have been under foreign domination, that "Irish history is something which Britishers should remember and Irishmen should forget." Nevertheless, it is simply not true that the Western countries have no moral responsibility or obligations to countries which have enabled them to a smaller or greater extent to build up their wealth and power.

Western Ideas and Asian Freedom Movements

European dominance over Asia had the effect of cutting off contacts among Asians and shifting their political relationships and economies to the West. But it was this very domination which generated in course of time a spirit of resistance against foreign rule and engendered the growth of nationalism in different countries of Asia. Yearning for freedom and movements for achieving national independence were inspired and stimulated in the nineteenth century by the impact of Western ideas—the English liberal philosophers, the French Encyclopedists and the French Revolution, and the American Revolution with its Declaration of Rights. Garibaldi and Mazzini's fight for independence of Italy and Ireland's struggle for Home Rule fired the imagination of the intelligentsia in my country. . . . It is of interest to mention that the British Prime Minister Sir Henry Campbell Bannerman's memorable words, "good government is no substitute for self-government," after the Boer War became a sheet anchor for those striving for self-rule. Asian peoples were thrilled by Japan's victory over Russia (1904-1905) which they hailed as the triumph of an Asian nation over a European power. Japan's development into a modern state was followed with keen interest until Japan's conquest of other Asian countries produced a feeling of revulsion. . . .

When, during World War I, President Woodrow Wilson enunciated the principle of national self-determination, countries in Asia were immensely enthused and demanded that this principle be applied not merely to the subject nations of Germany, the Austro-Hungarian Empire and the Ottoman Empire but also to those who were under the domination of the Allied Powers. There was a ferment in Asia towards the end of that war and it was then that the constitutional agitation for self-government in India became a dynamic mass movement. Leaders, like Mahatma Gandhi, Sun Yat-sen, Mustafa Kemal, and Nahas Pasha, became the pioneers of a resurgent Asia.

The freedom movement in Asian countries got a fillip during World War II. The ostensible objectives of that war such as safeguarding of democracy and liberty against fascism and nazism stimulated a demand for realization of these ideals in subject countries. The "four freedoms" proclaimed by the late President Roosevelt became a beacon for dependent and economically underdeveloped countries. National independence was demanded as implementing the principles for which the Allies fought Germany, Italy and Japan; and a desire for economic development received stimulus from the emphasis on "freedom from want." On the other hand and paradoxically, dramatic Japanese military successes were hailed by many in Asia, including those who detested militarism and Japanese chauvinism, as evidence of what an Asian country could achieve if it had the opportunity to develop its strength. Many Asians derive similar satisfaction from China's emergence as a powerful country; they look upon it less as a Communist phenomenon than as evidence of Asia's revival. . . .

The resurgence of Asia after the end of the war is, as Arnold Toynbee has observed, the most significant event of the present century and is "more explosive than the atom bomb." During the last ten years, over 600 million people of the world have emerged from their dependent status covering nearly 29 countries. These countries have achieved national freedom mainly through the enlightened policies of the ruling powers but partly also because of the collapse of imperial authority. In this ferment, there was a renewed desire to re-establish old contacts and make new ones within Asia. . . .

. . . The most important and organized expression of Asian consciousness was the Bandung Conference in April 1955 where the leading statesmen of 29 countries of Asia and Africa representing 56 per cent of the world's population met together. These countries have different political, social, and economic systems; some are members of mutually hostile military and political groupings while some are not aligned militarily to either power bloc. Nevertheless, the governments of these countries found enough in common to issue a unanimous declaration of principles, and the peoples of these lands were eager that mutual co-operation should be fostered despite differences in their ideologies or social systems. The Bandung declaration, it will be recalled, stressed respect for national sovereignty and integrity; equality of all races and nations, great and small; and the need for international co-operation. It has been evident that Asian countries are determined that they will no longer be under alien domination or permit themselves to be exploited because of their race or color. It is also significant that they are asserting themselves despite the fact that they lack economic strength or military power. This movement for equality and dignity is not simply negative, it is not only a revolt against political domination, economic exploitation, and racial discrimination. It is also a call for co-operation and partnership with the West on a free and equal basis.

The so-called Asian-African group at the United Nations now comprises 29 members. Even after some possible reduction as a result of recent mergers of some Arab States, its future strength is likely to be greater with the addition of new members. Thirty-one new members have joined the United Nations since its inception; 19 of these or over 60 per cent are from Asia and Africa. Further additions will be mostly from these two continents. Although members of this group are free to take their own decisions and frequently vote on different sides on important issues, their collective voice is becoming increasingly important and their views cannot be ignored on matters affecting Asia and Africa, colonialism, or racial tensions. Many of these countries also hold strong views about their being made helpless victims of a nuclear holocaust as a consequence of hostilities between great powers, and some of them have an aversion to military alliances or membership of any bloc. These countries taken as a whole account for the bulk of the world's population and their voice has to be heard on important international issues such as disarmament. Besides, most of these countries are underdeveloped and, although comprising the majority of the world's population, have only 15 per cent of the world's income; their common economic and social problems are, therefore, an additional link between them and engender similar approach on many economic questions. . . .

The independence of these Asian nations is incomplete until they can get rid of foreign bases as well as their stagnant, undiversified economies which, in part, are the legacy of alien rule. There is, in these countries, "a revolution of rising expectations," and the vast masses of these lands will no longer remain content with their lot. As Bertrand Russell has pointed out, it is "scientific technique" that "the East regards as important and distinctive in the West" and it is "this alone that the East is willing to learn from the West." It has been estimated, for instance, that less than 2 per cent of the world's armaments budget could provide Asia with more than three times her power capacity. Asia's transformation depends, in the last analysis, on removing gross poverty, drudgery, hunger, malnutrition, and disease; on eradicating illiteracy; and on providing better opportunities of employment—in other words, the emancipation of Asian nations is not complete until life is made more bearable for millions of people, giving them some sense of hope and confidence. It is because communism claims to be able to remove the social and economic evils of poorer countries promptly, methodically, and completely that it appeals to many downtrodden peoples. . . .

In Asia, as in the rest of the world, there are many unresolved problems among countries. . . .

Frequently, there is discussion of rivalry among nations in Asia, as, for instance, competition between industrialized Japan and India or the "race" between India and China. The peoples of Asia like those in other countries closely follow economic developments, social trends, and political movements in neighboring countries and elsewhere in the whole region. But differences in the mode or rate of development need not necessarily be categorized in terms of the cold war. Social and economic evils exist in Asia irrespective of Marxism and have to be fought and removed with intelligence and determination. Different countries follow various paths to achieve the aim of social welfare and economic development. Provided again there is no attempt to impose one system or the other by force or by subversion, those who believe in democratic values should have enough confidence to meet the challenge. . . .

Freedom and Responsibility

The existence of a nation, said Renan, is a daily plebiscite. It has been in Asia an assertion of the right of a group of people to determine their destiny free from alien interference and domination. But it has been something more. It has been an awareness of an entity submerged or forgotten in the dim past: a consciousness of a new dignity and self-respect for a people.

We in Asia have also to realize that new freedoms bring new responsibilities, that the right of self-rule carries with it a moral obligation to be a responsible member of a world community.

►ASIAN ISOLATIONISM: JAPAN

To ward off foreign domination and exploitation, Asians have tried complete isolation as well as faithful imitation of Western European capitalist or Communist techniques, ideas, and patterns of conquest.

Japan is an early example of both extremes. In 1636 an edict (a portion of it is reproduced below) was issued to prevent any Japanese from going abroad, and, at the same time, to stop the spread of un-Japanese ideology, the Catholic faith in particular.

Three years later the military ruler of Japan closed the country to all foreigners except the Dutch and the Chinese, who were believed to be interested in trade only and not in proselytizing. They were allowed to trade at Nagasaki under strict surveillance.

Edict Closing Japan

1. No Japanese ships may leave for foreign countries.

2. No Japanese may go abroad secretly. If anybody tries to do this, he will be killed, and the ship and owner will be placed under arrest whilst higher authority is informed.

3. Any Japanese now living abroad who tries to return to Japan will be put to death.

4. If any Christian (*Kirishitan*) believer is discovered, you (the authorities at Nagasaki) will make a full investigation.

5. Any informer revealing the whereabouts of a Jesuit (*bateren*) will be paid 200 or 300 pieces of silver. If any other categories of Christians (*Kirishitan*) are discovered, the informer will be paid at your discretion as hitherto. . . .

8. Strict search will be made for *bateren* [Jesuits] on all incoming ships.

9. No offspring of Southern Barbarians will be allowed to remain. Anyone violating this order will be killed, and all relatives punished according to the gravity of the offense.

10. If any Japanese have adopted the offspring of Southern Barbarians they deserve to die. Nevertheless, such adopted children and their foster-parents will be handed over to the Southern Barbarians for deportation.

11. If any deportees should try to return or to communicate with Japan by letter or otherwise, they will of course be killed if they are caught, whilst their relatives will be severely dealt with, according to the gravity of the offense.

This selection is from C. R. Boxer, *The Christian Century in Japan, 1549-1650* (Berkeley: University of California Press, 1951), pp. 439-40.

From the first half of the seventeenth century until July 14, 1853, when the bluff American commodore Matthew Calbraith Perry defiantly dropped anchor in Tokyo Bay, the Japanese rulers managed to keep the West at arm's length. "Then in the course of a few years," writes an American authority[1] on Japan, "they became convinced by the demonstration of Western naval superiority that Japan could defend itself only by adopting Western military techniques, and long before Occidentals had penetrated far into Japan, much less established colonial enclaves, the Japanese reacted with such energy and violence that within a few decades (that is, in 1904-1905) they were able to defeat Russia, one of the chief imperialist powers of the West."

►ASIAN ISOLATIONISM: CHINA

CHIANG KAI-SHEK

In the middle of the nineteenth century, China's isolation was forcibly interrupted by the Western imposition of trade contacts. The result was a number of the so-called "unequal treaties," which forced on the Chinese several limitations of their sovereignty: "treaty ports" were opened to foreign trade; the Chinese government was not allowed to fix its own tariffs on foreign goods or prohibit the importation of opium; inland waterways were opened to foreign shipping; foreigners owned factories in the "treaty ports" and were granted concessions which permitted them to lease land and carry on business without being subject to Chinese laws and administration.

The "unequal treaties" were renounced by the United States and Great Britain in 1942, one hundred years after their humiliating imposition on China (Opium War, 1839-1842). In a bitter commentary, Chiang Kai-shek deplores the unequal treaties and the resulting contact with the West for their effects on Chinese government, law, economics, ethics, and psychology. The author is the President of Nationalist China, and has lived on the island of Taiwan since the Communist conquest of China mainland in 1950.

For the last hundred years, Western science has greatly benefited Chinese civilization. This cannot be denied. After the Opium War, in the belief that the Western powers were rich and strong because of their guns and ships, the Chinese people began to study the technique of making guns and ships. After the War of 1894, the Chinese people also began to study foreign social and political institutions. Famous works of Western social science were translated into Chinese. Discussion of Western social and political theories began to appear in magazines and newspapers. For several decades after this, as a result of discussion, popular study, comparison, and observation, China's applied science, natural science, and social science all made progress. In

[1] Edwin O. Reischauer, *Wanted: An Asian Policy* (New York: Alfred A. Knopf, 1955), p. 50.

The selection is from *China's Destiny* (New York: Roy Publishers, copyright 1947).

some fields, we even made important new contributions to human knowledge. The power and prestige of science was fully recognized in Chinese thought and learning.

On the other hand, during the past hundred years, China's civilization showed signs of great deterioration. This was because, under the oppression of the unequal treaties, the Chinese people reversed their attitude toward Western civilization from one of opposition to one of submission, and their attitude toward their own civilization changed from one of pride to one of self-abasement. Carried to extremes, this attitude of submission [to Western theories] became one of ardent conversion and they openly proclaimed themselves loyal disciples of this or that foreign theory. Similarly, the attitude of self-abasement was carried to such an extreme that they despised and mocked the heritage of their own civilization. We should bear in mind that from the Opium War down to the Revolution of 1911, the unanimous demand of the people was to avenge the national humiliation and make the country strong, and all efforts were concentrated on enriching the country and strengthening the army. In other words, it was our unwillingness to become slaves that first caused us to study Western civilization. It follows that we should also study Western civilization for the purpose of winning our independence and making China strong. Unfortunately, after the Revolution of 1911, the will to avenge our national humiliation and make the country strong perished with the failure of the Revolution, and the effects of the unequal treaties were further deepened after this failure. Unconsciously, the people developed the habit of ignoring their own traditions and cultivating foreign ways; of respecting foreign theories and despising their native teachings; of depending upon others and blindly following them. Thus, although the Chinese people originally studied Western civilization because of their unwillingness to become slaves, the result was that they unconsciously became the slaves of foreign theories because of their studies of Western civilization.

After the May 4th [1919] Movement,[1] the ideas of Liberalism [Democracy] and Communism spread throughout the country. But those that advocated these ideas had no real knowledge of the enduring qualities of Chinese culture; they were simply looking for something new. Moreover, they merely endeavored to copy the superficial aspects of Western civilization without attempting to adopt its basic principles for the benefit of the Chinese economy and the people's livelihood. As a result, the educated classes and scholars generally lost their self-respect and self-confidence. Wherever the influence of these ideas prevailed, the people regarded everything foreign as right and everything Chinese as wrong. . . . They worshiped this or that foreign country in a similar manner. Different cliques existed among them only because there was more than one country and more than one foreign theory in the world.

[1] The May 4th Movement of 1919 was a great movement of students and intellectuals that marked the beginning of China's modern revolutionary history. It was both anti-imperialist and antifeudal, and represented the reaction of Chinese intellectuals to the turbulent new forces unleashed by the First World War. In specific protest against the terms of the Versailles Treaty as they affected China, and against the terms of Japan's infamous "Twenty-One Demands," huge student demonstrations were held in Peking on May 4, 1919 to denounce the pro-Japanese Peking Government.

Each clique imitated one particular country and worshiped one particular theory, forming a group around its particular one, and declaring that all who belonged to that clique were right and all who did not were wrong. Since the theories of the various countries were constantly changing, each of these cliques had to change its theories repeatedly in accordance with these foreign changes. Their ideas circulated widely and disturbed the people. But from an objective point of view, their ideas and proposals did not coincide with our nation's psychology and character, and from the subjective point of view, they lacked a solid foundation, since they were based on foreign theories and were constantly having to change. Thus, all the movements led by them lasted only a short time.

If we examine the theories and political proposals put forward since the Revolution, we find that all of them were copies of foreign theories. In 1913, the arguments for a parliamentary system, a cabinet system, and a presidential system in reality reflected the differences between the British, the French, and the American political systems. In 1920, the opposing theories of a centralized as against a federal state reflected the differences between the French and the American systems of local government. The theoretical basis of the monarchy of Yuan Shih-k'ai was provided by an American editorial, and the constitution of Tsao K'un was an exact copy of the Weimar Constitution of Germany.

As for the struggle between Liberalism and Communism, it was merely a reflection of the opposition of Anglo-American theories to those of Soviet Russia. Not only were such political theories unsuited to the national economy and the people's livelihood, and opposed to the spirit of China's own civilization, but also the people that promoted them forgot that they were Chinese and that they should study and apply foreign theories for the benefit of China. As a result, their copying [of Western theories] only caused the decay and ruin of Chinese civilization, and made it easy for the imperialists to carry on cultural aggression. China's theoreticians and political leaders, either directly or indirectly, intentionally or unintentionally, adopted the theories and interests of the imperialists as their own, and forgot their own origin and the purpose of their study. They even maintained this attitude in social propaganda and education, thus causing the people to accept without question the unequal treaties and the aggression and exploitation of the imperialists. This is the greatest single danger of cultural aggression, and the greatest threat to the nation's spirit. We citizens must wake up in time and correct this attitude. Only thus can we save our country and make China strong and independent, with a position of equality among the other nations of the world. . . .

For the past hundred years under the oppression of the unequal treaties, the people fell into decadent habits and evil practices in their daily life. Each person took his own selfish interest as the basis for determining right or wrong. . . . As a result, depraved and frivolous persons attained power in the villages, and scheming citizens pursued their lawless way in the towns and cities, sacrificing public welfare and other people's happiness for their own selfish end. Furthermore, literary theories and political writings were used to conceal, or even to justify the evils of this way of life. These writings glorify selfish desires and the quest for profit in order to incite social struggle. The tradition of emulating the sages, worshipping the heroes, and following the precept of our forefathers not only tended to perish but was despised by the people. They even praised foreign figures and scorned the history of their country. . . . As a consequence, the nation became like a pan of loose sand, and the state fell into disintegration and disunity; the people failing to realize that when the nation and the state are in danger of dismemberment, there is nothing that the individual can depend upon for his own existence.

The ancient sages said: "Propriety, righteousness, modesty, and honor are the four pillars of a state. If the four pillars are not strong, the state will perish." When we think and speak of the future, must we not tremble? Must we not be ashamed and disturbed?

►"THE EAST MUST BECOME WESTERN"

SUTAN SJAHRIR

Unlike Chiang, who claimed that China's philosophy was "superior to any other philosophy in the world," Sutan Sjahrir expresses his admiration for the rationality and vitality of the West.

Paradoxically, Sjahrir's interesting thoughts on the subject were written during eight years of confinement by the Dutch, beginning in 1934.

"There has been no specific accusation, no mention of an oral or written offense; in point of fact they have not been able to charge me with any misdemeanor," wrote Sjahrir when, at the age of twenty-five, he was notified that by virtue of the Netherlands Indies Government Ordinance he was sentenced to the Boven Digoel prison camp on New Guinea "for spreading hate and endangering public tranquillity and order."

Sjahrir is an Indonesian nationalist, founder of the Socialist Party of Indonesia and later the Prime Minister of his country, following its liberation from the Dutch after World War II.

The following lines were written during Sjahrir's exile at Banda Neira in the Moluccas Islands where he had been transferred after one year's imprisonment at Digoel camp. As he notes in his book, Out of Exile, *he was still a prisoner but his prison had increased in size and comfort.*

December 31, 1936.

For me, the West signifies forceful, dynamic, and active life. It is a sort of Faust that I admire, and I am convinced that only by a utilization of this dynamism of the West can the East be released from its slavery and subjugation.

The West is now teaching the East to regard life as a struggle and a striving, as an active movement to which the concept of tranquillity must be subordinated. Goethe teaches us to love striving for the sake of striving, and

The selection is from *Out of Exile* by Sutan Sjahrir, copyright © 1949 by The John Day Company, by permission of The John Day Company, Inc., publisher.

in such a concept of life there is progress, betterment, and enlightenment. The concept of striving is not, however, necessarily connected with destruction and plunder as we now find it. On the contrary, even in Faust, striving and struggle have the implication of constructive work, of undertaking great projects for the benefit of humanity. In this sense, they signify a struggle against nature, and that is the essence of struggle: man's attempt to subdue nature and to rule it by his will. The forms that the struggle take indicate the development and refinement of the individuals who are engaged in the effort.

What we need is not rest—or death—but a higher form of living and of striving. We must extend and intensify life, and raise and improve the goals toward which we strive. This is what the West has taught us, and this is what I admire in the West despite its brutality and its coarseness. I would even take this brutality and coarseness as accompanying features of the new concept of life that the West has taught us. I would even accept capitalism as an improvement upon the much famed wisdom and religion of the East. For it is precisely this wisdom and religion that make us unable to understand the fact that we have sunk to the lowest depths to which man can descend: we have sunk to slavery and to enduring subjugation.

What we in the East admire most in the West is its indestructible vitality, its love for life and for the fulfillment of life. Every vital young man and young woman in the East ought to look toward the West, for he or she can learn only from the West to regard himself or herself as a center of vitality capable of changing and bettering the world.

The East must become Western in the sense that it must acquire as great a vitality and dynamism as the West. Faust must reveal himself to the Eastern man and mind, and that is already going on at present.

It is, I suppose, not so unusual that I am sometimes called a "half Westerner," and I am often distrusted by those who are fanatically inclined toward Eastern civilization and culture, and who reject Western "materialism." It is true that I hate self-deception and submissiveness, and that instead I support the desire and courage to live that the West represents.

This does not, however, mean that I idealize the West as it now is. On the contrary, I am quite aware that there is deceit and decay in the West as well, but I nevertheless feel that it represents an improvement over what is generally and commonly implied by the term "Eastern." What I value most highly in the West is its resilience, its vitality, its rationality—and it is only rationality that can possibly control human life.

The following two documents make direct references to the American Revolution. Such references partly express admiration for the triumph of the thirteen colonies, which were successful in their revolution against the English and finally emerged as a more powerful nation than their former masters; partly they attempt to drive a wedge between the United States and its West European Allies, with their colonial interests in Asia.

▶VIET-NAM TO BE FREE FROM THE FRENCH

HO CHI MINH

The author is a former secretary to Michael Borodin (the Russian Comintern agent in China), founder of the Communist movement of Viet-nam, leader of its revolutionary activities, and President of Communist North Viet-nam.

"All men are created equal. They are endowed by their Creator with certain inalienable rights, among these are Life, Liberty, and the Pursuit of Happiness."

This immortal statement was made in the Declaration of Independence of the United States of America in 1776. Now if we enlarge the sphere of our thoughts, this statement conveys another meaning: All the peoples on the earth are equal from birth, all the peoples have a right to live, be happy and free.

The Declaration of the Rights of Man and the Citizen of the French Revolution in 1791 states: "All men are born free and with equal rights, and must always be free and have equal rights." Those are undeniable truths.

Nevertheless for more than eighty years, the French imperialists deceitfully raising the standard of Liberty, Equality, and Fraternity, have violated our fatherland and oppressed our fellow citizens. They have acted contrarily to the ideals of humanity and justice.

In the province of politics, they have deprived our people of every liberty.

They have enforced inhuman laws; to ruin our unity and national consciousness, they have carried out three different policies in the north, the center and the south of Viet-nam.

They have founded more prisons than schools. They have mercilessly slain our patriots; they have deluged our revolutionary areas with innocent blood. They have fettered public opinion; they have promoted illiteracy.

To weaken our race they have forced us to use their manufactured opium and alcohol.

In the province of economics, they have stripped our fellow citizens of everything they possessed, impoverishing the individual and devastating the land. . . .

We are convinced that the Allied nations which have acknowledged at Teheran and San Francisco the principles of self-determination and equality of status will not refuse to acknowledge the independence of Viet-nam.

A people that has courageously opposed French domination for more than eighty years, a people that has fought by the Allies' side these last years

The selection is from *The Declaration of Independence of the Republic of Viet-nam*, September 2, 1945, published by the Government of the Democratic Republic of Vietnam, *Documents*. Quoted in *Conflict in Indo-China and International Repercussions, A Documentary History, 1945-1955* (ed. Allan B. Cole; Ithaca: Cornell University Press, 1956), pp. 19-21.

against the fascists, such a people must be free, such a people must be independent.

For these reasons, we, members of the provisional government of Viet-nam, declare to the world that Viet-nam has the right to be free and inde-pendent, and has in fact become a free and independent country. We also declare that the Viet-namese people are determined to make the heaviest sacrifices to maintain its independence and its liberty.

►THE SHOT AT LEXINGTON HEARD IN INDONESIA

SUKARNO

. . . I have come here to learn something from America—from America not merely as a place, not merely as a nation, but America as a state of mind, America as the centre of an idea.

It was this very America which was in fact the first product of national-ism, of anti-colonialism and of the principle of independence. It is this America which, as the hot-house of American technology, surpassed the de-velopment of older sister-nations and became a great power—nay, one of the most powerful nations in the world today. Present-day America as a world phenomenon, with all its impact on the peoples of the earth, was the child of a marriage between the revolutionary America of Washington, Jefferson and Lincoln and, the technological America imbued with the prodigious technical spirit of Edison and Ford.

The shot that was fired at Lexington on the nineteenth of April 1775 was heard around the world. It echoes still in the hearts of all who have re-cently won their independence, and it echoes still in the hearts of peoples who still struggle against their colonial bonds.

Over half the world the burning words which fired the American War of Independence have been closely studied as a source of inspiration and a plan of action. Yes, this period is the period of Asian and African resurgence.

If we could see the passage of history as yesterday I saw your country from the windows of an aeroplane, we could have no doubt that the world is passing through the period of Asian and African nationalism.

I hesitate at using that word "nationalism," for I know that in many countries and in many nations nationalism is an out-of-date political doctrine. Please remember, Mr. Speaker, that for us of Asia and Africa nationalism is a young and progressive creed. We do not equate nationalism with chauvin-ism, and we do not interpret nationalism as meaning the superiority of our peoples over others. No! For us, nationalism means the rebuilding of our nations; it means the effort to provide equal esteem for our peoples; it means the determination to take the future into our own hands. For us, nationalism

The selection is from Sukarno's address before the United States Congress, "On the Aims of Indonesia," May 17, 1956.

is the love of country and the determination to improve it which, not so very long ago, illumined the actions of the founders of your nation. Nationalism may be an out-of-date doctrine for many in this world; for us of Asia and Africa, it is the mainspring of our efforts. Understand that, and you have the key to much of post-war history. Fail to understand it, and no amount of thinking, no torrent of words, and no Niagara of dollars will produce anything but bitterness and disillusionment.

We who are living in Asia and Africa during this period of Asian and African nationalism, and particularly those of us who have been called upon to guide the destiny of nations, we ask that the rest of the world should show understanding and sympathy. . . . Our efforts and the sacrifices we have made have been for the release of our people from a colonial tyranny lasting for generations and centuries. It has been a struggle—it is still a struggle—for the simple human demands which the rest of the world has long taken for granted.

▶DIFFERENT LANGUAGES—A THREAT TO INDIAN UNITY?

P. KODANDA RAO

India has been split into three by religious antagonisms. Is it going to be further shaken by language differences? The present Indian constitution recognizes fourteen major languages of India as official. In many areas of the world language has proved the most important heritage of the past. It influences the political thinking of the masses and their leaders. Will this be the case of India? An Indian nationalist expresses that fear. He is P. Kodanda Rao, who was a member of India's delegations to two Round Table conferences between India and South Africa in 1926 and 1932.

Linguism

Currently, linguism has come to occupy the center of the stage. It is based on the community of language and the claim that Indians speaking the same language should have a state: *one language, one state.* At present some of the States in India, corresponding to the States in the United States, are largely unilingual, but some are bilingual or multilingual. Under British rule one state or province, Orissa, was carved out to make it unilingual, while the unilingual Province of Bengal was in 1905 partitioned to create a Moslem province. The latter was subsequently cancelled to restore the unilingual province. Since independence, the Andhra state was carved out from the multilingual Madras Province to constitute a unilingual state.

Its creation stimulated the demand for the reorganization of the whole of India on a unilingual basis. The States Reorganization Commission, ap-

The selection is from an article, "Communalism in India," *Current History,* February, 1956, p. 84.

pointed by the Government of India, . . . was distressed by the linguistic rivalries and fissiparous tendencies, which might weaken the unity of India. Nevertheless, it conceded the linguistic demand, but sought to keep fissiparous tendencies in check by proposing expedients to strengthen the Central Government. . . .

There are those who fear that linguism, like communalism, might end in the break-up of India and the creation of linguistic sovereignties, in spite of hopes and assurances to the contrary. They suggest that the only effective way to retain and strengthen the unity of India, on which there is unanimity of opinion, is to abolish the autonomous States and establish India as a single unitary state. The fissiparous linguistic communalism of today, when there is no British overlord to stoke it, is somewhat disillusioning to the ardent Indian nationalist.

TOPIC 4

Nationalism and Communism—Conflict or Alliance?

The Marxist economic interpretation of history and its concept of the decisive importance of the class struggle—the struggle between the exploited and the exploiters—has logically led to the concept of proletarian internationalism. If, according to Marxism, membership in a given social-economic class is the decisive factor, and if capitalism is an international phenomenon, then, indeed, it follows that the "workingman has no fatherland." His membership in the class of the exploited must take precedence over his loyalty to the instrument of bourgeois exploitation, the national state. "Proletarians of all countries, unite!"—the slogan of the Communist Manifesto of 1848 which still appears more than a century later on the first page of every legitimate Communist publication—expresses the idea of the opposition to nationalism.

Lenin and Stalin believed in the theory but they were confronted with the realities of the revolutionary struggle against the Tsarist government. The weakness of the internationalist socialist movement in Russia could, so it seemed, be offset by the dynamism of the nationalist revolt among the non-Great-Russian nationalities of Tsarist Russia: Ukrainians, Georgians, Turkmens, etc. Although the revolt of these peoples against cultural oppression did not fit the internationalist and economic dogma of Marxism, it appeared useful to the Communist efforts to weaken the Tsarist government. The colonial revolts, although not Marxist in their orientation or leadership, could be supported because their effectiveness meant an indirect weakening of the capitalist front in Europe and therefore aided the Communists in Russia. This was in accordance with Lenin's theory on imperialism as the final phase of advanced capitalism on a world scale (see p. 270).

On December 17, 1917, the following appeal was addressed to the Moslems of Russia and the East:

> The rule of the robbers and enslavers of the peoples of the earth is about to end. . . . A new world is being born, a world of workers and free men. . . .
>
> Moslems of Russia, Tartars of the Volga and the Crimea, Kirghiz and Sarts of Siberia and Turkestan, Turks and Tatars of the Transcaucasia, Chechens and Mountaineers of the Caucasus—all those whose mosques and chapels have been destroyed, whose beliefs and customs have been trampled under foot by the Tsars and oppressors of Russia. Henceforth, your beliefs and customs, your national and cultural institutions, are free and inviolable. Build your national life freely and unhindered. You have a right to do so.
> [Etc. . . .]

> (Signed)   DZUGASHVILI (STALIN)
> V. ULYANOV (LENIN)

The potential conflict between nationalism, the right of national self-determination and sovereign independence on one side, and the demand for a proletarian, international discipline, on the other, was a matter of speculation and concern for the Communist leaders even prior to the emergence of the first Communist national state, the Russian Federal Republic. In the early 1920's Lenin and Stalin tended to distinguish between nationalism of ethnic groups composing the former Tsarist multinational empire and that of potential future Communist states which might emerge outside the confines of Soviet Russia proper.

Recommending finally a tight federal union for Ukrainians, Byelorussians and Georgians, the Communist leaders seemed to visualize Communist East Central Europe as a loose form of confederation. Stalin, writing to Lenin, considered inadvisable an outright incorporation of a future Soviet Germany, Poland and Hungary into the Soviet Union:

> It is doubtful whether these people, with their own states, armies, finances, would—once Soviet—consent to enter into direct federal union with Soviet Russia as the Bashkirs or Ukrainians did . . . because they would see in a Soviet type of federation a device of reducing their political independence, [and] a violation of this independence . . . the most expedient form . . . would be a confederation, a union of independent states.[1]

Until the end of World War II, this problem was a subject for only theoretical discussion. In 1945, it became a matter of practical politics. While the European Communist Parties were in the opposition and in need of Soviet money, guidance and encouragement, it was relatively simple for the Soviet Union to suppress nationalist deviations as they had appeared, here and there, within the German, French or other Communist Parties. The experience, power and monopoly in success gave the Motherland of Socialism and the Land of October Revolution an easy upper hand.

[1] V. l. Lenin, *Sochineniia,* 3rd edition, Vol. XXV, p. 624.

After the Second World War, however, the European Communist Parties emerged from their obscure status of outlawed or permanent opposition parties and in East Central Europe became leading partners in different forms of National Front coalition governments. Underground agitators became prime ministers, ministers of finance, police and defense, secretaries of the treasury. Operating within a national environment which at the end of a long war against German oppression may be described as emotionally patriotic, these Communist leaders and their partners in Moscow had to find a new formula for mutually satisfactory relationships between the Soviet Union and the Communist national states. . . . They are still in search of such a formula.

The clash between local economic and other interests, on one hand, and the central will in Moscow, on the other, formed the background not only for the first major crisis in 1948 (Yugoslavia), but equally for the 1956 crisis (Hungary and Poland). In the middle of the Cominform's dispute with Tito in 1948 the Bulgarian Communist leader Vulko Chervenkov coined the slogan:

> There cannot be true love for one's fatherland if the love is in one way or another opposed to the love of the Soviet Union.

This was an answer to Tito's assertion:

> No matter how much each of us love the land of Socialism, the Soviet Union, he can in no case love his country less which is also developing socialism.[2]

Albeit expressed in terms of somewhat "erotic" dialectic, this is the core of the matter—and the main source of conflict, past and future, within the Soviet bloc. Chervenkov's dictum was easy to formulate. Its implementation proves difficult, as it does not quite suggest what to do when the economic, trade and other interests of a people's democracy point one way, and Soviet policy considerations point the opposite way.

As in other areas of the world, nationalism and the desire for national self-determination in Eastern Europe represent a powerful force—the more so as the Soviet controls stand not only for foreign rule and foreign interests but also for totalitarian elimination of civil liberties.

►MARXISM AND THE NATIONAL AND COLONIAL QUESTION

JOSEPH STALIN

Stalin's lectures at Sverdlovsk University summarize the Communist rationalization with regard to nationalism: a nationalist revolt is to be supported if

---

[2] Royal Institute of International Affairs, 1948, *The Soviet Yugoslav Dispute,* "CPSU to CPY," May 4, 1948, p. 38.

The selection is from *Marxism and the National and Colonial Question* (London: Lawrence and Wishart, Ltd., 1936). It is there headed: "Extract from a Series of Lectures on the Foundations of Leninism Delivered at the Sverdlov University—April 1924."

*it weakens capitalism, but condemned as reactionary and counter-revolu-
tionary if it weakens the cause of socialism. In 1920, Stalin illustrated his
theory by the following concrete example:*

We are *for* the separation of India, Arabia, Egypt, Morocco and other
colonies from the Entente, for the separation in this case means the freeing
of these oppressed countries from imperialism, the weakening of imperialist
positions, the strengthening of revolutionary positions. We are *against* the
separation of the border-territories from Russia, because separation in this
case means imperialist slavery for the border-territory, the weakening of the
revolutionary capabilities of Russia, the strengthening of the imperialist
positions. . . . the question of separation is to be decided in dependence on
concrete international conditions, in dependence on the interests of the revolution. [Stalin's italics.]

*Joseph Stalin was the head of the Communist Party of the Soviet Union
until his death in 1953. His position was unchallenged after the elimination
in 1927 of Trotsky, his main opponent in the struggle for Lenin's mantle.*

*World War II and its aftermath have contradicted Stalin's thesis, which
is reprinted below. According to Stalin oppressed nationalities have only two
ways open to them: either to free themselves from the Western domination
by means of a revolution and amalgamate with the Communist orbit, or remain subjugated by capitalism.*

*Actually most of the British and French colonies have obtained, or are
about to obtain, their national independence peacefully. Only a very few
amalgamated with the Communist orbit. The majority have chosen either to
remain within the British Commonwealth or French Community, or decided
on the neutralist course of nations uncommitted to either bloc. On the other
hand, East Central Europe has been amalgamated with the Soviet orbit forcibly, with the more or less open assistance of the Soviet Army. Thus the stage
was set for a new—Communist—version of colonial and national oppression.*

1. The Presentation of the Problem

Formerly, the national question was usually confined to a small group
of questions chiefly affecting "cultured" nationalities. The Irish, the Hungarians, the Poles, the Finns, the Serbs and several other nationalities in
Europe made up the list of non-sovereign nations in whose fate the heroes of
the Second International were interested. The countless millions of Asiatic
and African peoples who were suffering under the yoke of national oppression
in its crudest and most brutal form usually remained outside their field of
vision. They could not make up their minds to put white and black, "cultured" and "uncultured" on the same plane. Two or three meaningless, luke-
warm resolutions, which carefully evaded the question of colonial emancipation, were all the leading spirits of the Second International could boast of.
Such a dual and half-hearted attitude to the national question must now be
considered a thing of the past. Leninism laid bare this crying incongruity,
broke down the wall between whites and blacks, between Europeans and
Asiatics, between the "cultured" and "uncultured" slaves of imperialism and
thus linked the national question with the question of the colonies. In this
way the national question was transformed from a partial and internal question of a particular state into a general and international question, into the

world question of the emancipation of the oppressed peoples in the dependent countries and colonies from the yoke of imperialism. . . .

Leninism has broadened the conception of self-determination, interpreting it as the right of the oppressed peoples in dependent countries and colonies to complete secession, as the right of nations to independent political existence. . . .

Formerly, the national question was regarded in a reformist way, it was regarded as an independent question separate from the general question of capitalist rule, of the overthrow of imperialism and the proletarian revolution. It was tacitly assumed that the victory of the proletariat in Europe was possible without a direct alliance with the movement for emancipation in the colonies, that the national and colonial question could be solved surreptitiously, that it would solve itself, off the highroad of the proletarian revolution, without a revolutionary struggle against imperialism. Now this anti-revolutionary point of view must be considered exposed. Leninism has proved, and the imperialist war and the revolution in Russia have confirmed, that the national question can be solved only in connection with and on the basis of the proletarian revolution, and that the road to the victory of the revolution in the West lies through a revolutionary alliance with the liberation movement of the colonies and dependent countries against imperialism. The national question is part and parcel of the general question of the proletarian revolution, part and parcel of the question of the dictatorship of the proletariat.

The question is as follows: are the revolutionary possibilities inherent in the revolutionary movement for emancipation of the oppressed countries *already exhausted* or not; and if not, is there any hope, any basis for believing that these possibilities may be utilized for the proletarian revolution, that the dependent and colonial countries may be transformed from a reserve of the imperialist bourgeoisie into a reserve of the revolutionary proletariat, into an ally of the latter?

Leninism replies to this question in the affirmative, that is, it recognizes that there are revolutionary capabilities inherent in the national liberation movement of the oppressed countries, and that they can be utilized for the purpose of overthrowing the common enemy, for the purpose of overthrowing imperialism. The mechanics of the development of imperialism, the imperialist war and the revolution in Russia entirely confirm the deductions made by Leninism in this respect.

Hence the necessity for the proletariat supporting, vigorously and actively supporting, the national liberation movement of the oppressed and dependent peoples.

This of course does not mean that the proletariat must support *every* national movement, everywhere and always, in every single, concrete instance. The point is that support must be given to those national movements which tend to weaken imperialism and bring about the overthrow of imperialism, and not to strengthen and preserve it. Cases occur when the national movements in certain oppressed countries come into conflict with the interests of the development of the proletarian movement. In such cases, of course, support is entirely out of the question. The rights of nations are not an isolated and self-contained question, but part of the general question of the proletarian revolution, a part which is subordinate to the whole and which must be dealt with from the point of view of the whole. In the forties of the last century, Marx favored the national movement of the Poles and the Hungarians and was opposed to the national movement of the Czechs and the Southern Slavs. Why? Because the Czechs and the Southern Slavs were at that time "reactionary nations," "Russian outposts" in Europe, outposts of absolutism, whereas the Poles and the Hungarians were "revolutionary nations" which were fighting absolutism; because to give support to the national movement of the Czechs and Southern Slavs at that time would have been to give indirect support to tsarism, a most dangerous enemy of the revolutionary movement in Europe.

> "The various demands of democracy," writes Lenin, "including self-determination, are not an absolute, they are *particles* of the general democratic (at present general socialist) *world* movement. In individual concrete cases, a particle may contradict the whole; if it does, then it must be rejected." ("The Discussion on Self-Determination Summed Up," *Collected Works,* Vol. XIX.)

Such is the position with regard to the various national movements, with regard to the possible reactionary character of these movements, that is, of course, if they are examined concretely, from the point of view of the interests of the revolutionary movement and not from the formal point of view, from the point of view of abstract rights.

The same must be said of the revolutionary character of national movements in general. The unquestionably revolutionary character of the overwhelming majority of national movements is as relative and specific as the possible reactionary character of certain national movements. The revolutionary character of a national movement in the conditions of imperialist oppression does not necessarily presuppose the existence of proletarian elements in the movement, the existence of a revolutionary or a republican programme of the movement, the existence of a democratic basis for the movement. The struggle which the Emir of Afghanistan is waging for the independence of his country is objectively a *revolutionary* struggle, despite the monarchist views of the Emir and his entourage, for it weakens, disintegrates and undermines imperialism, whereas the struggle waged by "desperate" democrats and "Socialists," "revolutionaries" and republicans, like, for example, Kerensky . . . during the imperialist war, was a *reactionary* struggle, for it resulted in the embellishment, the reinforcement and the victory of imperialism. For the same reason, the struggle which the Egyptian merchants and bourgeois intellectuals are waging for the independence of their country is objectively *revolutionary* despite the bourgeois origin and bourgeois calling of the leaders of the Egyptian national movement and despite the fact that they are opposed to socialism; whereas the fight the British Labor Government is waging to perpetuate Egypt's state of subjection is for the same reason a *reactionary* struggle, despite the proletarian origin and the proletarian calling of the members of that government and despite the fact that they are "for" socialism. I will not even mention the national movement in other, more extensive, colonial and dependent countries like India and China, every step of which along the road to liberation, even though it runs counter to the formal demands of democracy, is a steam hammer blow at imperialism, *i.e.,* is undoubtedly a *revolutionary* step.

Lenin was right in saying that the national movement of the oppressed countries should be judged not from the point of view of formal democracy, but from the point of view of the actual results in the sum total of the struggle against imperialism, that is to say, "not in an isolated way, but on a world scale." ("The Discussion on Self-Determination Summed Up," *Collected Works,* Vol. XIX.)

2. The Liberation Movement of the Oppressed Peoples and the Proletarian Revolution

In its solution of the national question Leninism proceeds from the following propositions:

a) The world is divided into two camps: the camp of a handful of civilized nations which possess finance capital and exploit the vast majority of the population of the globe, and the camp of the oppressed and exploited peoples of the colonies and dependent countries that comprise that majority;

b) The colonies and the dependent countries, oppressed and exploited by finance capital, constitute an enormous reserve power and a most important source of strength for imperialism;

c) The revolutionary struggle of the oppressed peoples in the dependent and colonial countries against imperialism is the only road that leads to their emancipation from oppression and exploitation;

d) The principal colonial and dependent countries have already entered on the path of the national liberation movement, which is bound to bring about a crisis in world capitalism.

e) The interests of the proletarian movement in the advanced countries and of the national liberation movement in the colonies require the fusion of these two aspects of the revolutionary movement into a common front against the common enemy, imperialism;

f) The victory of the working class in the developed countries and the liberation of the oppressed peoples from the yoke of imperialism are impossible without the formation and the consolidation of the common revolutionary front;

g) The formation of a common revolutionary front is impossible unless the proletariat of the oppressor nations renders direct and determined support to the liberation movement of the oppressed peoples against the imperialism "of its own country," for "no nation can be free if it oppresses other nations" (Marx);

h) This support implies the advocacy, defense and realization of the slogan of the right of nations to secession and to independent political existence;

i) Unless this slogan is put into effect, the amalgamation and collaboration of nations within a single world system of economy, which constitutes
the material basis for the victory of socialism, will be impossible;

j) This amalgamation can only be a voluntary one and must be based
on mutual confidence and fraternal relations between the nations.

Hence the two aspects, the two tendencies in the national question: the
tendency towards political emancipation from imperialist fetters and the
formation of an independent national state, arising out of imperialist oppression and colonial exploitation; and the tendency towards closer economic
relations between the nations resulting from the formation of a world market
and a world economic system.

> "Developing capitalism," says Lenin, "knows of two historical tendencies
> in the national question. The first is the awakening of national life and of
> national movements, the struggle against all national oppression, the creation
> of national states. The second is the development and growing frequency of
> all sorts of relations between nations, the breaking down of national barriers,
> the creation of the international unity of capital, and of economic life in
> general, of politics, of science, and so forth. Both tendencies are the univer-
> sal law of capitalism. The first predominates at the beginning of its develop-
> ment, the second characterises capitalism mature and approaching its trans-
> formation into a socialist society." ("Critical Remarks on the National
> Question," *Collected Works*, Vol. XVII.)

For imperialism these two tendencies represent irreconcilable contradictions because imperialism cannot subsist without the exploitation of colonies
and their forcible retention within the framework of "one integral whole,"
for imperialism can bring the nations closer to each other only through annexations and the seizure of colonies, without which it is generally speaking,
inconceivable.

For communism, on the contrary, these tendencies are only two sides of
a single cause—that of the emancipation of the oppressed peoples from the
yoke of imperialism; for communism knows that the amalgamation of the
nations into a single world economic system is possible only on the basis of
mutual confidence and voluntary agreement; that the formation of a voluntary
amalgamation of nations must be preceded by the separation of the colonies
from the "integral" imperialist "whole," by the transformation of the colonies
into independent states. . . .

This is what Lenin says of the two-fold work that Communism performs
in educating the workers in the spirit of internationalism:

> " . . . Can this education . . . be *concretely identical* in large oppressing
> nations and in small oppressed nations, in annexing nations and in annexed
> nations?
>
> "Obviously not. The way to the one goal: to complete equality, to the
> most intimate contact and to the subsequent *fusion of all* nations obviously
> proceeds here by different roads in each concrete case—in the same way, let
> us say, as the direction to a point in the middle of this page is towards the
> left from one side, and towards the right from the other. If a Socialist be-
> longing to a large, oppressing, annexing nation, in advocating the fusion of

nations in general, were to forget even for one moment that 'his' Nicholas II, 'his' Wilhelm, George, Poincaré, etc., *also stands for fusion* with the small nations (by means of annexations)—Nicholas II for 'fusion' with Galicia, Wilhelm II for 'fusion' with Belgium, etc.—such a Socialist would prove to be a ridiculous doctrinaire in theory and an abettor of imperialism in practice.

"The weight of emphasis in internationalist education for the workers in the oppressing countries must necessarily be that they must preach and uphold the right of secession for the oppressed countries. Without this there can be *no* internationalism. It is our right and duty to treat every Socialist of an oppressing nation who *fails* to conduct such propaganda as an imperialist and a scoundrel. This is an unconditional demand, even if the *chance* of secession being possible and 'feasible' before the introduction of socialism is only one in a thousand. . . .

"On the other hand, a Socialist belonging to a small nation must concentrate the weight of his agitation on the *second* word of our general formula: 'voluntary *amalgamation*' of nations. Without violating his duties as an internationalist he may be in favor of *either* the political independence of his nation *or* its inclusion in the neighboring state, X, Y, Z, etc. But in all cases he must fight *against* small-nation narrow-mindedness, reserve and aloofness, he must fight for the recognition of the general and the whole, for the subordination of the interests of the particular to the interests of the general.

"Those who have not thought over the question thoroughly think there is a 'contradiction' in Socialists of oppressing nations insisting on the 'right of *secession*' while Socialists of oppressed nations insist on the 'right to *amalgamation*.' A little reflection, however, will show that from *this* position there is not, nor can there be, any *other* road towards internationalism and the fusion of nations." ("The Discussion on Self-Determination Summed Up," *Collected Works*, Vol. XIX.)

►CAN A COMMUNIST BE A PATRIOT?

MAO TSE-TUNG

The answer by the leader of Chinese Communism is: yes. It is contained in a report submitted by Mao Tse-tung to the plenary session of the Central Committee of the Communist Party of China in October 1938, that is, in the second year of the Sino-Japanese War. Mao Tse-tung was the President of Communist China until 1959.

In leading the masses to struggle against the enemy, Communists should view things by taking into account the whole situation, the majority and the allies who are working together. They should grasp the principle of subordinating the needs of a part to the needs of the whole. If a certain idea seems practicable from a partial view of the situation but is impracticable from the

The selection is from Mao's *Selected Works*, Vol. II (New York: International Publishers, 1954).

over-all view, we should subordinate the part to the whole. Conversely, if it seems impracticable from a partial view of the situation but is practicable from the over-all view, we should also subordinate the part to the whole. This is taking into account the whole situation. . . .

Can a Communist, who is an internationalist, be at the same time a patriot? We hold that he not only can but also ought to be one. The specific content of patriotism is determined by historical conditions. There is the "patriotism" of the Japanese aggressors and of Hitler, and there is our own patriotism. Communists must resolutely oppose the so-called "patriotism" of the Japanese aggressors and of Hitler. The Communists in Japan and Germany are all defeatists in the wars of their respective countries. It suits the interests of the Japanese and German people to ensure by every means that the Japanese aggressors and Hitler are defeated in their wars, and the more complete the defeat, the better. The Japanese and German Communists should do this and they are doing this. For the wars launched by the Japanese aggressors and Hitler are, besides doing harm to the people of the world, doing harm to their own people as well. China's case is different because she is a victim of aggression. The Chinese Communists must therefore combine patriotism with internationalism. We are at once patriots and internationalists, and our slogan is to fight in defense of the motherland against the aggressors. For us defeatism is a crime, and to win the War of Resistance is a duty that we cannot shirk. For only by fighting in defense of the motherland can we defeat the aggressors and achieve national liberation. And only by achieving national liberation will it be possible for the proletariat and the toiling-masses to achieve their own liberation. The victory of China and the defeat of the imperialists invading China will also be a help to the people of foreign countries. Thus patriotism is simply an application of internationalism in the war of national liberation. For this reason every Communist must put forth all his activity, march valiantly and resolutely to the front of the war of national liberation, and train his gun on the Japanese aggressors. For this reason our Party, since the Incident of September 18, has issued the call for a war of national self-defense to resist the Japanese aggressors, and later on proposed an Anti-Japanese National United Front, ordered the reorganization of the Red Army as a part of the Anti-Japanese National Revolutionary Army and its march to the front, and instructed its members to go to the forefront of the Anti-Japanese War and be ready to defend the mother land to the last drop of their blood. All these patriotic actions are proper; they are the application of internationalism in China and do not in any way run counter to it. Only people who are politically muddle-headed or who have ulterior motives will be so foolish as to call this a dictate or an abandonment of internationalism.

►NATIONAL COMMUNISM IS COMMUNISM IN DECLINE

MILOVAN DJILAS

Communism necessarily becomes national communism in the course of its development within a given national environment. But when communism reflects national tradition and starts making concessions to it, it is communism in decline, particularly in non-communist states. This is the thesis of Milovan Djilas, former Vice-President of Yugoslavia and friend of Tito, who was expelled from the Yugoslav Communist Party in 1954. In 1956 Djilas was sentenced to prison for his public criticism of Tito's regime.

1.

In essence, Communism is only one thing, but it is realized in different degrees and manners in every country. Therefore it is possible to speak of various Communist systems, i.e., of various forms of the same manifestation.

The differences which exist between Communist states—differences that Stalin attempted futilely to remove by force—are the result, above all, of diverse historical backgrounds. Even the most cursory observation reveals how, for example, contemporary Soviet bureaucracy is not without a connecting link with the Czarist system in which the officials were, as Engels noted, "a distinct class." Somewhat the same thing can also be said of the manner of government in Yugoslavia. When ascending to power, the Communists face in the various countries different cultural and technical levels and varying social relationships, and are faced with different national intellectual characters. These differences develop even farther, in a special way. Because the general causes which brought them to power are identical, and because they have to wage a struggle against common internal and foreign opponents, the Communists in separate countries are immediately compelled to fight jointly and on the basis of a similar ideology. International Communism, which was at one time the task of revolutionaries, eventually transformed itself, as did everything else in Communism, and became the common ground of Communist bureaucracies, fighting one another on nationalistic considerations. Of the former international proletariat, only words and empty dogmas remained. Behind them stood the naked national and international interests, aspirations, and plans of the various Communist oligarchies, comfortably entrenched.

The nature of authority and property, a similar international outlook, and an identical ideology inevitably identify Communist states with one another. Nevertheless, it is wrong to ignore and underestimate the significance of the inevitable differences in degree and manner between Communist states. The degree, manner, and form in which Communism will be realized, or its

The selection is from *The New Class, An Analysis of the Communist System* (New York: Frederick A. Praeger, 1957).

purpose, is just as much of a given condition for each of them as is the essence of Communism itself. No single form of Communism, no matter how similar it is to other forms, exists in any way other than as national Communism. In order to maintain itself, it must become national.

The form of government and property as well as of ideas differs little or not at all in Communist states. It cannot differ markedly since it has an identical nature—total authority. However, if they wish to win and continue to exist, the Communists must adapt the degree and manner of their authority to national conditions.

The differences between Communist countries will, as a rule, be as great as the extent to which the Communists were independent in coming to power. Concretely speaking, only the Communists of three countries—the Soviet Union, China, and Yugoslavia—independently carried out revolutions or, in their own way and at their own speed, attained power and began "the building of socialism." These three countries remained independent as Communist states even in the period when Yugoslavia was—as China is today—under the most extreme influence of the Soviet Union; that is, in "brotherly love" and in "eternal friendship" with it. In a report at a closed session of the Twentieth Congress, Khrushchev revealed that a clash between Stalin and the Chinese government had barely been averted. The case of the clash with Yugoslavia was not an isolated case, but only the most drastic and the first to occur. In the other Communist countries the Soviet government enforced Communism by "armed missionaries"—its army. The diversity of manner and degree of the development in these countries has still not attained the stage reached in Yugoslavia and China. However, to the extent that ruling bureaucracies gather strength as independent bodies in these countries, and to the extent that they recognize that obedience to and copying of the Soviet Union weaken themselves, they endeavor to "pattern" themselves on Yugoslavia; that is, to develop independently. The Communist East European countries did not become satellites of the U.S.S.R. because they benefited from it, but because they were too weak to prevent it. As soon as they become stronger, or as soon as favorable conditions are created, a yearning for independence and for protection of "their own people" from Soviet hegemony will rise among them.

With the victory of a Communist revolution in a country a new class comes into power and into control. It is unwilling to surrender its own hard-gained *privileges,* even though it subordinates its *interests* to a similar class in another country, solely in the cause of ideological solidarity.

Where a Communist revolution has won victory independently, a separate, distinct path of development is inevitable. Friction with other Communist countries, especially with the Soviet Union as the most important and most imperialistic state, follows. The ruling national bureaucracy in the country where the victorious revolution took place has already become independent in the course of the armed struggle and has tasted the blessings of authority and of "nationalization" of property. Philosophically speaking, it has also grasped and become conscious of its own essence, "its own state," its authority, on the basis of which it claims equality.

This does not mean that this involves only a clash—when it comes to that—between two bureaucracies. A clash also involves the revolutionary elements of a subordinated country, because they do not usually tolerate domination and they consider that relationships between Communist states must be as ideally perfect as predicted in dogma. The masses of the nation, who spontaneously thirst for independence, cannot remain unperturbed in such a clash. In every case the nation benefits from this: it does not have to pay tribute to a foreign government; and the pressure on the domestic government, which no longer desires, and is not permitted, to copy foreign methods, is also diminished. Such a clash also brings in external forces, other states and movements. However, the nature of the clash and the basic forces in it remain. Neither Soviet nor Yugoslav Communists stopped being what they are—not before, nor during, nor after their mutual bickerings. Indeed, the diverse types of degree and manner with which they insured their monopoly led them mutually to deny the existence of socialism in the opposite camp. After they settled their differences, they again acknowledged the existence of socialism elsewhere, becoming conscious that they must respect mutual differences if they wanted to preserve that which was identical in essence and most important to them.

The subordinate Communist governments in East Europe can, in fact must, declare their independence from the Soviet government. No one can say how far this aspiration for independence will go and what disagreements will result. The result depends on numerous unforeseen internal and external circumstances. However, there is no doubt that a national Communist bureaucracy aspires to more complete authority for itself. This is demonstrated by the anti-Tito processes in Stalin's time in the East European countries; it is shown also by the current unconcealed emphasis on "one's own path to socialism," which has recently come to light sharply in Poland and Hungary. The central Soviet government has found itself in difficulty because of the nationalism existing even in those governments which it installed in the Soviet republics (Ukraine, Caucasia), and still more so with regard to those governments installed in the East European countries. Playing an important role in all of this is the fact that the Soviet Union was unable, and will not be able in the future, to assimilate the economies of the East European countries.

The aspirations toward national independence must of course have greater impetus. These aspirations can be retarded and even made dormant by external pressure or by fear on the part of the Communists of "imperialism" and the "bourgeoisie," but they cannot be removed. On the contrary, their strength will grow.

It is impossible to foresee all of the forms that relations between Communist states will assume. Even if cooperation between Communist states of different countries should in a short time result in mergers and federations, so can clashes between Communist states result in war. An open, armed clash between the U.S.S.R. and Yugoslavia was averted not because of the "socialism" in one or the other country, but because it was not in Stalin's interest to risk a clash of unforeseeable proportions. Whatever will happen between Communist states will depend on all those factors which ordinarily affect political events. The interests of the respective Communist bureaucracies, expressed variously as "national" or as "united," along with the unchecked tendency toward ever increasing independence on a national basis, will, for the time being, play an important role in the relationships among the Communist countries. . . .

Today national Communism is a general phenomenon in Communism. To varying degrees all Communist movements—except that of the U.S.S.R. against which it is directed—are gripped by national Communism. In its time, in the period of Stalin's ascendancy, Soviet Communism also was national Communism. At that time Russian Communism abandoned internationalism, except as an instrument of its foreign policy. Today Soviet Communism is compelled, even if indefinitely, to acknowledge a new reality in Communism.

Changing internally, Soviet imperialism was also compelled to alter its views toward the external world. From predominantly administrative controls, it advanced toward gradual economic integration with the East European countries. This is being accomplished by means of mutual planning in important branches of economy, in which the local Communist governments today mainly voluntarily concur, still sensing themselves weaker externally and internally.

Such a situation cannot remain for long, because it conceals a fundamental contradiction. On the one hand national forms of Communism become stronger, but on the other, Soviet imperialism does not diminish. Both the Soviet government and the governments of the East European countries, including Yugoslavia, by means of accords and cooperation, are seeking solution to mutual problems which influence their very nature—preservation of a given form of authority and of property ownership. However, even if it is possible to effect cooperation with respect to property ownership, it is not possible with respect to authority. Although conditions for further integration with the Soviet Union are being realized, those conditions which lead to the *independence* of the East European Communist governments are being realized even more rapidly. The Soviet Union has not renounced authority in these countries, nor have the governments of these countries renounced their craving to attain something similar to Yugoslav independence. The degree of independence that will be attained will depend on the state of international and internal forces.

Recognition of national forms of Communism, which the Soviet government did with clenched teeth, has immense significance and conceals within itself very considerable dangers for Soviet imperialism.

It involves freedom of discussion to a certain extent; this means ideological independence too. Now the fate of certain heresies in Communism will depend not only on the tolerance of Moscow, but on their national potentialities. Deviation from Moscow that strives to maintain its influence in the Communist world on a "voluntary" and "ideologic" basis cannot possibly be checked.

Moscow itself is no longer that which it was. It single-handedly lost the monopoly of the new ideas and the moral right to prescribe the only permissible "line." Renouncing Stalin, it ceased to be the ideological center. In

Moscow itself the epoch of great Communist monarchs and of great ideas came to an end, and the reign of mediocre Communist bureaucrats began.

"Collective leadership" did not anticipate that any difficulties and failures were awaiting it in Communism itself—either externally or internally. But what could it do? Stalin's imperialism was exorbitant and overly dangerous, and what was even worse, ineffective. Under him not only the people generally, but even the Communists, grumbled, and they did so at the time of a very strained international situation.

The world center of Communist ideology no longer exists; it is in the process of complete disintegration. The unity of the world Communist movement is incurably injured. There are no visible possibilities whatsoever that it can be restored. However, just as the shift from Stalin to "collective leadership" did not alter the nature of the system itself in the U.S.S.R., so too national Communism has been unable, despite ever increasing possibilities for liberation from Moscow, to alter its internal nature, which consists of total control and monopoly of ideas, and ownership by the party bureaucracy. Indeed, it significantly alleviated the pressure and slowed down the rate of establishment of its monopoly over property, particularly in the rural areas. But national Communism neither desires nor is able to transform itself into something other than Communism, and something always spontaneously draws it toward its source—toward the Soviet Union. It will be unable to separate its fate from that which links it with the remaining Communist countries and movements.

National modifications in Communism jeopardize Soviet imperialism, particularly the imperialism of the Stalin epoch, but not Communism either as a whole or in essence. On the contrary, where Communism is in control these changes are able to influence its direction and even to strengthen it and make it acceptable externally. National Communism is in harmony with non-dogmaticism, that is, with the anti-Stalinist phase in the development of Communism. In fact, it is a basic form of this phase. . . .

National Communism similar to that in Yugoslavia could be of immense international significance in Communist parties of non-Communist states. It could be of even greater significance there than in Communist parties which are actually in power. This is relevant above all to the Communist parties in France and Italy, which encompass a significant majority of the working class and which are, along with several parties in Asia, the only ones of major significance in the non-Communist world.

Until now, the manifestations of national Communism in these parties have been without major significance and impetus. However, they have been inevitable. They could, in the final analysis, lead to profound and essential changes in these parties.

These parties have to contend with the Social Democrats—who are able to channel the dissatisfied masses toward themselves by means of their own socialist slogans and activity. This is not the only reason for the eventual deviation of these parties from Moscow. Lesser reasons may be seen in the periodic and unanticipated reversals of Moscow and of the other ruling Communist parties. Such reversals lead these and other nonruling Communist parties into a "crisis of conscience"—to spit on what until yesterday they extolled, then suddenly to change their line. Neither oppositionist propaganda nor administrative pressure will play a fundamental role in the transformation of these parties.

The basic causes for deviation of these parties from Moscow may be found in the nature of the social system of the countries in which they operate. If it becomes evident—and it appears likely—that the working class of these countries is able through parliamentary forms to arrive at some improvement in its position, and also to change the social system itself, the working class will abandon the Communists regardless of its revolutionary and other traditions. Only small groups of Communist dogmaticists can look dispassionately at the disassociation of the workers; serious political leaders in a given nation will endeavor to avoid it even at the cost of weakening ties with Moscow.

Parliamentary elections which give a huge number of votes to Communists in these countries do not accurately express the actual strength of Communist parties. To a significant degree they are an expression of dissatisfaction and delusion. Stubbornly following the Communist leaders, the masses will just as easily abandon them the moment it becomes obvious to them that the leaders are sacrificing national institutions, or the concrete prospects of the working class, to their bureaucratic nature, or to the "dictatorship of the proletariat" and ties with Moscow.

Of course, all of this is hypothesis. But even today these parties are finding themselves in a difficult situation. If they really wish to be adherents of parliamentarianism, their leaders will have to renounce their anti-parliamentary nature, or change over to their own national Communism which would, since they are not in control, lead to disintegration of their parties.

The leaders of Communist parties in these countries are driven to experiment with the idea of national Communism and national forms by all of these factors: by the strengthening of the possibility that the transformation of society and the improvement of position of the workers will be attained by democratic means; by Moscow's reversals, which by the down-grading of the cult of Stalin ultimately resulted in destruction of the ideologic center; by concurrence of the Social Democrats; by tendencies toward unification of the West on a profound and enduring social basis as well as a military one; by military strengthening of the Western bloc which offers increasingly fewer prospects for "brotherly aid" for the Soviet army; and by the impossibility of new Communist revolutions without a world war. At the same time fear of the inevitable result of a transition to parliamentarianism, and of a breaking off with Moscow, prevents these leaders from doing anything of real significance. Increasingly deeper social differences between the East and the West work with relentless force. The clever Togliatti is confused, and the robust Thorez is wavering. External and internal party life is beginning to bypass them.

Emphasizing that today a parliament can serve as a "form of transition to socialism," Khrushchev intended at the Twentieth Congress to facilitate manipulation of the Communist parties in "capitalist countries," and to stimulate the cooperation of Communists and Social Democrats and the formation of "People's Fronts." Something like this appeared realistic to him, according to his words, because of the changes which had resulted in the strengthening of Communism and because of peace in the world. With that he tacitly acknowledged to everyone the obvious impossibility of Communist revolutions in the developed countries, as well as the impossibility of further expansion of Communism under current conditions without the danger of a new world war. The policy of the Soviet state has been reduced to a status quo, while Communism has descended to gradual acquisition of new positions in a new way.

A crisis has actually begun in the Communist parties of the non-Communist states. If they change over to national Communism, they risk forsaking their very nature; and if they do not change over, they face a loss of followers. Their leaders, those who represent the spirit of Communism in these parties, will be forced into the most cunning manipulations and unscrupulous measures if they are to extricate themselves from this contradiction. It is improbable that they will be able to check disorientation and disintegration. They have reached a state of conflict with the real tendencies of development in the world and in their countries that obviously lead toward new relationships.

National Communism outside of the Communist states inevitably leads toward renunciation of Communism itself, or toward the disintegration of the Communist parties. Its possibilities are greater today in the non-Communist states, but obviously, only along the lines of separation from Communism itself. Therefore, national Communism in these parties will emerge victorious only with difficulty and slowly, in successive outbursts.

In the Communist parties that are not in power it is evident that national Communism—despite its intent to stimulate Communism and strengthen its nature—is simultaneously the heresy that nibbles at Communism as such. National Communism per se is contradictory. Its nature is the same as that of Soviet Communism, but it aspires to detach itself into something of its own, nationally. In reality, national Communism is Communism in decline.

TOPIC 5

Through Fear to World Unity?

The discovery of nuclear fission and fusion has made conflicts between nation-states potentially apocalyptic. Is there an effective way to prevent nations from pursuing policies which could destroy mankind?

Some are convinced that the time has come to establish world government on the basis of world unity, as the world finally has one common denominator: fear. The division of the world into territorial states and ideological blocs appears not only outdated but potentially suicidal. Different methods are being suggested to achieve this aim. Some express the hope that if a nation were to take the initiative and renounce violence, others would follow suit; its acts would be manifestly in the interest of mankind. The United States, for instance, should disarm unilaterally without waiting for agreement with Russia. The risk of such U.S. action seems to be less than the hazard of nuclear annihilation, which humanity has to face now. This is the view of Lewis Mumford, an American writer and philosopher. In his *The Human Way Out* (Pendle Hill Pamphlet, 1958) Mumford expresses the hope that the example of the United States' unilateral disarmament would prove so irresistible that others would follow.

In their pamphlet, *Speak Truth to Power, A Quaker Search for an Alternative to Violence* (American Friends Committee, 1955), Quakers condemn two aspects of present policies among nations: their reliance on the ultimate test of force; and self-righteousness of both sides in the conflict. The pamphlet proposes the method of non-violence. Quakers also fear that the West might resort to the enemy's immoral methods in its search for unity and strength against external dangers. Individual rights might be submerged in the interest of national security ("Military power is as corrupting to the man who possesses it as it is pitiless to its victims"). In the Quaker view, only if nations recognize that evil is in Man and not in any particular System can peace and harmony follow.

The critics of this school of thought do not doubt the sincerity and selflessness of such proposals. They raise doubts as to the practical aspects. How to convince Communist leaders, for example, that evil exists not only in the capitalistic Man but also in the anticapitalistic one. Furthermore, adoption of non-violence does not guarantee any absence of violence or injustice. Nonviolence may mean two things: noncooperation or nonresistance. The aim of noncooperation (such as strike or boycott) may be coercion, that is, *violence* to other people's interests or feelings. The result of nonresistance may be *submission*. Should we adopt nonresistance and submit to slavery rather than risk lives in order to secure freedom?

These dilemmas as well as the question of whether the time has come at last to replace narrow nationalist attitudes with more universalist ones will be critically examined by two American scholars on the following pages.

►THE DEMISE OF THE TERRITORIAL STATE

J O H N H . H E R Z

In the following selection the author proclaims the inevitable demise of nation-states in the era of hydrogen interdependence. He expresses the hope that the common interest of mankind in its own sheer survival will force nationalist attitudes to recede. His hope is cautiously expressed: "it is perhaps not utopian to expect the ultimate spread of an attitude of universalism

This selection is the second part of an article, "Rise and Demise of the Territorial State," *World Politics,* Vol. IX, July 1957, No. 4.

through which a rational approach to world problems would at last become possible" (emphasis added).

The author is Professor of Government at the City College of New York. He is also author of Political Realism and Political Idealism, International Politics in the Atomic Age *(in which the thesis of the article below is further elaborated), and numerous other articles and studies on comparative government and politics among nations.*

Students and practitioners of international politics are at present in a strange predicament. Complex though their problems have been in the past, there was then at least some certainty about the "givens," the basic structure and the basic phenomena of international relations. Today one is neither here nor there. On the one hand, for instance, one is assured—or at least tempted to accept assurance—that for all practical purposes a nuclear stalemate rules out major war as a major means of policy today and in the foreseeable future. On the other hand, one has an uncanny sense of the practicability of the unabated arms race, and a doubt whether reliance can be placed solely on the deterrent purpose of all this preparation. We are no longer sure about the functions of war and peace, nor do we know how to define the national interest and what its defense requires under present conditions. As a matter of fact, the meaning and function of the basic protective unit, the "sovereign" nation-state itself, have become doubtful. On what, then, can policy and planning be built?

In the author's opinion, many of these uncertainties have their more profound cause in certain fundamental changes which have taken place in the structure of international relations and, specifically, in the nature of the units among which these relations occur. This transformation in the "statehood" of nations will be the subject of this article.

Basic Features of the Modern State System

Traditionally, the classical system of international relations, or the modern state system, has been considered "anarchic," because it was based on unequally distributed power and was deficient in higher—that is, supranational—authority. Its units, the independent, sovereign nation-states, were forever threatened by stronger power and survived precariously through the balance-of-power system. Customarily, then, the modern state system has been contrasted with the medieval system, on the one hand, where units of international relations were under higher law and higher authority, and with those more recent international trends, on the other, which seemed to point toward a greater, "collective" security of nations and a "rule of law" that would protect them from the indiscriminate use of force characteristic of the age of power politics.

From the vantage point of the atomic age, we can probe deeper into the basic characteristics of the classical system. What is it that ultimately accounted for the peculiar unity, compactness, coherence of the modern nation-state, setting it off from other nation-states as a separate, independent, and sovereign power? It would seem that this underlying factor is to be found neither in the sphere of law nor in that of politics, but rather in that substratum of statehood where the state unit confronts us, as it were, in its physical, corporeal capacity: as an expanse of territory encircled for its identification and its defense by a "hard shell" of fortifications. In this lies what will here be referred to as the "impermeability," or "impenetrability," or simply the "territoriality," of the modern state. The fact that it was surrounded by a hard shell rendered it to some extent secure from foreign penetration, and thus made it an ultimate unit of protection for those within its boundaries. Throughout history, that unit which affords protection and security to human beings has tended to become the basic political unit; people, in the long run, will recognize that authority, any authority, which possesses the power of protection.

Some similarity perhaps prevails between an international structure consisting of impenetrable units with an ensuing measurability of power and comparability of power relations, and the system of classical physics with its measurable forces and the (then) impenetrable atom as its basic unit. And as that system has given way to relativity and to what nuclear science has uncovered, the impenetrability of the political atom, the nation-state, is giving way to a permeability which tends to obliterate the very meaning of unit and unity, power and power relations, sovereignty and independence. The possibility of "hydrogenization" merely represents the culmination of a development which has rendered the traditional defense structure of nations obsolete through the power to by-pass the shell protecting a two-dimensional territory and thus to destroy—vertically, as it were—even the most powerful ones. Paradoxically, utmost strength now coincides in the same unit with utmost vulnerability, absolute power with utter impotence.

This development must inevitably affect traditional power concepts. Considering power units as politically independent and legally sovereign made sense when power, measurable, graded, calculable, served as a standard of comparison between units which, in the sense indicated above, could be described as impermeable. Under those conditions, then, power indicated the strategic aspect, independence the political aspect, sovereignty the legal aspect of this selfsame impermeability. With the passing of the age of territoriality, the usefulness of these concepts must now be questioned.

Thus the Great Divide does not separate "international anarchy," or "balance of power," or "power politics," from incipient international interdependence, or from "collective security"; all these remain within the realm of the territorial structure of states and can therefore be considered as trends or stages *within* the classical system of "hard shell" power units. Rather, the Divide occurs where the basis of territorial power and defensibility vanishes. It is here and now. . . .

The Decline of the Territorial State

Beginning with the nineteenth century, certain trends became visible which tended to endanger the functioning of the classical system. Directly or indirectly, all of them had a bearing upon that feature of the territorial state which was the strongest guarantee of its independent coexistence with other states of like nature: its hard shell—that is, its defensibility in case of war.

Naturally, many of these trends concerned war itself and the way in which it was conducted. But they were not related to the shift from the limited, duel-type contests of the eighteenth century to the more or less unlimited wars that developed in the nineteenth century with conscription, "nations in arms," and increasing destructiveness of weapons. By themselves, these developments were not inconsistent with the classical function of war. Enhancing a nation's defensive capacity, instituting universal military service, putting the economy on a war footing, and similar measures tended to bolster the territorial state rather than to endanger it.

Total war in a quite different sense is tied up with developments in warfare which enable the belligerents to overleap or by-pass the traditional hard-shell defense of states. When this happens, the traditional relationship between war, on the one hand, and territorial power and sovereignty, on the other, is altered decisively. Arranged in order of increasing effectiveness, these new factors may be listed under the following headings: (a) possibility of economic blockade; (b) ideological-political penetration; (c) air warfare; and (d) atomic warfare.

(a) *Economic warfare.* It should be said from the outset that so far economic blockade has never enabled one belligerent to force another into surrender through starvation alone. Although in World War I Germany and her allies were seriously endangered when the Western allies cut them off from overseas supplies, a very real effort was still required to defeat them on the military fronts. The same thing applies to World War II. Blockade was an important contributing factor, however. Its importance for the present analysis lies in its unconventional nature, permitting belligerents to by-pass the hard shell of the enemy. Its effect is due to the changed economic status of industrialized nations.

Prior to the industrial age, the territorial state was largely self-contained economically. Although one of the customary means of conducting limited war was starving fortresses into surrender, this applied merely to these individual portions of the hard shell, and not to entire nations. Attempts to starve a belligerent nation in order to avoid having to breach the shell proved rather ineffective, as witness the Continental Blockade and its counterpart in the Napoleonic era. The Industrial Revolution made countries like Britain and Germany increasingly dependent on imports. In war, this meant that they could survive only by controlling areas larger than their own territory. In peacetime, economic dependency became one of the causes of a phenomenon which itself contributed to the transformation of the old state system: imperialism. Anticipating war, with its new danger of blockade, countries strove to become more self-sufficient through enlargement of their areas of control. To the extent that the industrialized nations lost self-sufficiency, they were driven into expansion in a (futile) effort to regain it. Today, if at all, only control of entire continents enables major nations to survive economically in major wars. This implies that hard-shell military defense must be a matter of defending more than a single nation; it must extend around half the world.

(b) *Psychological warfare,* the attempt to undermine the morale of an enemy population, or to subvert its loyalty, shares with economic warfare a by-passing effect on old-style territorial defensibility. It was formerly practiced, and practicable, only under quite exceptional circumstances. Short periods of genuine world revolutionary propaganda, such as the early stages of the French Revolution, scarcely affected a general practice under which dynasties, and later governments, fought each other with little ideological involvement on the part of larger masses or classes. Only in rare cases—for instance, where national groups enclosed in and hostile to multinational empires could be appealed to—was there an opening wedge for "fifth column" strategies.

With the emergence of political belief-systems, however, nations became more susceptible to undermining from within. Although wars have not yet been won solely by subversion of loyalties, the threat involved has affected the inner coherence of the territorial state ever since the rise to power of a regime that claims to represent, not the cause of a particular nation, but that of mankind, or at least of its suppressed and exploited portions. Bolshevism from 1917 on has provided the second instance in modern history of world revolutionary propaganda. Communist penetration tactics subsequently were imitated by the Nazi and Fascist regimes and, eventually, by the democracies. In this way, new lines of division, cutting horizontally through state units instead of leaving them separated vertically from each other at their frontiers, have now become possible.

(c) *Air warfare* and (d) *nuclear warfare.* Of all the new developments, air warfare, up to the atomic age, has been the one that affected the territoriality of nations most radically. With its coming, the bottom dropped out —or, rather, the roof blew off—the relative security of the territorial state. True, even this new kind of warfare, up to and including the Second World War, did not by itself account for the defeat of a belligerent, as some of the more enthusiastic prophets of the air age had predicted it would. Undoubtedly, however, it had a massive contributory effect. And this effect was due to strategic action in the *hinterland* rather than to tactical use at the front. It came at least close to defeating one side by direct action against the "soft" interior of the country, by-passing outer defenses and thus foreshadowing the end of the frontier—that is, the demise of the traditional impermeability of even the militarily most powerful states. Warfare now changed "from a fight to a process of devastation."

That air warfare was considered as something entirely unconventional is seen from the initial reaction to it. Revolutionary transition from an old to a new system has always affected moral standards. In the classical age of the modern state system, the "new morality" of shooting at human beings from a distance had finally come to be accepted, but the standards of the age clearly distinguished "lawful combatants" at the front or in fortifications from the civilian remainder of the population. When air war came, reactions thus differed significantly in the cases of air fighting at the front and of air war carried behind the front. City bombing was felt to constitute "illegitimate" warfare, and populations were inclined to treat airmen engaging in it as "war criminals." This feeling continued into World War II, with its large-scale area bombing. Such sentiments reflected the general feeling of helplessness in the face of a war which threatened to render obsolete the concept of territorial power, together with its ancient implication of protection.

The process has now been completed with the advent of nuclear weapons. For it is more than doubtful that the processes of scientific invention and technological discovery, which not only have created and perfected the fission and fusion weapons themselves but have brought in their wake guided missiles with nuclear warheads, jet aircraft with intercontinental range and supersonic speed, and the prospect of nuclear-powered planes or rockets with unlimited range and with automatic guidance to specific targets anywhere in the world, can in any meaningful way be likened to previous new inventions, however revolutionary. These processes add up to an uncanny absoluteness of effect which previous innovations could not achieve. The latter might render power units of a certain type (for instance, castles or cities) obsolete and enlarge the realm of defensible power units from city-state to territorial state or even large-area empire. They might involve destruction, in war, of entire populations. But there still remained the seemingly inexhaustible reservoir of the rest of mankind. Today, when not even two halves of the globe remain impermeable, it can no longer be a question of enlarging an area of protection and of substituting one unit of security for another. Since we are inhabitants of a planet of limited (and, as it now seems, insufficient) size, we have reached the limit within which the effect of the means of destruction has become absolute. Whatever remained of the impermeability of states seems to have gone for good.

What has been lost can be seen from two statements by thinkers separated by thousands of years and half the world; both reflect the condition of territorial security. Mencius, in ancient China, when asked for guidance in matters of defense and foreign policy by the ruler of a small state, is said to have counseled: "Dig deeper your moats; build higher your walls; guard them along with your people." This remained the classical posture up to our age, when a Western sage, Bertrand Russell, in the interwar period could still define power as something radiating from one center and growing less with distance from the center until it finds an equilibrium with that of similar geographically anchored units. Now that power can destroy power from center to center, everything is different.

It is beyond the compass of this article to ask what the change in the statehood of nations implies for present and future world relations; whether, indeed, international relations in the traditional sense of the term, dependent as they have been on a number of basic data (existence of the nation-state, measurable power, etc.) and interpreted as they were with the aid of certain concepts (sovereignty, independence, etc.), can survive at all; and, if not, what might take their place. Suffice it to remark that this question is vastly complex. We cannot even be sure that one and only one set of conclusions derives from what has happened or is in the process of happening. For, in J. Robert Oppenheimer's words, one of the characteristics of the present is "the prevalence of newness, the changing scale and scope of change itself. . . . "[1] In the field of military policy, this means that since World War II half a dozen military innovations "have followed each other so rapidly that efforts at adaptation are hardly begun before they must be scrapped."[2] The scientific revolution has been "so fast-moving as to make almost impossible the task of military men whose responsibility it is to anticipate the future. Military planning cannot make the facts of this future stay long enough to analyze them."[3]

If this applies to military planning, it must apply equally to foreign policy planning, and, indeed, the newness of the new is perhaps the most significant and the most exasperating aspect of present world relations. Hardly has a bipolar world replaced the multipower world of classical territoriality than there loom new and unpredictable multipower constellations on the international horizon. However, the possible rise of new powers does not seem to affect bipolarity in the sense of a mere return to traditional multipower relations; since rising powers are likely to be nuclear powers, their effect must be an entirely novel one. What international relations would (or will) look like, once nuclear power is possessed by a larger number of power units, is not only extremely unpleasant to contemplate but almost impossible to anticipate, using any familiar concepts. Or, to use another example: We have hardly drawn the military and political conclusions from the new weapons developments, which at one point seemed to indicate the necessity of basing defense on the formation and maintenance of pacts like NATO and the establishment of a network of bases on allied territory from which to launch nuclear weapons "in case" (or whose existence was to deter the opponent from doing so on his part), and already further scientific and technological developments seem to render entire defense blocs, with all their new "hard shells" of bases and similar installations, obsolete.

To complicate matters even more, the change-over is not even uniform and unilinear. On the contrary, in concepts as well as in policies, we witness the juxtaposition of old and new (or several new) factors, a coexistence in theory and practice of conventional and new concepts, of traditional and new policies. Part of a nation's (or a bloc's) defense policy, then, may proceed on pre-atomic assumptions, while another part is based on the assumption of a preponderantly nuclear contest. And a compounding trouble is that the future depends on what the present anticipates, on what powers now think and how they intend to act on the basis of their present thinking; and on the fact that each of the actors on the scene must take into consideration the assumptions of the others.

There then evolves the necessity of multilevel concepts and of multilevel policies in the new era. In this we have, perhaps, the chief cause of the confusion and bewilderment of countries and publics. A good deal in recent

[1] *The Open Mind,* New York, 1955, p. 141.
[2] Roger Hilsman, "Strategic Doctrines for Nuclear War," in William W. Kaufmann, ed., *Military Policy and National Security,* Princeton, N. J., 1956, p. 42.
[3] Thomas K. Finletter, *Power and Politics: US Foreign Policy and Military Power in the Hydrogen Age,* New York, 1954, p. 256.

foreign policies, with their violent swings from one extreme to another, from appeasement or apathy to truculence and threats of war, and also much in internal policies, with their suspicions and hysterias, may be reflections of world-political uncertainties. Confusion, despair, or easy optimism have been rampant; desire to give in, keep out, or get it over with underlies advocacy of appeasement, neutralism, or preventive war; mutually exclusive attitudes follow each other in rapid succession.

One radical conclusion to be drawn from the new condition of permeability would seem to be that nothing short of global rule can ultimately satisfy the security interest of any one power, and particularly any superpower. For only through elimination of the single competitor who really counts can one feel safe from the threat of annihilation. And since elimination without war is hardly imaginable, destruction of the other power by preventive war would therefore seem to be the logical objective of each superpower. But—and here the security dilemma encounters the other great dilemma of our time—such an aim is no longer practical. Since thermonuclear war would in all likelihood involve one's own destruction together with the opponent's, the means through which the end would have to be attained defeats the end itself. Pursuance of the "logical" security objective would result in mutual annihilation rather than in one unit's global control of a pacified world.

If this is so, the short-term objective must surely be mutual accommodation, a drawing of demarcation lines, geographical and otherwise, between East and West which would at least serve as a stopgap policy, a holding operation pending the creation of an atmosphere in which, perhaps in consequence of a prolonged period of "cold peace," tensions may abate and the impact of the ideologies presently dividing the world diminish. May we then expect, or hope, that radically new attitudes, in accordance with a radically transformed structure of nationhood and international relations, may ultimately gain the upper hand over the inherited ones based on familiar concepts of old-style national security, power, and power competition? Until recently, advocacy of policies based on internationalism instead of power politics, on substituting the observance of universal interests for the prevalence of nation interests, was considered utopian, and correctly so. National interests were still tied up with nation-states as units of power and with their security as impermeable units; internationalist ideals, while possibly recognized as ethically valid, ran counter to what nations were able to afford if they wanted to survive and prosper. But the dichotomy between "national self-interest" and "internationalist ideals" no longer fits a situation in which sovereignty and ever so absolute power cannot protect nations from annihilation.

What used to be a dichotomy of interests and ideals now emerges as a dichotomy between two sets of interests. For the former ideal has become a compelling interest itself. In former times, the lives of people, their goods and possessions, their hopes and their happiness, were tied up with the affairs of the country in which they lived, and interests thus centered around nation and national issues. Now that destruction threatens everybody, in every one of his most intimate, personal interests, national interests are bound to recede behind—or at least compete with—the common interest of all mankind in sheer survival. And if we add to this the universal interest in the common solution of other great world problems, such as those posed by the population-resources dilemma (exhaustion of vital resources coupled with the "population explosion" throughout the world), or, indeed, that of "peacetime" planetary pollution through radio-active fallout, it is perhaps not entirely utopian to expect the ultimate spread of an attitude of "universalism" through which a rational approach to world problems would at last become possible. . . .

▶THE ILLUSION OF WORLD GOVERNMENT

REINHOLD NIEBUHR

Forces operating to integrate nations are limited. While fear of a common enemy has often acted as a factor of unification, no community has yet been established because nations fear each other. The United States and the Soviet Union fear not only their own simultaneous destruction but also the destruction or domination of one by the other. The hopes for a world community and a world state are critically examined by Reinhold Niebuhr, who emphasizes the need to preserve not only peace but also our civilization against possible totalitarian tyranny.

Reinhold Niebuhr, Professor of Applied Christianity at Union Theological Seminary, is author of Christian Realism and Political Problems, The Nature and Destiny of Man, The Structure of Nations and Empires, *and other books.*

The tragic character of our age is revealed in the world-wide insecurity which is the fate of modern man. Technical achievements, which a previous generation had believed capable of solving every ill to which the human flesh is heir, have created, or at least accentuated, our insecurity. For the growth of technics has given the perennial problems of our common life a more complex form and a scope that has grown to be world-wide.

Our problem is that technics have established a rudimentary world community but have not integrated it organically, morally or politically. They have created a community of mutual dependence, but not one of mutual trust and respect. Without this higher integration, advancing technics tend to sharpen economic rivalries within a general framework of economic interdependence; they change the ocean barriers of yesterday into the battlegrounds of today; and they increase the deadly efficacy of the instruments of war so that vicious circles of mutual fear may end in atomic conflicts and mutual destruction. To these perplexities an ideological conflict has been added, which divides the world into hostile camps.

The selection is from *Christian Realism and Political Problems* (New York: Charles Scribner's Sons, 1953); copyright 1953 Reinhold Niebuhr; reprinted with the permission of Charles Scribner's Sons).

It is both necessary and laudable that men of good will should, in this situation, seek to strengthen every moral and political force which might give a rudimentary world community a higher degree of integration. It was probably inevitable that the desperate plight of our age should persuade some well meaning men that the gap between a technically integrated and politically divided community could be closed by the simple expedient of establishing a world government through the fiat of the human will and creating world community by the fiat of world government. It is this hope which adds a touch of pathos to already tragic experiences. The hope not only beguiles some men from urgent moral and political responsibilities. It tempts others into irresponsible criticisms of the necessarily minimal constitutional structure which we have embodied in the United Nations and which is as bad as its critics aver only if a better one is within the realm of possibilities.

Virtually all arguments for world government rest upon the simple presupposition that the desirability of world order proves the attainability of world government. Our precarious situation is unfortunately no proof, either of the moral ability of mankind to create a world government by an act of the will, nor of the political ability of such a government to integrate a world community in advance of a more gradual growth of the "social tissue" which every community requires more than government.

Most advocates of world government also assume that nations need merely follow the alleged example of the individuals of another age who are supposed to have achieved community by codifying their agreements into law and by providing an agency of some kind for law enforcement. This assumption ignores the historic fact that the mutual respect for each other's rights in particular communities is older than any code of law; and that machinery for the enforcement of law can be efficacious only when a community as a whole obeys its laws implicitly, so that coercive enforcement may be limited to a recalcitrant minority.

The fallacy of world government can be stated in two simple propositions. The first is that governments are not created by fiat (though sometimes they can be imposed by tyranny). The second is that governments have only limited efficacy in integrating a community. . . .

. . . While a single sovereignty may be the final and indispensable instrument of a common community, it is not possible to achieve unity by the power of government alone. Government may be the head of the body, which without a single head could not be, or become, a single body; but it is not possible for a head to create a body. . . .[1]

The fact is that even the wisest statecraft cannot create social tissue. It can cut, sew and redesign social fabric to a limited degree. But the social fabric upon which it works must be "given."

The international community is not totally lacking in social tissue; but it is very scant, compared with that of particular states. Let us briefly assess the various factors in it. Most important as a force of social cohesion in the world community is the increasing economic interdependence of peoples of

---

[1] This and the five concluding paragraphs are from *The Children of Light and the Children of Darkness* by Reinhold Niebuhr, copyright 1944 Charles Scribner's Sons, with the permission of Charles Scribner's Sons.

the world. But it is important to contrast this economic interdependence immediately with the wide disparity in the economic strength of various nations. At the climactic dinner of the World Republic convention, held in Chicago in October, 1948, Professor Urey, the atomic scientist, expressed the conviction that the "inclusion of the illiterate, poverty-stricken, overnumerous masses of the Far East" constituted the major problem of the world state. He believed that the white race would not tolerate being outvoted by Asiatics. He therefore proposed a system of weighted votes in favor of nations with high literacy and abundance of raw materials and industrial production. He felt certain that the more "enlightened" Orientals would not object to this procedure. But an objection, from Thomas Tchou, sitting two places to the left of Professor Urey, was immediately forthcoming. Weighted representation, he declared, was immoral.[2] Thus the real problems have an inconvenient habit of peeking through, even at a dinner of a World Republic convention.

A second factor in the social tissue of the world community is the fear of mutual annihilation, heightened in recent years by the new dimension which atomic discoveries have given to mankind's instruments of death. We must not underestimate this fear as a social force, even as we must recognize that some culturally pluralistic communities of past history have achieved some cohesion through the minimal conviction that order is to be preferred to anarchy. But the fear of destruction in itself is less potent than the fear of specific peril from a particular foe. There is no record in history of peoples establishing a common community because they feared each other, though there are many instances when the fear of a common foe acted as the cement of cohesion.

The final and most important factor in the social tissue of the world community is a moral one. Enlightened men in all nations have some sense of obligation to their fellow-men, beyond the limits of their nation-state. There is at least an inchoate sense of obligation to the inchoate community of mankind. The desperate necessity for a more integrated world community has undoubtedly increased this sense of obligation, inculcated in the conscience of mankind since the rise of universal, rather than parochial, philosophies and religions. This common moral sense is of tremendous importance for the moral and religious life of mankind; but it does not have as much immediate political relevance as is sometimes supposed. Political cohesion requires common convictions on particular issues of justice; and these are lacking. If there is a "natural law" which is "self-evident" to all men, it certainly does not contain very much specific content beyond such minimal rules as the prohibition of murder and theft and such general principles of justice as the dictum that each man is to have his due. There is little agreement on the criteria by which the due of each man is to be measured.

There is a special irony in the fact that the primary differences in the conceptions of justice in the world do not, however, spring from religious and cultural differences between east and west. They can therefore not be resolved by elaborate efforts at cultural syncretism between east and west. The primary

[2] *Common Cause*, December, 1948, p. 199.

differences arise from a civil war in the heart of western civilization, in which a fanatical equalitarian creed has been pitted against a libertarian one. This civil war has become nationally localized. Russia has become the national center of the equalitarian creed, while America is the outstanding proponent of the libertarian one. The common use of the word "democracy," together with the contradictory interpretations of the meaning of that word, is the semantic symbol of the conflict. The idea that this conflict could be resolved by greater semantic accuracy is, however, one of the illusions of a too rationalistic culture which fails to understand the power of the social forces expressed in contradictory symbols.

In short, the forces which are operating to integrate the world community are limited. To call attention to this fact does not mean that all striving for a higher and wider integration of the world community is vain. That task must and will engage the conscience of mankind for ages to come. But the edifice of government which we build will be sound and useful if its height is proportionate to the strength of the materials from which it is constructed. The immediate political situation requires that we seek not only peace, but also the preservation of a civilization which we hold to be preferable to the universal tyranny with which Soviet aggression threatens us. Success in this double task is the goal; let us not be diverted from it by the pretense that there is a simple alternative. . . .

. . . We may well designate the moral cynics, who know no law beyond their will and interest, with a scriptural designation of "children of this world" or "children of darkness." Those who believe that self-interest should be brought under the discipline of a higher law could then be termed "the children of light." . . . the "children of light" may thus be defined as those who seek to bring self-interest under the discipline of a more universal law and in harmony with a more universal good.

According to the scripture "the children of this world are in their generation wiser than the children of light." This observation fits the modern situation. Our democratic civilization has been built, not by children of darkness but by foolish children of light. It has been under attack by the children of darkness, by the moral cynics, who declare that a strong nation need acknowledge no law beyond its strength. It has come close to complete disaster under this attack, not because it accepted the same creed as the cynics; but because it underestimated the power of self-interest, both individual and collective, in modern society. The children of light have not been as wise as the children of darkness.

The children of darkness are evil because they know no law beyond the self. They are wise, though evil, because they understand the power of self-interest. The children of light are virtuous because they have some conception of a higher law than their own will. They are usually foolish because they do not know the power of self-will. They underestimate the peril of anarchy in both the national and the international community. Modern democratic civilization is, in short, sentimental rather than cynical. It has an easy solution for the problem of anarchy and chaos on both the national and international level of community, because of its fatuous and superficial view of man. It does not know that the same man who is ostensibly devoted to the "common good" may have desires and ambitions, hopes and fears, which set him at variance with his neighbor.

It must be understood that the children of light are foolish not merely because they underestimate the power of self-interest among the children of darkness. They underestimate this power among themselves. The democratic world came so close to disaster not merely because it never believed that Nazism possessed the demonic fury which it avowed. Civilization refused to recognize the power of class interest in its own communities. It also spoke glibly of an international conscience; but the children of darkness meanwhile skilfully set nation against nation. . . .

. . . Clearly it has become necessary for the children of light to borrow some of the wisdom of the children of darkness; and yet be careful not to borrow too much. Pure idealists underestimate the perennial power of particular and parochial loyalties, operating as a counter force against the achievement of a wider community. But the realists are usually so impressed by the power of these perennial forces that they fail to recognize the novel and unique elements in a revolutionary world situation. The idealists erroneously imagine that a new situation automatically generates the resources for the solution of its problem. The realists erroneously discount the destructive, as well as the creative, power of a revolutionary situation. A catastrophic period of history may not create all the resources required for the solution of its problems; but it does finally destroy some false solutions and some of the inertial obstacles to advance. A view more sober than that of either idealists or realists must persuade us that,

"If hopes are dupes,
Fears may be liars."

Part II

THE STRUGGLE FOR POWER AND ORDER

What Is Power?

Individuals, elites, pressure groups, political parties, and national governments try to promote what they consider either their own interest or that of the whole. They succeed in proportion to their ability to influence or control the minds and actions of others.

The capacity to produce intended effects—to realize one's will—*is called power*. The competition for influence or control over the minds and actions of other men constitutes the essence of politics.

Sometimes the search for power is offensive: the aim is to increase one's power in order to impose one's concept on others. Sometimes the search for an increase of power may be defensive: the aim is to escape the power of others, that is, to become more resistant to the imposition of alien concepts or standards.

The capacity to gain another man's consent consists of many elements, some material, some spiritual. Threat of violence may be one of them. So may persuasive argument; reputation based on past performance or success; appealing plans of political or economic reform; a record of justice, truthfulness, selflessness, foresight, exceptional ability; material wealth and might. All are included in the broad meaning of the term "political power."

Some people refer to and condemn so-called "power politics." They actually use a redundant term inasmuch as politics is, by definition, the pursuit and exercise of power. Some use the derogatory term "power politics" to express their objection to politics in general; others may use it to condemn a political action which either relies on violence or seems to seek power for power's sake.

Power is a *means* to an end and practically never an end in itself. While it may sometimes appear to an observer to be the only aim, in reality it

129

acts as a tool for reaching an end that is not so obvious: satisfaction of some inner drive, seeing one's name in history, etc. A man may, for instance, try to increase his status and powers in the community in order to enjoy the idea of power, or only to impress his family, his friends, or his mistress, and to derive some satisfaction from it. Frederick the Great, King of Prussia (1740-1786), who made his country the foremost military power in Europe, once described his motives for seeking power as follows:

"My youth, the fire of passions, the desire for glory, yes, to be frank, even curiosity, finally a secret instinct has torn me away from the delights of tranquility. The satisfaction of seeing my name in the papers and later in history has seduced me."[1]

As a means to an end, power may be used to attain either noble or evil aims. These may be achieved by the use of spiritual, nonviolent, or violent components of power (or their combination). A humanitarian leader struggles for power over the minds and actions of other men in order to discourage them from using violence, spying on each other, and being self-centered. His aim is a more humane world. A religious person may pray for the realization of these ends and may refer to the *power* of sincere prayer.

When some people recommend a unilateral initiative on the part of the United States in the field of atomic disarmament and a nonnational approach to world problems, they rely on the irresistible power of humane example. They hope it may prove stronger than such forces as nationalism or fear of the enemy.

"If we dare to speak and act on behalf of the human race," claims Lewis Mumford, "as brothers helping brothers, who will oppose us?" Here, the power of human appeal is expected to balance and then outweigh the power of nationalism. The element of "nonviolent coercion" is dominant.

When the appeal to ethics and reason does not yield results, people may try to realize their aims, even the humane ones, by the threat or use of physical violence. Thus, military power is often mobilized or used to make the world allegedly safe for: Christianity, democracy, communism, fascism, monarchy, Moslemism, and—most frequently—for a particular portion of mankind, America or Russia, Israel or Egypt, and India or Pakistan.

The Organization of Power

A well-regulated, peaceful national community is often contrasted with the society of nations or with a jungle. The difference between a civilized national society on one hand, and a jungle (to which international society is often compared) on the other is not that power is present in the first and absent in the second. Power is present in both. The real difference is between the anarchic and the organized struggle for, and exercise of, power.

In a jungle or other form of anarchic society brute force often successfully asserts itself. "The powerful exact what they can," as Thucydides said, "and the weak grant what they must."

[1] Quoted by G. P. Gooch, *Frederick the Great* (New York: Alfred A. Knopf, 1947), p. 12.

But when the weak combine to increase their collective resistance against the powerful, the taming of power has begun. "The eternal problem of politics," writes Louis J. Halle, "is not to do away with power but to control it." Thus, dividing and opposing power with power has proved, in practice, a more efficient method of checking violence than relying on such restraints as the power-holder's conscience, religious belief, or morality, which lack the possibility of an ultimate physical coercion.

"The moralists, both religious and secular," writes the Protestant theologian Niebuhr, " . . . imagine that the egoism of individuals is being progressively checked by the development of rationality or the growth of a religiously inspired goodwill and that nothing but the continuance of this process is necessary to establish social harmony between all the human societies and collectives. . . . They completely disregard the political necessities in the struggle for justice in human society by failing to recognize those elements which belong to the order of nature and can never be brought completely under the dominion of reason or conscience. . . . What is lacking among all these moralists . . . is an understanding of the brutal character of the behavior of all human collectives, and the power of self-interest and collective egoism in all intergroup relations. . . . The world of history, particularly in man's collective behavior, will never be conquered by reason, unless reason uses tools, and is itself driven by forces which are not rational. . . . Since it is impossible to count on enough moral goodwill among those who possess irresponsible power to sacrifice it for the good of the whole, it must be destroyed by coercive methods. . . . [The moralists] do not recognize that when collective power, whether in the form of imperialism or class domination, exploits weakness it can never be dislodged unless power is raised against it." [2]

National communities have devised different systems of checks and balances in order to curb or divide power which could become irresponsible or oppressive. In a *unitary* form of government, as opposed to a federal form of government, power is concentrated in one central government which may delegate portions of it to provincial or municipal governments. If the unitary form of government is a democracy, the legislative body, free press, and public opinion *check* the executive branch of the central government. This system exists in contemporary England, France, Sweden, and Denmark. If the unitary form of government is a dictatorship, it is a relatively *unchecked* exercise of totally centralized power, usually in the hands of party oligarchy or one single dictator. In this sense, the difference between democracy and dictatorship lies in whether the central power is being checked or not.

In a *federal* form of government the people, through a constitution, distribute powers between one central government and a series of local governments. The power of the central government is checked, not only by the federal legislature, but also by the power of local governments—state, provincial, or regional, whatever the case may be.

A real federation means a high degree of decentralization of power. For

[2] Reprinted from *Moral Man and Immoral Society* by Reinhold Niebuhr, copyright 1932 Charles Scribner's Sons, with the permission of Charles Scribner's Sons.

this reason federation is incompatible with dictatorship, which, by definition, represents maximum centralization of power.

The constitutions of two Communist states (U.S.S.R. and Yugoslavia) claim to be federations. They describe various checks and balances which are typical of real federations or even go beyond what, for instance, the U.S. Constitution has reserved to the states. Major ethnic groups in the U.S.S.R. are said to be the components of the Soviet Federation (union and autonomous republics; or autonomous regions and districts). Unlike the American states, the Soviet republics have the right of secession, separate foreign policies and foreign services, and separate armed forces. In practice, however, the Ukrainians, Byelorussians, Kazakhs, or Tadzhiks, and others [3] do not possess or exercise any political power of their own. Their only national right is the use of their own languages within their territories. Such systems are federations only on paper, because all power is completely centralized. The governmental machinery exists only to record or implement the will of the "house of the first jurisdiction"—the monolithic party itself. Its inner structure is not federal.

We often hear that dictators use force, and only force, to maintain themselves in power. Yet, totalitarian practices confirm the existence of other ingredients which, besides the threat of violence, compose the whole of political power. While dictatorship obtains the population's compliance by the omnipresent secret political police and other forms of control, censorship and a constant avalanche of propaganda indicate the dictator's effort to elicit consent also by other means. (The means of governmental controls were discussed on p. 22.)

Although the line between forcible and non-compulsory methods of eliciting consent is quite fluid (see Topic 6), we may observe that too frequent threats of violence may not only alienate consent but may induce people into revolutionary mood and action. This is why wise dictators alternate threats with promises, and periods of strictness with periods of relaxation.

In conclusion it should be said once more that power is ever present in all types of human society. The choice is really not between a world with power and a world without power. Rather, it is a choice between the organized use of power and an anarchic one. When society attempts to confine the exercise of power to more or less organized channels, the choice is between different forms of power distribution. We have just illustrated this by pointing out the differences between the federal and unitary systems and between the democratic and dictatorial ones.

International Checks and Balances

International society so far has failed to establish a central political

---

[3] The major subdivisions of the Soviet Union are fifteen constituent Union republics. Their ethnic majorities determine their names. The largest republic, extending from Moscow to the Pacific, is itself federated: the Russian Socialist Federated Soviet Republic, R.S.F.S.R. The names of the other fourteen Soviet Socialist Republics are: Ukrainian, Byelorussian, Turkmenian, Uzbek, Tadzhik, Azerbaidzhan, Kazakh, Kirghiz, Georgian, Armenian, Estonian, Latvian, Lithuanian, and Moldavian (former Rumanian province of Bessarabia).

authority (unitary or federal) based either on world consent or on world conquest. The main device for preserving an approximation of peace and order has been checking power with power. This device has been somewhat inaccurately called *the balance of power*. It has not always proved entirely successful nor has it been completely unsuccessful.

"A balance of power is in fact a kind of managed anarchy," notes Reinhold Niebuhr (see Topic 5). "A policy which holds all factors of the world in the most perfect possible equipoise, can undoubtedly mitigate anarchy."

"In the absence of a common world superior and a common world morality," writes another authority, Herman Finer, "peace and justice can be sustained only by the intimidatory force supplied by individual nations." [4]

The terms "balance," "equilibrium," or "equipoise" suggest mathematical equality. Webster's International Dictionary defines equilibrium as a state of balance "between opposing forces or actions, either *static,* as in the case of a body acted on by forces whose resultant is zero, or *dynamic,* as in a reversible chemical reaction when the velocities in both directions are equal."

This image borrowed from science has been adopted by practitioners and theoreticians in the field of national and international politics. Two opposing forces are pictured as constituting roughly equal weights on a scale. In such a state of almost perfect equilibrium neither side may be absorbed by the other one. They may achieve the ideal zero, that is, absence of violence and disorder.

The term "balance" or "equilibrium" in the world of *politics* should not be interpreted as meaning an actual mathematical equation. In the American constitutional system, for example, the checking of the different elements is only approximate. While the veto power of the President is said to balance the power of Congress, it may be overridden by a two-thirds majority of the Congress. The Supreme Court may declare an act of the Congress or the President unconstitutional, but a constitutional amendment (by the Congress and the States) may eliminate the Supreme Court as a whole from the system. The balance between the federal government and the state governments (which share some powers although others are exercised solely by one or the other) certainly does not represent a mathematical equation. As in the American political system, so on the world scale, the balance of power rarely means equality of its components. It usually means a distribution of power which is politically acceptable to the participants in the system. They accept it as long as it preserves their autonomous existence and renders the hegemony of one over the others highly improbable. Balance is then the opposite of dominance (actual or potential) and absorption of one element by another.

The survival of individuals and groups as autonomous units was one of the earliest causes of participation in a power-balancing system. The alternative to the balance was either to submit to the domination of others or to impose one's own domination on others. This has been attempted often in the past and may be undertaken again in the future. To conquer the world by eliminating all rivals would mean an absolute security and a guarantee of

---

[4] Herman Finer, *America's Destiny* (New York: Macmillan Co., 1947), p. 367.

survival for the conquering group. Soviet leaders refer to the future peaceful world, free of capitalist rivals, who are to be buried. This shows that the concept of absolute security is not alien to world communism.

Because we have not been able to obtain absolute security in a world free of rivals, and because nations as independent units often have conflicting aims, the balance represents the second best approach to the desire for security. Through the balancing process nations settle for a *relative* security.

"The main purpose of a state seeking to establish or maintain a balance of power is to protect its vital rights and interests," notes Vernon Van Dyke.[5] "Vital rights and interests are those for which the state is willing to wage war if necessary. Thus, the desire for a balance of power becomes a desire for a distribution of power that will permit a state to avoid defeat, if not win victory in war. Stated in more general terms, the object of the balancing of power is to establish and maintain such a distribution of power among states as will prevent any one of them from imposing its will upon another by the threat or use of violence."

Domestic and International Balancing

The parallel between the checks and balances within a nation-state and among nation-states on the international scene is illustrative; yet it should not be carried too far. Checking power with power has often succeeded in maintaining long periods of *internal* peace but often failed to do so internationally. There are obvious reasons for the difference.

In the United States and other nation-states, the constitutional checks and balances have proved successful because the balancing process is the result of (a) a common consensus that all elements within the system should be preserved; (b) the organizing and equilibrating force of government.

On the international scene there is no such consensus as to the need to preserve all nations and their identities within the system, nor is there an organizing central authority. (The desire for a "world without Communist Russia" is mutually exclusive with the desire for a "world without capitalist America.")

"An equilibrium of power without the organizing and equilibrating force of government is potential anarchy which becomes actual anarchy in the long run. . . . It is a system in which anarchy inevitably overcomes the management at the end."[6] The author of this pessimistic appraisal, Reinhold Niebuhr, does not specify how long the run may be.

In the meantime, however, an approximation of peace and order has often been achieved for quite long periods. The uncertain peace following World War II is an example as is the nineteenth century when the five major powers were at general war only eighteen months during the era. The balance of power has achieved this result. It remains the only available method in a

[5] Vernon Van Dyke, *International Politics* (New York: Appleton-Century-Crofts, Inc., 1957), pp. 199-200.
[6] Reinhold Niebuhr, *The Children of Light and the Children of Darkness* (New York: Charles Scribner's Sons, 1944), p. 174.

world characterized by the absence of a single government and by the presence of oftentimes mutually exclusive aims—the very opposite of common consensus. If a perfect balance of power between opposing groups could be reached, the time limit, characteristic of the "managed anarchy" could be extended practically into eternity.

But here we encounter two additional difficulties:

The first is the impossibility of measuring accurately and reliably the power of a nation, that is, its total capacity to realize its will in international politics. Some elements of national power are measurable. Others—especially nonmaterial factors such as national character, quality of leadership, or national morale—are elusive and defy accurate measurement.

The second problem is accurate analysis of the intentions of other nations. A powerful nation may be peaceful while a less powerful nation may have aggressive intentions.

Two mathematically equal powers would probably fail to approximate a balanced stability if one nation was led by a Gandhi or a Quaker while the other nation was led by a power-fanatic or a statesman of the Hitler type.

The problem of balancing the equation of power and intentions may be illustrated by the failure of the 1932 Disarmament Conference at Geneva.

France went to Geneva to argue that an armed equality with Germany would actually mean inferiority as (1) France lacked a natural strategic boundary with Germany; (2) Germany had greater manpower and industrial capacity; and (3) within the last century, France had fallen victim to German aggressiveness three times while she had never attacked her neighbor. Thus, the *tradition* of German aggressive intentions toward France was brought into the picture as an element of the equation. In counterargument Germany pointed to the then important value of the French colonial empire as a source of additional manpower and natural resources; the quantity and quality of French military strength built in the period of Germany's disarmament; and German vulnerability since she was encircled by France's military allies. How can one *mathematically* balance such an elusive factor as "traditional German intentions" with so relatively tangible a factor as the "intensity and duration of military training" in France?

Disarmament conferences usually fail when their participants find themselves unable to agree on a mathematical formula which would express their relative military powers. The size and number of armored divisions, ships, aircraft, bombs and missiles are all quite meaningless unless we take into account also the facts of geography, economic development, as well as intentions. (Disarmament negotiations are also discussed in Part V.) In conclusion, we may note that peace among nations primarily depends either on the balance of power (in spite of opposite goals); or on the "balance" of mutual estimates of intentions (in spite of difference in power).

If no nation *can,* or if no nation *wishes* to dominate others, international peace and order may ensue—provided all concerned have reached similarly reassuring conclusions as to the other nations' capacities or intentions to dominate.

Assessment of Power

A nation's total capacity to make its will effective internationally—the power of a nation—can be measured only partly.

The *size* or *quantity* of some material components of national power (such as: geographic position, natural resources, manpower, productive capacity, or military establishment) can usually be assessed more reliably than their *quality*. The quality of many of them represents a combination of some material and many nonmaterial and elusive factors. It is not easy to evaluate, for instance, another nation's character, morale, or the quality of its leadership and foreign policy.

There is another difficulty. Different elements of national power undergo constant change. No evaluation of one's own or other nations' power is really meaningful unless probable future changes are taken into account. A change in one component of national power may profoundly affect all the rest. Then there are changes which, at the time of analysis, cannot be foreseen: death of a national leader; unexpected results of elections; civil war; invention of a new weapon or defense against it; or, an epidemic or natural disaster.

In spite of these difficulties approximate estimates of national power may be and are being made.

For the purpose of analysis we shall divide national power into its major components, following the pattern adopted by the pioneering work of Harold and Margaret Sprout and Hans J. Morgenthau.[7] It should be borne in mind, however, that the following categories have been arbitrarily created. On paper, one is neatly separated from the other. In reality, they are interlocked. One element conditions (or issues from) another.

The following nine components of national power will be discussed below:

    A. Physical elements of national power
        1. The geographic position
        2. The natural resources
        3. The productive capacity
        4. The military establishment
        5. The population
    B. Nonphysical elements of national power
        1. The national character
        2. The national morale
        3. The quality of national leadership
        4. The appeal of national politics to other nations

Physical Elements of National Power

The Geographic Position. The limits and possibilities of a territorial state's policies are profoundly influenced by its geography.

---

[7] Hans J. Morgenthau, *Politics Among Nations* (New York: Alfred A. Knopf, 1948, 1954, 1959); Harold and Margaret Sprout, *Foundations of National Power* (New York: Van Nostrand, 1945, 1951).

In evaluating this component of national power due importance should be attached to such factors as the state's size, general shape, topography, climate, boundaries (defensible or vulnerable) and relative location, that is, relative to other nations. Two nations of identical size, shape and climate would have different political preoccupations if the one lived in the shadow of an aggressive nation, and the other in the shadow of a peaceful power.

Some authors—geopoliticians like Sir Halford J. Mackinder in England [8] or Karl Haushofer in Germany—suggest that geography determines not only the limits and possibilities but the whole of a nation's policy.

Sir Halford J. Mackinder, for instance, interpreted history basically as the struggle for the conquest of territories. He argued that the major wars of history have been fought by central land powers against enveloping sea powers in a continuous effort to conquer more and more territory. Mackinder took into account that modern transportation and communication were to shrink the continents of Europe, Asia, and Africa into one land mass, "The World Island," which would be ruled by he who first succeeded in dominating Eastern Europe and the Middle East. Some German expansionists considered German domination of the area between Berlin and Baghdad an essential stepping stone to world domination.

Halford Mackinder expressed the succession of conquests in the following, often quoted statement:

"Who rules East Europe commands the Heartland. Who rules the Heartland commands the World Island. Who rules the World Island commands the world."

We may have some doubts as to the validity of several aspects of this theory—which the Germans labelled "Geopolitik"—yet one cannot deny the importance of the geographic factors in analyzing a nation's feelings of security or insecurity and its policies corresponding to such fears or ambitions. Geography should not be raised into an absolute, but should be evaluated in relation to other factors such as manpower, organization of territory, communications, or new weapons. In the late Nicholas Spykman's apt phrase, one cannot explain everything from the fourth symphony to the fourth dimension by geography. The highly advantageous geographic position of the United States (separated by oceans from the main areas of tension in Asia and Europe, and having only two weak neighbors, one in the north and one in the south) has a less reassuring meaning today than it had at the time of George Washington's "farewell" to Europe. The invention of the aircraft and later Soviet mastery in rocketry, as demonstrated by the first sputnik and lunar probes, has diminished the advantages of the U.S. geographic position.

The Natural Resources. The political influence of a nation in times of peace and its survival in times of war are partly determined by the capacity of the government to supply its national industries adequately with raw materials and to feed its population.

The relative importance of industrial raw materials varies from one period to another, although deposits of iron ore seem to have been a constant

[8] Halford J. Mackinder, *Democratic Ideals and Reality* (New York: Henry Holt & Co., 1919, 1942).

requirement since the end of the Bronze age. The nineteenth-century emphasis on coal as a primary requisite of a great power was partly replaced by emphasis on oil in the first half of the twentieth century and on uranium and plutonium—the chief sources of atomic energy—in the second half of our century. In addition to iron, copper, aluminum, sulphur and zinc, the age of jet engines and missiles has increased the demand for certain metals which had previously been only sparsely used.

The United States and the Soviet Union are superpowers also because they represent the nearest approximation of self-sufficiency in almost all essential raw materials. Great Britain has adequate resources only in combination with other portions of the Commonwealth in general, and with Canada and South Africa in particular. England's isolation from its Commonwealth partners is her weakness in times of war. But even the two industrial giants, Russia and America, lack certain essential raw materials. The United States has to rely on imports for asbestos, chromium, manganese, nickel, rubber and tin.[9]

The importance of the food supply does not need elaboration. German submarines which tried to starve England into surrender during World War I; the British system of elaborate convoys protecting the allied supply lines in both wars; the United States capacity to export surplus food and make it an instrument of policy in Asia and other undernourished parts of the world; Khrushchev's exhortations about cultivating the virgin lands of Soviet Asia and imitating the corn-and-hog economy of Iowa—these examples illustrate the importance of food supplies for any calculation of a nation's capacity to resist the will of others.

The Productive Capacity. In order to evaluate the productive capacity of one's rivals or allies one has to know not only a great deal about their national resources (their actual as well as potential development), but also about many other things. A few samples of typical inquiries follow:

What is the productive capacity of a nation's industrial establishment, mines, and agriculture now and what will it be in the foreseeable future? In this connection one should inquire into the organization of work and managerial capacity; the degree of modernization of industry or agriculture; the skill and number of engineers, research workers, scientists; the number, efficiency, and equipment of research laboratories; the ability of the government to mobilize the best brains for priority projects; the quality of scientific training and general education. After accompanying Vice-President Nixon to Russia and Poland in 1959, Admiral Hyman G. Rickover, the "Father of the Atomic Submarine," said: "Our really great race with the Soviet Union is in education. . . . The nation that wins this race will be the potentially dominant power. . . . I searched far and wide in Russia and Poland and could not find a single drum majorette. Nor did I hear of a single school where the principal was an ex-athletic coach. . . . Students in Poland do not spend their time collecting milk bottles . . . or taking courses in How to Find a Mate. . . . In 1957, 1,600,000 secondary school graduates in Russia passed an examina-

[9]A detailed study of this problem may be found in Alan M. Bateman, *Economic Mineral Deposits* (New York: Wiley, 1942).

tion which only about 2 percent of American high school graduates would have been able to pass." [10]

While the size of the labor force is a relevant factor in itself, one should further inquire into its skills, working morale, (e.g. absenteeism, a widespread phenomenon in Communist countries), management-labor relations, and the proportion between skilled, semiskilled, and unskilled workers, etc.

How efficient and how organized is a nation's transport and communication system? This is also meaningful in relation to the geographic location of industry and its vulnerability to aerial attacks.

In addition to the previous inquiries of a specific and often technical character, additional questions as to the general nature of a nation's economic system have to be asked: Is its system capable of avoiding economic crises, inflationary trends, social unrest, unemployment and other phenomena which may disturb smooth economic progress? How good and efficient is national planning? Is there a sound relationship between capital and consumer goods production? What is the gross national product and how much capital is available for investment? What is the rate of savings and how large are the yet untapped financial and economic reserves?

The Military Establishment. Its actual or potential use hardly need be stressed. The respective powers of rival nations may be subject to the ultimate test of force. The deterring or blackmail aspect of the military establishment may serve good or evil purposes. "If you wish to obtain your political objectives by force," Adolph Hitler once said, "you must be strong. If you want to obtain them by negotiation, you must be stronger still."

In some situations military strength may be the most important element of political power. The Chinese Communist leader Mao Tse-tung once wrote: *"Political power grows out of the barrel of a gun. . . .* Chiang Kai-shek succeeded Sun Yat-sen and brought about the heyday of the Kuomintang's military power. . . . He has looked upon the army as his very life. The Chiang Kai-shek of the last ten years [1927-1937] has been a counterrevolutionary. He created a huge "Central Army" for counterrevolutionary purposes. *Whoever has an army has power,* for war settles everything: he has firmly grasped this crucial point. In this respect we ought to learn from him. And in this respect both Sun Yat-sen and Chiang Kai-shek are our teachers." [11]

Mao's final triumph over Chiang only seems to confirm his emphasis on the army as the decisive instrument of a political struggle. While the advent of communism in China was largely due to superior military organization, planning, and strategy on the part of the Communist generals, the final Communist victory was a military victory in *combination* with many other equally relevant factors. It was the quality of political and military organization, frustration and fatigue of the population caused by a long war against the Japanese, political and military errors on the part of communism's opponents, the lack of appeal of Kuomintang's program, etc.

[10] The *New York Times,* August 9, 1959.
[11] Mao Tse-tung, *Selected Works* (New York: International Publishers, 1956), Vol. II (1937-1938), p. 271. (Italics added.)

An inquiry concerning a rival military establishment must avoid two errors:

First, a military establishment should never be evaluated in isolation from other factors such as national morale, geography, productive capacity, etc.

Second, the inquiry should not limit itself to the problem of size (the number of divisions, weapons, ships or aircraft). Size may prove actually a less important element than many others. Some of the important elements of military strength are listed below:

(a) Organization of the military establishment; training; over-all readiness and geographic disposition, including readiness and disposition of bases; suitability of weapons in view of the wars which may conceivably be fought; fire-power of combat units; the proportion of men at the combat level as opposed to those in logistics and other services; the mobility of different elements; the state of reserves and their training; adequacy of transportation and merchant marine; the quality and morale of officers and men and their mutual relationship; the presence or absence of interservice rivalries; the understanding between civilian and military leaders, or the lack of it.

(b) It is very important to estimate our rival's tactical and strategic planning as to the kind of war he may prepare—local or general, atomic or conventional, massive or jungle-guerrilla type. We may make the mistake of planning a local jungle war while our adversary prepares for an atomic conflict; or we may concentrate on atomic weapons while the immediate threat is a local war combined with civil strife. Failures in military estimate and subsequent wrong planning will increase the rival's chances for pressure or blackmail. The quality of tactical and strategic planning partly depends on the quality of military, naval, and air intelligence and counterintelligence. Two equally strong nations would be militarily unequal if one of them succeeded in piercing its adversary's secrets while fully protecting its own. During his official visit to the United States in 1959, N. S. Khrushchev met Allen W. Dulles, director of the Central Intelligence Agency. Khrushchev greeted Dulles at a White House dinner with what Washington sincerely hoped was a joke: "I know you. I read the same reports you do." Mr. Dulles replied: "I hope you get them legally." The Premier then proposed that the two countries save money by pooling their intelligence networks "so we don't have to pay twice for the same information."

Whatever may be the source and reliability of secret information received, the most important problem is its realistic as well as timely evaluation at the highest level.

False or planted information may become the basis for a wrong decision. Military planners sometimes plant elaborate false information in order to divert their rivals' attention from one particular area. Today some people fear an unintentional type of false rumor: a nervous commander may mistake some unclear spots on a radar screen for enemy missiles, push the button, and initiate a chain of retaliatory measures which might conceivably result in atomic extermination of most of humanity. A correct and important piece of information, on the other hand, may not be channelled to policy-makers in time or they may disbelieve it. During World War II one Nazi agent in Turkey reported accurately on the date and place of the Anglo-American invasion of Europe, yet in Berlin his report was not believed and was discarded. Also during World War II the United States overestimated the strength and quality of Japanese forces in Manchuria. Consequently, Soviet support of the war against Japan seemed more desirable than it actually was.

(c) Another aspect of military power is the efficiency as well as financial and moral support of research in military laboratories that are improving weapons or developing new ones.

(d) Industrial capacity is the backbone of modern military power. Therefore, adequate peacetime stockpiling of strategic materials and civil defense preparation (which would guarantee industrial and food supplies during a protracted war) also partly determine the quality of a military establishment.

(e) Finally, in view of the global aspects of possible modern military conflicts, correct evaluation of interallied military and other cooperation and coordination facilitates an approximate estimate of a military establishment.

The Population. The demographic basis of national power belongs only partly to what we have called the physical components of national power. It is important to know the size of a rival population as well as its expected changes in the future (that is, its rate of increase, or decrease, as well as the relationship of such trends to economic resources); its physical health, life expectancy, and record of physical endurance in times of strain; the distribution of age groups within a nation (do the old or young groups predominate?). But it is equally important to know about many nonphysical aspects of this element of national power, such as the degree of literacy, general education and technical skill, weight of tradition, historical experience and resulting idiosyncrasies, etc. We will now examine some of these aspects.

Nonphysical Elements of National Power

It is impossible to separate completely the physical from the nonphysical factors of national power. The morale of the labor and the military force has already been mentioned. More should be said about the general problem of the spiritual fibre of a nation. This factor consists of two major components: the national character and the national morale.

National character is the product of ages and their cumulative affect. ("There is such a thing as national character . . . " wrote the Spanish statesman and historian Salvador de Madariaga.[12] "Race, climate, economic conditions may enter for a greater or lesser part in [its] inception and development.") National morale, in its narrower sense, means the actual identification of a nation with its government and its policies. This latter is a product of much shorter spans of time; it may change with the rise and fall of political elites and their short-term programs.

The National Character. If one can prove that a hundred Russians will

[12] Salvador de Madariaga, *Englishmen, Frenchmen, Spaniards* (London: Oxford University Press, 1928), p. xi.

display certain defined characteristics more frequently than a hundred Americans or a hundred Chinese, comparably distributed as to age, sex, social class, and vocation (to paraphrase the well-known statement made by the American anthropologist, Clyde Kluckhohn), some of these characteristics occurring within the Russian group but absent within the American group would be highly significant in determining the power of their respective national communities. A tendency to submit to political authority; or to quarrel with one; fertile imagination which sharpens the awareness of danger; or the lack of it which may dull such awareness; a tendency to muddle through, or, on the contrary, to react to an adverse situation boldly and even irresponsibly—all these trends would be relevant to our evaluation of a nation's power if they could be proved to be national characteristics.

The American historian Henry Steele Commager, in reviewing Max Lerner's book *America as a Civilization,* recalled that in the nineteenth century historians were so fascinated by the concept of national character that some went so far as to consider it the only subject worth study. Then, following the brutal excesses of nationalism—excesses committed by all nations —historians became increasingly wary of generalizations about national character. But later, in the last twenty years, "the stone which the builders refused has become the head stone of a new history. As the historians vacated the field of historical nationalism, the cultural anthropologists, sociologists, psychiatrists, economists—in short, the "behavioral scientists" moved in and took over. If there was no national character, there were national characteristics, national habits and practices."[13]

Professor Gabriel Almond examines some of the claims made by the anthropologists, and stresses both their usefulness and limitations in his review of Kluckhohn's and Leighton's books (Topic 9).

Almond's own book, *The American People and Foreign Policy,* analyzes some American characteristics relevant to the conduct of a nation's foreign policy. Almond's emphasis is on the instability and extreme fluctuation of the national mood concerning international politics.

In the United States, Almond notes, "the characteristic response to questions of foreign policy is one of indifference. A foreign policy crisis, short of the immediate threat of war, may transform indifference to vague apprehension, to fatalism, to anger; but the reaction is still a mood, a superficial and fluctuating response. . . . The orientation of most Americans toward foreign policy is one of mood, and mood is essentially an unstable phenomenon." Professor Almond proposes that American attitudes constantly alternate between extreme poles such as

withdrawal and intervention (that is, "over-reaction to threat and over-reaction to temporary equilibria in world politics.");
optimism and pessimism;
idealism and cynicism ("Americans would appear to be happiest when they can cloak an action motivated by self-interest with an aura of New Testament selflessness, when an action which is 'good business,' or 'good

[13] *New York Times Book Review,* December 8, 1957, p. 1.

security' can be made to 'look good,' too. Similarly there is resistance among Americans over the straightforward expression of conscience-motivated behavior, what is 'good' has to be represented as satisfying the criteria of self-interest.");

superiority and inferiority ("America . . . being self-made produces a certain buoyancy, a sense of mastery, but it leaves the individual somewhat doubtful as to his social legitimacy. This sense of insecurity and uncertainty may add a strident note to American claims for recognition. . . . Americans typically overreact in their self-evaluations. They over- and under-estimate their skills and virtues, just as they over- and under-estimate the skills or/and virtues of other cultures and nations. . . . American artists, writers, and intellectuals have historically tended to manifest inferiority feelings in the form of imitativeness, or in expatriation. It has been asserted that members of the American foreign service have tended to assimilate themselves too readily to foreign cultures and aristocratic 'sets,' perhaps at the expense of their American perspective.")[14]

It is not the purpose of this chapter to confirm or challenge the accuracy of the preceding observations. Nevertheless, if these characteristics can be confirmed as representing typical American attitudes (as distinguished from Russian, English, or Chinese), they should certainly be taken into account as an influence on policy-making.

"Cultural arrogance" could impair confidence in the United States among its allies and uncommitted nations while "cultural subservience"—to use Almond's term—might result in unnecessary sacrifices of national interest.

The National Morale. National morale is one of the most complex and elusive, yet important elements of national power. It is defined by Hans J. Morgenthau as "the degree of determination with which a nation supports the foreign policies of its government in peace and war."[15]

National morale appears to be the end-product of some long-term factors and some short-term influences. The degree of national morale varies according to the harmony or conflict between the long-term and short-term factors as well as according to the successes or failures of national performance.

Among the long-term factors we would include the national character as previously discussed, the weight of traditions, and historical experience which colors and often distorts popular attitudes to present day problems. Traditional European distrust of Germany (democratic or Communist), manifested by its neighbors (democratic or Communist), and Korean misgivings with regard to Japan are classic examples of the long-term impact of history on popular attitudes.

Among short-term factors is the government's ability to elicit its nation's general consent to the aims and methods of its foreign policy.

In a democracy the gap between the government and the people is usu-

---

[14] From *The American People and Foreign Policy,* by Gabriel A. Almond; copyright, 1950, by Harcourt, Brace and Company, Inc.; pp. 53-65, *passim.*
[15] Hans J. Morgenthau, *Politics Among Nations* (New York: Alfred A. Knopf, 1954), p. 124.

ally minimal provided the government keeps the people informed of its foreign policy and that the people are interested and give their consent.

In a dictatorship the government may also succeed in narrowing a possible gap between its aims and those of the people by isolating them from all but its own sources of information. If, however, such a state is invaded by foreign troops and foreign information, the fabric of national morale may dissolve more quickly than in the case of a democracy. This may take the form of people's support of an alien government which their own government opposes or fights.

History offers several cases of such collapse of national consensus. In World War I, the Slavic majority of the multinational Austro-Hungarian empire did not identify itself with the domestic and foreign policies of the Hapsburg government. As a result, the whole empire dissolved internally even before the military defeat.

In World War II the inhabitants of the Soviet Ukraine greeted the German armies as their liberators not only from Communist but also Great Russian domination.

In 1956 the lack of the Hungarian people's identification with their Communist regime led to open revolt.

If the masses do not identify themselves with their government in some respects, it does not mean that they cannot support it in others. Popular dissatisfaction with governmental economic and social policies in peace, for instance, may be temporarily forgotten in a common struggle against a foreign enemy. (This was mentioned in our discussion of nationalism, pp. 23-24.)

In World War II the Ukrainians, having finally discovered the true nature of their Nazi "liberators" and their application of racial policies with regard to the Slavic "subhumans," fought the Germans alongside the Communists and Great Russians in a newly found—or newly imposed—unity. Their choice was to die under Hitler or perhaps survive by fighting him.

The gap and enmity between the Communist leaders and Eastern European peoples makes the Polish, Czechoslovak, and Hungarian armed forces a very doubtful asset in Soviet military calculations. Yet, the attitude of those forces would vary greatly according to circumstances, i.e., whether, in a war, these Communist-led armies were confronted by American, British, Canadian or French forces (viewed by Eastern Europe as traditional friends); or by West German components of the NATO forces (Eastern European suspicion of Germany's policies are still strong); or if their countries were exposed to actual explosion or threat emanating from the West.

Any forecast as to the concrete expression of national morale under different circumstances is extremely difficult and usually not too reliable.

The Quality of National Leadership. National character and national morale largely determine the quality of national leadership, another nonphysical element of national power. While recognizing the intimate relationship of these three elements of national power, several very specific questions should be answered before an estimate of a rival power can be completed. Some samples of such questions follow:

(a) How intimate is the link between the government and its people?

Does the government understand, and is it sensitive to, the fundamental aspirations of the people? Do the people understand, and approve of, the policies and methods of their government? Is there an appropriate balance between available resources and objectives as pursued by national leadership?

(b) If there is a gap between the government and the people, as to the aims and methods of policy, is it adequately bridged by common faith, ideology, all-permeating nationalism and antiforeignism? Such sentiments may temporarily overshadow dissatisfaction with one's government. (See Part I, pp. 23-24.)

(c) Is the constitutional and institutional system in harmony with a given challenge and era?

The provisions of the United States Constitution, e.g., concerning the conduct of foreign policy, necessarily reflect the slow pace of the era in which they were conceived. The U. S. Senate was to be associated with the conduct of foreign policy not only indirectly (the approval or disapproval of international treaties and confirmation of ambassadors) but also directly. Theoretically this seemed possible at a time when the Senate was a small aristocratic body of twenty-six Senators. Today there are one hundred of them. Such a huge body, with its long debates, does not seem adequate in an era that has seen the end of America's political and physical isolation from the world; an era that requires quick answers to the "blitz" decision-making processes of rivals of the United States. Even the Senate Foreign Relations Committee often seems too large.

(d) What are the personal qualities or liabilities of national leaders and personnel involved in the determination and execution of foreign policy? The problem of gathering and evaluating intelligence data has been already mentioned.

Exceptionally gifted statesmen, diplomats, and negotiators may compensate for many of their nation's deficiencies through their skill, training, brilliance, and foresight. An inept foreign secretary, on the other hand, may decrease his nation's effectiveness in international affairs to the point of catastrophe. Diplomats who do not understand the history, fears, and ambitions as well as the language of the country to which they have been appointed may dangerously diminish their ability to influence others in a direction favorable to their nation's interest.

It was under the chairmanship of J. W. Fulbright, Democrat of Arkansas, that the Senate's U.S. Foreign Relations Committee proposed, and the Senate approved (September 8, 1959), a bill which requires language training for certain positions in the Foreign Service. Prior to that time, as the committee noted, about 70 percent of those entering the United States Foreign Service did not have knowledge of any foreign language. Some 50 percent of those already in the service had the same deficiency. In its report the committee said that American representatives abroad should have "to the maximum practicable extent, a useful knowledge of the principal language or dialect of the country in which they are to serve, and knowledge and understanding of the history, culture, the economic and political institutions."

In 1958, in the whole United States Foreign Service there was only one

man who was able to converse in Urdu, official language of the largest
Moslem state in the world, Pakistan, a member of SEATO, and an ally of
the United States. Only one United States ambassador assigned to a Communist country spoke the language of that country (Llewellyn E. Thompson
in Russia). Only two ambassadors out of nine appointed to Arab countries
could speak Arabic (Raymond Hare in Egypt and Parker T. Hart in Jordan).

(e) How effective or ineffective, useful or obnoxious, frequent or
sporadic, is the influence on foreign policy of different pressure groups? They
all usually claim that their particular interest is identical with the interest of
the whole nation. Labor unions claim that what is good for them is good for
democracy; manufacturers suggest that what serves their interests serves also
the interests of the national struggle against communism. In Chicago the
interests of America are often equated with those of Poland and Czechoslovakia as many Chicagoans originally came from these countries and retain a
sentimental link to them. In New York the interests of Israel, Ireland,
Catholic Spain, revolutionary Cuba, and many other countries are frequently
identified with those of the United States.

The opposite may also occur. Former political exiles may attempt to
translate their own extreme opposition to the governments of their original
countries into official United States policy. In this category we find mainly the
activities of American citizens of Chinese, Russian, Central and South American, or East European descent. In 1959 the United States government tried
to discourage excessive forms of demonstration against Premier Khrushchev's
visit to the United States. Open protests were planned by groups whose members had originally come from countries under Soviet domination.

Another interesting development in the United States concerns the attitude of American negroes to an emerging free Africa. The traditional Negro
aversion to this may be replaced by an active sympathy, similar to other
sentimental links described above. As a possible sign of impending change
we may quote the 1959 conference of the American Society of African culture,[16] whose assistant executive director, James T. Harris, declared: "Our
fundamental assumption is that Africa must and will be free. Americans of
African descent have a special interest in fulfilment of this goal." At the same
conference, Dr. Horace Mann Bond, Dean of Atlanta University's School of
Education, said that the American Negro's "traditional aversion to Africa and
things African as a humiliating part of his heritage was quickly changing to
intense interest and sympathy." (Italics added.)

The general problem of the possible usurpation of national interest by
subnational or other-than-national groups is discussed in Morgenthau's analysis of "What is the National Interest" (Topic 11).

The Appeal of National Policies to Other Nations. Although still examining the elements which compose the total of national effectiveness in international politics, we cannot avoid touching on the nature of national objectives as they are reacted to and understood by foreign audiences.

As political power means the ability to realize one's will, a nation which

[16] The *New York Times,* June 27, 1959.

is liked, respected, or admired for its technology, art, literature, educational achievements, or scientific inventions *or* for its *foreign policy aims and methods,* may obtain a voluntary assent to its policies more easily than a nation which is disliked, its aims and methods resented, and its might feared —or not even feared. "Ideals are as much an instrument of national power," wrote Robert Endicott Osgood,[17] "as the weapons of war. . . . The strength of America's moral reputation and the persuasiveness of the American mission are as vital a factor in power equation as planes, ships, and tanks. . . . Ideals and self-interest are so closely interdependent that even on ground of national expediency, there are cogent arguments for maintaining the vitality of American idealism. . . . The effectiveness of the American foreign policy depends heavily upon winning the moral and intellectual allegiance of vast numbers of people in the throes of social and nationalistic revolution."

It is evident that a positive image of a nation in the minds of other nations is an important addition to its capacity to realize its aims on the international scene. If positive traits prevail and the negative ones are minimal, national power is enhanced.

Negative aspects of a nation's aims or a disparity between professed ideals and actual performance diminish a nation's international influence. The Soviets' professed ideal of peaceful coexistence is bound to be compared and contrasted with Soviet intervention in Hungary; or with the Communists' incapacity to coexist peacefully among themselves (Stalin's bloody, and Khrushchev's somewhat subtler, purges of their respective adversaries).

Similarly, foreign audiences compare America's professed ideals with performances both at home and abroad: Asians tend to contrast the United States' use of an atomic bomb against a civilian population with the professed goals of American economic and cultural help to Asia; advocacy of free elections in Germany and Eastern Europe is sometimes examined in the light of electoral practices in the Deep South; the American concern for refugees from communism is compared to legal hurdles in actual immigration.

"Few Americans are aware of the intense and sceptical scrutiny to which our domestic affairs are subjected by the outside world," wrote George F. Kennan in 1950, "and the beneficial effect produced on both our friends and enemies by evidence that we are seriously tackling the problems of our own society. This is not just a question of material prosperity. What the outside world is more eager to know is whether we are capable of coping with the sociological and spiritual strains placed upon us by all this abundance."[18]

Living in abundance in a world beset by misery and backward economic conditions imposes a great burden of responsibility on the United States, not only with regard to domestic social and economic problems, but on the international plane as well. The Marshall Plan, followed by the general Economic Aid and Technical Assistance programs indicate an awareness of this respon-

[17] Robert Endicott Osgood, *Ideals and Self-interest in America's Foreign Relations* (Chicago: University of Chicago Press, 1953), pp. 446-451.
[18] George F. Kennan, "Is War with Russia Inevitable?" *Reader's Digest,* March, 1950, p. 9.

sibility. They are manifestations of both American foresight and generosity. Yet many a critic does not consider that enough is being done. Criticizing the senatorial reluctance to appropriate enough funds for different aid and assistance programs, the chairman of the Foreign Relations Committee, J. W. Fulbright, Democrat of Arkansas, made the following statement on this subject:

"We look as if we are determined to end up the richest, fattest, most smug and complacent people who ever failed to meet the test of survival. In air-conditioned and air-suspensioned splendor, we may be heading for the last roundup; the real hope and expectation of the Soviets is not that the United States will spend itself into bankruptcy, but that it will suffocate in its own fat." [19]

The forceful tone of this statement, made in the middle of a heated debate, indicates the violence of clash between the economy-minded senators and their opponents who stress the international and political aspects of the American situation. But it also shows that Fulbright, like many keen political observers before him, is aware of the simple fact that a nation's over-all position is stronger if it is (or at least appears to be) in harmony with the fundamental needs and aspirations of mankind. The ideological wrappings of real national objectives will be discussed later. At this point we may conclude by quoting historical evidence of the fact that great material wealth and power—which is dreaded, resented, and opposed—may be detrimental to political influence.

On January 1, 1907, Sir Eyre Crowe (1864-1925), at the time head of the Western Department of the British Foreign Office, wrote a memorandum regarding the foundations of British foreign policy. In that memorandum he laid down an axiom that England must maintain the mastery of the seas against any possible enemy—a clear national security aim. "Yet he added an important corollary," writes a British historian. "He pointed out that this maritime supremacy would, if abused, arouse feelings of resentment and jealousy throughout the world. Our power, he said, must therefore be exercised with the utmost benevolence and with the minimum of provocation. Our policy must be 'closely identified with the primary and vital interests of the majority of nations.' And what were these primary interests? The first was independence and the second was trade. Sir Eyre Crowe therefore laid it down that British policy must maintain free trade and must at the same time display 'a direct and positive' interest in the independence of small nations." [20]

In the times of Sir Eyre Crowe these primary interests of the majority were the independence of small nations and trade. Today one might add to them also economic aid and technical assistance to underdeveloped nations. Sir Eyre's description of two fundamental requirements for a sound policy on the part of a Great Power, however, needs no editing. It still is: strength *and* identification with the "primary and vital interests of the majority of nations."

[19] *New York Times,* July 9, 1959, p. 1.
[20] Harold Nicolson, *The Meaning of Prestige* (Cambridge: Cambridge University Press, 1937), p. 33.

Summary

The capacity to realize one's will is called power. It is a means to either worthy or unworthy ends.

One of the important ingredients of power over the minds and action of men is the ultimate ability to coerce.

Politics is usually defined as the pursuit and exercise of power.

Power of a nation is composed of some material elements which are more or less concrete and may be evaluated, and some nonmaterial ones which are elusive.

The material elements are: geographic position, resources, productive capacity, military preparedness, and manpower.

National character, national morale, quality of leadership, and the world appeal of national policy constitute the second, more elusive, category of elements of national power.

TOPIC 6

Power, the Heart of Politics

The competition for power over the minds and actions of men is the essence of politics, domestic and international. The problem is not to do away with power, which is the very expression of life, but to confine it to legitimate channels. Power without restraint often becomes tyrannical.

While moral or religious restraints upon the exercise of power should not be overlooked, experience shows that the effectiveness of checks on power depends on the implicit or explicit ultimate threat of coercion.

Checking power with power seems as old as humanity. Throughout history it has been the means of preventing hegemony.

In domestic societies hegemony of one political faction or economic class is prevented by a balancing process. There is common agreement on the broad terms of this process. The visible sign of this agreement is common government. Within it, the distribution of power and its checks varies from nation to nation.

In international society, which is deeply divided and does not form a real community, there is no common world authority with the power to enforce law. The United Nations majority may exercise some moral influence through its power to condemn or recommend actions or policies. Their execution, however, depends either on the willingness of nations to abide by such recommendations or on the improbable unanimity of all five great powers.

Under these conditions, peace and order are still approximated mainly by mutually balancing the power of nations and thus preventing conquest and domination of all by some.

It is admittedly a shaky foundation for peace and order.

One reason for the lack of stability is the difficulty which nations experience when they try to measure their own and other nations' power. Accuracy is almost never possible. Yet, how can one balance if one cannot reliably estimate the weight of elements to be balanced?

►CIVILIZED LIFE RESTS ON POWER

NICHOLAS JOHN SPYKMAN

In case of opposition or conflict, individuals or nations may adopt either indirect or direct use of power. A group or a nation uses power indirectly *when it appeals to the coercive force of a superior authority with the aim of directing it against those who cooperation or compliance is demanded. This is usual within nation-states with their central authority. A group or nation uses power* directly *when it relies on its own strength to achieve the compliance or cooperation of other groups or nations. This is usual in international relations where we do not find a central authority with the power to enforce law. In the subsequent essay this thesis is illustrated and analyzed by N. J. Spykman, late Professor of International Relations at Yale University, one of the pioneering thinkers in the study of international policy.*

Without mechanical power—the ability to move mass—there can be no technology. Without political power—the ability to move men—technology cannot serve a social purpose. All civilized life rests, therefore, in the last instance on power. . . .

Distrust of the moral character of power which echoes out of the Christian conscience has not prevented man from pursuing it with a wholehearted devotion. Books with twelve easy lessons on how to become powerful are eternal best sellers, and the posts that carry power are sought as eagerly as those that carry only financial rewards. In the striving for positions of influence the struggle often becomes fierce and unrefined, and many a campaign for the presidency of a ladies' sewing circle or a Christian Endeavor Society has been embellished with all the Machiavellian[1] tactics that the Florentine writer recommended for the conduct of princes. . . .

Human beings have invented a great variety of techniques designed to win friends and influence people. These different methods can be classified under four broad headings: persuasion, purchase, barter, and coercion, although this does not mean that every endeavor to make others do our bidding can be neatly pigeonholed into one of these categories. On the contrary it will be found that most successful policies are a judicious mixture of all four. The relative amount of each of the ingredients differs from case to case, from

[1] See an excerpt from *The Prince* on p. 452.

The selection is from *America's Strategy in World Politics,* by Nicholas John Spykman; copyright, 1942, by Harcourt, Brace and Company, Inc.

individual to individual, from community to community, and it is the community which defines what is acceptable and what is condemned. Where freedom and individual dignity are cherished, persuasion is more acceptable than coercion and the use of the latter is usually restricted as between individuals. The state alone, not the citizen, can legally coerce by means of the night stick, tear gas bomb, and sub-machine gun.

From an ethical point of view power can be considered only as a means to an end. It is, therefore, important that the use which is made of it should be constantly subjected to moral judgments, but to hope for a world that will operate without coercion and to decry man's desire to obtain power is an attempt to escape from reality into a world of dreams. Man creates society through co-operation, accommodation, and conflict, and all three are essential and integral parts of social life. He works together with others for common ends and creates the instruments of government for that very purpose. He accommodates himself to his fellows by shaping his conduct in conformity to common values and by accepting the normative pressure of custom and the rules of law. But he also accepts conflict for personal gain or impersonal ideal. Strife is one of the basic aspects of life and, as such, an element of all relations between individuals, groups, and states. A world without struggle would be a world in which life had ceased to exist. An orderly world is not a world in which there is no conflict, but one in which strife and struggle are led into political and legal channels away from the clash of arms; are transferred from the battlefield to the council chamber and the court room.

For groups as for individuals there are two forms of approach to desired objectives in case of opposition and conflict, direct action and "political action." The first means that the group acts directly upon the individuals whose co-operation is necessary to achieve the desired result. The second means that the group tries to achieve success through the use of the coercive power of the state. A great deal of modern economic life involves group struggle in the form of direct action: share croppers against landowners, farmers against milk distributors, industrial unions against trade unions, labor unions against employers, and industrial corporations among themselves. Many a western railroad and pipeline owes its present right-of-way not to a court decision but to the successful outcome of a bloody battle at strategic points between the forces of opposing companies.

An industrial dispute may start with a negotiation between an employer and a labor union. If negotiation fails, the parties may attempt mediation or accept arbitration. They may, on the other hand, refuse the peaceful solution and declare war in the form of a strike or a lockout. In that case the opponents will have tried all the possible methods of influencing each other's behavior, including persuasion, purchase, barter, and coercion. The strength of the group will obviously influence its choice of method, but it would be a mistake to assume that power is important only in the case of coercion. On the contrary, the fact that the labor union is powerful may make a test of strength unnecessary and successful negotiation that much easier.

The union and every other group is, therefore, forced to devote itself not merely to the pursuit of its objectives but also to the constant improvement of its strength. Any association, however simple its purpose, which depends for the realization of its objectives on the actions of other men or other groups becomes involved in the struggle for power and must make not only self-preservation but also improvement of its power position a primary objective of both internal and external policy.

Labor unions, like all groups operating within the state, have an alternative method to their objective. If the direct approach is too difficult, they can try an indirect route through the legislature and attempt to obtain the use of the law-making power of the state. It is sometimes possible to achieve rewards for labor through legislative definitions of minimum standards which cannot possibly be obtained by direct action on employers. The Woman's Christian Temperance Union may act directly through persuasion and the picketing of saloons, or it can act indirectly through the "Eighteenth Amendment." It is to this technique in the national sphere that the term "political activity" is applied, the struggle for control of the government for the purpose of serving individual or group interest.

To the extent that private groups intend to work through government agencies they must add to their broad power objective the specific task of increasing political strength. For one particular kind of group, the political party, political power is the main object and *raison d'être*. It exists for the purpose of influencing public policy, and it can achieve its aim only by winning elections in competition with other political parties. The struggle for power is here so near the surface that it is easily visible, and everybody is, therefore, willing to agree that for the political party the improvement of its relative power position must be a constant endeavor. When the war chest is depleted more quickly than filled, when loyalty weakens, when organization and discipline deteriorate, the party will be on its way out, to be replaced by one of its competitors.

There are a great many instances when political action in the form of indirect pressure through the legislature is not possible. The group may be without political power because sex or property qualifications have disfranchised its members. The issue may be one in which the government cannot act because of constitutional restrictions, budget limitation, or lack of administrative agencies. In that case the group will have to choose between direct action and political activity of a special kind aimed at constitutional amendments, the extension of government power, changes in the distribution of authority, and the creation of new agencies. Political activity is then directed not at the use of the existing instruments of government but at their modification and the creation of new ones.

Groups which must operate within the power organization called the state must conduct their external policy within the limits of the permissible methods. In theory the state reserves to itself the legal monopoly of physical force, and only those forms of coercion which are free from physical violence are permitted. There are obviously wide differences in the ability or willingness of different states to enforce this principle and great variations in the same state at different times, running all the way from "perfect order" to "complete anarchy." . . .

Order and governmental control are elements of the environment within which groups operate, and exert direct influence on their external policy. When there exists a strong government with wide powers, able to enforce its decisions, there will be effective limits on the forms which inter-group struggles can take. The indirect method through legislation will be as important as the method of direct action, and the struggle for power will not only be a struggle for direct power over groups but also a struggle for political power over government. When there is no government with wide authority and ability to enforce its decisions, there will be little restraint on the forms which inter-group conflict may take. It will then be useless to try to influence the government, and direct action must become the preferred approach until such time as the government has changed. Under those conditions the struggle for power will be primarily a struggle for direct power over other groups and only indirectly a struggle for power over the government above the groups.

Power in International Relations

In international society, as in other social groupings, there are observable the three basic processes of co-operation, accommodation, and opposition. Not only individuals and groups but also states maintain the three types of social relations. They have co-operated for common ends and created the instruments of international administration in the fields of communication and transportation without which modern international intercourse would be impossible. They have, through acceptance of common values, developed modes of accommodation by building out of custom and precedent a body of rules called international law. States have often obeyed these rules voluntarily and have been willing to adopt peaceful procedures for the settlement of disputes. But they have also accepted conflict and used coercion including war for the achievement of their national objectives.

The situation which characterizes the relations of groups within a state only in periods of crisis and breakdown of central authority is normal for the relations of states within the international society. It is the so-called sovereign independence of states, the absence of higher authority, and the freedom from external restraints that give to interstate relations their peculiar character of anarchy.

This historical state system consisting of sovereign independent units has been subject to two processes, conquest and confederation, which, if successful, might have changed its basic character. But neither process could ever achieve more than partial success. There have been strong and vigorous states which conquered their neighbors and enslaved the weak, but not even the gigantic empires of antiquity managed to absorb the states beyond their regional control and integrate them into simple hegemonic systems. Equally unsuccessful has been the process of the delegation of power from below. There have been confederations in all historical periods, but they were always partial and limited, partial in the sense that they included only a small number of states and limited in the sense that the interstate organizations were formed for specific and usually administrative purposes. Illustrations of international co-operation and limited confederation are many, but there has never been a case of the actual transfer of military power and political authority from individual states to the organs of an international community.

The essential difference between the international community and the national community as conditioning environments for group behavior is, therefore, the absence in the former of a governmental organization capable of preserving order and enforcing law. The international community has never, in fact, guaranteed the member states either life, liberty, property, or the pursuit of happiness, whatever the paper provisions of international conventions may have stipulated. Each individual state has continued to depend for its very existence, as much as for the enjoyment of its rights and the protection of its interests, primarily on its own strength or that of its protectors.

Self-preservation used in connection with states has a special meaning. Because territory is an inherent part of a state, self-preservation means defending its control over territory; and, because independence is of the essence of the state, self-preservation also means fighting for independent status. This explains why the basic objective of the foreign policy of all states is the preservation of territorial integrity and political independence.

In addition to the primary task of survival, the foreign policy of states is directed at a great many specific objectives which can be classified in different ways.[2]

The same two methods which are used in the national sphere for promoting group interests are used in the international sphere for promoting state interests. States may use the direct method, acting immediately upon other states; they may use such international organizations as exist; or they may devote their foreign policy to the creation of new instruments. The relative importance of each of these methods is, however, very different from that which prevails in the national sphere. The character of international society today makes direct power over other states far more useful than ability to influence international organizations.

At the time of the founding of the League of Nations and during its early history when it was still expected that the new organization might develop into an important agency of international government, there were many struggles for control between the large and the small powers and competition between individual states for seats on the council and the important committees. It looked for a while as if the struggle for power on the battlefield might really be transformed into a struggle for power in the council room. But when it became clear that the council room was merely a place for deliberation and the League only a forum for debate, interest lagged. It was futile to try to control a government that had no power. The foreign ministers sent their assistant secretaries and finally even these stayed home. The edifice that was to house the parliament of nations became an expensive symbol of a forlorn hope.

Direct action from state to state has remained the normal and most prevalent form of approach. It represents the most characteristic expression

[2] See Part III, starting on p. 223.

of foreign policy. Absence of international government is responsible not only for the significance of direct action but for the fact that there is no community restraint on the methods used. In international society all forms of coercion are permissible, including wars of destruction. This means that the struggle for power is identical with the struggle for survival, and the improvement of the relative power position becomes the primary objective of the internal and the external policy of states. All else is secondary, because in the last instance only power can achieve the objectives of foreign policy. Power means survival, the ability to impose one's will on others, the capacity to dictate to those who are without power, and the possibility of forcing concessions from those with less power. Where the ultimate form of conflict is war, the struggle for power becomes a struggle for war power, a preparation for war.

The statesman who conducts foreign policy can concern himself with values of justice, fairness, and tolerance only to the extent that they contribute to or do not interfere with the power objective. They can be used instrumentally as moral justification for the power quest, but they must be discarded the moment their application brings weakness. The search for power is not made for the achievement of moral values; moral values are used to facilitate the attainment of power.

In this kind of a world states can survive only by constant devotion to power politics. Because power is in the last instance the power to wage war, states have always devoted considerable effort to the building of military establishments. But the relative power of states depends not only on military forces but on many other factors—size of territory, nature of frontiers, size of population, absence or presence of raw materials, economic and technological development, financial strength, ethnic homogeneity, effective social integration, political stability, and national spirit. In the struggle for power these items become important secondary objectives. They have value in themselves, and they are means to power.

The power position of a state, however, depends not only on its own military strength but also on that of its potential enemies. This means that there is a second approach to power apart from the enlargement of one's own war equipment. Its purpose is to influence directly the power position of other states, to weaken some, to strengthen others. To achieve this aim, states are willing to use their military power not only for the protection of their own territory but also for the protection of the territory of others, not for any altruistic reasons but because the continued existence of the third state contributes to their own security.

Far back into antiquity goes the practice of strong states protecting small countries on their border against invasion from states beyond. This policy of protecting "buffer states" is a development and improvement on the old type of territorial defense by means of the creation of special frontier zones. When states have neighbors that are not weak but strong, it is the neighbor that represents the potential threat. Under such circumstances, nations have usually been willing to make an alliance with the country beyond the neighbor, to fight for the protection of that country's territory in exchange for a reciprocal obligation. But willingness to support other states has not been motivated solely by a desire for the security of a frontier or a zone of special strategic significance, but also by a desire to stop the expansion of some great state which after further growth might become a menace. The policy is then directed at the prevention of hegemony, a power position which would permit the domination of all within its reach.

▶FORCE AND THE ETHICAL ORDER

HERBERT BUTTERFIELD

In view of human nature, individual or collective willfulness has to be reduced by rules and an appropriate authority which enforces them. Both within nations and in their mutual relations a healthy disposition of forces makes human nature better than it really is.

The relation between power and order, and justice and peace, is explained in the following selection. Its author is professor of modern history and Vice Chancellor of the University of Cambridge, and editor of the Cambridge Historical Journal. *Among his major books are:* History and Human Relations, Christianity in European History *and* Christianity and History.

Granted the flaws in human nature, then the orderings and arrangements of a healthy society seem to help out man's imperfections, conspiring with quiet inducements and concealed checks to keep the surface of life comparatively respectable; though down below there slumbers all the time the volcano that lies in human nature, and an unexpected cataclysm may bring it into activity. On the operation of certain safeguards which in normal times work so quietly that the superficial observer may miss them altogether, depends all the difference between civilization and barbarism. In this connection we may say indeed that the difference between civilization and barbarism is a revelation of what is essentially the same human nature when it works under different conditions. . . . Some of us have become so accustomed to a humane form of society, which cushions the conflicts between men and mitigates the self-aggression, that we imagine its virtues to spring straight out of nature with no more cultivation than the wild flowers on the bank of a stream. . . . The virtues of Western society in modern times were in reality the product of much education, tradition and discipline; they needed centuries of patient cultivation. Even without great criminality in anybody—merely by forgetting certain safeguards—we could lose the tolerance and urbanities, the respect for human life and human personality, which are in reality the late blossoms of a highly developed civilization. . . . In the eighteenth century . . . though the writers of theoretical books in that period might talk of human perfectibility,

Reprinted from *Christianity and History* by Herbert Butterfield; copyright 1949 Charles Scribner's Sons, with the permission of Charles Scribner's Sons. The book is an amplified version of six broadcast lectures delivered between April 2 and May 7, 1949, on the Third Programme, BBC, London.

the statesmen were much too wary to gamble on such illusions when the issue was a matter of life and death. It was clearly understood in those days, for example, that if you placed a great power in a position to act with impunity over a considerable part of Europe, then though it had been righteous hitherto—kept on the rails by the general balance of the world and by its calculation of what was prudent—it would now become an unrighteous power. Either it would be dazzled by new vistas of temptation or it would be desperately nervous to find itself the object of general suspicion. Granted an approximately reasonable disposition of forces on the map, they argued, and then—to something like that same degree—not only would wrong-doers be checked but in fact they would be less likely to emerge, and the statesmen concerned would actually be well-intentioned, and would get into the habit of being so. In other words, what is infirm in human nature may be helped out or concealed by the actual play of forces in an international order. On the footing of such ideas it was possible in times past for men to have what our own age has so tragically lacked—namely, something like a considered view of the relations between force and the existence of an ethical order; because what is important in this respect is not the strength actually necessary to put down crime, for example—not the weight of the policeman's truncheon —but the subtle disposition of the latent force which exists in a healthy society, where the police are said to be doing their work properly because they had eliminated the conditions in which crime flourishes—they most justify their existence when they are able to stand at street-corners doing nothing at all.

From all this the fact emerges that, both within a nation and in the larger realm of a whole international order, a healthy disposition of forces can be attained for long periods which, so to speak, makes human nature better than it really is, so then with good fortune and in quiet times certain aspects of it will hardly even be put to the test. In quiet times, indeed, people even come to be locked in illusions on this question, and to imagine that certain things cannot happen nowadays or cannot happen here—as though a superficial observer were to say, "There is little crime. See, the police have nothing to do. Why should we not cut down such a redundant service?" The infirmities of human nature are always with us and the twentieth century can hardly complain to high heaven that the basic human material with which the world is endowed is any worse nowadays than it was in other periods. The trouble is that the world has lost so many of the safeguards, and if there is an aspect of the modern tragedy which is to be regretted, because it might conceivably have been avoided, it is that the last generation suffered so much from the superficiality of its idealists and the spiritual impoverishment of its self-styled prophets. . . . We have gambled very highly on what was an over-optimistic view of the character of men. It is not social institutions that make men worse than they might have been, as people used to say—social institutions, however bad, are better than nothing, and have the effect of making men appear a little more virtuous than they really are. If we had no rule of the road a nasty side of human nature would make its appearance amongst motorists more often than it does at the moment. By having a rule of the road we reduce the manifestation of human willfulness, not that men inherently have any less of it in their composition, but we reduce the number of the occasions that bring it out.

►WHAT CONSTITUTES POWER?

LOUIS J. HALLE

Whatever the source or nature of power, its effect is the compliance of men. This may be a willing compliance or an enforced one. The line between the two is fluid in spite of the mutually exclusive sound of both terms.

The illegitimate use of force is resented and opposed. Yet, what is legitimate and what is illegitimate? From whose point of view? This question is examined in several of its aspects by L. J. Halle, former member of the U.S. Policy Planning Staff and now Professor at the Institut Universitaire des Hautes Etudes Internationales in Geneva, Switzerland.

One might say that power, at least for the purposes of this examination, is the ability to get one's way. It is related to will—related, that is, to the desire to attain particular objectives. An infant crying because it is hungry exerts power toward its mother, and if the power is sufficient the mother will respond by feeding it. When the infant has grown to be a child it may exert power through the use of sheer force to take food away from smaller children. Or it may exercise the power to charm a rich man into giving it food. Power is its ability to realize its will, to get what it wants by whatever means—by annoying others, by making them uneasy, by eloquence, by arousing pity, by threats, by bluff, by trade, by the application of force, or by any other methods that work. . . .

Napoleon was not physically the biggest and strongest man in Europe, but he had qualities of mind and character that, by the expression he gave them, induced armies to submit to his will, and those armies conquered Europe for him under his direction. The greatest power is not that which is exercised visibly, materially, and at first hand. More powerful than the butting elephants are those in whose service they butt each other. If the pen is mightier than the sword it may be only because it commands the sword.

We may ask, then, whether sheer physical might is not the ultimate manifestation of power in all its forms. Are the powers of eloquence, personal bearing, wisdom, virtue, knowledge, and custom all reducible, at last, to the firepower of armies?

One way or another all sources of power in human society manifest themselves, certainly, in the compliance of men. Napoleon's power was represented by the compliance of the men who constituted his armies and the compliance of those who in turn submitted to his armies. The compliance of

From *Civilization and Foreign Policy,* by Louis J. Halle, copyright 1952, 1955, by Louis Joseph Halle, Jr., reprinted by permission of Harper & Brothers.

the men who constituted his armies was, essentially, a willing compliance, a compliance that did not correspond to his own physical strength; while the secondary compliance of those who submitted to his armies was, essentially, a forced compliance. We find the same distinction, here, as that between the power of the girl who prevails upon the bully and the power of the bully who prevails upon the child. The bully's compliance is unforced, the child's is forced. If the girl had been able to exercise her power as effectively on the child, directly, as on the bully that transaction might have been accomplished altogether without force. One may similarly imagine a case in which the compliance of those men who had to be compelled by the force of Napoleon's armies was accorded voluntarily on the same basis as that on which his soldiers accorded their compliance. A leader could theoretically arise who was so universally respected that all men in the orbit of his will gave him their unforced accord.

Napoleon ruled through love and fear, the love of his soldiers and the fear of those who faced his soldiers. The proportion of fear was higher in the rule of Caligula than in that of Napoleon; it was lower in the rule of Queen Victoria. Confucius conceived of a rulership so wise and so virtuous that even the barbarians submitted voluntarily and it needed no armies to realize its will.

Custom is one of the most significant components of power. Established authority elicits an accustomed recognition and submission. Queen Victoria's power came only in small part from her personal attributes, its main source being her identification by birth and ceremonial investiture with an office that the British people had long been accustomed to respect. Her domestic authority did not, therefore, need the support of such force and fear as were needed to maintain the domestic authority, unsanctioned by established law and custom, of a usurper like Adolf Hitler.

One may conclude that power is most secure and effective when it has the willing consent of those who serve it, and that it is to be maintained by supplementary force only to the extent that unforced consent is lacking. In terms of the ideal, at least, reliance on force is a sign of inadequacy in the relying power.

We shall do well to fix this dichotomy of willing consent and forced compliance firmly in our minds, for it may prove to be the principal key to the understanding of power in its relation to foreign policy. . . .

Force and Consent

The distinction we have to make, then, is between forcible methods and other methods for which, in their collectivity, our language lacks a positive term. We could call these others the "non-forcible" or "non-compulsory" methods, thus defining them negatively, but the element of force or compulsion, as we shall quickly see, is not altogether absent from many of them; . . . it may, in fact, be merely less overt or less predominant in them.

Perhaps the reason why clear and simple linguistic terms are lacking for our dichotomy is that it is not, when examined closely, a categorical dichotomy in reality. In many cases where action is undertaken for the realization of a purpose one cannot say whether the action is of the one kind or the other. It has in it something of both, as is the case when the diplomat, gentle and reasonable as he may be in his demeanour, gets a more friendly response from those who deal with him because they have an impression of guns in the background. They may be more willing to accord their genuine consent because the force of the government for which he speaks commands their respect.

The fact that black and white may be separated by a transitional zone of grey, which is neither, does not mean, however, that black is indistinguishable from white. Recognizing that there is a grey zone between voluntary consent at one extreme and compelled acquiescence at the other, we may still find it useful to think in terms of a choice that governments may make, in their foreign affairs, between policies calculated to gain the willing consent of others and policies involving the use of force to compel their acquiescence.

Our extended semantic discussion has been justified if it has tended to fix in our minds the nature of the reality for which we have nevertheless been unable to find an adequate formula of words. It makes it safer at this point arbitrarily to introduce short-hand terms that we may use from now on, understanding that in themselves they are neither descriptive nor quite logical. We may hereafter talk about "force" and "consent" in international relations, meaning compulsion by the first, the eliciting of willing consent by the second. The first means the methods we use when we undertake to make somebody do something whether he likes it or not; the second means the methods we use when we undertake to get somebody freely to agree to do something.

The relationship between force and consent, between these two general approaches to the problem of attaining national objectives, is a reciprocating relationship of considerable delicacy and complexity. When a government uses force in international relations it is bound, one way or another, to affect the disposition of others to accord their consent. When the use of force is resented, potential consent is diminished by so much. Where it arouses respect the potential of consent may be increased. It is human to admire the strong when they display their strength; it is also human to resent them. Which reaction you get, and in what degree or in what mixture, depends on the circumstances. . . .

If a big man, previously a power in his community, strikes a child and injures it he is likely to find that he has, in consequence, lost his power in the community. He is likely to find, as well, that the sympathy of the community has at the same time enhanced the power of the child. All this may be so in spite of the fact that the child had provoked the man's assault by unjustifiable and injurious actions. . . .

A government may find that, without exerting any pressure, it has the spontaneous and eager consent of another country to what it wants to do. When we decided that we wanted to develop the St. Lawrence Seaway, for example, we found Canada more than willing to allow it and to co-operate in it. In another case a government may gain the consent of another country only by granting reciprocal favors: we might tell the Swiss, for instance, that if they buy more American automobiles we will buy more Swiss cheese. In still another case a government may gain the acquiescence of the other country by threatening to take actions injurious to it. Finally, it may force acquiescence by dropping bombs.

Only the last two cases could properly be said to represent policies of force. The trading of automobiles for cheese seems clearly in the category of consent, even though we pay a price to overcome the hypothetical reluctance of the Swiss to buy our automobiles. What would the case be, however, if we threatened to exclude Swiss production from our markets unless the Swiss bought our automobiles? Here, by only a slight transition, we find ourselves in the grey border zone. The element of compulsion begins to appear.

This element of compulsion would be conspicuous here if, to take the extreme hypothetical case, the exclusion of Swiss production from our markets might well entail the collapse of the Swiss economy and the starvation of the Swiss people. In such a case the Swiss would surely resent our threat, even though it involved action by us within our own domestic jurisdiction. . . . They might feel that to accede to this compulsion would be to acknowledge a *de facto* jurisdiction exercised by us over an area under their own legal sovereignty, with all the consequences implied for their future independence. This might lead them, in turn, to desperate measures and the acceptance of economic sacrifices in order to resist our pressure, even though they might otherwise have been willing to buy our cars. Our compulsion, in such a case, would have generated resistance. In other words, we would have lost consent by it. . . .

Suppose, now, that one of the great powers, having the physical capability, should undertake actual military operations against the Swiss . . . in order to realize its will with respect to them. Suppose that French troops should march into Switzerland to gain Swiss acceptance of a treaty of friendship proposed by France, . . . "the whole world," as our orators say, would be shocked and deeply angered, France . . . would be execrated by the spokesmen of virtually all nations, and "the aggressor" would suffer an immense loss in the potential of consent that contributed to the support of its position in the world.

The world would manifest no comparable sense of outrage, however, if the French, responding to some civil disturbance in Corsica, should declare martial law there and send troops in to enforce their will. . . . The inclusion of Corsica in the jurisdiction of France . . . is recognized, and the enforcement of order in these territories is therefore regarded as a legitimate function and even an obligation of the metropolitan power. Force is legitimately used by the French . . . here, where its use by them against Switzerland . . . would be regarded as illegitimate.

The principle of legitimacy, . . . turns up as a key, perhaps the key, to solving the force-consent equation. Where force is used illegitimately it alienates consent.

And what constitutes legitimacy? . . .

We may say, then, that general consent based on traditionally accepted procedures constitutes legitimacy. Or we may generalize still further, making room for exceptions to the exclusive sanction of custom, by simply equating general acceptance in principle with legitimacy.

At this point it is apparent that we have come close to the intellectual sterility of a circular argument. Are we merely saying, here, that the basis of consent is legitimacy and that legitimacy is represented by whatever has consent? I think two qualifying words used above prevent the circle from closing. Acceptance "in principle" is not necessarily identical with consent. A particular President of the United States may exercise his powers in spite of my opposition as a citizen, which I manifest in my vote at the polls, but I accept his authority because I accept the principle of minority acquiescence in the decision of the majority. I might get him out of office if I could do so legitimately—that is, in accordance with procedures accepted by me and my fellow citizens—but I recognize that he holds the office legitimately and I therefore accept his authority and submit willingly to it as an expression of my duty. The case would be quite different if he were a usurper, one who had seized power by unagreed and therefore unsanctioned procedures, and although I might have a higher regard for the personal character of the usurper than for that of the legitimate President I would not acquiesce in his authority except to the extent that I felt myself outwardly compelled to do so by the intimidation of force.

Our American Revolution was not sanctioned in the eyes of those who conducted it merely by the personal shortcomings and tyrannical acts of the individual who occupied the British throne, but by a finding that the principle of a rule exercised in the name of a distant and increasingly dissociated crown was unacceptable because it made impossible the discharge of the ruler's responsibility (under the eighteenth-century concept of the "social contract") for the welfare of those whom he ruled, thus violating the "Law of Nature and of Nature's God." In other words, the British connection was illegitimate because it was at odds with accepted principle, not because it was inconvenient and unpleasant.

Similarly, the increasing unacceptability in principle of the British rule in Catholic Ireland, quite aside from which persons exercsed it and how, gave it an increasing aspect of illegitimacy that made it advisable for the British at last to withdraw it. . . .

Legitimacy, which is a magic wand for eliciting consent, is itself a function of cultural evolution, and in periods of transition may itself be in question. In the thirteenth century the authority of Rome over all Christendom had the sanction of legitimacy. It later lost that sanction, not abruptly but gradually, as a result of the cultural development which we call the Reformation. In the sixteenth and seventeenth centuries the principle of legitimacy sanctioned the divine right of kings, but the development of eighteenth-century thought tended to illegitimatize what had been a legitimate right. This resulted in the overthrow of monarchies and the establishment of representative democratic governments, based on a new and up-to-date legitimacy, in their stead.

A century ago it was still generally considered legitimate for advanced and civilized powers like Great Britain to exercise a paternalistic authority over the relatively childlike peoples of Africa, of Persia, of India, and of other "colonial" or "semicolonial" areas. When the British landed troops in Egypt to enforce their will or when we landed troops in Santo Domingo to enforce our will no general sense of outrage ensued in the world at large, or even among the Egyptians and Dominicans, for such action accorded with the general view of what constituted normal and, therefore, legitimate relationships between peoples. "The white man's burden" or the paternalistic responsibility of our enlightened civilization, which we generally regard as illegitimate today, was legitimate then. It was based on an extension to international relations of the concept of social inequality. Just as all national populations tended to be divided into a lower class, a middle class, and an aristocracy or governing class, so nations were divided into colonial dependencies, spheres of influence, and dominant great powers. . . .

The central problem of foreign policy, however, is that of relations among great or, at least, substantial powers, powers that tend to be in approximate balance with one another. Japan's surprise attack on Pearl Harbor in 1941 was not the attack of a man on a child, yet it violated the moral sense of that part of the world which was still uncommitted in the power struggles of the day, with a resultant loss of the consent which Japan might otherwise have enjoyed. Many of the previously uncommitted were among our own people, and we may recall how our divided nation became, overnight, a nation united against Japan and her allies. Virtually the whole of Latin America, moreover, reacted against the Japanese attack and rallied to our defense with such swiftness that some of the Latin American states declared war against Japan even before we had a chance to do so ourselves. Surely nothing like this would have occurred if the Pacific War had opened, rather, with an American attack on Japan.

Japan's attack represented her use of force beyond the limits of her own jurisdiction for the purpose of subjecting us to her will, thereby extending her jurisdiction to include part or all of our own. The word for such a use of force is aggression, and aggression, like usurpation, is commonly regarded in our times as illegitimate. What shocked and antagonized the community of nations was Japan's use of force in contempt of legitimacy.

We may conclude, for the moment, that the consent enjoyed by a great power tends to diminish when its force is used in ways that are regarded as illegitimate, whether against a small state or another great power. The validity of this conclusion is attested by the efforts which virtually all states make today, through their diplomacy and propaganda, to identify any use of their armed forces with legitimacy. Adolf Hitler, who as a usurper necessarily attached more value to force than consent (thereby missing the exceptional opportunity which was offered him of appearing as a liberator in the Ukraine), was at pains to persuade the world that he was saving and protecting Austria by his occupation, that in his attacks on Czechoslovakia and Poland he was responding to their aggression against German nationals, and that his occupation of Norway was undertaken to defend her against British attack. The Soviet Union has made similar efforts to persuade the world that her enslavement of Eastern Europe by force was a legitimate liberation based on the consent of the people. We ourselves were concerned to leave no doubt about the legitimacy of our entry into Korea in 1950 as agents of the United Nations to repel an aggression by the North Koreans; but the North Koreans and their associates put the best face they could on a claim that it was the defenders in the southern half of Korea who had committed the aggression. Both sides were properly concerned with the maintenance or acquisition of consent, based on legitimacy,[1] as an element of power.

TOPIC 7

Checking Power with Counterpower

Modern and ancient authors whose essays are reproduced on the following pages agree on one fundamental point: The use of power for evil purposes can and should be checked effectively.

Methods of doing so may be different. Attempts were made to tame power through use of a piece of paper, a pledge of good intentions, or an oath. These methods have usually proved less effective than checking power with counter-power. This method is usually described by the shorthand expression: the balance of power.

The main purpose of this balance is to preserve a unit and its power and prevent its absorption or domination by another unit and power.

►CHECKS AND BALANCES

LOUIS J. HALLE

Clashes of interests and ensuing strife reflect the dynamism of life. The problem is not to do away with power but to use it in such a way that strife and struggle among individuals or nations may be transferred from the battlefield to the council chamber or courtroom. Relying on pledges of good intentions or a single central authority may be more dangerous to safety and freedom than a system of balance of power.

. . . Christendom or Western civilization was once under one governmental authority, that of Rome. This authority did not maintain a universal

[1] Cf. L. F. L. Oppenheim's similar statement on page 568 concerning the frequent violations of international law and the effort, on the part of violators, to prove the law to be on their side.

From *Civilization and Foreign Policy,* by Louis J. Halle, copyright 1952, 1955, by Louis Joseph Halle, Jr., reprinted by permission of Harper & Brothers.

and continuing order such as is suggested by the phrase *Pax Romana,* but it provided the basis for resolving chaos in the area between the Tigris River and what is now Scotland. It gave this area political coherence; it prevented or mitigated anarchy.

With the fragmentation of this empire and its replacement by a cluster of sovereign nation-states acknowledging no common authority other means had to be found for the prevention or mitigation of anarchy. What took the place of the imperial authority, then, was the European Balance of Power. This European Balance of Power did not maintain an unbroken order any more than the authority of Rome had, but like its predecessor it provided the basis for resolving chaos.

One talks of the European Balance of Power "system" as if it had been deliberately designed by European statesmanship, was operated by means of duly constituted political machinery, and provided statutory authority for the maintenance of order. A balance-of-power system, however, like a feudal system or like the system of natural selection in nature is just something that comes into being where no artificial system has been established for regulating the conflicting interests of a community.

If a number of men are thrown together in a restricted area and, having conflicting interests, find themselves in competition they may establish a single government and laws to regulate their mutual relations. Failing the construction of such a political entity, however, they may find in the initial chaos of their rivalries that they are grouping themselves automatically in response to certain common interests that transcend their differences. Many may come together to resist overweening claims put forward by the strongest among them. If each man is seeking the greatest possible freedom for himself virtually all of them will find it advisable to prevent any one man or group from becoming so strong relative to the others as to be able to control them. They will therefore associate themselves in groups to balance off one another's power, constantly readjusting their groupings to compensate for power shifts, and they may thus achieve, eventually, that precarious, dynamic equilibrium of the whole society which we have previously compared to the equilibrium of two elephants butting against each other. The classic Balance of Power, however, is multiple, encompassing a cluster of conflicting and mutually compensating pressures. Nobody plans it that way, perhaps, but so it happens in the absence of any plan.

We, the American people, could not allow ourselves to take a realistic view of what we were doing because we had grown up believing that "power politics" and "the Balance of Power" were evil in themselves, representing the nefarious policies of monarchs bent only on their own imperial aggrandizement. The terms stood for a cynical game that the crowned heads of the old world played among themselves with their armies, at the expense of the masses that languished under their feudal sway. We saw power supporting evil, and it was not difficult for us to take the step from this view to the view that power was evil. We thought, moreover, that we had proved it to be an unnecessary evil by ourselves developing a continent-wide organization of government among diverse and often conflicting interests that dispensed with its use. We had substituted the arbitrament of a single law for the arbitrament of arms, and only the old world's addiction to ancient evil kept it from doing likewise.

To think of power as being of itself evil, however, is tantamount to thinking of life as being of itself evil. Life is dynamic by nature, it is animated by kinetic energy, it expresses itself in power. The expectant mother feels the power of new life while it is still in the womb and from the moment of an infant's birth adjustments have to be made in the old environment to its new power. It must be controlled by swaddling or cajoled into co-operation or appeased with food. The conflicting pressures that exist even in the intimacy of a harmonious family have to shift in their mutual relationships to accommodate the addition and still preserve the stability of the family.

The eternal problem of politics, national or international, domestic or foreign, is not to do away with power but to tame it, to control it, to confine it within legitimate channels. Power was not less essential to the single government of Rome than to the multiple Balance of Power system. It was organized differently, that is all. Nor is it clear that peace, freedom, and the general welfare of mankind were better served by the single rule of Rome than by the balance of forces which came after. The Roman legions marched and counter-marched over the agonized body of Europe under the *Pax Romana* as the national armies of Europe marched and counter-marched in a later day. A close analysis might show, I think, that the balance of power tends, in fact, to be inimical to tyranny and to provide certain safeguards for freedom. If the alternative to a balance of power is a concentration of power we ought to hesitate before preferring the latter. . . .

►THE GROWTH OF ATHENIAN POWER HAS TO BE CHECKED

THUCYDIDES

Thucydides, probably born about 455 B.C., describes the application of the balance of power in Grecian wars. His distinction between the unrealizable ideal of absolute security and the attainable aim of relative security through the balancing process reads like a modern essay: "Your aim, no doubt, should be, if it were possible, to prevent anyone else having a navy at all; the next best thing is to have on your side the strongest navy there is." About 2,500 years ago, the navy was the essential element of the Greek cities' power. The following excerpt contains an exchange of views which had taken place at Sparta, the leading city of southern Greece (Peloponnesos—peninsula). It led to the military decision to oppose a further growth of the Athenian power in spite of many warnings as to the unpredictability of the outcome of a major war, and in spite of the advice that all the avenues of diplomatic negotiations should be explored before an irrevocable action is taken. Many

This selection is from Thucydides' major work, *History of the Peloponnesian War*. Translated by Rex Warner, Penguin Books, Ltd., 1954.

of the arguments which modern statesmen have used with respect to the growth of the Nazi or Communist power were heard then, too; some stressed the need to stop an expansion in its early stages, and others advocated a long-term policy of strength and containment ("when they see that our actual strength is keeping pace with the language that we use, they will be more inclined to give way"). The English philosopher, Thomas Hobbes, described Thucydides as "the most Politick Historiographer that ever writ."

Both the Athenians and the Peloponnesians had already grounds of complaint against each other. . . .

Now, however, Corinth brought matters into the open. Potidaea[1] was under blockade, some of her own citizens were inside, and she feared that the place might be lost. She therefore immediately urged the allies to send delegates to Sparta. . . . The Spartans also issued an invitation to their own allies and to anyone else who claimed to have suffered from Athenian aggression. They then held their usual assembly, and gave an opportunity there for delegates to express their views. Many came forward with various complaints. . . . The Corinthians were the last to come forward and speak, having allowed the previous speakers to do their part in hardening Spartan opinion against Athens. The Corinthian speech was as follows:

'Spartans, what makes you somewhat reluctant to listen to us others, if we have ideas to put forward, is the great trust and confidence which you have in your own constitution and in your own way of life. This is a quality which certainly makes you moderate in your judgements; it is also, perhaps, responsible for the kind of ignorance which you show when you are dealing with foreign affairs. Many times before now we have told you what we were likely to suffer from Athens, and on each occasion, instead of taking to heart what we were telling you, you chose instead to suspect our motives and to consider that we were speaking only about our own grievances. The result has been that you did not call together this meeting of our allies before the damage was done. . . .

'If there were anything doubtful or obscure about this aggression on the whole of Hellas, our task would have been to try to put the facts before you and show you something that you did not know. As it is, long speeches are unnecessary. You can see yourselves how Athens has deprived some states of their freedom and is scheming to do the same thing for others, especially among our own allies; and that she herself has for a long time been preparing for the eventuality of war. . . .

'And it is you who are responsible for all this. It was you who in the first place allowed the Athenians to fortify their city and build the Long Walls after the Persian War. Since then and up to the present day you have withheld freedom not only from those who have been enslaved by Athens but even from your own allies. When one is deprived of one's liberty one is right in blaming not so much the man who puts the fetters on as the one who had the power to prevent him, but did not use it—especially when such a one rejoices in the glorious reputation of having been the liberator of Hellas.

[1] Corinth's colony, but Athens' ally.

'Even at this stage it has not been easy to arrange this meeting, and even at this meeting there are no definite proposals. Why are we still considering whether aggression has taken place instead of how we can resist it? Men who are capable of real action first make their plans and then go forward without hesitation while their enemies have still not made up their minds. As for the Athenians, we know their methods and how they gradually encroach upon their neighbors. Now they are proceeding slowly because they think that your insensitiveness to the situation enables them to go on their way unnoticed; you will find that they will develop their full strength once they realize that you do see what is happening and are still doing nothing to prevent it.

'You Spartans are the only people in Hellas who wait calmly on events, relying for your defense not on action but on making people think that you will act. You alone do nothing in the early stages to prevent an enemy's expansion; you wait until your enemy has doubled his strength. Certainly you used to have the reputation of being safe and sure enough: now one wonders whether this reputation was deserved. The Persians, as we know ourselves, came from the ends of the earth and got as far as the Peloponnese before you were able to put a proper force into the field to meet them. The Athenians, unlike the Persians, live close to you, yet still you do not appear to notice them; instead of going out to meet them, you prefer to stand still and wait till you are attacked, thus hazarding everything by fighting with opponents who have grown far stronger than they were originally. . . .

'You will not see that the likeliest way of securing peace is this: only to use one's power in the cause of justice, but to make it perfectly plain that one is resolved not to tolerate aggression.

'Your inactivity has done harm enough. Now let there be an end of it. Give your allies, and especially Potidaea, the help you promised, and invade Attica at once. . . . Do not force the rest of us in despair to join a different alliance. If we did so, no one could rightly blame us—neither the gods who witnessed our oaths nor any man capable of appreciating our situation. The people who break a treaty of alliance are the ones who fail to give the help they swore to give, not those who have to look elsewhere because they have been left in the lurch. But if you will only make up your minds to act, we will stand by you. It would be an unnatural thing for us to make a change, nor could we find other allies with whom we have such close bonds. You have heard what we have to say. Think carefully over your decision. From your fathers was handed down to you the leadership of the Peloponnese. Maintain its greatness.'

This was the speech of the Corinthians. There happened to be already in Sparta some Athenian representatives who had come there on other business. When they heard the speeches that had been made, they decided that they, too, ought to claim a hearing. Not that they had any intention of defending themselves against any of the charges that had been made against Athens by the various cities, but they wished to make a general statement and to point out that this was an affair which needed further consideration and ought not to be decided upon at once. They wanted also to make clear how powerful their city was, to remind the elder members of the assembly of facts that were known to them, and to inform the younger ones of matters in which they were ignorant. In this way they hoped to divert their audience from the idea of war and make them incline towards letting matters rest. They therefore approached the Spartans and said that, if there was no objection, they, too, would like to make a speech before the assembly. The Spartans invited them to do so, and they came forward and spoke as follows:

'This delegation of ours did not come here to enter into a controversy with your allies, but to deal with the business on which our city sent us. We observe, however, that extraordinary attacks have been made on us, and so we have come forward to speak. We shall make no reply to the charges which these cities have made against us. Your assembly is not a court of law, competent to listen to pleas either from them or from us. Our aim is to prevent you from coming to the wrong decision on a matter of great importance through paying too much attention to the views of your allies. . . . We shall not be speaking in the spirit of one who is asking a favor, but of one who is producing evidence. Our aim is to show you what sort of a city you will have to fight against, if you make the wrong decision.

'This is our record. At Marathon we stood out against the Persians and faced them single-handed. In the later invasion, when we were unable to meet the enemy on land, we and all our people took to our ships, and joined in the battle at Salamis. It was this battle that prevented the Persians from sailing against the Peloponnese and destroying the cities one by one; for no system of mutual defense could have been organized in face of the Persian naval superiority. The best proof of this is in the conduct of the Persians themselves. Once they had lost the battle at sea they realized that their force was crippled and they immediately withdrew most of their army. That, then, was the result, and it proved that the fate of Hellas depended on her navy. Now, we contributed to this result in three important ways: we produced most of the ships, we provided the most intelligent of the generals, and we displayed the most unflinching courage. . . .

'Surely, Spartans, the courage, the resolution, and the ability which we showed then ought not to be repaid by such immoderate hostility from the Hellenes—especially so far as our empire is concerned. We did not gain this empire by force. It came to us at a time when you were unwilling to fight on to the end against the Persians. At this time our allies came to us of their own accord and begged us to lead them. It was the actual course of events which first compelled us to increase our power to its present extent: fear of Persia was our chief motive, though afterwards we thought, too, of our own honor and our own interest. Finally there came a time when we were surrounded by enemies, when we had already crushed some revolts, when you had lost the friendly feelings that you used to have for us and had turned against us and begun to arouse our suspicion: at this point it was clearly no longer safe for us to risk letting our empire go, especially as any allies that left us would go over to you. And when tremendous dangers are involved no one can be blamed for looking to his own interest.

'Certainly you Spartans, in your leadership of the Peloponnese, have arranged the affairs of the various states so as to suit yourselves. And if, in the years of which we were speaking, you had gone on taking an active part in the war and had become unpopular, as we did, in the course of exercising your leadership, we have little doubt that you would have been just as hard upon your allies as we were, and that you would have been forced either to govern strongly or to endanger your own security.

'So it is with us. We have done nothing extraordinary, nothing contrary to human nature in accepting an empire when it was offered to us and then in refusing to give it up. Three very powerful motives prevent us from doing so —security, honor, and self-interest. And we were not the first to act in this way. Far from it. It has always been a rule that the weak should be subject to the strong; and besides, we consider that we are worthy of our power. Up till the present moment you, too, used to think that we were; but now, after calculating your own interest, you are beginning to talk in terms of right and wrong. . . .

'Take time, then, over your decision, which is an important one. . . . Think, too, of the great part that is played by the unpredictable in war: think of it now, before you are actually committed to war. The longer a war lasts, the more things tend to depend on accidents. Neither you nor we can see into them: we have to abide their outcome in the dark. And when people are entering upon a war they do things the wrong way round. Action comes first, and it is only when they have already suffered that they begin to think. We, however, are still far removed from such a mistaken attitude; so, to the best of our belief, are you. And so we urge you, now, while we are both still free to make sensible decisions, do not break the peace, do not go back upon your oaths; instead let us settle our differences by arbitration, as is laid down in the treaty. If you will not do so, we shall have as our witnesses the gods who heard our oaths. You will have begun the war, and we shall attempt to meet you in any and every field of action that you may choose.'

The Athenians spoke as I have described. Now the Spartans had heard the complaints made by their allies against Athens and also the Athenian reply. They therefore requested all outsiders to leave and discussed the situation among themselves. Most people's views tended to the same conclusion— namely, that Athens was already acting aggressively and that war should be declared without delay. However, the Spartan King Archidamus, a man who had a reputation for both intelligence and moderation, came forward and made the following speech:

'Spartans, in the course of my life I have taken part in many wars, and I see among you people of the same age as I am. They and I have had experience, and so are not likely to share in what may be a general enthusiasm for war, nor to think that war is a good thing or a safe thing. And you will find, if you look carefully into the matter, that this present war which you are now discussing is not likely to be anything on a small scale. When we are engaged with Peloponnesians and neighbors, the forces on both sides are of the same type, and we can strike rapidly where we wish to strike. With Athens it is different. Here we shall be engaged with people who live far off, people also who have the widest experience of the sea and who are extremely well equipped in all other directions, very wealthy both as individuals and as a state, with ships, and cavalry and hoplites,[2] with a population bigger than that of any other place in Hellas, and then, too, with numbers of allies who pay tribute to them. How, then, can we irresponsibly start a war with such a people? What have we to rely upon if we rush into it unprepared? Our navy? It is inferior to theirs, and if we are to give proper attention to it and build it up to their strength, that will take time. Or are we relying on our wealth? Here we are at an even greater disadvantage: we have no public funds, and it is no easy matter to secure contributions from private sources. Perhaps there is ground for confidence in the superiority which we have in heavy infantry and in actual numbers, assets which will enable us to invade and devastate their land. Athens, however, controls plenty of land outside Attica and can import what she wants by sea. And if we try to make her allies revolt from her, we shall have to support them with a fleet, since most of them are on the islands. What sort of war, then, are we going to fight? . . .

'Not that I am suggesting that we should calmly allow them to injure our allies and should turn a blind eye to their machinations. What I do suggest is that we should not take up arms at the present moment; instead we should send to them and put our grievances before them; we should not threaten war too openly, though at the same time we should make it clear that we are not going to let them have their own way. In the meantime we should be making our own preparations by winning over new allies both among Hellenes and among foreigners—from any quarter, in fact, where we can increase our naval and financial resources. No one can blame us for securing our own safety by taking foreigners as well as Greeks into our alliance when we are, as is the fact, having our position undermined by the Athenians. At the same time we must put our own affairs in order. If they pay attention to our diplomatic protests, so much the better. If they do not, then, after two or three years have passed, we shall be in a much sounder position and can attack them, if we decide to do so. And perhaps when they see that our actual strength is keeping pace with the language that we use, they will be more inclined to give way, since their land will still be untouched and, in making up their minds, they will be thinking of advantages which they still possess and which have not yet been destroyed.

'Let no one call it cowardice if we, in all our numbers, hesitate before attacking a single city. They have just as many allies as we have, and their allies pay tribute. And war is not so much a matter of armaments as of the money which makes armaments effective: particularly is this true in a war fought between a land power and a sea power. So let us first of all see to our finances and, until we have done so, avoid being swept away by speeches from our allies. It is we who shall bear most of the responsibility for what happens later, whether it is good or bad. . . .

'Let us not be hurried, and in one short day's space come to a decision which will so profoundly affect the lives of men and their fortunes, the fates of cities and their national honor. . . .'

---

[2] A heavy-armed infantry soldier.

After this speech of Archidamus, Sthenelaidas, one of the ephors[3] of that year, came forward to make the final speech, which was as follows:

'I do not understand these long speeches which the Athenians make. Though they said a great deal in praise of themselves, they made no attempt to contradict the fact that they are acting aggressively against our allies and against the Peloponnese. And surely, if it is the fact that they had a good record in the past against the Persians and now have a bad record as regards us, then they deserve to pay double for it, since, though they were once good, they have now turned out bad. We are the same then and now, and if we are sensible, we shall not allow any aggression against our allies and shall not wait before we come to their help. They are no longer waiting before being ill treated. Others may have a lot of money and ships and horses, but we have good allies, and we ought not to betray them to the Athenians. And this is not a matter to be settled by law-suits and by words: it is not because of words that our own interests are suffering. Instead we should come to the help of our allies quickly and with all our might. Therefore, Spartans, cast your votes for the honor of Sparta and for war! Do not allow the Athenians to grow still stronger! Do not entirely betray your allies! Instead let us, with the help of heaven, go forward to meet the aggressor!'

After this speech he . . . put the question to the Spartan assembly. . . . The great majority were of the opinion that the treaty had been broken.

They then summoned their allies to the assembly and told them that they had decided that Athens was acting aggressively, but that they wanted to have all their allies with them when they put the vote, so that, if they decided to make war, it should be done on the basis of a unanimous resolution. . . .

The Spartans voted that the treaty had been broken and that war should be declared not so much because they were influenced by the speeches of their allies as because they were afraid of the further growth of Athenian power, seeing, as they did, that already the greater part of Hellas was under the control of Athens.

►THE BALANCING PROCESS: AN ANCIENT WISDOM

DAVID HUME

The principle of the balance of power is probably as old as humanity, although it has been fully defined and described only in the last three hundred years. This is discussed in the classic essay on the balance of power by one of the greatest English philosophers, David Hume (1711-1776). Hume also shows that the disregard of a cool and dispassionate concept of the balance of power has led to costly peace and long and cruel wars.

[3] One of the body of five Spartan magistrates.

The selection is from *Essays and Treatises on Several Subjects* (Edinburgh: Bell & Bradfute, and W. Blackwood, 1825), Vol. I.

It is a question, whether the *idea* of the balance of power be owing entirely to modern policy, or whether the *phrase* only has been invented in the later ages? . . .

In all the politics of Greece, the anxiety, with regard to the balance of power, is apparent, and is expressly pointed out to us, even by the ancient historians. Thucydides [1] represents the league which was formed against Athens, and which produced the Peloponnesian war, as entirely owing to this principle. And after the decline of Athens, when the Thebans and Lacedemonians disputed for sovereignty, we find that the Athenians (as well as many other republics) always threw themselves into the lighter scale, and endeavored to preserve the balance. They supported Thebes against Sparta, till the great victory gained by Epaminondas at Leuctra; after which they immediately went over to the conquered, from generosity, as they pretended, but in reality from their jealousy of the conquerors.

Whoever will read Demosthenes's oration for the Megalopolitans, may see the utmost refinements on this principle that ever entered into the head of a Venetian or English speculatist. And upon the first rise of the Macedonian power, this orator immediately discovered the danger, sounded the alarm throughout all Greece, and at last assembled that confederacy under the banners of Athens which fought the great and decisive battle of Chaeronea.

It is true, the Grecian wars are regarded by historians as wars of emulation rather than of politics; and each state seems to have had more in view the honor of leading the rest, than any well-grounded hopes of authority and dominion. If we consider, indeed, the small number of inhabitants in any one republic, compared to the whole, the great difficulty of forming sieges in those times, and the extraordinary bravery and discipline of every freeman among that noble people; we shall conclude, that the balance of power was, of itself, sufficiently secured in Greece, and need not to have been guarded with that caution which may be requisite in other ages. But whether we ascribe the shifting of sides in all the Grecian republics to *jealous emulation* or *cautious politics,* the effects were alike, and every prevailing power was sure to meet with a confederacy against it, and that often composed of its former friends and allies.

The same principle, call it envy or prudence, which produced the *Ostracism* [2] of Athens, and *Petalism* [2] of Syracuse, and expelled every citizen whose fame or power overtopped the rest; the same principle, I say, naturally discovered itself to foreign politics, and soon raised enemies to the leading state, however moderate in the exercise of its authority.

The Persian monarch was really, in his force, a petty prince compared to the Grecian republics; and therefore, it behoved him, from views of safety more than from emulation, to interest himself in their quarrels, and to support the weaker side in every contest. This . . . prolonged, near a century, the date of the Persian empire; till the neglect of it for a moment, after the

---

[1] See p. 166.
[2] The Athenian or Syracusan method of temporary banishment by popular vote without a trial or specific accusation.

first appearance of the aspiring genius of Philip, brought that lofty and frail edifice to the ground, with a rapidity of which there are few instances in the history of mankind. . . .

The reason why it is supposed that the ancients were entirely ignorant of the *balance of power,* seems to be drawn from the Roman history more than the Grecian; and as the transactions of the former are generally more familiar to us, we have thence formed all our conclusions. It must be owned, that the Romans never met with any such general combination or confederacy against them, as might naturally have been expected for their rapid conquests and declared ambition, but were allowed peaceably to subdue their neighbors, one after another, till they extended their dominion over the whole known world. Not to mention the fabulous history of the Italic wars, there was, upon Hannibal's invasion of the Roman state, a remarkable crisis, which ought to have called up the attention of all civilized nations. It appeared afterwards (nor was it difficult to be observed at the time) that this was a contest for universal empire; yet no prince or state seems to have been in the least alarmed about the event or issue of the quarrel. Philip of Macedon remained neuter, till he saw the victories of Hannibal; and then most imprudently formed an alliance with the conqueror, upon terms still more imprudent. He stipulated, that he was to assist the Carthaginian state in their conquest of Italy; after which they engaged to send over forces into Greece, to assist him in subduing the Grecian commonwealth.

. . . And what may be esteemed still a stronger proof, that this maxim was not generally known in those ages, no ancient author has remarked the imprudence of these measures, nor has even blamed that absurd treaty above mentioned, made by Philip with the Carthaginians. Princes and statesmen, in all ages, may, beforehand, be blinded in their reasonings with regard to events: But it is somewhat extraordinary, that historians, afterwards, should not form a sounder judgment of them.

Massinissa, Attalus, Prusias, in gratifying their private passions, were all of them the instruments of the Roman greatness, and never seem to have suspected, that they were forging their own chains, while they advanced the conquests of their ally. A simple treaty and agreement between Massinissa and the Carthaginians, so much required by mutual interest, barred the Romans from all entrance into Africa, and preserved liberty to mankind.

The only prince we meet with in the Roman history, who seems to have understood the balance of power, is Hiero, king of Syracuse. Though the ally of Rome, he sent assistance to the Carthaginians during the war of the auxiliaries; "Esteeming it requisite," says Polybius, "both in order to retain his dominions in Sicily, and to preserve the Roman friendship, that Carthage should be safe; lest by its fall the remaining power should be able, without control or opposition, to execute every purpose and undertaking. And here he acted with great wisdom and prudence: For that is never, on any account, to be overlooked; nor ought such a force ever to be thrown into one hand, as to incapacitate the neighboring states from defending their rights against it." Here is the aim of modern politics pointed out in express terms.

In short the maxim of preserving the balance of power is founded so much on common sense and obvious reasoning, that it is impossible it could altogether have escaped antiquity, where we find, in other particulars, so many marks of deep penetration and discernment. If it was not so generally known and acknowledged as at present, it had at least an influence on all the wiser and more experienced princes and politicians. And indeed, even at present, however generally known and acknowledged among speculative reasoners, it has not, in practice, an authority much more extensive among those who govern the world.

After the fall of the Roman empire, the form of government, established by the northern conquerors, incapacitated them, in a great measure, for farther conquests, and long maintained each state in its proper boundaries. But when vassalage and the feudal militia were abolished, mankind were anew alarmed by the danger of universal monarchy, from the union of so many kingdoms and principalities in the person of the Emperor Charles. But the power of the house of Austria, founded on extensive but divided dominions; and their riches, derived chiefly from mines of gold and silver, were more likely to decay of themselves, from internal defects, than to overthrow all the bulwarks raised against them. In less than a century, the force of that violent and haughty race was shattered, their opulence dissipated, their splendor eclipsed. A new power succeeded, more formidable to the liberties of Europe, possessing all the advantages of the former, and laboring under none of its defects, except a share of that spirit of bigotry and persecution, with which the house of Austria was so long, and is still so much infatuated.

In the general wars maintained against this ambitious power, Great Britain has stood foremost, and she still maintains her station. Beside her advantages of riches and situation, her people are animated with such a national spirit, and are so fully sensible of the blessings of their government, that we may hope their vigor never will languish in so necessary and so just a cause. On the contrary, if we may judge by the past, their passionate ardor seems rather to require some moderation; and they have oftener erred from a laudable excess than from a blameable deficiency.

In the *first* place, we seem to have been more possessed with the ancient Greek spirit of jealous emulation, than actuated by the prudent views of modern politics. Our wars with France have been begun with justice, and even perhaps from necessity, but have always been too far pushed, from obstinacy and passion. The same peace, which was afterwards made at Ryswick in 1697, was offered so early as the year ninety-two; that concluded at Utrecht in 1712 might have been finished on as good conditions at Gertruytenberg in the year eight; and we might have given at Frankfort, in 1743, the same terms which we were glad to accept of at Aix-la-Chapelle in the year forty-eight. Here then we see, that above half of our wars with France, and all our public debts, are owing more to our own imprudent vehemence, than to the ambition of our neighbors.

In the *second* place, we are so declared in our opposition to French power, and so alert in defense of our allies, that they always reckon upon our force as upon their own; and expecting to carry on war at our expense, refuse all reasonable terms of accommodation. . . .

In the *third* place, we are such true combatants, that, when once engaged, we lose all concern for ourselves and our posterity, and consider only how we may best annoy the enemy. To mortgage our revenues at so deep a rate in wars where we were only accessaries, was surely the most fatal delusion that a nation, which had any pretensions to politics and prudence, has ever yet been guilty of. That remedy of funding, if it be a remedy, and not rather a poison, ought, in all reason, to be reserved to the last extremity; and no evil, but the greatest and most urgent, should ever induce us to embrace so dangerous an expedient.

These excesses, to which we have been carried, are prejudicial, and may, perhaps, in time, become still more prejudicial another way, by begetting, as is usual, the opposite extreme, and rendering us totally careless and supine with regard to the fate of Europe. The Athenians, from the most bustling, intriguing, warlike people of Greece, finding their error in thrusting themselves into every quarrel, abandoned all attention to foreign affairs; and in no contest ever took part on either side, except by their flatteries and complaisance to the victor.

Enormous monarchies are probably destructive to human nature in their progress, in their continuance, and even in their downfall, which never can be very distant from their establishment.

▶THE BALANCING PROCESS: IS IT OUTDATED?

ARNOLD WOLFERS

The balance of power, like peace and order, is not the result of natural forces but of conscious and constant effort. There is nothing natural or automatic about it. This is stressed in the following essay by Arnold Wolfers, Director of the Washington Center of Foreign Policy Research at Johns Hopkins University, author of a number of books and articles on law, economics, and international relations.

. . . I shall speak of the balance of power as implying an equilibrium or a distribution of power between two opponents in which neither side has attained a position of superiority or supremacy. Such a definition points to the opposite of hegemony or domination. To make such a distinction between balanced and unbalanced power does not suggest that there is any sure way of measuring and comparing the relative power of nations and, thus, of deciding how great the unbalance or how close the balance is. Even the extent

The selection is an abridged version of a lecture, "The Balance of Power in Theory and Practice," delivered at the Naval War College on September 17, 1957. Reprinted in *Naval War College Review,* Vol. XI, No. 5 (January 1959).

of a nation's military power, which is only part of its over-all power, can only be tested in war, but such a test means that the balance of power process has failed in its purpose of preserving the peace. However, it makes sense to speak of an existing balance of power—or of a fair approximation of such a balance—whenever there are indications that two opposing nations, or blocs of nations, are being deterred from putting their opponents' total power to the test. In peacetime, one can speak of a balance of "mutual deterrence" which today, when nuclear power is involved, has been called a "balance of terror." It presupposes that according to their respective estimates the other side possesses not less than equal power.

With this definition of the balance of power in mind, one can inquire into theories on the chances or merits of an equilibrium of power among adversaries and on the process by which such equilibrium is established, preserved or upset. I shall distinguish and discuss four theories—three of long standing, one of recent vintage—and inquire into their significance for contemporary foreign policy. One theory regards the balance of power as the ideal distribution of power; a second considers it the automatic outcome of developments inherent in the multistate system; to a third, the balance of power represents a goal of foreign policy which some policy-makers find useful to pursue; according to a fourth theory of mid-twentieth century origin, it has become an obsolete notion, which can be misleading to anyone concerned with contemporary international affairs.

Very few people in this country can be persuaded, I presume, to take seriously the kind of glorification of balanced power among adversaries that often found expression in earlier centuries. While the idea of "checks and balances," intimately associated with the American Constitution, is still considered a valuable device in domestic affairs, equilibrium on the world stage arouses grave misgivings because it implies today the continued coexistence of a free world and a communist world, with each side holding the other in check. Such a concept could hardly be more remote from our ideals of the kind of world in which we would wish to live. At best, then, a balance of power between the two main opponents of today's world may be the least objectionable or evil distribution of power presently attainable.

Even if it were not for the Cold War, many people in the West would refuse to consider international equilibrium as the ideal distribution of power. Strong current predilections run in the direction of what is called "collective security." This theory assumes that the peace of the world depends not on having the power of all nations balanced and checked by the power of others, but, on the contrary, on making overwhelming power available to those who are ready to oppose potential aggressor nations or to punish actual aggressors. By the rules of collective security, the peace-loving nations of the world cannot have too much power since they can be expected never to abuse their superior power position. The stronger they are, collectively, the better their chances of deterring or, if necessary, of punishing potential violators of the peace. On this premise, the ideal situation is one in which the "defenders of the peace and law of the world community" enjoy unchallengeable hegemony. . . .

It has been said that equilibrium was never really regarded as an ideal, even by those statesmen who have been its foremost verbal champions. The British, in particular, have been accused of hypocrisy for advocating the balance of power as a universally beneficial principle, when they have derived unique benefits from its observance. It is pointed out that Britain was seeking an equilibrium between her continental rivals, not between herself and her potential enemies. Britain could then assume the role of the "balancer" with all the advantages of that position.

But preference for equilibrium need not be a mere rationalization of national interest. In fact, it is deeply rooted in what today would be called conservative thought. Characteristic of such thought, which found its classical expression in the writings of Machiavelli and Hobbes, is a pessimistic view of human nature. It sustains Lord Acton's expectation that "power corrupts and absolute power corrupts absolutely." Men with a conservative bent of mind need find nothing shocking, therefore, in the suggestion that all nations, including their own, should be restrained by counter power. They will thereby be spared many temptations as well as being prevented from abusing their power.

The suggestion that all nations need the restraint of the balance of power does not mean that the same amount of power is required to deter an aggressive would-be empire builder or megalomaniac dictator from initiating violence as is required to prevent a satisfied nation, especially a democratic nation that operates under strong internal restraints, from seeking to cash in on the weaknesses of others. In any "balance of deterrence," different estimates of the power distribution and variations in the willingness to take risks have to be taken into account. A fanatical government bent on conquest will tend to overestimate its own power and underestimate that of its "decadent" opponents. Nobody could seriously praise a balance of power, therefore, except on the assumption that it is of a kind that promises to place effective restraints even on the least self-restrained of the parties.

It is the all-round potential restraining effect of the balance that turns conquerors—the Napoleons and Hitlers—into its most violent critics, making them strange bedfellows of the idealistic exponents of collective security who share their hostility towards the concept of the balance of power. The Nazis were vociferous in their accusation that Britain espoused the "ideal" of a balance of power merely in order to hold down potential continental rivals who challenged her predominance. Quite generally, countries in revolt against the *status quo* are opposed to balanced power as barring the way to change. Equilibrium tends to prevent "revision" by means of force, which is usually the only means through which major changes can be brought about.

For the exponents of the second theory of balance of power, the controversy between those who contend that the balance of power is a good thing and those who condemn it makes no sense. They say that equilibrium of power is not a matter of choice; instead, it tends to result from a competition for power among nations that is inherent in the multistate system. In this view, a mechanism is at work, similar to the "invisible hand" operating in a market economy that tends to produce an equilibrium between supply and demand. Theorists have construed a model of a multistate system, in which equilibrium automatically results without the assistance of deliberate choice in favor of equilibrium by the actors. While today such a model is not regarded as more than an abstract initial working hypothesis, the conditions existing in the 19th century gave it the character of a rather striking portrait of reality. After the end of Napoleon's Continental hegemony, world power came to be distributed among five or six major European nations. All of them were jealous of their relative power positions, all keenly aware of any change in the distribution of power, and all eager to prevent any one of the others from stepping into the shoes of Napoleonic France. Therefore, in order to render impossible or to defeat any incipient hegemony, two or more powers could be counted upon to line up almost intuitively against any ascending power that threatened to become their superior. In their game of power politics, they were united by their common interest in not allowing the balance to be tipped against them. Competition for allies and competition in armaments were the chief instruments of a balancing process in which the realities of European power politics came close to resembling an automatic balancing system.

However, even in that period, the flaws in the expectation that an equilibrium of mutual deterrence would actually come about without deliberate and intelligent efforts on the part of governments were only too visible. Again and again, a country which believed it had attained a position of superiority struck out against its rivals, or another country which feared an increasingly adverse balance initiated war before the balance had tilted too far against it. In such instances, war was the instrument by which breakdown of equilibrium was overcome or prevented, a method of adjustment hardly comparable with the relatively smooth-working price mechanism of the market economy. Innumerable historical cases could be cited to show the extent to which the success of the balancing process depended on the choices made by statesmen of the countries involved. British statesmen were faced with a momentous choice when, prior to the outbreak of war in 1914, they had to decide whether or not to give full British backing to France and Russia as a means of deterring the Central Powers. There was no automatism in operation to prevent them from making the wrong choice. Similarly, when three years later Germany had hegemony almost within her grasp, there was nothing automatic about the decision of the United States to enter on the side of the hard-pressed Allies; in fact, by resuming unrestricted submarine warfare early in 1917, Germany was largely responsible for speeding up a decision that might have been reached too late to right the balance of power.

While it makes little sense, then, to use the term "automatic" in a literal way, as if human choices and errors have no effect upon the process of establishing or upsetting a state of equilibrium, there is nevertheless a significant element of truth in the theory of "automatism," and one that is valid even today. If it is correct to assume that any government in its senses will be deeply concerned with the relative power position of hostile countries, one is justified in concluding that efforts, to keep in step with such opponents in the competition for power, or even to outdo them, will almost certainly be forthcoming. If almost all nations react in this way, a tendency towards equilibrium follows as a consequence—it comes into play if both sides aim at equilibrium, but it also operates if the more aggressive side strives for superiority, thereby provoking his opponent to match his moves. In the latter case, which is the most frequent, it makes some sense to say that there are forces at work behind the backs of the human actors that seem to push them in the direction of balanced power irrespective of their preferences.

It is also worth noting, particularly in the light of recent events, how nations seem to be drawn into the balancing process almost without conscious choice or deliberation. The policy of the United States since World War II offers a particularly striking illustration. Despite its long-established policy of resisting all pressures and temptations toward involvement in the peace-time balancing of power, the United States reversed its traditional stand without hesitation when in 1946 no other country was in a position to contain the ascending Soviet Empire and to restrain it with at least equal counterpower.

One could point to other countries that have reluctantly become concerned about the world balance of power in recent years. Yugoslavia, for instance, although strongly committed by the ideology of her regime to remain on the Soviet side, has repeatedly given signs of appreciating the security she enjoys through the existence of Western counterpower. . . .

The question is whether, as a matter of expediency, nations, under certain circumstances, do or should make power equilibrium rather than power superiority the target of their efforts. . . . Frequently, one would suppose, the intention will be to achieve superiority until the competitive race proves it to be unattainable. Then equilibrium—or stalemate as it is often called today— may become the accepted goal. Both sides, in fact, may come to realize that a superiority is leading nowhere except to exhaustion, and agree, tacitly at least, to settle for the less ambitious and less costly goal of balanced power. Such a realization has been the rationale of most attempts to bring about disarmament through agreement, although the success of such attempts has been quite exceptional.

Frequently, as indicated earlier, when governments make the balance of power their aim, what they desire to bring about is a balance between the power of other nations that will place their country in the enviable position of a "balancer." Countries too weak to become active balancers are usually hopeful that an equilibrium will be established between their stronger neighbors, but they can do little to promote it. Up to 1914, the United States was one of the passive beneficiaries of the balance of power which Britain did so much to maintain on the Continent. Today, the United States stands out as the country that can do most to keep other nations, especially those within the free world, in a state of equilibrium. Not a few American moves have been directed towards this goal. The United States is interested in the maintenance of the peace between its many non-Communist friends and allies. It acts true to the traditions of the state system, therefore, when seeking, for instance, to keep Israel and its Arab neighbors in a condition approximating balanced power. . . .

No country faced with grave external danger, as is the United States today, would willingly forego superiority of power over its opponent if it were attainable at acceptable costs. Unquestionably, a sigh of relief would go up if a technical break-through in the arms race were suddenly to give this country military supremacy. Equilibrium, however carefully estimated and maintained, can give nothing like the security that would flow from undoubted supremacy. Nevertheless, with most of its allies, the United States can afford to resign itself to a policy of mere equilibrium if supremacy or a marked degree of superiority over its opponent proves to be an unattainable goal. It is possible for the United States and other like-minded countries, if they are rightly classified as *status quo* powers, to adopt a policy of equilibrium with its minimum power requirements.

Status quo powers are those states which seek to preserve the established order or which have renounced the use of force as a method of changing that order. Presumably, therefore, they can achieve their objective of deterring or stopping their opponent only if they possess defensive counterpower no less than equal to the power of their opponent. Success does not require superiority of power.

Although the United States may be thoroughly dissatisfied with a world order in which some countries suffer under partition, bondage as satellites, or despotism, it nevertheless qualifies as a *status quo* power because it has renounced the use of force as a means of remedying the iniquities of the *status quo*. Therefore, acceptance of power equilibrium as the goal of American policy does not mean that the United States has sacrificed its defensive objective, but only that it has forfeited the greater security that *status quo* powers can obtain from a position of superior power.

The other category of nations—the so-called "revisionist" countries, those bent on changing the *status quo,* if necessary by force—are in a less favorable position. They can resign themselves to a policy of balanced power only in despair, since they are well aware that only with rare exceptions can the established order be seriously modified without the threat or use of a force so preponderant that it will overcome the resistance of the opposing side. Thus, for these states to give up pursuit of superior power in favor of balanced power means, in effect, their renunciation of their ultimate national goal: a substantial change in the existing world order. Therefore, if it is correct to assume that the Soviet Union and Red China fall into the category of revisionist countries, it can be concluded that their power goal will be superiority rather than balanced power.

There are many Americans who deplore the acquiescence of their country in the policies of a *status quo* power. But their demands for a more offensive policy, one that would seek—by the use of force if necessary—to break Soviet resistance to unfavorable changes, must nevertheless face the practical question whether American superiority of power of the kind required for such a policy could be brought within practical reach.

Even the preservation or establishment of mere equilibrium is far from being an easy task. Democratic states suffer from severe handicaps in their competition with a totalitarian regime that can spend an exceedingly high proportion of its national product on armaments and mobilize impressive economic and ideological power for external purposes. Most of the governments of the non-Communist world, the United States included, find it difficult politically in contrast to the Soviets to maintain even their present inadequate military budgets and their present expenditure for foreign aid. Moreover, public opinion in the United States and throughout the West in general is content with a *status quo* policy which can be adequately served by balanced power between the East and the West. It is quite unlikely, therefore, that the additional sacrifices necessary to achieve a level of superiority *vis-a-vis* the Soviets would be found palatable. Fortunately, a quest for mere equilibrium may offer some advantages that will partly compensate for the failure, serious even for *status quo* powers, to attain the kind of security that only a safe margin of superiority can offer.

If a country is able to give convincing evidence of seeking only equilibrium, it will not usually be suspected of aggressive intentions, since it is obvious that the attainment of its relatively modest power goal can give it defensive capabilities at best. Its attitude, therefore, will tend to appeal to all friends and allies that belong in the category of *status quo* powers, though it will disappoint its "revisionist" friends. There is a chance, too, that the more modest power goal will have some effect on the behavior of the opposing side —in this case on the Soviet Union. If the Soviets feel secure from threats of external aggression and, at the same time, are suffering from the heavy burden of the arms race, they too may resign themselves, temporarily at least, to the continuation of the *status quo* and to the maintenance of a mere balance of power. Although we do not want to make too much of a virtue of necessity, the acceptance by the United States of the balance of power as the avowed goal of policy may have certain other advantages. Such a policy will remove unfounded public expectations of future superiority and eliminate temptations to conduct policy as if the United States could soon expect to impose its will on an inferior opponent.

This suggestion—that the United States might do well to make a reasonable balance of power between East and West a target of its foreign policy and the standard by which to measure its efforts in the power field—runs counter to the last of the theories mentioned earlier. The whole notion of a balancing of power policy, according to the exponents of this theory, has been rendered obsolete by the emergence of new forces that have radically changed the conditions of international politics. While, in former times, the balance may have been a condition both of peace and of the continued independence of many nations, it has ceased, they say, to be a practiced goal today, because of the impact of a number of new factors with which statesmen did not formerly have to contend.

One of these factors, strongly emphasized at the close of World War II, was the rise of the United States to a leading position in world politics. Many argued that the newcomer was little fitted for the task of playing the balancing game. Was it possible to expect that a country so little accustomed to, or inclined towards, power calculations in foreign affairs would be able to switch sides from former friends to former enemies if such a move were necessary for the restoration of the world balance of power? Would the United States agree to "entangling" itself in alliances? The record of American policies since World War II has laid these misgivings to rest and has thoroughly disproved the alleged ineptitude of the United States in the matter of the balancing of power process. With a speed that came as a shock even to many Europeans supposedly reared in the traditions of the power game, America's enemies of World War II became her military allies, and soon the United States was to emerge as the center of a peace-time alliance system of unprecedented breadth. Statesmen in Washington became quickly aware of the need for establishing and maintaining a balance between the power of the East and the West. Concepts such as containment and deterrence, which soon became the catch-words of the day, pointed to equilibrium as a minimum American objective. Therefore, it may be suggested that, rather than confirming the theory of obsolescence, this first factor demonstrates the continuing primacy of balancing-of-power considerations.

A second new factor, the so-called "bipolarity" of the postwar world, was thought to be of even greater consequence. After all, the so-called balance of power system of the 19th century rested on the simultaneous existence of five or six major powers. Now only two were left, while the remaining lesser powers were able to throw so little into the scales against a potential ascending state that their influence could be discounted. Here, too, however, experience in the era of the two superpowers has merely added weight to the contention that whenever there is more than one sovereign power in the world, the balancing process will begin to operate. Even had it been true that all significant power was to remain vested in the USA and the USSR, as it was at the close of World War II, their competition in armaments and in economic development could have led to a balance of power between them which might have been maintained by their efforts alone. But the condition of the extreme bipolarity of 1945 has been steadily on the decline as other centers of not inconsiderable power have arisen or reasserted themselves in many parts of the world. As the situation stands today, these lesser powers could, if they wanted, throw their weight to one side or another and significantly affect the distribution of power between the two main opposing camps. Moreover, regional balancing of power is under way among some of the lesser countries: for instance, between the Arab countries and Israel, or between Pakistan and India. Neither bipolarity nor the rise of new states, then, has resulted in the disappearance of traditional policies of power. On the contrary, one of the striking characteristics of the present situation is the manner in which some of the new states, which one might have expected would be preoccupied with their thorny internal problems, have come to throw their weight around in the world balancing process, sometimes, as in the case of Yugoslavia, for the obvious purpose of preventing one of the superpowers from becoming too mighty in a particular area.

A third novelty which has rightly attracted attention is the ideological note that has been introduced into the world's major power struggle. Some observers predicted that ideological affinities and antagonisms would become so strong that nations would become unwilling, whatever the requirements of the balancing process, to leave the camp of their ideological preference. If this had occurred, the distribution of power in the world would have been at the mercy of ideological competition. Ideological appeals have, undoubtedly, affected the orientation of some countries toward East or West, but in such cases one cannot necessarily say that efforts to establish a balance of power have ceased. Indeed, whenever ideological power has shown a tendency to gain the upper hand over other forms of power, competition between East and West does not disappear but is transferred to the field of ideology, propaganda and subversion. We can see evidence of this competition on all sides today, and we may well conclude that the United States will be unable to balance Soviet power if it fails to remain or establish itself as an ideological alternative no less attractive than the Soviet Union.

Ideology has not, however, come to reign supreme. There have been instances of recent date to show that the "blood" of military power considerations can still run thicker than the "water" of ideological sympathy. . . . Communist Yugoslavia lined up with the West when it felt threatened by Soviet military superiority, and countries with no Communist bias like Nasser's Egypt have taken full advantage of opportunities to swing toward the Soviet side when, for reasons of national interest, they wished to weaken or restrain the Western camp. If ideology interferes with the relatively smooth functioning of the traditional balancing process, it is most likely to do so by blinding ideologically fanatical leaders and elites to threats emanating from the camp of their ideological preference. When statesmen jeopardize national security interests in this way, one can speak of a kind of "ideological stickiness" which may lead to alignments that run counter to the requirements of equilibrium.

Finally, there is the new factor of nuclear weapons. The question has been raised whether the conditions of the nuclear age, with its weapons of unprecedented destructiveness and its revolutionary developments in weapons technology, does not defeat all efforts at rational power calculation and comparison. If it does, governments would be unable to establish any particular world power distribution or to know even approximately whether equilibrium exists at any given time. Thus, it would be hopeless to attempt to rely on the balance of power for the security of their countries or for the preservation of peace.

No one can deny that the art of estimating power—one's own and that of an adversary—which has been the source of many tragic errors even in prenuclear days, has been immensely complicated by the introduction of even new and untried instruments of war. Yet, despite this new element of uncertainty, there has probably never been a time in which more efforts have been exerted towards estimating comparative military power, strategic nuclear striking power included. All the talk of a stalemate on the strategic plane would be meaningless if these estimates had become a matter of sheer guesswork. It must be remembered, in this connection, that in time of peace it is the balance of mutual deterrence that is important, and deterrence rests not on the *actual* relative strengths of the two sides—which only war can reveal—but on what governments *believe to be* the existing distribution of power. In fact, the more both sides overestimate the relative power position of their opponent, the more likely it is that they will be deterred from using their power. Since the chief danger has always been an underestimation of enemy strength and determination, the advent of nuclear weapons has had the effect of buttressing the deterrent value of the balancing process. Even a megalomaniac will not easily discount enemy nuclear retaliatory power, provided it is creditable to him that his opponent will use that power to counter his moves. If credible, the threat of retaliation with less than equal nuclear force may suffice for deterrence provided the lesser force is enough to cause unacceptably great damage. The problem, today, therefore, is not so much equality of nuclear power, but the difficulty of creating equilibrium on other levels, so that one is ready to meet various types of attack and can convince an opponent that his attacks will actually be met.

It is particularly difficult and costly for the United States to balance the Soviet Union today precisely because a "balance of terror" on the level of strategic nuclear force is not enough to assure what might be called an "overall equilibrium" involving all levels of power competition. The respective strategic nuclear capabilities of the United States and the Soviet Union have a marked tendency to neutralize each other, which means that they drop out of the scales as a positive balancing factor. The balance then depends on power relationships all the way down the ladder from somewhere below massive retaliatory power to the respective capacities for limited war, for conventional war, for subversion and for ideological or economic appeal. On these less elevated rungs of the ladder, the Soviet bloc appears to be superior at this time. One may conclude, then, that the nuclear factor, while unable to end the balancing of power process or to rob it of its former functions, merely adds to the difficulties of manipulating the process in such a way that a reasonable degree of equilibrium can be attained, preserved and ascertained.

One last remark about the alleged obsolescence of the balance of power and balancing process is necessary. Those who accept the obsolescence theory must have asked themselves what alternative course is open to nations in the present era. An organization like the United Nations, despite its provisions for collective security, cannot put the balancing process to rest because it leaves all coercive power in the hands of its members. There can be only one alternative—the elimination of all military power from the control of individual nations, which, if it occurred, would obviously relieve governments of the need to concern themselves with the world distribution of power among nations. With the monopoly of military power by a single world authority, and only with such a monopoly, international power politics itself—and with it the whole balancing of power process—would disappear. Nations, even if embroiled in conflict with one another, would have no more reason to worry about the power position of other nations than a Rhode Island or an Oklahoma about the power of larger and potentially more powerful neighboring States of the Union. Unfortunately for those who would like to see such a world authority established, it must be said that there is not the slightest chance of its establishment in the foreseeable future. Can anyone imagine the United States or the Soviet Union, for that matter, subordinating themselves voluntarily to an authority over which their chief opponent might come to exercise supreme control? If they did, they would make themselves as impotent as is any State in the Union compared to the Federal Government. If ever the two superpowers had enough confidence in each other not to mind being ruled by a world authority which was controlled by the other, there would be no need for such a world authority anymore! Under such ideal conditions of mutual confidence, the two together could, and probably would, rule supreme in the world, but one must add that their chances of preserving their mutual confidence and of agreeing on the use of their power would be greater if they preserved a high degree of equilibrium between themselves. Rather than to make a world authority more practical today than it was in earlier periods, ideological conflict, concentration of power in the hands of two antagonistic superpowers, and the introduction of nuclear weapons have deepened the gulf between groups of nations and made world unity more remote. Under these circumstances the balance of power, while far from ideal, suggests itself as an acceptable and practical substitute for the supremacy in the world that the United States with all its potential power cannot presently hope to attain for itself.

TOPIC 8

Collective Security

By collective security we mean a distribution of power by which the overwhelming portion is in the hands of protectors of peace and order. Thus a potential aggressor would not dare to disturb peace. If he did, he would be crushed.

Collective security has been presented often not only as the opposite of the balance of power but as a concept which would mean "the end of the use of power in politics." If the balance of power is understood not as a mathematical equation, but as a distribution of power which deters aggression and domination, then the concept of collective security does not essentially differ from the principle that aggressive power should be checked by counterpower.

Professor Hans J. Morgenthau actually argues that "collective security . . . reaffirmed the balance of power in the form of a universal alliance against any potential aggressor . . . the presumption being that such an alliance would always outweigh any potential aggressor."[1] If, however, there is no overwhelming power on the side of law-abiding nations and if there is no agreement as to what constitutes aggression and what constitutes a justified defense, then "a device intent upon making war impossible ends by making

[1] Hans J. Morgenthau, *Politics Among Nations* (New York: Alfred A. Knopf, 1954), p. 175.

war universal. . . . Any war anywhere in the world then is potentially a world war." [2]

A similar conclusion was reached by Walter Lippmann, who believes that the principle of collective security was made inoperative by the probability that every local police action might degenerate into a major conflict—at terrifying cost. "When the issue is less than the survival of the *great* nations, the method of collective security will not be used because it is just as terrifying to the policeman as it is to the lawbreaker. It punishes the law-enforcing states, at least until they have paid the awful price of victory, as much as the law-breaking states. . . . The principle of collective security . . . in practice is not collective and does not bring security." [3]

It should be noted that the term "collective security" has a very definite meaning, not to be confused with the idea of multilateral alliances like NATO or the Warsaw Pact, which claim to insure security for collectivities of nations. Rather, such specific collective arrangements or alliances should be referred to as "collective self-defense." They are typical arrangements within the framework of the traditional balance of power.

▶THE IDEA OF "WORLD POLICE" AND ITS FALLACIES

KENNETH W. THOMPSON

The working of collective security depends on the following assumptions: (1) that there is a maximum disparity of power between peace-loving nations as opposed to would-be aggressors; (2) that peaceful nations always reach identical conclusions as to the source and nature of a threat to, or breach of, peace; (3) that they are willing and ready to use their power for the purpose of collective security anywhere and at any time.

But do these assumptions correspond to reality? This is critically examined by Kenneth W. Thompson, formerly of Northwestern University, author of several studies on international politics, lecturer at the Army War College, and author of such books as Christian Ethics and the Dilemmas of Foreign Policy, *and* Political Realism and the Crisis of World Politics.

From one standpoint it is a truism to say that collective security is something new under the sun. In past eras and especially in the eighteenth and nineteenth centuries, war was conceived of as a duel in which contestants should be isolated and restrained by the rest of international society. When nations engaged in armed conflict their neighbors sought to localize the struggle and alleviate its poisonous effects. However short-sighted their actions in not meeting the conflict directly and turning back aggression at its source, the

[2] *Op. cit.,* p. 393.

[3] Walter Lippmann, *New York Herald Tribune,* January 15, 1951.

The selection is from the article, "Collective Security Reexamined," *The American Political Science Review,* Vol. XLVII, No. 3 (Sept., 1953), pp. 753-766.

nations pursuing these policies were sometimes successful for varying periods of time in preserving islands of peace in a warring world.

On August 8, 1932, however, Secretary of State Henry L. Stimson proclaimed the revolutionary fact that the modern state system was entering a new era in which warring powers were no longer entitled to the same equally impartial and neutral treatment by the rest of society. He announced to the New York Council of Foreign Relations that in future conflicts one or more of the combatants must be designated as wrong-doer and added: "We no longer draw a circle about them and treat them with the punctilios of the duelist's code. Instead we denounce them as lawbreakers."

This is the cornerstone of the universally recognized theory of collective security to which most Western statesmen profess loyalty today. It is said that Mr. Stimson's memoirs, *On Active Service,* have become the "bible" of the Department of State, and in Britain we have the word of *The Times* (London) in a recent editorial that collective security " . . . indeed, is the view to which this country, like most others, is committed by its membership in the United Nations. . . ." . . .

In his first speech to the Senate, Harry S. Truman of Missouri declared: "The breaking of the peace anywhere is the concern of peace-loving nations everywhere." Senator Arthur H. Vandenberg announced following the San Francisco Conference in a dramatic speech to the Senate that he would support the ratification of the Charter with all the resources at his command. For, he explained: "peace must not be cheated of its collective chance. . . . We must have collective security to stop the next war, if possible, before it starts; and we must have collective action to crush it swiftly if it starts in spite of our organized precautions." Thus, the American President whose course in foreign policy was to be charted boldly and unambiguously according to the abstract principles of collective security, and the reputed architect of the bipartisan foreign policy were from the beginning unequivocally committed by their words to support of the United Nations. . . .

It is important that we ask at the outset, then: What is collective security in theory? What are its precepts and main tenets? What, in simplest terms, is the philosophy of collective security? The rock bottom principle upon which collective security is founded provides that an attack on any one state will be regarded as an attack on all states. It finds its measure in the simple doctrine of one for all and all for one. War anywhere, in the context of Article 11 of the League of Nations, is the concern of every state.

Self-help and neutrality, it should be obvious, are the exact antithesis of such a theory. States under an order of neutrality are impartial when conflict breaks out, give their blessings to combatants to fight it out, and defer judgment regarding the justice or injustice of the cause involved. Self-help in the past was often "help yourself" so far as the great powers were concerned; they enforced their own rights and more besides. In the eighteenth and nineteenth centuries this system was fashionable and wars, although not eliminated, were localized whenever possible. In a more integrated world environment, a conflict anywhere has some effect on conditions of peace everywhere. A disturbance at one point upsets the equilibrium at all other points, and the adjustment of a single conflict restores the foundations of harmony at other points throughout the world.

This idea of collective security is simple, challenging and novel. It would do for the international society what police action does for the domestic community. If the individual is threatened or endangered in municipal society, he turns to the legitimate agents of law enforcement, the police. The comparatively successful operation of this system has meant relative peace and tolerable harmony for most local communities. Through the action of police or "fire brigades" on a world scale, collective security has as its goal two comparable objectives. It would *prevent* war by providing a deterrent to aggression. It would *defend* the interests of peace-loving states in war if it came, by concentrating a preponderance of power against the aggressor. These two ends have been the goals of both the League and the United Nations. . . .

Article 16 of the Covenant provided that any member resorting to war contrary to the Covenant had committed *ipso facto* an act of aggression against all other members. It was intended that first economic measures and then overt force should be applied against any offender. But although the international obligations of members were less ambiguous than in the Charter, there was no clear provision for their implementation or organization by a central enforcement agency. Each nation had full freedom to provide what troops it saw fit. The Council could then advise on additional measures. In contrast, Article 39 of the Charter of the United Nations commissions the Security Council to determine the existence of a threat to the peace or act of aggression and Articles 43-47 obligate the members, upon the completion of agreements, to supply troops to the Military Staff Committee. . . .

From the beginning, however, the real issue concerning collective security has had little to do with charters or compacts. The real issue has been the question of why the implementation of a system logically so flawless, and enjoying such impressive official devotion and popular support, should have been accompanied by a period of virtually unprecedented collective insecurity. It is a sobering fact that the nineteenth century was perhaps the most peaceful of modern centuries; the twentieth, by contrast, has been an epoch of unparalleled bloodshed. From 1815 to 1914 a system of old-fashioned balance of power contributed to the achievement of nearly a full century of uninterrupted peace. The past forty years have witnessed in rapid succession two great wars which the historian Arnold J. Toynbee compares to the double wars of the Romans and the Carthaginians and the two struggles of the Peloponnesian War which wrecked Hellenic Civilization. He has observed that quite possibly we have dealt ourselves the same "knockout blows" that these wars represented for the older civilizations. There were only eighteen months in the nineteenth century when France, Russia, Austria, Prussia, England and Spain found themselves at war with one another (excluding the Crimean War as a colonial struggle). By contrast, our experience thus far with the novel machinery of collective security has hardly warranted the unqualified postwar optimism of men like Mr. Hull that, with the new international organization, power politics and war were being left far behind in our progress toward utopia.

Instead the recent decades have been years of unceasing war or threats of war. What are the causes of this state of affairs? What are the reasons for the enormous gap between the theory and practice, the promise and performance of collective security? The most popular and reassuring answer has been that the radical doctrines of National Socialism and Communism have undermined the ideal system, and that modern technology has shattered the earlier limitations on conflict. Yet an equally dynamic creed challenged peace and order in the nineteenth century and provided a fighting faith for imperialist France.

The serious observer must look more deeply at the substance of political reality. In so doing he will find that collective security yesterday and today has been viewed unrealistically, and that its executors have been asked to perform tasks which could be performed with complete success only if certain objective conditions were realized. The most vital questions regarding collective security have seldom been asked; the real problems have often been evaded. The fundamental issues and problems which should have been boldly and realistically confronted have been concealed and obscured in constitutional verbiage and formal legalistic arguments. The . . . basic problems responsible for the tragic predicament of collective security include the problem of its basic preconditions [and] the political problem. . . . The first is from one standpoint most basic, for the preconditions of collective security, being frequently misunderstood, have presented the most stubborn obstacle to the maintenance of international peace.

Preconditions of Collective Security. Manifestly, collective enforcement is unattainable in the absence of appropriate international machinery and binding obligations clearly set forth in recognized legal instruments. Yet every informed citizen knows from experience that a legal arrangement imposed upon political and social conditions incompatible with its fulfillment makes successful political action difficult. Therefore it is essential in considering the reality of collective security that we understand fully its assumptions and requirements.

First, collective enforcement assumes a status quo, or situation of peace, on which the nations with predominant strength agree. In practical terms, the peace which a collective system must defend is the territorial status quo existing at the time the system is brought into being. There is nothing in past experience to indicate that all nations, or even a combination sufficiently powerful to defy the rest, will agree on the meaning of a particular status quo. Following every war, the defeated powers who feel they have suffered most by the terms of peace come to oppose the established status quo. In the aftermath of World War II, however, the question of satisfaction or dissatisfaction with the status quo has largely been superseded by an earlier and prior question. Up to the present time, no practical arrangement has been worked out acceptable to the major powers, who in this case are primarily the Soviet Union and the United States, on which the postwar status quo could be founded. The unresolved conflict between East and West has prevented the establishment of peace, Consequently, the latest experiment in collective security presents us with the anomalous picture of a system created to defend a status quo which has not yet been brought into being.

Moreover, the absence of accepted conditions of peace has been interpreted by some as a positive virtue. The wartime Secretary of State Cordell Hull argued that the League had been destroyed on the floor of the American Senate because of its intimate relationship with the Peace Treaty of Versailles. Better to establish a general international organization, he urged, and then, with passions less inflamed, work out a just and reasonable peace. James F. Byrnes, one of Mr. Hull's successors as Secretary of State in the postwar period, said that he was convinced, based upon his studies as a congressman of the proceedings of the Paris Peace Conference, that a "new approach" was essential. The negotiators at Paris had tried to settle too many difficult problems when the spirit of conflict and revenge still dominated their counsels. Mr. Byrnes prescribed a schedule of discussions in which the less controversial treaties, such as the Italian and Balkan settlements, would be negotiated first. Then the negotiators might turn from their initial successes to the more difficult questions of a German and a Japanese settlement. All agreements arrived at in this order would be introduced in the United Nations, where great and minor powers might participate in considering and amending them. In order to prevent the historic division of the nations into opponents and supporters of the postwar status quo, Mr. Byrnes reached the ingenious conclusion that: "We had to devise a system that would facilitate agreement among the major powers and at the same time provide the smaller states with ample opportunities to express their views." The newly created collective organization would intervene directly in the establishment of the postwar status quo.

In retrospect the problem inherent in the "new approach" has become plain for all to see. Its author, Mr. Byrnes, has observed: "It was a good theory. But it was faulty in one assumption." It assumed that the claims of the Soviet Union could be more readily accommodated to the vital interests of the West than has been the case. While this faulty assumption was shared by the majority of those responsible for the conduct of Soviet-American relations, there were at least three prominent leaders who at various times expressed misgivings about the priority accorded the founding of the United Nations. In 1941 President Roosevelt declared that he "would not be in favor of the creation of a new Assembly of the League of Nations, at least until after a period of time had passed . . . ," during which the major powers, and Britain and the United States in particular, had been successful in establishing and maintaining peace.

Secretary of War Henry L. Stimson maintained, in opposition to Mr. Byrnes, that the breakdown of peace after World War I was due primarily to the lack of political foundations from which the League of Nations had suffered. He held that " . . . the mistake was made of not securing that guarantee [of French security] before the second step of creating the League of Nations. . . . " was taken. In the preparatory discussions on the United Nations Mr. Stimson accordingly warned: "we should not put the cart before the horse." He urged that attention not be diverted from the paramount need for a settlement among the major powers by too much premature concern over blueprints for world organization. For the international organization would gain power and authority only if outstanding political problems had been adjusted. He advised: "We should by thorough discussion between the three or four great powers endeavor to settle . . . fundamental problems." If a general settlement based on mutual guarantees could be worked out, the new instruments of international organization would stand on more viable foundations.

A third distinguished American statesman supported the views of Secretary Stimson. In the Senate debate in 1944 on postwar plans, Senator Arthur H. Vandenberg insisted that the United States must not subscribe to collective security " . . . until we know more about what the new status quo will be. It is my argument that we should go ahead and perfect a plan for collective security; but that we should make it wholly contingent . . . the new 'league' must be *contingent* upon the *character* of the *peace*."

Second, collective security demands that nations subscribing to the status quo be willing and able at all times to muster overwhelming strength for collective defense at successive points of conflict. In theory, the supporters of the status quo might be capable in particular emergencies of mobilizing effective and decisive power against the single aggressor who sought to defy them. Or, by pooling the resources of all the nations in a permanently organized international force, collective enforcement could be made automatic, instantaneous, and preponderant. The former condition, however, is practically impossible of fulfillment, inasmuch as the threat to the status quo comes historically from more than one dissatisfied power or aggressor. The second condition would call for the unprecedented practice of international contingents operating under an international agency empowered to decide conclusively when and how they should be used.

The United Nations Charter seems to take a long step toward this objective by providing that all members are "to make available to the Security Council, on its call and in accordance with a special agreement or agreements, armed forces, assistance and facilities. . . ." (Article 43, Paragraph 1.) Through this provision, the incurable weakness of decentralized enforcement by which past international systems have been rendered impotent is ostensibly rectified. For the Achilles' heel of the earlier experiments was the decentralized character of the enforcement process; separate nations retained the right to determine whether or not military forces would be made available to meet particular crises. In 1942, Cordell Hull had urged that "some international agency must be created which can—by force, if necessary—keep the peace. . . ." Yet Mr. Hull's proposition and Articles 43ff of the Charter, by which this historic difficulty apparently had been surmounted, in practice have remained a dead letter. No special agreements have been concluded by Members with the Security Council; talks in the Military Staff Committee soon reached an impasse. The Soviet Union has opposed proportionate contributions to an international air and naval force, which would leave it particularly vulnerable to forces overwhelmingly more powerful than its own. The United

States has been concerned to make the United Nations Armed Force as strong as possible against the military preponderance of the Soviet Army in Europe and Asia, while the Russians have sought to keep it as weak as possible. It should be noted that the Russians have no monopoly on opposition to a powerful world police force. Senator Vandenberg declares in his Memoirs: "I am opposed to what is generally understood by the term 'international police force.' So, I believe, are the President, Secretary Hull and most realistic students of this problem. To be adequate, an international police force would have to be larger than the regular army and navy of any other power on earth. I think it is fantastic to believe that the people would long consent to the maintenance of any such enormous concentration of power in the postwar peace; and I also think that the temptation to reach for its ultimate control could become the greatest possible threat to peace in years to come." [Vandenberg, *Private Papers,* pp. 120-21.] The stalemate in the Military Staff Committee is fundamentally a symptom of the struggle between the two great powers and between supporters and opponents of the undefined status quo. In practice, the realization of the second condition of overwhelming strength for collective enforcement has constantly run afoul of special national demands for military security and supremacy.

There is a *third* and final prerequisite of collective security, however, to which we now turn, that was widely assumed to be in existence at the time preparations for the United Nations were first being made. It is essential to collective security in a world of unequal powers that at least the major powers enjoy a minimum of political solidarity and moral community. On October 13, 1944, Premier Stalin asked himself, in an article appearing in the Soviet *Information Bulletin,* if the world organization could be effective. He predicted that it would "be effective if the Great Powers, which have borne the brunt of the war against Hitler-Germany continue to act in a spirit of unanimity and accord."

The effectiveness of the United Nations and of the Security Council in particular was predicated upon the unanimity of the five great powers. It was an article of political faith in the Roosevelt Administration that trustworthiness and good will on the part of Americans would inspire the same qualities among the Russians. In a particularly revealing memorandum for President Harry S. Truman dated September 11, 1945, Mr. Stimson explained: "The chief lesson I have learned in a long life is that the only way you can make a man trustworthy is to trust him; and the surest way to make him untrustworthy is to distrust him and show your distrust." Unanimity among the great powers which alien ideologies and conflicting interests might otherwise undermine would be secured through the application of a code of social ethics that had in general been effective within the United States.

By October of 1947, Mr. Stimson, writing in *Foreign Affairs,* had cause to reformulate his proposition and to say: "I have often said that the surest way to make a man trustworthy is to trust him. But I must add that this does not always apply to a man who is determined to make you his dupe. Before we can make friends with the Russians, their leaders will have to be convinced that they have nothing to gain, and everything to lose, by acting on the assumption that our society is dying and that our principles are outworn." Thus the preconditions of collective security under the United Nations have either been wanting from the beginning, or have been corroded and destroyed by the all-consuming forces of the "cold war."

The Political Problem. The chief practical obstacle to collective security is the political problem deriving from the conflict of independent foreign policies. The loyalties and interests of nations participating in international organizations and collective security systems are of a different order from those of individuals taking part in the more intimate communities of the family and nation. Some years ago Monsieur Paul Henri Spaak in an address before the Foreign Press Union declared: "There must be a hierarchy in international obligations. The nations of the continent cannot be asked to consider with the same realism and sincerity of judgment affairs which directly concern them and events which are taking place thousands of kilometres away in regions where they have neither interests nor influence. Indivisible peace, mutual assistance, and even collective security are general ideas whose practical effect must be clearly explained and clearly limited." [Quoted in *Survey of International Affairs, 1936* (London, 1937), pp. 354-55.] Both individuals and nations pursue their own interests, but in some areas and on certain occasions the individual may forsake his egotistic motives for loyalty to some higher institution or nobler cause. There are institutions in integrated societies which provide common standards under which the individual can realize his aspirations. There need be no inherent conflict between an individual's private interests and his national loyalties, for the latter can often promote the realization of the former. On the other hand, conflicts are often inevitable between national and supranational loyalties, and when the projected policy of an international organization conflicts with that of a particular nation, at all times and in all places the national interest prevails.

In the debate between the so-called realists and idealists, the latter have often assumed that the conflict between national and supranational policies and purposes need not take the form the realists give it. Idealists have maintained that if two sets of objectives should be in conflict, the clash could always be resolved by taking "the long view." It should not be surprising that statesmen have been more disposed to approach the foreign policies of *other* nations with this as their "rule of thumb." For example, on January 10, 1945, in his momentous speech to the American Senate, Arthur H. Vandenberg assessed the objectives of the Soviet Union. He announced that the Soviet leaders appeared to contemplate the engulfment, directly or indirectly, of a surrounding circle of states on the Russian borders. Their defense of this sphere of influence policy was on grounds of security against German aggression. While finding this a perfectly understandable claim, Senator Vandenberg observed: "The alternative is collective security. . . . Which is better in the long view, from a purely selfish Russian standpoint: To forcefully surround herself with a cordon of unwillingly controlled or partitioned states, thus affronting the opinion of mankind . . . or to win the priceless asset of world-confidence in her by embracing the alternative, namely, full and whole hearted cooperation with and reliance upon a vital international organization."

Yet Senator Vandenberg and other American statesmen, while raising this standard for others, have by their actions and not infrequently their words appealed to another less lofty if more attainable political goal. Not all of our leaders have been as transparently candid as Senator Vandenberg in expressing the hope "that American spokesmanship at the peace table is at least as loyal to America's own primary interests as Mr. Stalin is certain to be in respect to Russian and Mr. Churchill . . . to the British Empire." Yet in his warning, the Senator appeared to employ a new "rule of thumb" based on the precept "that no one is going to look out for us . . . unless we look out for ourselves. . . ."

It is true that the ambivalence we have found in Senator Vandenberg's use of guides to action in foreign policy is sometimes accounted for by the role he played in American life. As a onetime arch-isolationist, he could be expected to cling to certain narrow standards and selfish nationalist principles. Yet Theodore and Franklin D. Roosevelt, who can hardly be placed under the same stricture, sensed instinctively the importance of American vital interests in the conduct of foreign policy. Theodore Roosevelt intervened to sustain a balance of power in Europe and Asia by offering American good offices at the Portsmouth Conference and by seeking to moderate the crisis over Morocco at the Conference of Algeciras in 1906. When asked at the time of the Russo-Japanese War of 1904-5 why he opposed England, though admiring its democracy, and why he favored Russia, though despising its despotism and mendacity, he replied: "Do you not understand that I am looking after America's interest, that and nothing more. . . . If anyone else views action taken in American interest from the standpoint of a foreign power, I shall be sorry, but it certainly will not alter my own conduct."

The nature of the first Roosevelt's concept of foreign policy may be less surprising than the private admission by Franklin D. Roosevelt that he approached foreign policy on essentially the same basis. In early 1941, when seeking a formula by which aid to Britain could be extended, Franklin Roosevelt received a letter from a well-known advertising man reporting that charges being made by the Nyes and Lindberghs that we were acting in foreign policy to save the British and not ourselves were taking a serious toll. The business man urged Mr. Roosevelt to tell the truth, namely, that we were not concerned primarily with the British Empire as such but with our own safety, the security of our trade, the future of our crops, the integrity of our continent, and the lives of our children in the next generation. The President replied: "That I think, is a pretty good line to take because it happens to be true and it is on that line itself that we must, for all the above purely selfish reasons, prevent at almost any hazard the Axis domination of the world." The American strategy of fighting World War II first on the Atlantic sea lanes and in Europe reflected the priority Mr. Roosevelt gave to our interests in Europe.

In short, it is untrue to imply that American statesmen have been free from concern for immediate strategic interests and have consistently taken "the long view." There is almost no evidence that in pursuing our national destiny we have been immune from the same basic considerations by which other members of the society of nations have been guided. One of the most significant documents in the annals of recent American foreign policy was the blueprint of strategic interests in World War II called the "Joint Board Estimate of United States Over-all Production Requirements." Dated September 11, 1941, it was signed by the Chiefs of Staff, General Marshall and Admiral Stark. Paragraph 5 provided: "Those major national objectives of the United States which are related to military policy may broadly be stated as: preservation of the territorial, economic and ideological integrity of the United States and of the remainder of the Western Hemisphere; prevention of the disruption of the British Empire; prevention of the further extension of Japanese territorial dominion; eventual establishment in Europe and Asia of balances of power which will most nearly ensure political stability in those regions and the future security of the United States; and, so far as practicable, the establishment of regimes favorable to economic freedom and individual liberty." This unequivocal statement of our basic objectives and interests puts to rest the illusion that World War II was conceived and conducted by American leaders who took no stock in the need for discriminating judgments respecting vital interests. [Quoted in Sherwood, *Roosevelt and Hopkins,* Vol. 1, p. 496.] When this principle has been disregarded, as in certain military decisions in 1945, American security has been gravely imperilled.

However, the pursuit of separate national interests by the various independent states presents the most troublesome issue we face in appraising collective security. The problem which impaired collective security under the League, and which was perhaps more decisive than the defection of the United States in causing its downfall, was the unresolved conflict in the foreign policies of the principal powers. The conceptions of the national interests of France and England clashed with one another and with the principles of the League. France had one overarching objective: the absolute security of its territory. In French eyes, the one conspicuous threat it faced was Germany, which bordered France and perpetually endangered its northeastern frontier. In 1935-36, the second attack on the integrity of the League was launched with Mussolini's cruel "Rape of Ethiopia," which Il Duce preferred to describe euphemistically as a "civilizing mission." The dilemma with which France was confronted provides us with the classic instance of the political problem.

For France the sole threat against which sanctions had been prepared was Germany. Italy's aggressive action represented the wrong threat, at the wrong time, at the wrong border. Italy was the natural ally of France for, aligned with the much publicized Italian army, France hoped to balance the preponderance of the land forces of Germany, especially after Germany had moved into the Rhineland. The character of French foreign policy made it highly improbable that France could support sanctions up to the point where French loyalty to the Covenant would cost France its recent *entente* with Italy against Germany. British opinion appeared to accept this fact and Mr. Churchill observed that "the Foreign Secretary [Mr. Eden] was *justified in going as far with the League of Nations against Italy as he could carry France;* but I added that he ought not to put any pressure upon France because of her military convention with Italy and her German preoccupations;

and that in the circumstances I did not expect France would go very far." In simplest terms, the choice for France was between the long range precedent which effective action might provide against the likelihood of German expansion and the immediately tangible results of not losing an ally against Germany. France compromised and sanctions were applied only half-heartedly.

The political problem also presents itself in regard to actual enforcement. Who is to apply sanctions? Who is to carry the burden of overt military action? In 1935-36, Britain alone was in a position to cut Mussolini's lines of communication and isolate his army. If genuine sanctions and force had been applied, the British navy would have shouldered the main burden. Yet there were murmurings by admirals and statesmen that the navy was ill-prepared, that there was ammunition for only about thirty minutes of fighting. British foreign policy, in contrast to that of France, directed that a stand should be taken. But the military component for action was lacking. In any enforcement action, since states are unequal, someone must bear more than his share. For this the British were unready in 1935-36.

The political problem has returned to plague Western society in the actions of the United Nations. The foreign policies of some nations have clashed periodically with the resolutions of that body. France and England are probably second and third-rate powers. England in particular has sensed this and has sought to husband her resources. Her first duty has been to her interests in Europe. She has maintained that a threat to her survival could come only from Europe. Any new action that would drain off a single drop of strength for efforts not in the national interest has been viewed with alarm. Moreover, England's policy has been one of watchful waiting in China. Under present conditions, the hope has been fostered that wise diplomacy could drive a wedge between the USSR and China, so that they would cease to march as members of a well-drilled team. The later phases of the UN's Korean policy have conflicted at every point with British Far Eastern policy. Is it surprising, therefore, that she has been a reluctant partner? The foreign policies of the member states, including those of the West, have diverged within the United Nations precisely as they did in 1935-36. Only the overwhelming power and material and political influence of the United States, made possible by the decline and exhaustion of postwar European and Asian powers, have prevented a repetition of the earlier experience. Unless nations have a margin of power beyond that essential to their survival, they can hardly be expected to share in the defense of a principle.

TOPIC 9

Why Do Men Fight?

The preceding readings were mainly concerned with the behavior and actions of territorial states and nations.

When we refer to the ways in which nations and states live, work, think, fight, or die, we actually speak of individual men who collectively compose the nation-states.

Exploration of forces which shape the attitudes and actions of individual men may help us analyze and perhaps predict the behavior of human collectives. Does human nature make war or peace ultimately inevitable? Can environment change human nature? Can men be diverted from violence quickly enough—in view of the dangers of our era?

Many psychologists, psychiatrists, psychoanalysts, and anthropologists have attempted to answer these questions. A few samples of their conflicting opinions are reproduced on the following pages.

►NATIONS SHOULD BE DEPRIVED OF THEIR SOVEREIGNTY

ALBERT EINSTEIN

One of the greatest scientists of our epoch suggested in a letter to Sigmund Freud that an authority should be created to deprive nations of their sovereignty and bring them to reason. Albert Einstein's suggestion was accompanied by disturbing questions addressed to the great psychoanalyst: Why does not reason have more power? How can instincts be overcome? How can we eliminate the need to hate, which degenerates into collective psychosis? Einstein's lines were written from Potsdam on the eve of the Nazi seizure of power in Germany. Later, during World War II, pacifist Einstein suggested to President Roosevelt that in view of the Nazi advances in atomic research the United States should concentrate on production of atomic weapons.

DEAR PROFESSOR FREUD:

The proposal of the League of Nations and its International Institute of Intellectual Co-operation at Paris that I should invite a person, to be chosen by myself, to a frank exchange of views on any problem that I might select affords me a very welcome opportunity of conferring with you upon a ques-

Both Einstein's letter and Freud's reply are reprinted with the permission of the International Institute for Intellectual Cooperation, UNESCO.

tion which, as things now are, seems the most insistent of all the problems civilization has to face. This is the problem: Is there any way of delivering mankind from the menace of war? It is common knowledge that, with the advance of modern science, this issue has come to mean a matter of life and death for civilization as we know it; nevertheless, for all the zeal displayed, every attempt at its solution has ended in lamentable breakdown. . . .

As one immune from nationalist bias, I personally see a simple way of dealing with the superficial (*i.e.* administrative) aspect of the problem: the setting up, by international consent, of a legislative and judicial body to settle every conflict arising between nations. . . . But here, at the outset, I come up against a difficulty; a tribunal is a human institution which, in proportion as the power at its disposal is inadequate to enforce its verdicts, is all the more prone to suffer these to be deflected by extrajudicial pressure. This is a fact with which we have to reckon; law and might inevitably go hand in hand. . . . At present we are far from possessing any supranational organization competent to render verdicts of uncontestable authority and enforce absolute submission to the execution of its verdicts. Thus I am led to my first axiom: the quest of international security involves the unconditional surrender by every nation, in a certain measure, of its liberty of action, its sovereignty that is to say, and it is clear beyond all doubt that no other road can lead to such security.

The ill-success, despite their obvious sincerity, of all the efforts made during the last decade to reach this goal leaves us no room to doubt that strong psychological factors are at work, which paralyze these efforts. . . . The craving for power which characterizes the governing class in every nation is hostile to any limitation of the national sovereignty. This political power-hunger is wont to batten on the activities of another group, whose aspirations are on purely mercenary, economic lines. I have specially in mind that small but determined group, active in every nation, composed of individuals who, indifferent to social considerations and restraints, regard warfare, the manufacture and sale of arms, simply as an occasion to advance their personal interests and enlarge their personal authority.

But recognition of this obvious fact is merely the first step toward an appreciation of the actual state of affairs. Another question follows hard upon it: How is it possible for this small clique to bend the will of the majority, who stand to lose and suffer by a state of war, to the service of their ambitions? . . .

An obvious answer to this question would seem to be that the minority, the ruling class at present, has the schools and press, usually the Church as well, under its thumb. This enables it to organize and sway the emotions of the masses, and make its tool of them.

Yet even this answer does not provide a complete solution. Another question arises from it: How is it these devices succeed so well in rousing men to such wild enthusiasm, even to sacrifice their lives? Only one answer is possible. Because man has within him a lust for hatred and destruction. In normal times this passion exists in a latent state, it emerges only in unusual circumstances; but it is a comparatively easy task to call it into play and raise it to the power of a collective psychosis. Here lies, perhaps, the crux of all the complex factors we are considering, an enigma that only the expert in the lore of human instincts can resolve.

And so we come to our last question. Is it possible to control man's mental evolution so as to make him proof against the psychoses of hate and destructiveness? Here I am thinking by no means only of the so-called un-cultured masses. Experience proves that it is rather the so-called 'intelligentzia' that is most apt to yield to these disastrous collective suggestions, since the intellectual has no direct contact with life in the raw, but encounters it in its easiest, synthetic form—upon the printed page.

To conclude: I have so far been speaking only of wars between nations; what are known as international conflicts. But I am well aware that the ag-gressive instinct operates under other forms and in other circumstances. (I am thinking of civil wars, for instance, due in earlier days to religious zeal, but nowadays to social factors; or, again the persecution of racial minorities.) But my insistence on what is the most typical, most cruel and extravagant form of conflict between man and man was deliberate, for here we have the best occasion of discovering ways and means to render all armed conflicts impossible.

I know that in your writings we may find answer, explicit or implied, to all the issues of this urgent and absorbing problem. But it would be of the greatest service to us all were you to present the problem of world peace in the light of your most recent discoveries, for such a presentation might well blaze the trail for new and fruitful modes of action.

Yours very sincerely,
A. EINSTEIN

Caputh, Near Potsdam,
July 30, 1932

►MIGHT IS NOT THE OPPOSITE OF RIGHT

SIGMUND FREUD

In his answer from native Vienna, Sigmund Freud stressed man's vital erotic (i.e., constructive) force as well as his death instinct. Humanity's aggressive tendencies cannot be suppressed but perhaps they may be channeled into forms other than war. Violence of one nation can be curbed only by the union of its prospective victims, "the alliance of many weaklings." In this sense, right requires might to be successful.

DEAR PROFESSOR EINSTEIN:

The question which you put me—what is to be done to rid mankind of the war menace?—took me by surprise. And, next, I was dumbfounded by the thought of my (of *our,* I almost wrote) incompetence; for this struck me as being a matter of practical politics, the statesman's proper study. But then

I realized that you did not raise the question in your capacity of scientist or physicist, but as a lover of his fellow men. . . . And I reminded myself that I was not being called on to formulate practical proposals, but, rather, to explain how this question of preventing wars strikes a psychologist. . . .

You begin with the relations between Might and Right, and this is assuredly the proper starting point for our enquiry. But, for the term "might," I would substitute a tougher and more telling word: "violence." In right and violence we have today an obvious antinomy. . . . Conflicts of interest between man and man are resolved, in principle, by the recourse to violence. It is the same in the animal kingdom. . . . To start with, brute force was the factor which, in small communities, decided points of ownership and the question which man's will was to prevail. Very soon physical force was implemented, then replaced, by the use of various adjuncts; he proved the victor whose weapon was the better, or handled the more skilfully. Now, for the first time, with the coming of weapons, superior brains began to oust brute force, but the object of the conflict remained the same; one party was to be constrained, by the injury done him or impairment of his strength, to retract a claim or a refusal. This end is most effectively gained when the opponent is definitively put out of action—in other words, is killed. This procedure has two advantages: the enemy cannot renew hostilities, and, secondly, his fate deters others from following his example. Moreover, the slaughter of a foe gratifies an instinctive craving—a point to which we shall revert hereafter. However, another consideration may be set off against this will to kill: the possibility of using an enemy for servile tasks if his spirit be broken and his life spared. Here violence finds an outlet not in slaughter but in subjugation. Hence springs the practice of giving quarter; but the victor, having from now on to reckon with the craving for revenge that rankles in his victim, forfeits to some extent his personal security.

Thus, under primitive conditions, it is superior force—brute violence, or violence backed by arms—that lords it everywhere. We know that in the course of evolution this state of things was modified, a path was traced that led away from violence to law. But what was this path? Surely it issued from a single verity; that the superiority of one strong man can be overborne by an alliance of many weaklings, that *l'union fait la force*. Brute force is overcome by union, the allied might of scattered units makes good its right against the isolated giant. Thus we may define "right" (*i.e.* law) as the might of a community. Yet it, too, is nothing else than violence, quick to attack whatever individual stands in its path, and it employs the selfsame methods, follows like ends, but with one difference: it is the communal, not individual, violence that has its way. But, for the transition from crude violence to the reign of law, a certain psychological condition must first obtain. The union of the majority must be stable and enduring. If its sole *raison d'etre* be the discomfiture of some overweening individual and, after his downfall, it be dissolved, it leads to nothing. Some other man, trusting to his superior power, will seek to reinstate the rule of violence and the cycle will repeat itself unendingly. Thus the union of the people must be permanent and well organized; it must enact rules to meet the risk of possible revolts; must set up machinery ensuring that its rules—the laws—are observed and that such acts of violence as the laws demand are duly carried out. This recognition of a community of interests engenders among the members of the group a sentiment of unity and fraternal solidarity which constitutes its real strength.

So far I have set out what seems to me the kernel of the matter: the suppression of brute force by the transfer of power to a larger combination, founded on the community of sentiments linking up its members. . . . But such a combination is only theoretically possible; in practice the situation is always complicated by the fact that, from the outset, the group includes elements of unequal power. . . . The most casual glance at world history will show an unending series of conflicts between one community and another or a group of others, between large and smaller units, between cities, countries, races, tribes and kingdoms, almost all of which were settled by the ordeal of war. Such wars end either in pillage or in conquest and its fruits, the downfall of the loser. No single all-embracing judgment can be passed on these wars of aggrandizement. Some, like the war between the Mongols and the Turks, have led to unmitigated misery; others, however, have furthered the transition from violence to law, since they brought larger units into being, within whose limits a recourse to violence was banned and a new regime determined all disputes. Thus the Roman conquests brought that boon, the *pax romana,* to the Mediterranean lands. The French kings' lust for aggrandizement created a new France, flourishing in peace and unity. Paradoxical as it sounds, we must admit that warfare well might serve to pave the way to that unbroken peace we so desire, for it is war that brings vast empires into being, within whose frontiers all warfare is proscribed by a strong central power. In practice, however, this end is not attained, for as a rule, the fruits of victory are but short-lived, the new-created unit falls asunder once again, generally because there can be no true cohesion between the parts that violence has welded. Hitherto, moreover, such conquests have only led to aggregations which, for all their magnitude, had limits, and disputes between these units could be resolved only by recourse to arms. For humanity at large the sole result of all these military enterprises was that, instead of frequent not to say incessant little wars, they had now to face great wars which, for all they came less often, were so much the more destructive.

Regarding the world of today the same conclusion holds good, and you, too, have reached it, though by a shorter path. There is but one sure way of ending war and that is the establishment, by common consent, of a central control which shall have the last word in every conflict of interest. . . . [But] obviously such notions as these can only be significant when they are the expression of a deeply rooted sense of unity, shared by all. It is necessary, therefore, to gauge the efficacy of such sentiments. History tells us that, on occasion, they have been effective. For example, the Panhellenic conception, the Greeks' awareness of superiority over their barbarian neighbors, which found expression in the Amphictyonies, the Oracles and Games, was strong enough to humanize the methods of warfare as between Greeks, though inevitably it failed to prevent conflicts between different elements of the Hellenic race or even to deter a city or group of cities from joining forces with their racial foe, the Persians, for the discomfiture of a rival. The solidarity of Christendom in the Renaissance age was no more effective, despite its vast authority, in hindering Christian nations, large and small alike, from calling in the Sultan to their aid. And, in our times, we look in vain for some such unifying notion whose authority would be unquestioned. It is all too clear that the nationalistic ideas, paramount today in every country, operate in quite a contrary direction. Some there are who hold that the Bolshevist conceptions may make an end of war, but, as things are, that goal lies very far away and, perhaps, could only be attained after a spell of brutal internecine warfare. Thus it would seem that any effort to replace brute force by the might of an ideal is, under present conditions, doomed to fail. Our logic is at fault if we ignore the fact that right is founded on brute force and even today needs violence to maintain it.

I now can comment on another of your statements. You are amazed that it is so easy to infect men with the war-fever, and you surmise that man has in him an active instinct for hatred and destruction, amenable to such stimulations. I entirely agree with you. I believe in the existence of this instinct and have been recently at pains to study its manifestations. In this connection may I set out a fragment of that knowledge of the instincts, which we psychoanalysts, after so many tentative essays and gropings in the dark have compassed? We assume that human instincts are of two kinds: those that conserve and unify, which we call "erotic" (in the meaning Plato gives to *Eros* in his *Symposium*), or else "sexual" (explicitly extending the popular connotation of "sex"); and, secondly, the instincts to destroy and kill, which we assimilate as the aggressive or destructive instincts. . . . Each of these instincts is every whit as indispensable as its opposite and all the phenomena of life derive from their activity, whether they work in concert or in opposition. . . . Thus the instinct of self-preservation is certainly of an erotic nature, but to gain its ends this very instinct necessitates aggressive action. In the same way the love-instinct, when directed to a specific object, calls for an admixture of the acquisitive instinct if it is to enter into effective possession of that object. . . .

If you will travel with me a little further on this road, you will find that human affairs are complicated in yet another way. Only exceptionally does an action follow on the stimulus of a single instinct, which is *per se* a blend of Eros and destructiveness. As a rule several motives of similar composition concur to bring about the act. . . . Thus, when a nation is summoned to engage in war, a whole gamut of human motives may respond to this appeal; high and low motives, some openly avowed, others slurred over. . . . Musing on the atrocities recorded on history's page, we feel that the ideal motive has often served as a camouflage for the lust of destruction; sometimes, as with the cruelties of the Inquisition, it seems that, while the ideal motives occupied the foreground of consciousness, they drew their strength from the destructive instincts submerged in the unconscious. . . .

You are interested, I know, in the prevention of war, not in our theories, and I keep this fact in mind. Yet I would like to dwell a little longer on this destructive instinct which is seldom given the attention that its importance warrants. . . . The living being . . . defends its own existence by destroying foreign bodies. But, in one of its activities, the death instinct is operative *within* the living being and we have sought to trace back a number of normal and pathological phenomena to this *introversion* of the destructive instinct. . . . Obviously when this internal tendency operates on too large a scale, it is no trivial matter, rather a positively morbid state of things; whereas the diversion of the destructive impulse toward the external world must have beneficial effects. Here is then the biological justification for all those vile, pernicious propensities which we now are combating. We can but own that they are really more akin to nature than this our stand against them, which, in fact, remains to be accounted for.

All this may give you the impression that our theories amount to a species of mythology and a gloomy one at that! But does not every natural science lead ultimately to this—a sort of mythology? Is it otherwise today with your physical science?

The upshot of these observations . . . is that there is no likelihood of our being able to suppress humanity's aggressive tendencies. In some happy corners of the earth, they say, where nature brings forth abundantly whatever man desires, there flourish races whose lives go gently by, unknowing of aggression or constraint. This I can hardly credit; I would like further details about these happy folk. The Bolshevists, too, aspire to do away with human aggressiveness by ensuring the satisfaction of material needs and enforcing equality between man and man. To me this hope seems vain. Meanwhile they busily perfect their armaments, and their hatred of outsiders is not the least of the factors of cohesion amongst themselves. In any case, as you, too, have observed, complete suppression of man's aggressive tendencies is not in issue; what we may try is to divert it into a channel other than that of warfare.

From our "mythology" of the instincts we may easily deduce a formula for an indirect method of eliminating war. If the propensity for war be due to the destructive instinct, we have always its counter-agent, Eros, to our hand. All that produces ties of sentiment between man and man must serve us as war's antidote. . . .

In your strictures on the abuse of authority I find another suggestion for an indirect attack on the war-impulse. That men are divided into leaders and the led is but another manifestation of their inborn and irremediable inequality. The second class constitutes the vast majority; they need a high command to make decisions for them, to which decisions they usually bow without demur. In this context we would point out that men should be at greater pains than heretofore to form a superior class of independent thinkers, unamenable to intimidation and fervent in the quest of truth, whose function it would be to guide the masses dependent on their lead. There is no need to point out how little the rule of politicians and the Church's ban on liberty of thought encourage such a new creation. The ideal conditions would obviously be found in a community where every man subordinated his instinctive life to the dictates of reason. Nothing less than this could bring about so thorough and so durable a union between men, even if this involved the severance of mutual ties of sentiment. But surely such a hope is utterly utopian, as things are. The other indirect methods of preventing war are certainly more feasible, but entail no quick results. They conjure up an ugly picture of mills that grind so slowly that, before the flour is ready, men are dead of hunger.

As you see, little good comes of consulting a theoretician, aloof from worldly contacts, on practical problems! Better it were to tackle each successive crisis with means that we have ready to our hands. However, I would like to deal with a question which, though it is not mooted in your letter, interests me greatly. Why do we, you and I and many another, protest so vehemently against war, instead of just accepting it as another of life's odious importunities? . . . I trust you will not be shocked by my raising such a question. For the better conduct of an inquiry it may be well to don a mask of feigned aloofness. The answer to my query may run as follows: Because every man has a right over his own life and war destroys lives that were full of promise; it forces the individual into situations that shame his manhood, obliging him to murder fellow men, against his will; it ravages material amenities, the fruits of human toil, and much besides. Moreover wars, as now conducted, afford no scope for acts of heroism according to the old ideals and, given the high perfection of modern arms, war today would mean the sheer extermination of one of the combatants, if not of both. This is so true, so obvious, that we can but wonder why the conduct of war is not banned by general consent. Doubtless either of the points I have just made is open to debate. It may be asked if the community, in its turn, cannot claim a right over the individual lives of its members. Moreover, all forms of war cannot be indiscriminately condemned; so long as there are nations and empires, each prepared callously to exterminate its rival, all alike must be equipped for war. But we will not dwell on any of these problems. . . . I pass on to another point, the basis, as it strikes me, of our common hatred of war. . . . We cannot do otherwise than hate it. Pacifists we are, since our organic nature wills us thus to be. Hence it comes easy to us to find arguments that justify our standpoint.

This point, however, calls for elucidation. Here is the way in which I see it. The cultural development of mankind (some, I know, prefer to call it civilization) has been in progress since immemorial antiquity. To this process we owe all that is best in our composition, but also much that makes for human suffering. Its origins and causes are obscure, its issue is uncertain, but some of its characteristics are easy to perceive. It well may lead to the extinction of mankind, for it impairs the sexual function in more than one respect, and even today the uncivilized races and the backward classes of all nations are multiplying more rapidly than the cultured elements. This process may, perhaps, be likened to the effects of domestication on certain animals—it clearly involves physical changes of structure—but the view that cultural development is an organic process of this order has not yet become generally familiar. The psychic changes which accompany this process of cultural change are striking. . . . They consist in the progressive rejection of instinctive ends and a scaling down of instinctive reactions. . . . On the psychological side two of the most important phenomena of culture are, firstly, a strengthening of the intellect, which tends to master our instinctive life, and, secondly, an introversion of the aggressive impulse, with all its consequent benefits and perils. Now war runs most emphatically counter to the psychic disposition imposed on us by the growth of culture; we are therefore bound to resent war, to find it utterly intolerable. With pacifists like us it is not merely an intellectual and affective repulsion, but a constitutional intolerance, an idiosyncrasy in its most drastic form. . . .

How long have we to wait before the rest of men turn pacifist? Impossible to say, and yet perhaps our hope that these two factors—man's cultural disposition and a well-founded dread of the form that future wars will take—may serve to put an end to war in the near future, is not chimerical. But by what ways or by-ways this will come about, we cannot guess. . . .

With kindest regards and, should this *exposé* prove a disappointment to you, my sincere regrets,

Yours,
SIGMUND FREUD

Vienna, September, 1932

►ANTHROPOLOGY AND INTERNATIONAL POLITICS

GABRIEL ALMOND

The following selection is a critique of two books which have been labelled "general statements of the contemporary anthropological credo." They are: Mirror for Man, *by Clyde Kluckhohn, and* Human Relations in a Changing World, *by Alexander H. Leighton. The anthropologists stress that if we are to avoid grave policy errors, it is important to be familiar with comparative culture. The reviewer raises the question, which has shaken many otherwise correct analyses and theories: How does one translate theoretical findings into political practice? Gabriel Almond is Professor of Political Science at Princeton University and a member of its Center of International Studies. He is the author of* American People and Foreign Policy, *and other studies.*

These two books . . . are general statements of the contemporary anthropological credo. They reject the earlier conception of anthropology as the study of prehistoric and primitive culture, and assert strong claims to its relevance in the solution of crucial problems of modern politics. Clyde Kluckhohn is a psychoanalytically trained anthropologist. Alexander Leighton is an anthropologically trained psychiatrist. Both have had distinguished academic and governmental careers. Leighton was chief and Kluckhohn co-chief of the Foreign Morale Analysis Division of the Office of War Information, an organization which pioneered in the application of psycho-anthropological insights and methods to problems of government policy.

The selection is part of an article, "Anthropology, Political Behavior, and International Relations," *World Politics,* Vol. II, No. 2 (January, 1950), pp. 277-284.

Leighton's general views are based on a detailed analysis of his experiences during the war in the Office of War Information and the United States Strategic Bombing Survey in Japan. Kluckhohn's book is a general statement of the nature and significance of modern anthropology directed at an informed lay audience.

Special interest for students of international relations attaches to propositions advanced by these writers about the usefulness of the modern anthropological approach in the study of problems of foreign policy and international order. While there is some difference in the treatment of these themes in the two books, there is such substantial agreement between them that there is no need for our purposes for a separate statement of individual views. We review these propositions in brief form.

1. Cultural-psychological differences are largely unconscious in character. The peculiar sentiments, values, and attitudes of the various cultures, in addition to being deeply embedded in the individual are perpetuated by the pressure of the cultural institutions. As a consequence, efforts to change culture and personality cannot be soundly based on a simple faith in human reason and expectations of quick results.

2. The political behavior manifested within cultures, subcultures, nations, social classes, and similar groups, is not only to be understood as rational effort directed at objective problem-solving, but as affected by these largely unconscious, culture-bound "views of the world," and the emotional tonus of the social environment.

3. The proposition that human nature is instinctively destructive has not been established. Present-day psychology leans more to the theory that situational and cultural factors provoke aggressive impulses which may spill over into the international sphere. Present-day psychology also demonstrates that aggressive impulses can be directed into "constructive" channels. Thus psychology cannot support propositions about any simple relationships between human instincts and organized aggression.

4. The proposition that war is an inherent element of intercultural or international relations is not supported by anthropological research. There are known instances of long-run intercultural stability. For the modern era these writers cite Switzerland, Sweden, and similar nations which have lived for long periods at peace with their neighbors. In other words, there is nothing inherent in human psychology and culture which makes organized violent conflict inevitable.

5. The efficiency of foreign policy in achieving peace, international order, or other national aspirations would be greatly increased through knowledge of one's own and other cultures. The tendency to project one's own cultural assumptions and expectations upon other cultures and nations is a common source of international misunderstanding. Genuine conflicts of interest might often be resolved "were not irrational emotional forces mobilized through culture-bound misinterpretations of motives."[1]

6. Cultural values are so deeply embedded that any adequate solution

[1] Kluckhohn, p. 272.

of the problem of world peace and world organization has to be based on the principle of unity in diversity, "agreement on a set of principles for world morality but respect and toleration for all activities that do not threaten world peace." [2]

The modern student of politics and international relations has for the most part fully accepted these propositions. While he might find them to be substantially less than clear directives for contemporary policy, he will offer wholehearted support to the efforts on the part of anthropologists to reach policy-makers and the public with these basic insights. Furthermore, he can only offer the fullest support to anthropologists in their efforts to apply their hypotheses and methods in the analysis of the social-psychological factors which affect policy-making in modern nations. The anthropologists are fully justified in stressing the overwhelming importance of thoroughgoing knowledge of comparative culture if we are to avoid the gravest policy errors. Certainly no serious scholar in the field of international relations would deny the enormous improvements in the observation, analysis, and understanding of individual and group behavior which have resulted from discoveries made by these newer social science disciplines.

But unfortunately even such modest and sober psycho-cultural practitioners as Kluckhohn and Leighton appear to be affected by the all too human tendency toward overselling. Thus Kluckhohn argues that "Its all-embracing character gives anthropology a strategic position for determining what factors will create a world community of distinct cultures and hold it together against disruption." [3] To be ardent in love is not the same as being successful in love, and to be all-embracing is not the same as having embraced all. In the sense in which Kluckhohn uses his term in the foregoing quotation there is no "all-embracing" anthropology. To say nothing of "all the distinct cultures," the anthropologists have not made a thorough analysis of a single modern culture, and furthermore with their present equipment they are probably incapable of doing so. The social sciences in their modern manifestations— with the exception of history—are all new sciences. The oldest and most complacent among them, economics, has only recently become aware of how much it failed to embrace. The psycho-anthropologists are newest among the new—vastly promising—but like the young they sometimes find it difficult to distinguish between aspiration and achievement.

The infancy of the kind of anthropology to which this discipline aspires becomes apparent at a number of points at which these writers draw inferences from their general hypotheses for the solution of crucial contemporary policy problems. Both writers make occasional references to the problem of East-West relations. Thus Kluckhohn touching for a brief moment on the problem of alleviating the American-Russian conflict argues:

> Even now there is common ground which could well be brought nearer the center of bitter political discussion. For example both the American people and the peoples of the Soviet Union are remarkable among the

[2] *Ibid.*, p. 273.
[3] *Ibid.*, p. 286.

nations of the world for their faith in man's capacity to manipulate his environment and control his fate.[4]

Assuming that this proposition is true, how could it be "brought nearer the center of bitter political discussion?" Discussion between whom, and by what means? This is not to suggest that Kluckhohn's proposition is totally lacking in relevance. But the suggestion is made without reference to the problems of communication and political structure, which in this case are the critical factors.

Leighton, similarly concerned with Russian-American relations, states:

> . . . when suspicious and hostile feelings are in the air, as they are with Russia, there is a trend toward "leaning over backward" in selecting persons who will not in any way favor the other party. This means that more and more individuals are chosen who are least likely to mitigate suspicion and develop understanding and most likely to be prejudiced and uncompromising and to make a bad situation worse. A sort of automatic social syphon is established that draws to the surface, interacting with Russia, a large percentage of those who have a high potential for anti-Russian decisions.[5]

This proposition is based on a simple assertion of fact; even casual memory suffices to raise serious doubts as to its truth. That it should be made by one of the ablest and most highly respected of the anthropologically trained psychiatrists is indicative of the state of anthropology as a policy science. In making applications of their hypotheses to the international relations of modern nations (as distinguished from their highly relevant contributions to policy toward "dependent areas" and non-Western cultures) the anthropologists simply lack professional knowledge of modern politics. They cannot make relevant policy proposals without such knowledge. Unless they acquire it they will have to be content with the formulation of general propositions such as those listed above, and leave to others the urgent task of applying them to policy problems. This would represent a serious loss, since there is urgent need for the introduction of psycho-cultural insights in the analysis of the policy-making process itself, a need which cannot be adequately served by political scientists familiar with comparative government and politics but untrained or half-trained in anthropology and psychology. . . .

▶THEORIES ON THE NATURE OF WAR

KENNETH W. THOMPSON

Three distinct theories about the nature of war among nations have been articulated in Western civilization, namely, the romanticist, idealist, and realist. Professor Kenneth W. Thompson describes them in the following selection.

[4] *Ibid.*, p. 273.
[5] Leighton, p. 196.

This is an excerpt from K. W. Thompson's article "Mr. Toynbee and World Politics: War and National Security," *World Politics*, Vol. VIII, No. 3 (April, 1956), pp. 383-391, *passim.*

The romanticists maintain that wars are inevitable or necessary. . . . German Romanticists [were] most brazen in their emphasis upon the intrinsic value of war. Thus their most outspoken protagonist, Heinrich von Treitschke, asserted: " . . . all movement and all growth would disappear with war, and . . . only the exhausted, spiritless, degenerate periods of history have toyed with the idea." The final word from this group of theorists is: "War . . . will endure to the end of history, as long as there . . . [are] States." The laws of society and the fundamental nature of man make it inevitable that war will continue without any foreseeable prospect of its eradication. . . .

The dominant theory of war, however, particularly in contemporary Western society, has maintained that war is not inevitable, but can be eliminated through the achievement of a new and better form of international relations. This has sometimes been called the idealistic or rationalistic theory of war. Its origin goes back to the Period of Enlightenment of the seventeenth · and eighteenth centuries. We may say that reason and science constitute the foundation upon which this utopian edifice is built and morality and democracy provide its façade. War is conceived of as an anachronism which international organization, social conditioning, and increased contacts among peoples of different nations will eliminate. Power politics and autocratic government are singled out as the primary causes of war. A handful of leaders or a nation or two which persist in disrupting international harmony are all that stand in the way of a peaceful world. . . .

The spokesman whose words carried greatest inspiration and weight in this connection was undoubtedly President Woodrow Wilson. He envisioned and declared that in the new age, "National purposes have fallen more and more into the background and the common purpose of enlightened mankind has taken their place." . . .

That was the expression of the hope that the evil aspects which were the result of the general character of power politics and were aggravated by the immoral conduct of certain "devils" in politics—whether munitions-makers or great power diplomats—[would be] mitigated, if not eliminated, by the new international organizations. . . .

Secondly, the idealist theory of war is a manifestation of a particular type of rationalist viewpoint which has sometimes served as a primary intellectual assumption of the modern mind. The philosopher of history Buckle expressed this view in the assertion: " . . . it must happen, that as the intellectual acquisitions of a people increase, their love of war will diminish. . . ." There is a natural ratio between peace and reason which preordains that wherever intellectual classes are weak, the military influence will be strong. This is the reason that Russia in the mid-nineteenth century embarked on such ventures as the Crimean War. He concludes: "Russia is a warlike country, not because the inhabitants are immoral, but because they are unintellectual." It is not strange that Buckle, writing in the nineteenth century at a time when Europe was enjoying a period of general peace, should have confused and equated the political condition of peace with the underlying intellectual assumptions of the age. . . .

A corollary to the rationalist philosophy is the belief in the existence of a natural harmony of interests between all nations and peoples. What is true in Mandeville's *Fable of the Bees* and Adam Smith's economic cosmos is said to be no less characteristic of the idealist cosmos of international affairs. This harmony of interests may be temporarily obscured by the specific actions of some arch-troublemaker or by the atavism of power politics in general. Informed by this view, Mr. Toynbee, writing in 1935, found that ". . . this supreme British interest was also the supreme interest of the whole World, inasmuch as international law and order were in the true interests of the whole of Mankind and all the parochial states among which the living generation was partitioned. . . ."

A third illustration of the idealist philosophy of international relations is the still popular belief that war can be decisively banished through contacts between nations and by programs of cultural understanding. A shrinking globe which facilitates trade and travel will gradually eliminate the seeds of ignorance and contempt from which wars grow. On a small scale, this has been true of England and France, as Buckle attempted to show. English conceptions of French morals and French notions of the Englishman's scorn of letters have altered: " . . . the progress of improvement, by bringing the two countries into close and intimate contact, has dissipated those foolish prejudices, and taught each people to admire, and, what is still more important, to respect each other. And the greater the contact, the greater the respect." . . .

Easily the most popular of idealist conceptions of war is that which believes there are no inherent instincts making for war. Modern psychology, anthropology, and biology have sought to show either that war is inevitable owing to inherent human characteristics, or, more frequently, that in the absence of any such basic instincts it is not inevitable. A few students have come to the conclusion that war is inevitable and that "It would serve no useful purpose to endeavor to define principles to eliminate causes of war, for war is inherent in human nature. . . ." The majority view, however, is reflected in the answers given to a questionnaire sent to 528 members of the American Psychological Association. To the question, "Do you as a psychologist hold that there are present in human nature ineradicable, instinctive factors that make war inevitable?" 346 answered, "No"; 10, "Yes"; 150 did not reply; and 22 were ambiguous in their answers. Most psychologists would probably agree with Mr. Julian Huxley's thesis that there are no specific human instincts which one can designate as "war instincts."

Only three kinds of animals practice war at all in the sense of organized conflict between groups of the same species. These are man and two kinds of social insects—certain bees and some ants. The motive force and driving power in these two cases are quite different. Among the insects, wars are based on a mechanical and instinctive foundation. In a particular kind of warfare, the tactics on both sides are identical in every respect. War among humans, however, lacks this mechanical and automatic character and numbers are not invariably the final arbiter. Rather, the real basis of wars is the impulse of "pugnacity," which merges with other impulses and attitudes such as patriotism whenever it is evoked by external conditions. It should be possible to create new and different external conditions to enable this instinct to find other outlets and express itself in more peaceful ways. Without examining the political means by which its goals can be attained or approached, this school of modern psychology finds its new conditions for peaceful relations in a world government and world system of law.

There is another form of idealism embodied in certain anthropological research, such as the work of Malinowski, who finds no evidence of any biological impulse toward war. Instead he shows that " . . . aggression is a derived impulse. It arises from the thwarting of one or the other of the basic psychological drives. . . . " Changing cultural conditions are capable of ameliorating aggression and eliminating war. The conflicting interests which are at the root of aggressive wars can be reduced and redirected by social engineering. One of the earliest suggestions in this field was that of William James. He recommended, as a "moral equivalent of war," the conscription of young men into a kind of glorified Civilian Conservation Corps where they would give vent to their aggressions in a struggle against nature rather than against alien nations. The more contemporary views of means by which aggressions and frustrations might be channeled have often been no less impractical and utopian than this original proposal. . . .

The third theory of war is formulated in terms fundamentally different from those of either romanticist or idealist philosophies. The realist approach gives neither a negative nor an affirmative answer to the question, "Is war inevitable?" Instead it starts with the assumption that international politics can be understood only as a perpetual and unceasing struggle for power. The normal condition of modern international society, and indeed of all human relations, is one in which rivalry, conflict, and strife coexist with good will, amity, and cooperation—perhaps until the end of history. This assumption is of greatest importance in determining the techniques of international relations. If one assumes that harmony and cooperation are the sole norm in relations between nations, then a state can pursue policies based on humanitarian and moral principles. If, on the other hand, one recognizes the existence of constant rivalry and competition, then a state can base its policy upon the national interest and follow a program aiming at temporary adjustments and arrangements which will prevent any antagonist from succeeding in dominating all the others. Under the realist theory of war, the goals and policies pursued must be more tentative, immediate, and practical in character. . . .

TOPIC 10

Instruments of Evaluation

Successes and failures of foreign policy largely depend on the estimate of rival and allied capabilities and their relation to one's own.

Other nations' power and changes in that power are being constantly observed, registered, analyzed, and assessed by a network of trained officers.

Some of the elements of other nations' power are easily ascertained by merely reading newspapers and statistics. Others are concealed from foreign inquiry. Many elements may be in their embryonic stage and largely unknown even to the government which has been placed under close observation—such as growing maturity or discontent of the population.

Policy-makers evaluate the sum of various estimates and reports as to their relevancy to foreign policy. Mistakes may occur at any stage of the process: from the gathering of the original information to evaluation by the intelligence chief and foreign secretary.

►ELEMENTS OF POWER DO NOT STAY PUT

NICHOLAS JOHN SPYKMAN

The author warns against the frequent fallacy of believing that a weak or strong nation may remain such forever.

It is easy to balance mechanical forces because they can be measured, but there is no measuring stick for political power. Are two states balanced, is their power equal, is the relationship between the two sets of alliances in equilibrium? On that question there is usually profound disagreement. The relative power remains a purely subjective judgment. Each state always feels that the other one needs balancing. In so far as the power concerned is in the last instance a power to wage war, it might be assumed that the military men would know the answer, but theirs is an opinion equally subjective, even if a little more expert. The most learned generals have disagreed as often as the statesmen. The only objective test of relative strength is to fight the war and see who wins, but this is hardly a helpful guide to the state that wants to decided whether to fight or not.

The second difficulty lies in the fact that the elements contributing to strength are not static but dynamic; they do not stay put. A new economic development, a new raw material, a new weapon, a new martial spirit may produce the most profound inequality between states that only a few years before had been approximately equal. Besides, in a world of states of equal strength, what is there to prevent the combination of two of them against a third? . . .

From *America's Strategy in World Politics,* quoted previously on pp. 150-156. Copyright, 1942, by Harcourt, Brace and Company, Inc.

►HOW STRONG IS THE U.S.S.R.?

ALLEN W. DULLES

The military, economic, and subversive capabilities of the U.S.S.R. are the subject of many careful and detailed analyses. Following is a public estimate of Soviet power, made by Allen W. Dulles, head of the Central Intelligence Agency. He tried here to reassure his audience and at the same time to prevent any relaxation of effort. He also attempted here to project the evaluation of Soviet power into the foreseeable future.

The challenge of Soviet power presents today a triple threat: first, military; second, economic; and third, subversive.

This challenge is a global one. As long as the principles of international communism motivate the regimes in Moscow and Peiping, we must expect that their single purpose will be the liquidation of our form of free society and the emergence of a Sovietized, communized world order.

They change their techniques as circumstances dictate. They have never given us the slightest reason to hope that they are abandoning their overall objective.

We sometimes like to delude ourselves into thinking that we are faced with another nationalistic power struggle, of which the world has seen so many. The fact is that the aims of the Communist International with its headquarters in Moscow are not nationalistic; their objectives are not limited. They firmly believe and eloquently preach that communism is the system which will eventually rule the world, and each move they make is directed to this end. Communism, like electricity, seeks to be an all-pervasive and revolutionary force.

To promote their objectives they have determined—cost what it may—to develop a military establishment and a strong national economy which will provide a secure home base from which to deploy their destructive foreign activities.

Soviet Military Establishment

To achieve this objective they are devoting about twice as much of their gross national product to military ends as we do. The U.S.S.R. military effort as a proportion of GNP is greater than that of any other nation in the world. Their continuous diversion of economic resources to military support is without any parallel in peacetime history.

We estimate that the total value of their current annual military effort is roughly equivalent to our own. They accomplish this with a GNP which is now less than half of our own.

From the address "The Challenge of Soviet Power," made before the Edison Electric Institute at New Orleans, La., on April 8, 1959.

Here are some of the major elements which go into their military establishment. The Soviet Union maintains an army of 2½ million men, and the tradition of universal military training is being continued. The Soviet Army today has been fully reequipped with a post-World War II arsenal of guns, tanks, and artillery. We have reason to believe the army has already been trained in the use of tactical nuclear weapons.

They have the most modern types of aircraft for defense: night and day fighters, a very large medium-bomber force, and some long-range bombers. They have built less of these long-range bombers than we had expected several years ago and have diverted a major effort to the perfection of ballistic missiles.

Their submarine strength today is many times that with which Germany entered World War II. They have over 200 long-range, modernized submarines and a like number of less modern craft. They have made no boasts about nuclear powered submarines, and on all the evidence we are justified in concluding that we are ahead of them in this field. We must assume, however, that they have the capability to produce such submarines and will probably unveil some in the near future.

Ballistic Missile Situation

I would add a word on the ballistic missile situation.

When World War II ended the Soviet acquired much of the German hardware in the missile field—V-1 and V-2—and with them many German technicians. From that base, over the past 10 years, they have been continuously developing their missile capability, starting with short-range and intermediate-range missiles. These they have tested by the hundreds and have been in production of certain models for some time.

They also early foresaw that, in their particular geographical position, the long-range ballistic missile would become their best instrument in the power struggle with their great rival, the United States. As the size and weight of powerful nuclear weapons decreased with the improvement of the art, they became more and more persuaded of this. Hence they have concentrated on these weapons, have tested some, and assert that they now have ICBM's in serial production.

They hope in this way eventually to be able to hold the U.S. under the threat of nuclear attack by ICBM's while they consolidate their position in the fragile parts of the non-communistic world.

Before leaving the military phase of the Soviet threat, I want to dispel any possible misinterpretations. First, I do *not* believe that the Soviet now have military superiority over us; and second, I do *not* believe that they desire deliberately to provoke hostilities with the U.S. or the Western World at this time. They are well aware of our deterrent force. They probably believe that the risks to them, even if they resorted to surprise attack, would be unacceptable.

Taking into account our overall military strength and our strategic position vis-à-vis the Soviet Union, I consider that our military posture is stronger and our ability to inflict damage is today greater than that of the Soviet Union.

Furthermore, we have allies. The strength, the dependability, and the dedication of our allies put them in a very different category than the unwilling and undependable allies of Moscow, even including the Chinese Communists.

But as the Soviet military capabilities and their nuclear power grow, they will feel that their foreign policy can be somewhat more assertive. In 1956, during the Suez crisis, we had the first Soviet missile-rattling as a new tactic of Moscow diplomacy. Since then there have been the Taiwan Straits and Berlin crises and today the aggressive Communist penetration of Iraq. Hence we must assume that they will continue to probe and to test us, and they may even support other countries in aggression by proxy. They will put us to the test.

There are two points to keep in mind as we view the military future. Firstly, with a much lower industrial base than we, they are producing a military effort which is roughly equivalent to our own; and secondly, they have conditioned their people to accept very real sacrifices and a low standard of living to permit the massive military buildup to continue. If the Soviet should decide to alter their policy so as to give their own people a break in the consumer field with anything like the share in their gross national product which we, as a people, enjoy, the prospects of real peace in our time would be far greater.

Soviet "Economic Order of Battle"

I will turn now to some of the highlights of the economic aspect of the Soviet challenge.

The new confidence of Khrushchev, the shrewd and vocal leader of the Soviet Communist Party and incidentally Head of Government, does not rest solely on his conviction that he, too, possesses a military deterrent. He is convinced that the final victory of communism can be achieved mainly by non-military means. Here the Soviet economic offensive looms large.

The proceedings of the recent 21st Party Congress laid out what we might call the Soviet economic order of battle.

Khrushchev explained it in these words, to summarize the 10 hours of his opening and closing remarks:

> The economic might of the Soviet Union is based on the priority growth of heavy industry; this should insure the Soviet victory in peaceful economic competition with the capitalist countries; development of the Soviet economic might will give communism the decisive edge in the international balance of power.

In the short space of 30 years the Soviet Union has grown from a relatively backward position into being the second largest industrialized economy in the world. While their headlong pace of industrialization has slowed down moderately in the past few years, it still continues to be more rapid than our own. During the past 7 years, through 1958, Soviet industry has grown at the annual rate of 9½ percent. This is not the officially announced rate, which is somewhat larger. It is our reconstruction and deflation of Soviet data.

Our own industrial growth has been at the annual rate of 3.6 percent for the 7 years through 1957. If one included 1958, the comparison with the rate of Soviet growth would be even less favorable.

Investment for National Policy Purposes

I do not conclude from this analysis that the secret of Soviet success lies in greater efficiency. On the contrary. In comparison with the leading free-enterprise economies of the West the Communist state-controlled system is relatively inefficient.

The secret of Soviet progress is simple. It lies in the fact that the Kremlin leaders direct a far higher proportion of total resources to national policy purposes than does the United States. I define national policy purposes to include, among other things, defense and investment in heavy industry.

With their lower living standards and much lower production of consumer goods, they are in effect plowing back into investment a large section of their production—30 percent—while we in the United States are content with 17 to 20 percent. Soviet investment in industry as planned for 1959 is about the same as U.S. investment in industry during 1957, which so far was our best year.

Although the Soviets in recent years have been continually upping the production of consumer goods, their consuming public fares badly in comparison with ours. Last year, for example, Soviet citizens had available for purchase barely one-third the total goods and services available to Americans. Furthermore, most of the U.S. output of durable consumer goods is for replacement, while that of the U.S.S.R. is for first-time users. In summary, the Soviet economy is geared largely to economic growth and for military purposes; ours is geared largely to increasing consumer satisfactions and building a higher standard of living.

While the Soviets last year were producing only 1 automobile for every 50 we produced, they were turning out 4 machine tools to our 1. . . .

Our housing investment is roughly twice that of the Soviet, even though living space per capita in the U.S. is already four times that of the U.S.S.R.

Industrial Production Trends

What of the future? In Khrushchev's words, "The Soviet Union intends to outstrip the United States economically. . . . To surpass the level of production in the United States means to exceed the highest indexes of capitalism."

Khrushchev's ambitious 7-year plan establishes the formidable task of increasing industrial production about 80 percent by 1965.

Steel production, according to the plan, is to be pushed close to 100 million net tons. Cement output is set at a level somewhat higher than industry forecasts place United States production in 1965.

The energy base is to be revolutionized. Crude oil and natural gas will constitute more than one-half of the total energy supply, and relatively high-cost coal will be far less important than now.

By 1965 the U.S.S.R. plans to produce about 480 billion kilowatt hours of electricity. As a study comparing U.S. and U.S.S.R. electric power production prepared by a leading industrial research group pointed out, this means that the absolute gap between the U.S. and U.S.S.R. in the quantities of electricity generated will increase somewhat in our favor over the next 7 years.

This interesting study received a considerable amount of deserved publicity. We agree with its conclusion. However, what is true about electric power is not true across the board, as some commentators concluded.

For example, compare primary energy production trends in the two countries. Soviet production of coal, petroleum, natural gas, and hydroelectric power, expressed in standard fuel units, amounted to 45 percent of the U.S. production in 1958. By 1965 it will be close to 60 percent. The absolute gap in primary energy has been closing since 1950. At the present pace it will continue to narrow over the next 7 years.

Similarly, the absolute gap in steel *production* has been shrinking over the past 5 years. The maximum gap in steel *capacity* apparently was reached in 1958.

The comforting illusion spread by the "disciples of the absolute gap" should not serve as a false tranquilizer.

Soviet Exaggerations

At the same time it is important not to exaggerate Soviet prospects in the economic race. In the propaganda surrounding the launching of the 7-year plan, Khrushchev made a number of statements about Soviet economic power which were nothing more than wishful thinking. Specifically he stated that "after the completion of the 7-year plan, we will probably need about 5 more years to catch up with and outstrip the United States in industrial output." "Thus," he added, "by that time [1970], or perhaps even sooner, the Soviet Union will advance to first place in the world both in absolute volume of production and in per capita production."

First of all, to reach such improbable conclusions the Kremlin leaders overstate the present comparative position. They claim U.S.S.R. industrial output to be 50 percent of that of the U.S. Our own analyses of Soviet industrial output last year concluded that it was not more than 40 percent of our own.

Secondly, Khrushchev forecasts that our future industrial growth will be only 2 percent a year. If this is true, the United States will be virtually committing economic suicide. This prediction I regard as unrealistic.

A saner projection would place 1965 Soviet industrial production at about 55 percent of our own. By 1970, assuming the same relative rates of growth, U.S.S.R. industrial output as a whole would be about 60 percent of that in the United States.

Further, when Khrushchev promises his people the world's highest standard of living by 1970, this is patently nonsense. It is as though the shrimp had learned to whistle, to use one of his colorful comments.

Implications of Soviet Economic Progress

These Soviet exaggerations are a standard tool of Communist propaganda. Such propaganda, however, should not blind us to the sobering implications of their expected economic progress.

First of all, rapid economic growth will provide the Kremlin leaders with additional resources with which to intensify the arms race. If recent trends and present Soviet policies continue, Soviet military spending could increase by over 50 percent in the next 7 years without increasing the relative burden on their economy.

Secondly, some additional improvement can be made in the standards of living of the Russian people, even with continued emphasis on heavy industry and armaments. It is only since the death of Stalin in 1953 that serious attention has been given to improving living standards. The moderate slowdown in the headlong growth of heavy industry which then ensued has been caused in large part by the diversion of more resources to housing, to agriculture, and to consumer goods.

Living standards, based on present Soviet plans, are expected to increase about one-third over the next 7 years. This level, if achieved, will still be far below that which our own citizens are now enjoying, but it will look good to people who for long have been compelled to accept very low standards.

Finally, the Soviet 7-year plan, even if not fully achieved, will provide the wherewithal to push the expansion of trade and aid with the uncommitted and underdeveloped nations of the free world. By 1965 Soviet output of some basic raw materials and some industrial products will be approaching, and in a few cases exceeding, that of the United States. Most prominently, these products will be the kind that are needed for industrialization in the less developed countries.

The outcome of this contest—the Communist challenge in underdeveloped areas—is crucial to the survival of the free world.

Communist Trade-and-Aid Programs

This is an unprecedented epoch of change. Within little more than 10 years, over three-quarters of a billion people in 21 nations have become independent of colonial rule. In all of these newly emergent countries there is intense nationalism coupled with the determination to achieve a better way of life, which they believe industrialization will bring them.

The leaders of world communism are alert to the opportunity which this great transformation provides them. They realize the future of communism can be insured only by expansion and that the best hope of such expansion lies in Asia and Africa. While they are attempting to focus all our concern on Berlin, they are moving into Iraq with arms, economic aid, and subversion and giving added attention to Africa.

The Communist bloc trade-and-aid programs in undeveloped countries moved into high gear during 1958. The equivalent of over $1 billion in new credits was extended to underdeveloped countries by the bloc in this year. In the 4-year period ending 1958 the total of grants and credits totaled $2.5 billion, of which $1.6 billion came from the U.S.S.R. and the balance from the satellites and China. Three-fifths of the total delivered to date has been in the form of arms to the U.A.R.—Egypt and Syria—Yemen, Iraq, Afghanistan, and Indonesia. These same countries, plus India, Argentina, Ceylon, Burma, and Cambodia, have received the bulk of the economic aid.

Over 4,000 bloc technicians have been sent to assist the development of nations in the free world. About 70 percent of these technicians are engaged in economic activities. Others are reorganizing local military establishments and teaching bloc military doctrine to indigenous personnel.

The bloc also has a well-developed program for training students from underdeveloped countries. About 3,200 students, technicians, and military specialists have now received such training behind the Iron Curtain.

While these figures are still well below the total of our own aid, loan, and training programs, this massive economic and military aid program is concentrated in a few critical countries, and of course these figures do not include Soviet aid and trade with the East European satellites and Communist China.

India, which has received over $325 million of bloc grants and credits, is a primary recipient. The Soviet economic showplace here is the Bhilai steel mill, being built by the Russians. The U.A.R. over the past 4 years received over $900 million in aid and credits. This investment today does not seem quite as profitable to the Soviet as it did last year.

Iraq provides a prime example of the opportunistic nature of the bloc's aid program. Prior to the coup d'etat on July 14th last year, Iraq's economic involvement with Communist nations had been negligible. In the past few months the U.S.S.R. has provided over $250 million in military and economic development credits. The Iraq Development Board has dropped its two Western advisers. Western technicians are also being dismissed and contracts with many Western firms canceled. Increasingly, Moscow is pressuring the Iraq Government to accept dependence on Communist support, and the number of fellow travelers in high government posts is growing.

Communist Campaign of Subversion

The Soviet policy of economic penetration fits like a glove into their worldwide campaign of subversion, which is the third main element of the triple Soviet challenge: military, economic, and subversive.

International communism has not changed its operating procedure since the days of the Comintern and the Cominform. The Communist Party of the

U.S.S.R., of which Khrushchev is the leader, is the spearhead of the movement. It has a worldwide mission, formulated by Lenin and Stalin and now promoted by Khrushchev but with more subtle techniques than those of Stalin. This mission continues to be the subversion of the entire free world, starting of course with those countries which are most vulnerable.

Its arsenal of attack is based, first of all, on the Communist Parties of the Soviet Union and Communist China. These in turn direct the hard-core Communist organizations which exist in practically every country of the world. Every Communist Party maintains its secret connections with Moscow or, in case of certain of the Communist parties in the Far East, with Peiping.

These parties also have an entirely overt association with the international Communist movement. At the 21st meeting of the Soviet Party Congress there were present representatives of some 60 Communist parties throughout the world, including two representatives of the U.S. Communist Party. The single theme of these Communist leaders was their confidence in the eventual worldwide triumph of the Communist movement. . . .

In addition to its worldwide penetration through Communist Party organizations, the Communists in Moscow and Peiping have set up a whole series of front organizations to penetrate all segments of life in the free countries of the world. These include the World Federation of Trade Unions, which claims some 90 million members throughout the world. International organizations of youth and students stage great festivals at frequent intervals. . . .

They have the Women's International Democratic Federation, the World Federation of Teachers Unions, the International Association of Democratic Lawyers, and Communist journalists and medical organizations. Then cutting across professional and social lines, and designed to appeal to intellectuals, the Communists have created the World Peace Council, which maintains so-called peace committees in 47 countries, gaining adherents by trading on the magic word of "peace."

To back up this massive apparatus the Soviet has the largest number of trained agents for espionage and secret political action that any country has ever assembled. In Moscow, Prague, and Peiping, and other Communist centers, they are training agents recruited from scores of other countries to go out as missionaries of communism into the troubled areas of the world. Much of the Middle East and Southeast Asia, and particularly black Africa, are high on their target list. . . . Their basic purpose is to destroy all existing systems of free and democratic government and disrupt the economic and political organizations on which these are based. Behind their Iron Curtain they ruthlessly suppress all attempts to achieve more freedom—witness Hungary and now Tibet.

The task of destruction is always easier than that of construction. The Communist world, in dealing with the former colonial areas and the newly emerging nations of the world, has appealing slogans to export and vulnerable economic conditions to exploit. The fragile parliamentary systems of new and emerging countries are fertile ground for these agitators.

Also under the heading of subversion we must not overlook the fact that the Communist leaders have sought to advance their cause by local wars by proxy—Korea, Viet-nam, Malaya are typical examples.

In conclusion I wish to emphasize again the pressing need for a clearer understanding of the real purpose of the Sino-Soviet program. There is no evidence that the present leaders of the Communist world have the slightest idea of abandoning their goal or of changing the general tactics of achieving them.

Those who feel we can buy peace by compromise with Khrushchev are sadly deluded. Each concession we give him merely strengthens his position and prestige and the ability of the Soviet regime to continue its domination of the Russian people, whose friendship we seek.

Our defense lies not in compromise but in understanding and firmness, in a strong and ready deterrent military power, in the marshaling of our economic assets with those of the other free countries of the world to meet their methods of economic penetration, and finally in the unmasking of their subversive techniques.

The overall power of the free world is still vastly superior to that under the control of the leaders of international communism. If they succeed and we fail, it will only be because of our complacency and because they have devoted a far greater share of their power, skill, and resources to our destruction than we have been willing to dedicate to our own preservation.

Part III

EVALUATION OF INTENTIONS

We have seen how difficult it is to evaluate other nations' power. It is even more difficult to estimate what they intend to do with the power they have. Nations, like individuals, often conceal their intentions in polite or deceptive phrases. Yet accurate assessment of the *real* intentions of other nations in international politics may be a question of life or death.

The fundamental task of foreign policy is usually defined as a continuous process of assessing one's own and other nations' capacities and intentions. It means:

1. Determining one's own objectives in the light of one's own and allied power that is actually and potentially available for the pursuit of these objectives;

2. Evaluating the objectives of unfriendly, neutral, and friendly nations as well as their actual and potential capacity to realize them.

An error in either or both of these processes may lead to disaster. Wars may start because the opposite power was underestimated or one's own power was overestimated. Some wars could have been avoided, or fought at lesser cost, had an earlier *wrong* estimate of other nations' real intentions not occurred. (Appeasing a conqueror who pretends not to be one is an example of a policy based on a wrong estimate.)

The term "intention" is used here as the conception of objectives plus a plan for realization of the objectives.

It is never easy to detect the real motives, ends, and intentions of men and nations.

In international politics three general assumptions can be made:

1. The first is that the nature of a nation's power suggests possibilities and sets limitations to what national leaders might do with the power they have at their disposal.

Intentions may be more modest than the national power allows. Or they may be overambitious and extend far beyond the limits set by available

223

means. Error in calculation or fanaticism may induce statesmen to conceive of unrealistic aims. More will be said about the imperative need to balance ends and means in Part IV.

Whatever a nation's intentions, the simple existence of power may bring a reaction. Other nations may believe great power not only permits but generates great designs. "I dread our being too much dreaded," wrote the British statesman and philosopher Edmund Burke at the end of the eighteenth century. "We may say that we shall not abuse this astonishing and hitherto unheard-of power. But every other nation will think we shall abuse it."

After Hiroshima the Soviet Union apparently believed that the United States intended to abuse its "astonishing and hitherto unheard-of power." The United States atomic monopoly, while it lasted, could have been used to blackmail Russia into political concession. This was not intended or attempted. The Baruch plan for world control of atomic energy was proof of that. Yet the United States' refusal to communicate atomic secrets to the Russians prior to establishment of effective international controls was taken by the Russians as evidence of evil intention.

Some Americans, on the other hand, could interpret the Soviet shot at the moon, occurring significantly on the eve of N. S. Khrushchev's official arrival in the United States, as an instrument of blackmail, whatever the intentions behind this demonstration of the Soviet missile supremacy might have been.

2. The second assumption which can be made in international politics is that nations usually pursue what is primarily their own interest rather than what would be in the interest of others. In their own actions, individuals often may be capable of altruism. This is rarely so in the case of nations.

"A sharp distinction must be drawn," suggests Protestant theologian Reinhold Niebuhr," between the moral and social behavior of individuals and of social groups, national, racial, and economic, and . . . this distinction justifies and necessitates political policies, which a purely individualistic ethic must always find embarassing . . . Individual men may be moral in the sense that they are able to consider interests other than their own in determining problems of conduct, and are capable, on occasion, of preferring the advantages of others to their own. . . . But all these achievements are more difficult, if not impossible, for human societies and social groups. In every human group there is less reason to guide and to check impulse, less capacity for self-transcendence, less ability to comprehend the needs of others and therefore more unrestrained egoism than the individuals, who compose the group, reveal in their personal relationships. . . ." [1]

Our previous analysis of the territorial state and the force of modern nationalism has already indicated that the collective interest of a nation—and none other—is the primary determinant of its conduct in relation to other nations and their interests.

The various national leaders' concept of their national interests guides

[1] Reinhold Niebuhr, *Moral Man and Immoral Society* (New York: Charles Scribner's Sons, 1932).

their decisions and actions. They may take into consideration also other-than-national interests (humane, ideological, religious and other concepts which transcend national boundaries). If they do so, they pursue such other-than-national interests only if these are in harmony with the national interest, or, at least, do not conflict with it.

3. The third assumption concerns two possible *intermediary* objectives (whatever the ultimate objectives may be):

Nations may be satisfied with the international situation as is; then their immediate objective is to maintain the *status quo;*[2] or, in case of dissatisfaction, they will challenge the *status quo* with the aim of changing it.

National Interest

The concept of national interest, like many other terms in the field of politics, is a shorthand expression rather than a well-defined term. It is elusive, relative, and subject to a variety of interpretations.

While circumstances may alter several aspects of the national interest, its hard core seems to be the *desire to secure the survival of the nation.* "Safety from external danger," in Alexander Hamilton's words, "is the most powerful dictator of national conduct." In our world, which is as in the time of Alexander Hamilton divided into sovereign nations, "the foreign policies of all nations must necessarily refer to their survival as their minimum requirement." (H. J. Morgenthau on "What is the National Interest" in Topic 11.)

The term "survival" has different and often conflicting meanings to different people. What kind of survival do we mean? The survival of the physical substance of nation, that is, people? Or the survival of the nation's spiritual substance: culture, values, language, and ideals as well as way of life and standard of living?

Two extreme examples may be suggested. The physical survival of the American people could be achieved by merging the United States with a world-wide Soviet Union. The number of Americans who would die in forced labor camps or otherwise for opposition to Communism conceivably might be smaller than the number of Americans who would die opposing the extension of the Soviet system in an atomic war. Complete submission may, indeed, guarantee the physical survival of many.

The opposite suggestion may postulate the elimination of any actual or potential threat to the preservation of the American way of life, now and in the future. The conquest of the world would guarantee national survival as long as the world remained conquered.

Between these two extremes—complete submission or complete conquest—we find a great variety of proposals and suggestions to secure national survival in less absolute terms. This is referred to as the quest for *relative* security in contrast to the ideal of absolute security, that is, complete elimination of all rivals.

---

[2] *Status quo:* Latin for "situation as it now exists."

Preserving the Status Quo

Nations adopt the policy of the *status quo* because they are either satisfied with the situation or, while dissatisfied with it, they fear that a change may bring a worse situation.

The policy of the *status quo* in international politics is similar to conservative policy on the domestic scene. Neither of these policies objects to the concept of some change. But both are willing to accept only slow, organic and non-violent changes which would not disturb the main characteristics of a given system.

A policy of the *status quo* may be sometimes preferred only because of abhorrence of violence as an instrument for introducing changes. Peacefulness is its main attraction. We must note, however, that a policy which aims at preservation of a given situation may actually mean a preservation of a highly unjust and oppressive state of affairs.

A policy which aims at preservation of a colonial empire is a typical policy of the *status quo,* although those who condemn colonialism in the name of humanity, justice, and peace, refer to it as a policy of imperialism. When, during World War II, Winston Churchill proclaimed that he would not preside over the liquidation of the British empire, he spoke as a typical conservative and *status quo* politician. Briefly, the conservative policy in international relations, with its stress on peace and legality, may mean good or evil, depending on what one wants to conserve: democracy, justice, national independence, or dictatorship, oppression, colonies.

Conquerors often become conservative leaders when future conquests seem improbable and when their former conquests are challenged by demands for change. Thus, in January, 1958, N. S. Khrushchev made a speech in which he defended peaceful preservation of the *status quo.* He excluded any discussion concerning the fate of East Central Europe from the agenda of any future summit meeting. Speaking in Minsk, Khrushchev proclaimed: "What then do Messrs. Eisenhower and Dulles want? . . . They evidently want us to give up socialist construction (in East Central Europe) and to restore the capitalist order. Some people go so far as to suggest a public opinion poll in the socialist countries as to whether they are for socialism or for capitalism . . . If the *status quo* (!) is not recognized, if the socialist states are ignored . . . and their domestic affairs interfered in, then it is, of course, absolutely (!) impossible to come to terms."

The *status quo* policy is sometimes equated with the balance of power. The balancing process may often be the method of the *status quo* policy. But it is, of course, conceivable that a certain state of affairs may be preserved by the very opposite of a balance, that is, by complete imbalance. If one power conquered the whole world, its overwhelming might could protect the new *status quo* against demands for change.

The Challenge to the Status Quo

The opposite to the conservative policy in international relations is the policy of challenge to the *status quo.* This category includes policies that (a) aim at a new power superiority; (b) attempt to reverse a given power distribution; (c) start an empire (instead of merely preserving what has been built); or (d) engage in territorial expansion.

Not all policies which challenge a given distribution of power may be labelled imperialistic.

A nation may, for instance, aim at a balance of power in order to end its inferior position and, thus, terminate a superior position of another nation. Many colonial revolts or challenges to imperial situations represent such challenge to the *status quo*. The Indian and Pakistani struggle for independence belonged to this category.

One can also conceive of a situation in which a nation may wish to challenge the *status quo* not because it actually is inferior, but because it feels that it might become so in the future.

In 1933 and 1934 (following Adolph Hitler's seizure of government in Germany) some people feared that the Nazi Reich might become so powerful and expansionist as to be able to blackmail the world into surrender. They thought preventive war at the beginning of the Nazi buildup could preserve the balance of power in Europe and that the restoration of such balance at a later stage might prove either too costly or impossible. The concept of a preventive war against Nazi Germany was allegedly that of Marshal Pilsudski of Poland.

In the late forties, some people similarly voiced their opinion that atomic blackmail should be directed against the Soviet Union in order to prevent the Soviets from gaining a superior position, which they would achieve if their conquests were left unchallenged. Communist literature itself refers to the expected position of future power to dictate. It speaks of the future "socialist encirclement of capitalism" which will replace the former "capitalist encirclement of socialism."

Similar to the policy of the *status quo,* the policy which challenges a given situation and may even envisage the use of violent methods, is neither good or evil *per se;* its merit depends on what it wants to achieve: freedom or oppression, justice or injustice, national independence or colonial exploitation.

In theory, a policy of the *status quo* is clearly contrasted with a policy that advocates radical and fundamental change. In practice, however, the line cannot be so easily drawn. The problem is not academic. Our survival may depend on our ability to distinguish one from the other and to react accordingly.

A conservative policy (whether in the domestic or international sphere) is not opposed to a change as such; it emphasizes the desirability of organic, slow, non-violent and nonrevolutionary transformation. The major problem is to distinguish an organic and evolutionary change from a radical or revolutionary one.

The British Conservative Party considered the previous nationalization of the steel industry by the Labour Party to be a nonorganic and revolutionary change. Consequently, when the Labour Party had been defeated at the elections, the Conservative Party "conserved" the nature of the British economy by voiding the Labour measures with regard to steel. On the other hand, the

Conservative Party did not consider the Labour nationalization of medicine, transport, and power as representing a nonorganic change of British society and preserved these changes following its electoral victory over the Labour Party.

Similarly, in 1959, one could ask whether the Soviet proposal to "internationalize" West Berlin represented a challenge to the postwar *status quo* in Europe, or only the removal of one of the major irritants between the East and the West within the *status quo*.

In 1956, the United States chose to consider the reassertion of Soviet power in Hungary as being part of the *status quo* in East Central Europe. To have challenged it would have involved the risk of a major armed conflict with the U.S.S.R.

On the other hand, in 1958, the United States and Great Britain opposed the threat of the extension of Soviet influence to the Middle East, in particular to Jordan and Lebanon. The dispatch of American and British troops to the area notified the Russians that a change of the *status quo* in that particular area was considered a major challenge and would be prevented even at the risk of a major conflict.

These examples demonstrate how vital, yet difficult, it is to analyze the real substance of other nations' objectives and select appropriate responses to them.

An accurate analysis is, furthermore, complicated by the following five problems:

1. Unattractive ultimate goals are often disguised in terms which have general appeal.

2. Ideology or creed is sometimes the cause of policy; often it is only a front for it.

3. The human mind—the fountain of evaluations and decisions—is unfathomable, especially its emotional part.

4. Not only words but also acts may be misinterpreted.

5. Any policy, whatever its original assumptions and aims, may be transformed under the impact of counter-power and counter-policies.

These five problems now deserve to be examined in more detail.

1. *Disguise of Objectives.* Nations and their leaders tend to justify their policies in broader-than-national terms. They refer to their policies as those of peace, justice, historical rights, place in the sun, equal opportunity, and, above all, of defense. A national leader would hardly refer to his policy as aiming at depriving other nations of their rights. The aim is said to be the defense of his own nation's rights. The fact that their defense may require the elimination of others' rights would not be mentioned.

Even such a crude conqueror as Adolf Hitler considered it useful to wrap up his aims in justifications which could appeal at least to some observers outside the Nazi borders. His outbursts against the *Versailles Diktat* (unilaterally imposed terms of peace upon Germany at Versailles in 1919) were to appeal to those individuals or nations who had reached a similar conclusion with regard to post-Versailles arrangements in Europe. Thus, some groups in the West were induced to believe that Hitler's objective was to terminate discrimination against Germany, and not to start conquest of Europe.

The aim of his anti-Semitism was not to make the world "safe for the Aryans" but to subject it to the rule of one particular segment of the Aryan race, the Nazis. Anti-Semites of the world were asked to unite to help Hitler achieve his aim.

At this point, it may be mentioned that the defensive tone of all programs which proclaim the need to make the world safe for something (democracy, communism, Christianity) implies that such a world would not be very safe for the opposite doctrines.

Defense is an aim which always evokes sympathy, at least at first sight. Defense of rights, defense of positions lost, defense of justice, defense against attack, they all appear justified. The assailant is always wrong.

Perhaps this is why offense so often assumes the mask of defense. Once, Lenin approvingly quoted Clausewitz (part of this Prussian military thinker's writing is reproduced on p. 438): "The conqueror is always peaceful, as Bonaparte claimed. He would just as soon march into our state. Since he cannot do this, *we* must want war and also prepare for it."

On the eve of attack, the assailant usually accuses his victim of provocation: the victim merely braces himself for the forthcoming assault.

On the eve of Nazi expansion in Eastern Europe, first Czechoslovakia (1938), then Poland (1939) were accused of aggressive dispositions toward Germany. Their defensive treaties with France were labelled by Hitler as aggressive. And when Czechoslovakia and Poland were occupied, the Nazis tried to present the liquidation of the Czechoslovak and Polish states as defensive measures aimed at protecting German minorities against Polish and Czechoslovak hatred.

The Soviet Union, similarly, "protected" the Communist minority in Hungary in 1956. The North Atlantic Treaty Organization, which was created in response to the Soviet threat, is now labelled as aggressive and provocative by the Soviets.

The aggressive aspects of Communist doctrine are couched almost exclusively in defensive terms. The term "capitalist encirclement" suggests an aggressive intent on the part of capitalism and defense on the part of socialism. This is in tune with Lenin's analysis of the inevitably aggressive nature of modern capitalism (Topic 12). Capitalism is, by definition, aggressive. Socialism is pacific and defensive. Consequently, to initiate destruction of aggressive capitalism could be construed as justified defense against an attack which would come in any case.

We may like to think that democracies never disguise or distort their policy aims or methods in this fashion. Yet democratic governments need favorable support for their foreign policy at home and abroad. This may induce the national leaders to *pretend* to be acting in harmony with professed ideals. This happens when the need to choose between the two different kinds of evil does not permit democracies to act as their ethics require. During World War II, the general tendency to depict Stalin's Russia as a "democracy after all" was only partly a result of wishful thinking or error; many of those who knew better abstained from voicing their objections. The desire to achieve victory against a common enemy relegated, understandably, some disturbing aspects of a democratic alliance with communism to a secondary position.

Restoration of past positions or glories has a less general appeal than the argument of defense. Yet many an offensive program has been presented as a "defense of the past" and gained at least some support and sympathy for that reason.

In the nineteenth century, for instance, many Pan-Slavists presented the program of Slavic unity as a defense against Pan-Germanism. In part, this was true, especially in the case of smaller Slavic nations at that time living under the domination of the German, Austrian, or Turkish empires. In Russia, however, Pan-Slavism was leavened with Orthodox Messianism asking for the restoration of Constantinople to the world of Christian orthodoxy, that is Russia. This combination of religious Messianism with racial overtones, and of defense with the need to expand was noted and condemned by the co-author of the Communist Manifesto of 1848, Friedrich Engels, in unmistakable terms: "Behind this comical theory [of Pan-Slavism] there stood the terrible reality of the Russian empire, of that Empire which by every movement manifested a pretension to consider the whole of Europe the property of the Slavic tribe and, in particular, of its only energetic part— Russia. That Empire which, with two such capitals as Petersburg and Moscow, is unable to find its center of gravity until Constantinople [Tsargrad, the City of the Tsar, in Russian], in which every Russian peasant sees the true focus of his religion and nation, becomes the residence of the Russian emperor . . ." [3]

Some writers and poets in Russia were probably sincere in their sentimental advocacy of Slavic unity and hopes for a Constantinople free of the Moslem infidels. But they unwittingly supplied attractive arguments for those Russian politicians who did not particularly strive to enhance the glory of God and orthodoxy but wanted to control Constantinople and its straits (Bosporus, Sea of Marmara, and the Dardanelles) to the strategic advantage of the Russian navy operating from the ports in the Black Sea.

Similarly, the Spanish falangist movement looked for inspiration to the period between 1580-1640 when, as one Pan-Hispanic writer expressed it in the thirties, "all peoples of the Hispanidad were ruled by the same monarchs." [4] The official program of the Fascist party of Spain, *Falange Española,* proclaims quite clearly: "Our aim is the Empire . . . Spain will seek its glory and its riches across the seas."

During the Anglo-French-Israeli invasion of Egyptian territory some Zionist papers claimed the right to expand Israeli boundaries to their biblical limits.

Mussolini, proclaiming his aim to transform the Mediterranean Sea into

---

[3] Quoted by Waclaw Lednicki in *European Ideologies,* ed. Feliks Gross (New York: Philosophical Library, 1948), p. 808.
[4] Ramiro de Maeztú, quoted by Stephen Naft in *European Ideologies,* ed. Feliks Gross (New York: Philosophical Library, 1948), p. 714.

an Italian lake referred to the defense and restoration of the old glory of the Roman empire.

After World War II some Czechoslovak Communists claimed portions of German territory (Glatz area) in the name of medieval Bohemian kings.

2. *Ideological Justification.* The Communist doctrine is internationalist. Yet, a territorial state, Soviet Russia, constantly invokes this doctrine in its relations with the non-Communist states. Is it a disguise for the national policies of the Soviet state? What is the relationship of that doctrine to real Soviet aims? Is it their basis or only a pretext? Or is it only a Marx-Leninist wrapping, necessary to sell the Soviet national interest to foreign consumers? Do the Soviet leaders believe in their ideology? And if they do, do they act accordingly? Their beliefs may differ from their actions, as the Communists, like everybody else, must take into consideration not only their aims but also the practical possibility of achieving them.

Furthermore, is the ideology on which the Soviet leaders base their decisions and actions so clear that it indicates to them what to do and what not to do?

The writings and speeches by V. I. Lenin, J. V. Stalin, and N. S. Khrushchev (excerpts are in Topics 12 and 13) indicate that, according to their ideology, a war among the Capitalists, and also between the Capitalist and Socialist blocs, is inevitable because of the nature of capitalism. The war is inevitable in the long run, according to Lenin and Stalin, but a temporary peaceful coexistence between two opposed systems is possible.

In his early writings, Stalin expressed this idea that increased strength and success of the Socialist camp might reduce the chances of a war with capitalism.

"If the present Capitalist encirclement is replaced by a Socialist encirclement, then a peaceful path is quite possible for certain Capitalist countries whose Capitalists will consider it expedient voluntarily to make substantial concessions to the proletariat." [5]

In 1956, Nikita S. Khrushchev suggested that while capitalism exists, this theory of the inevitability of war is still true but the new deterring strength of the Communist bloc makes it less "fatally inevitable."

Where does all that leave us? The "holy" writings of Lenin, Stalin, and Khrushchev, by which all the Communist leaders from Prague to Peking seem to swear, proclaim the final goal: a world safe only for communism. This is clear enough yet the same writings are not committed to either violent or non-violent methods of action. Furthermore we are not certain whether the Soviet leaders believe in their dogmas; and even if they do they may be ready to deviate from them when the circumstances suggest a more pragmatic than messianic course of action.

The maximum goal proclaimed by the Soviet leaders—a Communist world—may not be a realistic program of action on their part but only a bluff. Nations as well as individuals often ask for more than they actually want in order to obtain at least something. On the other hand, nations may sometimes

[5] V. I. Lenin, *Voprosy Leninizma* (11th ed.; 1945), p. 32.

ask for less; their modest claim is then merely a trial balloon which is to test the resistance of their opponents. And at other times leaders may, of course, proclaim their final goals precisely and accurately and yet nobody may believe them. When Hitler wrote his *Mein Kampf,* he apparently meant every word he had put into it. At the beginning of his political career, however, only a few people took his program for the future seriously.

Two conclusions may be derived from the preceding observations: (a) it is dangerous to disbelieve an over-ambitious program merely because its aims appear to us as preposterous; and (b) it is equally dangerous to believe that a maximum program, however seriously conceived, will be pursued regardless of cost.

3. *The Depth of the Human Mind.* The third major difficulty in evaluating other nations' intentions lies in the simple but inescapable fact that motives are matters of human heart and mind. Motives, impulses "rising from some inner need or desire spur the mind into the exercise of will," says Charles Burton Marshall (Topic 13). Some of these inner needs and desires may be the result of an abnormal mind.

It is frightening to think in what hands the fate of mankind has often been. The Soviet Union, that is, one-sixth of the world, was ruled by J. V. Stalin for thirty-five years. His manias and disregard for facts were described by one of his close associates, N. S. Khrushchev, whose visit to the United States in 1959 and some of his reactions to observable facts suggested he had visions and illusions of his own:

> The sickly suspicion created in him [Stalin] a general distrust even toward eminent Party workers whom he had known for years. Everywhere and in everything he saw "enemies," "two-facers," and "spies." . . . He never acknowledged to anyone that he made any mistake, large or small, despite the fact that he made not a few mistakes in the matter of theory and in his practical activity. . . . Stalin became even more capricious, irritable and brutal; in particular his suspicion grew. His persecution mania reached unbelievable dimensions. Many workers were becoming enemies before his very eyes. . . . The willfulness of Stalin showed itself not only in decisions concerning the internal life of the country but also in the international relations of the Soviet Union. The July plenum of the Central Committee studied in detail the reasons for the development of conflict with Yugoslavia. It was a shameful role which Stalin played here. . . . This does not mean, however, that the Yugoslav leaders did not make mistakes or did not have shortcomings. But these mistakes and shortcomings were magnified in a monstrous manner by Stalin, which resulted in a break of relations with a friendly country. . . . Once, when I came from Kiev to Moscow, I was invited to visit Stalin who, pointing to the copy of a letter lately sent to Tito, asked me, "Have you read this?" Not waiting for my reply he answered, "I will shake my little finger—and there will be no more Tito. He will fall." We have dearly paid for this "shaking of the little finger." This statement reflected Stalin's mania for greatness, but he acted just that way. . . . No matter how much or how little Stalin shook, not only his little finger but everything else that he could shake, Tito did not fall. Why? The reason was that, in this case of disagreement with the Yugoslav comrades, Tito had behind him a state and a people

who had gone through a severe school of fighting for liberty and independence, a people which gave support to its leaders. You see to what Stalin's mania for greatness led. He had completely lost consciousness of reality; he demonstrated his suspicion and haughtiness not only in relations with individuals in the USSR, but in relation to whole parties and nations.[6]

In another portion of the same speech Nikita S. Khrushchev demonstrated more of Stalin's disregard for facts and realities. This concerned the beginning of the Nazi-Soviet War in 1941. Khrushchev told Party delegates that on April 3, 1941, more than two months before the beginning of the Nazi hostilities against the U.S.S.R., Churchill "through his ambassador to the U.S.S.R., Cripps, personally warned Stalin that the Germans had begun regrouping their armed units with the intent of attacking the Soviet Union." Although Premier Khrushchev considered it necessary to add that "Churchill did not do this at all because of his friendly feeling toward the Soviet nation," but in order "to bring Germany and the U.S.S.R. into a bloody war and thereby strengthen the position of the British Empire," Khrushchev admitted that it was correct information which Stalin had chosen to disregard. "Stalin took no heed of these warnings," said Khrushchev. "What is more, Stalin ordered that no credence be given to information of this sort, in order not to provoke the initiation of military operations." Then there were other warnings as to the impending Nazi attack against the Soviet Union from German army deserters, and some sources of secret information. Finally the Nazi armies invaded Soviet territory and military operations began. "At that time," Khrushchev relates, "Moscow issued the order that the German fire was not to be returned. Why? It was because Stalin, despite evident facts, thought that the war had not yet started, that this was only a provocative action on the part of several undisciplined sections of the German army, and that our reaction might serve as a reason for the Germans to begin the war. . . . After the first severe disaster and defeat at the front, Stalin thought that this was the end. In one of his speeches in those days he said: 'All that which Lenin created we have lost for ever.' . . . Even after the war began, the nervousness and hysteria which Stalin demonstrated, interfering with actual military operations, caused our army serious damage." [7]

Khrushchev's speech may have been only an effort to present himself as a completely different leader, while deep in his heart he may have agreed

[6] Secret speech of Nikita S. Khrushchev concerning the "Cult of the Individual," delivered at the Twentieth Congress of the Communist Party of the Soviet Union on February 25, 1956. On June 4, the U.S. Department of State released a text of the Khrushchev speech with the following introduction: "The Department of State has recently obtained from a confidential source a copy of a document which purports to be a version of the speech of Party First Secretary, N. S. Khrushchev, at a session of the XX. Party Congress of the Communist Party of the Soviet Union on February 25, 1956. This session was limited in attendance to the delegates from the USSR. The document is being released in response to many inquiries. This version is understood to have been prepared for the guidance of the Party leadership of the Communist Party outside of the USSR. The Department of State does not vouch for the authenticity of the document and in releasing it intends the document to speak for itself."

[It should be added that the speech was never denied by the Soviet Government.]
[7] From N. S. Khrushchev speech on Stalin.

with many aspects of Stalin's rule. But if we are to believe Khrushchev's description as a true measure of the man (his constant references to Stalin's "mania," "nervousness," "capriciousness," "irritability," and "suspiciousness") we realize that in the crucial period of modern European history one great power was led by a man whose mind can be described at least as highly unbalanced.

When Stalin's successor came to the United States, the *New York Herald Tribune* (Sept. 24, 1959) published an estimate of Khrushchev's mind on the basis of guesses made by four psychiatrists. All warned that they were not making a psychiatric diagnosis. But they saw, as the paper noted, "no mental derangement in that often-smiling, sometimes-scowling face."

One of the psychiatrists, Dr. Mortimer Ostow, listed the personality traits he had detected: personal warmth, alertness, vigor, quickness, self-confidence, pride, bluntness, sensitivity to criticism, eagerness to impress, use of temper to intimidate, failure to respond to arguments of reason, volatility, self-righteousness, and a tendency to be moralistic by petty criteria and to see himself, his government, and the Russian people as one. "Such a person will respond positively to affection and admiration and with vigorous aggression to criticism and hostility. He will respect those more powerful than he, but only grudgingly and with bad humor." Another psychiatrist, Dr. Brussel, classified the Prime Minister as a pyknic (a person with roundness of contour and face). A pyknic, Dr. Brussel said, is blunt, outgoing, capable of great warmth and great hate and responding instantly to environmental stimuli with action or words.

The psychiatrists' conclusion seemed to be that a man with these traits, contradictory as they are, can be a great and effective leader.

Similar observations could be made about other dictators—whose motives and aims lay buried deep in the unfathomable depth of their souls. Their latent drives may not be known to the masses, the outside world, close collaborators, and, in the case of maniacs, not even to themselves. If peace and order among nations depend on the balance of power and/or correct estimate of intentions, sickness of mind or body may upset the most careful and rational calculations.

Two weeks before the beginning of World War II, Italy's Minister of Foreign Affairs Galleazzo Ciano (1936-1943), made the following entry in his diary.[8] "The decision to fight is implacable. [Von Ribbentrop] rejects any solution which might give satisfaction to Germany and avoid the struggle. I am certain that even if the Germans were given more than they ask for, they would attack just the same, because they are possessed by the demon of destruction. . . . Hitler is very cordial, but he, too, is impassive and implacable in his decision. He speaks in the large drawing room of his house, standing in front of a table on which some maps are spread out. . . . He speaks with a great deal of calm and becomes excited only when he advises us to give Yugoslavia that *coup de grâce* as soon as possible. . . . He has decided to strike and strike he will. All our arguments will not in the least avail to stop him.

[8] *The Ciano Diaries, 1939-1943,* (Garden City, N. Y.: Doubleday & Co., Inc., 1946), pp. 119, 184.

He continues to repeat that he will localize the conflict with Poland, but his affirmation that the great war must be fought while he and the *Duce* are still young, leads me to believe once more that he is acting in bad faith."

After the war had broken out, Ciano described the behavior of Mussolini, his father-in-law, as follows: "A long conference with Bocchini [head of the Fascist secret police]. He complained about the restlessness of the *Duce,* which has already been noticed by all the collaborators, and he even went so far as to say that the *Duce* should take an intensive anti-syphilitic cure, because Bocchini claims that the psychic condition of Mussolini is due to a recurrence of this old illness.

"It surprised and annoyed me very much that Bocchini should have said this, although I myself recognize the fact that Mussolini's contradictory behavior is truly upsetting to anyone who works with him."

A reader of memoirs of any statesman is surprised at the number of seemingly unimportant, superficial, and often accidental elements which influence the final decision of a policy-maker. The remark which is so often heard in cocktail lounges, "If I were Nehru, Eisenhower, Hitler, Mao, or Khrushchev," illustrates the relativity of all evaluations. What appears as a dominant factor to some, may be viewed as a minor irritant by others. A sleepless night, a dispute with one's wife, a sentimental thought about one's youth, a superficial observation of the faces in the crowd, all may enter the final decision-making process.

When in June 1940, the Fascist government of Italy was about to invade France from the south, the original date of Italy's entry into World War II had to be postponed from June 5 to June 11. In Ciano's Diary (June 3) we read the following explanation: "Mussolini says that the King, too, finds the date of the 11th satisfactory perhaps because of the slight delay that will be granted to us, because it is his birthday, and because as a raw recruit he was given the number 1,111. Now that the sword is about to be unsheathed, the King, like all members of the House of Savoy, is preparing to be a soldier, and only a soldier." [9]

Here, an attitude worthy of a superstitious gypsy seemed to affect the circumstances which had led Italy into war.

Hitler's interpreter, Dr. Paul Schmidt (Topic 15), relates in his memoirs the cause of Hitler's change of tone during the Munich crisis in 1938. First he exclaimed: "War next week." Later he wrote a conciliatory letter to Chamberlain. This switch was perhaps due to "a significant sight he had seen late that afternoon. In dull autumn weather a motorized division passed along the Wilhelmstrasse. The completely apathetic and melancholy behavior of the Berlin populace, which Hitler observed from a window of the Chancellory, made a deep impression on him. I was told at the time by his adjutants that he found the scene most disillusioning." [10]

Various checks and balances usually prevent decision-makers in democracies from being too easily swayed in one direction or another on the spur of the moment. Yet even here, one must take into account the influence

[9] *Ibid.,* p. 260.
[10] Dr. Paul Schmidt, *Hitler's Interpreter* (New York: Macmillan Co., 1951).

of tiredness or ill-health on policy (Roosevelt at Yalta in 1945 or John Foster Dulles at the beginning of the Berlin crisis in 1958); irrational suspicion of leaders and masses; dedication to a traditional idea which has become outdated (adherence to the concept of isolationism in the era of missiles); the pressure of groups or personal friends.

In his *Memoirs*,[11] Harry S. Truman describes how—as President of the United States—he decided to avoid any contact with the advocates of the Zionist cause in the middle of the Palestinian crisis (1947-1948). His decision was changed by one single visit of a personal friend:

> The Jewish pressure on the White House did not diminish in the days following the partition vote in the U.N. Individuals and groups asked me, usually in rather quarrelsome and emotional ways, to stop the Arabs, to keep the British from supporting the Arabs, to furnish American soldiers, to do this, that, and the other. I think I can say that I kept my faith in the rightness of my policy in spite of some of the Jews. When I say "the Jews," I mean, of course, the extreme Zionists. I know that most Americans of Jewish faith, while they hoped for the restoration of Jewish homeland, are and always have been Americans first and foremost.
>
> As the pressure mounted, I found it necessary to give instructions that I did not want to be approached by any more spokesmen for the extreme Zionist cause. I was even so disturbed that I put off seeing Dr. Chaim Weizmann, who had returned to the United States and had asked for an interview with me. My old friend, Eddie Jacobson, called on me at the White House and urged me to receive Dr. Weizmann at the earliest possible moment. Eddie, who had been with me through the hard days of World War I, had never been a Zionist. In all my years in Washington he had never asked me for anything for himself. He was of the Jewish faith and was deeply moved by the sufferings of the Jewish people abroad. He had spoken to me on occasion, both before and after I became President, about some specific hardship cases that he happened to know about, but he did this rarely. On March 13 he called at the White House.
>
> I was always glad to see him. Not only had we shared so much in the past, but I have always had the warmest feelings toward him. It would be hard to find a truer friend. Eddie said that he wanted to talk about Palestine. I told him that I would rather he did not and that I wanted to let the matter run its course in the United Nations.
>
> I do not believe that in all our thirty years of friendship a sharp word had ever passed between Eddie and me, and I was sorry that Eddie had brought up the subject.
>
> Eddie was becoming self-conscious, but he kept on talking. He asked me to bear in mind that some of the pro-Zionists who had approached me were only individuals and did not speak for any responsible leadership.
>
> I told him that I respected Dr. Weizmann, but if I saw him, it would only result in more wrong interpretations.
>
> Eddie waved toward a small replica of an Andrew Jackson statue that was in my office.
>
> "He's been your hero all your life, hasn't he?" he said. "You have

[11] Harry S. Truman, *Years of Trial and Hope, 1946-1952, Memoirs,* (Garden City, N. Y.: Doubleday & Co., Inc., 1956), pp. 162-166. Copyright 1956 Time Inc.

probably read every book there is on Andrew Jackson. I remember when we had the store that you were always reading books and pamphlets, and a lot of them were about Jackson. You put this statue in front of the Jackson County Courthouse in Kansas City when you built it."

I did not know what he was leading up to, but he went on.

"I have never met the man who has been my hero all my life," he continued. "But I have studied his past as you have studied Jackson's. He is the greatest Jew alive, perhaps the greatest Jew who ever lived. You yourself have told me that he is a great statesman and a fine gentleman. I am talking about Dr. Chaim Weizmann. He is an old man and a very sick man. He has traveled thousands of miles to see you, and now you are putting off seeing him. That isn't like you."

When Eddie left I gave instructions to have Dr. Weizmann come to the White House as soon as it could be arranged.

Many other examples could be quoted. They all would confirm what Harold Nicolson once wrote, discussing the Congress of Vienna of 1815: "Nobody who has not watched 'policy' expressing itself in day-to-day action can realize how seldom is the course of events determined by deliberately planned purpose."

It does not mean that, in the conduct of foreign policy, no predictions are possible. Geographic position, history, the endurance and patience of the people, the power of the nation itself set certain predictable limits to the decision making process on the part of even an unbalanced dictator; the more so in the case of the leaders who either think rationally or are checked and controlled. Yet the influence of the unpredictable must never be excluded. Men in singular or plural are mixtures of rational and irrational elements, common sense and passion, patience and impatience, and firmness and flabbiness. It is sometimes said that the danger to peace in the pre-democratic era lay in the conspiratorial gambles of European courts. The danger to peace in our modern era lies in the mistaken estimates of statesmen and in erroneous preconceptions of the masses. Liberal democracies often project their optimism concerning human nature on the international scene, while dictators—pessimists with regard to men—may err by over-suspicion.

This leads us to the final point: the accuracy of our evaluation of another nation's intentions suffers by our tendency to project our own fears, ambitions, hopes, or predilections into our estimates. To assess another nation's power and direction is often as difficult as to measure the speed of one jet plane while riding in another.

4. *Known Factors and their Uncertain Meaning.* Plans and concepts defy detection while they lie deep in human minds. Is it any easier to analyze them when they come to the surface in the form of actions and systems?

According to some observers, (a) the nature of the internal political structure; (b) the economic system; or (c) actions—instead of words which may have a double meaning—may give us a key to the kind of foreign policy which a nation may follow. Others, on the contrary, maintain that these factors are not illuminating at all.

This controversy should now be examined.

(a) *Internal political structure* is sometimes said to determine the nature of foreign policy. Absolute monarchies and dictatorships are described as aggressive. Democracies, in which the public determines policies, are usually considered peaceful.

This seemed to be also the opinion of Woodrow Wilson, who argued:

> Cunningly contrived plans of deception or aggression . . . can be worked out and kept from the light only within the privacy of courts or behind the carefully guarded confidences of a narrow and privileged class. They are happily impossible where public opinion commands and insists upon full information concerning all the nation's affairs. A steadfast concept for peace can never be maintained except by a partnership of democratic nations. No autocratic government could be trusted to keep faith within it or observe its covenants.[12]

On the other hand, the eighteenth century observer of the political scene, Alexander Hamilton, seemed to fear the passion of the masses as much as that of the kings:

> The causes of hostility among nations are innumerable. There are some which have a general and almost constant operation upon the collective bodies of society. Of this description are the love of power, or the desire of pre-eminence and dominion—the jealousy of power, or the desire of equality and safety. There are others which had a more circumscribed, though an equally operative influence, within their spheres; such are the rivalships and competition of commerce between commercial nations. And there are others, not less numerous than either of the former, which take their origin entirely in private passions; in the attachments, enmities, interests, hopes, and fears, of leading individuals in the communities of which they are members. . . . There have been, if I may so express it, almost as many popular as royal wars.
>
> Have republics in practice been less addicted to war than monarchies? Are not the former administered by men as well as the latter? Are there not aversions, predilections, rivalships, and desires of unjust acquisition, that affect nations as well as kings? Are not popular assemblies frequently subject to the impulses of rage, resentment, jealousy, avarice, and of other irregular and violent propensities? Is it not well known, that their determinations are often governed by a few individuals in whom they place confidence, and that they are of course liable to be tinctured by the passions and view of those individuals? . . . Is not the love of wealth as domineering and enterprising a passion as that of power or glory?[13]

The general nature of an internal political structure does not seem to offer a reliable basis for a final estimate of a nation's foreign policy. Many other factors which have been already discussed (the personal qualities or idiosyncrasies of the elite, ideology, the link between the masses and the leadership) have to be added to our calculations.

At this point it is necessary to add that changes which occur within a given system, as a result of elections, revolutions, or the death of a statesman,

---

[12] Congress, April 2, 1917. Declaration of war against Germany.
[13] Alexander Hamilton, *The Federalist,* No. VI.

may offer a key to a better understanding of that nation's probable foreign policy. Internal opposition to the government often voices its criticism of current policy. Such criticism may indicate future policy trends, especially if the opposition subsequently takes over governmental duties.

In 1952, the Soviet leaders might have estimated that the Republican criticism of the Democratic Party in the United States, Eisenhower's promise to end the Korean War, and other aspects of the electoral fight would mean a substantial departure from the previous Truman era. That era had been marked by such energetic containment measures as aid to Greece and Turkey (1947), the Marshall Plan (1947), NATO (1949), and the U.S. intervention in Korea (1950).

Similarly, Khrushchev's criticism of the previous Stalin era always has been examined with the hope of probable changes in Soviet foreign policy.

Revolutionary changes which publicly and conspicuously negate the past seem to be particularly indicative of impending total change: e.g., the end of monarchy in Russia and its succession by the Bolsheviki in 1917; or the end of the German Weimar republic and its replacement by Hitler's Nazi Reich.

Yet, we often discover that the alterations of foreign policy after both revolutionary and evolutionary changes within nations are less notable than expected. Following the defeat of Churchill's party after World War II, the victorious Labour Party of England found itself confronted with the same problems of an insular and impoverished United Kingdom. The reaction was bound to be similar, even if there were noticeable nuances. The parliamentary or revolutionary opposition to the party in power is also bound to discover that responsibility for action is a much heavier burden than criticism without responsibility for results.

After 1952, the Soviet leaders often voiced disappointment that Eisenhower's foreign policy was not very different from that of his criticized predecessor, Harry S. Truman. Similarly, the United States discovered that Khrushchev is not only heir to Stalin's mantle but also to some of the pre-Bolshevik Russian aspirations.

(b) *The economic system* is, according to some observers, another of the determinants of national policies. According to others, it is the only one.

Economic motives are always present in political decisions. The problem is whether they solely determine them or only co-determine them. Nations pursuing a policy of *status quo* may be guided by their desire to preserve their markets, profits, investments, and standard of living. Nations that challenge a *status quo* may do so because they wish to increase their profits, expand their markets, open up new opportunities for investments, or improve their standard of living. Or, on the contrary, their challenge of the *status quo* may be the result of their dissatisfaction with the fact that they are being economically exploited. Internal changes within the economic structure may also lead to changes in foreign policies.

But what changes? Here again, known factors may have unpredictable results because so many other elements enter the picture. In one country economic depression may initiate a program of withdrawal and isolationism; in another, on the contrary, economic difficulties at home may lead to adventures abroad. Mussolini tried to divert the attention of the people from domestic economic ills to the world of dreams about a new Roman Empire. In the 1950's, President Sukarno of Indonesia was accused of instituting his anti-Dutch campaigns and his demand for annexation of Irian (Western New Guinea) to compensate for his incapacity to solve internal economic and social problems.

Similarly, prosperity may lead to contradictory conclusions in the field of foreign policy: a nation may attempt a bolder course of action because it is prosperous enough to afford it; or it may withdraw into its own shell so as not to threaten its prosperity by an adventure.

Marxian Socialists in general, and Communists in particular, consider aggression and imperialism the inevitable results of Capitalist economy. International peace, on the other hand, is the necessary result of Socialist economy, they believe.

In the eighteenth century, Alexander Hamilton argued that competition of commerce between commercial nations is only one of the reasons for wars. Other factors are "love of power, the desire of pre-eminence and dominion, or the desire of equality or safety." Communism considers the Capitalist system as the only source of all evil. (Lenin's theory on imperialism, as the last stage of capitalism; Khrushchev's redefinition of the inevitability of war under capitalism; and Raymond Aron's refutation are reproduced in Topic 12.)

In contrast to the assertion that politics is the chained prisoner of the economic structure, postwar developments within the Communist bloc suggest that such "capitalistic" characteristics as competition for power, struggle for prestige, suspicion and enmity appear also in relations between Communist states. Questions like "Will China or Yugoslavia be industrialized first?" or "Will Bulgaria be the raw material base for the more advanced comrade republics of East Germany and Czechoslovakia?" are inevitable in the collectivist world, as is suggested by John H. Herz in his study of political realism and political idealism: [14]

> There is no reason to assume that even in a system of socialist commonwealths all causes for friction among the various units would suddenly disappear. To believe, as collectivists usually do, that a feeling of common brotherhood between the masses of the various socialist countries would prevent any such friction from developing into major conflicts or wars, is as unwarranted an assumption as was the belief, in 1914, in the readiness and ability of the Second International to prevent the outbreak of the World War. If it be said that at that time the proletariat had not yet come into power in the respective countries, while in the assumed case of socialist commonwealths it would be the ruling and, therefore, policy-determining group, one might retort that this very fact, in itself, would tend to aggravate the feeling of responsibility for the survival and the security of one's "own" proletarian unit, so that the security dilemma would play its role to an even

[14] John H. Herz, *Political Realism and Political Idealism* (Chicago: University of Chicago Press, 1951), pp. 119-120. Reprinted by permission of The University of Chicago Press; copyright © 1951 by The University of Chicago.

higher degree. For there would still be conflicts of interests which would pit one unit against another. . . . Competition for riches such as raw materials, as a basis for planning and calculation in each unit, can be presumed to become the more violent, the more one unit, in a system of complete trade regulation, is able to shut out another unit from any access to its sphere. Economic rivalries over the "price" to be paid by a unit that has no access to some raw material to a unit that does possess it might easily turn into political conflicts over possession of territories with all their power-political and military implications. To assume that a solution in the spirit of "international" consciousness would then prevail over "nationalistic" solutions would be a rash conclusion. It would be realistic only if there were a complete change in individual and group attitudes concerning international relations.

(c) *Acts of foreign policy.* Just as facts of national internal policy and economy may have contradictory meaning, so may concrete acts in the field of foreign policy.

Many American statements concerning relations with the Soviet Union stress that Soviet words and pledges are not enough. Only deeds can convince the United States about the sincerity of a change in the Soviet attitude. Can they?

Acts of any foreign policy may be variously interpreted. They may be an indication of a real or impending change; or a means to gain time; or only a tactical maneuver: one step backward in preparation for two steps forward.

When a nation withdraws from some advanced position, is it a sign of peacefulness or a measure similar to those which military commanders undertake in order to shorten their lines and to prepare a more concentrated assault later on? If a nation announces unilateral disarmament and actually takes the first steps to implement it, is it proof of peaceful intentions? Or is it a clever move to induce the adversary to disarmament moves which, given the different nature of the rival's government and economy, would be more difficult to rescind in the future?

When in 1955 Soviet Russia agreed to withdraw its troops from Austria,[15] these were no words. It was an act for everybody to see and inspect. Austria became a neutral state, a buffer between NATO and the Communist zone in Europe. For the first time since 1945 the Soviet military line voluntarily receded eastward. But was the meaning clear?

Optimists interpreted it as clear proof of a profound change of policy, initiated by post-Stalin Russia. One good act would be followed by others.

Pessimists suggested that the Soviet withdrawal from Austria strangely coincided with a global Communist courtship addressed to uncommitted or neutral nations. It could be worth while to permit Vienna to embrace the West culturally if—in exchange—the Middle East and South East Asia would give a more sympathetic reception to Soviet policies.

Others could read into the Soviet move the first of Soviet pressures to force the military power of the United States out of Europe: first from Berlin,

---

[15] The four occupying powers, Russia, the United States, England, and France, signed the Austrian State Treaty on May 15, 1955, ten years after the end of World War II.

second from West Germany (in combination with so-called disengagement), and third from continental Europe. Austria could be the first step.

Which of these interpretations of one single Soviet act was correct? The future may tell. But will it? Whatever the real objectives and intentions of the U.S.S.R. were in 1955, they might have undergone profound change under the weight of counter-policies.

5. *Policy and Counter-Policy.* The psychological, political, economic, and power factors have been examined so far in isolation from counter-power and counter-policies. But the last and probably the most important problem in any evaluation of other nations' policies is the fact that their direction is the result of forces and influences as much within the nation's boundaries as outside them. No nation determines its foreign policy in the abstract. Policies are bound to change under the impact of counter-policies. At the beginning of this chapter we defined the two major tasks of any foreign policy: to determine one's own objectives, and those of other nations. Now we want to stress the interrelation of both tasks. We determine our own objectives in the light and under the pressure of other nations' objectives.

Policy aims may change when they encounter opposition or when they fail to meet it. A policy which has originally aimed at only some minor change within the *status quo* may transform itself into a policy which challenges the whole order of things. It may develop that a demand for a minor change was unjustly frustrated; or, on the other hand, the demand may have been so easily satisfied that it suggests unpreparedness or cowardice on the part of rivals and competitors.

An aggressive nation may re-evaluate its policy aims when it is confronted with a situation of strength. It may then adopt a policy of wait-and-see, a temporary coexistence which, if it lasts for a considerable length of time, may be regarded for all practical purposes as a really peaceful one. (The problem of such a balance is discussed under the heading of "Peaceful Coexistence" in Topics 13 and 14.)

The opportunity of expanding painlessly may corrupt and seduce a relatively peaceful nation; the impossibility of expanding may counsel prudence and peace to an otherwise adventurous and aggressive leadership.

Aims, methods, and results of foreign policy are determined by the foresight or stupidity, alertness or complacency, energy or weakness of not only one's own nation and leaders but also those who compose and lead our rivals.

This makes a definite evaluation of foreign policy results a matter of controversy, even after events have occurred and been recorded and analyzed.

One classical example may be noted:

Opposing revolutionary France at the end of the eighteenth century, William Pitt was not very successful at the beginning. Finally, however, his rival and the heir to the French revolution, Napoleon, was defeated. Was the original premise of William Pitt correct—or was it made subsequently correct by grave errors on the part of Napoleon? Writing more than half a century later, the first Earl Russell, British Prime Minister and Foreign Secretary, expressed the view that the coalition wars against Napoleon had been wrong and unsuccessful because Napoleon's rivals used the war against France in order to expand. "The military ruler of France, however, in his turn, abused his strength. . . . It seemed to be his object to extinguish the life of nations, and leave standing only one mighty despotism . . . The war, then, at length became successful, not because Mr. Pitt had been endowed with wisdom and foresight in 1793, but because Napoleon had made the empire of 1804 incompatible with the independence of the nations of Europe . . ." [16]

Instruments of Detection and Evaluation

The major instruments of the evaluating process usually are: the foreign office of a nation and its numerous branches abroad (embassies, etc.); an intelligence agency which engages in research and operations of a semi-secret, secret, or, occasionally, cloak-and-dagger type; military intelligence which tries to pierce the enemy's military and technical secrets; and different research institutes or *ad hoc* research projects which concentrate on specific countries or specific problems.

In the case of the United States the agencies which make professional estimates of other nations' power and policies and suggest appropriate measures are:

1. The National Security Council, which, under the chairmanship of the President, evaluates and determines major policies concerning the security of the United States;

2. The U.S. Department of State and the U.S. embassies, legations, missions and consulates in all parts of the world;

3. The Central Intelligence Agency and its different research branches, usually operating under inconspicuous cover names;

4. The military, naval and air intelligence, and military, naval and air attachés at U.S. embassies abroad;

5. Various counter-intelligence agencies, including a portion of the activities of the F.B.I. The tasks and intensity of enemy intelligence, as detected by counter-intelligence, are also an indication of other nations' intentions.

Summary

Evaluating other nations' power and intentions in the light of one's own capacity and goals is the fundamental task of foreign policy. It is not an occasional but a continuous process. It reflects the endless chain of developments within and among nations.

The diplomatic service, intelligence agents, and researchers prepare pertinent data on other nations' affairs for evaluation and decisions to be made by policy-makers.

[16] Earl Russell, *The Life and Times of Charles James Fox* (London: Richard Bentley, 1886), Vol. II, p. 380. Quoted by Hans J. Morgenthau and Kenneth W. Thompson in *Principles and Problems of International Politics* (New York: Alfred A. Knopf, 1950), p. 346-347.

The power of a nation opens possibilities and sets limits to policy aims. Wrong calculation may induce nations to take actions beyond or below their physical possibilities.

While we may be reasonably certain that, generally speaking, nations use their power in order to pursue their own interests rather than those of others, the national interest under given circumstances is unclear and subject to change. So is action that might be taken to protect the national interest.

Whatever their ultimate objectives may be, nations usually aim at either of two fundamental intermediary objectives: to conserve the *status quo,* or to change it.

A nation which tries to conserve the situation as is, does so because, on the whole, the situation satisfies that nation. Such a satisfactory situation for the one nation may be highly unsatisfactory to others. A *status quo* nation may, for instance, desire to preserve its colonial domination.

A nation which tries either to build an empire or to dissolve one pursues a policy of challenge to the *status quo.*

The yardstick of a correct foreign policy is ability to distinguish between different ultimate or intermediary objectives and find appropriate responses to them.

Five major difficulties complicate the task of evaluation of other nations' objectives:

1. Nations use attractive terms to explain or conceal their unattractive intentions.

2. The role of national ideology in foreign policy-making is unclear. Often national leaders cynically use ideology to further their non-ideological aims and interests. Sometimes leaders adhere to their creed and try to so base their policies and actions. At other times leaders betray what they believe in because the concrete situation does not allow them to realize their ideological goals.

3. Motives for political action lie deep in the hearts and minds of policy-makers. Human minds often prove impenetrable.

4. In contrast to the depth of human minds, ideological disguise of policies and the deceptive nature of words, observable acts appear as much more reliable evidence of policies and intentions. Experience, however, shows that often not only words but also acts may have a double meaning.

5. Policy is not only the result of one's own intentions and power but also that of counter-power and counter-policies. Whatever the original aims are, they may either contract under the weight of counterpressure or expand because of the lack of it.

TOPIC II

The Impenetrable Blank of the Future

The process of detecting and evaluating one's own and other nations' power is characterized by many uncertainties and few certainties.

One of the certainties is that governments are guided by their nations' interests, real or fancied, rather than by those of other nations. Nations, like individuals, are primarily interested in preserving their life, well-being and identity against a possible threat. This is the hard core of their national interest.

Uncertainties are numerous and fundamental. What does the national interest mean in terms of immediate objectives and methods of achieving them? What is its relation to policies for important problems and regions of the world? The national interest may be—or seem to be—compatible with the interests of other nations. Or it may be—or seem to be—in conflict with them.

"The policy-maker works in an uneasy world of prediction and probability," noted Robert R. Bowie,[1] Director of the U.S. Department of State Policy Planning Staff (1953-1957). His predecessor, George F. Kennan, wrote: "I can testify from personal experience that not only can one never know when one takes a far-reaching decision in foreign policy, precisely what the consequences are going to be, but almost never do these consequences fully coincide with what one intended or expected."[2]

This humble view of the accuracy in estimating other nations' intentions and correctly reacting to them reflects the simple fact that in international politics policy-makers confront situations largely shaped by factors beyond their direct control. Thus, for instance, nations which are beyond direct control by the United States constitute sixteen-seventeenths of mankind. This lack of direct control is one of the most significant characteristics of foreign policy.

►WHAT IS THE NATIONAL INTEREST?

HANS J. MORGENTHAU

Should a national government pursue only such aims and adopt such courses of action as are consonant with the universal rules of morality, however

---

[1] Robert R. Bowie, "Analysis of Our Policy Machine," *New York Times,* March 9, 1958.
[2] George F. Kennan, "Foreign Policy and Christian Conscience," *The Atlantic,* May, 1959.

From *Dilemmas of Politics* (Chicago: University of Chicago Press, 1958), pp. 58-86. Reprinted by permission of The University of Chicago Press; copyright © 1958 by The University of Chicago.

abstract they may be? Or should the preservation of a nation's identity be raised above all other considerations?

These are the problems with which the following essay will deal. Its author is Hans J. Morgenthau, Professor of Political Science at the University of Chicago and Director of its Center for the Study of American Foreign and Military Policy. Among his major books in the field of international politics are: Scientific Man vs Power Politics, Politics Among Nations, *and* Dilemmas of Politics.

. . . The history of modern political thought is the story of a contest between two schools which differ fundamentally in their conception of the nature of man, society, and politics. One believes that a rational and moral political order, derived from universally valid abstract principles, can be achieved here and now. It assumes the essential goodness and infinite malleability of human nature and attributes the failure of the social order to measure up to the rational standards to lack of knowledge and understanding, obsolescent social institutions, or the depravity of certain isolated individuals or groups. It trusts in education, reform, and the sporadic use of force to remedy these deficiencies.

The other school believes that the world, imperfect as it is from the rational point of view, is the result of forces which are inherent in human nature. To improve the world one must work with those forces, not against them. This being inherently a world of opposing interests and of conflict among them, moral principles can never be fully realized, but at best approximated through the ever temporary balancing of interests and the ever precarious settlement of conflicts. This school, then, sees in a system of checks and balances a universal principle for all pluralist societies. It appeals to historic precedent rather than to abstract principles, and aims at achievement of the lesser evil rather than of the absolute good. . . .

The character of a foreign policy can be ascertained only through the examination of the political acts performed and of the foreseeable consequences of these acts. Thus we can find out what statesmen have actually done, and from the foreseeable consequences of their acts we can surmise what their objectives might have been. Yet examination of the facts is not enough. To give meaning to the factual raw material of history, we must approach historical reality with a kind of rational outline, a map which suggests to us the possible meanings of history. In other words, we put ourselves in the position of a statesman who must meet a certain problem of foreign policy under certain circumstances and ask ourselves, what are the rational alternatives from which a statesman may choose who must meet this problem under these circumstances, presuming always that he acts in a rational manner, and which of these rational alternatives was this particular statesman, acting under these circumstances, likely to choose? It is the testing of this rational hypothesis against the actual facts and their consequences which gives meaning to the facts of history and makes the scientific writing of political history possible.

In the process of writing the history of foreign policy the interpretations by statesmen of their own acts, especially if they are made for public consumption, must needs have a strictly subsidiary place. The public self-interpretation by actors on the political scene is itself, of course, a political act which seeks to present a certain policy to its presumed supporters in terms of their moral and political folklore and to those against which it is directed in terms which intend to embarrass and deceive. Such declarations may indeed shed light upon the character and objectives of the policy pursued if they are considered in conjunction with, and in subordination to, rational hypotheses, actions, and likely consequences. Yet it is quite a different matter to interpret the American tradition of foreign policy in the light of a collection of official statements which, like most such statements, present humanitarian and pacifist justifications for the policies pursued. If anybody should be bold enough to write a history of world politics with so uncritical a method he would easily and well-nigh inevitably be driven to the conclusion that from Timur to Hitler and Stalin the foreign policies of all nations were inspired by the ideals of humanitarianism and pacifism. The absurdity of the result is commensurate with the defects of the method. . . .

One of the great experiences of our time which have impressed themselves upon the American mind is the emergence of the United States as a nation among other nations, exposed to the same opportunities, temptations, risks, and liabilities to which other nations have been traditionally exposed. This experience becomes the more shocking if it is compared with the expectation with which we fought the Second World War. We expected from that war a reaffirmaton of the secure, detached, and independent position in world affairs which we had inherited from the Founding Fathers and which we had been successful in preserving at least to the First World War. By avoiding what we thought had been Wilson's mistakes, we expected to emerge from that war if not more independent, certainly more secure than we were when we entered it. In fact, probably not even in the early days of the Republic were we more exposed to danger from abroad than we are today, and never had we less freedom of action in taking care of our interests than we have today.

It is naturally shocking to recognize that a happy chapter in the history of the nation and in one's own way of life has come to an end. There are those who reconcile themselves to the inevitable, albeit with sorrow rather than with glee, and try to apply the lessons of the past to the tasks at hand. There are others who try to escape from a disappointing and threatening reality into the realm of fantasy. Three such escapist fantasies have arisen in our midst in response to the challenge of American world leadership and power: the fantasy of needless American participation in war, the fantasy of American treason, and the fantasy of American innocence.

The first of these fantasies presumes that the present predicament is a result not of necessity but of folly, the folly of American statesmen who needlessly intervened in two world wars. The second of these fantasies attributes the present predicament to treason in high places whereby the fruits of victory were handed to the enemy. The third of these fantasies denies that the predicament is real and prefers to think of it as an intellectual fraud perpetrated upon the American people. To support this fictional denial of the actualities of the present, it draws upon a fictional account of the past. The United States does not need to bear at present the intellectual, moral, and political burdens which go with involvement in power politics and the maintenance of the balance of power; for it has never borne them in the past, never having been thus involved.

We have said that to present the American tradition in foreign policy as having been free from concern with power politics and the balance of power is not warranted by the facts of American history. Yet it might still be argued, and it is actually being argued, that, regardless of the evidence of history, the American people will not be reconciled to power politics and the balance of power and will support only policies based upon abstract moral principles. While in the past the United States might have pursued balance-of-power policies and while it might be a good thing if it did do so again, the American people will not stand for it. Here the emotional appeal to patriotic piety is joined by calculations of political expediency. Yet the case for misrepresenting American history has nothing to gain from either.

There is a strong tendency in all historiography to glorify the national past, and in popular presentations that tendency takes on the aspects of the jingoist whitewash. Even so penetrating a mind as John Stuart Mill's could deliver itself of an essay in which he proved, no doubt to the satisfaction of many of his English readers but certainly of few others, that Great Britain had never interfered in the affairs of European nations and had interfered in those of the Indian states only for their own good. Yet it is the measure of a nation's maturity to be able to recognize its past for what it actually is. Why should we not admit that American foreign policy has been generally hard-headed and practical and at times ruthless? Why should we deny Jefferson's cunning, say, in the Puget Sound affair, the cruelty with which the Indians were treated, and the faithlessness with which the treaties with the Indians were cast aside? We know that this is the way all nations are when their interests are at stake—so cruel, so faithless, so cunning. We know that the United States has refrained from seeking dominions beyond the seas not because it is more virtuous than other nations but because it had the better part of a continent to colonize. . . .

American history shows in abundance, that responsible statesmen can guide [the citizen] by awakening his latent understanding of the national interest.

Yet what is the national interest? How can we define it and give it the content which will make it a guide both for understanding and for action? . . .

It has been frequently argued against the realist conception of foreign policy that its key concept, the national interest, does not provide an acceptable standard for either thought or action. This argument is in the main based upon two grounds: the elusiveness of the concept and its susceptibility to interpretations, such as limitless imperialism and narrow nationalism, which are not in keeping with the American tradition in foreign policy. The argument has substance as far as it goes, but it does not invalidate the usefulness of the concept.

The concept of the national interest is similar in two respects to the "great generalities" of the Constitution, such as the general welfare and due process. It contains a residual meaning which is inherent in the concept itself, but beyond these minimum requirements its content can run the whole gamut of meanings that are logically compatible with it. That content is determined by the political traditions and the total cultural context within which a nation formulates its foreign policy. The concept of the national interest, then, contains two elements, one that is logically required and in that sense necessary, and one that is variable and determined by circumstances. The former is, then, of necessity relatively permanent while the latter will vary with circumstances.

The relative permanency of what one might call the hard core of the national interest stems from three factors: the nature of the interests to be protected, the political environment within which the interests operate, and the rational necessities which limit the choice of ends and means by all actors on the stage of foreign policy. Any foreign policy that operates under the standard of the national interest must obviously have some reference to the physical, political, and cultural entity which we call a nation. In a world where a number of sovereign nations compete with and oppose each other for power, the foreign policies of all nations must necessarily refer to their survival as their minimum requirement. Thus all nations do what they cannot help but do: protect their physical, political, and cultural identity against encroachments by other nations.

The nature of the threat to which the national interest is exposed remains equally constant over long periods of history. Throughout the centuries the main threat to Great Britain has come from the hegemonic aspirations of one or the other of the European nations. Russia has traditionally been threatened by a great power having access to the plains of eastern Europe. France and Germany, regardless of their changing political forms, have threatened each other throughout the ages.

The relative permanency of interest and threat is surpassed by the virtual immutability of the configurations through which the reason of man transforms the abstract concept of the national interest into foreign policy. Faced with the necessity to protect the hard core of the national interest, that is, to preserve the identity of the nation, all governments have resorted throughout history to certain basic policies, such as competitive armaments, the balance of power, alliances, and subversion, intended to make of the abstract concept of the national interest a viable political reality. Governments might have been wise or unwise in their choice of policies, successful or unsuccessful in their execution; they could not have escaped the rational necessity of selecting one of a limited number of avenues through which to bring the power of their nation to bear upon the power of other nations on behalf of the national interest.

The possibility both to reconstruct past foreign policies through the writing of history and to understand the contemporary foreign policies of one's own and other nations derives from this rational character of the national interest. If one could not assume that this rationality is identical throughout history and ubiquitous on the contemporary scene, however diminished and distorted by the irrationality of men and nations, one would be lost in a maze of unconnected data, to be explained perhaps in terms of psychology and sociology but not in terms conducive to the understanding of foreign policy. It is this assumption of the universality of the national interest in time and space which enables us to understand the foreign policies of Demosthenes and Caesar, of Kautilya and Henry VIII, of the statesmen of contemporary Russia and China. Regardless of all the differences in personality, social environment, convictions, and preferences, their thinking was predetermined and their actions could take place only within a narrow range, when they were faced with the task of protecting and promoting the rational core of the national interest. By thinking as they must have thought we can understand their thoughts, and by putting their thoughts into the context of their personalities and social environment we can understand their actions as well.

It has been suggested that this reasoning erects the national state into the last word in politics and the national interest into an absolute standard for political action. This, however, is not quite the case. The idea of interest is indeed of the essence of politics and, as such, unaffected by the circumstances of time and place. Thucydides' statement, born of the experiences of ancient Greece, that "identity of interest is the surest of bonds whether between states or individuals" was taken up in the nineteenth century by Lord Salisbury's remark that "the only bond of union that endures" among nations is "the absence of all clashing interests." The perennial issue between the realist and utopian schools of thought over the nature of politics, to which we have referred before, might well be formulated in terms of concrete interests versus abstract principles. Yet while the concern of politics with interest is perennial, the connection between interest and the national state is a product of history.

The national state itself is obviously a product of history and as such is destined to yield in time to different modes of political organization. As long as the world is politically organized into nations, the national interest is indeed the last word in international politics. When the national state has been replaced by another mode of organization, foreign policy must then protect the interest in survival of that new organization. For the benefit of those who insist upon discarding the national state and constructing supranational organizations by constitutional fiat, it must be pointed out that these new organizational forms will either come into being through conquest or else through consent based upon the mutual recognition of the national interests of the nations concerned; for no nation will forego its freedom of action if it has no reason to expect proportionate benefits in compensation for that loss. This is true of treaties concerning commerce or fisheries as it is true of the great compacts, such as the European Coal and Steel Community, through which nations try to create supranational forms of organization. Thus, by an apparent paradox, what is historically conditioned in the idea of the national interest can be overcome only through the promotion in concert of the national interest of a number of nations.

These reflections have been made particularly relevant by the atomic age. It has been said that the atomic age has rendered obsolete the idea of the national interest and the conception of foreign policy derived from it. This is too sweeping a statement to be correct. What has become obsolete is the historically conditioned connection between interest and a passing historic phenomenon, the nation state; what has not, and could not have, become obsolete is the logically required connection between interest and foreign policy. The point can indeed be made . . . that the technological revolutions of our age, of which the atomic revolution is the most spectacular one, have made the political organization of the world into nation states as obsolete as the first industrial revolution did the political organization based upon the feudal state. Yet the techniques by which new and wider interest must be given a politically viable expression have not been affected by those revolutionary changes. Thus the supranational control of atomic energy is today in the national interest of all nations; for while the present bipolarity of atomic power is dangerous to all nations, the acquisition of uncontrolled atomic power by an indefinite number of nations is likely to prove fatal to civilized life on this planet. In consequence, the nations of the world are faced with, and must overcome, the dilemma that the pursuit of their interests, conceived in national terms, is incompatible with modern technology, which requires supranational political organization.

The survival of a political unit, such as a nation, in its identity is the irreducible minimum, the necessary element of its interests vis-à-vis other units. Taken in isolation, the determination of its content in a concrete situation is relatively simple; for it encompasses the integrity of the nation's territory, of its political institutions, and of its culture. Thus bipartisanship in foreign policy, especially in times of war, has been most easily achieved in the promotion of these minimum requirements of the national interest. The situation is different with respect to the variable elements of the national interest. All the crosscurrents of personalities, public opinion, sectional interests, partisan politics, and political and moral folkways are brought to bear upon their determination. In consequence, the contribution which scientific analysis can make to this field, as to all fields of policy formation, is limited. It can identify the different agencies of the government which contribute to the determination of the variable elements of the national interest and assess their relative weight. It can separate the long-range objectives of foreign policy from the short-term ones which are the means for the achievement of the former and can tentatively establish their rational relations. Finally, it can analyze the variable elements of the national interest in terms of their legitimacy and their compatibility with other national values and with the national interest of other nations. We shall address ourselves briefly to the typical problems with which this analysis must deal.

The legitimacy of the national interest must be determined in the face of possible usurpation by subnational, other-national, and supranational interests. On the subnational level we find group interests, represented particularly by ethnic and economic groups, which tend to identify themselves with the national interest. Charles A. Beard has emphasized, however one-sidedly, the extent to which the economic interests of certain groups have been presented as those of the United States. Group interests exert, of course, constant pressure upon the conduct of our foreign policy, claiming their identity with the national interest. It is, however, doubtful that, with the exception of a few spectacular cases, they have been successful in determining the course of American foreign policy. . . .

The national interest can be usurped by other-national interests in two typical ways. The case of treason by individuals, either out of conviction or for pay, needs only to be mentioned here; . . . it is significant for psychology, sociology, and criminology, but not for the theory of politics. The other case, however, is important not only for the theory of politics but also for its practice, especially in the United States.

National minorities in European countries, ethnic groups in the United States, ideological minorities anywhere may identify themselves, either spontaneously or under the direction of the agents of a foreign government, with the interests of that foreign government and may promote these interests under the guise of the national interest of the country whose citizens they happen to be. The activities of the German-American Bund in the United States in the 'thirties and of Communists everywhere are cases in point. . . .

The genuine usurpation of the national interest by supranational interests can derive in our time from two sources: religious bodies and international organizations. The competition between church and state for determination of certain interests and policies, domestic and international, has been an intermittent issue throughout the history of the nation state. . . .

The more acute problem arises at the present time from the importance which the public and government officials, at least in their public utterances, attribute to the values represented and the policies pursued by international organizations either as alternatives or supplements to the values and policies for which the national government stands. It is frequently asserted that the foreign policy of the United States pursues no objectives apart from those of the United Nations, that, in other words, the foreign policy of the United States is actually identical with the policy of the United Nations. This assertion cannot refer to anything real in actual politics to support it. For the constitutional structure of international organizations, such as the United Nations, and their procedural practices make it impossible for them to pursue interests apart from those of the member states which dominate their policy-forming bodies. The identity between the interests of the United Nations and the United States can only refer to the successful policies of the United States within the United Nations through which the support of the United Nations is being secured for the policies of the United States. The assertion, then, is mere polemic, different from the one discussed previously in that the identification of a certain policy with an assumed supranational interest does not seek to reflect discredit upon the former but to bestow upon it a dignity which the national interest pure and simple is supposed to lack.

The real issue in view of the problem that concerns us here is not whether the so-called interests of the United Nations, which do not exist apart from the interests of its most influential members, have superseded the national interest of the United States, but for what kind of interests the United

States has secured United Nations support. While these interests cannot be United Nations interests, they do not need to be national interests either. Here we are in the presence of that modern phenomenon which has been variously described as "utopianism," "sentimentalism," "moralism," the "legalistic-moralistic approach." The common denominator of all these tendencies in modern political thought is the substitution for the national interest of an assumed supranational standard of action which is generally identified with an international organization. The national interest is here not being usurped by subnational or supranational interests which, however inferior in worth to the national interest, are nevertheless real and worthy of consideration within their proper sphere. What challenges the national interest here is a mere figment of the imagination, a product of wishful thinking, which is postulated as a valid norm for international conduct, without being valid either there or anywhere else. At this point we touch the core of the present controversy between utopianism and realism in international affairs; we shall return to it later.

The national interest as such must be defended against usurpation by non-national interests. Yet once that task is accomplished, a rational order must be established among the values which make up the national interest and among the resources to be committed to them. While the interests which a nation may pursue in its relation with other nations are of infinite variety and magnitude, the resources which are available for the pursuit of such interests are necessarily limited in quantity and kind. No nation has the resources to promote all desirable objectives with equal vigor; all nations must therefore allocate their scarce resources as rationally as possible. The indispensable precondition of such rational allocation is a clear understanding of the distinction between the necessary and variable elements of the national interest. Given the contentious manner in which in democracies the variable elements of the national interest are generally determined, the advocates of an extensive conception of the national interest will inevitably present certain variable elements of the national interest as though their attainment were necessary for the nation's survival. In other words, the necessary elements of the national interest have a tendency to swallow up the variable elements so that in the end all kinds of objectives, actual or potential, are justified in terms of national survival. Such arguments have been advanced, for instance, in support of the rearmament of Western Germany and of the defense of Formosa. They must be subjected to rational scrutiny which will determine, however tentatively, their approximate place in the scale of national values.

The same problem presents itself in its extreme form when a nation pursues, or is asked to pursue, objectives that are not only unnecessary for its survival but tend to jeopardize it. Second-rate nations which dream of playing the role of great powers, such as Italy and Poland in the interwar period, illustrate this point. So do great powers which dream of remaking the world in their own image and embark upon world-wide crusades, thus straining their resources to exhaustion. Here scientific analysis has the urgent task of pruning down national objectives to the measure of available resources in order to make their pursuit compatible with national survival.

Finally, the national survival of a nation that is conscious not only of its own interests but also of that of other nations must be defined in terms compatible with the latter. In a multinational world this is a requirement of political morality; in an age of total war it is also a condition for survival.

Two mutually exclusive arguments have been brought to bear upon this problem. On the one hand, it has been argued against the theory of international politics here presented that the concept of the national interest revives the eighteenth-century concept of enlightened self-interest, presuming that the uniformly enlightened pursuit of their self-interest by all individuals, as by all nations, will of itself be conducive to a peaceful and harmonious society. On the other hand, the point has been made that the pursuit of their national interest by all nations makes war the permanent arbiter of conflicts among them. Neither argument is well taken.

The concept of the national interest presupposes neither a naturally harmonious, peaceful world nor the inevitability of war as a consequence of the pursuit by all nations of their national interest. Quite to the contrary, it assumes continuous conflict and threat of war, to be minimized through the continuous adjustment of conflicting interests by diplomatic action. . . .

We have said before that the utopian and realist positions in international affairs do not necessarily differ in the policies they advocate, but that they part company over their general philosophies of politics and their way of thinking about matters political. It does not follow that the present debate is only of academic interest and without practical significance. Both camps, it is true, may support the same policy for different reasons. Yet if the reasons are unsound, the soundness of the policies supported by them is a mere coincidence, and these very same reasons may be, and inevitably are, invoked on other occasions in support of unsound policies. The nefarious consequences of false philosophies and wrong ways of thinking may for the time being be concealed by the apparent success of policies derived from them. You may go to war, justified by your nation's interests, for a moral purpose and in disregard of considerations of power; and military victory seems to satisfy both your moral aspirations and your nation's interests. Yet the manner in which you waged the war, achieved victory, and settled the peace cannot help reflecting your philosophy of politics and your way of thinking about political problems. If these are in error, you may win victory on the field of battle and still assist in the defeat of both your moral principles and the national interest of your country. . . .

. . . Abraham Lincoln was faced with a dilemma similar to that which confronts us today. Should he make the liberation of the slaves the ultimate standard of his policy even at the risk of destroying the Union, as many urged him to do, or should he subordinate the moral principle of universal freedom to considerations of the national interest? The answer Lincoln gave to Horace Greeley, a spokesman for the utopian moralists, is timeless in its eloquent wisdom. Lincoln wrote on August 22, 1862:

> If there be those who would not save the Union unless they could at the same time save slavery, I do not agree with them. If there be those who

would not save the Union unless they could at the same time destroy slavery, I do not agree with them. My paramount object in this struggle *is* to save the Union, and is *not* either to save or to destroy slavery. If I could save the Union without freeing *any* slave I would do it, and if I could save it by freeing *all* the slaves, I would do it; and if I could save it by freeing some and leaving others alone I would also do that. What I do about slavery, and the colored race, I do because I believe it helps to save the Union; and what I forbear, I forbear because I do *not* believe it would help to save the Union. I shall do *less* whenever I shall believe what I am doing hurts the cause, and I shall do *more* whenever I shall believe doing more will help the cause. I shall try to correct errors when shown to be errors; and I shall adopt new views so fast as they appear to be true views.

I have here stated my purpose according to my view of *official* duty; and I intend no modification of my oft-expressed *personal* wish that all men everywhere could be free. . . .

I have always maintained that the actions of states are subject to universal moral principles and I have been careful to differentiate my position in this respect from that of Hobbes. Five points basic to my position may need to be emphasized again.

The first point is what one might call the requirement of cosmic humility with regard to the moral evaluation of the actions of states. To know that states are subject to the moral law is one thing; to pretend to know what is morally required of states in a particular situation is quite another. The human mind tends naturally to identify the particular interests of states, as of individuals, with the moral purposes of the universe. The statesman in the defense of the nation's interests may, and at times even must, yield to that tendency; the scholar must resist it at every turn. For the light-hearted assumption that what one's own nation aims at and does is morally good and that those who oppose that nation's policies are evil is morally indefensible and intellectually untenable and leads in practice to that distortion of judgment, born of the blindness of crusading frenzy, which has been the curse of nations from the beginning of time.

The second point which obviously needs to be made again concerns the effectiveness of the restraints which morality imposes upon the actions of states:

> A discussion of international morality must guard against the two extremes either of overrating the influence of ethics upon international politics or else of denying that statesmen and diplomats are moved by anything else but considerations of material power.
>
> On the one hand, there is the dual error of confounding the moral rules which people actually observe with those they pretend to observe as well as with those which writers declare they ought to observe. . . .
>
> On the other hand, there is the misconception, usually associated with the general depreciation and moral condemnation of power politics, discussed above, that international politics is so thoroughly evil that it is no use looking for ethical limitations of the aspirations for power on the international scene. Yet, if we ask ourselves what statesmen and diplomats are capable of

doing to further the power objectives of their respective nations and what they actually do, we realize that they do less than they probably could and less than they actually did in other periods of history. They refuse to consider certain ends and to use certain means, either altogether or under certain conditions, not because in the light of expediency they appear impractical or unwise, but because certain moral rules interpose an absolute barrier. . . .[1]

The third point concerns the relations between universal moral principles and political action. I have always maintained that these universal moral principles cannot be applied to the actions of states in their abstract universal formulation, but that they must be, as it were, filtered through the concrete circumstances of time and place. The individual may say for himself: *"Fiat justitia, pereat mundus"*;[2] the state has no right to say so in the name of those who are in its care. Both individual and state must judge political action by universal moral principles, such as that of liberty. Yet while the individual has a moral right to sacrifice himself in defense of such a moral principle, the state has no moral right to let its moral disapprobation of the infringement of liberty get in the way of successful political action, itself inspired by the moral principle of national survival. . . .

Fourth, the realist recognizes that a moral decision, especially in the political sphere, does not imply a simple choice between a moral principle and a standard of action which is morally irrelevant or even outright immoral. A moral decision implies always a choice among different moral principles, one of which is given precedence over others. To say that a political action has no moral purpose is absurd; for political action can be defined as an attempt to realize moral values through the medium of politics, that is, power. The relevant moral question concerns the choice among different moral values, and it is at this point that the realist and the utopian part company again. If an American statesman must choose between the promotion of universal liberty, which is a moral good, at the risk of American security and, hence, of liberty in the United States, and the promotion of American security and of liberty in the United States, which is another moral good, to the detriment of the promotion of universal liberty, which choice ought he to make? The utopian will not face the issue squarely and will deceive himself into believing that he can achieve both goods at the same time. The realist will choose the national interest on both moral and pragmatic grounds; for if he does not take care of the national interest nobody else will, and if he puts American security and liberty in jeopardy the cause of liberty everywhere will be impaired.

Finally, the political realist distinguishes between his moral sympathies and the political interests which he must defend. He will distinguish with Lincoln between his *"official* duty" which is to protect the national interest and his *"personal* wish" which is to see universal moral values realized throughout the world. . . .

The contest between utopianism and realism is not tantamount to a contest between principle and expediency, morality and immorality, although

[1] H. J. Morgenthau, *Politics Among Nations,* pp. 210-216.
[2] Let justice be done though the world may perish.

some spokesmen for the former would like to have it that way. The contest is rather between one type of political morality and another type of political morality, one taking as its standard universal moral principles abstractly formulated, the other weighing these principles against the moral requirements of concrete political action, their relative merits to be decided by a prudent evaluation of the political consequences to which they are likely to lead.

►THE DESIRABLE AND THE POSSIBLE

WILLIAM T. R. FOX

While Hans J. Morgenthau seems to suggest that policy must be based either *on national interest* or *on moral principle, William T. R. Fox asserts that there is no escape from the need to reconcile them—just as there is no escape from the need to reconcile the desirable and the possible.*

The author is Professor of International Relations at Columbia University and Director of its War and Peace Institute. He is also member of the editorial board of World Politics, *a quarterly journal of international relations (Princeton).*

Can one successfully assert the irrelevance of "moral principle" to the conduct of foreign relations? This is what Professor Morgenthau says he is doing when he declares that "national interest" provides the sole valid criterion in making decisions in the field of foreign affairs.

A doctrine of this character will shock those many men of good will who believe the world is suffering from an excess of devotion to national interest rather than from the opposite. The doctrine will seem even more frightening to them because of the tone of pessimism which pervades the whole analysis. The casual reference to "those potentially unlimited power drives which are latent in all men" suggests that Power, Evil, and Original Sin are three names for the same thing, that the Kingdom of God is not to be brought down on this earth whatever we do, that peace on earth and good will to men is something to be sung about in Christmas carols and not to be translated into actuality.

The "men of little faith" have been the traditional objects of public scorn when things go amiss with the world. Professor Morgenthau instead turns his neo-Calvinist verbal artillery on the men of too great faith. It is perhaps time that they be put on the moral defensive. Serious students of politics will share with Professor Morgenthau a profound skepticism regarding any man whose faith in the virtue of his particular design for universal peace is so great that he would have us if necessary fight a third world war to make the Russians accept his plan.

From "The Reconciliation of the Desirable and the Possible," *The American Scholar,* Spring 1949.

There is a further difficulty. "Politics," says Max Weber, "is a slow boring of hard boards." Advocates of utopian programs almost invariably short-circuit the political process. Their faith in the virtue of a particular plan is buttressed by their faith in the possibility of its beng put into effect. Whether a given utopian plan would be put into effect by threatening war or by making a series of dramatic concessions, its supporters generally propose to avoid the necessity for painful negotiation and for the hard intellectual analysis that accompanies such negotiation. But neither the avenging God of the Old Testament, who would have us deal harshly with His enemies, nor the merciful God of the New, who would turn the other cheek however great the provocation, can furnish the model for the responsible politician who abjures both holy war and fatuous gesture.

The demagogues of the Right and of the Left can afford to offer simple solutions. Their freedom to criticize is unlimited by any substantial prospect that they will come to power. There is little chance that they will be forced to demonstrate how much passion and how little dispassionate analysis entered into their program-making. Advocacy of one-way atomic war is not yet socially acceptable, but some of the more extreme Russophobes who call for firmness without patience only imperfectly conceal their anxiety to have the United States begin dropping atomic bombs. At the other extreme, are the protagonists of patience without firmness, of unlimited concession, of choking Stalin with kindness. Such a course of action may conceivably evoke a complete change in the hearts of the men of the Kremlin. But if it did not, and all available historical evidence suggests that it would not, the United States would then be under the necessity of opposing a Russia which it had materially strengthened.

The patient exploration of every avenue for peace and the day-by-day assessment of the country's security position are twin tasks which the responsible leader cannot escape. Neither can be performed simply by imposing on a refractory world some moral principle of universal applicability. But how shall he decide when to be firm and when to be conciliatory?

According to Professor Morgenthau, war is never necessary solely to uphold a moral principle; but one must always be prepared to make war when a fundamental national interest is involved. National interest turns out to be another name for national security, and this in its turn is revealed to mean the maintenance of the state's territorial integrity *and* its basic institutions. Now which institutions are basic? Can this question be answered except in the language of moral principle?

Here, it seems to me, is a basic flaw in Professor Morgenthau's choice of language. The flaw appears to me to be more in his choice of words than in his underlying analysis. He protests too vehemently his amorality. His uncompromising support of national interest as *the* guiding principle does not wholly conceal the moral foundations of his position.

"Respect for the existence and the individuality of its members is," he declares, "of the essence of the Western state system." This is the principle of live and let live. It is the democratic principle which recognizes the equal integrity and right of autonomous and full development of *other* personalities or groups. It is a principle which determines when one is to be unyielding and when compliant. It is a moral principle.

One is not bound absolutely to respect the existence and the individuality of every other member of the state system, but only so long as the actions of the other do not threaten the existence and the individuality of one's "self." (The "self" of which we are here talking, in a world politics context, is the nation-state.) Stated in concrete present-day terms, Red totalitarianism is all right in Russia, provided its existence there does not threaten the American national interest. It must, of course, be in the national interest to frustrate the policies of another state if that state's national interest were defined in terms which menaced that of one's own state. Therefore, only compatible national interests ought to be recognized.

Is the national interest of any given state capable of objective determination except in terms of some explicitly declared set of value preferences? The camel's nose of moral principle is already under the tent when one admits that it is territorial integrity *plus* basic institutions which must "in the national interest" be protected. By the time the responsible leader has taken the next step and decided which foreign policies of other powers are compatible with this national interest he will be consulting his conscience as well as his intellect.

We are sometimes told that a responsible statesman would recognize that there really is no such thing as national interest. Charles Beard denounced the whole idea of national interest as a pious fraud to cloak the internal struggle between the trade-hungry merchants and the land-hungry planters for control of United States foreign affairs. He could see only sub-national interests. But he rejected the idea of supra-national interest even more emphatically than he did the idea of national interest. It was only, he maintained, because the American people became infected with a sense of world mission, that they have in the twentieth century blundered into other peoples' wars. Thus, even he, in a negative sort of way recognized an American national interest—in avoiding taking sides in "other peoples' wars."

To Woodrow Wilson, on the other hand, is attributed the belief that formulation of policy in terms of national self-interest is wrong per se. Wilson undoubtedly believed that what was good for the world was good for the United States, and he believed that democracy, national self-determination and a world commonwealth of nations would together usher in the reign of universal peace. But he was quite as ready to outbuild Britain in a naval arms race to crush "British navalism" as he had been to lead the United States to victory over Prussian militarism. Wilson clearly understood the need for protecting what he believed to be American interests in a stubborn and imperfect world.

That Wilson, in the Fourteen Points and at Versailles, may have been mesmerized by his own skill in phrase-making—some think he had been earlier when he coined the phrase "too proud to fight"—is more than possible. The moral effect of solemn invocations of principle uttered by Cordell Hull was negated by his recurring explicit warning that the United States would assume no risk of war or of political or military involvement in defense of these principles. In our own decade the too sweeping phraseology of the Atlantic Charter and the Truman Doctrine has aroused unfulfillable expectations in many parts of the world. All these point to the undesirability of careless, irresponsible and unconditional invocation of moral principle.

The chief task of the policy-maker lies in the reconciliation of the desirable and the possible. Moral principle is *not* irrelevant, but it can provide by itself no sure guide to policy. It is in weighing the risks and the gains—the value losses and the value increments to the self in whose name one is acting, i.e., the nation-state—that judgments about the possible emerge. It is in formulating this judgment that one arrives at a conception of the national interest.

What is judged to be absolutely impossible is the pursuit of a policy which endangers the very existence of the nation-state itself. Such a policy will be rejected, however imperative may appear the moral precept which gave rise to the policy. Thus if one arranges political objectives in hierarchical order, survival will take precedence over all the others. But it is not the survival of the individual, but of his state, for which the ultimate sacrifice of life is in our century ordinarily made. Stated in other language, the nation-state is the "survival self," but the self in whose name moral principle is invoked may be either broader or narrower in scope. . . .

The difference between the Morgenthau position and my own is partly but not wholly verbal. He contends that policy must be based *either* on national interest *or* on moral principle. My own view is that moral principle necessarily enters into any valid formulation of national interest, which must itself reconcile the desirable and the possible. Against the view that there can be no compromise, I assert that there can be no escape from compromise. This is what makes politics a vocation only for the mature, for the responsible, for the man who does not despair when he discovers incommensurate values placed in such a juxtaposition that one or another has to be sacrificed.

It is this to which Alexander Hamilton had reference when he pointed to the "disproportion" between the risk to which strict fulfillment of the French Alliance would have exposed the United States and the advantages either to the United States or to France which would have flowed from American intervention in that European war. Then as now, treaty observance depended upon continuing mutuality of interest.

These things must be said if only because stability and responsibility in American foreign policy require that the American people not appear to themselves as more generous than they really are. Leadership in the United Nations, Truman Doctrine and Marshall Plan are none of them exclusively the result of a developing sense of world citizenship in the United States or a manifestation of American belief in the brotherhood of man.

It was fear of the consequences for American security if Greece were overrun or if European recovery were longer delayed that has stimulated the military aid to Greece and the economic aid to Western Europe. The European Recovery Program appears unselfish in a context in which material values alone are considered; but it is more correctly assessed as based on *mutual* interest, including the American national interest, once the non-material values of freedom and survival are also brought into the analysis. . . .

That the American national interest seems to be in so little conflict with the interests of the other powers on the outer side of the Iron Curtain is fortunate indeed. It shows that the national interest of the United States is in our time formulated in terms which can be supported by any other power whose diplomatic watchword is "live and let live."

►CRITIQUE OF REALISM

STANLEY H. HOFFMAN

Morgenthau's theory of power and national interest allows us to eliminate those policies which would foolishly overlook the prerequisite of power. It does not explain why statesmen, although aware of national interest and power, act in one way rather than in another.

This is part of the critical examination of realism in politics written by Stanley H. Hoffman, Professor of Political Science at Harvard University. He is the author of several studies on the theory of international relations. He is also author and editor of Contemporary Theory in International Relations *(Prentice Hall, 1960).*

The theory which has occupied the center of the scene in this country during the last ten years is Professor Morgenthau's "realist" theory of power politics. It tries to give us a reliable map of the landscape of world affairs, to catch the essence of world politics. The master key is the concept of interest defined in terms of power. The theory succeeds in focusing attention on the principal actors in world affairs: the states, and on the factors that account for the autonomy of international relations: the differences between domestic and world politics which thwart the operation in the latter of ideas and institutions that flourish in the former, the drastic imperatives of survival, self-preservation, and self-help which are both the causes and the products of such differences.

However, as a general theory, the realist analysis fails because it sees the world as a static field in which power relations reproduce themselves in timeless monotony. The map is inadequate for two main reasons. First, the realist analysis of power is a very debatable one. The decision to equate politics and the effects of man's "lust for power," and the tendency to equate power and evil or violence, mutilate reality. A "power monism" does not account for all politics, when power is so somberly defined. Furthermore, the extent to which power as a carrier of evil and violence expresses a basic human instinct is questionable, for much of the international (or domestic)

From the article "International Relations: The Long Road to Theory," *World Politics,* Vol. XI, No. 3 (April, 1959), pp. 346-377.

evil of power is rooted not in the sinfulness of man but in a context, a constellation, a situation, in which even good men are forced to act selfishly or immorally. The discrimination between the inherent or instinctive aspects of the "power drive," and the situational or accidental ones, is an important task, neglected by the theory.

Also, it is dangerous to put in a key position a concept which is merely instrumental. Power is a means toward any of a large number of ends (including power itself): the quality and quantity of power used by men are determined by men's purposes. Now, the realist theory neglects all the factors that influence or define purposes. Why statesmen choose at times to act in a certain way rather than in another is not made clear. The domestic considerations that define national power are either left out or brushed aside. So is the role of internationally shared values and purposes. We get a somewhat mechanistic view of international affairs in which the statesmen's role consists of adjusting national power to an almost immutable set of external "givens." The realist world is a frozen universe of separate essences.

Even if the role of power were as determining as the theory postulates, the question arises whether any scheme can put so much methodological weight upon one concept, even a crucial one; for it seems to me that the concept of power collapses under the burden. Power is a most complex product of other variables which should be allowed to see the light of the theory instead of remaining hidden in the shadow of power. Otherwise, the theory is bound either to mean different things at different steps of the analysis (or when dealing with different periods), or to end by selecting for emphasis only one aspect of power: either military force or economic strength. Thus, instead of a map which simplifies the landscape so that we can understand it, we are left with a distortion.

There is a second reason for the inadequacy of the map. The clumsiness that comes from the timeless concept of power is compounded by the confusing use of other concepts that are dated in more ways than one, and which the theory applies to situations in which they do not fit. The model of the realists is a highly embellished ideal-type of eighteenth- and nineteenth-century international relations. This vision of the golden age is taken as a norm, both for empirical analysis, and for evaluation. A number of oddities of the theory are explained thereby. First, the lack of an adequate discussion of ends. For when all the actors have almost the same credo, it becomes easy to forget the effects of the common credo on the actors' behavior, and to omit from among the main variables of the theory a factor whose role seems constant. It is nevertheless an optical illusion to mistake a particular pattern for the norm of a scientific system. Secondly, the conception of an objective and easily recognizable national interest is one which makes sense only in a stable period in which the participants play for limited ends, with limited means, and without domestic kibitzers to disrupt the players' moves. In such a period, the survival of the main players is rarely at stake in the game, and a hierarchy can rather easily be established among the other and far less vital interests that are at stake. Today, survival is almost always in question, and the most divergent courses of action can be recommended as choices for survival. An attempt at using the theory as a key to the understanding of contemporary realities puts one in the position of a Tiresias who recognizes interests which the parties refuse to see, who diagnoses permanence where the parties find confusing change, and whose ex post facto omniscience is both irritating and irrelevant.

Thirdly, the idea that the national interest carries its own morality is also one which makes sense only in a stable period (although it is strangely phrased). For it is in such a period that an international consensus assures at least the possibility of accommodation of national objectives: the conflicts of interests which are involved are not struggles between competing international moralities. The philosophical pluralism implicit in the realist theory (which purports to be both normative and empirical) is hardly tolerable in periods of "nationalistic universalism," and it is unnecessary in periods of stability and moderation, which bloom only because of a basic agreement on values. Fourth, the emphasis on the rationality of foreign policy and the desire to brush aside the irrational elements as intrusions or pathological deviations are understandable only in terms of cabinet diplomacy, where such deviations appear (especially with the benefit of hindsight) to have been rare. There, rationality seemed like the simple adjustment of means to stable and generally recognized ends. These concepts are far less applicable to a period in which the political struggles involve primarily the determination of ends. Thus, behind the claim to realism, we find a reactionary utopia.

The consequence of this inadequacy of the map is that the theory's usefulness as a general theory for the discipline is limited. In the first place, from the point of view of systematic empirical analysis, the theory stresses the autonomy of international relations to the point of leaving beyond its pale the forces which work for change and which, cutting across the states, affect the states' behavior. We are presented both with a single key to the closed room of politics among nations, and with a warning that the room is in a house whose key we cannot have, or whose opening must be left to the "workman-like manipulation of perennial forces." We are not told what they are, or how they operate. We reach at this point one of the most fundamental ambiguities of the theory. The postulate of the permanence of power politics among nations as the core of international relations tends to become a goal. The static qualities of the theory lead to confusion between the phenomenon of power conflicts and the transitory forms and institutions in which such conflicts have been taking place in recent centuries. Why should the sound reminder that power is here to stay mean that the present system of nation-states will continue, or change only through forces that are of no concern to us? Such an attitude is a double evasion: from the empirical duty of accounting for change, and from the normative task of assessing whether the present system should indeed continue. One cannot help but feel that, in spite of Mr. Morgenthau's qualifying statements, there is behind his theory the old position that whatever has been, must continue.

This brings us to a second limitation, which concerns the usefulness of the scheme as a normative theory. It is something of a success philosophy. The criterion of a good foreign policy is its rationality, but the touchstone of rationality is success. Unfortunately the standards of success and failure are not made clear. First, how will we distinguish between the follies of straight utopianism and the fallacies of wrong realism—realism that did not work? Secondly, from what viewpoint shall we decide whether a statesman has succeeded or failed? Shall we turn to history alone? But at what stage? Metternich had succeeded by 1825, failed by 1848, and writers disagree as to whether he had succeeded or failed by 1914. If we set our standards outside and above history, we must avoid trying to prove that history will inevitably recompense policies that meet our standards. Otherwise, we become salesmen for a philosophical stand who travel the roads of history in search of a clientele of confirmations, rather than scholars testing a hypothesis or philosophers interested in an ideal which history cannot promise to bless at all times.

The former position we wish to avoid. It is particularly uncomfortable when one's basic postulate about human nature is such that history cannot be anything but a tale full of sound and fury, signifying nothing. This view makes it impossible to understand how there could be a rational theory of rational human behavior. This is not the last contradiction: the realist theory combines a Hobbesian image of naked power politics with an attempt to show that states are nevertheless not condemned to a life that is "nasty, brutish, and short." Realism thus puts its faith in voluntary restraints, moderation, and the underlying assumption of possible harmony among national interests —points scarcely admitted by the original postulate. Finally, there is a sharp contrast between this postulate, whose logic is a permanent clash of forces of evil, and the norm of eighteenth- and nineteenth-century international relations—the period in which the world's state of nature was most Lockian, and Morgenthau's view of human nature most unjustified.

With such flaws and contradictions, the policy guidance which the realist theory is able to afford is limited. Realism allows us to eliminate those policies that would foolishly forget the prerequisite of power; but it does not go much further. Too many factors are left out for realist advice to avoid the dilemma of homilies and admonishments, or suggestions inappropriate for revolutionary periods. The light that illuminated the landscape in the quiet obscurity of nineteenth-century politics is blown out by today's tempest.

▶FORESIGHT AND BLINDNESS IN FOREIGN POLICY

CHARLES BURTON MARSHALL

A wise policy-maker knows how little he knows about other nations' goals and their probable course of action.

This is the theme of the following essay written by a former member of the U.S. Department of State's Policy Planning Staff, and now research

The selection is from a series of five lectures given at Hollins College. They were published as a book, *The Limits of Foreign Policy,* copyright © 1954 by Henry Holt and Company, Inc. By permission of the publishers.

consultant of the Washington Center of Foreign Policy Research, affiliated with Johns Hopkins University.

I wish to stress [foreign policy's] limits rather than its magnitudes. . . .

A sound general understanding of foreign policy, avoiding excessive expectations and the sense of frustration incident to the disappointment of such expectations, is therefore essential to the conduct of a sound foreign policy. . . .

Those who govern and those who counsel them are subject to refractions of view and errors of judgment. The problem is neither how to endow them with unquestioned authority in foreign affairs nor how to render them entirely subservient to the whims and pressures of the particular interests which in sum constitute the public. The problem is how to acquaint Americans in general, whether in government or out of it, with the inherent limits respecting foreign policy so that issues may turn on questions of how best for the nation to fill the limits rather than on vain propositions of perfection and destructive self-reproach over failure to achieve it. . . .

The foreign policy of a state takes form in the courses of action undertaken by authority of the state and intended to affect situations beyond the span of its jurisdiction.

Do not construe too narrowly the meaning of the word *action*. In this field utterance is sometimes a form of action, and pronouncements are deeds when they convey meaning about things intended to be done rather than merely expressing abstractions and moralizations.

Let me emphasize the human and therefore finite character of the political institutions concerned in foreign policy.

The state is an abstract expression representing a body of people occupying a defined territory and politically organized so as to be capable of acting collectively with respect to matters both within that territory and beyond it. Government is the apparatus of decision and execution for such action.

The terms *state* and *government* convey ideas of hugeness, majesty, and impersonality. These overtones should not mislead us. The state—and this is true also of its agent, government—remains, in Plato's phrase, man written large.

It is only man. It is not superman. It is man written large, not limitless. The individual is multiplied in the frame of the state. The individual's limitations are not transcended. The institutions of political life do not add to the dimensions of the human mind. They have no insights denied to individuals. They produce no wisdom beyond the compass of man's mind. The intelligence operating in the lines of decision and execution is but human intelligence. It has the inherent attributes of contingency, fallibility, and subjectivity. Service to the state does not bring to the minds of the servants any additional endowments for perceiving the future. For all its majesty, the situation of the state is still the human situation.

Americans generally recognize the characteristics of intrinsic limitation in respect to the state's role in domestic affairs. Here indeed, in their precepts if not so much in their practices. the Americans are virtually singular among the nations for their skepticism about the wisdom and the efficacy of public authority. Americans tend to overlook these limitations—at least, many Americans tend to do so—in their attitudes toward the role of the United States in foreign affairs. In this range their perspectives tend to be thrown off. Americans, said Gertrude Stein, are brought up "to believe in boundlessness." With respect to nothing else is this so manifest as it is with respect to their views as to the inherent capability of the United States government to avail in matters actually external to its jurisdiction and therefore beyond its control.

I stress the obvious but often overlooked externalness of foreign policy. The fundamental circumstance giving rise to foreign policy is that most of the world is outside the United States. The areas in which our foreign policy has its effects are those lying beyond the range of our law. They include about fifteen-sixteenths of the world's land surface and contain about sixteen-seventeenths of its peoples. We cannot ordain the conditions there. The forces do not respond to our fiat. At best we can only affect them. We exercise only influence, not the sovereign power to dispose, in those ranges once described by the Supreme Court in a memorable opinion as "this vast external realm, with its important, complicated, delicate, and manifold problems."

I can recall from my own experience dozens of examples of the American tendency to disregard limitation of power precisely with respect to matters beyond the limits of our control.

An exigent lady in the audience in a Midwestern city about three years ago asked me to outline the course of United States foreign policy for the next ten years. I denied having a crystal ball. She reduced to five years the interval concerned in the request. I carefully restated my view of foreign policy as necessarily being in large part a response to situations arising beyond the national jurisdiction and therefore beyond our government's control and beyond my modest power to predict. She spurned that answer. She insisted on the predictability of the future in world affairs, given sufficient diligence on the part of those conducting policy. I told her the main surely predictable element of the future was trouble, which was bound to proliferate along our course, though I could not undertake to define all its forms and occasions. The lady answered with scorn for the Department of State for not having worked out a formula for eliminating trouble.

Such ideas abound within as well as outside the government. I recall, for example, a conference of a couple of years ago between a delegation from another office of the government and the members of the Policy Planning Staff of the State Department. The visitors wanted to mesh with foreign policy certain plans of their making. They asked us to unroll the secret scrolls of the future—at least for a twenty-year interval of it. They departed in dudgeon, disdain, and disbelief on hearing our disclaimer.

I call to mind being asked by a man in an audience in Texas a few months ago to explain the State Department's failure to foresee the rising clash in interest and purpose between metropolitan France and native elements of French North Africa. I assured him this had been foreseen. Then he asked for an accounting on the United States' failure to prevent it.

In the life of the state as in the life of the individual, problems foreseen may often be beyond the scope of one's power of ordaining. The situation in the conduct of foreign policy often reminds me of the story of the boastful pilot. While steering a ship into port, he remarked to the skipper, "I know every rock in this harbor." A rending contact between ship and reef interrupted him. Then he added, "That's one of them now." I related all this to my questioner in Texas but did not convince him that the fact of a falling out between North African Arabs and France was not due to some remissness in Washington. . . .

The same notion of the attainability of perfect foresight in the planning and perfect efficacy in the execution of foreign policy is an ingredient in the abundant schemes put forth by well-meaning groups for a variety of one-shot solutions of the problems of a difficult world.

. . . The sweep of its problems gives foreign policy a special attraction for those—in the words of Shelley's self-description—born with a passion to reform the world. . . . [Foreign policy's] complexities and subtleties are rich with opportunity for generalizers and obfuscators. . . .

Nothing comes more easily or does less good than the engaging pastime of thinking up bold and imaginative schemes for improvement in disregard of the means for realizing them. This is true in all human endeavor. Here I wish to apply the thought to the subject of foreign policy. . . .

Another influence on the American attitude toward foreign affairs might be called faith in engineering—confidence of a limitless power to transform situations by working on the material factors, faith in the achievability of great purposes through applying technics. This relates to our natural pride in the physical development of our country. . . .

This faith in capability to transform through material factors is relevant to a tendency to think loosely about the nature of force, which is physical, and its relation to power in general. By force I mean the capacity to transmit energy and so to expend it as to do vital harm to a foe and also the deterrent, compulsive effect produced by having that capacity. It is only one of many forms of power. For power let us use Count Tolstoi's definition of it as "merely the relation between the expression of someone's will and the execution of that will by others."

Wars occur when nations seek to impose their wills by effecting drastic changes in the ratios of power through radical action in the factors of force. The force factors are susceptible of precision in military planning. The elements are concrete. The speeds of ships, their capabilities for carrying men and cargo, the distances, the fuel requirements of planes and tanks, the fire power of divisions, and so on are knowable factors. The military planning process, insofar as it relates to the ponderables of real or hypothetical campaigns, turns out tidy and complete results. I do not mean that battles and campaigns are fought according to preconceived schedules. I mean only that insofar as advance planning is employed in the military field, the quotients are precise, the columns are even, and the conclusions concrete.

In a course of active hostilities force capabilities may be brought to a ratio of 100 to 0 as between one side and the other by the elimination of resistance in a particular place for a particular time, changing the relationship between antagonists to that between victor and vanquished. Surrender may be complete and unconditional. Victory may appear absolute.

It is easy for the unwary to jump to a conclusion that if all human affairs were laid out with the precision of military plans, then all problems could be brought to as complete solution as can the problem of force in the conduct of a victorious military campaign.

Victory's appearance of absoluteness is transitory. Victory itself is evanescent. It invariably has given way to a substitute unless the victors, like the Romans at Carthage, have obliterated the conquered or undertaken permanently to deprive them of will—in other words, to enslave them, an undertaking likely to prove burdensome and fearsome to the enslavers as well as to the enslaved.

Ascendancy based on force begins to diminish as soon as force ceases to be sole arbiter. The introduction of factors other than force modifies the relationship between conquerors and those conquered. The victor will ceases to be the only active will. The vanquished recover in some degree wills of their own. A mutuality of relationship begins to be renewed. The relationship recovers political character. Victory fades as a circumstance and becomes only a memory. Bold expectations identified with the moment of victory fade away with it.

This accounts for an ancient and recurring cliché—I am old enough to have heard it in the sequels to two world wars—about politicians' having dissipated the glories and benefits of victories achieved by violence. To my view a failure of events to confirm expectations shows something wrong about the expectations rather than something deficient in the facts. The failure of peace to live up to the high hopes of the moment of victory shows something to be deceptive about the hopes—indeed about the concept—of victory itself.

Use of force is an incident. The problems of power are endless. Wars occur. Politics endures. Let us identify as a persistent illusion about power in foreign policy the idea that by dint of planning and perseverance it can be realized in that degree of efficacy seemingly secured in the moment of victory. It is an illusion first in equating all power with force and second in exaggerating the enduring effectiveness of the latter.

In examining the urges and the claims of perfection of solution in foreign policy, let us take note of a characteristic tendency of our times to regard the whole field of human relations as substantively and entirely an aspect of science. This links with a notion of the capability of cumulative and organized knowledge to solve anything and an accompanying view of every problem as something by definition solvable. . . .

Anyone who has dealt responsibly with foreign policy must have felt the meaning of Whitman's lines:

How can I pierce the impenetrable blank of the future?
I feel thy ominous greatness, evil as well as good;
I watch thee, advancing, absorbing the present, transcending the past;
I see thy light lighting and thy shadows shadowing, as if the entire globe;
But I do not undertake to define thee—hardly to comprehend thee . . .

To perceive the great extent to which a foreign policy, attempting to cope with the future, must be speculative and chancy is not a source of weakness. To the contrary, in Edmund Burke's phrase, "We can never walk surely but by being sensible of our blindness." The gravest errors are consequent from deceiving oneself that it is possible by some prodigy of planning to overcome this inherent circumstance.

Something of this fallacy is basic to every proposition for a perfect, all-embracing solution of our problems in foreign relations. The young Gladstone's mentor advised him that politics was an unsatisfactory business and that he would have to learn to put up with imperfect results. That advice has wisdom akin to the lessons of *Faust* and *Paradise Lost:* that grace derives from a sense of one's limitations and that tragedy is the wage of losing that sense.

Not perfection but utility is the test of planning in a foreign policy, and utility is a modest virtue. . . . The Duke of Wellington once referred to the differences in concept and planning between his adversary and himself in the Peninsular Campaign. The French plans, he said, were made with logical perfection and completeness. He likened them to a fine leather harness—admirable and useful until some part broke, whereupon the whole was useless. His own plans, he said, were made on the principle of rope, and as portions broke under the stress of circumstance, he would just tie knots and go on. A foreign policy should be planned on that principle.

Foresight in foreign policy—the planning function, I might call it—is best if seasoned with contingency and a recognition of human limitation. . . .

TOPIC 12

The Economic System as an Indicator of Foreign Policy

According to Karl Marx, people must first of all satisfy their hunger and thirst and protect their bodies against the climate. Only then can they engage in political, ethical, or aesthetic endeavors. Thus, the Marxists maintain, man's material environment (especially the modes of production) determines man's thoughts and goals.

In the words of Friedrich Engels, who with Karl Marx wrote the *Communist Manifesto* of 1848, "economic relations . . . are those whose action is ultimately decisive, forming a red thread which runs through all the other relations and enables us to understand them. . . . The production of the immediate material means of subsistence, and consequently the degree of economic development attained by a given people or during a given epoch, form the foundation upon which State institutions, the legal institutions, the art and even the religious ideas of the people concerned must have been evolved, and in the light of which these things must be explained instead of vice versa as had hitherto been the case."

Communist leaders transfer this basic Marxian premise to the international scene and seem to base their estimates of other nations' policies on their respective economic structures. Thus, they bluntly equate capitalism with aggressive policies and socialism of the Communist type with peaceful policies.

►CAPITALISM EQUALS IMPERIALISM

VLADIMIR I. LENIN

In the following selection the spiritual leader and organizer of the Bolshevik Revolution (November 7, 1917) defines imperialism as an inevitable and final stage of the capitalist economic system. He engages in argument with another socialist view which held that capitalism did not necessarily result in imperialism.

If it were necessary to give the briefest possible definition of imperialism we should have to say that imperialism is the monopoly stage of capitalism. Such a definition would include what is most important, for, on the one hand, finance capital is the bank capital of a few big monopolist banks, merged with the capital of the monopolist combines of manufacturers; and, on the other hand, the division of the world is the transition from a colonial policy which has extended without hindrance to territories unoccupied by any capitalist power, to a colonial policy of monopolistic possession of the territory of the world which has been completely divided up.

But very brief definitions, although convenient, for they sum of the main points, are nevertheless inadequate, because very important features of the phenomenon that has to be defined have to be especially deduced. And so, without forgetting the conditional and relative value of all definitions, which can never include all the concatenations of a phenomenon in its complete development, we must give a definition of imperialism that will embrace the following five essential features:

1) The concentration of production and capital developed to such a high stage that it created monopolies which play a decisive role in economic life.

2) The merging of bank capital with industrial capital, and the creation, on the basis of this "finance capital," of a financial oligarchy.

3) The export of capital, which has become extremely important, as distinguished from the export of commodities.

From "Imperialism, the Highest Stage of Capitalism," *The Essentials of Lenin* (London: Lawrence & Wishart, 1947), Vol. I, pp. 708-713.

4) The formation of international capitalist monopolies which share the world among themselves.

5) The territorial division of the whole world among the greatest capitalist powers is completed. . . .

[Following his definition, Lenin entered into an argument with Karl Kautsky. This German Marxist led the Second Socialist International from its inception in 1889. At the end of World War I, its left (Bolshevik) wing seceded and created the Third International (the Comintern) under Lenin's leadership. The Second International continued as a federation of Socialist democratic parties while the Third International represented its totalitarian rivals. Like Lenin, Karl Kautsky condemned imperialism and annexation of one nation by another. But he viewed such phenomena as a preferred policy of capitalism and not as an unavoidable stage in its development.]

Kautsky's definition is not only wrong and un-Marxian. It serves as a basis for a whole system of views which run counter to Marxian theory and Marxian practice all along the line. . . . Kautsky detaches the politics of imperialism from its economics, speaks of annexations as being a policy "preferred" by finance capital, and opposes to it another bourgeois policy which, he alleges, is possible on this very basis of finance capital. According to this argument, monopolies in economics are compatible with non-monopolistic, non-violent, non-annexationist methods in politics. According to his argument, the territorial division of the world, which was completed precisely during the period of finance capital, and which constitutes the basis of the present peculiar forms of rivalry between the biggest capitalist states, is compatible with a non-imperialist policy. The result is a slurring-over and a blunting of the most profound contradictions of the latest stage of capitalism, instead of an exposure of their depth; the result is bourgeois reformism instead of Marxism. . . .

Kautsky writes:

from the purely economic point of view it is not impossible that capitalism will yet go through a new phase, that of the extension of the policy of the cartels to foreign policy, the phase of ultra-imperialism, *i.e.*, of a superimperialism, a union of world imperialism and not struggles among imperialisms; a phase when wars shall cease under capitalism, a phase of the joint exploitation of the world by internationally combined finance capital. . . .

Is "ultra-imperialism" possible "from the purely economic point of view" or is it ultra-nonsense? . . .

The only objective, *i.e.*, real, social significance Kautsky's "theory" can have, is that of a most reactionary method of consoling the masses with hopes of permanent peace being possible under capitalism, distracting their attention from the sharp antagonisms and acute problems of the present era, and directing it towards illusory prospects of an imaginary "ultra-imperialism" of the future. Deception of the masses—there is nothing but this in Kautsky's "Marxian" theory. . . .

Let us consider India, Indo-China and China. It is known that these three colonial and semi-colonial countries, inhabited by six to seven hundred million human beings, are subjected to the exploitation of the finance capital of several imperialist states: Great Britain, France, Japan, the U.S.A., etc....

We will assume that *all* the imperialist countries conclude an alliance for the "peaceful" division of these parts of Asia; this alliance would be an alliance of "internationally united finance capital." As a matter of fact, alliances of this kind have been made in the twentieth century, notably with regard to China. We ask, is it "conceivable," assuming that the capitalist system remains intact—and this is precisely the assumption that Kautsky does make—that such alliances would be more than temporary, that they would eliminate friction, conflicts and struggle in all and every possible form?

This question need only be stated clearly enough to make it impossible for any reply to be given other than in the negative, for there can be *no* other conceivable basis under capitalism for the division of spheres of influence, of interests, of colonies, etc., than a calculation of the *strength* of the participants in the division, their general economic, financial, military strength, etc. And the strength of these participants in the division does not change to an equal degree, for under capitalism the development of different undertakings, trusts, branches of industry, or countries cannot be *even*. Half a century ago, Germany was a miserable, insignificant country, as far as its capitalist strength was concerned, compared with the strength of England at that time. Japan was similarly insignificant compared with Russia. Is it "conceivable" that in ten or twenty years' time the relative strength of the imperialist powers will have remained *un*changed? Absolutely inconceivable.

Therefore, in the realities of the capitalist system, . . . "inter-imperialist" or "ultra-imperialist" alliances, no matter what form they may assume, whether of one imperialist coalition against another, or of a general alliance embracing *all* the imperialist powers, are *in*evitably nothing more than a "truce" in periods between wars. Peaceful alliances prepare the ground for wars, and in their turn grow out of wars; the one is the condition for the other, giving rise to alternating forms of peaceful and nonpeaceful struggle out of *one and the same* basis of imperialist connections and the relations between world economics and world politics. . . .

The question as to whether it is possible to reform the basis of imperialism, whether to go forward to the accentuation and deepening of the antagonisms which it engenders, or backwards, towards allaying these antagonisms, is a fundamental question in the critique of imperialism. As a consequence of the fact that the political features of imperialism are reaction all along the line, and increased national oppression, resulting from the oppression of the financial oligarchy and the elimination of free competition, a petty-bourgeois-democratic opposition has been rising against imperialism in almost all imperialist countries since the beginning of the twentieth century. And the desertion of Kautsky and of the broad international Kautskyan trend from Marxism is displayed in the very fact that Kautsky not only did not trouble to oppose, not only was unable to oppose this petty-bourgeois reformist opposition, which is really reactionary in its economic basis, but in practice actually became merged with it.

In the United States, the imperialist war waged against Spain in 1898 stirred up the opposition of the "anti-imperialists," the last of the Mohicans of bourgeois democracy. They declared this war to be "criminal"; they denounced the annexation of foreign territories as being a violation of the Constitution, and denounced the "Jingo treachery" by means of which Aguinaldo, leader of the native Filipinos, was deceived (the Americans promised him the independence of his country, but later they landed troops and annexed it). They quoted the words of Lincoln:

> When the white man governs himself, that is self-government; but when he governs himself and also governs others, it is no longer self-government; it is despotism.

But while all this criticism shrank from recognizing the indissoluble bond between imperialism and the trusts, and, therefore, between imperialism and the very foundations of capitalism; while it shrank from joining up with the forces engendered by large-scale capitalism and its development—it remained a "pious wish." . . .

►YES, CAPITALISM MEANS CONFLICTS

NIKITA S. KHRUSHCHEV

Lenin's thesis, that capitalist competition over world markets must lead to conflicts, was voiced once more by Joseph Stalin at the end of 1952, a few months before his death. Stalin then predicted crises and wars among capitalist nations.

In his report to the Twentieth Party Congress (February 14, 1956), Khrushchev, then Soviet Premier and successor to Stalin, illustrated the validity of Lenin's thesis by informing his party audience of the growing antagonism among the Capitalists, in particular between the United States and England, and between Germany and France.

We should closely follow the economies of capitalism, not accept Lenin's thesis of the decay of imperialism in a simplified fashion but study all the best that sciences and techniques yield in the world of capitalism, in order to use the achievements of the world technical progress in the interests of socialism.

On the basis of the present situation, talk about "prosperity" has been renewed in certain circles in the West. Efforts are made to prove that allegedly the Marxist theory of crises is "outmoded."

Bourgeois economists are silent about the fact that only a timely confluence of circumstances of a favorable nature in capitalism retarded the growth of economic crises.

From a speech to the Twentieth Congress of the Soviet Communist Party on February 14, 1956, published by the *New York Times,* February 15, 1956.

Even so, at the period of a brisker situation, even crises phenomena are showing themselves. The commodity stock and also consumer credits have reached dangerous proportions in the U.S.A.

Britain is displeased with the growing activity of West Germany and Japan. Western Germany and Japan are displeased with Britain barring them from its markets.

Altogether they have more than enough grounds to be displeased with the United States, which is disorganizing the world market by carrying on unilateral trade, fencing off its markets from foreign imports, banning trade with the East, and resorting to dumping of agricultural produce and other measures hitting hard at other countries.

The economic struggle between the capitalist countries is flaring up with ever-growing force. As hitherto, the main contradiction is between the United States and Great Britain. . . .

The revival of Western Germany's economic might particularly aggravates the situation on the world market. The lessons of the two world wars show that, in their struggle for world markets, the German monopolies stop short of nothing. . . .

Germany still remains split, Western Germany is being speedily rearmed. It is no secret that by restoring German militarism, each of the three Western powers pursues its own ends.

But who will gain from this short-sighted policy? First of all, the imperialist forces of Western Germany. First among the losers will be France, which by such a policy is being reduced to the position of a third-rate power.

There is emerging ever more clearly a new Washington-Bonn axis that is increasing the dangers of war. . . .

▶UNDER CAPITALISM IMPERIALISM WILL WITHER AND DIE

JOSEPH A. SCHUMPETER

Lenin's equation capitalism = imperialism = aggression has been refuted by many writers on two main grounds: (1) the economic interest of the leading group has demonstrably been only one of several motives for aggressive policies. Sometimes it has been the dominant one, at other times quite secondary if present at all. Wars have sometimes been waged though no concrete interest was to be served by them. (2) capitalism—in association with rationalism and democracy which it has helped to produce—is actually anti-imperialistic because rational.

This is the thesis of the economist Joseph A. Schumpeter. According to him aggressive tendencies under capitalism are remnants of the precapitalistic period which are bound to wither away.

From *Imperialism and Social Classes* (New York: A. M. Kelley, Inc., 1951), pp. 3, 7, 27, 33, 36, 45, 49, 55, 60, 84, 89, 93, 94, 118, 130. Copyright 1951 by Elizabeth Boody Schumpeter.

Imperialism is the objectless disposition on the part of a state to un-limited forcible expansion. . . .

Just as such expansion cannot be explained by concrete interest, so too it is never satisfied by the fulfillment of a concrete interest, as would be the case if fulfillment were the motive, and the struggle for it merely a necessary evil. . . .

Hence the tendency of such expansion to transcend all bounds and tangible limits, to the point of utter exhaustion.

Aggressive attitudes on the part of states—or of such earlier organizational structure as history may record—can be explained, directly and unequivocally, only in part by the real and concrete interests of the people. . . .

A concrete interest need not be economic in character. When a state resorts to aggression in order to unite its citizens politically, as was the case with Piedmont in 1848 and 1859, this likewise betokens a real, concrete interest, explaining its conduct. . . .

The imperialism of a warrior nation, a people's imperialism, appears in history when a people has acquired a warlike disposition and a corresponding social organization *before* it has had an opportunity to be absorbed in the peaceful exploitation of its definitive area of settlement. . . .

The Arabs were mounted nomads, a persistent warrior type, like the nomadic Mongol horsemen. At heart they have remained just that, despite all modifications of culture and organization. . . . We are here face to face with a "warrior nation." . . . War was the normal function of this military theocracy. . . . Their social organization needed war; without successful wars it would have collapsed. War, moreover, was the normal occupation of the members of the society. . . . Had an Arab been asked why he fought, he might, as a born warrior, on proper reflection have countered with the question as to why one lived. . . .

In order to exhibit a continual trend toward imperialism, a people must not live on—or at least not be absorbed by—its own labor. When that happens, the instincts of conquest are completely submerged in the economic concerns of the day. In such a case even the nobles—unless a special military class arises—cannot evade the economic pressure, even though they themselves may remain parasitical in an economic sense. . . .

No people and no ruling class today can openly afford to regard war as a normal state of affairs or a normal element in the life of nations. . . .

Every expansionist urge must be carefully related to a concrete goal. All this is primarily a matter of political phraseology, to be sure. But the necessity for this phraseology is a symptom of popular attitude. And that attitude makes a policy of imperialism more and more difficult—indeed, the very word of imperialism is applied only to the enemy, in a reproachful sense, being carefully avoided with reference to the speaker's own policies. . . .

Trained in economic rationalism, . . . people (under capitalism) left no sphere of life unrationalized, questioning everything about themselves, the social structure, the state, the ruling class. . . . Everything that is purely instinctual, everything insofar as it is purely instinctual, is driven into the background by this development. . . . The mode of life of the capitalist world does not favor imperialist attitudes. . . . The alignment of interests in a capitalist economy—even the interests of its upper strata—by no means points unequivocally in the direction of imperialism.

The interests of trade and everyday life in England had turned pacifist, and the process of social restratification that marked the Industrial Revolution brought these interests to the fore.

Our analysis of the historical evidence has shown, first, the unquestionable fact that "objectless" tendencies toward forcible expansion, without definite, utilitarian limits—that is, nonrational and irrational, purely instinctual inclinations toward war and conquest—play a very large role in the history of mankind. It may sound paradoxical, but numberless wars—perhaps the majority of all wars—have been waged without adequate "reason"—not so much from the moral viewpoint as from that of reasoned and reasonable interest. The most herculean efforts of nations, in other words, have faded into the empty air.

Our analysis, in the second place, provides an explanation for this drive to action, this will to war—a theory by no means exhausted by mere references to an "urge" or an "instinct." The explanation lies, instead, in the vital needs of situations that molded peoples and classes into warriors—if they wanted to avoid extinction—and in the fact that psychological disposition and social structures acquired in the dim past in such situations, once firmly established, tend to maintain themselves and to continue in effect long after they have lost their meaning and their life-preserving function. . . .

Imperialism thus is atavistic. It falls into that large group of surviving features from earlier ages that play such an important part in every concrete social situation. In other words, it is an element that stems from the living conditions, not of the present, but of the past—or, put in terms of the economic interpretation of history, from past rather than present relations in production. It is an atavism in the social structure, in individual, psychological habits of emotional reaction. . . . *It is a basic fallacy to describe imperialism as a necessary phase of capitalism, or even to speak of the development of capitalism into imperialism.* . . .

Our analysis, in the third place, has shown the existence of subsidiary factors that facilitate the survival of such dispositions and structures—factors that may be divided into two groups. The orientation toward war is mainly fostered by the domestic interests of ruling classes, but also by the influence of all those who stand to gain individually from a war policy, whether economically or socially. . . .

The precapitalist elements in our social life may still have great vitality; special circumstances in national life may revive them from time to time; but in the end the climate of the modern world must destroy them. [Warlike instincts, structural elements, and organizational forms oriented toward war] will be politically overcome in time, no matter what they do to maintain among the people a sense of constant danger of war, with the war machine forever primed for action. And with them, imperialisms will wither and die.

►THE LENINIST MYTH OF IMPERIALISM

RAYMOND ARON

The actual relationship between economic interests and diplomacy is more often the reverse of that accepted by the Leninist theory of imperialism: thus, in Aron's words, "diplomatic alignments are determined not by conditions of economic rivalry or solidarity, but by considerations of power, by racial or cultural affinities, by the passions of the masses."

A contemporary French philosopher of history applies this thesis to recent history, marked by Nazi imperialism. He is author of several books on international politics and problems of our era. Among them are: Opium of the Intellectuals, On War *and* The Century of Total War.

The Marxist theory of imperialism appears, in various forms, in the works of Rosa Luxemburg, Bukharin, Lenin, and others. But the ideas common to all of them may be reduced to a few propositions. First, capitalist economy cannot, because of its very structure, absorb its own production, and is therefore compelled to expand; the individual is not even aware of the mechanism that is carrying him away. Second, the race among the European nations to win overseas territories for colonial exploitation is a fatal consequence of competition. In Africa, in Asia, in Oceania, Europeans seek raw materials, markets, places to invest their surplus capital. The period of colonial expansion marks a stage of capitalist development characterized by the dominance of financial capital and the power of monopolies. Third, the European wars are the fatal result of imperialism: their real stake is the division of the planet, even though they may be set off by some European dispute. They are accelerated by the growing disparity between the mother countries and the colonial empires—by the advent of the era of the closed world. Having reached the limits of the planet, the will to power that has driven the capitalists to the remotest corners of the world now must turn upon itself.

This theory enjoys tremendous prestige even in non-Marxist circles. It is intellectually satisfying because it accounts for a variety of circumstances. The interest in the Near East manifested by Britain, and more recently by the United States, is measured in terms of the oil resources of this region. The Boer War is linked with the South African gold mines, and with the propaganda carried on in London by agents of large development companies. In the course of the last twenty years of the nineteenth century the European nations carved out empires in Africa for themselves, and simultaneously the foremost of these nations (with the exception of England) returned to protectionism. The great German coal and steel trusts financed a press campaign for an ambitious program of naval construction before 1914, just as they financed National Socialism before 1933; similarly, certain American trusts torpedoed the disarmament conferences. The First World War ended in a

From *The Century of Total War* by Raymond Aron. Copyright © 1958 by Martin Secker & Warburg, Ltd. Reprinted by permission of Doubleday & Company, Inc. Footnotes omitted.

partition of the German colonies among the victors, and if the Germans had won, they would have done the same thing. . . .

But the objections to these summary and superficial interpretations are as strong as the arguments adduced in their favor are plausible. There is no relation between the purely economic need for expansion, such as should have obtained according to theory, and the actual facts of colonial expansion. French capitalism was one of the least dynamic in Europe yet the African empire that France acquired at the end of the nineteenth century is second in importance only to that of Great Britain. Russia, which at that time was only entering upon its capitalistic career and whose immense territory was still undeveloped, was nevertheless diplomatically active both in Europe and in Asia. The Russian interest in Manchuria and in the Slavic peoples of Europe was not dictated by economic considerations, nor was it the result of capitalist machinations.

Neither the First nor the Second World War originated directly in a conflict over colonies. Morocco was provocation for several international crises, yet all were settled by diplomatic negotiations—it was as though none of the great powers regarded these remote rivalries as sufficient justification for resorting to arms. The twenty years preceding the first war were probably among the most prosperous in the history of capitalism. The prevailing protective tariffs remained moderate, the national income of Germany doubled in twenty years, international trade continued to grow. Therefore, the image of a Europe constrained by its economic contradictions to destroy itself is a myth.

It will not be denied that capitalism tends to incorporate undeveloped territories into its system. Nor is it to be denied that colonial conquest may be regarded as a function of economic expansion. But whatever the plausibility of such a view, two questions remain to be answered: Were the African colonial empires founded in accordance with this pattern? Were the European wars a consequence of these quarrels for the division of the planet? The facts, if invoked without bias, answer these two questions negatively.

During the period between 1870 and 1914, there were instances in which the diplomatic services of nations were mobilized on behalf of capitalists, and in which they vigorously defended certain private investments (as in Venezuela and Persia). Not that Foreign Ministers were manipulated by capitalists, but they felt there were valid reasons for defending certain economic positions. The fact is that under the system of private ownership, the ambitions of certain corporations are genuinely identical with national interests. But (except for the Boer War, which was largely the result of intrigues by a large development company) none of the colonial undertakings that caused important diplomatic conflicts in Europe was motivated by the quest for capitalist profits; they all originated in political ambitions that the chancelleries camouflaged by invoking "realistic" motives. In other words, the actual relationship is most often the reverse of that accepted by the current theory of imperialism: the economic interests are only a pretext or a rationalization, whereas the profounder cause lies in the nations' will to power. . . .

The celebrated Berlin-Baghdad railway was a political project, and the

German banks consented—with great reluctance—to interest themselves in it only under pressure from the Wilhelmstrasse. The Bank of Rome extended its operations in Tripoli at the instigation of the Italian Minister of Foreign Affairs. It was granted discount privileges on condition that it would invest capital in Tripoli. Once these interests had been created, the relationship was reversed and the banks campaigned in favor of an active policy. The diplomats created economic interests in the hope that the defense of these interests would result in territorial acquisitions.

The legendary interpretation can be accounted for quite readily. Colonialist statesmen, such as Jules Ferry, for instance, constantly invoked economic arguments—the prospect of acquiring naval bases, markets for products, reserves of raw materials, etc. Nothing was easier than to take such arguments literally and transform them into the real causes. It is of course possible that such long-range interests were among the motives of the statesmen. All that the documents disclose is that the initiative came from them. And it is a fact that in each epoch conquerors have found different formulas for masking the will to power, which appears to be one of the unchanging features of European communities.

It is certain that, once a territory has been acquired, enterprising individuals and companies seek to exploit the protected areas. While this exploitation is not the primary purpose of the governments, they conceive it as one of the advantages of conquest. More than that, at a time when thinking everywhere is dominated by economic considerations, the so-called colonialists can increase the popularity of their cause by using these considerations to justify it. The public might turn away from them or rebel if they spoke of glory or national greatness.

The central idea of Lenin's theory is this: Twentieth-century wars, though waged in Europe and precipitated by European conflicts, have as their stake and their meaning the division of the planet. The main difficulty in trying to refute this theory is that it is difficult to see how it can be proved and by the same token how it can be disproved. No one denies that the First World War broke out because of German-Slav rivalry in the Balkans. Nor does anyone deny that the victors did not return to Germany the colonies they had occupied during the hostilities, and that secret agreements had provided for the division of these colonies among the Allies. No one questions the fact that if Germany had been victorious she would have seized at least part of the French and British empires. It can therefore be taken for granted that the immediate cause of the war had nothing to do with overseas territories, and that the issue of the war inevitably implied a new division of the colonies. Beyond these facts, we are in the realm of interpretations.

The burden of proof obviously rests upon those who attribute to events a deep significance of which the protagonists were unaware. In neither of the two camps did statesmen believe that the acquisition of distant possessions justified a European war, or that the economic system had no choice but to expand. It is true that the victorious camp profited from the occasion to seize the colonies of the defeated camp; but this, of itself, does not introduce any new factor into the process of European history, and in no way proves that

Frenchmen, Englishmen, or Germans—though they thought they were fighting to preserve the power or prestige of their respective nations—really fought because the capitalists, having reached the ends of the earth, had finally no other choice but to resort to arms to enlarge their respective shares in the territory of the world.

In forming national alignments, as in unleashing international hostilities, it is easy to discover the influence of traditional or emotional conflicts; but they supply no proof of the allegation that in our time capitalist rivalries exercise sovereign sway over human fate. Though the French penetration of Morocco created an additional reason for discord, France and Germany, whose economies were to a far greater extent complementary than competing, had never become reconciled after 1870. The French, while not calling for a war to recover Alsace-Lorraine, had not morally ratified the amputation of its territory. Moreover, calculations of the most classic kind regarding the balance of forces made them reject the idea of joining their powerful neighbor. If France had allied herself to her incomparably stronger neighbor she would have lost almost all of her independence, while as an ally of a naval power or of a distant land power, she essentially retained it. Such diplomatic mechanisms mark all eras.

Nor does the conflict between Russia and Austria-Hungary or Germany seem to be essentially economic in origin. To be sure, their interests may have been in conflict at one point or another. But Russia's interests—which, incidentally, were more political than economic—clashed, in Persia and in Afghanistan, with those of Great Britain more than with those of any other European nation.

The only way of giving some plausibility to the interpretation espoused by Marxist sympathizers is to represent the war of 1914-18 as having been determined above all by German-British rivalry, and then to represent this rivalry as an effect of trade competition. Many German publicists defended this thesis out of other motives. Desiring to clear their country of all guilt, to represent it as a victim of jealous "have" nations, they made a great deal of articles published in the English press at the end of the nineteenth century and more especially the beginning of the twentieth century—articles fulminating against the expansion of Germany, which was described as a deadly threat to Britain, and suggesting a resort to arms as the only means of saving Old Albion's prosperity.

Actually such voices were isolated, and did not in any way reflect the opinion of leading banking, industrial, or political circles. It was rather the opposite concept, as developed by Norman Angell in his well-known book, *The Great Illusion,* that underlay the predominant opinion. Angell's central thesis was that modern war does not pay, that the annexation of provinces does not increase the wealth of the inhabitants of the victorious country. National wealth is increased by a certain amount, but this must be divided by a proportionately increased denominator; in the end everyone finds himself where he was before. One may try to eliminate a rival. But in doing so one loses a customer and a supplier, and the effect of the deprivation inflicted on one's neighbor rebounds upon oneself. Modern economy creates solidarity among the nations. The idea of sharing spoils, of seizing treasures, belongs to another age. In the century of industry and trade, war would deal a fatal blow to everyone, victors and vanquished; in the damage sustained by the capitalist system, no one would be spared.

This demonstration, which is valid on the whole if Angell's implicit assumptions are granted (the existence of a world system and of respect for individual property on the part of belligerents), holds true in regard to the relations between Britain and Germany, as became evident after 1918. Leading circles in the two countries were perfectly aware of the fact, even though the competition between them was very real. Germany and Britain were first-rank customers and suppliers for each other.

Economically, Britain's outstanding rival since the beginning of the century has consistently been the United States. Yet the two Anglo-Saxon powers have never been on the verge of going to war against each other. Hence this admirable statement in a recent Soviet publication: "The characteristic feature of this contradiction [between Britain and the United States] lies in the fact that it unfolds within the framework of close co-operation, both economic and diplomatic." The truth is that trade rivalries between nations are one thing, and life-and-death struggles another. There is little truth in the myth that millions of men were sent to their deaths to open up markets for industries.

The essential cause of the hostility between Britain and Germany was Germany's creation of a navy. By threatening or seeming to threaten British naval supremacy, Germany, perhaps without realizing it, precipitated a break that contributed to creating the diplomatic conjuncture out of which the explosion took place. The British people know that for them control of the seas is neither a matter of prestige nor a luxury, but a question of survival. The naval policy of Wilhelm II and Von Tirpitz could be interpreted only as a challenge, and it necessarily drove Britain into joining the Franco-Russian alliance.

It might be said that Britain would under no circumstances have tolerated the annihilation of France, and that she would have intervened whether Von Tirpitz built his fleet or not. We do not have to confirm or reject this consideration, because it is irrelevant to our main thesis—that military alignments are political in origin. It was not without bitterness that Britain yielded her hegemony in the air and on the seas to the United States. She would never have yielded it, without a fight to the end, to the Germany of the Kaiser or Hitler.

Whereas the First World War followed a period of rising prices and expanding international trade, the second broke out ten years after the beginning of the greatest depression in the history of capitalism. In most countries recovery had taken place several years before the war, and production levels were generally higher than before the depression. But this recovery had a special character: it had taken place within each nation. International trade, instead of continuing to develop as in the preceding century, had not recovered its pre-1929 volume, and the dominant economy, that of the United States, had not overcome a condition of underemployment that seemed chronic. One would have to be blind or fanatic to deny that there was a relation between the slump of 1929 and the war of 1939.

One of the immediate causes of National Socialism's rise to power was indisputably the unprecedented economic crisis, with its concomitant factor of millions of unemployed. But the exceptional acuteness of the crisis, particularly in Germany, cannot be attributed to the effects of the autonomous evolution of the capitalist system. A sequence of events, accidental in relation to world economic developments (the financial policy of Great Britain, the rate of exchange for the pound, the use of the gold exchange standard, the pyramiding of credits in the United States, the high level of world prices, which were made dependent on American prices following the wartime inflation, the German inflation, the accumulation of foreign loans, etc.), had brought about the situation of 1929 and the collapse that followed. It would be possible to show that many of these accidents originated directly or indirectly in the First World War and its aftermath. Nevertheless, it is a fact that the road from Versailles to the September aggression against Poland leads through the depression of 1929. Assuming that this depression was, in a way, a consequence of the First World War, it is even more certain that it was one of the causes of the second.

Between 1930 and 1933, the Germany of the Weimar regime, stricken by unemployment, had a choice between three possible orientations. She could adapt her domestic economy to world conditions; she could undertake total planning under the leadership of the workers' party, which was inclined to co-operate with Soviet Russia, or she could undertake planning under the leadership of the "national" parties, with rearmament and diplomatic aggressiveness. The second solution was ruled out by the existing balance of strength and by the popular passions. Moreover, by concentrating its attack on the "social traitors," the Communist Party was robbing the parties of the left of the small chances of success they might have had. Neither the masses nor the parties were willing to accept the sacrifices implied in the first solution. Adjustment to world economic conditions would probably have required a devaluation of the mark (which was unpopular because of memories of the inflation); failing that, a lowering of nominal wages (which was resisted by the trade unions) and a credit policy inspired by the theories of Keynes. Recovery under these conditions would have been slow and gradual. It would logically have implied a diplomatic armistice over a period of a few years. But nationalistic feeling among the people had been exacerbated by economic distress and by the propaganda against the Treaty of Versailles. Rightist circles were impatient to recover sovereignty with regard to armaments. The coalition of the Hitlerites and the nationalists, symbol of the rapprochement between the revolutionaries and the traditional conservatives, was founded on the common will to achieve certain objectives: liquidation of unemployment on a national basis, rearmament, and revision of the Treaty of Versailles.

We shall not contend that the former ruling classes unanimously desired this solution, and the share of responsibility of each group remains a matter of controversy—namely: How much individual responsibility is to be attributed to the financiers and captains of industry, who contributed money to the National Socialist movement; and to the Rhenish bankers and East Prussian landowners, who brought about the coalition of January 1933? All formulas ascribing a specific attitude to any single one of the ruling classes have always been semi-mythical in character. There was no want of conservatives who were uneasy about the brown-shirted demagogues. All that can be said is that in the seizure of power by the National Socialists, the prerequisite was the consent to this adventure given by a fraction of the former ruling classes. Apprentice sorcerers, these men expected the Führer to subject the masses to discipline, to reintegrate the millions of the unemployed into the Army or to absorb them in the factories, to restore sovereignty and power to Germany; they, no more than others, wanted the thing that came to an end in the bunker of Berlin, with the crushing of their homeland.

Unemployment—that is, the economic depression—was at the root of rearmament. The formula according to which unemployment was its cause greatly oversimplifies the truth. The United States had more than 12 million unemployed, yet neither the masses nor the leaders thought of mobilizing an army or building a war industry. The resort to a war economy was natural for the Germans, faithful to their military traditions and anxious to alter, if not to supersede, the status imposed by the Treaty of Versailles. In one way or another, a little sooner or a little later, Germany would have demanded and obtained equality, demanded if not obtained a revision of the treaties of peace. On the other hand, it was not implied in the permanent elements of the German situation that a man like Hitler and a party like the National Socialist must inevitably seize power. War was implied in the style and in the ambitions of the National Socialists, not in those of the traditional nationalists.

Once rearmament had begun and the theory of full employment on a national basis was applied, was war inevitable? Did rearmament lead to aggression, just as unemployment had led to rearmament? Did the economic system of the Third Reich rule out the peace or even the truce that, on the eve of the seizure of Prague, a British trade delegation once again offered to the Berlin rulers? These questions are abstract and, in a sense, unreal. Hitler and his companions had always thought in political and not in economic terms. What they wanted for their country was power, the reward of which would be to attain the wealth of a master nation. They never asked themselves whether they could ever call a halt from an economic standpoint, for from 1939 on they had not had the slightest intention of doing so. Occasionally, at least, Hitler directly wanted war, which he thought he alone could wage victoriously, and which he regarded as indispensable for the realization of his schemes. The National Socialist system itself derived from a will to empire.

Would not Hitler have been driven at all events, by force of the economic system that he erected, to attempt conquest? This thesis is advanced by pseudo-Marxists who allege that they discover in [the Nazi economic system] the same imperialist fatality they ascribe to monopoly capitalism. It is also advanced by other critics, according to whom National Socialism or Hitler himself would have been endangered by a peace, even a provisional one.

In the long run, from a philosophical point of view, it might be said that the choice between integration into world economy and a supranational economy based on a *Grossraum,* an expanded national territory, continued to present itself. But the need for decision was not urgent. The Western democracies were ready to appease by concessions. Once again, Hitler was not subjected to any economic restraint.

Would Hitler's authority or his regime have been shaken by a truce? Would Hitler have lost part of the prestige he had won by his peaceful triumphs? There is nothing to justify an affirmative answer to these questions. In September 1938 the German people dreaded a general war almost as much as the British and French peoples dreaded it. They would not have found fault with their Führer for saving the peace; rather they would have taken the contrary attitude. After Munich, Germany held a hegemony over Central Europe that was more complete than that which had been refused the Kaiser's Germany before 1914. But so long as there was the Soviet Union on one side, and the Franco-British alliance on the other, the hegemony over *Mitteleuropa* fell short of assuring a European empire. The truth, concealed under the allegations of political or economic necessity, is that Hitler was not content with his hegemony. He wanted to take advantage of his temporary superiority in armament at least to liquidate Poland. And therewith he unleashed the monster.

Inevitably, a partisan of National Socialism inclines to the theory of the *Grossraum.* The authoritarian organization of an economic whole develops the more smoothly, the fewer are the obstacles encountered by the will of the planners. By definition, the planners possess no authority over the people and the raw materials situated on the other side of the customs line. They cannot foresee the free prices of the raw materials they must import, nor can they foresee the changing tastes of those who, by buying their manufactured products, supply them from the outside with foreign currency. Compulsory subjection to the foreign customer means the survival of a principle which the planners are attempting to suppress at home. Subjection changes into sovereignty on the day when sellers and buyers have been reduced by force of arms to the common law of a planned economy. . . .

The ambition for conquest and the dream of rationalization are combined in the *Grossraum* theory.

Thus we are far from denying the imperialistic potentialities of the economic policy adopted by the National Socialists. We maintain only that the Third Reich was not driven to imperialism by residues of capitalism in its structure. If the private entrepreneurs or managers had been replaced by government-appointed managers, if the Ruhr had been nationalized, if the planning had been total, the imperialist temptation would not have been mitigated. Indeed, the opposite is true. If German heavy industry had become collective property, it would have been no less disproportionate to the needs of the domestic market for peaceful consumption. The need for outside purchase of supplies for the people and for the factories, the wish to include in the plan a territory as vast as possible, would have persisted. In short, the contradiction between the essence of modern economy and National Socialism, between political nationalism and the industrial system, would not have been overcome, and this contradiction is the ultimate cause of the suicide of Europe.

This contradiction, as we have seen, emerged only during the course of the First World War. A traditional conflict was amplified into a superwar because of the weapons that industry placed at the disposal of the combatants. In the years preceding 1939, the contradiction became more acute. The disturbances that followed the war, the depression of 1929, had thrown the states back upon the expedients of controlled trade, of planning in isolation from world economy. National Socialism marked the extreme form of this falling back on intranational resources. Such a structure is not favorable either to peaceful international trade, or to the peaceful coexistence of empires. Although the motives of the protagonists were political, although the conqueror was inspired by the will to power, Europe, before the Hitlerian adventure, was torn by an absurd situation. The European nations do not offer a rational framework for planned economy.

Modern industry and militarism have always been associated throughout the centuries of their simultaneous flowering. Although none of the fundamental discoveries that made the industrial revolution possible seems to have been occasioned by military needs, such discoveries have often accelerated progress or given rise to improvements in manufacturing methods. Assembly-line production in metallurgy and textiles was partly the effect of military requirements, and at the same time it determined the tempo of the battles.

Current expressions emphasize the analogies between the style of modern industry and that of the army. In order to create an army, thousands, hundreds of thousands, and finally millions of men must be uprooted from a communal, organic mode of life and subjected to a hierarchy organized in accordance with the sole imperative of collective action and performance. Industry gives rise to a similar process. Factory discipline is not the same as the discipline of the barracks; the worker, outside his shop, continues to have a family life. Nevertheless there is an unquestionable similarity between the two, and the labor camps of wartime Germany and of five-year plans in Russia stress this similarity to the point of horror.

The evolution of capitalism during the second half of the nineteenth century and the first years of the twentieth century had opened up a different perspective. Humanization of industrial work had seemed not impossible. Higher living standards had made it possible to restore to the worker the personal life of which he had been deprived during the stage of initial accumulation, the pioneer stage of the coal, textile, and metallurgic industries. The municipal workers' quarters in Sweden, in Germany—like those later erected in some English centers—no longer evoked the image of the "wretched of the earth." At least a part of the proletariat was gradually obtaining decent living conditions. Increasing access to middle-class comforts was mitigating the isolation of the worker and the amorphism of the masses. The industrial army was slowly returning to civilian life.

The wars did not halt the rise of the working class; in some respects, in some countries, they accelerated it. But they brought forth a danger that the bourgeoisie, during its time of glory, had never dreamed of—the subjection of all of society to the law of military organization. At the very moment when economic progress was helping to cure some of the evils chargeable to technology, war has brought about the total mobilization of collectivities. Tomorrow the rule of the bourgeoisie may seem like a precarious transition from the military order of the aristocracies to the military order of the technocracies.

TOPIC 13

Ideology and Foreign Policy

The *Communist Manifesto* of 1848 proclaims:

> The Communists disdain to conceal their views and aims. They openly declare their ends can be attained only by the forcible overthrow of all existing social conditions. Let the ruling classes tremble at a Communist revolution. The proletarians have nothing to lose but their chains. They have a world to win. Proletarians of all countries, unite!

Ideology which is openly committed to proselytizing on a world scale is usually associated with violent methods in foreign policy. A political system which advocates and practices the art of compromise at home is often equated with peacefulness abroad.

But is it all as simple as that? An ideology or a creed may be differently interpreted and translated into practice by believers and leaders. Thus American application of democratic theory differs from that of the French. Yugoslav and Chinese interpretations of communism differ from those of the Russians.

Furthermore, an aggressive ideology may postpone the realization of its goal, accept a temporary truce, and advocate coexistence or even a compromise when it encounters serious hurdles. Aggressive public statements may also aim at securing compliance. Yet they may not form the basis for actual actions if we refuse to comply.

Fanatic leaders, on the other hand, may proceed to the realization of their objectives, regardless of cost or risk involved.

In an era in which the Soviet Union challenges the free world and the doctrine of communism challenges that of democracy, it is useful to explore the possible relationship between communism and the Soviet foreign policy.

►COMMUNIST DOCTRINE ON WAR AND COEXISTENCE

HISTORICUS

Like generals, Soviet leaders cannot be expected to publicize details of their world strategy or their operational directives. Yet the public statements of the Communist trinity should be studied and analyzed for two reasons: (1) They may be the basis of Soviet actions; and (2) they are meant to be read, heard, and reacted to, by enemies, allies, and the Communists. The pronouncements of Lenin, Stalin, and Khrushchev remain the assigned reading of leaders and masses of the Sino-Soviet bloc of a billion people.

Following are Stalin's and Lenin's thoughts on war and coexistence with capitalism. They were ably translated from original sources by an anonymous American diplomat in Moscow. Some of his pertinent comments are also reproduced.

(Stalin defined[1] the strategy which world communism was to adopt after the October revolution as follows:)

"The goal is to consolidate the dictatorship of the proletariat in one country, using it as a base for the overthrow of imperialism in all countries. Revolution spreads beyond the limits of one country; the epoch of world revolution has begun."

The fundamental, not merely incidental, intention to use the Soviet Union as the base for world revolution has thus been on the record in Stalin's most important doctrinal work, repeatedly republished for mass circulation from 1924 to the present time. In another passage which has had similar authoritative distribution from 1924 to the present Stalin elaborates his view:

. . . the very development of world revolution . . . will be more rapid and more thorough, the more thoroughly Socialism fortifies itself in the first victorious country, the faster this country is transformed into a base for the further unfolding of world revolution, into a lever for the further disintegration of imperialism.

While it is true that the *final* victory of Socialism in the first country to emancipate itself is impossible without the combined efforts of the proletarians of several countries, it is equally true that the development of world revolution will be the more rapid and thorough, the more effective the aid rendered by the first Socialist country to the workers . . . of all other countries.

In what should this aid be expressed?

Excerpted by special permission from "Stalin on Revolution," *Foreign Affairs,* January, 1949. Copyright by Council on Foreign Relations, Inc., New York. (Footnotes omitted.)

[1] Quoted from *Ob osnovakh Leninizma* (1924 to present) and *Voprosy Leninizma,* 11th ed., 1945, p. 54. Italics added. The book *Voprosy Leninizma (Problems of Leninism)* is the basic collection of Stalin's writings in which Lenin's fundamental formulations are incorporated, stressed or elaborated on. Since the twenties it has been reprinted in millions of copies and studied by every new generation of Soviet citizens and their leaders. The majority of quotations in Historicus' article are from the above-mentioned book.

It should be expressed, first, in the victorious country "carrying out the maximum realizable in one country *for* the development, support, awakening of revolution in all countries" . . .

It should be expressed, second, in that the "victorious proletariat" of the one country . . . "after organizing its own Socialist production, should stand up . . . *against* the remaining, capitalist world, attracting to itself the oppressed classes of other countries, raising revolts in those countries against the capitalists, in the event of necessity coming out even with armed force against the exploiting classes and their governments" . . .

This passage deserves detailed comment. The supreme aim of world revolution is the logical outcome of Stalin's entire theoretical position [on imperialism and capitalism]—notably the thesis that capitalism is a single *world-system* fatally torn by contradictions which can be cured only by a consciously directed Socialist revolution. Granted these assumptions, the determination to use the foothold won in the Soviet Union as a base for world revolution is elementary common sense. . . .

The second paragraph in the long passage quoted above places the problem of the "final" victory of Socialism in one country within the wider context of world revolution, thus excluding the hypothesis that the more limited objective—involving merely enough additional revolutions to end "capitalist encirclement" and provide security for the Soviet Union—marks the outer limit of Stalin's program for Communist expansion. Further, the passage quoted indicates that the Soviet Union will first be prepared as a base, and only then, *"after* organizing its own Socialist production," will be used more aggressively to aid revolution abroad. This tallies with the predominant absorption of the Soviets with internal affairs during the earlier five-year plans. Further, the phrase does not define the stage at which production is to be considered adequately organized. Hence the prospect of three or more additional five-year plans, as announced in 1938 and again in 1946, may indicate that the base is still not ready for contemplated operations.

Finally, the passage definitely states that armed force will be used against capitalist governments if necessary. There thus is nothing except expediency to limit the aid which Stalin contemplates giving to revolutions abroad. However, the phrase "if necessary" indicates that armed force is not to be used by preference; ahead of it come propaganda and Communist Party control, by which is meant that the Soviet Union should attract to itself "the oppressed classes of other countries, raising revolts in these countries against the capitalists."

The ultimate resort to armed force is a logical development of the Leninist thesis that only consciously-led revolution can drive the capitalists from the stage of history [in Stalin's words to H. G. Wells in 1934: "Classes which had their day do not leave the stage of history voluntarily"]. The assumption that the world has been fundamentally divided into two camps since the October Revolution runs through Stalin's writings from his early days and is grounded in his Marxist philosophy. Stalin pictures the long-range evolution of the two camps as follows:

Most probably, in the course of development of the world revolution, side by side with the centers of imperialism in individual capitalist countries and the system of these countries throughout the world, centers of Socialism will be created in individual Soviet countries and a system of these centers throughout the world, and the struggle between these two systems will fill up the history of the development of the world revolution.

The systems are expected to be organized around two centers:

Thus in the course of further development of international revolution two centers will form on a world scale: a Socialist center, binding to itself the countries that gravitate to Socialism, and a capitalist center, binding to itself the countries that gravitate to capitalism. The struggle between these two centers for the possession of the world economy will decide the fate of capitalism and Communism in the whole world.

The plan to make the Soviet Union the base for world revolution implies that it will be one of the centers. [Stalin's writings offer evidence] that the United States is expected to be the other. The ultimate inevitability of war to the finish between the two camps is made clear in one of Stalin's favorite quotations from Lenin: "We live . . . not only in a state but in a system of states, and the existence of the Soviet Republic side by side with the imperialist states for a long time is unthinkable. In the end either one or the other will conquer. And until that end comes, a series of the most terrible collisions between the Soviet Republic and the bourgeois states is inevitable." Stalin appended to this forecast of inexorable wars a succinct, "Clear, one would think." Thus Stalin expects not merely one but several world wars before the end of capitalism.

At the very close of the struggle the forces of Socialism will be so superior that Stalin foresees an exception to the general rule that revolutionary violence is necessary to overthrow capitalism: "Of course, in the distant future, if the proletariat wins in the most important capitalist countries and if the present capitalist encirclement is replaced by a Socialist encirclement, a 'peaceful' path of development is fully possible for some capitalist countries, whose capitalists, in view of the 'unfavorable' international situation, will consider it expedient to make serious concessions to the proletariat 'voluntarily.' " . . .

On Flexible Tactics

In general, despite his comparatively rigid doctrinal framework, Stalin's conception of Communist strategy and tactics is highly flexible. It rests on a continual assessment of the status of forces in both the capitalist and the Socialist systems. Thus he writes: *"Tactics,* guiding itself by the directives of strategy and by experience of the revolutionary movement . . . calculating at every given moment the state of forces inside the proletariat and its allies (greater or less cultivation, greater or less degree of organization and class-consciousness, presence of particular traditions, presence of particular forms of movement, forms of organization, *basic* and *secondary*), as well as in the camp of the adversary, profiting by discord and every kind of confusion in the camp of the adversary—marks out those *concrete courses* for winning the wide masses to the proletarian side and leading them to battle stations on the social front . . . which most surely pave the way for strategic successes."

In view of this flexibility, and of the way in which Stalin expects Communist leadership to win control of many movements which originate spontaneously, it must be concluded that the "objective" conditions of revolution are not fixed quantities in Stalin's thinking, but rather interdependent variables which are to be manipulated to satisfy just one equation: revolution occurs where the Communist command concentrates superiority of forces at a point on the Capitalist front where the bourgeoisie can be isolated and overwhelmed. In other words, "revolutionary crises" do not have to be waited for; they can to some extent be organized; and an extremely favorable balance of outside aid can compensate to a considerable degree for a deficiency in favorable internal conditions.

For the period of world revolution, Stalin's grand strategy is to use the Soviet Union as a base linking the proletariat of the west with the movements for national liberation from imperialism in the east into "a single world front against the world front of imperialism." In this way he harnesses two of the major contradictions of capitalism to his chariot—contradictions between proletariat and bourgeoisie, and contradictions between capitalist and colonial countries. The front thus formed is to be used to exploit the third contradiction of capitalism—that between capitalist countries, whose rivalry for spheres of influence must lead periodically to war, the event most propitious for revolution. . . .

. . . Describing the skill shown by the Communist Party in Russia in 1917 in uniting "in one common revolutionary stream such different revolutionary movements as the general democratic movement for peace, the peasant democratic movement for seizure of the landed estates, the movement of the oppressed nationalities for national liberation and national equality, and the Socialist movement of the proletariat for the overthrow of the bourgeoisie and the establishment of the dictatorship of the proletariat," Stalin declares that "undoubtedly, the merging of these diverse revolutionary streams in one common, powerful revolutionary stream decided the fate of capitalism in Russia." . . .

One of the chief conditions to which tactics must be adjusted, according to Stalin, is the ebb and flow of the forces favoring revolution. Aggressive tactics should be timed with a rising tide; tactics of defense, the assemblage of forces, and even retreat go with an ebbing tide. The importance of gauging the direction of the tide is illustrated by Stalin's remarks in 1929 concerning a controversy with Bukharin, who apparently held that the "stabilization of capitalism" was persisting unchanged: "This question, comrades, is of decisive importance for the sections of the Comintern. Is the capitalist stabilization going to pieces or is it becoming more secure? On this the whole line of the Communist Parties in their day-to-day political work depends. Are we in a period of decline of the revolutionary movement . . . or are we in a period when the conditions are maturing for a new revolutionary rise, a period of preparing the working class for coming class battles—on this depends the tactical position of the Communist Parties." Stalin holds that it is a period of revolutionary upswing.

Stalin's insistence on flexibility of tactics is ground for a very important maxim in the interpretation of his public statements; one must avoid, if possible, mistaking a change in tactics for a change in fundamental doctrine and strategic objectives. The example of a change in tactics often thus mistaken is Stalin's remarks about peaceful coexistence of and coöperation between the Socialist and capitalist systems. . . .

On Peaceful Coexistence

Stalin first announced a period of "peaceful coexistence" for proletarian and bourgeois worlds in 1925, saying that the revolutionary movement was ebbing and capitalism achieving a temporary stabilization. But the context of his statement makes plain that he expected peaceful coexistence to be as temporary as the stabilization. In 1927 he stated that capitalist stabilization was coming to an end and that the period of "peaceful coexistence" was likewise giving way to one of imperialist attacks. But he added that the Soviet Union must continue to pursue a policy of maintaining peace for the following reason:

> We cannot forget the saying of Lenin to the effect that a great deal in the matter of our construction depends on whether we succeed in delaying war with the capitalist countries, which is inevitable but which may be delayed either until proletarian revolution ripens in Europe, or until the colonial revolutions come fully to a head, or, finally, until the capitalists fight among themselves over division of the colonies. Therefore the maintenance of peaceful relations with capitalist countries is an obligatory task for us.
> The basis of our relations with capitalist countries consists in admitting the coexistence of two opposed systems. . . .

The peace policy has another tactical function in Stalin's strategy of revolution. He notes how successfully the Communists capitalized on the general popular craving for peace during the October Revolution; accordingly he maneuvers the Soviet Union and the Communist Parties into position as apostles of peace, unmasking the imperialist "warmongers" in order to profit by popular sentiments for peace in the future. Particularly interesting in this connection is the way Stalin combines his peace stand with verbal onslaughts on Social Democratic pacifism as a mere mask of the warmongers.

Apart from their bearing on peace, the tasks of developing trade and obtaining technological assistance from capitalist countries have a direct relationship to building the industrial base of the Soviet Union, especially during the early stage of the five-year plans. Stalin makes several unsentimental and businesslike proposals for improved relations along these lines, particularly with the United States. His fullest and frankest statement on coöperation between Soviet and capitalist worlds is made in 1927, shortly before his announcement that the capitalist stabilization is coming to an end. To the American Workers' Delegation, who asked to what extent such coöperation is possible and whether it has definite limits, Stalin replies:

> The matter concerns, obviously, temporary agreements with capitalist states in the field of industry, in the field of trade, and, perhaps, in the field of diplomatic relations. I think that the presence of two opposed systems . . . does not exclude the possibility of such agreements. I think that such agreements are possible and expedient under conditions of peaceful development. . . .
>
> The limits of these agreements? The limits are set by the opposition of the two systems, between which rivalry and struggle go on. Within the limits permitted by these two systems, but only within these limits, agreements are fully possible. . . .
>
> Are these agreements merely an experiment or can they have more or less lasting character? That depends not only on us; that depends also on those who contract with us. That depends on the general situation. War can upset any agreement whatever. . . .

A few pages later the same interview reads: "Thus in the course of further development of international revolution two centers will form on a world scale: a Socialist center . . . and a capitalist center. . . . The struggle between these two centers for the possession of the world economy will decide the fate of capitalism and Communism in the whole world."

▶PEACEFUL COEXISTENCE—THE SOVIET VIEW

NIKITA S. KHRUSHCHEV

While generally agreeing with Lenin and Stalin that capitalism is incurable of its aggressive tendencies, Soviet Premier Khrushchev suggested at the Twentieth Party Congress in 1956, and has consistently repeated ever since, that the increased strength of the Communist bloc may deter capitalism from plunging the world into a new war. The strength of the Communist bloc is also supposed to facilitate peaceful introduction of communism into countries which have not developed a strong capitalist system. Civil war may be necessary in countries with strong capitalism. The United States is probably meant but is not mentioned by name.

Khrushchev's announcement that "there is no fatal inevitability of war" has evoked the following comment by Louis J. Halle, a prominent scholar in the field of foreign policy (his essays are reproduced in Topics 6 and 7): " . . . if what was inevitable gets over being inevitable, then it could not have been inevitable to begin with. Therefore to say that a great war is no longer inevitable is to deny the infallibility of Marxist 'science.' Does Mr. Khrushchev really mean to do this? Or is he simply pulling the wool over our eyes, trying to disarm us?" (The New York Times Magazine, November 15, 1959).

This selection is from the Speech to the Twentieth Congress of the Soviet Communist Party, in Moscow, February 14, 1956; published by the *New York Times*, February 15, 1956, p. 10.

. . . The principal feature of our epoch is the emergence of socialism from the confines of one country and its transformation into a world system. Capitalism has proved impotent to hinder this world-historic process. . . .

The Leninist principle of the peaceful coexistence of states with differing social systems was, and remains, the general line of our country's foreign policy.

It is alleged that the Soviet Union advocates the principle of peaceful coexistence exclusively from tactical considerations of the moment.

However, it is well known that we have advocated peaceful coexistence just as perseveringly from the very inception of Soviet power. Hence, this is not a tactical stratagem but a fundamental principle of Soviet foreign policy.

The foes of peace still allege that the Soviet Union intends to overthrow capitalism in other countries by "exporting" revolution. It goes without saying that there are no adherents of capitalism among Communists.

But this does not at all signify that we have interfered or intend to interfere in the internal affairs of countries where a capitalist system exists. It is ridiculous to think that revolutions are made to order.

When we say that in the competition between the two systems of capitalism and socialism, socialism will triumph, this by no means implies that the victory will be reached by armed intervention on the part of the Socialist countries in the internal affairs of the capitalist countries. . . .

We presume that countries with differing social systems cannot just simply exist side by side. There must be progress to better relations, to stronger confidence among them, to cooperation.

As will be recalled, there is a Marxist-Leninist premise which says that while imperialism exists, wars are inevitable. While capitalism remains on earth the reactionary forces representing the interests of the capitalist monopolies will continue to strive for war gambles and aggression, and may try to let loose war.

There is no fatal inevitability of war.

Now there are powerful social and political forces, commanding serious means capable of preventing the unleashing of war by the imperialists, and—should they try to start it—of delivering a smashing rebuff to the aggressors and thwarting their adventuristic plans.

To this end it is necessary for all the forces opposing war to be vigilant and mobilized. It is necessary for them to act in a united front and not to slacken their efforts in the fight to preserve peace. . . .

It is quite likely that the forms of the transition to socialism will become more and more variegated. Moreover, it is not obligatory for the implementation of these forms to be connected with civil war in all circumstances.

The enemies are fond of depicting us, Leninists, as supporters of violence always and in all circumstances. It is true that we recognize the necessity for the revolutionary transformation of capitalist society into Socialist society.

This is what distinguishes revolutionary Marxists from reformists and opportunists. There is not a shadow of doubt that for a number of capitalist countries the overthrow of the bourgeoise dictatorship by force and the connected sharp aggravation of the class struggle is inevitable.

But there are different forms of social revolution and the allegation that we recognize force and civil war as the only way of transforming society does not correspond to reality.

Leninism teaches us that the ruling classes will not relinquish power of their own free will. However, the greater or lesser degree of acuteness in the struggle, the use or not of force in the transition to socialism, depend not so much on the proletariat as on the extent of the resistance put up by the exploiters, and on the employment of violence by the exploiting class itself.

In this connection the question arises of the possibility of employing the parliamentary form for the transition to socialism. . . .

Of course in countries where capitalism is still strong and where it controls an enormous military and police machine, the serious resistance of the reactionary forces is inevitable. There the transition to socialism will proceed amid conditions of an acute class revolutionary struggle.

The political leadership of the working class, headed by its advance detachment, is the indispensable and decisive factor for all the forms of the transition to socialism. Without this, the transition to socialism is impossible. . . .

*   *   *

From its very inception the Soviet state proclaimed peaceful coexistence [1] as the basic principle of its foreign policy [G. F. Kennan disputes this particular point in Topic 14]. It was no accident that the very first act of the Soviet power was the decree on peace, the decree on the cessation of the bloody war.

What, then, is the policy of peaceful coexistence?

In its simplest expression it signifies the repudiation of war as a means of solving controversial issues. However, this does not cover the entire concept of peaceful coexistence. Apart from the commitment to non-aggression, it also presupposes an obligation on the part of all states to desist from violating each other's territorial integrity and sovereignty in any form and under any pretext whatsoever. The principle of peaceful coexistence signifies a renunciation of interference in the internal affairs of other countries with the object of altering their system of government or mode of life or for any other motives. . . .

It is often said in the West that peaceful coexistence is nothing else than a tactical method of the socialist states. There is not a grain of truth in such allegations. Our desire for peace and peaceful coexistence is not conditioned by any time-serving or tactical considerations. It springs from the very nature of socialist society [see Kennan's counterargument in Topic 14] in which there are no classes or social groups interested in profiting by war or seizing and enslaving other people's territory.

Peaceful coexistence does not mean merely living side by side in the absence of war but with the constantly remaining threat of its breaking out in the future. *Peaceful coexistence can and should develop into peaceful competition for the purpose of satisfying man's needs in the best possible way.*

We say to the leaders of the capitalist states: Let us try out in practice

---

[1] This and the following paragraphs are from the article "On Peaceful Coexistence," *Foreign Affairs*, October, 1959, reprinted by special permission. Copyright by Council on Foreign Relations, Inc., New York.

whose system is better, let us compete without war. This is much better than competing in who will produce more arms and who will smash whom. We stand and always will stand for such competition as will help to raise the well-being of the people to a higher level.

The principle of peaceful competition does not at all demand that one or another state abandon the system and ideology adopted by it. It goes without saying that the acceptance of this principle cannot lead to the immediate end of disputes and contradictions which are inevitable between countries adhering to different social systems. But the main thing is ensured: the states which decided to adopt the path of peaceful coexistence repudiate the use of force in any form and agree on a peaceful settlement of possible disputes and conflicts, bearing in mind the mutual interests of the parties concerned. In our age of the H-bomb and atomic techniques this is the main thing of interest to every man.

As for the social system in some state or other, that is the domestic affair of the people of each country. We always have stood and we stand today for non-interference in the internal affairs of other countries. We have always abided, and we shall abide, by these positions.

Displaying skepticism about the idea of peaceful competition, Vice President Nixon, in his speech over the Soviet radio and television in August 1959, attempted to find a contradiction between the Soviet people's professions of their readiness to coexist peacefully with the capitalist states and the slogans posted in the shops of our factories calling for higher labor productivity in order to ensure the speediest victory of Communism.   .

This was not the first time we heard representatives of the bourgeois countries reason in this manner. They say: The Soviet leaders argue that they are for peaceful coexistence. At the same time they declare that they are fighting for Communism and they even say that Communism will be victorious in all countries. How can there be peaceful coexistence with the Soviet Union if it fights for Communism?

People who treat the question in this way confuse matters, wilfully or not, by confusing the problems of ideological struggle with the question of relations between states. Those indulging in this sort of confusion are most probably guided by a desire to cast aspersions upon the Communists of the Soviet Union and to represent them as the advocates of aggressive actions. This, however, is very unwise.

The Communist Party of the Soviet Union at its Twentieth Congress made it perfectly clear and obvious that the allegations that the Soviet Union intends to overthrow capitalism in other countries by means of "exporting" revolution are absolutely unfounded. . . .

We Communists believe that the idea of Communism will ultimately be victorious throughout the world, just as it has been victorious in our country, in China and in many other states. Many readers of FOREIGN AFFAIRS will probably disagree with us. Perhaps they think that the idea of capitalism will ultimately triumph. It is their right to think so. We may argue, we may disagree with one another. *The main thing is to keep to the positions of ideological struggle, without resorting to arms in order to prove that one is right.*

The point is that with military techniques what they are today, there are no inaccessible places in the world. Should a world war break out, no country will be able to shut itself off from a crushing blow.

TOPIC 14

The Nature of the Soviet Challenge

The free world is confronted with three elements, which compose the totality of the Communist challenge:

1. The Communist doctrine, which tries to appeal to masses and nations by its promise of a better world, the end of capitalism, and the establishment of one Communist world. It also suggests the strategy and tactics of action.

2. The Communist parties, which are ideologically and politically attuned to the Soviet base of world communism. They rule over one billion people, from Berlin and Prague to Peking and Hanoi. Other Communist parties operate within democratic communities of Western Europe (France and Italy in particular; their voting strength in those two countries is between 20 and 28 percent of the total) and in the underdeveloped new nations of Asia and Africa (Indonesia, India, Ceylon, Iraq and the U.A.R., for example).

3. The economic and military power of the Soviet states, which might seduce or frighten nations into communism. The Soviet Union uses world communism in support of its national policies while, at the same time, the Russian state and its dependencies represent the most important instrument of world communism.

The Soviet leaders, speaking as high priests of Communism, do not conceal that their ultimate goal is a Communist world. "All the world will come to Communism," said Khrushchev in his interview with Tomoo Hirooka of the Japanese newspaper *Asahi Shimbun,* on June 18, 1957. "History does not ask whether you want it or not." Two years later, on May 31, 1959, at the Albanian city of Vlore, Khrushchev reiterated his conviction of the inevitable triumph of communism as follows: "No matter how much aging capitalism is to prolong its existence, it is doomed because it will be replaced by the new victorious system—communism. Some madmen in the camp of the imperialists threaten the world with their atomic and hydrogen bomb. They threaten with their strength. . . . To attack us is tantamount to suicide. One would be a madman to do it."

In their capacity as captains of the Soviet state the same leaders, however, do not seem to act as ideological fanatics for whom the world is the only limit. While desiring hegemony, they seem to chart their course cautiously, in relation to their estimates of the real or assumed hurdles to be overcome.

►SOVIET ADVANCES CAN BE CONTAINED

GEORGE F. KENNAN

If the Soviet system's advances depend on whether they are met with strength or weakness, then the West should consider the possibility of their containment. This is the theme of an article which was published by Foreign Affairs *in 1947. It was signed "X," but readers soon learned that its author was George F. Kennan, Director of the U.S. Department of State's Policy Planning Staff. His article has since become the classic statement of the policy of containing the Soviet Union.*

George F. Kennan, who was also U. S. Ambassador to the Soviet Union, is author of Soviet-American Relations, 1917-1920, Realities of American Foreign Policy, *and* Russia, the Atom and the West. *Presently at the Institute for Advanced Studies at Princeton, he is engaged in writing a multivolume history of the Bolshevik Revolution.*

The political personality of Soviet power as we know it today is the product of ideology and circumstances: ideology inherited by the present Soviet leaders from the movement in which they had their political origin, and circumstances of the power which they now have exercised for nearly three decades in Russia. There can be few tasks of psychological analysis more difficult than to try to trace the interaction of these two forces and the relative rôle of each in the determination of official Soviet conduct. Yet the attempt must be made if that conduct is to be understood and effectively countered.

It is difficult to summarize the set of ideological concepts with which the Soviet leaders came into power. Marxian ideology, in its Russian-Communist projection, has always been in process of subtle evolution. The materials on which it bases itself are extensive and complex. But the outstanding features of Communist thought as it existed in 1916 may perhaps be summarized as follows: (a) that the central factor in the life of man, the factor which determines the character of public life and the "physiognomy of society," is the system by which material goods are produced and exchanged; (b) that the capitalist system of production is a nefarious one which inevitably leads to the exploitation of the working class by the capital-owning class and is incapable of developing adequately the economic resources of society or of distributing fairly the material goods produced by human labor; (c) that capitalism contains the seeds of its own destruction and must, in view of the inability of the capital-owning class to adjust itself to economic change, result eventually and inescapably in a revolutionary transfer of power to the working class; and (d) that imperialism, the final phase of capitalism, leads directly to war and revolution.

The rest may be outlined in Lenin's own words: "Unevenness of economic and political development is the inflexible law of capitalism. It follows

Excerpted by special permission from "The Sources of Soviet Conduct," *Foreign Affairs,* July, 1947. Copyright by Council on Foreign Relations, Inc., New York.

from this that the victory of Socialism may come originally in a few capitalist countries or even in a single capitalist country. The victorious proletariat of that country, having expropriated the capitalists and having organized Socialist production at home, would rise against the remaining capitalist world, drawing to itself in the process the oppressed classes of other countries." It must be noted that there was no assumption that capitalism would perish without proletarian revolution. A final push was needed from a revolutionary proletariat movement in order to tip over the tottering structure. But it was regarded as inevitable that sooner or later that push be given. . . .

The circumstances of the immediate post-Revolution period—the existence in Russia of civil war and foreign intervention, together with the obvious fact that the Communists represented only a tiny minority of the Russian people—made the establishment of dictatorial power a necessity. . . .

Subjectively these men probably did not seek absolutism for its own sake. They doubtless believed—and found it easy to believe—that they alone knew what was good for society and that they would accomplish that good once their power was secure and unchallengeable. But in seeking that security of their own rule they were prepared to recognize no restrictions, either of God or man, on the character of their methods. And until such time as that security might be achieved, they placed far down on their scale of operational priorities the comforts and happiness of the peoples entrusted to their care.

Now the outstanding circumstance concerning the Soviet regime is that down to the present day this process of political consolidation has never been completed and the men in the Kremlin have continued to be predominantly absorbed with the struggle to secure and make absolute the power which they seized in November 1917. They have endeavored to secure it primarily against forces at home, within Soviet society itself. But they have also endeavored to secure it against the outside world. For ideology, as we have seen, taught them that the outside world was hostile and that it was their duty eventually to overthrow the political forces beyond their borders. The powerful hands of Russian history and tradition reached up to sustain them in this feeling. Finally, their own aggressive intransigence with respect to the outside world began to find its own reaction. . . . It is an undeniable privilege of every man to prove himself right in the thesis that the world is his enemy; for if he reiterates it frequently enough and makes it the background of his conduct he is bound eventually to be right. . . .

Of the original ideology, nothing has been officially junked. Belief is maintained in the basic badness of capitalism, in the inevitability of its destruction, in the obligation of the proletariat to assist in that destruction and to take power into its own hands. But stress has come to be laid primarily on those concepts which relate most specifically to the Soviet regime itself: to its position as the sole truly Socialist regime in a dark and misguided world, and to the relationships of power within it.

The first of these concepts is that of the innate antagonism between capitalism and Socialism. We have seen how deeply that concept has become imbedded in foundations of Soviet power. It has profound implications for Russia's conduct as a member of international society. It means that there can never be on Moscow's side any sincere assumption of a community of aims between the Soviet Union and powers which are regarded as capitalism. It must invariably be assumed in Moscow that the aims of the capitalist world are antagonistic to the Soviet regime and, therefore, to the interests of the peoples it controls. If the Soviet Government occasionally sets its signature to documents which would indicate the contrary, this is to be regarded as a tactical maneuver permissible in dealing with the enemy (who is without honor) and should be taken in the spirit of *caveat emptor*. Basically, the antagonism remains. It is postulated. And from it flow many of the phenomena which we find disturbing in the Kremlin's conduct of foreign policy: the secretiveness, the lack of frankness, the duplicity, the war suspiciousness, and the basic unfriendliness of purpose. These phenomena are there to stay, for the foreseeable future. There can be variations of degree and of emphasis. When there is something the Russians want from us, one or the other of these features of their policy may be thrust temporarily into the background; and when that happens there will always be Americans who will leap forward with gleeful announcements that "the Russians have changed," and some who will even try to take credit for having brought about such "changes." But we should not be misled by tactical maneuvers. These characteristics of Soviet policy, like the postulate from which they flow, are basic to the internal nature of Soviet power, and will be with us, whether in the foreground or the background, until the internal nature of Soviet power is changed.

This means that we are going to continue for a long time to find the Russians difficult to deal with. It does not mean that they should be considered as embarked upon a do-or-die program to overthrow our society by a given date. The theory of the inevitability of the eventual fall of capitalism has the fortunate connotation that there is no hurry about it. The forces of progress can take their time in preparing the final *coup de grâce*. Meanwhile, what is vital is that the "Socialist fatherland"—that oasis of power which has been already won for Socialism in the person of the Soviet Union—should be cherished and defended by all good Communists at home and abroad, its fortunes promoted, its enemies badgered and confounded. The promotion of premature, "adventuristic" revolutionary projects abroad which might embarrass Soviet power in any way would be an inexcusable, even a counter-revolutionary act. The cause of Socialism is the support and promotion of Soviet power, as defined in Moscow.

This brings us to the second of the concepts important to contemporary Soviet outlook. That is the infallibility of the Kremlin. The Soviet concept of power, which permits no focal points of organization outside the Party itself, requires that the Party leadership remain in theory the sole repository of truth. For if truth were to be found elsewhere, there would be justification for its expression in organized activity. But it is precisely that which the Kremlin cannot and will not permit.

The leadership of the Communist Party is therefore always right, and has been always right ever since in 1929 Stalin formalized his personal power by announcing that decisions of the Politburo were being taken unanimously.

On the principle of infallibility there rests the iron discipline of the Communist Party. In fact, the two concepts are mutually self-supporting. Perfect discipline requires recognition of infallibility. Infallibility requires the observance of discipline. And the two together go far to determine the behaviorism of the entire Soviet apparatus of power. But their effect cannot be understood unless a third factor be taken into account: namely, the fact that the leadership is at liberty to put forward for tactical purposes any particular thesis which it finds useful to the cause at any particular moment and to require the faithful and unquestioning acceptance of that thesis by the members of the movement as a whole. This means that truth is not a constant but is actually created, for all intents and purposes, by the Soviet leaders themselves. It may vary from week to week, from month to month. It is nothing absolute and immutable—nothing which flows from objective reality. It is only the most recent manifestation of the wisdom of those in whom the ultimate wisdom is supposed to reside, because they represent the logic of history.

The accumulative effect of these factors is to give to the whole subordinate apparatus of Soviet power an unshakeable stubbornness and steadfastness in its orientation. This orientation can be changed at will by the Kremlin but by no other power. Once a given party line has been laid down on a given issue of current policy, the whole Soviet governmental machine, including the mechanism of diplomacy, moves inexorably along the prescribed path, like a persistent toy automobile wound up and headed in a given direction, stopping only when it meets with some unanswerable force. The individuals who are the components of this machine are unamenable to argument or reason which comes to them from outside sources. Their whole training has taught them to mistrust and discount the glib persuasiveness of the outside world. Like the white dog before the phonograph, they hear only the "master's voice." And if they are to be called off from the purposes last dictated to them, it is the master who must call them off. Thus the foreign representative cannot hope that his words will make any impression on them. The most that he can hope is that they will be transmitted to those at the top, who are capable of changing the party line. But even those are not likely to be swayed by any normal logic in the words of the bourgeois representative. Since there can be no appeal to common purposes, there can be no appeal to common mental approaches. For this reason, facts speak louder than words to the ears of the Kremlin; and words carry the greatest weight when they have the ring of reflecting, or being backed up by, facts of unchallengeable validity.

But we have seen that the Kremlin is under no ideological compulsion to accomplish its purposes in a hurry. Like the Church, it is dealing in ideological concepts which are of long-term validity, and it can afford to be patient. It has no right to risk the existing achievements of the revolution for the sake of vain baubles of the future. The very teachings of Lenin himself require great caution and flexibility in the pursuit of Communist purposes. Again, these precepts are fortified by the lessons of Russian history: of centuries of obscure battles between nomadic forces over the stretches of a vast unfortified plain. Here caution, circumspection, flexibility and deception are the valuable qualities; and their value finds natural appreciation in the Russian or the oriental mind. Thus the Kremlin has no compunction about retreating in the face of superior force. And being under the compulsion of no timetable, it does not get panicky under the necessity for such retreat. Its political action is a fluid stream which moves constantly, wherever it is permitted to move, toward a given goal. Its main concern is to make sure that it has filled every nook and cranny available to it in the basin of world power. But if it finds unassailable barriers in its path, it accepts these philosophically and accommodates itself to them. The main thing is that there should always be pressure, increasing constant pressure, toward the desired goal. There is no trace of any feeling in Soviet psychology that that goal must be reached at any given time.

These considerations make Soviet diplomacy at once easier and more difficult to deal with than the diplomacy of individual aggressive leaders like Napoleon and Hitler. On the one hand it is more sensitive to contrary force, more ready to yield on individual sectors of the diplomatic front when that force is felt to be too strong, and thus more rational in the logic and rhetoric of power. On the other hand it cannot be easily defeated or discouraged by a single victory on the part of its opponents. And the patient persistence by which it is animated means that it can be effectively countered not by sporadic acts which represent the momentary whims of democratic opinion but only by intelligent long-range policies on the part of Russia's adversaries—policies no less steady in their purpose, and no less variegated and resourceful in their application, than those of the Soviet Union itself.

In these circumstances it is clear that the main element of any United States policy toward the Soviet Union must be that of a long-term, patient but firm and vigilant containment of Russian expansive tendencies. It is important to note, however, that such a policy has nothing to do with outward histrionics: with threats or blustering or superfluous gestures of outward "toughness." While the Kremlin is basically flexible in its reaction to political realities, it is by no means unamenable to considerations of prestige. Like almost any other government, it can be placed by tactless and threatening gestures in a position where it cannot afford to yield even though this might be dictated by its sense of realism. The Russian leaders are keen judges of human psychology, and as such they are highly conscious that loss of temper and of self-control is never a source of strength in political affairs. They are quick to exploit such evidences of weakness. For these reasons, it is a *sine qua non* of successful dealing with Russia that the foreign government in question should remain at all times cool and collected and that its demands on Russian policy should be put forward in such a manner as to leave the way open for a compliance not too detrimental to Russian prestige.

In the light of the above, it will be clearly seen that the Soviet pressure against the free institutions of the western world is something that can be contained by the adroit and vigilant application of counter-force at a series of constantly shifting geographical and political points, corresponding to the shifts and maneuvers of Soviet policy, but which cannot be charmed or talked out of existence. The Russians look forward to a duel of infinite duration, and they see that already they have scored great successes. It must be borne in mind that there was a time when the Communist Party represented far more of a minority in the sphere of Russian national life than Soviet power today represents in the world community. . . .

It is clear that the United States cannot expect in the foreseeable future to enjoy political intimacy with the Soviet regime. It must continue to regard the Soviet Union as a rival, not a partner, in the political arena. It must continue to expect that Soviet policies will reflect no abstract love of peace and stability, no real faith in the possibility of a permanent happy coexistence of the Socialist and capitalist worlds, but rather a cautious, persistent pressure toward the disruption and weakening of all rival influence and rival power.

Balanced against this are the facts that Russia, as opposed to the Western world in general, is still by far the weaker party, that Soviet policy is highly flexible, and that Soviet society may well contain deficiencies which will eventually weaken its own total potential. This would of itself warrant the United States entering with reasonable confidence upon a policy of firm containment, designed to confront the Russians with unalterable counter-force at every point where they show signs of encroaching upon the interests of a peaceful and stable world.

But in actuality the possibilities for American policy are by no means limited to holding the line and hoping for the best. It is entirely possible for the United States to influence by its actions the internal developments, both within Russia and throughout the international Communist movement, by which Russian policy is largely determined. This is not only a question of the modest measure of informational activity which this government can conduct in the Soviet Union and elsewhere, although that, too, is important. It is rather a question of the degree to which the United States can create among the peoples of the world generally the impression of a country which knows what it wants, which is coping successfully with the problems of its internal life and with the responsibilities of a World Power, and which has a spiritual vitality capable of holding its own among the major ideological currents of the time. To the extent that such an impression can be created and maintained, the aims of Russian Communism must appear sterile and quixotic, the hopes and enthusiasm of Moscow's supporters must wane, and added strain must be imposed on the Kremlin's foreign policies. For the palsied decrepitude of the capitalist world is the keystone of Communist philosophy. Even the failure of the United States to experience the early economic depression which the ravens of the Red Square have been predicting with such complacent confidence since hostilities ceased would have deep and important repercussions throughout the Communist world.

By the same token, exhibitions of indecision, disunity and internal disintegration within this country have an exhilarating effect on the whole Communist movement. At each evidence of these tendencies, a thrill of hope and excitement goes through the Communist world; a new jauntiness can be noted in the Moscow tread; new groups of foreign supporters climb on to what they can only view as the band wagon of international politics; and Russian pressure increases all along the line in international affairs.

It would be an exaggeration to say that American behavior unassisted and alone could exercise a power of life and death over the Communist movement and bring about the early fall of Soviet power in Russia. But the United States has it in its power to increase enormously the strains under which Soviet policy must operate, to force upon the Kremlin a far greater degree of moderation and circumspection than it has had to observe in recent years, and in this way to promote tendencies which must eventually find their outlet in either the break-up or the gradual mellowing of Soviet power. For no mystical, Messianic movement—and particularly not that of the Kremlin— can face frustration indefinitely without eventually adjusting itself in one way or another to the logic of that state of affairs.

Thus the decision will really fall in large measure in this country itself. The issue of Soviet-American relations is in essence a test of the over-all worth of the United States as a nation among nations. To avoid destruction the United States need only measure up to its own best traditions and prove itself worthy of preservation as a great nation.

Surely, there was never a fairer test of national quality than this. In the light of these circumstances, the thoughtful observer of Russian-American relations will find no cause for complaint in the Kremlin's challenge to American society. He will rather experience a certain gratitude to a Providence which, by providing the American people with this implacable challenge, has made their entire security as a nation dependent on their pulling themselves together and accepting the responsibilities of moral and political leadership that history plainly intended them to bear.

►RIVALS SHOULD NEGOTIATE

WALTER LIPPMANN

The columnist and political analyst for the New York Herald Tribune *criticizes the optimistic premise of the policy of containment (elucidated by George F. Kennan on pages 297-303): that is, the assumption of an inherent weakness of the Soviet system. He also considers a policy of patient and defensive containment to be a strategic "monstrosity" and a policy particularly unsuited for the United States' constitutional and economic system.*

An anonymous article on "The Sources of Soviet Conduct" appeared in the quarterly journal *Foreign Affairs* for July 1947 and shortly afterwards it was republished in *Life* magazine. By its quality alone it would have commanded wide attention. For it was manifestly the work of a man who had observed the Soviet regime closely with a trained eye and an educated mind, and had arrived at a theory as to why the conduct of the Soviet government

From *The Cold War* by Walter Lippmann, copyright 1947 by Walter Lippmann; reprinted by permission of Harper & Brothers.

reflects "no abstract love of peace and stability, no real faith in the possibility of a permanent happy coexistence of the socialist and capitalist worlds, but rather a continuous, persistent pressure towards the disruption and weakening of all rival influence and rival power." . . .

We must begin with the disturbing fact, which anyone who will reread the article can verify for himself, that Mr. X's conclusions depend upon the optimistic prediction that the "Soviet power . . . bears within itself the seeds of its own decay, and that the sprouting of these seeds is well advanced"; that if "anything were ever to occur to disrupt the unity and the efficacy of the Party as a political instrument, Soviet Russia might be changed overnight (*sic*) from one of the strongest to one of the weakest and most pitiable of national societies"; and "that Soviet society may well (*sic*) contain deficiencies which will eventually weaken its own total potential."

Of this optimistic prediction Mr. X himself says that it "cannot be proved. And it cannot be disproved" . . .

The best that Mr. X can say for his own proposal is that if for a long period of time we can prevent the Soviet power from winning, the Soviet power will eventually perish or "mellow" because it has been "frustrated." . . .

Now the strength of the western world is great, and we may assume that its resourcefulness is considerable. Nevertheless, there are weighty reasons for thinking that the kind of strength we have and the kind of resourcefulness we are capable of showing are peculiarly unsuited to operating a policy of containment.

How, for example, under the Constitution of the United States is Mr. X going to work out an arrangement by which the Department of State has the money and the military power always available in sufficient amounts to apply "counterforce" at constantly shifting points all over the world? Is he going to ask Congress for a blank check on the Treasury and a blank authorization to use the armed forces? Not if the American constitutional system is to be maintained. Or is he going to ask for an appropriation and for authority each time the Russians "show signs of encroaching upon the interests of a peaceful and stable world"? If that is his plan for dealing with the maneuvers of a dictatorship, he is going to arrive at the points of encroachment with too little and he is going to arrive too late. The Russians, if they intend to encroach, will have encroached while Congress is getting ready to hold hearings.

A policy of shifts and maneuvers may be suited to the Soviet system of government, which, as Mr. X tells us, is animated by patient persistence. It is not suited to the American system of government.

It is even more unsuited to the American economy which is unregimented and uncontrolled, and therefore cannot be administered according to a plan. . . .

I find it hard to understand how Mr. X could have recommended such a strategic monstrosity. For he tells us, no doubt truly, that the Soviet power "cannot be easily defeated or discouraged by a single victory on the part of its opponents," and that "the patient persistence by which it is animated" means that it cannot be "effectively countered" by "sporadic acts." Yet his own policy calls for a series of sporadic acts; the United States is to apply "counterforce" where the Russians encroach and when they encroach. . . .

The genius of American military power does not lie in holding positions indefinitely. That requires a massive patience by great hordes of docile people. American military power is distinguished by its mobility, its speed, its range and its offensive striking force. It is, therefore, not an efficient instrument for diplomatic policy of containment. It can only be the instrument of a policy which has as its objective a decision and a settlement. It can and should be used to redress the balance of power which has been upset by the war. But it is not designed for, or adapted to, a strategy of containing, waiting, countering, blocking, with no more specific objective than the eventual "frustration" of the opponent.

The Americans would themselves probably be frustrated by Mr. X's policy long before the Russians were.

The policy of containment, which Mr. X recommends, demands the employment of American economic, political, and in the last analysis, American military power at "sectors" in the interior of Europe and Asia. This requires . . . ground forces, that is to say reserves of infantry, which we do not possess. . . .

The policy can be implemented only by recruiting, subsidizing and supporting a heterogeneous array of satellites, clients, dependents and puppets. The instrument of the policy of containment is therefore a coalition of disorganized, disunited, feeble or disorderly nations, tribes and factions around the perimeter of the Soviet Union. . . .

The natural allies of the United States are the nations of the Atlantic community: that is to say, the nations of western Europe and of the Americas. The Atlantic Ocean and the Mediterranean Sea, which is an arm of the Atlantic Ocean, unite them in a common, strategic, economic, and cultural system. . . .

The nations of the Atlantic community are not occupied by the Red Army. They cannot be occupied by the Red Army unless the Kremlin is prepared to face a full scale world war, atomic bombs and all the rest. Though impoverished and weakened, the nations of the Atlantic community are incomparably stronger, richer, more united and politically more democratic and mature than any of the nations of the Russian perimeter.

If the Soviet Union is, nevertheless, able to paralyze and disorganize them, then surely it can much more readily paralyze and disorganize the nations of the perimeter. They are already paralyzed and disorganized. They have never, in fact, been organized and effective modern states.

It will be evident, I am sure, to the reader who has followed the argument to this point that my criticism of the policy of containment, or the so-called Truman Doctrine, does not spring from any hope or belief that the Soviet pressure to expand can be "charmed or talked out of existence." I agree entirely with Mr. X that we must make up our minds that the Soviet power is not amenable to our arguments, but only "to contrary force" that "is felt to be too strong, and thus more rational in the logic and rhetoric of power."

My objection, then, to the policy of containment is not that it seeks to confront the Soviet power with American power, but that the policy is misconceived, and must result in a misuse of American power. . . .

The policy concedes to the Kremlin the strategical initiative as to when, where and under what local circumstances the issue is to be joined. It compels the United States to meet the Soviet pressure at these shifting geographical and political points by using satellite states, puppet governments and agents which have been subsidized and supported, though their effectiveness is meager and their reliability uncertain. By forcing us to expend our energies and our substance upon these dubious and unnatural allies on the perimeter of the Soviet Union, the effect of the policy is to neglect our natural allies in the Atlantic community, and to alienate them. . . .

At the root of Mr. X's philosophy about Russian-American relations and underlying all the ideas of the Truman Doctrine there is a disbelief in the possibility of a settlement of the issues raised by this war. Having observed, I believe quite correctly, that we cannot expect "to enjoy political intimacy with the Soviet regime," and that we must "regard the Soviet Union as a rival, not a partner in the political arena," and that "there can be no appeal to common purposes," Mr. X has reached the conclusion that all we can do is to "contain" Russia until Russia changes, ceases to be our rival, and becomes our partner.

The conclusion is, it seems to me, quite unwarranted. The history of diplomacy is the history of relations among rival powers, which did not enjoy political intimacy, and did not respond to appeals to common purposes. Nevertheless, there have been settlements. Some of them did not last very long. Some of them did. For a diplomat to think that rival and unfriendly powers cannot be brought to a settlement is to forget what diplomacy is about. There would be little for diplomats to do if the world consisted of partners, enjoying political intimacy, and responding to common appeals.

►PEACEFUL COEXISTENCE—A WESTERN VIEW

GEORGE F. KENNAN

In the seventeenth century the Peace of Westphalia recognized the right of European states to determine the creed of their subjects and their way of life: Catholic or Protestant. Thus Europe was fragmented yet pacified. Religious conflicts remained; their clash, however, shifted from the battlefield to the pulpits. Unreconciled, Catholicism and Protestantism began peacefully to coexist.

Is it possible to adapt the Westphalian formula to the unreconcilable conflict of Democracy and crusading Communism in our atomic age and on a world scale?

Excerpted by special permission from "Peaceful Coexistence—a Western View," *Foreign Affairs,* January, 1960. Copyright by Council on Foreign Relations, Inc., New York.

In his article in Foreign Affairs *(reprinted in part on pp. 292ff.) Nikita S. Khrushchev seems to recommend such a neo-Westphalian formula to the world. In his view, the present division of the world into two ideological blocs should be maintained and combined with peaceful competition which, as he maintains, must ultimately result in a world-wide victory of the Communist creed.*

The author of the following selection replies to Khrushchev's assertions in the January 1960 issue of Foreign Affairs *under the title "Peaceful Co-existence—A Western View."*

Almost thirteen years after the publication of his first article on containment of, and competition with, the Soviet Union, George F. Kennan returns to his theme of 1947. He has to take into account two facts: while the Communist ideology has changed little if at all, other aspects of the Communist world have changed considerably: the rigid rule of Stalin has been replaced by the more flexible one of Khrushchev; China and all of East Central Europe have been included in the Soviet orbit; and Russia has not only acquired a formidable thermonuclear arsenal but has overtaken the United States in the art of rocketry. In 1947 Kennan could describe the Soviet Union as "still by far the weaker party;" this description would obviously not fit Russia of 1960.

The conflict between Democracy's goals and method and those of Communism remains, however, unchanged; the question of whether it can be shifted from a potential atomic battlefield to the "pulpits" has become even more acute than ever.

While in his reply to Khrushchev Kennan does not exclude the possibility of a less strained relationship with the Soviet Union, two obstacles, in his opinion, block the way to peaceful coexistence: the fact of the Soviet expansion into the heart of Europe which, irrespective of the ideology prevailing in Moscow, is "a matter of most serious interest to the world at large"; and the Soviet insistence on depicting Western democracies as the source of all evil. "If the Soviet leaders really think us to be as evil as they depict us to their people," asks George F. Kennan, "how can they seriously believe in the possibility of coexisting peacefully with us? If on the other hand, they are deliberately misleading their own people, how can we, on our side, have confidence in them?"

A portion of Kennan's article follows.

In the public debate that has marked the progress of what is called the cold war, no term has been used more loosely, and at times unscrupulously, than the word "coexistence." In the article under his name, published in the last issue of *Foreign Affairs,* Mr. Khrushchev has given us an interesting definition of what he understands by this term. Peaceful coexistence, he says, signifies in essence the repudiation of war as a means of solving controversial issues. It presupposes an obligation to refrain from every form of violation of the territorial integrity and sovereignty of another state. It implies renunciation of interference in the internal affairs of other countries. . . .

Not only has Mr. Khrushchev given us this definition but he has made it plain that he considers that the Soviet Union abides by these principles, has abided by them ever since the revolution of the autumn of 1917 and cannot help but abide by them in view of its social foundation; whereas there are still important elements in the Western countries who, in his view, do not abide by these principles, who "believe that war is to their benefit," who want to inflict "capitalism" by violent means on unwilling peoples and whose opposition must be overcome before peaceful coexistence can really be said to prevail.

There could be few propositions more amazing than the assertion that the Soviet state "from its very inception . . . proclaimed peaceful coexistence as the basic principle of its foreign policy," and that the initial Communist leaders in Russia were strong partisans of the view that peaceful coexistence could and should prevail among states with different social systems. . . .

If reference is to be taken prominently on the Communist side to the attitudes of Soviet leaders in 1917, as proof of the inviolable and inevitable attachment of Russian Communism to such principles as the repudiation of violence as a means of solving controversial political issues, the renunciation of interference in the internal affairs of other countries and the predominance of peaceful competition as between states of different social systems, then the Western scholar cannot refrain from registering his amazement and protest. It is surprising that there should be so little respect for the true history of the Russian revolutionary movement on the part of those who profess today to be its custodians and protagonists that they are willing to pervert it in this way for the sake of their own tactical convenience. One shudders to think what Lenin would have said to these preposterous distortions. Do the present leaders of the Russian Communist Party really profess to have forgotten that Lenin regarded himself outstandingly as an *international* socialist leader? Who was it wrote, on October 3, 1918, "The Bolshevik working class of Russia was always internationalist not only in words, but in deeds, in contrast to those villains—the heroes and leaders of the Second International. . . ."? . . .

The proposition that the political power dominant in the Soviet Union has always been on the side of coexistence, as defined by Mr. Khrushchev, also calls upon us to forget the long and sinister history of the relationship between Moscow and the foreign Communist Parties in the Stalin era. There is ample documentation to show for what purposes foreign Communist Parties were used during those years, by whom, and by what methods. There are many of us in the West who, again, would be happy to disregard these recollections when it comes to the political discussion of the present day. But it is another thing to suffer insult to one's intelligence. . . .

These statements of mine are not to be taken as implying a disposition to believe that the attachment of Mr. Khrushchev and certain of his colleagues to the principles of coexistence, as he has now defined them, is insincere and conceals sinister motives. This does not necessarily follow. The purpose is merely to point out that people in Moscow are not likely to strengthen belief outside Russia in the sincerity of their attachment to liberal and tolerant principles of international life by distorting the history of the Lenin or Stalin eras or by pleading that such an attachment flows inevitably from the nature of the social and political system prevailing in the Soviet Union. It is possible to conceive that the Soviet attitude in such questions may have changed; it is not possible to accept the proposition that it did not need to change in order to meet the requirements of peaceful coexistence, as Mr. Khrushchev has defined them.

*

In the statement of the Soviet view of coexistence, much stress has been laid on the attachment of people in the West to capitalism and on their alleged desire to see it triumph as a world system.

The Westerner of this day experiences a certain bewilderment when he hears the term "capitalism" used in this way. What is it that is meant by this expression? One notices that whatever the reality may be which it purports to symbolize, it is one which in Russian Communist eyes has not changed appreciably since the Russian Social Democratic Party came into being at the turn of the century. If there is any recognition in official Soviet thought of the fact that changes in the economic practices and institutions of non-Communist countries over this past half-century have been such as to affect in any way the elements of the classic Marxist view of Western capitalism, I am not aware of the place where this has found expression. Contemporary Soviet ideological material seems to suggest that there exists outside the Communist orbit a static and basic condition—a set of practices known as "capitalism" and expressed primarily in the private ownership of the means of production —which has undergone no essential alteration over the past 50 years, or indeed since the lifetime of Karl Marx; which continues to be the dominant reality of Western society; belief in which constitutes the essence of all non-Communist political philosophy; and to which the Western governments and "ruling circles," in particular, remain, as a matter of pride and tenacious self-interest, profoundly committed. It would presumably be to "capitalism" in this sense that Mr. Khrushchev was referring when he wrote that many readers of *Foreign Affairs* would perhaps think that capitalism will ultimately triumph. . . .

There is today not *one* social and economic system prevailing outside the Communist orbit: there are almost as many such systems as there are countries; and many of them are closer to what Marx conceived as socialism than they are to the laissez faire capitalism of his day. In each of them furthermore, the balance between private and social influences is everywhere in a state of flux and evolution which makes it quite impossible to predict from the aspect it assumes today what aspect it is going to assume tomorrow.

This means that in the non-Communist world, where it is customary to attempt to relate the meaning of words to objective phenomena, the term "capitalism" no longer has any generic and useful meaning. It is only in Russia, where theoretical concept can still be spared the test of relevance to objective reality, that a meaning for this term still exists. Not only this, but there are numbers of issues of public life which today appear to most people in the non-Communist world as having a higher importance, from the standpoint of their general effect on the human condition, than the issues of the ownership of the means of production and the distribution of wealth with which the Marxist doctrine was preoccupied.

How absurd, in the light of these facts, to picture Western non-

Communists as the passionate protagonists and devotees of something called "capitalism," and to suggest that there are influential people in the West who desire to bring upon the earth the miseries of another world war in the hope of being able to inflict the capitalist system on great masses of people who do not desire it. The question of who owns the machines is not the one that today dominates the thoughts and discussions of Western society and Western "ruling circles;" it is primarily the question of human freedom—of the right of people to choose and alter their own social and political systems as they like, to select those who shall govern them within the framework of those systems, and to enjoy, within that same framework, the civil liberties which relieve them of the fear of arbitrary injustice, permit them to practice freedom of the mind and enable them to walk with their heads up. . . .

We decline . . . , to be depicted as the passionate protagonists of something called "capitalism" waging an ideological competition with the protagonists of something called "socialism." Least of all can we in America accept the charge of wishing to impose something called capitalism on other peoples. Several European countries have changed their social and economic institutions over the course of recent decades in ways that carry them very far from those prevailing in the United States. In this, they have not encountered the slightest opposition or hindrance from the American side. The basic ideological issue, as seen in the United States today, is not capitalism versus socialism but freedom versus its opposite. The disagreement between Moscow and the "leading circles" of the non-Communist world is not really a disagreement about which form of social system is most productive; it is rather a disagreement about what is most important, in the first place, in the lives of peoples.

*

The fact that an ideological disagreement of this nature exists is in itself no reason why peaceful coexistence, as Mr. Khrushchev defines it, should not prevail. There is nothing new in the prolonged peaceful residence, side by side, of ideologically antagonistic systems. Many of the present peaceful relationships of international life, outside the Communist orbit, have evolved from ones which were originally relationships of profound ideological antagonism. There was, for that matter, no ideological affinity but rather a sharp ideological conflict between the Tsarist system in Russia and the world of American political thought. This did not prevent the two powers from existing in the same world, without hostilities, for more than a hundred years.

There are no doubt individuals scattered here and there throughout the Western countries who find intolerable this present antagonism of outlook as between the Soviet Government and the Western peoples and who cannot see how it can be either resolved or endured by means short of a world war. If one searches, one can even find, for quotation, public utterances of this view. But it would be generally agreed, I think, that these people are few and not very influential. The general attitude throughout the West would unquestionably be—and this goes for governments as well as for individuals—that while the social and political system now dominant in Russia is one that may not commend itself to us, its existence and prevalence there is not our responsibility; it is not our business to change it; it constitutes in itself no reason why a relationship of peaceful coexistence should not prevail.

But the Soviet Union is not only an ideological phenomenon. It is also a great power, physically and militarily. Even if the prevailing ideology in Russia were not antagonistic to the concepts prevailing elsewhere, the behavior of the government of that country in its international relations, and particularly any considerable expansion of its power at the expense of the freedom of other peoples, would still be a matter of most serious interest to the world at large.

And it is, let us recall, precisely such an expansion that we have witnessed in recent years. So far as Europe is concerned, this expansion had its origin in the advance of Soviet armies into Eastern and Central Europe in 1945. This advance was not only accepted at the time—it was generally welcomed in the West as a very important part of the final phase of the struggle against Hitler. But it has had a consequence which few people in the West foresaw in 1945 and which fewer still desired: the quasipermanent advancement of the effective boundaries of Moscow's political and military authority to the very center of Europe.

The discussion of the question of coexistence on the Communist side is cast in terms which take no account of this situation and which ask us, by implication, either to ignore it or to pretend that it does not exist. The problem, we are told, is to "liquidate the consequences of the Second World War;" but this particular consequence, we are left to infer, is one which is neither to be liquidated nor to be spoken about. . . . The fact is that this extension of Russia's political and military power into the heart of Europe represents a major alteration in the world strategic and political balance, and one that was never discussed as such with Western statesmen, much less agreed to by them.

It is not just the *fact* of this situation which is of importance to the Western peoples; there is also the question as to *how* it came into existence and *how* it is being maintained. The truth is that it did not come into existence because the majority of the people in the region affected became convinced that Communism, as Mr. Khrushchev has put it, was "the more progressive and equitable system." This peaceful competition for the minds of men which the Communists today ask us to accept as the concomitant and condition of peaceful coexistence had precious little to do with the means by which socialist governments, on the pattern approved by Moscow, were established in the countries of Eastern Europe in 1944 and 1945 or with the means by which their rule was subsequently consolidated there. In the view of the West, formed on the strength of overwhelming historical evidence, these régimes were imposed by the skillful manipulations of highly disciplined Communist minorities, trained and inspired by Moscow, and supported by the presence or close proximity of units of the Soviet armed forces. They have been maintained in power by similar means. . . .

There is one kind of peace that is compatible with the true security of peoples; and this is one which is based on the principles of genuine national freedom. There is another kind of peace which represents the silence that reigns where the instruments of coercion are simply too formidable to be challenged by those against whom they are aimed. . . .

The Soviet leaders seem either unwilling or unable to take any proper account of the true measure of the shock wrought to the Western public by their exploitation, for purposes of political aggrandizement, of their military position in Eastern and Central Europe in the period 1945 to 1948; by their failure to match the demobilization of the Western armies; by the political attack launched by the Communists in Western Europe in the years 1947 and 1948; by the imposition of the Berlin blockade, and above all by the launching of the Korean War. To people in the West these actions seemed to reflect a hostility no less menacing in intent than would have been threats of overt military aggression by Soviet forces. Coming as they did on the heels of the Second World War, affecting as they did nerves already frayed and minds already prone to anxiety as a result of these fresh experiences, it is not surprising that they produced on a great many people in the West the impression that the security of Western Europe, having just withstood one fearful challenge, was now confronted by another one of scarcely smaller dimensions. Neither is it surprising that peoples' reaction to this impression should have been the intensive effort to re-create, within the framework of a Western alliance, something of the armed force which had been so hastily and trustingly demobilized in the immediate aftermath of the war. . . .

Mr. Khrushchev is right in viewing the weapons race of this day as inconsistent with any satisfactory form of coexistence. But the prospects for bettering this situation will not be promising so long as Moscow persists in viewing the military policies pursued in the Western coalition in recent years as solely the products of the lust of Western financiers and manufacturers thirsting for another war in the hopes of greater profits, and refuses to recognize that these policies, however misconceived or overdrawn, represent in large measure the natural and predictable reactions of great peoples to a situation which Moscow itself did much to create. . . .

Propaganda is propaganda; but surely, like everything else in life, it has its limits. What are we to conclude from the propagation of these fantastic misapprehensions about the United States?—that the Soviet leaders really believe them? or that, knowing them to be misapprehensions, they nevertheless find it in order that Soviet citizens should be encouraged to accept them as true? Either variant would have most questionable implications from the standpoint of the prospects for peaceful coexistence. . . .

Is it too much to ask the Soviet leaders to drop today this Byzantine dogmatism of political thought and utterance, for which a case might have been made in the early days of the revolutionary militancy of the Party, when it was still fighting for its ascendancy in Russia, but which is out of place on the part of a great government which asks for acceptance as a mature and responsible force in world affairs? Scarcely anyone, surely, is deceived today by these absurd extremisms. But there are many people in the non-Communist world to whom these recurring evidences of irresponsibility in the attitude toward truth are a constant source of misgiving about the prospects of any sound and enduring coexistence between Communist and non-Communist 'worlds. What can be the value of specific understandings, these people ask, if the underlying assumptions and beliefs are so grotesquely different? If the Soviet leaders really think us to be as evil as they depict us to their own people, how can they seriously believe in the possibility of co-existing peacefully with us? If, on the other hand, they are deliberately misleading their own people, how can we, on our side, have confidence in them? . . .

The road to peaceful coexistence lies, admittedly, through many gates; but one of these is the abandonment by Russian Communists of the absurd contention that theirs is a party which has always had a perfect understanding of the human predicament and has never made a mistake.

TOPIC 15

Foresight and Hindsight—Errors of the Democracies

Is war with Russia inevitable? Writing in 1950, George F. Kennan suggested that a war which is avoidable may still occur. Wars can arise by accident. Or a war can occur because the Russians may think someone is going to attack them. Or, finally, as George F. Kennan humbly added, our analysis may be wrong.[1]

The readings that follow depict two wrong analyses made by the Democracies: Munich in 1938 and Yalta in 1945. In both cases the intentions of the Democracies' rivals were wrongly interpreted.

In 1938 England and France abandoned an important military and political position in the heart of Europe—Czechoslovakia—its forty divisions and fortifications, in the hope that Czechoslovakia was Hitler's last territorial demand. The Nazis cleverly exploited the Wilsonian slogan of national self-determination for the German minorities in Czechoslovakia. Their right to union with Germany was to be realized at the cost of the unity and defensibility of Czechoslovakia.

In 1945, at Yalta, the Western estimate of Stalin's desire to live in friendship with his wartime partners was equally unrealistic. In his *Triumph and Tragedy* (vol. VI of *The Second World War*) Winston Churchill noted: "The impression I brought back from the Crimea [where the City of Yalta is located], and from all my other contacts, is that Marshal Stalin and the Soviet leaders wish to live in honorable friendship and equality with the Western democracies. I feel also that their word is their bond. I know of no Government which stands to its obligations, even in its own despite, more solidly

[1] George F. Kennan, "Is War With Russia Inevitable?" *Reader's Digest,* March, 1950, pp. 1-9.

than the Russian Soviet Government. . . . Sombre indeed would be the fortunes of mankind if some awful schism arose between the Western democracies and the Russian Soviet Union."

This was what Churchill told the House of Commons in 1945. Now he adds this melancholy afterthought:

"Our hopeful assumptions were soon to be falsified. Still, they were the only ones possible at the time."

►MUNICH, 1938

PAUL SCHMIDT

The Nazi Government's official interpreter describes events preceding the summit conference at Munich and the negotiations during the conference, on the basis of his personal experience.

Right from the beginning of 1938 it was clear, despite what Hitler had said in 1937, that the period of surprises was by no means over. First came the internal crisis of February, in the course of which Neurath was sacked and succeeded by Ribbentrop at the Foreign Office. Then the entry of German troops into Austria, and finally the Czech crisis of September, when for many days Europe hovered on the brink of war. . . .

During the summer my interpreting activity slowed down ominously. The tone of the German Press on Czecho-Slovakia became more and more violent. . . .

At the beginning of September I was again on duty at the Party Rally. Foreign countries were even more strongly represented than in the previous year. . . . From the conversations I translated I sensed the daily increasing tension that prevailed throughout Europe in September, 1938. Rarely had I translated so much about war and the danger of war as during those days. . . .

The news that reached Nuremberg from abroad was also alarming. I can still see the anxious faces of some of my colleagues when they handed to me, to translate for Hitler, a statement by the British Government that German aggression against Czecho-Slovakia would be ground for intervention by the Western Powers. At almost the same time I had to translate for Hitler a report from London stating that Britain might be prepared to give military support of Czecho-Slovakia. That was on September 11th.

"I can only tell the representatives of these democracies that, if these tormented creatures (the Sudeten Germans) cannot themselves obtain justice and help, they will receive both from us," Hitler shouted in a speech full of threats against the Czechs on September 12th, the last day of the Party Rally. "The Germans in Czecho-Slovakia are neither defenseless nor deserted!" I heard it on the loud speaker at the airport as I left Nuremberg.

From *Hitler's Interpreter*. Used with permission of The Macmillan Company.

With Hitler's threats still ringing in my ears, I got back to Berlin, where I found not only in the Foreign Office but also amongst friends and acquaintances generally, profound depression at what was generally felt to be the imminence of war. . . .

On the morning of September 14th events took a dramatic and sensational turn. I had to translate for Hitler a seven-line message: "Having regard to the increasingly critical situation, I propose to visit you immediately in order to make an attempt to find a peaceful solution. I could come to you by air and am ready to leave tomorrow. Please inform me of the earliest time you can receive me, and tell me the place of meeting. I should be grateful for a very early reply. Neville Chamberlain.". . .

Next day at noon I met Chamberlain at the Munich airport with Ribbentrop, whom Hitler had sent for the purpose.

We lunched in Hitler's dining car on the way to Berchtesgaden. The scene is still very clear in my memory. During almost the whole of the three-hour journey troop transports rolled past, making a dramatic background, with soldiers in new uniforms and gun barrels pointing skywards. "Peace Envoy Chamberlain," as he was then called in Germany, formed a curious contrast to this warlike picture.

Shortly before we reached Berchtesgaden it began to rain, and as we drove up with Chamberlain to the Berghof the sky darkened and clouds hid the mountains. Hitler received his guests at the foot of the steps leading up to the house. . . .

The conversation (between Hitler and Chamberlain), on which hung the issue of peace or war, was not conducted in an exactly serene atmosphere, and sometimes became quite stormy. It lasted nearly three hours. Hitler, the Party Rally just over, was apparently still attuned to long speeches, and from time to time he was so carried away by his rage against Benes and Czecho-Slovakia that his harangues went on interminably.

Hitler began fairly quietly by presenting in full the list of complaints against Germany's neighbors which he always brought forward. The Versailles Treaty, the League of Nations, and disarmament were discussed in detail, as well as economic difficulties, unemployment and National Socialist reconstruction. Chamberlain was reproached in rising tone with the attitude of the British Press, with Britain's "interference" in German affairs, and in the Reich's relations with South-East Europe, including Austria.

Chamberlain listened attentively, looking frankly at Hitler. Nothing in his clear-cut, typically English features, with their bushy eyebrows, pointed nose and strong mouth, betrayed what went on behind his high forehead. His brother, Sir Austen, sitting opposite Stresemann at Locarno had always looked like that; but Neville Chamberlain had nothing of his brother's aloof frigidity. On the contrary, he dealt in lively manner with individual points brought up by Hitler, giving the stock answer about the freedom of the Press with a friendly, almost conciliatory smile. Then, looking Hitler full in the face, he emphasized that he was prepared to discuss every possibility of righting German grievances, but that in all circumstances the use of force must be excluded.

"Force!" Hitler exclaimed. "Who speaks of force? Herr Benes applies force against my countrymen in the Sudetenland, Herr Benes mobilized in May, not I." Outside it was pouring with rain, and the wind was howling. "I shall not put up with this any longer. I shall settle this question in one way or another. I shall take matters into my own hands." This was the first time, in a discussion with a foreign statesman, that the phrase "in one way or another" had been used—a phrase which I observed then and later to be an extreme danger signal. I rightly translated it "one way or another," but its meaning now and on later occasions amounted to: "Either the other side gives in, or a solution will be found by means of the application of force, invasion, or war."

Now Chamberlain, who had hitherto listened to everything that was said with serious calm, also became excited. "If I have understood you aright," he said, "you are determined to proceed against Czecho-Slovakia in any case." After pausing for a second, he added: "If that is so, why did you let me come to Berchtesgaden? Under the circumstances it is best for me to return at once. Anything else now seems pointless."

Hitler hesitated. If he really wants it to come to war, I thought, now is the moment; and I looked at him in agonized suspense. At that moment the question of peace or war was really poised on a razor's edge. But the astonishing happened: Hitler recoiled.

"If, in considering the Sudeten question, you are prepared to recognize the principle of the right of peoples to self-determination," he said in one of those sudden changes from raging to complete calm and collectedness, "then we can continue the discussion in order to see how that principle can be applied in practice."

I thought that Chamberlain would immediately assent. The principle of self-determination had always played an important part in English political thought, and its relevance to the Sudeten question had been generally admitted by the British Press and by prominent British visitors to Germany. But Chamberlain at once raised an objection—though whether this was because he had been angered by Hitler's aggressive manner, or because, as a practical administrator, he recognized the complications in applying this principle to Czecho-Slovakia, it is difficult to say.

"If, in the application of the right of self-determination in Czecho-Slovakia, a plebiscite were held among the Sudeten Germans, the practical difficulties would be enormous," he replied. Even so Hitler did not get indignant. Had Chamberlain's threat to return home frightened him? Was he really recoiling from the prospect of a war?

"If I am to give you an answer on the question of self-determination," said Chamberlain, "I must first consult my colleagues. I therefore suggest that we break off our conversation at this point, and that I return to England immediately for consultation, and then meet you again." When I translated these words about breaking off the discussion, Hitler looked up uneasily; but when he understood that Chamberlain would meet him again, he agreed with obvious relief. The atmosphere had suddenly become friendly again, and

Chamberlain at once availed himself of this change to secure a promise from Hitler that in the interval no aggressive action would be taken against Czecho-Slovakia. Hitler unhesitatingly gave this assurance, but added that it would not apply if any particularly atrocious incident occurred.

Thus the discussion ended. . . .

Next morning we drove with Chamberlain to Munich, where he took the plane for London exactly twenty-four hours after his arrival. The same evening I returned to Berlin. . . . Profound pessimism still prevailed, . . . in Berlin as a result of the Press stories of clashes between Germans and Czechs in the Sudeten territory. Gœbbels stepped up the tone of the German Press day by day. He had almost reached the limit of indignant abuse when, five days later, I left for Cologne by the night train. Chamberlain arrived at noon on September 22nd. We escorted him to his hotel beside the Rhine, opposite Godesberg, and the same afternoon he held his first conversation with Hitler at the Hotel Dreesen, Godesberg.

Hitler met Chamberlain at the hotel entrance with very friendly inquiries about his journey and his accommodation at the Hotel Petersberg. The conference room had a glorious view over the Rhine and the Siebengebirge. But the statesmen had no eyes for natural scenery and without a glance out of the window they sat down at the end of the long conference table. Owing to the incident about my report, Chamberlain had brought with him Sir Ivone Kirkpatrick, . . . who speaks excellent German.

Chamberlain opened the session with an account of his talks in London, recalling that he had agreed to get the Cabinet's views on the recognition of the Sudetenland's right to self-determination. The Cabinet had agreed to this, and so had the French Ministers, who had come to London at his invitation. Even the Czecho-Slovak Government had expressed its agreement. Together with the French, he had drawn up a plan in London whereby the territories inhabited by Sudeten Germans were to be transferred to Germany. Even the details of a new frontier were provided for in the plan. Chamberlain then outlined a comprehensive and complicated system of agreements providing for relatively protracted handing over periods. He concluded by announcing the guarantee which France and Britain were prepared to give to the new German-Czecho-Slovak frontier. Germany, on her side, was to conclude a non-aggression pact with Czecho-Slovakia.

Chamberlain leant back after this exposition with an expression of satisfaction, as much as to say: "Haven't I worked splendidly during these five days?" That was what I felt, too, for the agreement of the French, and still more of the Czecho-Slovaks, to a definite cession of territory seemed to me an extraordinary concession. I was the more surprised to hear Hitler say quietly, almost regretfully, but quite definitely: "I am exceedingly sorry, Mr. Chamberlain, but I can no longer discuss these matters. This solution, after the developments of the last few days, is no longer practicable."

Chamberlain sat up with a start. He flushed with anger at Hitler's attitude, at the ingratitude for his pains. I noticed that his kindly eyes could gleam very angrily under their bushy brows. Chamberlain was extremely surprised and indignant: he said he could not understand why Hitler should now suddenly say that the solution was no longer practicable, when the demands he had made at Berchtesgaden had been met.

Hitler at first evaded a direct reply, saying that he could not conclude a non-aggression pact with Czecho-Slovakia while the claims of Poland and Hungary on that country remained unsatisfied. Then, speaking relatively very calmly, he criticized the individual points of the plan elaborated by Chamberlain. Above all, the period of transfer contemplated was far too long. "The occupation of the Sudeten territories to be ceded must take place forthwith," he stated.

Chamberlain justly pointed out that this constituted a completely new demand, going far beyond the request put forward at Berchtesgaden; but Hitler continued to demand the immediate occupation of the Sudeten territories. As the conversation proceeded, he became more and more excited, more and more violent in his abuse of Benes and Czecho-Slovakia: Chamberlain became more reserved and withdrawn.

"The oppression of the Sudeten Germans and the terror exercised by Benes admit of no delay," Hitler declared hoarsely, and propounded the settlement he himself envisaged. This amounted to almost unconditional capitulation by Czecho-Slovakia.

Thus that first meeting in the ill-starred Godesberg conference room ended with complete discord. Chamberlain returned angrily to his hotel. The only ray of hope was that another meeting had been agreed upon. . . . Hitler, at Chamberlain's express request, had renewed his Berchtesgaden promise not to take any action against Czecho-Slovakia during the course of the negotiations. . . .

The following day Chamberlain asked Hitler to let him have these proposals in the form of a Memorandum, and he announced that he proposed to return to London to make the necessary preparations for passing them on.

During the discussion with Ribbentrop it was agreed that Chamberlain should be asked to come again that evening to receive the Memorandum and hear Hitler's explanatory remarks on it.

This discussion with Chamberlain, which began just before eleven that night of September 23rd, was one of the most dramatic in the whole of the Sudeten crisis. As there were to be a larger number of people present it took place in a small dining room of the hotel. . . . Present were Wilson, Henderson, Ribbentrop, Weizsäcker, and the head of the Legal Department of the Foreign Office. They sat informally in a semi-circle round Hitler and Chamberlain. I opened the session by translating the Memorandum (from Hitler to Chamberlain).

"The news of hourly increasing incidents in the Sudetenland proves that the condition of the Sudeten Germans is quite intolerable, and has therefore become a danger to European peace," I read. The main demand was: Withdrawal of all Czech armed forces from an area shown on an accompanying map, "evacuation of which will start on September 26th, and which will be ceded to Germany on September 28th." "The evacuated territory to be handed over in its present condition," "the Czech Government to release all prisoners of German origin arrested for political offenses," "voting (in certain areas) under the supervision of an International Commission"—these were some of the other points in the brief document.

The effect on Chamberlain and the other Englishmen was devastating. "But that's an ultimatum!" exclaimed Chamberlain, lifting his hands in protest. "Ein Diktat," interjected Henderson, who always liked to introduce German words into a discussion. Speaking forcibly, Chamberlain declared that it was quite out of the question for him to transmit such an ultimatum to the Czecho-Slovak Government. Not only the content, but also the tone of the document, on its becoming known, would arouse violent indignation in neutral countries. "With the most profound regret and disappointment, Chancellor, I have to state that you have made no effort to assist my attempts to secure peace."

Hitler seemed surprised by the violence of the reaction. He was put on the defensive. He clumsily tried to counter the reproach that he had handed in an ultimatum by saying that it was headed "Memorandum," not "ultimatum." Chamberlain, Wilson and Henderson returned to the attack, pointing out that his proposals would certainly fail, if only because of his suggested time-table. It would allow the Czecho-Slovak Government scarcely forty-eight hours to give the necessary orders, and the whole territory was to be evacuated in four days. The danger that these circumstances would lead to violence was enormously increased. The consequences of hostilities between Germany and Czecho-Slovakia were unpredictable. A European war would certainly result.

Negotiations had thus come to an absolute deadlock. At that moment, the door opened and an adjutant handed a note to Hitler. After reading it he gave it to me, saying: "Read this to Mr. Chamberlain."

I translated: "Benes has just announced over the wireless general mobilization of the Czecho-Slovak forces."

The room was dead still. "Now war is unavoidable," I thought; and all present probably thought the same. Although Hitler had promised Chamberlain he would make no move against Czecho-Slovakia, he had always added the proviso: "Unless any exceptional action by the Czechs forces me to act." Had such an eventuality now arisen?

Afterwards, when telling friends of this dramatic scene, I often used the analogy of the kettle-drum beat in a symphony. After the drum beat of "Czech mobilization" there was silence for a few bars; then the violins lightly took up the melody again. In a scarcely audible voice, Hitler said to the frozen Chamberlain: "Despite this unheard-of provocation, I shall of course keep my promise not to proceed against Czecho-Slovakia during the course of negotiations—at any rate, Mr. Chamberlain, so long as you remain on German soil."

Tension began to relax. Discussion was resumed, in a more subdued quieter tone. All seemed somehow to be relieved at the postponement of the catastrophe. Negotiations were continuing. That was the great thing.

Hitler was suddenly prepared to discuss the question of evacuation dates, which Chamberlain had cited as the chief difficulty. "To please you,

Mr. Chamberlain," he said, "I will make a concession over the matter of the time-table. You are one of the few men for whom I have ever done such a thing. I will agree to October 1st as the date for evacuation." He wrote the relevant correction in his memorandum, adding a few other minor alterations which, so far as I recollect, affected the form rather than the content of the document, which was then sent out for a fair copy to be made.

In the course of further conversation Hitler pointed out that he had supported Chamberlain's endeavors for peace inasmuch as the boundaries of the areas to be ceded were quite different in his proposal from those which he would seize if he had used force against Czecho-Slovakia. Finally Chamberlain said that he was prepared to transmit the German Memorandum to the Czech Government. The crisis had cleared the air like a thunderstorm, and at two o'clock in the morning Chamberlain and Hitler parted in a thoroughly amiable atmosphere, after talking alone, with my assistance, for a short time. In the course of their conversation, Hitler thanked Chamberlain, in words which seemed sincere, for his work on behalf of peace, and said that the Sudeten question was the last great problem which, as far as he was concerned, required solution. He also spoke about closer relations between Germany and England, and about their cooperation. It was evident how much store he set on good relations with the English. He returned to his old theme. "There need be no differences between us," he said. "We shall not get in the way of the exercise of your extra-European interests, while you can leave us a free hand in Central and South-Eastern Europe without harm." Some time the colonial question would have to be settled, too, but there was no hurry about that, and they certainly need not go to war about it. Chamberlain returned to London later that morning.

Two days later, on September 26th, Sir Horace Wilson arrived in Berlin with a personal letter from Chamberlain to Hitler. Accompanied by Henderson and Kirkpatrick, he was received by Hitler at the Chancellery. At this session Hitler, for the first and only time in my presence, completely lost his nerve.

I do not recollect whether the Englishmen brought a German translation of Chamberlain's letter with them, or whether I had to translate it. In any case, the letter produced one of the most stormy meetings that I have ever experienced.

"The Government of Czecho-Slovakia has just informed me," Chamberlain wrote, "that it regards the proposals contained in your Memorandum as wholly unacceptable." In the course of the letter Chamberlain more or less said "I told you so," and he appeared to support the Czech position. Hitler, who had been listening with growing restlessness, suddenly leapt up, shouting: "There's no point at all in going on with negotiations," and rushed to the door. It was an exceptionally painful scene, especially as Hitler seemed to realize when he reached the door how impossible his behavior was, and returned to his seat like a defiant boy. He had himself now sufficiently under control, and I was able to continue reading out the letter. When I had ended, however, he let himself go more violently than I ever saw him do during a diplomatic interview. Nevertheless it in no way resembled the legendary fits of rage so frequently described. In the course of my duties I never saw anything which suggested them.

A very confused discussion followed, at which everybody talked at once, except Kirkpatrick and myself. It was one of the rare occasions when I failed to assert myself as an interpreter against Hitler. At other stormy meetings, especially during the conference of the Big Four held at Munich a few days later, I succeeded in restoring order by calling the attention of Hitler, or of some other speaker who had interrupted heatedly, to the fact that I had not finished my translation. Sir Horace Wilson's quiet efforts to persuade Hitler to be reasonable only increased his fury; Henderson combated Ribbentrop's excited talk of Benes as a terrorist and the Czechs as war mongers.

It was in this mood that Hitler made his famous speech at the Sports Palace a few hours later. "The question which has stirred us most deeply these last few weeks is known to you all," he said. "It is called not so much Czecho-Slovakia as Herr Benes. In this name is summed up all the emotion of millions of people today, that makes them despair or fills them with fanatical determination! . . . He is now driving the Germans out! But that's where his little game must stop. . . . The decision now rests with him. Peace or war! Either he accepts this offer, and at last gives freedom to the Germans, or we will come and fetch that freedom for ourselves!"

But there were other tones in the speech. Hitler spoke in a friendly way about Chamberlain, and added the much quoted, significant sentence: "I have assured Mr. Chamberlain that as soon as the Czechs have settled with their minorities . . . I shall have no further interest in the Czech state. I will guarantee him that. We want no Czechs."

The next day I was again summoned to the Chancellery. There I met Wilson, who had received a new message from Chamberlain during the night for transmission to Hitler. In this the Prime Minister offered a British guarantee to see that Czech evacuation was carried out if Germany, on her side, would abstain from using force.

Hitler refused to discuss this proposal, even when Wilson asked what he was to report back to Chamberlain. Hitler kept saying that there were now only two possibilities open to the Czech Government—acceptance or refusal of the German proposal. "And if they choose to refuse I shall smash Czecho-Slovakia!" he shouted angrily. "If the Czechs have not accepted my demands by 2 p.m. on Wednesday September 28 I shall march into the Sudeten territory on October 1st with the German army." That morning it was quite impossible to talk to Hitler reasonably. Abuse of the Czechs and dark threats were all he would utter. Wilson and his associates sat there helpless: they were not equal to such violence.

Suddenly Wilson rose to his feet. In a firm voice, slowly weighing each word, he said: "In these circumstances, there is a further commission from the Prime Minister that I must carry out. I must request you, Chancellor, to take note of the following communication." Then he read out a short but pregnant message, which I translated to Hitler as slowly and emphatically as possible, so that he could appreciate its significance. "If France, in fulfilment of her treaty obligations, should become actively involved in hostilities against Germany the United Kingdom would deem itself obliged to support France."

Hitler replied furiously that he took note of the communication. "It means," he added, "that if France chooses to attack Germany, England feels it her duty to attack Germany also." Raising his voice he went on: "If France and England want to unleash war, they can do so. It's a matter of complete indifference to me. I am prepared for all eventualities. I can only take note of the position. So—next week we'll all find ourselves at war with each other." That was his last word to Wilson, and his answer to Chamberlain.

The same evening I had to translate a letter to Chamberlain, which Hitler phrased in a rather more conciliatory manner. This was the second time in these critical days that I had the impression that Hitler shrank from the extreme step. Had Wilson's final statement caused him to change his course? In this letter, I still particularly remember, the German dictator said that he was prepared to participate in an international guarantee for the remaining part of Czecho-Slovakia, as soon as the minorities question had been settled.

Hitler's change of tone between exclaiming "war next week" and the writing of the conciliatory letter was perhaps due to a significant sight he had seen late that afternoon. In dull autumn weather a motorized division passed along the Wilhelmstrasse. The completely apathetic and melancholy behavior of the Berlin populace, which Hitler observed from a window of the Chancellery, made a deep impression on him. I was told at the time by his adjutants that he found the scene most disillusioning.

Next day, September 28th, there was an almost uninterrupted coming and going of ambassadors. François-Poncet, Henderson and the Italian Ambassador Attolico, passed each other at the door of Hitler's office, and in the neighboring rooms and passages there was the high-pressure activity of a time of crisis. Ministers and Generals, with their train of Party members, A.D.C.'s officers and Heads of Departments, who had hurried round to consult Hitler, were sitting or standing everywhere. None of these discussions were held as part of formal meetings. Hitler strolled the rooms, speaking now to one, now another. Whoever happened to be near could get at him, but nobody could actually get a word in. To anyone who wanted, or did not want, to listen, Hitler made long harangues about his view of the situation. It was just a series of shorter Sports Palace speeches. Only now and then Hitler withdrew to his office for a longer discussion with Ribbentrop, Göring, or one of the Generals—Keitel in particular.

The first Ambassador to appear that morning was François-Poncet. He spoke excellent German, but I was called in "just in case." As it was, having nothing to do, I could listen quietly to a conversation which I often recalled in later years for the statesmanlike wisdom and the extraordinary diplomatic ability with which François-Poncet conducted it. The French Ambassador wrestled for peace. "You deceive yourself, Chancellor," he said, "if you believe that you can confine the conflict to Czecho-Slovakia. If you attack that country you will set all Europe ablaze." He chose his words well, with characteristic thoughtfulness, and spoke a grammatically perfect German, whose faintly French accent somehow contributed to the impressiveness of what he said. "You are naturally confident of winning the war," he continued, "just as we believe that we can defeat you. But why should you take this risk when your essential demands can be met without war?"

Hitler gave no sign of agreement as he abused Benes once again, stressed his endeavors for peace, and stated emphatically that he could wait no longer. François-Poncet was not to be side-tracked; he continued, with great diplomatic skill, to demonstrate the senselessness of the action Hitler proposed to take. . . .

Again a door opened and an adjutant came in. I wondered whether this was to be another startling announcement. Had the Czechs perhaps started striking out on their own? I only caught the name Attolico mentioned, and was at once relieved, for I knew that the Italian Ambassador was one of the friends of peace. He belonged to the group, which at that time included Göring, Neurath and Weizsäcker, of those who were doing all they could to divert Hitler from his war plans. Attolico wanted to speak to Hitler at once "on an urgent matter." I left the room with Hitler, as Attolico spoke little German.

The slightly stooping Attolico was breathless, his face flushed with excitement. "I have an urgent message to you from the Duce, Führer!", he shouted unceremoniously from some way off. I then translated his message— "The British Government has just let it be known through its Ambassador in Rome that it will accept the Duce's mediation in the Sudeten question. It regards the area of disagreement as relatively narrow." He made an interesting addition. "The Duce informs you that whatever you decide, Führer, Fascist Italy stands behind you." But he quickly went on: "The Duce is, however, of the opinion that it would be wise to accept the British proposal, and begs you to refrain from mobilization." Hitler, already reflective after his talk with François-Poncet, was clearly impressed by Mussolini's message. Attolico watched him intently.

It was at this moment that the decision in favor of peace was made. It was just before noon on September 28th, two hours before the expiry of Hitler's ultimatum. Hitler replied: "Tell the Duce that I accept his proposal." . . .

We went back to his office, where François-Poncet was still waiting with Ribbentrop. "Mussolini has just asked whether I will accept his mediation," Hitler said briefly. . . .

François-Poncet had scarcely left when Henderson appeared. He had another message from Chamberlain, which I translated. "After reading your letter," he wrote, "I feel certain that you can get all that is essential without war and without delay. I am ready to come to Berlin myself at once to discuss arrangements for the transfer of territory with you and representatives of the Czech Government, together with representatives of France and Italy if you so desire. . . . I cannot believe that you will take the responsibility of starting a world war which may end civilization for the sake of a few day's delay in settling this long-standing problem." Hitler replied that he must contact

Mussolini about this proposal. "I have postponed German mobilization for twenty-four hours to meet the wishes of my great Italian ally," Hitler told Henderson. The latter took his leave after a perfectly friendly interview.

The same afternoon Hitler telephoned to Mussolini, and the conversation resulted in the greatest sensation of the interwar period—the decision that Hitler should invite Chamberlain, Daladier and Mussolini to a conference at Munich. That night I went south by special train.

The Munich Conference was regarded at the time as the decisive turning point in the Sudeten crisis. Actually this had occurred the day before, in Hitler's talk with Attolico, after the vital preparatory work carried out by François-Poncet. . . .

The course of the Munich Conference, held in the new Führer building in the Konigsplatz, was described in such detail at the time that it would be redundant for me to write at length about it. It was not in any case the actual peak of the crisis.

Soon after my arrival at Munich I drove with Hitler to Kufstein. There he boarded the Italian special train and talked to Mussolini during the journey —a conversation which confirmed my assumption that peace was assured. Mussolini, in words similar to those used by François-Poncet, emphatically advocated a peaceful solution.

Shortly before two o'clock I took my seat at a round table in the Führer building at Munich (now the Amerikahaus), with the Big Four, Hitler, Chamberlain, Mussolini and Daladier. Ribbentrop, Ciano, Wilson and Alexis Léger, head of the French Foreign Office, were also there. The historic Munich Conference had begun. Its course was far less sensational than was then universally assumed, for, as I have said, the actual decision had already been taken.

The four principals first briefly expounded the attitude of their respective countries. They all spoke against a solution by force, even Hitler emphasizing that he was all for a peaceful settlement of the matter. An atmosphere of general goodwill prevailed, broken only once or twice when Hitler violently attacked Benes and Czecho-Slovakia and Daladier took up the challenge.

Daladier was still an unknown figure in that circle. A short man, he sat silent most of the time. He was clearly perturbed by the fact that decisions were being taken about the cession of territory by an ally of France, Czecho-Slovakia, without that country being represented at the conference. I noticed that Alexis Léger several times spoke to him, apparently urging him to oppose some point or other. But Daladier did not react, except on the occasions already mentioned, when he took up a fairly stiff attitude towards Hitler. . . .

There was also a slight clash with Chamberlain at Munich. He persistently raised a question which, by and large, was of very minor significance. It concerned the transfer of Czecho-Slovak public property to Germany in the ceded territory. Chamberlain kept on asking who would compensate the Czecho-Slovak Government for the buildings and installations which would pass to Germany with the Sudeten territory? It was obvious that here not the Prime Minister and politician, but the former Chancellor of the Exchequer and business man was speaking. Hitler became more and more restive. "These installations and buildings are the result of taxes paid by the Sudeten Germans," he kept saying with growing impatience, "and so there can be no question of indemnification." But this failed to satisfy Chamberlain's sense of tidiness in matters affecting property. Hitler finally exploded. "Our time is too valuable to be wasted on such trivialities," he shouted at Chamberlain. This was when Chamberlain, for full measure, also raised the question of whether cattle were to remain in Sudeten territory or whether some of the livestock might not be driven into what remained of Czecho-Slovakia. . . .

After Mussolini had submitted a written proposal for the solution of the Sudeten question, the Conference adjourned for a short lunch interval at about three o'clock. . . .

Negotiations continued somewhat disjointedly after lunch. The meeting was no longer confined to the Big Four with their Foreign Ministers or diplomatic advisers; gradually Göring, François-Poncet, Henderson, Attolico, von Weizsäcker, legal advisers, secretaries and adjutants came into the room and formed a tense audience round the heads of Governments who sat in the middle. Mussolini's draft Agreement had in the meantime been translated into the three Conference languages and from it eventually emerged, with a few minor alterations, the famous Munich Agreement, which was finally signed between 2 and 3 a.m. on September 30th. . . .

Hitler about nine o'clock had invited everyone to dine with him in the banquet room at the Führer building. Chamberlain and Daladier excused themselves, saying they had to telephone to their Governments; they were obviously not in the mood to attend a banquet. They had secured peace, but at the price of a serious loss of prestige. Under pressure from Hitler they had arranged for an ally of France to cede part of its territory to Germany. As we now know, considerable pressure had to be brought to bear on Czecho-Slovakia both by France and England; it was therefore understandable that Chamberlain and Daladier seemed decidedly depressed that evening. . . .

An exclusively Italo-German company, therefore, sat down with Hitler at a banqueting table that was much too long. It was on this occasion that Mussolini made his statement about the catastrophic consequences that would have ensued for Italy at the time of the Abyssinian war, if the League of Nations had extended its sanctions to oil, even if only for a week.

As far as I was concerned, the Munich Conference lasted without respite for nearly thirteen hours, for I also had to interpret during lunch and dinner. I had to translate everything that was said continuously into three languages, and so spoke literally twice as many words as the Big Four put together. . . .

"I am now going to a dying man to give him supreme unction," François-Poncet had very aptly said as, in the small hours of September 30th, he went to tell the Czechs, France's allies, of the verdict passed on them in their absence. "But I have not even got oil with me," he added, "to pour on his wounds."

The British Prime Minister had flown three times to Germany; step by step he had allowed Hitler to push him into a solution which contributed very little to the prestige of the Western Powers.

Hitler was astonished and indignant that the two great countries, after their transitory relief at the maintenance of peace, were not exactly congratulating themselves on the price they had had to pay for it, and that they were naturally determined to do everything possible to see that they were never again in such a helpless position.

It once again became startlingly clear to me during those days how little Hitler understood the mentality of Western Europe.

Despite these unpleasant impressions I, and my colleagues at the Foreign Office, retained up to the end of that eventful year the feeling of relief that the great slaughter had been prevented.

►THE YALTA CONFERENCE

RAYMOND J. SONTAG

A relatively thorough and detailed preparation through diplomatic channels preceded the wartime summit meeting of President Franklin D. Roosevelt, Prime Minister Winston Churchill and Premier Joseph V. Stalin. The author of the subsequent evaluation of confidential and public documents relating to Yalta is Professor of History at the University of California. He is author of European Diplomatic History *and numerous studies relating to World War II. The article was written in 1955 after the United States Department of State had published most of the confidential material concerning the preparation and proceedings of the Yalta Conference.*

Sontag's study is followed by the protocol of proceedings at Yalta, as published by official United States sources.

The foreign policy objectives of the United States in 1944-45, as set forth in the pre-conference papers, can still be studied with pride by Americans; and they should be placed by the rest of the world in contrast to Soviet policy as it has unfolded over the last decade. . . .

Through every statement of policy in the period preparatory to the conference there is evident the conviction that American interests would be best served by the independence and the economic revival of other nations, by the liberation of subject peoples, by the spread of social reform, and by the free coöperation of all countries in the United Nations. And throughout it is evident that the one central problem was believed to be to obtain Soviet support for the attainment of these objectives. That support obtained, the conviction was general that the world would enjoy peace.

Yalta was the supreme effort of the United States Government to obtain Soviet support for these objectives, an effort which ended in disastrous failure. . . .

In the winter of 1944-45 the duration of the war was uncertain. For

Excerpted by special permission from "Reflections on the Yalta Papers," *Foreign Affairs*, July, 1955. Copyright by Council on Foreign Relations, Inc., New York.

planning purposes, it was assumed that the European war would be over, at the earliest, by July 1, 1945. At the time of the Yalta Conference, the Russian armies seemed to have a clear road ahead of them across the great European plain; the Western armies had not yet crossed the Rhine. In this situation, it was possible that the end of the war would find the Russians in possession of most of Germany, as they were already in possession of nearly all of what we now call the satellites.

Beyond the ending of the European war, there stretched the unknown duration of the Pacific war. For planning purposes, the end of the war against Japan was set at 18 months after the defeat of Germany. While this date was tentative and set merely for logistical purposes, there is clear evidence that the Joint Chiefs saw a hard fight ahead, as indeed there was. The probability that one atomic bomb would be ready by July 1, 1945, and more by the end of the year, was known. But there is no evidence that the military had yet assessed the probable effect of atomic weapons on the length of the war, either in Europe or Asia.

If the war developed in this way, the whole strength of the United States would be concentrated in Asia for some time after the ending of the war in Europe, and if, during this time, the Russians were in undisturbed occupation of most of Europe north of the Alps and east of the Rhine, how would they use this time? Ambassador Harriman reported that, "the overriding consideration in Soviet foreign policy is the preoccupation with 'security.' . . . The Soviet Union seeks a period of freedom from danger during which it can recover from the wounds of war and complete its industrial revolution. The Soviet conception of 'security' does not appear cognizant of the similar needs or rights of other countries and of Russia's obligation to accept the restraints as well as the benefits of an international security system." This was ominous.

The situation in Asia was even more ominous. Within China, according to the Briefing Book Papers of the Department of State, "there is now Kuomintang China, Communist China, and puppet [*i.e.* Japanese dominated] China. Kuomintang China is being weakened by dissident elements and widespread popular discontent. Communist China is growing in material and popular strength. Puppet China is filled with pockets of Communist guerilla resistance." A continuance of this situation would be "detrimental to our objective of a united, progressive China capable of contributing to security and prosperity in the Far East." There was an even more dangerous possibility. If the U.S.S.R. entered the Far Eastern war, one line of attack might be from Outer Mongolia; Soviet troops could strike east and take over all of north China and Manchuria. The Department believed that as yet there was little to substantiate the fear that Russia intended "to establish an independent or autonomous area in north China and Manchuria," but an open break between the Kuomintang and the Chinese Communists would tempt Russia to abandon her declared policy of nonintervention in the internal affairs of China. "It is our task to bring about British and Russian support of our objective of a united China which will coöperate with them as well as with us."

Reading these documents, one sees clearly that the American policymakers, civil or military, had no confidence in their ability, while the war continued, to *compel* the U.S.S.R. to accept the American plans for the organization of the Asiatic mainland. Moreover, our Government was eager to secure early Soviet military intervention in the war against Japan, and recognized the necessity to pay for it. The problem as seen in Washington was both to ensure early Soviet intervention and to bring the U.S.S.R. to recognize that "a strong and friendly China" was the best guarantee of Soviet security in Asia.

Even after victory over Japan, in the view of American policy-makers, the power of the United States directly to shape the future would be very limited. The strategic situation expected after the war is most clearly outlined in a letter which Admiral Leahy wrote to Secretary Hull on May 16, 1944, giving the view of the Joint Chiefs of Staff on a British proposal for the disposition of the Italian colonies. While this letter was written many months before Yalta, it was accepted as the basis for policy by the Department of State in the Briefing Book for the conference, and, so far as can be determined from the available evidence, the views of the Joint Chiefs had not altered during the intervening months. The central theme of the letter was the "revolutionary changes in relative national military strengths" resulting from the war, and particularly the "phenomenal development" of Soviet strength, absolutely, and relative to the impaired strength of Britain. The situation which was expected to result from this shift now seems so remote that it is almost forgotten, but it must be recalled if American policy in 1945 is to be understood. Admiral Leahy wrote:

> It would seem clear that there cannot be a world war, or even a great war, which does not find one or more of the great military powers on each side. At the conclusion of the present war, there will be, for the foreseeable future, only three such powers—the United States, Britain and Russia. Since it would seem in the highest degree unlikely that Britain and Russia, or Russia alone, would be aligned against the United States, it is apparent that any future world conflict in the foreseeable future will find Britain and Russia in opposite camps. . . .
>
> In a conflict between these two powers the disparity in the military strengths that they could dispose upon that continent [*i.e.* Europe] would, under present conditions, be far too great to be overcome by our intervention on the side of Britain. Having due regard to the military factors involved—resources, manpower, geography and particularly our ability to project our strength across the ocean and exert it decisively upon the continent—we might be able to successfully defend Britain, but we could not, under existing conditions, defeat Russia. In other words, we would find ourselves engaged in a war which we could not win even though the United States would be in no danger of defeat and occupation.
>
> It is apparent that the United States should, now and in the future, exert its utmost efforts and utilize all its influence to prevent such a situation arising and to promote a spirit of mutual coöperation between Britain, Russia and ourselves. So long as Britain and Russia coöperate and collaborate in the interests of peace, there can be no great war in the foreseeable future.
>
> The greatest likelihood of eventual conflict between Britain and Russia would seem to grow out of either nation initiating attempts to build up its strength, by seeking to attach to herself parts of Europe to the disadvantage

and possible danger of her potential adversary. Having regard to the inherent suspicions of the Russians, to present Russia with any agreement on such matters as between the British and ourselves, prior to consultation with Russia, might well result in starting a train of events that would lead eventually in [to] the situation we most wish to avoid.

Seen in the light of Admiral Leahy's letter, much that is puzzling in the Yalta period becomes understandable: Mr. Roosevelt's elaborate efforts to avoid the appearance of intimacy with Britain, even to create the impression of friction between Britain and the United States; American opposition to the delimitation of Anglo-Soviet spheres of influence in Southeastern Europe; what seems now the shortsighted preoccupation of the Department of State with the possibility that the British and Soviet Zones in Germany might be administered along divergent lines. These and other aspects of American policy should be seen in relation to the conviction that, in the future, war between the U.S. and U.S.S.R. was "in the highest degree unlikely," that Anglo-Russian enmity was the one likely cause of war, and that the United States must avoid appearing to line up with Britain on questions of direct interest to Russia "lest postwar disunity of the three great powers be thereby fostered with all the possibility of ultimate impact upon the military position of the United States which such a disaster would entail."

What requires explanation is the fact that, at the end of the Yalta Conference, the American delegation was convinced (so far as can be determined from evidence set down at the time, and not from undocumented afterthought) that Soviet support had in fact been won. In the last days a note of relief, even of rejoicing, breaks through the cold summaries of the proceedings.

To understand this rejoicing it is necessary to stress, not the concessions made by the Americans and the British, but the attitude and the promises of the Russians. On Poland, the Americans and the British stood firm until Stalin said that free elections could be held in about one month; then agreement was quickly achieved. On Germany, what seemed important at the time was that the Soviet Union agreed to a single administration for all the zones, thus apparently eliminating the possibility of disastrous friction between the occupying Powers. On the Far East, the concessions to Russia in Manchuria, Sakhalin and the Kuriles seemed justified not only because they insured Soviet military intervention in the war against Japan; these concessions also set limits to Soviet expansion in an area where there was no effective force to oppose Soviet expansion; finally, these concessions brought a Soviet promise to support the government of Chiang Kai-shek. When Molotov agreed to accept the American proposal that in the United Nations the veto should not be used in questions involving the peaceful adjustment of disputes, Mr. Roosevelt "felt that this was a great step forward" and Mr. Churchill echoed the President's words, adding that the decision "would bring joy and relief to the peoples of the world."

Over and above concrete concessions, there were Marshal Stalin's repeated protestations of his determination to "create for the future generation such an organization as would secure peace for at least fifty years," and, in contrast to earlier exchanges between the Allied Governments, his disarming friendliness and apparent eagerness to continue the wartime coöperation into the years of peace which lay ahead. Even Mr. Churchill, whose detestation of Communism went back to 1917, was persuaded to hope that "we were all standing on the crest of a hill with the glories of future possibilities stretching before us," while Mr. Roosevelt felt that the atmosphere "was as that of a family, and it was in those words that he liked to characterize the relations that existed between our three countries."

Seldom in history has deception been so successful and so decisive as that perpetrated at Yalta by the Soviet leaders at the expense of Britain and the United States. Immediately after the conference closed, evidence began to accumulate that the Soviet promises were worthless. If the Americans alone had been deceived, one would be driven to conclude that they were deceived only because they were blind to the nature of their antagonists. Blind they certainly were. Nowhere in this volume is there anything which suggests that American statesmen were conscious that they were dealing, not with Russian national leaders, but with Communist revolutionaries determined to outwit and eventually destroy their allies, allies not from choice but because of the mad decision of Hitler to attack the Soviet Union.

Even those who urged a firmer policy in dealings with the U.S.S.R. did not make it clear that Russia was now, not a national state pursuing national interests, but the center of a revolutionary movement dedicated to the creation of a Communist world ruled from Moscow. General John R. Deane believed that for the United States always to be "at the same time the givers and the supplicants" was "neither dignified nor healthy for U.S. prestige." But he also believed "we have few conflicting interests, and there is little reason why we should not be friendly now and in the foreseeable future." Ambassador Harriman shared General Deane's views on the need for tougher bargaining with the U.S.S.R., but he also felt strongly "that the sooner the Soviet Union can develop a decent life for its people the more tolerant they will become. . . . I am satisfied that the great urge of Stalin and his associates is to provide a better physical life for the Russian people, although they will retain a substantial military establishment." Such statements did little to undermine the belief, dominant in Washington, that Russian and American interests were identical, and that the only problem was to bring the Soviet leaders to a recognition of this fact.

But it was not just the Americans who were deceived at Yalta. Churchill also was deceived, and that was indeed a triumph for Soviet duplicity, for Churchill's denunciations of "the foul baboonery of Bolshevism" are among the most magnificent examples of sustained invective in the English language. Here we touch the real root of Soviet success at Yalta: British and American consciousness of the consequences of failure to reach agreement with the Soviet Union. Churchill stated the case with his customary precision when he presented the Yalta agreements to the Commons: "I decline absolutely to embark here on a discussion about Russian good faith. It is quite evident that these matters touch the whole future of the world. Sombre indeed would be the fortunes of mankind if some awful schism arose between the Western democracies and the Russian Soviet Union."

That awful schism did arise. . . . At Yalta, the professions and promises of Stalin and Molotov convinced the American negotiators that Soviet friendship had been won, that Soviet good faith was assured. Almost immediately after Yalta the conviction was shaken, and slowly, much too slowly, it was destroyed by Soviet aggression. But if that honest and desperate effort had not been made at the outset it is hard to believe that we could now accept unflinchingly the tragically unfolding consequences of the schism between East and West.

The schism is not of our making. So much consolation we can derive from our failure at Yalta. Farther we need not go, and should not go.

►THE YALTA AGREEMENTS

PROTOCOL OF PROCEEDINGS, FEBRUARY 11, 1945

The Crimea Conference of the Heads of the Governments of the United States of America, the United Kingdom, and the Union of Soviet Socialist Republics which took place from February 4th to 11th came to the following conclusions:

I. WORLD ORGANIZATION

It was decided: (1) that a United Nations Conference on the proposed world organization should be summoned for Wednesday, 25th April, 1945, and should be held in the United States of America.

(2) the Nations to be invited to this Conference should be: (a) the United Nations as they existed on the 8th February, 1945; and (b) such of the Associated Nations as have declared war on the common enemy by 1st March, 1945. (For this purpose by the term "Associated Nation" was meant the eight Associated Nations and Turkey.) When the Conference on World Organization is held, the delegates of the United Kingdom and United States of America will support a proposal to admit to original membership two Soviet Socialist Republics, i.e., the Ukraine and White Russia.

(3) that the United States Government on behalf of the Three Powers should consult the Government of China and the French Provisional Government in regard to decisions taken at the present Conference concerning the proposed World Organization.

(4) that the text of the invitation to be issued to all the nations which would take part in the United Nations Conference should be as follows:

[Invitation] "The Government of the United States of America, on behalf of itself and of the Governments of the United Kingdom, the Union of Soviet Socialist Republics, and the Republic of China and the Provisional

Government of the French Republic, invite the Government of   to send representatives to a Conference of the United Nations to be held on 25th April, 1945, or soon thereafter, at San Francisco in the United States of America to prepare a Charter for a General International Organization for the maintenance of international peace and security.

"The above named governments suggested that the Conference consider as affording a basis for such a Charter the Proposals for the Establishment of a General International Organization, which were made public last October as a result of the Dumbarton Oaks Conference, and which have now been supplemented by the following provisions for Section C of Chapter VI:

"C. *Voting.* 1. Each member of the Security Council should have one vote.

"2. Decisions of the Security Council on procedural matters should be made by an affirmative vote of seven members.

"3. Decisions of the Security Council on all other matters should be made by an affirmative vote of seven members including the concurring votes of the permanent members; provided that, in decisions under Chapter VIII,[1] Section A and under the second sentence of paragraph 1 of Chapter VIII, Section C, a party to a dispute should abstain from voting.

"Further information as to arrangements will be transmitted subsequently.

"In the event that the Government of —— desires in advance of the Conference to present views or comments concerning the proposals, the Government of the United States of America will be pleased to transmit such views and comments to the other participating Governments."

Territorial Trusteeship. It was agreed that the five Nations which will have permanent seats on the Security Council should consult each other prior to the United Nations Conference on the question of territorial trusteeship.

The acceptance of this recommendation is subject to its being made clear that territorial trusteeship will only apply to (a) existing mandates of the League of Nations; (b) territories detached from the enemy as a result of the present war; (c) any other territory which might voluntarily be placed under trusteeship; and (d) no discussion of actual territories is contemplated at the forthcoming United Nations Conference or in the preliminary consultations, and it will be a matter for subsequent agreement which territories within the above categories will be placed under trusteeship.

II. DECLARATION ON LIBERATED EUROPE

The following declaration has been approved:

"The Premier of the Union of Soviet Socialist Republics, the Prime Minister of the United Kingdom and the President of the United States of America have consulted with each other in the common interests of the peoples of their countries and those of liberated Europe. They jointly declare their mutual agreement to concert during the temporary period of instability in liberated Europe the policies of their three governments in assisting the

[1] Chapter VI and paragraph 3 of Article 52 in the differently organized final version of the Charter.

peoples of the former Axis satellite states of Europe to solve by democratic means their pressing political and economic problems.

"The establishment of order in Europe and the re-building of national economic life must be achieved by processes which will enable the liberated peoples to destroy the last vestiges of Nazism and Fascism and to create democratic institutions of their own choice. This is a principle of the Atlantic Charter—the right of all peoples to choose the form of government under which they will live—the restoration of sovereign rights and self-government to those peoples who have been forcibly deprived of them by the aggressor nations.

"To foster the conditions in which the liberated peoples may exercise these rights, the three governments will jointly assist the people in any European liberated state or former Axis satellite state in Europe where in their judgment conditions require (a) to establish conditions of internal peace; (b) to carry out emergency measures for the relief of distressed peoples; (c) to form interim governmental authorities broadly representative of all democratic elements in the population and pledged to the earliest possible establishment through free elections of governments responsive to the will of the people; and (d) to facilitate where necessary the holding of such elections.

"The three governments will consult the other United Nations and provisional authorities or other governments in Europe when matters of direct interest to them are under consideration.

"When, in the opinion of the three governments, conditions in any European liberated state or any former Axis satellite state in Europe make such action necessary, they will immediately consult together on the measures necessary to discharge the joint responsibilities set forth in this declaration.

"By this declaration we reaffirm our faith in the principles of the Atlantic Charter, our pledge in the Declaration by the United Nations, and our determination to build in cooperation with other peace-loving nations world order under law, dedicated to peace, security, freedom and general well-being of all mankind.

"In issuing this declaration, the Three Powers express the hope that the Provisional Government of the French Republic may be associated with them in the procedure suggested."

III. DISMEMBERMENT OF GERMANY

It was agreed that Article 12 (a) of the Surrender Terms for Germany should be amended to read as follows:

"The United Kingdom, the United States of America and the Union of Soviet Socialist Republics shall possess supreme authority with respect to Germany. In the exercise of such authority they will take such steps, including the complete disarmament, demilitarization and dismemberment of Germany as they deem requisite for future peace and security."

The study of the procedure for the dismemberment of Germany was referred to a Committee, consisting of Mr. Eden (Chairman), Mr. Winant and

Mr. Gousev. This body would consider the desirability of associating with it a French representative.

IV. ZONE OF OCCUPATION FOR THE FRENCH
AND CONTROL COUNCIL FOR GERMANY

It was agreed that a zone in Germany, to be occupied by the French Forces, should be allocated to France. This zone would be formed out of the British and American zones and its extent would be settled by the British and Americans in consultation with the French Provisional Government.

It was also agreed that the French Provisional Government should be invited to become a member of the Allied Control Council for Germany.

V. REPARATION

The Heads of the three governments agreed as follows:

1. Germany must pay in kind for the losses caused by her to the Allied nations in the course of the war. Reparations are to be received in the first instance by those countries which have borne the main burden of war, have suffered the heaviest losses and have organized victory over the enemy.

2. Reparations in kind are to be exacted from Germany in three following forms:

(a) Removals within 2 years from the surrender of Germany or the cessation of organized resistance from the national wealth of Germany located on the territory of Germany herself as well as outside her territory (equipment, machine-tools, ships, rolling stock, German investments abroad, shares of industrial, transport and other enterprises in Germany, etc.), these removals to be carried out chiefly for purpose of destroying the war potential of Germany.

(b) Annual deliveries of goods from current production for a period to be fixed.

(c) Use of German labor.

3. For the working out on the above principles of a detailed plan for exaction of reparation from Germany an Allied Reparation Commission will be set up in Moscow. It will consist of three representatives—one from the Union of Soviet Socialist Republics, one from the United Kingdom and one from the United States of America.

4. With regard to the fixing of the total sum of the reparation as well as the distribution of it among the countries which suffered from the German aggression the Soviet and American delegations agreed as follows:

"The Moscow Reparation Commission should take in its initial studies as a basis for discussion the suggestion of the Soviet Government that the total sum of the reparation in accordance with the points (a) and (b) of the paragraph 2 should be 20 billion dollars and that 50% of it should go to the Union of Soviet Socialist Republics."

The British delegation was of the opinion that pending consideration of the reparation question by the Moscow Reparation Commission no figures of reparation should be mentioned.

The above Soviet-American proposal has been passed to the Moscow Reparation Commission as one of the proposals to be considered by the Commission.

VI. MAJOR WAR CRIMINALS

The Conference agreed that the question of the major war criminals should be the subject of inquiry by the three Foreign Secretaries for report in due course after the close of the Conference.

VII. POLAND

The following Declaration on Poland was agreed by the Conference:

"A new situation has been created in Poland as a result of her complete liberation by the Red Army. This calls for the establishment of a Polish Provisional Government which can be more broadly based than was possible before the recent liberation of Western part of Poland. The Provisional Government which is now functioning in Poland should therefore be reorganized on a broader democratic basis with the inclusion of democratic leaders from Poland itself and from Poles abroad. This new Government should then be called the Polish Provisional Government of National Unity.

"M. Molotov, Mr. Harriman and Sir A. Clark Kerr are authorized as a commission to consult in the first instance in Moscow with members of the present Provisional Government and with other Polish democratic leaders from within Poland and from abroad, with a view to the reorganization of the present Government along the above lines. This Polish Provisional Government of National Unity shall be pledged to the holding of free and unfettered elections as soon as possible on the basis of universal suffrage and secret ballot. In these elections all democratic and anti-Nazi parties shall have the right to take part and to put forward candidates.

"When a Polish Provisional Government of National Unity has been properly formed in conformity with the above, the Government of the USSR, which now maintains diplomatic relations with the present Provisional Government of Poland, and the Government of the United Kingdom and the Government of the United States of America will establish diplomatic relations with the new Polish Government of National Unity, and will exchange Ambassadors by whose reports the respective Governments will be kept informed about the situation in Poland.

"The three Heads of Government consider that the Eastern frontier of Poland should follow the Curzon Line with digressions from it in some regions of five to eight kilometres in favor of Poland. They recognize that Poland must receive substantial accessions of territory on the North and West. They feel that the opinion of the new Polish Provisional Government of National Unity should be sought in due course on the extent of these accessions and that the final delimitation of the Western frontier of Poland should thereafter await the Peace Conference."

VIII. YUGOSLAVIA

It was agreed to recommend to Marshal Tito and to Dr. Subasic: (a) that the Tito-Subasic Agreement should immediately be put into effect and a new Government formed on the basis of the Agreement (b) that as soon as the new Government has been formed it should declare:

(i) that the Anti-Fascist Assembly of National Liberation (AVNOJ) will be extended to include members of the last Yugoslav Skupstina who have not compromised themselves by collaboration with the enemy, thus forming a body to be known as a temporary Parliament and

(ii) that legislative acts passed by the Anti-Fascist Assembly of National Liberation (AVNOJ) will be subject to subsequent ratification by a Constituent Assembly; and that this statement should be published in the Communique of the Conference.

IX. ITALO-YUGOSLAV FRONTIER; ITALO-AUSTRIA FRONTIER

Notes on these subjects were put in by the British delegation and the American and Soviet delegations agreed to consider them and give their views later.

X. YUGOSLAV-BULGARIAN RELATIONS

There was an exchange of views between the Foreign Secretaries on the question of the desirability of a Yugoslav-Bulgarian pact of alliance. The question at issue was whether a state still under an armistice regime could be allowed to enter into a treaty with another state. Mr. Eden suggested that the Bulgarian and Yugoslav Governments should be informed that this could not be approved. Mr. Stettinius suggested that the British and American Ambassadors should discuss the matter further with M. Molotov in Moscow. M. Molotov agreed with the proposal of Mr. Stettinus.

XI. SOUTHEASTERN EUROPE

The British Delegation put in notes for the consideration of their colleagues on the following subjects:

(a) the Control Commission in Bulgaria

(b) Greek claims upon Bulgaria, more particularly with reference to reparations

(c) Oil equipment in Rumania.

XII. IRAN

Mr. Eden, Mr. Stettinius and M. Molotov exchanged view on the situation in Iran. It was agreed that this matter should be pursued through the diplomatic channel.

XIII. MEETINGS OF THE THREE FOREIGN SECRETARIES

The Conference agreed that permanent machinery should be set up for consultation between the three Foreign Secretaries; they should meet as often as necessary, probably about every three or four months.

These meetings will be held in rotation in the three capitals, the first meeting being held in London.

XIV. THE MONTREUX CONVENTION AND THE STRAITS

It was agreed that at the next meeting of the three Foreign Secretaries to be held in London, they should consider proposals which it was understood the Soviet Government would put forward to relation to the Montreux Convention and report to their Governments. The Turkish Government should be informed at the appropriate moment.

The foregoing Protocol was approved and signed by the three Foreign Secretaries at the Crimean Conference, February 11, 1945.

E. R. STETTINIUS, JR.
V. MOLOTOV
ANTHONY EDEN

Agreement Regarding Japan, February 11, 1945

The leaders of the three Great Powers—the Soviet Union, the United States of America and Great Britain—have agreed that in two or three months after Germany has surrendered and the war in Europe has terminated the Soviet Union shall enter into the war against Japan on the side of the Allies on condition that:

1. The status quo in Outer-Mongolia (The Mongolian People's Republic) shall be preserved;

2. The former rights of Russia violated by the treacherous attack of Japan in 1904 shall be restored, viz: (a) the southern part of Sakhalin as well as all the islands adjacent to it shall be returned to the Soviet Union, (b) the commercial port of Dairen shall be internationalized, the preeminent interests of the Soviet Union in this port being safeguarded and the lease of Port Arthur as a naval base of the USSR restored, (c) the Chinese-Eastern Railroad and the South-Manchurian Railroad which provides an outlet to Dairen shall be jointly operated by the establishment of a joint Soviet-Chinese Company it being understood that the preeminent interests of the Soviet Union shall be safeguarded and that China shall retain full sovereignty in Manchuria;

3. The Kuril Islands shall be handed over to the Soviet Union.

It is understood, that the agreement concerning Outer-Mongolia and the ports and railroads referred to above will require concurrence of Generalissimo Chiang Kai-shek. The President will take measures in order to obtain this concurrence on advice from Marshal Stalin.

The Heads of the three Great Powers have agreed that these claims of the Soviet Union shall be unquestionably fulfilled after Japan has been defeated.

For its part the Soviet Union expresses its readiness to conclude with the National Government of China a pact of friendship and alliance between the USSR and China in order to render assistance to China with its armed forces for the purpose of liberating China from the Japanese yoke.

JOSEPH V. STALIN
FRANKLIN D. ROOSEVELT
WINSTON S. CHURCHILL

February 11, 1945

TOPIC 16

How Dictators Err

At the end of World War II Anglo-American forces in defeated Germany succeeded in capturing a major part of the German secret archives. Thus was gained an unprecedented insight into the secret decision-making processes of two great European powers, Nazi Germany and Communist Russia.

An unbiased and scholarly study of captured German documents reveals that the outbreak of World War II at the particular period of September, 1939 was largely caused by Hitler's overconfidence in his proficiency in the art of brinkmanship. In the light of his personal experience with the Western democracies at Munich, he underestimated their determination to assist Poland. Until the last moment Hitler hoped to isolate his war with Poland and postpone the world conflict at least until a later date. His agreement with Russia was meant as a device to frighten the Western democracies into passivity.

While Hitler underestimated the West, Stalin overestimated the possibility of harmonizing Soviet and Nazi territorial ambitions. "Peaceful" co-existence between the dictators, initiated in 1939 at the cost of the existence of Poland and peace in Europe, collapsed in 1941. Unable to eliminate England, and suspicious of Russia's growing territorial appetite, Hitler decided to transform the partnership with the Russians into a bitter and fatal war. Russia's unpreparedness for Hitler's shift in thinking greatly facilitated deep Nazi penetration into the heart of Russia.

►THE LAST MONTHS OF PEACE

RAYMOND J. SONTAG

In the following selection a scholar who was in charge of the United States Department of State study of German secret documents (1946-1949), describes the series of successful Nazi bluffs and fatal errors which led to the outbreak of World War II. His article is followed by quotes from original diplomatic notes, decodified cables, and ambassadors' reports on secret conversations at the Soviet-Nazi summit. They illustrate the process by which two arch-enemies, always suspecting each other's intentions, were able to initiate a period of mutually advantageous coexistence, maintain it for some time, and then, when the problem of delimitation of zones of influence had arisen, return to the previous enmity; finally they engaged in a life-or-death struggle.

Excerpted by special permission from "The Last Months of Peace, 1939," *Foreign Affairs*, April, 1957. Copyright by Council on Foreign Relations, Inc., New York.

Only one who has had the oppressive feeling of being buried under the sheer mass of the captured German Foreign Ministry archives can appreciate the achievement of the editors of the papers relating to the last months of peace in 1939.[1] Despite their bulk, the captured archives are not complete. Much was lost by destruction, deliberate or accidental. Parts of the archives remained in Berlin or Eastern Germany, and the fate of these parts is still uncertain. Above all, few in the German Government knew with certainty what was in Hitler's mind, and Hitler's own words were often designed to obscure, not clarify, his intentions. In these circumstances, the pencilled notes for a private conference within the Foreign Ministry may tell more than a score of formal diplomatic papers, and a private letter in the files of an ambassador may be needed to correct the impression left by the instructions he received through official channels. The editors of the "Documents on German Foreign Policy" have not only tracked down every shred of evidence in the captured archives; they have also related this evidence to the enormous body of published evidence from other archives, to the testimony offered at the war crimes trials, and to the memoirs and biographies of participants in the events of these months.

From the tangle of evidence, one theme emerges, a theme which has relevance to our own day. It is the way in which a succession of diplomatic moves, intended only as preparatory to a still distant trial of strength, developed into a diplomatic crisis involving all of Europe, and eventually precipitated a world war which at the outset Hitler had no thought of starting and which to the end he hoped to avoid.

To see that story in proper perspective, and to appreciate its present relevance, it is necessary to push aside the legend that Hitler was either a fool or a reckless gambler. Leaving moral values to one side, Hitler's achievements during his first six years as chancellor compel reluctant acknowledgment. He had come to power in a distracted, impoverished, disarmed country. He had enforced unity at home. He had revived and increased German industrial power. He had built armed forces before which all Europe trembled. He had reoccupied the Rhineland and constructed formidable defenses in the west. He had annexed Austria and the strategically decisive Sudeten districts. What was left of Czechoslovakia lay helpless under the shadow of German power. As German industrial and military strength expanded, and as he moved from success to success, his favor was courted by those who had treated the Weimar Republic with scant respect. With Japan and Italy his relations were intimate. Poland, while retaining the alliance with France, was in practice closer to Germany. The Baltic States and the states of southeastern Europe were tacitly acknowledged to be within the German sphere of influence. The Governments of Britain and France were desperately eager to appease their formidable neighbor. Even the U.S.S.R. was showing a desire not to provoke the sworn enemy of Communism. In the light of his amazing successes, the warning voices of those of his advisers who feared he was carrying

---

[1] "Documents on German Foreign Policy, 1918-1945." Series D (1937-1945). v. 6, "The Last Months of Peace, March-August 1939;" v. 7, "The Last Days of Peace, August 9-September 3, 1939." (London: H.M. Stationery Office, 1956.)

Germany headlong to destruction were silenced by dismissal, by fear or by conversion to the belief that his judgment was, in fact, infallible.

Hitler freely admitted that his successes in the foreign field had been won by bluff. The conviction was general in Europe that the First World War had dangerously undermined European society and that another war would bring the structure to ruin, with Communism as the only gainer. The Soviet Union, sharing this conviction, was eager to stand clear so that it would not be involved in the general ruin. By exploiting fear of war Hitler had won much. He was confident that still more must be won by diplomacy before he could safely embark on war with the West.

Some day, Hitler recognized, Britain and France would be tempted to set limits to German power, even by war. In preparation for that day, he argued, Germany must not only strain her resources in military preparations; she must also win territory sufficient to feed her people during a long war— for war with the Western democracies would be both long and hard. Colonies would be of no value; their resources would be lost by blockade just when they were needed. The territory must be won in Eastern Europe. There, German skill could increase agricultural production, and the non-German population would provide a labor pool for farm and factory. The moment was, he believed, auspicious. Russia could not interfere: the purges had shaken the country and deprived the Red Army of its leaders; Stalin must fear a victorious army no less than military defeat. Fear of Russia would hold Poland on the side of Germany so long as exactions from Poland were counterbalanced by concessions to Polish territorial greed. Italy and Japan were so completely estranged from the Western democracies that they must follow the German lead. British and especially French rearmament was only beginning, and was encountering opposition unavoidable where the press was unmuzzled. Above all, Britain and France were ruled by men who had already retreated before the threat of war. Hitler was convinced that they lacked the resolution to precipitate a war or conduct it to the death.

The moves of March 1939 were, like the annexation of Austria and the Sudeten districts of Czechoslovakia, merely preliminary to the task of winning "living space." They would provide better frontiers and advanced military bases in the east, jumping-off places for future action. They would not bring the enlarged agricultural base needed for the future long war of annihilation with the Western democracies. Hitler made no diplomatic or military preparations which would suggest that even local opposition of any importance was anticipated. In one sense he envisioned the moves of March 1939 as the logical completion of the campaign against Czechoslovakia; in another sense, they were moves preparatory to the winning of the desired agricultural base.

II

In the early morning hours of March 15, 1939, after a stormy interview with Hitler, President Hácha wearily signed away the independence of what was left of Czechoslovakia. German troops had already crossed the frontier, and by afternoon Hitler was in Prague. The following Monday, March 20, the

Lithuanian Foreign Minister was received by Ribbentrop and told that Memel must be surrendered to Germany. Even before this demand was accepted on Thursday, the next move was made.

On Tuesday, March 21, Ribbentrop asked the Polish Ambassador, Lipski, to call on him. The Ambassador said that the German protectorate over Slovakia had hit Poland hard. Ribbentrop [indicated that] . . . the Führer was troubled by anti-German feeling in Poland. The Poles must surely recognize that unless they coöperated with Germany they would be absorbed by Communist Russia. It was necessary to put German-Polish relations on a sound and lasting basis. To this end, Danzig must return to Germany, and Germany must be granted extra-territorial rail and road connections between the Reich and East Prussia. Then Hitler would be prepared to guarantee the Polish Corridor. . . . Ribbentrop suggested that Lipski take these proposals to Warsaw. Possibly the Polish Foreign Minister, Beck, would come to Berlin to discuss them; Hitler would warmly welcome such a discussion.

Lipski did go to Warsaw, and while he was away Hitler informed his army commander that a military solution of the problem of Danzig was not desired, because this would drive Poland into the arms of Britain. . . . While he did not wish to solve the Polish question militarily unless especially favorable political conditions arose, Hitler continued, plans should be made, with the objective of beating the Poles so thoroughly that they would not be a political factor for some decades. . . .

The Polish reply was presented by Lipski on Sunday, March 26. In form it was most conciliatory, but it did not meet the German demands. . . .

Already signs were multiplying that the crisis was not, in fact, at its climax, and that Prague, Memel and Danzig had violently shaken world diplomatic alignments. In Britain and France the annihilation of Czechoslovakia produced a strong popular reaction against the policy of appeasement. Chamberlain and Daladier had wavered and then fallen in with the popular mood. Recognition of the German action in Czechoslovakia was refused, and the British and French Ambassadors in Berlin were ordered home for consultation. When there were rumors of new German moves in Central Europe, there was a flurry of diplomatic activity from which emerged, on March 31, a declaration by Chamberlain in the House of Commons that Britain and France would aid Poland in resisting any action clearly threatening Polish independence. Hard on this declaration, the Polish Foreign Minister arrived in London, and at the conclusion of his visit Chamberlain stated on April 6 that a permanent alliance would be negotiated between Britain and Poland. . . .

More ominous, negotiations began in mid-April for drawing the Soviet Union into what the Germans called the British encirclement program; someone kept the German Embassy in London fully and promptly informed of these negotiations. Finally, even the United States Government assumed a more active rôle. At the onset of the March crisis, the German chargé in Washington warned that the Roosevelt Administration was determined to support Britain and France in any war with Germany and that, while American opinion was opposed to war, this opposition would collapse on the first news of air attacks on British or French cities. On April 15, President Roosevelt appealed directly to Hitler and Mussolini, asking for assurance against armed attack on a long list of states.

Even within the Axis, the occupation of Prague produced a violent re-action. As usual, the Italian Government had received no advance notice of the German action, and repetition intensified Italian resentment against such cavalier treatment. Now, however, the Italians were not only humiliated; they were frightened. Austria and Czechoslovakia were completely under German control, and Hungary was a dependent of the Reich. . . . German assurances that the Mediterranean, including the Adriatic, was an Italian sphere of influence, did not disarm Italian fears. On Good Friday, Mussolini moved to solidify the Italian position by seizing Albania, and he did not forewarn Germany. . . . Italian policy was assuming an unaccustomed and potentially dangerous independence of German leadership.

III

There is no evidence that all this activity caused Hitler any alarm, and much evidence that he continued confident of success. As the weeks passed, German policy towards Poland changed, and by May 23 Hitler was resolved to attack her at the first suitable opportunity; but this was to be an isolated operation, from which other Powers would remain aloof.

By April 3, when Beck arrived in London, it was already obvious that the German plan to hold Poland away from Britain had failed. On the same day, the high command of the Wehrmacht was instructed to prepare plans for an attack on Poland in such a way that the operation could begin at any time from September 1. In the amplification of these instructions issued on April 11, the war with Poland was still described as a possibility to be avoided if possible; in any case, every precaution must be taken to limit the war to Poland only. The proposal made by Ribbentrop to Lipski was withdrawn on April 6; German missions abroad were instructed not to discuss the proposal or the Polish counter-offer.

The war of nerves was begun, with full confidence of victory. Ribbentrop was convinced that "not one British soldier would be mobilized in the event of a German-Polish conflict." Göring and Hitler expressed the same conviction. Public excitement, the Nazis argued, had pushed Beck, Chamberlain and Daladier into foolish threats and promises, but, as Hitler said, "one could only yell for a certain time." When passions cooled, and reason reasserted itself, it would become obvious that the German position was overwhelmingly strong. In the German view, British and French rearmament had only begun, and the German West Wall was impregnable; therefore no effective help could come to Poland from the west. Russia would not fight, and in any case the Poles knew that the Russians, if they ever entered their country, would never leave. . . . The German chargé in Moscow stressed Soviet "mistrust and reserve" in relations with the West, and on April 17 the Soviet Ambassador in Berlin suggested that so far as the U.S.S.R. was concerned, Nazi-Soviet relations could easily be improved. And so Hitler was probably quite honest when he said that he "had a great deal of time for theatres and concerts" and that he "regarded the whole course of events calmly."

Through four weeks after Chamberlain's promise of assistance to the Poles, the Germans kept their own counsel. Then, on Friday, April 28, Hitler spoke. The British encirclement policy and the Polish military agreement had, he said, destroyed the Anglo-German naval agreement of 1935 and the German-Polish political understanding of 1934. With irony verging on ridicule, he dismissed Roosevelt's peace appeal as meaningless. About Russia he said nothing. . . .

A week after Hitler's speech the strength of the German position was dramatized by a meeting in Milan between Ribbentrop and the Italian Foreign Minister, Ciano. In the communiqué issued at the conclusion of the meeting, on May 7, emphasis was placed on the "perfect identity of views" between Germany and Italy, and on the intention of the two Governments to conclude a political and military pact—the pact which was grandiloquently to be called "The Pact of Steel."

Actually, the pact which was announced on May 7 and concluded on May 22 was thought a poor and temporary substitute for the alliance of Germany, Italy and Japan for which the Germans had been pressing. The Japanese were willing to conclude an alliance against Russia; they were as yet unwilling to promise military assistance against Britain and the United States. Since the alliance was wanted by Hitler as a means of bringing the British to a more "reasonable" attitude, the proposal of an alliance against Russia was rejected. As an alternative, Ribbentrop touched lightly in his discussion with Ciano on the possibility of improving relations with the Soviet Union. Ciano thought such a move desirable; but felt that for domestic political reasons Mussolini would not wish too great an improvement.

At this stage in the developing crisis, the Germans also showed no great eagerness to strengthen their position by bidding for the support of the Soviet Union, despite clear indications of the importance which the British and French attached to a political agreement with the U.S.S.R. . . .

The Russians did their best to elicit a German offer. On May 3 Molotov replaced Litvinov as Foreign Secretary and the Soviet chargé in Berlin intimated that the change could facilitate improvement in Nazi-Soviet relations. Two weeks later he again suggested that an improvement in relations would not be difficult to achieve. The German Government did bring Schulenburg, the Ambassador in Moscow, home for consultation; but he returned to Russia with instructions only to suggest the reopening of economic negotiations which had been interrupted earlier in the year. Schulenburg talked with Molotov for over an hour on May 20, but found him unwilling to reopen the economic discussions until a "political basis" had been found. After some wavering, the German Government decided to make no definite political proposals.

On May 23, Hitler reviewed the international situation with his military advisers. Now, two months after his first demands on Poland, he had enlarged his objective. Poland was to be attacked at the first suitable opportunity, and destroyed. "It is not Danzig that is at stake. For us it is a matter of expanding our living space in the East and making food supplies secure and also solving the problem of the Baltic States." The campaign against Poland could be a success only if Britain and France stood aside. There were indications that "Russia might disinterest herself in the destruction of Poland," but to restrain Russia it might be necessary to have closer ties with Japan. In any case, the task was to isolate Poland, and there must not be a simultaneous showdown with France and Britain. That showdown would come, but later. It would be a hard, and probably a long fight, involving the very existence of Germany; it was time to begin preparations for that fight. He was, therefore, setting up a small planning staff, which would work in complete secrecy, and which would study all aspects of the problem of preparing for the life and death battle with Britain. He gave no date for the war with the West, but in response to a question from Göring he stated that the armaments program would be completed by 1943 or 1944.

IV

For two months the Polish, British and French Governments had been trying to convince Hitler that further advances to the east by the threat or use of force would precipitate a general war which Germany was bound to lose. The only effect of these warnings had been to convince Hitler that Poland would not give up without a fight, as Austria and Czechoslovakia had done, and that Poland must therefore be destroyed. He refused to believe that the rulers of Britain and France would, after preaching the blessings of peace for so long, accept the terrors of general war, which they themselves described in such despairing language. Yet, while the British and French continued to proclaim their dread of war and their eagerness for a reconciliation with Germany, they also continued to affirm their determination to preserve Polish independence. In the German view, these contradictory positions could be reconciled only by the assumption that the Soviet Union would shoulder the burden of defending Poland.

The Germans were convinced that Russia neither could nor would defend Poland. At the same time it was thought probable in Berlin during the last days of May that some sort of agreement would be made between Russia, Britain and France. If agreement was achieved, the illusory conviction of the British and French that they could support Poland without peril to themselves would be strengthened. Therefore, as the State Secretary in the Foreign Ministry, Weizsäcker, wrote privately, "in the days before Whitsun [May 28] and during the holidays, deliberations on whether and by what means one could still try to put a spoke into the Anglo-Russian conversations have been going to and fro.". . .

The course of action finally adopted on May 30 was a "private" conversation between the State Secretary and the Russian chargé in which Weizsäcker made clear the German desire for improved political as well as economic relations with the U.S.S.R., and hinted that an Anglo-Russian agreement would prevent this improvement. On the following day, Molotov publicly denied that an Anglo-Russian agreement impended and intimated that trade negotiations between Russian and Germany would soon begin. From London, Dirksen[1] reported a few days later that even in Labor circles alarm was spreading over the price Russia was now asking for an agreement with Britain.

A spoke had indeed been put in the Anglo-Russian negotiations, and again the German Government settled back, waiting for the long, unremitting strain to have its effect. . . .

Meanwhile, through June the Anglo-Russian negotiations limped along. . . . At the end of the month, Weizsäcker was unable to guess what the outcome of the talks would be, although the British seemed disposed to make every concession to the Russians. He was equally uncertain whether anything would come of German offers to resume trade discussions with Russia. . . . The Russians continued to drop hints that they would welcome political discussions. Schulenburg, during a two weeks' stay in Berlin, attempted to move the discussions in this direction, but he found Ribbentrop not greatly concerned about the problem of Russia. . . . Hitler had impatiently ordered even the trade discussions with Russia stopped.

V

From this point it is necessary to grope one's way through the maze of Nazi diplomacy, without certain documentary guidance. So far, through 15 tense weeks, if German diplomatists at home or abroad did not believe Britain and France would stand aside while Poland was crushed, they kept their heretical views to themselves. By July, however, it was becoming difficult to believe German pressure on Poland would not, in the end, lead to a general war. . . . The German press had ever more stridently called for . . . the right of Danzig to become a part of Germany. As the clamor grew, the attitude of Britain and France perceptibly stiffened. On July 1 the French Foreign Minister, Georges Bonnet, formally declared that "any action, whatever its form, which would tend to modify the status quo in Danzig, and so provoke armed resistance by Poland, would bring the Franco-Polish Agreement into play and oblige France to give immediate assistance to Poland." The British position, Dirksen reported on July 3, was equally firm. If war with the West did come, it was problematical how much support Germany would receive from Italy: with suspicious frequency, the Italians pointed out that they would not be ready for a general war for at least three years. . . .

While Hitler and Ribbentrop continued to assert that the courage of Britain and France would, in the end, collapse and while there is no evidence of open dissent from this view among the officials of the German Foreign Ministry, there is evidence that in Berlin, and in the Moscow embassy, there was recognition that Russia was becoming of central importance in the war of nerves. No sooner had Hitler ordered negotiations with Russia ended than arguments were presented not only for the continuance of the negotiations but also for greater concessions to Russian views. . . .

[1] The German ambassador in London, Herbert von Dirksen.

[In July] Mussolini believed the tension had become so intolerable that the world would prefer war to continued uncertainty. He was convinced that this was the moment for an international conference; such a conference would, he believed, disrupt the unity of the front opposing Germany and Italy. Ribbentrop rebuffed this suggestion with vigor: any peace initiative by the Axis would be interpreted as a sign of weakness. The Axis was bound to win the war of nerves, he argued, because the Axis had steadier nerves than its opponents. Britain was not militarily prepared for war, and Britain had not been able to conclude the alliances necessary for war. Therefore the Axis must hold firm. "Time was on our side."

The difficulty was that time was running out. When Hitler had ordered the Wehrmacht to be ready for war with Poland by September 1, that date had been five months away. When, on May 23, he had announced his determination to crush Poland, there had seemed ample time to insure the isolation of Poland which he said was essential for the success of that operation. Now, however, less than six weeks remained before September 1, and by now the German Government had decided that September 1 was not the earliest, but almost the last day upon which operations could begin. By late September heavy rains were likely to make mechanized warfare in Poland impossible. To be on the safe side, the timetable had been advanced so that operations could begin by August 20, less than a month away. If the British and French Governments were not to be forced into war by the pressure of public opinion when the German armies struck, then the futility of war must be brought home to the peoples of Britain and France.

One cannot say with certainty that Hitler was forced to revise his policy towards Russia by recognition that time was running out. What is certain is that while Hitler had ordered efforts to secure even a trade agreement stopped on June 29, and while opinion within the German Government was still fluctuating two weeks later, the pace was rapidly accelerated in the days following the uproar in Britain over the supposed offer of a huge loan to Germany by the Chamberlain government. The official in charge of the economic negotiations, Schnurre, wrote privately on August 2 that, from about July 23, he had at least one conversation daily about Russia with Ribbentrop who was also constantly exchanging views with Hitler. "The Foreign Minister is concerned to obtain some result in the Russian question as soon as possible, not only on the negative side (disturbing the British negotiations) but also on the positive side (an understanding with us)."

VI

During the weeks which followed, the Nazis were driven, step by step, to meet every Soviet demand. The first step, on July 26, was a long dinner conversation, extending past midnight, between Schnurre, the Soviet chargé and the Soviet trade representative. Emphasizing that he was speaking on Ribbentrop's instructions, Schnurre declared that there was no real conflict of interest between Germany and the U.S.S.R. at any point from the Baltic to the Black Sea and on to the Far East, and said he "could imagine a far-reaching arrangement of mutual interests" in all these areas. However, he warned, the opportunity to effect such an arrangement would be lost if the U.S.S.R. allied itself with Britain. The Russians expressed surprise and pleasure at these remarks; they reciprocated Schnurre's desire for improved relations, but emphasized that improvement could come only slowly. . . .

During the days which followed, the German representatives repeatedly sought to draw from the Russians a definite statement of willingness to enter negotiations on political problems, but without success. At last, on August 10, Schnurre came to the point. He stressed the impossibility of any agreement if the U.S.S.R. concluded a military pact with Britain. Beyond that, however, he made it plain that war against Poland impended, and that a demarcation of spheres of interest in Poland was desirable before war came. This produced results. Two days later, the chargé reported that his government was interested in a discussion of political problems, including Poland, and wished the negotiations to take place in Moscow.

To Hitler it seemed that the road ahead was now clear. In a conference at Obersalzberg on August 14 he stated categorically that Russia would keep out of the war. Britain would, in the end, draw back: "the men I got to know in Munich are not the kind that start a new World War." Without Britain, France would not move.

That evening, Ribbentrop telegraphed new proposals to Schulenburg, proposals which he wished Stalin to receive in as exact a form as was possible without putting an incriminating document into Soviet hands. He proposed a linking of the Soviet and German economies, "which are complementary in every sphere." He proposed political coöperation. He affirmed "that there is no question between the Baltic Sea and the Black Sea which cannot be settled to the complete satisfaction of both countries." To secure speedy agreement, he was prepared to come to Moscow himself "to lay the foundations for a final settlement of German-Russian relations."

By then, the September 1 deadline was less than three weeks away and the propaganda campaign preparatory to war with Poland was already approaching its strident climax. Foreign observers in Berlin were freely predicting that the question of Danzig if not the fate of Poland would be settled before the month was over. Hitler encouraged these prophets. In the past he had carefully concealed his plan of action from the indiscreet Italians. This time, he was very explicit. War against Poland might come any day, he told Ciano, and would come by the end of August unless Poland not only surrendered Danzig but altered "her general attitude."

German need was Russian opportunity. Even while they had suggested ever more plainly their desire for a political agreement with Germany, the Russians had continued their negotiations with the British and French. At the time that he had announced the opening of trade negotiations with Germany, Molotov had also suggested the sending of an Anglo-French military mission to Moscow as a means of speeding agreement with the Western democracies. The discussions of this mission with the Soviet military leaders were begun on the very day, August 12, that the Germans were told of Soviet willingness to begin political discussions. Now, on August 15, when Schulenburg presented Ribbentrop's proposal that he come to Moscow, Molotov stressed the need for "adequate preparation" before the arrival of so distinguished a visitor and asked whether Germany was prepared to conclude a nonagression pact and to influence Japanese policy in the direction of better relations with the Soviet Union.

Two days later—and even this short interval seemed long to Ribbentrop —Schulenburg was back with fresh instructions. Germany would conclude a nonaggression pact. Germany was willing to influence Japanese policy in the desired direction. But speed was essential because "of the possibility of the occurrence, any day, of serious events." Ribbentrop was prepared to come to Moscow by airplane at any time after August 18. Molotov refused to be hurried, and laid out a timetable: first the economic agreement must be concluded; then "after a short interval" a political agreement could be made; however, there might now be an exchange of drafts of the proposed political agreement, and the Soviet Government would await with interest the German draft.

Promptly, Schulenburg received new instructions, which he executed in two interviews with Molotov on August 19. With only the thinnest covering of diplomatic verbiage, the Russians were told that war was imminent and that a delineation of spheres of influence was essential before the fighting started. In the first interview Molotov refused to set a date for Ribbentrop's visit. In the second, Molotov (apparently on new instructions from Stalin) agreed that Ribbentrop might come on August 26 or 27. Meanwhile, in Berlin, the trade agreement was finally signed.

Hitler now intervened with a letter to Stalin. Polish presumption, said Hitler, had produced intolerable tension which might lead to war any day. There was no time to lose. He asked that Ribbentrop be received on August 22, or at the latest on August 23; Ribbentrop would have full powers to draw up and sign the nonaggression pact and the political agreement. The letter was delivered on August 21. On the same day Stalin replied, agreeing to the arrival of Ribbentrop on August 23. That night, the German Government issued a communiqué telling of the impending conference for the purpose of concluding a nonaggression pact.

The final card had been played. It was a costly move. At the end of May, consideration for Soviet interests in Poland had been the highest price mentioned for a pact with the U.S.S.R. As late as August 16 Ribbentrop offered, so far as the Baltic States were concerned, only a joint guarantee of their independence. Now, in the pact of August 23, Finland, Estonia and Latvia were to be an exclusively Soviet sphere of influence. Russia was also to receive a large share of Poland. As for southeastern Europe, the Soviet claim to Bessarabia was acknowledged, while "the German side declares complete political *désintéressement* in these territories." In the search for "living space," a search which had seemed so easy in the spring, Hitler had been forced to surrender his claim to hegemony in the Baltic and in southeastern Europe.

The cost was high, but again Hitler was confident that he could now crush Poland without provoking general war. On August 22, before Ribbentrop reached Moscow, Hitler called his military leaders together once more. Most of what he said was an elaborate demonstration of the necessity for war with Poland, together with instructions for the ruthless conduct of the war. So far as Britain and France were concerned, his arguments were those he had used so often before: neither had really rearmed, both were obsessed by the frightful risks entailed by war, neither had strong leaders. He said the German attack would probably be launched on Saturday, August 26.

Momentarily, Hitler's optimism seemed justified by reports of the confusion caused in Britain and France by the Nazi-Soviet pact. On Wednesday, August 23, the attack on Poland was definitely set for Saturday, and on August 24 the first of the moves by which war was to be provoked was made by the Germans in Danzig. On August 25, however, there came two heavy blows: the Anglo-Polish Mutual Assistance Agreement was signed, and Mussolini made it plain that he would not intervene if Germany became involved in war with France and Britain. In the evening, the order to attack was cancelled.

There followed a week of desperate maneuvering. Much has been written of the "offers" made by Hitler in those last days of peace, but it is now clear that the offers were intended only to shake the determination of the British Government. Hitler had gone too far to retreat, and time had run out. On September 1, the German invasion began, with Hitler still vainly hoping that the political leaders of Britain and France would, at the last moment, lose their nerve.

VII

Over and over, through the spring and summer of 1939 the British and French Governments had said they would fight if Germany attacked Poland. These warnings went unheeded. In justification for his refusal to heed the warnings from London and Paris, Hitler invariably came back to the same arguments: Britain and France were militarily unprepared for war, and certainly for a war to protect Poland; they had threatened before, and had drawn back at the end; the men in power in 1939 were the same men whose will had collapsed in face of firm resistance. As he repeatedly boasted, he had bluffed and won before; what he had done when Germany was weak he could do again with confidence now that Germany was strong.

These boasts had an increasingly hollow sound from the last week of July. But by then the whole world had come to regard the question of Danzig as a decisive test of strength. Through the years since 1933 he had advanced from one victory to another by convincing his opponents that if they did not surrender he would annihilate them. . . . Now Hitler was confronted by the despised Poles; they not only remained steady through the war of nerves, but, despite all provocation, they avoided rash action which would place the onus of aggression on them. If they were able to defy him with impunity, the tide which had carried him from success to success would turn. In a last desperate effort to break the will of his opponents, he promised the hated Communists more for neutrality than he could win from war against Poland. Even under this pressure the courage of the Poles did not collapse. Retreat was now more impossible than ever. And so the diplomatic moves of March, intended at the outset only to advance Germany another stage along the road to supremacy in Europe, led inexorably, step by step, to war against the West in which the very existence of Germany was at stake.

►NAZI-SOVIET COEXISTENCE, 1939-1941

The Nazi-Soviet rapprochement began one month after the Nazi occupation (March 15, 1939) of what had been left of Czechoslovakia after Munich. The Soviet Ambassador in Berlin initiated Soviet-Nazi discussions concerning Soviet contracts with the Skoda works in Czechoslovakia and suggested the possibility of improving Soviet-Nazi political relations. Only after the Nazi Government realized the seriousness of the Western commitment to Poland, the prospective victim of Nazi aggression, did Hitler reply with haste and eagerness to the original Soviet initiative.

The first Nazi diplomatic note on the subject follows.

THE REICH FOREIGN MINISTER TO THE GERMAN AMBASSADOR
IN THE SOVIET UNION (SCHULENBURG)—TELEGRAM

MOST URGENT   BERLIN, August 14, 1939—10:53 p.m.
                            Received Moscow, August 15, 1939—4:40 a.m.

No. 175 of August 14

For the Ambassador personally.

I request that you call upon Herr Molotov personally and communicate to him the following:

1) The ideological contradictions between National Socialist Germany and the Soviet Union were in past years the sole reason why Germany and the U.S.S.R. stood opposed to each other in two separate and hostile camps. The developments of the recent period seem to show that differing world outlooks do not prohibit a reasonable relationship between the two states, and the restoration of cooperation of a new and friendly type. The period of opposition in foreign policy can be brought to an end once and for all and the way lies open for a new sort of future for both countries.

2) There exist no real conflicts of interest between Germany and the U.S.S.R. The living spaces of Germany and the U.S.S.R. touch each other, but in their natural requirements they do not conflict. Thus there is lacking all cause for an aggressive attitude on the part of one country against the other. Germany has no aggressive intentions against the U.S.S.R. The Reich Government is of the opinion that there is no question between the Baltic and the Black Seas which cannot be settled to the complete satisfaction of both countries. Among these are such questions as: the Baltic Sea, the Baltic

From *Nazi-Soviet Relations, 1939-1941* (Department of State Publication 3023), *passim.*

area, Poland, Southeastern questions, etc. In such matters political cooperation between the two countries can have only a beneficial effect. The same
applies to German and Soviet economy, which can be expanded in any
direction.

3) There is no doubt that German-Soviet policy today has come to an
historic turning point. The decisions with respect to policy to be made in the
immediate future in Berlin and Moscow will be of decisive importance for the
aspect of relationships between the German people and the peoples of the
U.S.S.R. for generations. On those decisions will depend whether the two
peoples will some day again and without any compelling reason take up arms
against each other or whether they pass again into a friendly relationship. It
has gone well with both countries previously when they were friends and
badly when they were enemies.

4) It is true that Germany and the U.S.S.R., as a result of years of
hostility in their respective world outlooks, today look at each other in a
distrustful fashion. A great deal of rubbish which has accumulated will have
to be cleared away. It must be said, however, that even during this period
the natural sympathy of the Germans for the Russians never disappeared.
The policy of both states can be built anew on that basis.

5) The Reich Government and the Soviet Government must, judging
from all experience, count it as certain that the capitalistic Western democracies are the unforgiving enemies of both National Socialist Germany and of
the U.S.S.R. They are today trying again, by the conclusion of a military alliance, to drive the U.S.S.R. into the war against Germany. In 1914 this policy
had disastrous results for Russia. It is the compelling interest of both countries
to avoid for all future time the destruction of Germany and of the U.S.S.R.,
which would profit only the Western democracies.

6) The crisis which has been produced in German-Polish relations by
English policy, as well as English agitation for war and the attempts at an
alliance which are bound up with that policy, make a speedy clarification of
German-Russian relations desirable. Otherwise these matters, without any
German initiative, might take a turn which would deprive both Governments
of the possibility of restoring German-Soviet friendship and possibly of clearing up jointly the territorial questions of Eastern Europe. The leadership in
both countries should, therefore, not allow the situation to drift, but should
take action at the proper time. It would be fatal if, through mutual lack of
knowledge of views and intentions, our peoples should be finally driven
asunder.

As we have been informed, the Soviet Government also has the desire
for a clarification of German-Russian relations. Since, however, according to
previous experience this clarification can be achieved only slowly through the
usual diplomatic channels, Reich Foreign Minister von Ribbentrop is prepared to make a short visit to Moscow in order, in the name of the Führer,
to set forth the Führer's views to Herr Stalin. Only through such a direct discussion, in the view of Herr von Ribbentrop, can a change be brought about,
and it should not be impossible thereby to lay the foundations for a definite
improvement in German-Russian relations. . . .

MEMORANDUM BY THE GERMAN AMBASSADOR IN THE SOVIET UNION
(SCHULENBURG)
SECRET

I began the interview with Molotov on August 15 about 8:00 p.m. by stating that according to information which had reached us the Soviet Government was interested in continuing the political conversations, but that it preferred that they be carried on in Moscow.

Molotov replied that this was correct.

Then I read to Herr Molotov the contents of the instruction which had been sent to me and the German text was immediately translated into Russian, paragraph by paragraph. . . .

Molotov then declared that in view of the importance of my communication he could not give me an answer at once but he must first render a report to his Government. He could state at once, however, that the Soviet Government warmly [lebhaft] welcomed the intention expressed on the German side to bring about an improvement in relations with the Soviet Union. . . .

Molotov repeated that he was interested above everything else in an answer to the question of whether on the German side there was the desire to make more concrete the points which had been [previously] outlined. So, for example, the Soviet Government would like to know whether Germany saw any real possibility of influencing Japan in the direction of a better relationship with the Soviet Union. "Also, how did things stand with the idea of the conclusion of a nonaggression pact? Was the German Government sympathetically inclined to the idea or would the matter have to be gone into more deeply?" were Molotov's exact words. . . .

Moscow, August 16, 1939

COUNT VON DER SCHULENBURG

Ribbentrop to Moscow

THE REICH FOREIGN MINISTER TO THE GERMAN AMBASSADOR IN THE
SOVIET UNION (SCHULENBURG)—TELEGRAM

URGENT   BERLIN, August 16, 1939—4:15 p.m.

Received Moscow, August 17, 1939—1 a.m.

No. 179 of August 16

For the Ambassador personally.

I request that you again call upon Herr Molotov with the statement that you have to communicate to him, in addition to yesterday's message for Herr Stalin, a supplementary instruction just received from Berlin, which relates to the questions raised by Herr Molotov. Please then state to Herr Molotov the following:

1) The points brought up by Herr Molotov are in accordance with German desires. That is, Germany is ready [bereit] to conclude a nonaggression pact with the Soviet Union and, if the Soviet Government so desires, one which would be irrevocable [unkündbar] for a term of twenty-five

years. Further, Germany is ready to guarantee the Baltic States jointly with the Soviet Union. Finally, it is thoroughly in accord with the German position, and Germany is ready, to exercise influence for an improvement and consolidation of Russian-Japanese relations.

2) The Führer is of the opinion that, in view of the present situation, and of the possibility of the occurrence any day of serious incidents (please at this point explain to Herr Molotov that Germany is determined not to endure Polish provocation indefinitely), a basic and rapid clarification of German-Russian relations and the mutual adjustment of the pressing questions are desirable. For these reasons the Reich Foreign Minister declares that he is prepared to come by plane to Moscow at any time after Friday, August 18, to deal on the basis of full powers from the Führer with the entire complex of German-Russian questions and, if the occasion arises [*gegebenenfalls*], to sign the appropriate treaties.

ANNEX: I request that you read these instructions to Herr Molotov and ask for the reaction of the Russian Government and Herr Stalin. Entirely confidentially, it is added for your guidance that it would be of very special interest to us if my Moscow trip could take place at the end of this week or the beginning of next week.

RIBBENTROP

THE GERMAN AMBASSADOR IN THE SOVIET UNION (SCHULENBURG)
TO THE GERMAN FOREIGN OFFICE—TELEGRAM
VERY URGENT   Moscow, August 21, 1939—7:30 p.m.
SECRET

No. 200 of August 21
   Supplementing my telegram No. 199 of August 21.
   Text of Stalin's reply:
   "August 21, 1939. To the Chancellor of the German Reich, A. Hitler. I thank you for the letter. I hope that the German-Soviet nonaggression pact will mark a decided turn for the better in the political relations between our countries.
   The people of our countries need peaceful relations with each other. The assent of the German Government to the conclusion of a nonaggression pact provides the foundation for eliminating the political tension and for the establishment of peace and collaboration between our countries.
   The Soviet Government has authorized me to inform you that it agrees to Herr von Ribbentrop's arriving in Moscow on August 23. J. Stalin."

SCHULENBURG

FULL POWERS—TO THE REICH FOREIGN MINISTER,
HERR JOACHIM VON RIBBENTROP

   I hereby grant full power to negotiate, in the name of the German Reich, with authorized representatives of the Government of the Union of Soviet Socialist Republics, regarding a nonaggression treaty, as well as all related questions, and if occasion arises, to sign both the nonaggression treaty and other agreements resulting from the negotiations, with the proviso that this treaty and these agreements shall enter into force as soon as they are signed.

ADOLF HITLER

Obersalzberg, August 22, 1939.

The Nazis and the Communists at the Kremlin

MEMORANDUM OF A CONVERSATION HELD ON THE NIGHT OF AUGUST 23D TO 24TH, BETWEEN THE REICH FOREIGN MINISTER, ON THE ONE HAND, AND HERR STALIN AND THE CHAIRMAN OF THE COUNCIL OF PEOPLE'S COMMISSARS MOLOTOV, ON THE OTHER HAND
VERY SECRET!
STATE SECRET

The following problems were discussed:

1) Japan:

The REICH FOREIGN MINISTER stated that the German-Japanese friendship was in no wise directed against the Soviet Union. We were, rather, in a position, owing to our good relations with Japan, to make an effective contribution to an adjustment of the differences between the Soviet Union and Japan. Should Herr Stalin and the Soviet Government desire it, the Reich Foreign Minister was prepared to work in this direction. He would use his influence with the Japanese Government accordingly and keep in touch with the Soviet representative in Berlin in this matter.

HERR STALIN replied that the Soviet Union indeed desired an improvement in its relations with Japan, but that there were limits to its patience with regard to Japanese provocations. If Japan desired war, it could have it. The Soviet Union was not afraid of it and was prepared for it. If Japan desired peace—so much the better! Herr Stalin considered the assistance of Germany in bringing about an improvement in Soviet-Japanese relations as useful, but he did not want the Japanese to get the impression that the initiative in this direction had been taken by the Soviet Union. . . .

2) Italy:

HERR STALIN inquired of the Reich Foreign Minister as to Italian aims. Did not Italy have aspirations beyond the annexation of Albania—perhaps for Greek territory? Small, mountainous, and thinly populated Albania was, in his estimation, of no particular use to Italy.

The REICH FOREIGN MINISTER replied that Albania was important to Italy for strategic reasons. Moreover, Mussolini was a strong man who could not be intimidated.

This he had demonstrated in the Abyssinian conflict, in which Italy had asserted its aims by its own strength against a hostile coalition. Even Germany was not yet in a position at that time to give Italy appreciable support.

Mussolini welcomed warmly the restoration of friendly relations between Germany and the Soviet Union. He had expressed himself as gratified with the conclusion of the Nonaggression Pact. . . .

4) England:

HERREN STALIN and MOLOTOV commented adversely on the British Military Mission in Moscow, which had never told the Soviet Government what it really wanted.

The REICH FOREIGN MINISTER stated in this connection that England had always been trying and was still trying to disrupt the development of good relations between Germany and the Soviet Union. England was weak and wanted to let others fight for its presumptuous claim to world domination.

HERR STALIN eagerly concurred and observed as follows: the British Army was weak; the British Navy no longer deserved its previous reputation. England's air arm was being increased, to be sure, but there was a lack of pilots. If England dominates the world in spite of this, this was due to the stupidity of the other countries that always let themselves be bluffed. It was ridiculous, for example, that a few hundred British should dominate India.

THE REICH FOREIGN MINISTER concurred and informed Herr Stalin confidentially that England had recently put out a new feeler which was connected with certain allusions to 1914. It was a matter of a typically English, stupid maneuver. The Reich Foreign Minister had proposed to the Führer to inform the British that every hostile British act, in case of a German-Polish conflict, would be answered by a bombing attack on London.

HERR STALIN remarked that the feeler was evidently Chamberlain's letter to the Führer, which Ambassador Henderson delivered on August 23 at the Obersalzberg. Stalin further expressed the opinion that England, despite its weakness, would wage war craftily and stubbornly.

5) France:

HERR STALIN expressed the opinion that France, nevertheless, had an army worthy of consideration.

The REICH FOREIGN MINISTER, on his part, pointed out to Herren Stalin and Molotov the numerical inferiority of France. While Germany had available an annual class of more than 300,000 soldiers, France could muster only 150,000 recruits annually. The West Wall was five times as strong as the Maginot Line. If France attempted to wage war with Germany, she would certainly be conquered.

6) Anti-Comintern Pact:

The REICH FOREIGN MINISTER observed that the Anti-Comintern Pact was basically directed not against the Soviet Union but against the Western democracies. He knew, and was able to infer from the tone of the Russian press, that the Soviet Government fully recognized this fact.

HERR STALIN interposed that the Anti-Comintern Pact had in fact frightened principally the City of London and the small British merchants.

The REICH FOREIGN MINISTER concurred and remarked jokingly that Herr Stalin was surely less frightened by the Anti-Comintern Pact than the City of London and the small British merchants. What the German people thought of this matter is evident from a joke which had originated with the Berliners, well known for their wit and humor, and which had been going the rounds for several months, namely, "Stalin will yet join the Anti-Comintern Pact."

7) Attitude of the German people to the German-Russian Nonaggression Pact:

The REICH FOREIGN MINISTER stated that he had been able to determine that all strata of the German people, and especially the simple people, most warmly welcomed the understanding with the Soviet Union. The people felt instinctively that between Germany and the Soviet Union no natural conflicts of interests existed, and that the development of good relations had hitherto been disturbed only by foreign intrigue, in particular on the part of England.

HERR STALIN replied that he readily believed this. The Germans desired peace and therefore welcomed friendly relations between the Reich and the Soviet Union.

The REICH FOREIGN MINISTER interrupted here to say that it was certainly true that the German people desired peace, but, on the other hand, indignation against Poland was so great that every single man was ready to fight. The German people would no longer put up with Polish provocation.

8) Toasts:

In the course of the conversation, HERR STALIN spontaneously proposed a toast to the Führer, as follows:

"I know how much the German nation loves its Führer; I should therefore like to drink to his health."

HERR MOLOTOV drank to the health of the Reich Foreign Minister and of the Ambassador, Count von der Schulenburg.

HERR MOLOTOV raised his glass to Stalin, remarking that it had been Stalin who—through his speech of March of this year, which had been well understood in Germany—had brought about the reversal in political relations.

HERREN MOLOTOV and STALIN drank repeatedly to the Nonaggression Pact, the new era of German-Russian relations, and to the German nation.

The REICH FOREIGN MINISTER in turn proposed a toast to Herr Stalin, toasts to the Soviet Government, and to a favorable development of relations between Germany and the Soviet Union.

9) When they took their leave, HERR STALIN addressed to the Reich Foreign Minister words to this effect:

The Soviet Government takes the new Pact very seriously. He could guarantee on his word of honor that the Soviet Union would not betray its partner.

HENCKE

Moscow, August 24, 1939.

AUGUST 23, 1939.

TREATY OF NON AGGRESSION BETWEEN GERMANY AND THE UNION OF SOVIET SOCIALIST REPUBLICS

The Government of the German Reich and
the Government of the Union of Soviet Socialist Republics
desirous of strengthening the cause of peace between Germany and the

U.S.S.R., and proceeding from the fundamental provisions of the Neutrality Agreement concluded in April 1926 between Germany and the U.S.S.R., have reached the following agreement:

Article I. Both High Contracting Parties obligate themselves to desist from any act of violence, any aggressive action, and any attack on each other, either individually or jointly with other powers.

Article II. Should one of the High Contracting Parties become the object of belligerent action by a third power, the other High Contracting Party shall in no manner lend its support to this third power.

Article IV. Neither of the two High Contracting Parties shall participate in any groupings of powers whatsoever that is directly or indirectly aimed at the other party.

Article VII. The present treaty shall be ratified within the shortest possible time. The ratifications shall be exchanged in Berlin. The agreement shall enter into force as soon as it is signed.

Done in duplicate, in the German and Russian languages.

Moscow, August 23, 1939.

For the Government	With full power of the
of the German Reich:	Government of the U.S.S.R.:
v. RIBBENTROP	V. MOLOTOV

SECRET ADDITIONAL PROTOCOL

On the occasion of the signature of the Nonaggression Pact between the German Reich and the Union of Socialist Soviet Republics the undersigned plenipotentiaries of each of the two parties discussed in strictly confidential conversations the question of the boundary of their respective spheres of influence in Eastern Europe. These conversations led to the following conclusions:

1. In the event of a territorial and political rearrangement in the areas belonging to the Baltic States (Finland, Estonia, Latvia, Lithuania), the northern boundary of Lithuania shall represent the boundary of the spheres of influence of Germany and the U.S.S.R. In this connection the interest of Lithuania in the Vilna area is recognized by each party.

2. In the event of a territorial and political rearrangement of the areas belonging to the Polish state the spheres of influence of Germany and the U.S.S.R. shall be bounded approximately by the line of the rivers Narew, Vistula, and San.

The question of whether the interests of both parties make desirable the maintenance of an independent Polish state and how such a state should be bounded can only be definitely determined in the course of further political developments.

In any event both Governments will resolve this question by means of a friendly agreement.

3. With regard to Southeastern Europe attention is called by the Soviet side to its interest in Bessarabia. The German side declares its complete political disinterestedness in these areas.

4. This protocol shall be treated by both parties as strictly secret.
Moscow, August 23, 1939.

For the Government   Plenipotentiary of the
of the German Reich: Government of the U.S.S.R.:
v. RIBBENTROP   V. MOLOTOV

Russia Attacks Poland

THE REICH FOREIGN MINISTER TO THE GERMAN AMBASSADOR
IN THE SOVIET UNION (SCHULENBURG)—TELEGRAM

No. 253 of September 3   BERLIN, September 3, 1939—6:50 p.m.
                          Received MOSCOW September 4, 1939—12:30 a.m.

Very Urgent! Exclusively for Ambassador. Strictly secret! For Chief of
Mission or his representative personally. Top secret. To be decoded by himself. Strictest secrecy!

We definitely expect to have beaten the Polish Army decisively in a few
weeks. We would then keep the area that was established as German sphere
of interest at Moscow under military occupation. We would naturally, however, for military reasons, also have to proceed further against such Polish
military forces as are at that time located in the Polish area belonging to the
Russian sphere of interest.

Please discuss this at once with Molotov and see if the Soviet Union does
not consider it desirable for Russian forces to move at the proper time against
Polish forces in the Russian sphere of interest and, for their part, to occupy
this territory. In our estimation this would be not only a relief for us, but also,
in the sense of the Moscow agreements, in the Soviet interest as well.

In this connection please determine whether we may discuss this matter
with the officers who have just arrived here and what the Soviet Government
intends their position to be.

RIBBENTROP

THE GERMAN AMBASSADOR IN THE SOVIET UNION (SCHULENBURG)
TO THE GERMAN FOREIGN OFFICE—TELEGRAM

Pol. V 8924   Moscow, September 6, 1939—5:46 p.m.
No. 279 of September 6   Received September 6, 1939—8:15 p.m.

Reference your telegram No. 267 of the 5th.

Since anxiety over war, especially the fear of a German attack, has
strongly influenced the attitude of the population here in the last few years,
the conclusion of a nonaggression pact with Germany has been generally received with great relief and gratification. However, the sudden alteration in
the policy of the Soviet Government, after years of propaganda directed expressly against German aggressors, is still not very well understood by the
population. Especially the statements of official agitators to the effect that
Germany is no longer an aggressor run up against considerable doubt. The
Soviet Government is doing everything to change the attitude of the popula-

tion here toward Germany. The press is as though it had been transformed. Attacks on the conduct of Germany have not only ceased completely, but the portrayal of events in the field of foreign politics is based to an outstanding degree on German reports and anti-German literature has been removed from the book trade, etc.

The beginning of the war between Germany and Poland has powerfully affected public opinion here, and aroused new fear in extensive groups that the Soviet Union may be drawn into the war. Mistrust sown for years against Germany, in spite of effective counterpropaganda which is being carried on in party and business gatherings, cannot be so quickly removed. The fear is expressed by the population that Germany, after she has defeated Poland, may turn against the Soviet Union. The recollection of German strength in the World War is everywhere still lively.

In a judgment of conditions here the realization is of importance that the Soviet Government has always previously been able in a masterly fashion to influence the attitude of the population in the direction which it has desired, and it is not being sparing this time either of the necessary propaganda.

SCHULENBURG

THE GERMAN AMBASSADOR IN THE SOVIET UNION (SCHULENBURG)
TO THE GERMAN FOREIGN OFFICE—TELEGRAM
VERY URGENT   Moscow, September 9, 1939—12:56 a.m.
No. 300 of September 8   Received September 9, 1939—5 a.m.

I have just received the following telephone message from Molotov:
"I have received your communication regarding the entry of German troops into Warsaw. Please convey my congratulations and greetings to the German Reich Government. Molotov."

SCHULENBURG

THE GERMAN AMBASSADOR IN THE SOVIET UNION (SCHULENBURG)
TO THE GERMAN FOREIGN OFFICE—TELEGRAM
VERY URGENT   Moscow, September 16, 1939.
STRICTLY SECRET
No. 371 of September 16

Reference your telegram No. 360 of September 15.
I saw Molotov at 6 o'clock today and carried out instructions. Molotov declared that military intervention by the Soviet Union was imminent—perhaps even tomorrow or the day after. Stalin was at present in consultation with the military leaders and he would this very night, in the presence of Molotov, give me the day and hour of the Soviet advance.

Molotov added that he would present my communication to his Government but he believed that a joint communiqué was no longer needed; the Soviet Government intended to motivate its procedure as follows: the Polish State had collapsed and no longer existed; therefore all agreements concluded with Poland were void; third powers might try to profit by the chaos which had arisen; the Soviet Union considered itself obligated to intervene to protect

its Ukrainian and White Russian brothers and make it possible for these unfortunate people to work in peace.

The Soviet Government intended to publicize the above train of thought
by the radio, press, etc., immediately after the Red Army had crossed the
border, and at the same time communicate it in an official note to the Polish
Ambassador here and to all the missions here.

Molotov conceded that the projected argument of the Soviet Government contained a note that was jarring to German sensibilities but asked that
in view of the difficult situation of the Soviet Government we not let a trifle
like this stand in our way. The Soviet Government unfortunately saw no possibility of any other motivation, since the Soviet Union had thus far not concerned itself about the plight of its minorities in Poland and had to justify
abroad, in some way or other, its present intervention. . . .

SCHULENBURG

THE GERMAN AMBASSADOR IN THE SOVIET UNION (SCHULENBURG)
TO THE GERMAN FOREIGN OFFICE—TELEGRAM
VERY URGENT   Moscow, September 17, 1939
SECRET

Reference my telegram No. 371 of September 16.

Stalin received me at 2 o'clock at night at the presence of Molotov and
Voroshilov and declared that the Red Army would cross the Soviet border
this morning at 6 o'clock along the whole line from Polozk to Kamenetz-
Podolsk.

In order to avoid incidents, Stalin urgently requested that we see to it
that German planes as of today do not fly east of the Bialystok-Brest-Litovsk-
Lemberg Line. Soviet planes would begin today to bomb the district east of
Lemberg.

I promised to do my best with regard to informing the German Air
Force, but asked in view of the little time left that the Soviet planes do not
approach the abovementioned line too closely today.

SCHULENBURG

THE GERMAN AMBASSADOR IN THE SOVIET UNION (SCHULENBURG)
TO THE GERMAN FOREIGN OFFICE—TELEGRAM
STRICTLY SECRET   Moscow, September 20, 1939—2:23 a.m.
No. 395 of September 19   Received September 20, 1939—4:55 a.m.

Molotov stated to me today that the Soviet Government now considered
the time ripe for it, jointly with the German Government, to establish definitively the structure of the Polish area. In this regard, Molotov hinted that
the original inclination entertained by the Soviet Government and Stalin personally to permit the existence of a residual Poland had given way to the
inclination to partition Poland along the Pissa-Narev-Vistula-San Line. . . .

SCHULENBURG

THE GERMAN AMBASSADOR IN THE SOVIET UNION (SCHULENBURG)
TO THE GERMAN FOREIGN OFFICE—TELEGRAM
VERY URGENT   MOSCOW, September 25, 1939—10:58 p.m.
STRICTLY SECRET   Received September 26, 1939—12:30 a.m.
No. 442 of September 25

Stalin and Molotov asked me to come to the Kremlin at 8 p.m. today. Stalin stated the following: In the final settlement of the Polish question anything that in the future might create friction between Germany and the Soviet Union must be avoided. From this point of view, he considered it wrong to leave an independent Polish rump state. He proposed the following: From the territory to the east of the demarcation line, all the Province of Lublin and that portion of the Province of Warsaw which extends to the Bug should be added to our share. In return, we should waive our claim to Lithuania.

Stalin designated this suggestion as a subject for the forthcoming negotiations with the Reich Foreign Minister and added that, if we consented, the Soviet Union would immediately take up the solution of the problem of the Baltic countries in accordance with the Protocol of August 23, and expected in this matter the unstinting support of the German Government. Stalin expressly indicated Estonia, Latvia, and Lithuania, but did not mention Finland.

I replied to Stalin that I would report to my Government.

SCHULENBURG

The Dictators Divide the World—Berlin 1940

MEMORANDUM OF THE FINAL CONVERSATION BETWEEN REICH FOREIGN MINISTER VON RIBBENTROP AND THE CHAIRMAN OF THE COUNCIL OF PEOPLE'S COMMISSARS OF THE U.S.S.R. AND PEOPLE'S COMMISSAR FOR FOREIGN AFFAIRS, HERR MOLOTOV, ON NOVEMBER 13, 1940
SECRET
RM 42/40

Duration of conversation: 9:45 p.m. until 12 midnight.

Because of the air raid alert that had been ordered, Reich Minister for Foreign Affairs von Ribbentrop and Herr Molotov went into the Reich Foreign Minister's air raid shelter after the supper at the Embassy of the U.S.S.R. at 9:40 p.m. on November 13, 1940, in order to conduct the final conversation.

The Reich Foreign Minister opened the conversation with the statement that he wanted to take the opportunity to supplement and give more specific form to what had been discussed thus far. . . . He had to stress explicitly, however, that this was merely a matter of ideas which were still rather rough, but which might perhaps be realized at some time in the future. By and large, it was a matter of achieving future collaboration between the countries of the Tripartite Pact—Germany, Italy, and Japan—and the Soviet Union, and he believed that first a way must be found to define in bold outlines the spheres of influence of these four countries and to reach an understanding on the problem of Turkey. . . . He conceived the future developments as follows:

Herr Molotov would discuss with Herr Stalin the issues raised in Berlin; then, by means of further conversations, an agreement could be reached between the Soviet Union and Germany; thereupon the Reich Foreign Minister would approach Italy and Japan in order to find out how their interests with respect to the delimitation of spheres of influence could be reduced to a common formula. He had already approached Italy as to Turkey. The further *modus procedendi* between Italy, the Soviet Union, and Germany would be to exert influence upon Turkey in the spirit of the wishes of the three countries. If they succeeded in reducing the interests of the four countries concerned to a common denominator—which, given good will, was entirely possible—it would undoubtedly work to the advantage of all concerned. The next step would consist in attempting to record both sets of issues in confidential documents. If the Soviet Union entertained a similar view, that is, would be willing to work against the extension, and for the early termination of the war (the Reich Foreign Minister believed that Herr Molotov had indicated his willingness in the previous discussions), he had in mind as the ultimate objective an agreement for collaboration between the countries of the Tripartite Pact and the Soviet Union. He had drafted the contents of this agreement in outline form and he would like to inform Herr Molotov of them today, stressing in advance that he had not discussed these issues so concretely either with Japan or with Italy. He considered it necessary that Germany and the Soviet Union settle the issue first. This was not by any means a matter of a German proposal, but—as already mentioned—one of still rather rough ideas, which would have to be deliberated by both parties and discussed between Molotov and Stalin. It would be advisable to pursue the matter further, particularly in diplomatic negotiations with Italy and Japan, only if the question had been settled as between Germany and the Soviet Union.

Then the Reich Foreign Minister informed Herr Molotov of the contents of the agreement outlined by him in the following words:

> The Governments of the states of the Three Power Pact, Germany, Italy, and Japan, on the one side, and the Government of the U.S.S.R. on the other side, motivated by the desire to establish in their natural boundaries an order serving the welfare of all peoples concerned and to create a firm and enduring foundation for their common labors toward this goal, have agreed upon the following:
>
> *Article 1.* In the Three Power Pact of September 27, 1940, Germany, Italy, and Japan agreed to oppose the extension of the war into a world conflict with all possible means and to collaborate toward an early restoration of world peace. They expressed their willingness to extend their collaboration to nations in other parts of the world which are inclined to direct their efforts along the same course as theirs. The Soviet Union declares that it concurs in these aims and is on its part determined to cooperate politically in this course with the Three Powers.
>
> *Article 2.* Germany, Italy, Japan, and the Soviet Union undertake to respect each other's natural spheres of influence. In so far as these spheres of influence come into contact with each other, they will constantly consult each other in an amicable way with regard to the problems arising therefrom.

Article 3. Germany, Italy, Japan, and the Soviet Union undertake to join no combination of powers and to support no combination of powers which is directed against one of the Four Powers.

The Four Powers will assist each other in economic matters in every way and will supplement and extend the agreements existing among themselves.

The Reich Foreign Minister added that this agreement was intended for a period of ten years, with the provision that the Governments of the Four Powers, before the expiration of this term, were to reach an understanding regarding the matter of an extension of the agreement.

The agreement itself would be announced to the public. Beyond that, with reference to the above-mentioned agreement, a confidential (secret) agreement could be concluded—in a form still to be determined—establishing the focal points in the territorial aspirations of the Four Countries.

As to Germany, apart from the territorial revisions to be made in Europe at the conclusion of the peace, her territorial aspirations centered in the Central African region.

The territorial aspirations of Italy, apart from the European territorial revisions to be made at the conclusion of the peace, centered in North and Northeast Africa.

The aspirations of Japan would still have to be clarified through diplomatic channels. Here too, a delimitation could easily be found, possibly by fixing a line which would run south of the Japanese home islands and Manchukuo.

The focal points in the territorial aspirations of the Soviet Union would presumably be centered south of the territory of the Soviet Union in the direction of the Indian Ocean.

Such a confidential agreement could be supplemented by the statement that the Four Powers concerned, except for the settlement of individual issues, would respect each other's territorial aspirations and would not oppose their realization.

The above-mentioned agreements could be supplemented by a second secret protocol, to be concluded between Germany, Italy, and the Soviet Union. This second secret protocol could perhaps read that Germany, Italy, and the Soviet Union, on the occasion of the signing of the agreement between Germany, Italy, Japan, and the Soviet Union, were agreed that it was in their common interest to release Turkey from her previous ties and win her progressively to a political collaboration with them.

They declare that they would pursue this aim in close contact with each other, in accordance with a procedure to be established. . . .

[A thorough discussion of every aspect of Nazi propositions followed.]

. . . Molotov stated that the Germans were assuming that the war against England had already actually been won. If, therefore, as had been said in another connection, Germany was waging a life and death struggle against England, he could only construe this as meaning that Germany was fighting "for life" and England "for death." As to the question of collaboration, he quite approved of it, but he added that they had to come to a thorough understanding. This idea had also been expressed in Stalin's letter. A delimitation of the spheres of influence must also be sought. On this point, however, he (Molotov) could not take a definitive stand at this time, since he did not know the opinion of Stalin and of his other friends in Moscow in the matter. However, he had to state that all these great issues of tomorrow could not be separated from the issues of today and the fulfillment of existing agreements. The things that were started must first be completed before they proceeded to new tasks. The conversations which he—Molotov—had had in Berlin had undoubtedly been very useful, and he considered it appropriate that the questions raised should now be further dealt with through diplomatic channels by way of the ambassadors on either side.

Thereupon Herr Molotov cordially bade farewell to the Reich Foreign Minister, stressing that he did not regret the air raid alarm, because he owed to it such an exhaustive conversation with the Reich Foreign Minister.

HILGER

Moscow, November 18, 1940.

Russia Asks for a Too Large Slice of the World

THE GERMAN AMBASSADOR IN THE SOVIET UNION (SCHULENBURG)
TO THE GERMAN FOREIGN OFFICE—TELEGRAM
VERY URGENT   Moscow, November 26, 1940—5:34 a.m.
STRICTLY SECRET   Received November 26, 1940—8:50 a.m.
No. 2362 of November 25

For the Reich Minister in person.

Molotov asked me to call on him this evening and in the presence of Dekanosov stated the following:

The Soviet Government has studied the contents of the statements of the Reich Foreign Minister in the concluding conversation on November 13 and takes the following stand:

"The Soviet Government is prepared to accept the draft of the Four Power Pact which the Reich Foreign Minister outlined in the conversation of November 13, regarding political collaboration and reciprocal economic [support] subject to the following conditions:

"1) Provided that the German troops are immediately withdrawn from Finland, which, under the compact of 1939, belongs to the Soviet Union's sphere of influence. At the same time the Soviet Union undertakes to ensure peaceful relations with Finland and to protect German economic interests in Finland (export of lumber and nickel).

"2) Provided that within the next few months the security of the Soviet Union in the Straits is assured by the conclusion of a mutual assistance pact between the Soviet Union and Bulgaria, which geographically is situated inside the security zone of the Black Sea boundaries of the Soviet Union, and by the establishment of a base for land and naval forces of the U.S.S.R. within range of the Bosporus and the Dardanelles by means of a long-term lease.

"3) Provided that the area south of Batum and Baku in the general direction of the Persian Gulf is recognized as the center of the aspirations of the Soviet Union.

"4) Provided that Japan [renounces] her rights to concessions for coal and oil in Northern Sakhalin.

"In accordance with the foregoing, the draft of the protocol concerning the delimitation of the spheres of influence as outlined by the Reich Foreign Minister would have to be amended so as to stipulate the focal point of the aspirations of the Soviet Union south of Batum and Baku in the general direction of the Persian Gulf.

"Likewise, the draft of the protocol or agreement between Germany, Italy, and the Soviet Union with respect to Turkey should be amended so as to guarantee a base for light naval and land forces of the U.S.S.R. on [am] the Bosporus and the Dardanelles by means of a long-term lease, including— in case Turkey declares herself willing to join the Four Power Pact—a guarantee of the independence and of the territory of Turkey by the three countries named. . . .

In conclusion Molotov stated that the Soviet proposal provided for five protocols instead of the two envisaged by the Reich Foreign Minister. He would appreciate a statement of the German view.

SCHULENBURG

Hitler Decides to Destroy Russia

THE FÜHRER AND COMMANDER-IN-CHIEF OF THE GERMAN ARMED FORCES
MILITARY SECRET
TOP SECRET   FÜHRER'S HEADQUARTERS
BY OFFICER ONLY   December 18, 1940
DIRECTIVE NO. 21—OPERATION BARBAROSSA

The German Armed Forces must be prepared *to crush Soviet Russia in a quick campaign* (Operation Barbarossa) even before the conclusion of the war against England.

For this purpose the *Army* will have to employ all available units, with the reservation that the occupied territories must be secured against surprise attacks.

For the *Air Force* it will be a matter of releasing such strong forces for the eastern campaign in support of the Army that a quick completion of the ground operations may be expected and that damage to Eastern German territory by enemy air attacks will be as slight as possible. This concentration of the main effort in the East is limited by the requirement that the entire combat and armament area dominated by us must remain adequately protected against enemy air attacks and that the offensive operations against England, particularly her supply lines, must not be permitted to break down.

The main effort of the *Navy* will remain unequivocally directed against *England* even during an eastern campaign.

I shall order the *concentration* against Soviet Russia possibly eight weeks before the intended beginning of operations.

Preparations requiring more time to start are to be started now—if this has not yet been done—and are to be completed by May 15, 1941.

It is to be considered of decisive importance, however, that the intention to attack is not discovered. . . .

THE GERMAN AMBASSADOR IN THE SOVIET UNION (SCHULENBURG)
TO THE GERMAN FOREIGN OFFICE—TELEGRAM

No. 1368 of June 13   Moscow, June 14, 1941—1:30 a.m.
                                       Received June 14, 1941—8 a.m.

People's Commissar Molotov has just given me the following text of a Tass despatch which will be broadcast tonight and published in the papers tomorrow:

Even before the return of the English Ambassador Cripps to London, but especially after his return, there have been widespread rumors of "an impending war between the U.S.S.R. and Germany" in the English and foreign press. These rumors allege:

1. That Germany supposedly has made various territorial and economic demands on the U.S.S.R. and that at present negotiations are impending between Germany and the U.S.S.R. for the conclusion of a new and closer agreement between them;

2. That the Soviet Union is supposed to have declined these demands and that as a result Germany has begun to concentrate her troops on the frontier of the Soviet Union in order to attack the Soviet Union;

3. That on its side the Soviet Union is supposed to have begun intensive preparations for war with Germany and to have concentrated its troops on the German border.

Despite the obvious absurdity of these rumors, responsible circles in Moscow have thought it necessary, in view of the persistent spread of these rumors, to authorize Tass to state that these rumors are a clumsy propaganda maneuver of the forces arrayed against the Soviet Union and Germany, which are interested in a spread and intensification of the war.

Tass declares that:

1. Germany has addressed no demands to the Soviet Union and has asked for no new closer agreement, and that therefore negotiations cannot be taking place;

2. According to the evidence in the possession of the Soviet Union, both Germany and the Soviet Union are fulfilling to the letter the terms of the Soviet-German Nonaggression Pact, so that in the opinion of Soviet circles the rumors of the intention of Germany to break the Pact and to launch an attack against the Soviet Union are completely without foundation, while the recent movements of German troops which have completed their operations in the Balkans, to the eastern and northern parts of Germany, must be explained by other motives which have no connection with Soviet-German relations;

3. The Soviet Union, in accordance with its peace policy, has fulfilled

and intends to fulfill the terms of the Soviet-German Nonagression Pact; as a result, all the rumors according to which the Soviet Union is preparing for a war with Germany are false and provocative;

4. The summer calling-up of the reserves of the Red Army which is now taking place and the impending maneuvers mean nothing but a training of the reservists and a check on the operations of the railroad system, which as is known takes place every year; consequently, it appears at least nonsensical to interpret these measures of the Red Army as an action hostile to Germany.

SCHULENBURG

THE REICH FOREIGN MINISTER TO THE GERMAN AMBASSADOR
IN THE SOVIET UNION (SCHULENBURG)—TELEGRAM
VERY URGENT   BERLIN, June 21, 1941.
STATE SECRET
By radio

For the Ambassador personally.

1) Upon receipt of this telegram, all of the cipher material still there is to be destroyed. The radio set is to be put out of commission.

2) Please inform Herr Molotov at once that you have an urgent communication to make to him and would therefore like to call on him immediately. Then please make the following declaration to him.

"The Soviet Ambassador in Berlin is receiving at this hour from the Reich Minister for Foreign Affairs a memorandum giving in detail the facts which are briefly summarized as follows:

"I. In 1939 the Government of the Reich, putting aside grave objections arising out of the contradiction between National Socialism and Bolshevism, undertook to arrive at an understanding with Soviet Russia. Under the treaties of August 23 and September 28, 1939, the Government of the Reich effected a general reorientation of its policy toward the U.S.S.R. and thenceforth adopted a cordial attitude toward the Soviet Union. This policy of goodwill brought the Soviet Union great advantages in the field of foreign policy.

"The Government of the Reich therefore felt entitled to assume that thenceforth both nations, while respecting each other's regime and not interfering in the internal affairs of the other partner, would arrive at good, lasting, neighborly relations. Unfortunately it soon became evident that the Government of the Reich had been entirely mistaken in this assumption.

"II. Soon after the conclusion of the German-Russian treaties, the Comintern resumed its subversive activity against Germany, with the official Soviet-Russian representatives giving assistance. Sabotage, terrorism, and espionage in preparation for war were demonstrably carried out on a large scale. In all the countries bordering on Germany and in the territories occupied by German troops, anti-German feeling was aroused and the German attempt to set up a stable order in Europe was combated. Yugoslavia was gladly offered arms against Germany by the Soviet Russian Chief of Staff, as proved by documents found in Belgrade. The declarations made by the U.S.S.R. on conclusion of the treaties with Germany, regarding her intention to collaborate with Germany, thus stood revealed as deliberate misrepresentation and deceit and the conclusion of the treaties themselves as a tactical maneuver for obtaining arrangements favorable to Russia. The guiding principle remained the weakening of the non-Bolshevist countries in order the more easily to demoralize them and, at a given time, to crush them.

"III. In the diplomatic and military fields it became obvious that the U.S.S.R.—contrary to the declaration made at the conclusion of the treaties that she did not wish to Bolshevize and annex the countries falling within her sphere of influence—was intent on pushing her military might westward wherever it seemed possible and on carrying Bolshevism further into Europe. The action of the U.S.S.R. against the Baltic States, Finland, and Rumania, where Soviet claims even extended to Bucovina, showed this clearly. The occupation and Bolshevization by the Soviet Union of the sphere of influence granted to her clearly violated the Moscow agreements, even though the Government of the Reich for the time being accepted the facts.

"IV. When Germany, by the Vienna Award of August 30, 1940, settled the crisis in Southeastern Europe resulting from the action of the U.S.S.R. against Rumania, the Soviet Union protested and turned to making intensive military preparations in every field. Germany's renewed effort to achieve an understanding, as reflected in the exchange of letters between the Reich Foreign Minister and Herr Stalin and in the invitation to Herr Molotov to come to Berlin, brought demands from the Soviet Union which Germany could not accept, such as the guarantee of Bulgaria by the U.S.S.R., the establishment of a base for Soviet Russian land and naval forces at the Straits, and the complete abandonment of Finland. Subsequently, the policy of the U.S.S.R. directed against Germany became more and more obvious. The warning addressed to Germany regarding occupation of Bulgaria and the declaration made to Bulgaria after the entry of German troops, which was of a definitely hostile nature, were as significant in this connection as was the promise to protect the rear of Turkey in the event of a Turkish entry into the war in the Balkans, given in March 1941.

"V. With the conclusion of the Soviet-Yugoslav Treaty of Friendship of April 5 last, which was intended to stiffen the spines of the Yugoslav plotters, the U.S.S.R. joined the common Anglo-Yugoslav-Greek front against Germany. At the same time she tried *rapprochement* with Rumania, in order to induce that country to detach itself from Germany. It was only the rapid German victories that caused the failure of the Anglo-Russian plan for an attack against the German troops in Rumania and Bulgaria.

"VI. This policy was accompanied by a steadily growing concentration of all available Russian forces on a long front from the Baltic Sea to the Black Sea, against which countermeasures were taken by Germany only later. Since the beginning of the year this has been a steadily growing menace to the territory of the Reich. Reports received in the last few days eliminated the last remaining doubts as to the aggressive character of this Russian concentration and completed the picture of an extremely tense military situation. In addition to this, there are the reports from England regarding the negotiations of Ambassador Cripps for still closer political and military collaboration between England and the Soviet Union.

"To sum up, the Government of the Reich declares, therefore, that the Soviet Government, contrary to the obligations it assumed,

1) has not only continued, but even intensified its attempts to undermine Germany and Europe;

2) has adopted a more and more anti-German foreign policy;

3) has concentrated all its forces in readiness at the German border. Thereby the Soviet Government has broken its treaties with Germany and is about to attack Germany from the rear, in its struggle for life. The Führer has therefore ordered the German Armed Forces to oppose this threat with all the means at their disposal."

End of declaration.

Please do not enter into any discussion of this communication. It is incumbent upon the Government of Soviet Russia to safeguard the security of the Embassy personnel.

RIBBENTROP

Part IV

CHOICE OF RESPONSES

The previous readings have shown that estimating other nations' power and objectives is a complex problem which cannot be solved with perfect accuracy and certainty. When a statesman must select appropriate means of action and response, he is seriously handicapped by uncertainty as to his rival's intentions and might. A certain amount of guesswork, experimentation, and improvisation is necessary, as in the case of a man who finds his way along a dark and unfamiliar road.

How effective can be our response if we are not quite sure of our rival's intentions? How are we to distinguish a threat cloaked in an apparent offer of amity from genuine friendship darkened by a show of force?

Furthermore, there is the additional problem of a balance between *aims* and *means*. Even if we know where to aim, we may not be able to do it. Lack of adequate means often prevents us from achieving our aims. "The capacity of the mind to conceive *ends* is limitless. The *means* at hand are invariably limited," says Charles Burton Marshall (p. 392).

Thus, political action depends on the *analysis of objectives and power* as well as on the *means* at hand. Concrete forms of such action may range from no action at all to the violent method of war.

Nonaction Is Also a Policy

If a nation were to decide that other nations' challenges or offers should not be met except by silence and prayer, such a nonpolicy would still be a policy, although probably a suicidal one. A nation which decides not to use its power to promote its interests, and retreats into its own shell, actually adopts a policy that leaves the decisions to other nations, or to time. Policies of other nations may have such an impact on the passive nation's security and prosperity that it will have to abandon isolation from international tensions. The entry of an isolationist U.S. into both World Wars is an example. Or, even though action is not taken, some of a nation's problems may be mitigated with the passage of time.

Other concrete measures and policies which nations may adopt to promote their interests may be divided, for the purpose of systematic analysis, into two broad categories: negotiations and balancing measures.

Negotiations aim at discovering whether respective national objectives are compatible or incompatible and suggesting terms of compromise. Such compromise would make it possible to diminish or eliminate balancing measures.

Balancing measures are based on one's own analysis of the objectives of rival nations. These measures may be of violent or nonviolent nature. They may be taken also in conjunction with and support of negotiations.

The process of negotiations among nations will be the subject of analysis in Part V. The body of rules binding upon nations, known as the Law of Nations, as well as different forms of international organization will be discussed in Part VI. In this section our attention will be focused on the balancing measures.

There are *five major balancing devices*. Nations usually adopt more than one category of measures at the same time. They are:

1. Increase of one's strength
2. Declaration of policy aims and methods
3. Cooperative agreements
4. Division of rival power and coalition
5. Military movements and activities

A brief description of these devices follows.

1. *Increase of one's strength* for the purpose of either resisting the will of a rival or imposing one's will on others. *Armament,* that is, an increase of the purely military component of national power, is the most frequent, crude, but efficient form. Maintaining a military posture which, in Theodore Roosevelt's words, makes fighting against us "too expensive and dangerous a task to be undertaken lightly by anybody" is the first requirement of national security. A new and more complex dimension has been recently added to this aspect of national power by the advent of missiles and hydrogen and atomic warheads.

However, a statesman would be ill-advised to rely solely on military preparedness as the source of national power. For example, Nazi Germany, Fascist Italy, and Imperial Japan possessed superior military power at the outset of the last war. The early and continuous Axis concentration on armaments gave Germany, Italy, and Japan an impressive lead and brought a series of early major victories. At that time the United States, Russia, and Great Britain were either unprepared or only partly so. Yet, they were able not only to catch up but to defeat one Axis nation after another. This shows that the relation between the levels of national armaments is not constant; it is subject to relatively rapid changes when necessary. Furthermore the experience of Nazi Germany indicates that military preparedness is but one of the many factors which constitute the power of a nation (as discussed in Part III).

2. *Declarations of policy aims and methods.* Unilateral proclamations

are often contained in more or less solemn speeches or addresses to the people, journalists, or to assembled legislators. These serve the purpose of publicly fixing a line of policy and notifying friends, neutrals, and enemies of aims and means.

These proclamations, often referred to as doctrines, may announce either

(a) A policy of *isolation* and/or *neutrality*. Such was the case of George Washington's Farewell Address announcing the intention to avoid entangling alliances, and President Monroe's address, later known as the Monroe Doctrine, which announced U.S. isolation from Europe and the government's primary interest in excluding European powers from the Western Hemisphere; or

(b) A policy of partial or total, occasional or permanent, *involvement* in other areas of the world. Such were the Truman and Eisenhower Doctrines, the Marshall speech announcing the willingness of the United States to help Europe, as well as proclamations of policies the Soviet leaders occasionally direct at the world at large through different intermediaries.

3. *Cooperative agreements with other nations* aim at adding to one's power the strength of other nations which may have reached a similar conclusion as to the source and kind of danger to be met. A great power may sometimes offer its protection to a small nation whose power is negligible or actually demands bolstering. In the short run, such alliances may be costly in terms of money or extension of lines of defense. Nevertheless, the small nation's area may be strategically important as with a buffer area between the zones of the great powers, or its survival may be symbolically meaningful, and (in the long run) it may be of major importance to include such a nation in a cooperative agreement. Strategic and other advantages are thus denied to the rival power.

In practice, there are no substantial material differences between a *multilateral* alliance and a *unilateral* declaration when either is initiated by a great power. Formalities are different: in the case of a multilateral alliance a great power and a number of smaller nations go through a ritual of mutual pledges and solemn signatures of documents. A unilateral declaration is *publicly* presented as a proclamation of one nation. In reality it may be the result of previous negotiations or agreements of several partners. In both cases, however, it is the pledge and readiness of a *great power* which gives the alliance or unilateral declaration its substance.

The traditional forms of cooperative agreements among nations are military alliances. They may be bilateral, like the treaties between the United States and Japan, or the Soviet Union and China; or multilateral, like such modern collective-defense alliances as the North Atlantic Treaty Organization (NATO), the South East Asia Pact (SEATO), the Organization of American States (Rio Pact), or the Warsaw Pact.

Then there are agreements concluded with nations which are not formally allies. Such agreements may concern the establishment of naval, air, or rocket bases, as well as radio propaganda installations on foreign territories. Other agreements may deal with military missions or programs of military training within foreign military establishments. These arrangements, if concluded in the absence of formal alliance treaties, are in their practical consequences alliances without the name.

This applies also to some economic aid, technical assistance, and cultural exchange programs which may be either an aspect of political and military alliances or a second-best substitute for them.

It should be noted that some economic and cultural cooperative arrangements seem to have no political strings attached. Closer observation, however, reveals that a certain amount of political interest is present even in the seemingly most unselfish programs of economic or technical assistance. It may be, for instance, the minimum aim of preventing a needy nation from feeling grateful in only one direction (Ceylon toward Russia, for instance).

Economic cooperation and cultural or scientific exchanges may be arranged also between highly competitive and fundamentally inimical nations. In 1959, during a major political crisis in connection with the West Berlin issue, the Soviet Union and the United States exchanged cultural and technical exhibits, a great number of good-will delegations, as well as mutual visits not only of the New York Philharmonic and the Bolshoi Theater, but also of Premier Khrushchev to the United States and planned reciprocation by President Eisenhower in 1960. Each party to these agreements obviously considered the results to work in its own favor.

4. *Dividing rival strength* is another device which aims at increasing one's own power by weakening a rival. The ancient advice, "Divide and rule" *(divide et impera)*, has its counterpart in modern politics: divide your rival internally or disintegrate the opposing coalition—in order to increase your relative power.

Different means, used to implement this aim, may be divided into three broad categories: (a) the economic method; (b) the psychological and cultural method; (c) the subversive method.

(a) *The economic method* is a manipulation of trade, tariffs, financial arrangements, transportation facilities, and raw materials which results in harming rival interests and in advancing the economic situation of one's own nation or one's allies. Freezing financial assets of the enemy; granting or withdrawing financial support (the Aswan Dam project in Egypt); denying rivals access to raw materials, hard currency, markets (U.S. restriction on trade with Communist China), transportation facilities (Arab refusal to let Israeli cargo pass through the Suez Canal)—these are concrete examples of such economic manipulations for the purpose of policy.

Offers of loans and other forms of assistance that sometimes have the quality of economic bribes are often used as pressure against the solidarity of a multinational coalition. It is hoped that one or another key nation may be lured away from the rival camp. When on June 5, 1947, the Marshall Plan was offered to Europe, the West attempted to seduce Poland and Czechoslovakia away from the economic embrace of the Soviet Union. By politico-military threats the U.S.S.R. was able to prevent its two westernmost satellites from succumbing to the dollar temptation.

Both the Soviet Union and the United States have used economic assistance to prevent smaller nations from drifting into the adversary's camp.

When a great power cannot gain a nation as an ally, it may succeed in keeping it neutral with the help of economic aid. In this context a neutral nation is sometimes rewarded for not being an ally of either side. Many African and Asian nations are in a position to draw economic assistance from both Communist and capitalist sources. They may even increase the contributions of both by playing one against the other. Needy allies obviously resent such rewarding of political noncommitment.

(b) *The psychological and cultural method* consists in the use of a great variety of mass communication media and exchanges of ideas and persons to advance policy. The objective of propaganda and psychological warfare is to induce the target audience to adopt a certain viewpoint and to behave in a manner which would benefit the propaganda source. The term "propaganda" which originally (in the Roman Catholic Church) meant a relatively limited dissemination of information and creed, is now used with special stress on the mass communication media.

Propaganda is a method in itself as well as an ingredient of other balancing devices. In all these cases its effectiveness bears a direct relation to its truthfulness. The celebrated "Big Lie" tactic may work only as long as the audiences cannot compare words with facts. The contact of captive audiences with contrary reality will deflate any propaganda.

The same applies to the relation of propaganda and the will to implement proclaimed policies. The United States proclamation of a policy of liberation of East Central Europe lost much of its appeal during the Hungarian revolution in 1956. Although Central Europeans can still identify themselves with the aim (liberation), they have come to the conclusion that the American aim of liberation is a hope rather than a policy; it is not going to be implemented by *acts*. The Soviet counter-policy of nonliberation had the determined support of Soviet armed forces and their tanks.

In principle, propaganda should always be one of the instruments of actual foreign policy and should be subordinated to its needs.

On the other hand, in our era of mass communications, foreign policy should not deprive itself of the modern methods and skills of propaganda. The best intentions may evoke hostility if they are presented in a clumsy manner or if they are ill-timed. A generous answer to a needy nation's call for help may be so phrased that it offends that nation's pride. A new policy is not proclaimed but almost inaudibly whispered if its announcement misses the morning papers in the target area.

Nevertheless, evil plans may be made to look better by attractive and well-timed presentation.

Some of the psychological and cultural methods are: radio propaganda; circulation of books, magazines, and newspapers; distribution of pamphlets by mail or by air drop; exchange of television and radio programs, artistic performances, technical and cultural exhibits; exchange of artists, scientists, students, professors, technicians, or politicians; tourism in the traditional sense of the word; and other forms and methods which facilitate the circulation of persons and ideas among nations.

Similar to the economic and technical assistance programs, these exchanges have an intrinsic value *per se*. Enrichment of culture through contacts with other cultural environments is a laudable aim irrespective of its political context. Here, however, we are concerned with possible uses and abuses of cultural contacts in policy. The real aim of psychological and cultural methods is to create misunderstanding between the target audience and its own government. While the propaganda source claims to promote understanding among governments, it often aims at establishing some form of tacit agreement between itself and the target audience.

For example: one of the aims of the American exhibition in Moscow in 1959 was to make the Russian people think well of the United States and its cultural and technical achievements and less well of their own government. The purpose of the Soviet exhibit in New York was not to enrich the American way of life but to persuade Americans that the Communist system is better and more efficient than the democratic one.

In order to reach the audience, most devices of cultural and psychological pressure require some degree of cooperation on the part of the receiving country and its government. Governments distribute the mail, control the issuance of visas to visitors, and supervise—or directly administer—the media of mass entertainment. In such government-controlled cultural exchanges as fairs, exhibits, and other people-to-people programs the propaganda aim must be either nearly imperceptible or appear acceptable to the rival government whose cooperation is required.

As in the case of the American and Soviet exhibits, each of the two governments must arrive at the conclusion that the impact of the exchange works to its own advantage. The possibility of realizing such programs under the control of competing governments then depends on what we may call a "balance of explicit and implicit aims."

Other devices of political and cultural propaganda escape the control of the receiving country almost completely. This is true of propaganda material smuggled in or distributed by air. In such propaganda the real purpose and aim of the policy may be bluntly stated. In war, leaflets and safe-conduct passes distributed by air incite enemy personnel to desert their army and join the opposite side. In peace, this device was used by the Free Europe Committee, a private anti-Communist organization in the United States, which succeeded in the balloon distribution of a weekly magazine in the Czech, Slovak, Polish, and Hungarian languages to the target areas.

Radio propaganda is the most usual form of psychological warfare which can reach foreign audiences without the knowledge and consent of their governments. In this sense, any radio propaganda beamed at foreign audiences without the consent of the government concerned represents an act of interference in the domestic affairs of a sovereign state. However, all nations engage in this interference. The waves carrying different political broadcasts through the air, night and day, present a picture of an astonishing battle between ideas and symbols. The London BBC, Radio Paris, The Voice of America, Radio Moscow, and also Radio Belgrade, Radio Prague, Radio Vatican and the Swiss Radio compete with each other, presenting their points of view in almost all languages of the world, from Russian and English to Urdu and Tadzhik.

The Voice of America is part of the United States Information Agency, which is also in charge of many cultural exhibits, exchanges, television programs, publications, U.S. information centers and libraries abroad. The Voice of America directs its broadcasts to friendly as well as unfriendly nations. In addition to the propaganda agencies of the federal government, private organizations in the United States run Radio Free Europe, Radio Free Asia, and Radio Liberation, which address their specific messages to audiences behind the Iron and Bamboo Curtains.

The appeal of American and British broadcasts to nations behind the Iron Curtain is indirectly confirmed by strenuous Communist efforts to discourage their populations from listening to them, by penalties or jamming. Some Communist governments appear to employ the same number of technical personnel for jamming as they do to broadcast their own propaganda to their people.

(c) *The subversive method* is the use of psychological and other pressures in order to (1) infiltrate the rival government apparatus with disloyal elements, transform loyal into disloyal elements, and spread a web of conspiratorial activities throughout the country; or (2) eliminate the hostile government entirely by internal revolutionary activities, incited, guided, organized, or militarily supported from abroad.

Here we shift from the field of psychological warfare, fought mostly in printed and spoken words and symbols, to a gray zone where words may be replaced by weapons. The concept of indirect aggression and indirect warfare belongs to this gray zone. The gray zone between psychological warfare on one hand and military warfare on the other cannot be clearly defined. Propaganda (softening up the enemy and recruiting support among local populations) may be used to pave the way for a military invasion. On the other hand, the use of military forces may serve to make the arguments of psychological warfare more effective. If a nation, for instance, mobilizes its armed forces in order to use them *only* if an ultimate demand is not complied with—where does psychological warfare end the actual war begin?

5. *Military movements and activities* represent another device of policy among nations which try to realize their ambitions. It is a crude, yet rather frequent and effective instrument, and is thus closely related to another balancing measure, armament. However, there is a difference. The armament race (see pp. 139ff. and 498ff.) evolves around the creation, maintenance, increase and improvement of a military establishment. In this section we are concerned with the *uses* of a military establishment. The terms "military movements and activities" is employed here to cover other movements than those which are normally required for the purpose of training and organizing armed forces.

A military establishment may be used for *violent* or *nonviolent* imposition of one's will on others. Violent use of a military establishment results in war. General Karl von Clausewitz (1780-1831), Prussian writer on military strategy and the theory of war, defines war as "an act of violence intended to compel our opponent to our will." [1]

Samples of some nonviolent uses of a military establishment follow: (a) elaborate military parades, impressive war games, naval visits, sputniks, or lunar probes; (b) partial or general mobilization, introduction of general draft or intensive military training schools, or other indications of an intensified militarism; (c) movements of troops and weapons to specific geographic areas, siege, blockade, occupation of territory, and other forceful actions which still do not constitute war. Such steps may be taken either to provoke or prevent war.

Statesmen may also demonstrate military power to gain prestige or to impress their own nation. Dictators often display military might to discourage active internal opposition.

War

War represents maximum acceleration and intensification of military activity and movement. Quincy Wright (in Topic 20) defines war as "a legal condition which equally permits two or more hostile groups to carry on a conflict by armed force," and states that its "most obvious manifestation . . . is the accelerated movement and activity of armies and navies." [2] Today we would add aircraft, and preparation of missiles and their warheads.

Wars among nations may be classified according to different criteria: (1) weapons used, (2) the number of nations or the area involved, and (3) the nature of the war (a war may be defensive or aggressive; aggression may be direct or indirect).

1. Future wars may be fought with either the so-called *conventional* weapons or with *atomic* weapons, or both. The distinction between the two kinds of weapons may not suggest a real choice in practice. The terms "conventional" and "atomic" do not actually suggest contrast but evolution and perfection of weapons of mass destruction.

Some hope that the possession of atomic weapons by both camps will prevent their use, so that new wars will be fought only with the perfected conventional weapons of mass destruction that had been used during World War II.

Others fear that any minor or limited war fought even with the most primitive weapons may degenerate into a major conflict if the losing side uses the hydrogen bomb as the only alternative to its defeat. A near-suicidal atomic risk might then appear preferable to the certainty of nonatomic defeat and destruction. Atomic bombs may be outlawed and destroyed but not the knowledge and skill to produce them when needed.

2. A conflict in which all, or practically all, major powers are involved and the globe itself is the battlefield represents *a general war*. In contrast, a

[1] Karl von Clausewitz, *On War* (London: Kegan Paul, Trench, Trubner & Co., Ltd., 1940), Vol. I, p. 2.
[2] Quincy Wright, *A Study of War* (Chicago: University of Chicago Press, 1942), Vol. II, pp. 698, 685.

limited or *local war* concerns a limited number of participants or a limited geographic area.

But it is not easy to draw a definite line between a general war and a limited one. Often what seems to be a local conflict may represent a major conflict in disguise. While in theory the Korean War was a local war between North Korea and South Korea, in practice it was a conflict between Russia and Red China on the one hand and the United States on the other. At other times a genuinely local war may degenerate into an international conflict. A similarly fluid line often separates a civil war from an international one, whether local or general.

Revolutionary factions within a nation may appeal for help and assistance from a sympathetic foreign source. Other domestic insurrections may elicit interest, support, intervention, and even full participation of a major power if certain political shifts might affect balance of power in a given area. Many civil wars, insurrections, colonial revolts, and local wars thus acquire international connotation and resemble international wars, although their original causes were local.

In the eighteenth century, both the French and American revolutions finally involved the interest and support of major powers. Royal France seized the opportunity to assist American republican revolutionaries in order to weaken her main rival, England.

A local war may sometimes be cynically used as an experimental laboratory in preparation for a major conflict. The Spanish Civil War of 1936 was, true enough, a struggle for power between Franco and the Republicans. But in some respects it was also a prelude to and preparation for World War II. Many German weapons, the all-purpose 88-mm,[3] for instance, were tried against Spanish Republicans before they were used against Poland, France and Anglo-American forces. The Spanish Civil War was also part of the Nazi-Fascist struggle for dominant position in the western Mediterranean in preparation for World War II.

Here, again, it is not easy to draw a clear line between a civil war which transforms itself into an international one, and a civil war which has been fomented from the outside and, from the outset, has been an international war in disguise.

This will be apparent in the subsequent analysis of defensive and directly or indirectly aggressive wars.

3. There are individuals and organizations that consider any war evil, irrespective of its cause and objectives. A war always means violence and sacrifices of many important values. A moral perfectionist applies the principle "Thou shall not kill" to any situation, even that of self-defense or overthrow of a dictator.

Others consider the *purpose* before they approve or condemn violence. They accept the exercise of violence for a good purpose, like punishing or

---

[3] In his report, "The Winning of War in Europe and the Pacific," General George C. Marshall testified: "When we first encountered it (German 88-mm gun), it was serving all three purposes (anti-tank, anti-aircraft, and anti-personnel) with deadly effect. . . . The Wehrmacht held an advantage with its 88-mm gun almost to the end of the war."

preventing a criminal from committing other crimes, or a nation from per-
petuating acts of inhumanity. The use of violence for unjust and evil purposes
is to be condemned and, if necessary, stopped by counter-violence.

The problem is that in the absence of universal standards among nations
rivals rarely agree on the quality of purpose. What appears as the quintes-
sence of evil to one leader and his nation may seem to be a just aim to a
rival. Hitler's concept of ends and means was in contradiction to that of
Roosevelt. According to Marxism-Leninism, wars which promote the interests
of capitalism are evil and unjust. Wars which promote the interests of socialism are "legitimate and holy." In his book *Left-Wing Childishness and Petty
Bourgeois Mentality,* Lenin wrote: "If war is waged by the exploiting class
with the object of strengthening its class rule, such a war is a criminal war. . . .
If war is waged by the proletariat after it has conquered the bourgeoisie in its
own country, and is waged with the object of strengthening and extending
socialism, such a war is legitimate and 'holy'." The same distinction between
wars may be found in Stalin's letter to Maxim Gorky in 1930: "On the
market there is a multitude of publications . . . filling people with disgust
toward any war, not only an imperialist one but any war whatsoever. These
are bourgeois publications of no great value. . . . We are not against every
war. We are against an imperialist war, as a counter-revolutionary war. But
we are for a liberating, anti-imperialist, revolutionary war, although such a
war, as is well known, is not only not free from the 'horrors' of bloodshed but
abounds in them." (*Sochineniia,* Vol. 12, 1950, p. 176.)

This concept of war, which is either good or evil depending on its causes
and aims, is relatively new. According to international law of the nineteenth
century, war was a *legal condition,* as opposed to the legal condition of peace.
It was not an outbreak of lawlessness. Hence the definition by Quincy Wright
(quoted above) as a "legal condition which *equally* permitted two or more
hostile groups to carry on a conflict by armed force. . . . War was a duel the
results of which determined the justice of the claims of the participants." [4]

The concept of equality of belligerents is fully consonant with the principle of neutrality of non-participants. If a war was only a continuation of
diplomacy by other means, if all participants were equally responsible for it,
and if its results determined the justice of the participants' claims, it was
morally and legally inacceptable for outsiders to influence the final outcome.
The Hague convention of 1907 held that neutrals must be impartial except if
they can justify reprisals because of injuries resulting from illegal behavior
by one of the belligerents.

Collective Security vs. Neutrality

The 19th-century concept of equality of belligerents and the accompanying neutrality of non-participants is incompatible with the 20th-century concept of collective security. This principle is based on maximum inequality of
the belligerents and on partiality of nonparticipants. The League of Nations

---

[4] Quincy Wright, *Contemporary International Law: A Balance Sheet* (Garden City,
N. Y.: Doubleday & Co., Inc., 1955), pp. 17, 18. (Italics added.)

and the United Nations Organization have proclaimed the legal-moral obligation of members to participate in just war in order to defend the principles
of the organizations. Members are committed to collective intervention and
discrimination against the aggressor. (Under certain circumstances, five
permanent members and two temporary members of the UN Security Council
could obligate the remaining seventy-five nations—minus the aggressor—to
participate in a defensive war.)

"War and neutrality," writes Quincy Wright, "no longer exist as legal
institutions. A state that resorts to armed force is either an aggressor who
should be suppressed, a defender who should be assisted, or a participant in
international sanctions permitted or authorized by the United Nations. . . .
Impartiality is forbidden. . . . Discrimination against the aggressor . . . is
obligatory." [5]

This is why Switzerland, a neutral country in the traditional sense of the
word, is not a member of the United Nations. The neutrality of some members of the United Nations (India, Ceylon, Burma, Austria, Sweden, and
others) would be better described as a policy of non-commitment or non-
participation in alliances. According to the charter these "neutral" nations
are committed to policies of discrimination and even to action against another
nation which has been declared an aggressor.

Who Attacked Whom?

In order to implement the policy of collective security, it is necessary to
distinguish between an offensive and a defensive war. This is often difficult.
Nations which engage in military activities always claim that their purpose is
defense. Even Hitler considered it necessary to justify his invasion of Poland
(1939) and Russia (1941) as basically *defensive* moves against alleged violations of, or threats against, German interests. In 1950, the North Koreans
justified their invasion across the 38th parallel as a defense against provocative and aggressive actions on the part of South Koreans. It is understood that
these were obvious disguises for offensive action. However, both sides adhere
to contradictory and mutually exclusive claims, and there is no arbiter whose
objective findings they would accept.

In other cases even an objective arbiter would have some difficulty in
determining who started what. If an atomic bomb were dropped on a concentration of enemy submarines apparently about to launch atomic missiles,
would the user of the bomb engage in an "offensive defensive" against unbearable provocation or a "defensive offensive"? War is usually the result of
many complex situations and tensions. Even historians, with the benefit of
hindsight, cannot agree as to what really caused a war. [6]

As to World War I, historians and writers have declared its cause to
have been "the Russian or the German mobilization; the Austrian ultimatum;
the Sarajevo assassination; the aims and ambitions of the Kaiser, Poincaré,

[5] *Op. cit.*, p. 19.
[6] We differentiate here "efficient causes," which precede a war, from war aims, which
may change during the progress of the war.

Berchtold, or someone else; the desire of France to recover Alsace-Lorraine or of Austria to dominate the Balkans; the European system of alliances; the activities of the munition-makers, the international bankers, or the diplomats; the lack of an adequate European political order; armament rivalries; colonial rivalries; commercial policies; the sentiment of nationality; the concept of sovereignty; the struggle for existence; the tendency of nations to expand; the unequal distribution of population, of resources, or of planes of living; the law of diminishing returns; the value of war as an instrument of national solidarity or as an instrument of national policy; ethnocentrism or group egotism; the failure of the human spirit; and many others." [7]

Future historians of a hypothetical World War III (if left to write such history) might list just as many of its causes: communism, democracy, nationalism, capitalism and competition for the vital areas in the Middle East, Asia, and Africa; divisions of Germany and Berlin; Soviet domination of East Central Europe; the American failure to communicate the secret of the atomic bomb to the Russians, which would have alleviated their suspicions and minimized their countermeasures; Soviet failure to live up to war-time agreements; Stalin; or—even further back—the German decision of 1917 to send Lenin to Russia.

What Is Aggression?

The modern concept of collective security further presupposes a definition of aggression as opposed to justified defense. Such a definition would then have to be applied to concrete situations. Neither the League of Nations in its twenty years of existence nor the United Nations in an almost equally long period have succeeded in finding a definition of aggression which would be acceptable to all. Various members of these organizations continue to interpret the nature of concrete wars and the merit or guilt of their participants according to their own national standards and interests.

Perhaps it is objectively impossible to include all aspects and forms of aggression in one comprehensive definition. Yet such an all-embracing definition is an important part of the concept of collective security.

Indirect Aggression

The relationship between international tension and civil strife which might affect the international balance of power has already been noted. Nations often instigate, militarily or morally support, or advise and guide, subversion, guerilla warfare, or civil wars on other nations' territory.

In international wars such activities are usually part of over-all military planning. Before the outbreak of World War II, Nazi Germany organized, mobilized, and ordered into different activities German minorities in Central

[7] Quincy Wright, *A Study of War* (Chicago: University of Chicago Press, 1942), Vol. II, pp. 727-728. Copyright 1942 by The University of Chicago.

Europe which were really fifth columns of Nazism. On the eve of conflict the Soviet Union can be expected to do the same with its fifth columns, the Communist parties that operate within democratic nations.

During World War II partisan activities behind the Nazi lines in France, Yugoslavia, and the Ukraine were advised and supplied by the general staffs of the great allied powers.

A particularly successful use of an internal explosive situation for the purpose of international war marked the third year of World War I.

In March, 1917, the German Imperial General Staff took advantage of the revolutionary atmosphere in Russia to eliminate fighting on the eastern front and to concentrate on the final onslaught against the western front. The Germans sent V. I. Lenin from his exile in Switzerland back to Russia where he would bring on the Bolshevik revolution. Lenin delivered the promised revolution of a size, intensity, and duration far beyond the expectations of the Kaiser's Germany.

Governments also may initiate or merely support (morally or materially) civil strife within other nations in times of peace. This may constitute a more or less serious act of interference in domestic affairs of other nations. A milder form of such an interference is radio propaganda (discussed on p. 376). A more serious case is represented by radio propaganda which is inflammatory and incites to assassination and civil war. The extreme form of interference is "indirect aggression," that is, fomenting of civil strife in the interest of a foreign power. Its objective is the overthrow of the legitimate government.

If, on the other hand, one foreign government assists another in quelling civil strife, this is not considered interference or indirect aggression provided the support is rendered in response to a request made by the legitimate authority. The problem is, in civil war, the conflict evolves precisely around the question of who the legitimate authority is. In the Spanish Civil War the Nazi and Fascist governments considered and treated General Franco as the legitimate authority in Spain. Soviet Russia did the same with respect to the Republican government in Madrid. In the unfinished civil war in China, the United States recognizes Chiang Kai-shek and Soviet Russia recognizes Mao Tse-tung as heads of legitimate governments of China.

The United Nations "Peace through Deeds" resolution of 1950 proclaims: "Whatever the weapons used, any aggression, whether committed openly, or by fomenting civil strife in the interests of a foreign power, or *otherwise* is the gravest of all crimes against peace and security in the world."

This resolution was passed with Korea on the minds of those who voted for it. The tone is forceful; the meaning obscure (Italics were added to the word "otherwise" which means nothing and everything at the same time).

The international origins or aspects of civil wars, the problem of great power protection of a government faced with internal revolt (both sides claiming legitimacy and authority to represent the "true interests of the people") are particularly important because potentially so dangerous in our atomic era of sharp competition between communism and democracy. John

Foster Dulles, the late Secretary of State, dealt with this problem several times:

> Indirect aggression is nothing new. But the art has been greatly perfected in recent years. Through use of inflammatory radio broadcasts; through infiltration of weapons, personnel and bribe money; through incitement to murder and assassination, and through threats of personal violence, it becomes possible for one nation to destroy the genuine independence of another.
>
> It was in order to help to halt such practices that the United States responded to the urgent plea of the freely elected Government of Lebanon and sent United States forces to Lebanon to assist that democratic country to retain its independence.
>
> The United Kingdom acted similarly in relation to Jordan. . . .
>
> The United States is convinced that if indirect aggression, in the form of fomenting civil strife or subverting foreign governments, is now tolerated as an instrument of international policy, events will indeed follow the tragic pattern which led to World War II, and this time with even more disastrous consequences.
>
> We must of course recognize that this issue of indirect aggression is a delicate one. On the one hand it is clear, beyond a possibility of a doubt, that nations are free to seek, and to get help as against a genuine external threat. On the other hand we must be careful not to encourage or condone armed intervention which of itself may subvert the will of a foreign people. We saw that occur when the Soviet Union sent its armed divisions into Hungary in order to repress what the United Nations found to be a spontaneous uprising of the Hungarian people.
>
> We believe that the task of dealing with indirect aggression should so far as possible be assumed by the United Nations itself. That will eliminate the hazard that individual nations might use armed intervention under circumstances that were self-serving rather than serving the principles of the Charter. But in order that the United Nations should act effectively, several things are needed.
>
> First of all it is necessary that public opinion be more alert to the dangers which come from efforts short of actual war to destroy the independence and security of another nation. Too often it is assumed that so long as armies do not march openly across borders the situation is tolerable. The fact is that if indirect aggression were to be admitted as a legitimate means of promoting international policy, small nations would be doomed and the world become one of constant chaos, if not of war. . . .
>
> President Eisenhower also proposed a system which would enable the United Nations to monitor, and if need be condemn, the transmission by radio from one country to another of propaganda which seeks to foment civil strife.[8]

The next month, Mr. Dulles said this:

> You have to use, you might say, a rule of reason in trying to decide whether, in fact, a situation is a civil war, or whether it involves a threat to

[8] From an address by John Foster Dulles before the national convention of the Veterans of Foreign Wars, August 18, 1958.

international peace. The Communists made the argument in the case of Korea, that that was purely a civil war, an effort by the North Koreans to reunite their country, that they had the right to do it, and that the United Nations and the United States were aggressors when they came in there to stop this effort of the Korean people to reunite their own country. Similar positions could be made in the case of other countries. You could say, if the Federal Republic of Germany tried to reunite Germany, that it was a civil operation. But none of us treat it that way. . . . The Chinese Communists, with a treaty alliance with the Soviet Union, [make a similar claim that a forceful reunification of Taiwan with Communist China is an internal matter]. And the Soviet Union says they are prepared to back them up to the hilt. Here you have the Republic of China (Taiwan), which has a treaty of collective self-defense with the United States, which we are prepared to live up to.

Now when those two forces come to clash, nobody in his senses could say, 'This is purely a civil war and does not affect international peace.' It does. And, therefore, it is properly a matter to be dealt with from the standpoint of international peace and the welfare of the world. You cannot treat it purely as a civil war matter.[9]

Do Ends Justify Means?

We have a natural urge to answer this question in the negative. It is perhaps because of our tendency to associate the practice of justifying any means by political ends with nazism, fascism, communism, or moral cynicism in general, and not with democracies and their Judean-Christian ethics.

However, in practice we observe that democratic leaders and democratic majorities, too, justify concrete measures and methods of action in relation to their aims. Policy-makers are confronted with difficult and highly disturbing ethical and moral dilemmas. Choices have to be made—and "choice is simply the selection of one possibility to the exclusion of others when no more than one is feasible. Choice inevitably involves renunciation."[10]

In principle we abhor violence and do not approve of destruction of human lives. Yet, we accept war as an instrument to attain certain ends. We approve of a defensive war, for example.

In daily life individuals as well as groups have to make their choices and accept, in the process, renunciations and sacrifices of values which they sincerely cherish. These may be peace, non-violence, truth, justice, ideological or ethical principles, etc. Thus parents sometimes withhold the truth from their prematurely inquisitive children; governments keep some of their plans (like currency reform) secret from their people in order to prevent speculation; criminal use of force is punished by legitimate use of force (capital punishment, for instance).

It may be considered ethically wrong to spy on other nations. Woodrow Wilson seemed to believe that democracies should abstain from secret intelligence to prove the superiority of their ethics. In his address, explaining the

[9] September 30, 1958. Reproduced in the *New York Times,* October 1, 1958.
[10] Charles B. Marshall in Topic 17.

declaration of war against Germany (April 2, 1917) he said: "Self-governed nations do not fill their neighbors' states with spies." Does this mean that democracies should base their policies on incorrect information and thus endanger their own existence?

Human life, survival of an individual or a nation, has been raised to the position of an overwhelming priority in our scale of values. But how many or what portion of *other* important values can be renounced if they conflict with such a primary objective? "Men, statesmen, and private individuals," answers Arnold Wolfers, "are morally required to choose among the roads open to them the one which under the circumstances promises to produce the least over-all destruction of values." It would seem that cost in values has to be accepted. The problem is how to limit the absorption of all important values by the primary value of "survival."

A statesman is faced with an often superhuman task when he tries to find the correct path through the complex labyrinth of conflicting values: he has to sacrifice some in order to preserve others. In the name of the survival of a nation, should one avoid war and preserve peace at *all* cost or just *some* cost? One can indeed avoid war by submitting to the will of the potential aggressor. Or one may appease his appetite by the sacrifice of freedom of *one* small nation so that *many* great and small nations may, perhaps, enjoy peace. And if war is imposed on us and cannot be avoided, should we try to win it at the price of some unholy alliance with a political system which we consider evil by our ethical standards? Or should we rather die in an uncompromising pose of ideological purity?

Winston Churchill might have asked this question in 1941 when Nazi Germany attacked the Soviet Union and made a totalitarian dictatorship an ally of Western democracies. Should the democracies have rather continued to fight Hitler in isolation and perhaps lose the war, or should they have tried to win it in alliance with the Communists?

And finally—should one try to shorten a war by using a particularly inhumane yet effective weapon? Can inhumanity serve humanity?

Such disturbing questions have to be asked and some answers found. Following are four examples of such dilemmas in concrete situations, and their actual solutions:

1. *Should great powers try to preserve peace by sacrificing a small nation?* The Munich agreement of 1938 is a classic example (Topic 15). It threw Czechoslovakia, France's ally, into the hands of Nazi Germany, the common enemy of both France and Czechoslovakia. The Munich policy was condemned on two counts: it was *unwise* and it was *immoral*.

The lack of wisdom was confirmed by subsequent events. Munich became a symbol of the folly of appeasement.

A policy of *appeasement* may be defined as an error in the estimate of the rival's intentions. While the rival's policy aims at a complete reversal of the balance of power, it may present itself as a policy of the *status quo*. It pretends to aim only at minor changes within the current framework and it may be very convincing to those who are exposed to the pressure for change. Hitler presented his demand for the annexation of parts of Czechoslovakia as a slight change in the post-Versailles *status quo* in Europe. Neville Chamberlain committed an error of judgment when he did not recognize Hitler's demands as links in a chain which would end in the demand for control of all Europe. On March 15, 1939, Czechoslovakia was occupied by Germany; in September of the same year the long and costly World War II started. The folly of appeasement was demonstrated.

Even twenty years after, the evaluation of Munich in England is not unanimous. The defenders of Munich still maintain that the agreement was not unwise, as it postponed the outbreak of war and allowed Great Britain to speed up its re-militarization program. Without that delay the battle of Britain in 1940 could not have been won. World War II might have been lost.

The Munich agreement was condemned also because it was immoral. It was an attempt to buy peace for Western Europe at the expense of a small democratic nation. The definition in the American College Dictionary suggests a condemnation of appeasement on moral grounds: "To appease means to accede to the belligerent demands (of a country, government, etc.) by a sacrifice of justice."

In this case the immorality of the Munich agreement coincided with lack of wisdom and foresight, so quickly demonstrated by World War II. But what would have been the judgment of history if it had turned out to be an immoral but wise decision? How would we regard it today if Czechoslovakia had been really Hitler's last territorial demand and if slavery and destruction of twelve million Czechs and Slovaks had to be weighed against the life and prosperity of several hundred million Western Europeans, Russians and Americans? How, in the labyrinth of values, can we compare enslavement of twelve million with the peace and freedom of many times that number? Or what if, after Munich, the West had so increased its power that Hitler curbed his expansionist aims?

It was not only in 1938 that such a dilemma has confronted Western statesmen. In 1875 the Turkish government quelled a revolt against Turkish rule in Bulgaria by a cruel mass killing. In a private letter, Disraeli, then the British Prime Minister, refused to "avenge atrocities (in Bulgaria) by the butchery of the world." His main concern was to keep the Russians away from the Mediterranean so they could not exploit internal strife in Turkey for their own purposes. Gladstone, head of the opposition and Disraeli's successor, criticized him for subordinating philanthropy to the British national interest. In 1877 war between Russia and Turkey broke out. Two years later, Lord Salisbury, Disraeli's Foreign Secretary, stated in an address to his party in Middlesex:

"Anyone who has followed the history for the past three years, who has counted up the lives that were lost on the field of battle, and who has studied the reports of our representatives abroad, will agree that if all the misery inflicted by these atrocities [committed by the Turks in Bulgaria] had been repeated every year for thirty years, it would not have involved the miseries which this philanthropic war has entailed upon the human race."[11]

[11] Quoted in H. J. Morgenthau's and K. W. Thompson's *Principles and Problems of International Politics* (New York: Alfred A. Knopf, 1956), p. 57.

Here we have another difficult equation: one mass killing which justly causes extreme moral indignation over acts of inhumanity—weighed against an avenging war which may mean thirty times more misery.

A similar dilemma confronted the West in 1956. Western democracies could have stopped Soviet atrocities during the suppression of the Hungarian revolution, at the cost of a major "philanthropic" war. An atomic war between the great powers would most certainly entail upon the human race more than thirty times the amount of misery that the Russians inflicted upon the Hungarian people.

Yet, such horrifying equations can hardly offer reliable guidance for practical action. If so, major nations could then be successfully blackmailed into assenting to any aggression or inhumanity which would not concern them too directly.

2. *Does a noble aim justify an alliance with the devil?* The Western alliance with the Soviet Union has already been mentioned. As the aims and ideologies of democracy and communism are basically inimical and mutually incompatible, this alliance was certainly unholy from the point of view of both the West and the Soviet Union. Yet, they temporarily put their common conflict with nazism above the basic conflict between democracy and socialist totalitarianism. It was, however, bound to re-emerge soon after the common enemy was defeated.

General Eisenhower's arrangement with a pro-Nazi French admiral in 1943 is another example of sacrificing some principle for the sake of victory at lesser cost. This case was in connection with the Anglo-American invasion of French North Africa, which the French troops would have strongly resisted had they not been ordered to do otherwise. Information and the experience of the first few days of the invasion indicated that the only man who could order French Africa not to resist (and thus reduce great losses on both sides) was Admiral Darlan, who just happened to be in North Africa visiting his son at that time. The deal was made, despite its repugnance to the American personnel involved, and Admiral Darlan issued the appropriate order. Many American and French lives were saved at the cost of a moral compromise on the part of the American military authorities. Dwight D. Eisenhower describes this arrangement in his *Crusade in Europe* (Topic 22). The interplay of the term "crusade" and the actuality of such a compromising deal is interesting.

3. *Can inhumane action serve humane ends?* In 1945 the United States decided to use the atomic bomb against two Japanese cities and their military installations, as well as the civilian population. The purpose was to shorten the long war. One single blast, which killed fifty to one hundred thousand people in a matter of seconds, would prevent the killing of five to ten times that number in case of a full-fledged invasion of Japan.

Ten years later, the city council of Hiroshima passed a resolution condemning the American action. President Truman, responsible for the decision of August 1945, wrote a letter to the city council, which—in part—reads as follows:

Our military advisors had informed the Prime Minister of Great Britain, Generalissimo Chiang Kai-shek, and the President of the United States that it would require at least 1,500,000 allied soldiers to land in the Tokio plain and on the south island of Japan.

On July 16, 1945, before the demand for Japan surrender was made, a successful demonstration of the greatest explosive force in the history of the world had been accomplished.

After a long conference with the Cabinet, the military commanders, and Prime Minister Churchill it was decided to drop the atomic bomb on two Japanese cities, devoted to war work for Japan. The two cities selected were Hiroshima and Nagasaki. When Japan surrendered a few days after the bomb was ordered dropped, on August 6, 1945, the military estimated that at least 250,000 of the invasion forces in Japan and 250,000 Japanese had been spared complete destruction and that twice that many on each side would, otherwise, have been maimed for life.

To look for the right solution to this dilemma and the implied equations is a stupendous task. What is worse: the atomic death of several thousands in one moment or the same number killed during weeks and months of conventional fighting, as was the case in Germany?

In the case of Hiroshima and Nagasaki the mathematical equation seems to point in only one direction: it is more humane to sacrifice 100,000 instead of 500,000 human lives. But was it really the *only* choice?

Some argue today that atomic destruction was not necessary because Japan was defeated anyway.

Others allege that an invasion of Japan might have been necessary *in addition* to the use of the two atomic bombs that America had at its disposal. If the suicide-oriented elements had prevailed over the realistic influences in Japanese politics, Japan would not have surrendered even after atomic bombardment.

The history of the United States' decision is contained in Topic 22.

4. *An individual* vs. *the war machine.* Our last example is a postscript, rather than a problem comparable in magnitude to the previous ones where statesmen, nations, and millions of lives were involved. Yet, it is comparable to those dilemmas as an illustration of severely limited choices when physical survival is involved.

In 1957, the *New York Times* published a short report under the heading *Jews Here Honor Hitler Arms Aid.* The report told the story of Oscar Schindler, a Catholic German national, who saved many Jews during the war by employing them in his factory. He was permitted to employ Jewish workers, who would have been otherwise sent to the Nazi extermination camps, only because his factory belonged in the "essential industry" category. Although he was opposed to nazism and its cause, his factory produced ammunition for Hitler's army. The absurdity of his and his Jewish employees' situation is obvious.

This and similar problems and dilemmas are present in any life-or-death situation. It is not only Machiavellian diplomats, statesmen, or immoral men who sacrifice principles. The question of survival often makes men adopt or approve measures that they would consider totally unacceptable under a different set of circumstances.

Summary

1. Nations try to protect their interests and security either by negotiation with others which are deemed to challenge their interests, or by taking some concrete measures, singly or in cooperation with other nations which share their estimate of the challenge to be met.

2. The purpose of such balancing measures is usually either to increase a nation's resistance against the potential imposition of a rival will or to increase its power to be able to impose its will on others.

3. The most usual steps taken for either of the two purposes are:

(a) Increasing one's strength, most frequently through armaments;

(b) Declarations of policy aims and methods;

(c) Cooperative agreements of a military, economic, scientific or cultural nature;

(d) Dividing rival power and coalition, most frequently through psychological warfare and subversion;

(e) Military movements and activities, ranging from intimidatory bluffs to actual wars.

4. In life-or-death situations the understandable desire to survive may lead men and statesmen to adopt measures which, under a different set of circumstances, would be considered morally or ideologically condemnable.

TOPIC 17

The Art of the Possible

The foreign-policy process is composed of three major phases:

1. The *formulation* phase[1]—a creative process in which policy is suggested and a program of action proposed. This is usually the role of the executive branch of the government (the cabinet in most countries; the National Security Council in the U.S.; the party presidium in Russia or China, etc.). On the basis of available intelligence and in view of immediate or ultimate objectives, alternate courses of action are considered and one of them is chosen.

2. The *decision* phase—a process of marshaling support to ensure policy's eventual execution. Sometimes even a dictator must convince his

[1] Terminology used by Paul H. Nitze in his article "National Policy-Making Techniques," *SAIS Review*, Vol. III, No. 3, is adopted here. His article on brinkmanship forms part of this Topic.

generals, solve interservice rivalries and interallied jealousies. In democracies the process is more complex and includes the effort to obtain the support of legislators and private (industrial) interests. Policy is often modified during this phase.

3. The *execution* phase—the final and difficult process of putting the chosen policy and program into action. This includes the problems, in Paul H. Nitze's words, "of meeting unforeseen obstacles and of capitalizing on unforeseen possibilities. This final phase of execution often takes on continuing elements of the first and second phases. Objectives and methods are modified in the light of actual practice. Action builds a measure of consensus among those who are acting together."

►ERRORS IN THE CALCULATION OF MEANS

CHARLES BURTON MARSHALL

It is easier to postulate a balance of means than to apply this principle in practice. The author of the following observations experienced this difficulty while he served as a member of the U.S. Policy Planning Staff.

The situation of the state—substitute the term *government* or *nation* if you will—is that of having some, but only some, capability. That is the situation of responsibility. It lies between the extremes of omnipotence and powerlessness. Each of these extremes alike carries no responsibility.

The situation of responsibility involves the necessity of choice. Choice is simply the selection of one possibility to the exclusion of others when no more than one is feasible. Choice inevitably involves renunciation. In the view of the scholastic philosophers, even an infinite being is compelled to make choices because of being unable to will into existence simultaneously inherently contradictory things. Finite entities have to make choices not only as between inherently contradictory possibilities but also as between things which together are practicably unfeasible within the means at hand.

One knows this from the daily circumstances of his own life—the continuing necessity of allocating one's time and rationing one's money, one's inability to spend the same two hours in both studying and going to the movies, and the incapacity to obtain together the rewards of diligence and the comforts of indolence. One must repeatedly put aside one desirable thing in preference for another thing also desirable. This circumstance distinguishes the real life from the myths treasured in childhood with their seven-league boots, lamps of Aladdin, magic carpets, and open sesames.

The situation of the state in its external responsibilities is that of the limits of adult reality, notwithstanding that many Americans persist in talking of foreign policy in a frame of reference akin to the wishful tales of child-

This selection is from *The Limits of Foreign Policy,* quoted before on p. 265. Copyright © 1954 by Henry Holt and Company, Inc. By permission of the publishers.

hood. Let us apply then to the state in its external relations the simple concepts about will applicable to other human endeavors.

Will is the faculty for making choices. The difference between a weak and a determined will is simply a difference in steadfastness in carrying through with the renunciations inescapably involved in making choices. This is as true in the frame of the state as it is in other human affairs.

An exercise of will is a volition. A volition unfolds at three levels. The first of these concerns motives. By that term I mean those impulses rising from some inner need or desire and spurring the mind to volition. The second level involves ends. By an end I mean that which the mind conceives as representing the satisfaction of the need or desire identified as the source of motivation. The third level involves intentions. At this level the mind adds to the conception of ends the projection of action in pursuit of them.

Note that I say pursuit, not attainment. The capacity of the mind to conceive ends is limitless. The means at hand are invariably limited. The level of intention involves above all the establishment of a balance between ends and means—that is, if one is responsible in his undertakings. Balancing ends and means requires at any juncture the selection of some feasible fraction of one's ends to be acted upon and the deferment of the rest. The portions of one's ends selected for action let us call purposes.

All this applies to foreign policy.

The formulation of foreign policy, if done responsibly, must be regarded as the forming of our intentions—as distinguished from our ends—regarding the world external to our national jurisdiction. The distinction makes a difference. The sum of the foreign policy is the sum not of things we should like to achieve but of the things we do or are going to set about doing in the world. . . .

Many—one finds them in government as well as out of it—regard foreign policy as a set of good wishes and high aspirations about the world, as that and nothing more. . . .

I do not mean to decry the essentiality of a set of goals in foreign policy. Ultimate purposes have a value in serving as a standard for knowing how to proceed, problem by problem, in this field. Moreover, the good is not always beyond reach, though the way to it is arduous, long, and charged with paradoxes.

A few years ago one of our most distinguished military leaders, one typifying in the best sense the combination of soldiery and statesmanship, made a speech about the criteria for our relationships with the rest of the world. His peroration was a plea for the nation to guide by the eternal stars instead of steering by the lights of each passing ship. The sweep and grandeur of his metaphor impressed me. I said so in a conversation with a seafaring friend. "Obviously you don't know much about the sea," he told me. "One of the easiest parts of seamanship is celestial navigation. That never keeps you awake on the bridge all night. The test of seamanship is the shoals, the fogs, the storms that blow and yet you can't do anything to stop them, and the passing ships. Just try to imagine sailing under a skipper who thinks the big part of his job is star-gazing."

That anecdote makes my point. The goal aspect of foreign policy is essential. It is also easy. It is the easiest part of the business. The difficult part comes not in figuring out what one would do if one could do everything one may wish to do. It comes in deciding what to do in the circumstances of being able to do only part of what one may wish to do. That is the task of handling dilemmas and of rationing means. Here the making of foreign policy reaches the vital level. Here success is courted. Here failure is risked.

From this concept of the making of foreign policy as essentially involving not the mere conceiving of ends but the establishment of purposes of action and the allocation of means comes a recognition of the determinative importance of means. We know this well in the frame of individual lives. Probably not one of all the men in Sing Sing set Sing Sing as his goal in life. They all arrived there because of grievous errors in the calculation of means.

Let us then apply to foreign policy a few simple ideas relating to the economy of means. . . .

History is replete with . . . instances of governments which committed themselves overtly to undertakings which they could not fulfill but from which they could not back away and in consequence incurred war.

Once begun, the process of inflating the purposes is most difficult to stop. A government proclaims aims in excess of its means to effect them. Becoming anxious over the disparity between what it can do and what it has proclaimed, it seeks to redress the disparity by even wider assertions of aims still more stridently proclaimed. Eventually the range of assertions and the range of achievements are so obviously and widely disparate that the nation's policy faces imminent disintegration. Here the temptation to resort to coercion by threat and display of force rises, bringing on the danger of counter-threat and counterdisplay, and finally the plunge into general violence. Thus the course of proclaiming goals beyond the margins of capability provided by calculable means tends toward war. This course no nation can afford to begin. We must not presume for our nation any exemption from the penalties imposed for mistaking pronouncement for policy. . . .

The use of means involves cost. The achievement of purposes represents gain. It is easy to wish a gain. The difficult part is the envisaging of the cost. The cost aspects of a foreign policy are the aspects despite which a course of action is undertaken. The gain aspects are those because of which a course of action is undertaken.

In the balancing between these two aspects every important policy issue officially familiar to me has been also a close one. The merits in argument for and against an acceptable line of action never occur in ratios of 100 to 0 or even of 80 to 20. They tend rather to occur in the order of 55 to 45 or even 51 to 49. Even at best, the arguments against a line of action in foreign policy tend to be almost as weighty as the considerations in favor. Yet these small margins of difference constitute the distinction between success and failure and are all-important.

I did not find the issues so closely balanced in a former time when I used to write newspaper editorials about foreign policy. Then I could arrive at solutions plain as day and overwhelmingly cogent for even the most serious issues. The process usually took only about forty-five minutes. I did almost equally well with solving the great problems of policy in teaching international relations. In the line of responsibility, however, things look quite different.

Whatever his shortcomings as a philosopher, Jeremy Bentham was surely right in this: the forming of an intention includes the acceptance of the cost as well as the entertaining of the gain.

►A SHAKY BALANCE OF BRINKMANSHIP

PAUL H. NITZE

The author warns against the art of brinkmanship if it is not backed up by overwhelming superiority. He advises maintenance of nuclear retaliatory capability (second-strike capability) in a world in which the art of brinkmanship may be used by the Soviet leaders.

Paul H. Nitze is Chairman of the Executive Committee of the Washington Center of Foreign Policy Research, Johns Hopkins University. He is also President of the Foreign Service Educational Foundation, and a former Director of the U.S. State Department's Policy Planning Staff. He has written several books and studies on the conduct of foreign policy.

On January 11, 1956, James Shepley, one of *Life* Magazine's able reporters, published an article on "How Mr. Dulles Averted War." The article created a furor. It was bitterly attacked by many here and abroad. Others as vigorously supported the propositions it advanced. From that debate the word "brinkmanship" came to have a new and special meaning in the English language. It now suggests a particular approach to the conduct of foreign policy. What is that approach and what today, after the experience of [several] years, can be said about it?

Shepley said that in the conduct of his office Mr. Dulles had done two things: he had radically revised the "containment" policy of the Truman administration and he had altered drastically the concept of the job of Secretary of State.

He quotes Mr. Dulles as saying, "You have to take chances for peace, just as you have to take chances in war. Some say we were brought to the verge of war. Of course we were brought to the verge of war. The ability to get to the verge without getting into the war is the necessary art. If you cannot master it, you inevitably get into war. If you try to run away from it, if you are scared to go to the brink, you are lost. We've had to look it square in the face—on the question of enlarging the Korean war, on the question of getting into the Indochina war, on the question of Formosa. We walked to the brink and we looked it in the face. We took strong action."

The selection is from the article "Brinkmanship and the Averting of War," *Military Policy Papers* (Washington, D. C.: The Washington Center of Foreign Policy Research, December, 1958).

None but the most visionary take issue with the view that risks must be run to maintain any kind of acceptable peace and that in today's world the unavoidable risks in standing up to the Soviet-Chinese-Communist drive for world hegemony are very great indeed.

The issue of "brinkmanship" is not then one of willingness to accept necessary risks. The issue is rather one of the policy and method used in selecting and managing the risks which are to be taken—what Mr. Dulles calls "the necessary art."

We can get an insight into Mr. Dulles' conception of "the necessary art" from other portions of the Shepley article, those portions which describe the new policy, the policy of "deterrence," developed by Mr. Dulles to take the place of the policy of "containment." Shepley says that the policy of deterrence is based on the proposition that wars are caused by miscalculation. He then quotes from Mr. Dulles' famous January, 1954, speech before the Council on Foreign Relations. "Local defense must be reinforced by the further deterrent of massive retaliation power. A potential aggressor must know that he cannot always prescribe battle conditions that suit him. . . . The way to deter aggression is for the free community to be willing and able to respond vigorously at places and with means of its own choosing."

Shepley goes on to explain that Mr. Dulles was not thinking of attacks on Moscow but of such retaliation as would make a Communist military venture of any size unprofitable. It was his intention to make the punishment fit the crime. He quotes Mr. Dulles as saying that the best example of what he meant was the retaliation planned, if necessary, against the Chinese Communists, either in connection with Korea or Indochina. "They were specific targets reasonably related to the area. They did not involve massive destruction of great population centers like Shanghai, Peking or Canton. Retaliation must be on a selective basis. The important thing is that the aggressor know in advance that he is going to lose more than he can win. He doesn't have to lose *much* more. It just has to be *something* more. If the equation is clearly going to be against him, he won't go in."

On another occasion Mr. Dulles indicated that a nuclear attack upon the new industrial complex in Manchuria was the type of punishment he had in mind.

Now what are the essential elements of this "necessary art," the art of brinkmanship as it was conceived by Mr. Dulles in January, 1956? They are the following: (1) the drawing of a line to avoid miscalculation by the enemy; (2) deterrence, letting the enemy know that we are prepared to take strong action if he violates that line, and (3) retaliation, the ability and will to punish the aggressor by making him lose more by his aggression than he can possibly win. The assertion was that this policy had prevented not only the "big hydrogen war but the littler wars as well." The implication was that it would continue to do so over the "long haul."

Serious questions can be raised as to the historical accuracy of the assertion. Did the heroic defense of the Republic of Korea forces, supported by our Army, Navy and Air Forces using conventional weapons, have no role in bringing about the Korean armistice? Did the threat of retaliation save

Dien Bien Phu or prevent the partition of Indochina? Was Formosa not defensible without the threat of a nuclear attack on Manchuria? The Korean war, however, was brought to an end, the fighting in Indochina ceased and Formosa was not attacked. It cannot be demonstrated that Mr. Dulles' diplomacy had no part in these results. It is highly debatable, however, that it would have been wise or moral for the United States to have initiated a nuclear attack on Manchuria had those results not been achieved. In any case, it would seem to have been unwise to boast of the successes of a policy of threats the seriousness of which one did not expect to be called upon to demonstrate by action. Such boasts encourage the enemy to test and challenge the policy and thus tend to undercut any prospect that the policy will continue to be effective in the future.

But the important question is not the reconstruction of past history. The problem now is whether the policy of brinkmanship is, under today's conditions, "the necessary art." And what of the future?

The interesting thing is that today it is not we but the Russians who seem to be pursuing a policy of brinkmanship. During the [1958] Quemoy-Matsu crisis, Mr. Eisenhower and Mr. Dulles were silent about deterrence and about retaliation. They condemned the use of force in the pursuit of aggressive aims. They emphasized their determination that the Chinese Nationalists not be driven from Quemoy and Matsu by force of arms. But there were no threats of punishment of aggression by nuclear attack "on targets reasonably related to the area" such as the Manchurian industrial complex. Admiral Burke stated that Quemoy and Matsu could be re-supplied and defended against conventional attack for the indefinite future. This would suggest that in the Quemoy-Matsu crisis we were pretty well back to a policy of "containment" and local defense at the point of attack with conventional weapons.

Mr. Khrushchev, on the other hand, in the letter to Mr. Eisenhower, which Mr. Eisenhower properly rejected as being offensive beyond the limits of acceptable diplomatic discourse, drew lines, made threats and suggested targets for retaliatory attack reasonably related to the area. In referring to United States naval forces Mr. Khrushchev said, "In the age of nuclear and rocket weapons of unprecedented power and rapid action these once formidable warships are fit, in fact, for nothing but courtesy visits and gun salutes, and can serve as targets for the right types of rockets." This suggests that Mr. Khrushchev believes his lead in ICBM's has now turned the tables on Mr. Dulles and that it is he who can play at brinkmanship.

Brinkmanship is one kind of policy if it is backed up by an overwhelming superiority in nuclear weapons and means for their accurate and selective delivery. For then it is unlikely that the threats necessarily implied by deterrence will be tested, the possibility that one will in fact have to retaliate is low, and it is possible to draw arbitrary lines not closely related to the political and military realities. But brinkmanship is quite a different policy if it is not backed up by overwhelming superiority. The game ceases to be analogous to cops and robbers. It becomes a contest combining the principles of chess and those of stud poker played for enormous stakes. The prospect that threats will in fact be tested rises. The retaliation necessary to demonstrate that the threat was serious may have to be carried out. Otherwise, if the threat is tested and is abandoned under pressure, it will be revealed as having been a bluff.

Under today's conditions, where brinkmanship is no longer our unilateral prerogative, modifications in the "necessary art" would seem to be in order. What modifications come to mind?

In the first place, greater care is called for, under the new conditions, in the determination of the issues and places which merit the full commitment of United States prestige and power. It is important that the issues so backed be clearly definable and that they lend themselves to rational and consistent explanation. As reliance upon the threat of the use of purely physical power becomes more dubious as a policy, it becomes more important to assure ourselves of wide and convinced support in the minds of men. Certain issues of principle command wide support of peoples and governments across the noncommunist world. One of these principles is that military force, across recognized international boundaries, shall not be used as an instrument of policy. The principle that indirect aggression should not be condoned, and that it is proper to use direct military means to counter it, has far less support. The islands of Quemoy and Matsu, in the minds of many people in the world, do not logically fall within a recognized boundary. An attack upon them does not therefore appear to be aggression and their defense does not command widespread support.

Similarly it becomes important to consider, in addition to the issues involved, the location, importance, and military defensibility of the places to be defended. Formosa and Japan are easier to defend, particularly if only nonnuclear weapons are to be used, than are Quemoy and Matsu or Nepal. No simple formula is available for determining the proper weight to be given to issues of principle as against considerations of military defensibility. Berlin, though militarily defended against Russian divisions only through the use of nuclear weapons, if then, must be defended. We could hardly live with ourselves if we permitted the two million West Berliners, who have shown exceptional courage in standing up to the pressure of surrounding communism, to be overrun by military attack or surrender because of the threat of attack. The history of the Berlin situation is such that there is wide understanding of why the West must support this militarily unsound position with the full commitment of its power and prestige. But where the history of the situation is not so clear, more weight has to be given to the military defensibility of the local position through means other than nuclear retaliation. The suppression of the Hungarian revolution was as offensive to the sensibilities of mankind as would be the invasion of West Berlin. But the history of that situation was not such as to give a foundation of political support to our threatening to use nuclear weapons in support of the Hungarian freedom fighters.

Two further corollaries flow from these considerations of a world in which brinkmanship can be played by more than one player. One is that we should be wise to rebuild our non-nuclear military capabilities. The other is that we must develop the necessary fortitude to stand up against the brink-manship threats of the Soviet Union and do what we can to decrease the effectiveness of these threats in influencing the policy of others.

Our military planning over recent years contemplated that, if Quemoy and Matsu were attacked in such a manner as to persuade the President that the attack was a prelude to an attack on Formosa, nuclear weapons would be used in their defense. Little advance attention was given to the problem of re-supplying the islands to carry out a protracted defense against concentrated artillery or air attack using conventional weapons. When the artillery attack came the unwisdom of our initiating the use of nuclear weapons was evident. The loss of prestige involved in retreating under fire was also evident. The upshot was a rapidly improvised, but at least temporarily effective, resupply effort. The chance of avoiding, on the one hand, retreat under fire and, on the other, the initiating by us of nuclear war rested on our ability to take effective non-nuclear action. The implication would seem to be clear that a reversal of our policy of the last few years of shrinking our conventional military capabilities is called for.

The other side of the equation is fortitude in standing firm in the face of Soviet nuclear threats and blackmail, in other words, Soviet brinkmanship. This requires that we maintain nuclear retaliatory capabilities—second strike capabilities—that cannot be taken out by surprise attack and whose solid power make Soviet threats to use nuclear weapons unconvincing. If we were ever to surrender positions of major importance under such threats, Mr. Dulles' "falling domino" theory could in fact have substance.

The final point about brinkmanship played by more than one nation is that it can introduce a general instability into the equations of international strategy. Threats and counter-threats, in the age of nuclear weapons systems requiring reaction in a matter of minutes, can become intolerably danger-ous. . . .

TOPIC 18

What Is to Be Done?

We have seen that it is not easy to define policy goals, to suggest steps which give promise of leading to them, or to estimate the cost and effort required.

With regard to the Soviet challenge, the United States has no difficulty in stating its goals in *negative* terms. The United States does *not* want (1) to engage in war with the Soviet Union (a preventive war is and always has been out of question); or (2) to permit further advances of the Sino-Soviet bloc aiming at world hegemony; submission to their will is also out of question.

The difficulty arises with the question what can be done *positively* to prevent either of these alternatives. If war or submission are ruled out, any favorable change in the present situation seems to require either (a) the consent of the Communist bloc; or (b) absence of its opposition.

Internal crisis disrupting the strength and solidity of the Sino-Soviet bloc would facilitate favorable changes. But initiation of such an occurrence, while possible, is beyond the immediate means of the United States.

►MINIMUM REQUIREMENTS

HENRY L. ROBERTS

If the conflict with Russia can be resolved without general war or acceptance of Communist hegemony, the basic requirement for American foreign policy is to maintain our ability to negotiate, to communicate, and to propose a settlement while checking the expansion of the Communist bloc.

This emphasis on firmness combined with flexibility is the theme of the following essay. Its author is Professor of History and Director of the Russian Institute of Columbia University.

For a number of policy questions, primarily those not involving our immediate dealings with the Soviet bloc, there is a reasonably close correspondence between objectives and methods. We are able to define our goal, to indicate steps which give promise of leading to it, and to have some idea of the effort required. In such cases it is both possible and profitable to arrive at a fairly precise policy statement. Differences, and they may be serious, chiefly concern techniques and costs. By and large, however, such precision is confined to the defense of the vital interests of the United States and the free world and to the averting of certain evils.

In contrast to this area of relative stability and clarity, there are a number of policy questions, primarily those arising from our direct relations with the Soviet bloc, which are not, so far as we can see, amenable to precise or clear-cut solution. The ultimate purposes of policy may escape definition. The means of realizing them may be lacking. Or the consequences of the actions which are open to us may currently be unforeseeable. In such cases the formulation and execution of policy must necessarily be tentative. Goals which are set as aspirations may have to wait upon the discovery or arrival of appropriate means. The results of actions must be tested in practice.

This distinction is of real importance if we are to keep the necessary stability of our national policy from degenerating into dogmatism and rigidity and its equally necessary flexibility from degenerating into wobbling and opportunism. [Here] we deal with what we take to be the first class of policy questions: those for which the purposes are reasonably clear and for which

From *Russia and America,* published for the Council on Foreign Relations by Harper & Brothers, New York. Pp. 79-90.

the requisite means appear to be at hand, if often extremely difficult to apply.

From our discussion of the potentialities of thermonuclear weapons and the nature of Soviet Communism we conclude that a general war, whether we won it or not, or the world-wide establishment of Communism, whether through general war or by other means, would each constitute a disaster of terrible magnitude. Yet we cannot simply make the avoidance of *both* war and Communist hegemony an absolute policy requirement, since avoiding the one might, under certain circumstances, mean accepting the other. If the choice is put in these narrow terms, the answer has to be that the United States must prevent the world-wide establishment of Soviet Communism—even at the cost of general war. This answer may not be self-evident to all. It would not be acceptable to the Communist, nor to the absolute pacifist, nor even to those who feel that there are limits to frightfulness beyond which no nation can go, even in its own defense, without destroying its own moral being. Debate over the relative inhumanity of labor-camp slavery and genocide as against the obliteration of millions through burning and radiation cannot be conclusive, though each person may have no doubt as to his own preference. The reason for the choice must be on other grounds: willingness to accept war is to accept means which may lead to an incalculable disaster as the outcome; willingness to accept the defeat implicit in Communist hegemony is to accept the outcome in advance, with the consequent relinquishment of all means, not merely those of war. That is, the decision to avoid general war at *all* costs simultaneously destroys whatever other means there are, or may be, for averting the disaster of Communist world hegemony. The game is up.

Having said this, however, we must stress the function of our willingness to accept general war as a means of keeping the door open for possibilities *other* than the frightful choice between such a war and the global ascendancy of Communism. Under conditions of thermonuclear conflict a general war as an instrument to advance the national interest, or indeed to achieve any positive objective, is most probably a self-contradiction. A decision for general war is reasonable only as a necessity to avoid our succumbing to the Communist bloc. This also may not seem self-evident to all, particularly to those who believe that a justifiable war is a war in a righteous cause, such as the liberation of enslaved peoples or the vanquishing of the evil of Communist totalitarianism. In circumstances, however, where the liberation of the enslaved is at the cost of their lives, and the vanquishing of evil at the cost of unlimited and indiscriminate suffering by wicked and innocent alike, such justification for general war, as for pacifism, transcends politics and is not a subject for political debate or decision.

Hence we may formulate our limiting requirements as follows: preventing at whatever cost the world-wide imposition of Soviet Communism, and avoiding general war as a means of achieving positive political goals. It is the task, then, of policy not to foreclose on the future either by backing into a total defeat or by pressing forward to a general war.

The state of prolonged and uneasy suspension indicated in these require= ments inevitably raises the question whether another requirement is not called for, one that takes account of time. When we consider the prospects for the future, the constantly growing production, stockpiling and development of atomic and thermonuclear weapons; the promised advent of intercontinental ballistic missiles; the likelihood of continuing Communist efforts to undermine other societies, including our own, and to prepare for their absorption into the Communist world; the absence of positive confidence in any self-induced change in the nature and aims of the Soviet regime; the continuing strain upon our own society of meeting, without taking on the attributes of our opponents, a situation that is neither war nor peace—when we consider these prospects, we may be impelled to conclude that such a state of affairs cannot go on indefinitely, that each year our room for maneuver and decision narrows, and hence that within a limited period of time some kind of resolution or showdown is absolutely necessary. Under this view, in which the alternatives of a holocaust or Communist global victory seem increasingly to be the only ones, it is urged that despite present perils an all-out effort to resolve the crisis must be made, since it will be harder to achieve with each year that passes.

Depending upon one's estimate and apprehensions for the future course of events, this demand for a termination of the conflict may take several forms. It may seek a showdown by means of either 1) a sudden preventive atomic strike against the Soviet Union; 2) an ultimatum on such matters as arms control, Soviet domination of other lands and the activities of international Communism, to be followed by war in case of its nonacceptance by the Soviet leaders; or 3) serious efforts for a limited period of time to negotiate a general settlement on these matters, but resort to war if the negotiations fail. In contrast to a showdown, the termination may be sought in transcending the conflict: an effort to establish a world government or some other type of supranational organization possessing the power and authority to compose and settle the conflict.

These views must be taken seriously; the problem they envisage is real and grave. While there is little to be gained from lamenting the past, the experience of the last 30 years does appear to provide a number of examples of situations which might have been saved, catastrophes which might have been avoided, had there been a willingness to deal with a growing menace in its early stages. More vigorous intervention in the Russian Civil War might have kept the Bolsheviks from consolidating their power; universal and full support of the League of Nations in its early stages might have averted some of the disasters of the 1930's; firm dealing with Hitler between 1933 and 1936 might have checked the plunge into war in 1938 and 1939; it is tempting to feel that we would have done well to have had a showdown (which might not have been as violent as now) with the Soviet Union while the Second World War was coming to an end. Certainly our present plight is related to the many things that were not done in the past, though we cannot rewrite history and know how things might have turned out otherwise. (What, for example, would have been the course of German-Russian relations between 1919 and 1945 had there been no Soviet regime?)

Nevertheless, we cannot accept as a *requirement* this need for an early termination or resolution of the conflict. In the present situation it appears impossible to force a general showdown without bringing about a general war. While it is conceivable that for reasons quite unknown to us the Soviet regime might yield to the demands of an American ultimatum on such critical issues as arms control and international Communism, the chances of such an outcome are exceedingly slight. Given the nature of the antagonism and the nature of the Soviet regime, one's expectation would have to be that such steps, if forced through, could only lead to a general war.

It may, however, be argued that the real choice may be between risking a general war in the near future or facing either sure defeat without a fight or a worse war under even more unfavorable circumstances later on. One cannot deny that this could be the case—that a future generation, if there is one, might heartily regret an American failure to drive for an early showdown. It may be thought that it is a matter of balancing risks and uncertainties. Nonetheless, there is a real and, in our view, decisive difference between the risks and uncertainties involved in pressing for an immediate showdown and those involved in waiting for the future. In the first instance the risks and uncertainties are those of a poker game, but the steps by which this pressing for a showdown could, if the opponent did not yield, lead to a general war are perfectly concrete and apparent. In the second case, the risks and uncertainties are those inherent in any effort to forecast the future; they include not only the unavoidable uncertainties of any effort to derive the future from past and present trends, but also, and most important, the element of real novelty, the things presently unknown and unknowable which might enter the picture and influence it to an entirely unpredictable degree. In other words, while it is not difficult to see precisely how pressure for a showdown could precipitate a war, the same cannot be said for the movement of events into the future. To be sure, in 1936 Churchill was able to state with extraordinary precision the moves by which Hitler, after the reoccupation of the Rhineland, would be able to establish his positions for the events of 1938 and 1939. And we should certainly try to be as foresighted in our estimates of the consequences of particular moves and crises that occur throughout the world. But this is quite different from the much more general and casually imprecise expectation underlying the assertion that a showdown in the near future is a necessary requirement for American policy.

If such a showdown by force or threat of force promises only to engulf us in general war, or presents so great a risk that we could not reasonably embark on such a course, the opposite means of trying to terminate the conflict—by transcending it—carries the other danger of undermining our own security against Communist hegemony. An effort to force the creation of "one world" with the existing radical incompatibility of interests and intentions still festering within it would be disastrous in creating an internecine struggle of an even more desperate and obscure sort. From our previous experience with coalitions of which the Communist Party was a member, as well as from our experience in the United Nations, it is not to be believed that the Communist world could be absorbed into a supranational organization without attempting to turn it to its own ends. This is not to argue against international organizations as such but against the effort to place on them the task of bringing off an early termination to the conflict. Even worse than this incompatibility of interests and intentions would be our forgetting or disregarding its existence.

Our requirements, then, with respect to time should be put somewhat differently: we must maintain over time our ability to act appropriately in the event there should develop a real possibility to resolve the conflict without general war or acceptance of Communist hegemony. We must also try to create such a possibility. More concretely, this means maintaining our ability to negotiate, to communicate, to propose. We cannot become so exclusively concerned with checking the expansion of the Communist bloc's power and influence—though we must do that, too—that we are at any time unable to explore and assess in the international scene the prospects, which may remain nonexistent, which may arise suddenly, or which may emerge slowly, for bringing about the termination or radical alteration of the present antagonistic relationship. That we are unable at this point to envisage these prospects or even to define a "resolution" with any precision does not affect the fact that we must be ready to grasp and utilize the new and the unforeseen. Even though we cannot count with any assurance on a more propitious future we must not deny ourselves the potentialities that might reside in it.

On the basis of these very general requirements a number of corollaries may be established:

A. *The maintenance of American strength.* That strength must be both adequate and flexible. Without adequate strength we are inviting defeat. Unless we possess the ability to exert our strength flexibly according to the particular requirements of a situation we may unintentionally precipitate a general war.

American and Soviet strengths take a number of forms, ranging from the brute power of the thermonuclear explosion to the subtler and less tangible but very real manifestations of political and psychological strength. Which of these forms will come into play depends upon the circumstances. Reduction of strength to just one component and reliance upon it alone could force the United States into an extremely rigid position in which it either would fail to have the requisite type of strength to avert a disastrous defeat or would have to rely upon the mutual mauling of a strategic atomic exchange. Consequently, we must accept as a general requirement for policy the building up of all the relevant types of strength to the extent necessary to prevent Communist hegemony.

It follows from this that the United States must develop its own strength [along all the lines discussed in Part II and Topic 14]: atomic, military, economic, political. It cannot afford to say that because the issue *may* be settled on one level—nuclear warfare, political warfare, etc.—the other factors of strength can be disregarded. Because of the wide-ranging nature of the conflict, any such simple-minded approach would only lead, through the actions and responses of the Soviet leaders, to a shifting of the contest to a different level of power. It must be said, however, that creating strength is not just a matter of choice; it involves expenditures and allocation of resources. Very real and difficult decisions must be made in determining the best distribution of our energies. The only point to be made here is that such decisions be made within the framework of the need for a balanced and modulated development of our strength, however that may be worked out in actual practice.

B. *Allies*. While strength in a situation of conflict cannot always be measured by simple addition (for example, the importance of United States strength as compared with that of Western Europe is not adequately brought out by a comparison of national incomes or manpower), in the present situation, in which power and strength of all types may, under certain circumstances, play an important role in the defense of the United States, it is indispensable that the United States regard its own strength as a part of the total strength available to defend the non-Soviet world. It is quite true that there might be situations in which, say, Europe's strength could not come into play; but there are others in which it might be decisive (if, for example, both the United States and the Soviet Union were badly disabled after a mutually destructive atomic interchange). Consequently, a requirement of United States policy must be to couple its strength with that of allies. There is ample room for legitimate debate concerning alliance policy, the extent to which allies aid us, the amount of aid which should be granted them, the degree to which a coordination of policies is required. . . . But this debate must be within the framework of the general need to make as much of this potentiality as possible.

C. *Territory*. Though it may not be true in every case, in general each time a piece of territory and its inhabitants are brought into the Soviet orbit the free world suffers a loss of strength and the Communists enjoy a corresponding gain. This strength may be primarily in manpower or resources, or it may represent strategic position, or it may comprise a political advantage in terms of prestige and posture. A general requirement of our policy, therefore, must be to oppose any further absorption of territory into the Soviet or Communist system. Here, too, there is legitimate area for debate when it comes to specific policy decisions. It may be that a certain piece of territory is politically important to the United States but a military liability. Such was the case of Berlin; in that instance the political considerations were clearly, and correctly, regarded as the more important: the airlift resulted from the decision to support the city despite the logistic and strategic difficulties. Debates are bound to arise in such cases, and the decisions may reasonably differ under different circumstances. But there must be general recognition that the absorption of territories within the Soviet orbit is far from being a matter of indifference to the security of the United States, since each such loss not only alters the balance of forces but reduces the area of freedom in the world. It is in our interest to have this area as large as possible.

This requirement that we oppose further territorial expansion by the Soviet bloc runs counter, of course, to the view that American interests would best be served by a withdrawal of our forces and commitments from Europe and Asia. This view is worth considering briefly. In so far as it is not just a symptom of impatience or of disinclination to face the problems of the contemporary world, the most persuasive case that can be made for it would probably rest on some such argument as the following:

While advocates of withdrawal must admit the possibility that the entire resources of the Eastern Hemisphere will fall as a consequence to the Soviet bloc, to be developed and disciplined as it sees fit, they might contend that this does not weaken our military position, or does not weaken it more than the costs and risks incurred in attempting to defend overseas areas. If it is conceded that any general war will be won by atomic blows against the heart of the opponent and that the advent within the decade of intercontinental ballistic missiles will have rendered overseas air bases relatively unimportant, then it can be argued that if we maintain and protect a massive retaliatory force in the Western Hemisphere, capable of knocking out any power attempting a knockout blow against us, we shall be as safe as we could be under any other arrangement, and should not be wasting money in more vulnerable areas abroad or getting into foreign crises which might develop into a general war. In any event, as things stand now, we cannot be sure that overseas areas can be defended except by the employment of atomic weapons, and while a conflict might start with their limited tactical employment, a build-up to intercontinental strategic attacks is distinctly possible. The loss of no overseas area, it might be urged, is militarily worth the damage we would suffer through such a chain reaction.

Finally, it could be argued that American morale would be much better with such a withdrawal. We would know where we stood, there would be unanimous agreement that we must defend our homeland, and any attack upon it would be so clear in intent that we would be fully united in resisting it. Any commitment beyond this line, however, threatens to confront us with an endless series of agonizing decisions: shall we hold the Communist powers at this point or shall we make a limited withdrawal. While we may repeatedly declare, "Thus far and no farther," we would never know, under the awful threat of the consequences, whether we, or public opinion, would hold any outlying line. Piecemeal retreats would be altogether demoralizing, and it would be much better to state in advance that it is not our intent to defend overseas areas.

These arguments are not without some weight, nor are they wholly disposed of by counterarguments concerning our commitments to our allies and to the United Nations, or the damaging effect upon American morale at witnessing the destruction of freedom and culture elsewhere in the world. For, it might be maintained, if these are to be defended only at the cost of an atomic holocaust, all values may be reduced to cinders; we would be of greater service to humanity as a free island, no matter how beleaguered.

Even on its own terms, however, this argument for withdrawal has a fatal defect which, in our view, effectively removes it from the range of our policy choices. *It involves an irrevocable loss of the power of decision.* If its worst implications are accepted—i.e., willingness to accede to Soviet domination over the rest of the globe—there is no way to reverse this decision at a later date. We are perforce committed to whatever consequences may ensue.

Hence, unless the following questions can be answered categorically in the affirmative, and in the nature of things they cannot, this view must be rejected:

Can we afford to accept as beyond our control or influence whatever may happen (politically, economically, scientifically, militarily and culturally) in the rest of the world over an unlimited period of time, including our encirclement by a more powerful Soviet bloc?

Is the revolution in arms and military strategy such that the coupling of the non-Soviet world's strength with our own will not, under any circumstances, be of decisive significance to our national security?

Is it certain that the American people will in fact acquiesce in the progressive Communization of the rest of the world, were that to take place?

We would answer, no, to each of these questions; in any event they certainly cannot be affirmed without qualification, which they would have to be if a policy of hemispheric withdrawal were to be considered tenable.

Beyond this, however, it is worth observing that this view—and in this respect it bears a close resemblance to advocacy of an early showdown by forceful means or preventive war—demonstrates a complete, and in our view wholly unwarranted, pessimism about even the possibility of managing or mastering the present international crisis by means other than war. The great area of political action, including diplomacy and economic and social measures, is entirely dismissed, and in desperation we either toss in our chips and go home, or start shooting. . . .

At this point . . . , it may be useful to enumerate in review those positions which, for the reasons indicated in the preceding paragraphs, we reject. . . .

1. A policy of avoiding war at all costs, whether explicitly stated or implicit in a series of actions which deprive the United States of its military capabilities.

2. A policy of preventive general war, whether stated explicitly, or implicit in a set of actions which can only detonate such a war.

3. A policy of territorial retrenchment and withdrawal, which will invite the Soviet Union and Communist China to take over more and more countries and eventually to dominate and exploit all areas outside North America.

4. A policy which disregards or fails to utilize the strengths available in the non-Soviet world.

5. A policy which places exclusive reliance upon any one form of strength—whatever it may be—and is indifferent to the creation of other components of American strength.

In our view each of these policies would, if acted upon consistently, promote either the eventual victory of Soviet Communism or the convulsive catastrophe of a thermonuclear war. We cannot be positive that the policies to be considered later may not do the same. There are no safe bets in these times. But in the above-mentioned policies such disasters seem inherent, and at the very least they reduce our ability to respond with flexible strength to the many forms the challenge to us may take.

TOPIC 19

Alliances

When nations have interests in common, they may add legal precision to them and establish machinery for common execution of their policies by concluding an alliance. An alliance represents an expression of a pre-existing community of interests. An alliance without common interests is a scrap of paper. The aim of any operative alliance is to protect common interests or pursue common policies through a common effort.

Common policies may be pursued without a formal alliance. This occurs when nations are so fully aware of the general harmony of their interests that they act as if they were allies. This has been the case of Great Britain and the United States from the proclamation of the Monroe Doctrine in 1823 to the attack on Pearl Harbor in 1941.

►AMERICAN AND SOVIET ALLIANCE POLICIES

HANS J. MORGENTHAU

Alliances may be of different types: mutual or one-sided; general or limited; economic, military, or ideological; operative or inoperative.

And, alliances may be also monolithic or in the process of dissolution. The author of the following essay believes that Soviet and American alliances are in the process of loosening but not breaking up.

Alliances are a necessary function of the balance of power operating within a multiple-state system. Nations A and B, competing with each other, have three choices in order to maintain and improve their relative power positions. They can increase their own power, they can add to their own power the power of other nations, or they can withhold the power of other nations from the adversary. When they make the first choice, they embark upon an armaments race. When they choose the second and third alternatives, they pursue a policy of alliances.

Whether or not a nation shall pursue a policy of alliances is, then, not a matter of principle but of expediency. A nation will shun alliances if it believes that it is strong enough to hold its own unaided or that the burden of the commitments resulting from the alliance is likely to outweigh the ad-

A part of this selection was presented to the Annual Meeting of the American Political Science Association in 1957 and published in the Winter issue of *Confluence*, Vol. 6, No. 4, pp. 311-34. Also appeared as a chapter in *Alliance Policy in the Cold War*, ed. Arnold Wolfers, (Baltimore: The Johns Hopkins Press, 1959).

vantages to be expected. It is for one or the other or both of these reasons that, throughout the better part of their history, Great Britain and the United States have refrained from entering into peacetime alliances with other nations. . . .

Not every community of interests, calling for common policies and actions, also calls for legal codification in an explicit alliance. Yet, on the other hand, an alliance requires of necessity a community of interests for its foundation. Thucydides said that "identity of interest is the surest of bonds whether between states or individuals." . . . Under what conditions, then, does an existing community of interests require the explicit formulation of an alliance? What is it that an alliance adds to the existing community of interests?

An alliance adds precision, especially in the form of limitation, to an existing community of interests and to the general policies and concrete measures serving them. Glancing through the treaties of alliance of the seventeenth and eighteenth centuries, one is struck by the meticulous precision with which obligations to furnish troops, equipment, logistic support, food, money, and the like were defined. The interests nations have in common are not typically so precise and limited as to geographic region, objective, and appropriate policies as has been the American and British interest in the preservation of the European balance of power. Nor are they so incapable of precision and limitation as concerns the prospective common enemy. For while a typical alliance is directed against a specific nation or group of nations, the enemy of the Anglo-American community of interests could in the nature of things not be specified beforehand, since whoever threatens the European balance of power is the enemy. As Jefferson shifted his sympathies back and forth between Napoleon and Great Britain according to who seemed to threaten the balance of power at the time, so during the century following the Napoleonic Wars Great Britain and the United States had to decide in the light of circumstances ever liable to change who posed at the moment the greatest threat to the balance of power. This blanket character of the enemy, determined not individually but by the function he performs, brings to mind a similar characteristic of collective security, which is directed against the abstractly designed aggressor, whoever he may be.

The typical interests that unite two nations against a third are both more definite as concerns the determination of the enemy and less precise as concerns the objectives to be sought and the policies to be pursued. . . .

We can distinguish alliances serving identical, complementary, and ideological interests and policies. We can further distinguish mutual and one-sided, general and limited, temporary and permanent, operative and inoperative alliances.

The present Anglo-American alliance within NATO provides the classic example of an alliance serving identical interests; the objective of one partner, the preservation of the balance of power in Europe, is also the objective of the other. The alliance between the United States and Pakistan is one of many contemporary instances of an alliance serving complementary interests. For the United States it serves the primary purpose of expanding the scope of the policy of containment; for Pakistan it serves primarily the purpose of increasing her political, military, and economic potential *vis-à-vis* her neighbors.

The pure type of an ideological alliance is presented by the Treaty of the Holy Alliance of 1815 and the Atlantic Charter of 1941. Both documents laid down general moral principles to which the signatories pledged their adherence, and general objectives whose realization they pledged themselves to seek. The Treaty of the Arab League of 1945 provides a contemporary example of an alliance expressing, since the war against Israel of 1948, primarily ideological solidarity.

Much more typical is the addition of ideological commitments to material ones in one and the same treaty of alliance. Thus the Three Emperors League of 1873 provided for military assistance among Austria, Germany, and Russia in case of attack on any of them and at the same time emphasized the solidarity of the three monarchies against republican subversion. In our times, the ideological commitment against Communist subversion, inserted in treaties of alliance, performs a similar function. The ideological factor also manifests itself in the official interpretation of an alliance, based upon material interests, in terms of an ideological solidarity transcending the limitations of material interests. The conception of the Anglo-American alliance, common before the British invasion of Egypt in 1956, as all-inclusive and world-embracing, based upon common culture, political institutions, and ideals, is a case in point.

As concerns the political effect of this ideological factor upon an alliance, three possibilities must be distinguished. A purely ideological alliance, unrelated to material interests, cannot but be stillborn; it is unable to determine policies and guide actions and misleads by giving the appearance of political solidarity where there is none. The ideological factor, when it is superimposed upon an actual community of interests, can lend strength to the alliance by marshaling moral convictions and emotional preferences to its support. It can also weaken it by obscuring the nature and limits of the common interests that the alliance was supposed to make precise and by raising expectations, bound to be disappointed, for the extent of concerted policies and actions. For both these possibilities, the Anglo-American alliance can again serve as an example.

The distribution of benefits within an alliance should ideally be one of complete mutuality; here the services performed by the parties for each other are commensurate with the benefits received. This ideal is most likely to be approximated in an alliance concluded among equals in power and serving identical interests; here the equal resources of all, responding to equal incentives, serve one single interest. The other extreme in the distribution of benefits is one-sidedness, a *societas leonina* in which one party receives the lion's share of benefits while the other bears the main bulk of burdens. In so far as the object of such an alliance is the preservation of the territorial and political integrity of the receiving party, such an alliance is indistinguishable from a treaty of guarantee. Complementary interests lend themselves most easily to this kind of disproportion, since they are by definition different in substance and their comparative assessment is likely to be distorted by subjective interpretation. A marked superiority in power is bound to add weight to such interpretations.

The distribution of benefits is thus likely to reflect the distribution of power within an alliance, as does the determination of policies. A great power has a good chance to have its way with a weak ally as concerns benefits and policies, and it is for this reason that Machiavelli warned weak nations against making alliances with strong ones except by necessity. The relationship between the United States and South Korea exemplifies this situation.

However, this correlation between benefits, policies, and power is by no means inevitable. A weak nation may be able to exploit its relations with a strong ally by committing the latter to the support of its vital interests, which may mean nothing to the latter or may even run counter to its interests. In return, the weak nation may offer the strong ally its support, which typically is much less important to the latter than the latter's support is to the former. Historically, the relationship between Germany and Austria-Hungary before World War I was of this kind; the present relations of the United States with Pakistan and the regime of Chiang Kai-shek belong to the same type.

However, it is possible that a weak nation possesses an asset that is of such great value for its strong ally as to be irreplaceable. Here the unique benefit the former is able to grant or withhold may give it within the alliance a status completely out of keeping with the actual distribution of material power. The relationships between the United States and Iceland with regard to bases and between Great Britain and Iraq with regard to oil come to mind. . . .

A typical alliance attempts to transform a small fraction of the total interests of the contracting parties into common policies and measures. Some of these interests are irrelevant to the purposes of the alliance, others support them, others diverge from them, and still others are incompatible with them. Thus a typical alliance is imbedded in a dynamic field of diverse interests and purposes. Whether and for how long it will be operative depends upon the strength of the interests underlying it as over against the strength of the other interests of the nations concerned. The value and the chances of an alliance, however limited in scope, must be considered within the context of the overall policies within which it is expected to operate.

General alliances are typically of temporary duration and most prevalent in wartime. For the overriding common interest in winning the war and securing through the peace settlement the interests for which the war was waged is bound to yield, once victory is won and the peace treaties are signed, to the traditionally separate and frequently incompatible interests of the individual nations. On the other hand, there exists a correlation between the permanency of an alliance and the limited character of the interests it serves; for only such a specific, limited interest is likely to last long enough to provide the foundation for a durable alliance. The alliance between Great Britain and Portugal, concluded in 1703, has survived the centuries because Portugal's interest in the protection of her ports by the British fleet and the British interest in the control of the Atlantic approaches to Portugal have endured. Yet it can be stated as a general historical observation that while

alliance treaties have frequently assumed permanent validity by being concluded "in perpetuity" or for periods of ten or twenty years, they could not
have been more durable than the generally precarious and fleeting configurations of common interests that they were intended to serve. As a rule, they
have been short-lived.

The dependence of alliances upon the underlying community of interests
also accounts for the distinction between operative and inoperative alliances.
For an alliance to be operative, that is, to be able to co-ordinate the general
policies and concrete measures of its members, the latter must agree not only
on general objectives but on policies and measures as well. Many alliances
have remained scraps of paper because no such agreement was forthcoming,
and it was not forthcoming because the community of interests did not extend
beyond general objectives to concrete policies and measures. The Franco-
Russian alliances of 1935 and 1944 and the Anglo-Russian alliance of 1942
are cases in point. The legal validity of a treaty of alliance and its propagandistic invocation can easily deceive the observer about its actual operational value. The correct assessment of this value requires the examination of
the concrete policies and measures that the contracting parties have taken in
implementation of the alliance.

II

It is obvious that the alliance systems as they exist today on either side
of the Iron Curtain are different from what they were during the first decade
following World War II. While a decade ago they opposed each other as two
monolithic blocs, they are today beset by problems that threaten their internal
cohesion. While these problems do not at present threaten these alliance systems with outright dissolution, they may well do so in a not-too-distant future.
But they already put into question the unity of effective action that is the very
purpose of all alliances. This holds true in different degrees of the three major
alliance systems existing today: the Atlantic Alliance (NATO), the Western
alliances with nations outside Europe, and the Communist alliances. They
have all been subject to the same eroding forces that have in different ways
affected the mutual interests and policies of the members of the different alliance systems.

The vital interest of the United States in the protection of the nations of
Western Europe against Russian domination is identical with the interest of
these nations in preserving their national independence. Yet this foundation
of the Atlantic Alliance has undergone a change both subtle and drastic. The
Atlantic Alliance is beset by a crisis that the events of November 1956 have
made obvious but not created. The beginnings of that crisis antedate the
autumn of 1956 by several years; for the conditions that created the Atlantic
Alliance during World War II and maintained it during the first decade following it have changed.

Seen from the perspective of the nations of Western Europe, three factors sustained the Atlantic Alliance in the decade following World War II:
the atomic monopoly of the United States, the economic weakness of the nations of Western Europe, and the intransigence of Stalinist policies. The con-

junction of these factors confronted the nations of Western Europe with the choice between suicide and the acceptance of the political, economic, and military support of the United States. In other words, the Atlantic Alliance was for the nations of Western Europe a prerequisite of national survival.

This connection between national survival and the Atlantic Alliance is no longer as close nor as obvious as it used to be. The atomic monopoly of the United States provided the nations of Western Europe with absolute protection against Russian conquest. With the Soviet Union having become an atomic power equal to the United States, the Atlantic Alliance is no longer for the nations of Western Europe solely a protection, but has become also a liability. The atomic stalemate threatens not only the two superpowers, but also their allies, with total destruction. The nations of Western Europe do not take it for granted that the United States, being thus threatened, is willing to commit suicide on their behalf.

Paradoxical as it may seem, the drastically increased threat of Soviet power has thus drastically weakened the Atlantic Alliance. The Soviet Union has not been slow to point out, and the man in the street in Western Europe has not been slow to understand, that if there is a chance for the nations of Western Europe to survive in an atomic war, it may lie in not being too closely identified, or perhaps not being identified at all, with the United States. Thus a latent neutralism has had a slowly corrosive influence upon the Atlantic Alliance. The rise of this neutralism in Western Europe as a popular movement is not primarily the result of Communist propaganda, or of faintness of heart, or political decadence, but of the new objective conditions under which the nations of Western Europe must live in the age of the atomic stalemate.

Second, the distribution of power within the Atlantic Alliance has greatly changed since the beginning of the fifties. The weak nations have grown stronger and the nations defeated in World War II are in the process of growing very strong indeed. Ten years ago, the nations of Western Europe had either to join the United States or go bankrupt economically and disintegrate socially. The economic recovery of the nations of Western Europe has greatly diminished their dependence upon the United States. The Coal and Steel Community, Euratom, the Common Market, and the development of East-West trade are likely to decrease it still more. Thus while the nations of Western Europe are still in need of American economic aid, that aid is no longer a question of life and death as it was ten years ago. Today, they have, or at least have evidence that they soon will have, an alternative. They can stand on their own feet again and look beyond the wall of containment for new outlets for their energies and products.

These factors affect with particular intensity West Germany's attitude to the Atlantic Alliance. Their effect is strengthened by the political issue that has the widest, and is likely to have a lasting and ever-deepening, emotional appeal: unification. The Atlantic Alliance has been presented to West Germany, both by American and German official spokesmen, as the instrument through which unification would be achieved. While this view was from the outset open to serious doubts on theoretical grounds, the historic experience of its failure has led to a crisis of confidence that is likely to deepen as time goes on without, despite German membership in the Atlantic Alliance, bringing unification closer. The Atlantic Alliance, far from being supported as the instrument of unification, is ever more loudly and widely blamed as the main obstacle to unification.

The Soviet Union has been eager to use these new political, military, and economic conditions under which the nations of Western Europe live for the purpose of weakening and ultimately destroying the Atlantic Alliance. What has been called the "new look" of Soviet foreign policy is essentially a new flexibility that has taken the place of the monotony of the Stalinist threats. In the face of these threats, no nation that wanted to survive as a nation had any choice; thus Stalin was really the architect of the Atlantic Alliance. The new Soviet foreign policy alternately threatens and tempts, as the occasion seems to require, but always seeks to hold before the eyes of Western Europe an acceptable or even preferable alternative to the Atlantic Alliance. In consequence, the Atlantic Alliance has lost much of its urgency and even vitality. Great Britain and France, for instance, no longer feel that they have to subordinate their separate national interests to the common defense against the Soviet Union, and they have begun, in different degrees, to pursue those interests regardless, and sometimes at the expense, of the common interests of the alliance; they have also begun to vent openly their resentment at their lack of great-power status and to allow their policies to be influenced by it. The rise of Germany to a position of political, military, and economic eminence, with all the fears and expectations this rise must cause in both Western and Eastern Europe, cannot help but add to the opportunities of the new Soviet foreign policy.

As viewed from the vantage point of the United States, the Atlantic Alliance is also in the process of undergoing a subtle change, which in the end is bound to be a drastic one. For the United States, the Atlantic Alliance is the political and military implementation of its perennial interest in the maintenance of the European balance of power. However, the military implementation of this interest is likely to change under the impact of a new technology of warfare. As long as the main deterrent to Russian aggression remains the atomic bomb delivered by plane, the military strategy of the United States requires military installations in Western Europe; and the nations of Western Europe have a corresponding interest in providing them. To the extent that intercontinental and navy-borne missiles will replace airplanes as the means of atomic attack, the interest in American military installations in Western Europe will diminish on both sides of the Atlantic. This interest will decrease still further when some of the nations of Western Europe have atomic weapons and, hence, a deterrent of their own. When this day comes, the Atlantic Alliance will take on a new complexion, probably losing some of its specific military aspects and tending to revert to an implicit community of interests similar to that which tied the United States to Great Britain from 1823 to 1941. It is to this contingency that the British Minister of Defense, Mr. Duncan Sandys, appears to have been referring when he justified in April 1957, in the House of Commons, the British emphasis on atomic armaments by asking: "When the United States has developed the five-thousand-mile intercontinental ballistic rocket can we really be sure that every American Administration will go on looking at things in the same way?"

However, the interests of the United States and the nations of Western Europe are not limited to that continent. Those of the United States and Great Britain are world-wide, and France is engaged in Africa. While the interests of the United States and of the nations of Western Europe indeed coincide in the preservation of the latter's independence, they do not necessarily coincide elsewhere. The coincidence or divergence of these non-European interests has had, as it was bound to have, a strengthening or debilitating effect upon the Atlantic Alliance itself; and the vital interest of all concerned in this alliance has, in turn, limited their freedom of action outside Europe.

The United States in particular, dealing with the colonial revolutions, which are directed primarily against Great Britain and France, has been continuously confronted with a painful and inherently insoluble dilemma. The horns of that dilemma are the interest of the United States in the continuing strength of Great Britain and France as its principal allies and the American interest in preventing the colonial revolutions from falling under the sway of communism. If the United States underwrites the colonial position of Great Britain or France, as it did in Indochina, it may, at best, strengthen temporarily its principal European allies, but it will impair its standing with the anticolonial peoples of Asia and Africa. If the United States sides unreservedly with the Afro-Asian bloc, as it did in the United Nations on the occasion of the Suez Canal crisis of the autumn of 1956, it weakens Great Britain and France and, in consequence, the Atlantic Alliance.

Faced with this dilemma, which can be solved only at the price of impairing the vital interests of the United States in one or the other respect, the United States has inevitably been reduced to straddling the fence by supporting halfheartedly on one occasion one side and on another occasion the other side, or else keeping hands off altogether. Algeria and Cyprus exemplify at present the dilemma and its evasion. In such situations, then, the Atlantic Alliance does not operate at all; for there are no common interests that could support its operation.

This has always been obviously true of Western policies toward Communist China. The policy of the United States has been one of implacable hostility, while Great Britain has sought accommodation. The Atlantic Alliance is here not only not operating, but the policies of its two principal members have been consistently at cross-purposes. The success of one would of necessity mean the failure of the other.

That such divergencies of interest and policy have not imposed greater stresses upon the Atlantic Alliance and have left it essentially unimpaired testifies to its inherent strength. But that strength cannot be taken for granted. The common interests underlying the Atlantic Alliance have thus far prevailed over the divergent ones only because of the conviction of the members of the alliance that they have a greater stake in their common than in their divergent interests. The paramountcy of the common interests has thus far kept the divergent ones in check. But in recent years the latter have grown stronger and the former, weaker. If this trend should continue unchecked, it would indeed put in jeopardy the very survival of the Atlantic Alliance.

Common interests are the rock on which all alliances are built. Yet upon this rock all kinds of structures may be erected, some solid and spacious, others crumbling and confining. In other words, there are good and bad alliances, some that work smoothly and are enthusiastically supported, others that are cumbersome and are grudgingly accepted as a lesser evil. While the existence of an alliance depends upon a community of interests, its quality is determined by the manner in which common interests are translated into concrete policies and day-by-day measures.

It is in this latter respect that the Atlantic Alliance must cause concern. Here, too, the crisis of November 1956 has made obvious defects that antedate that crisis. Three such defects have, continuously and to an ever-increasing degree, impaired the operation of the Atlantic Alliance: its organizational structure; the policies, domestic and international, of its leading members; and the prestige enjoyed by some of its leading statesmen.

The common interest of the members of the Atlantic Alliance in the military protection of their independence has found its organizational expression in the North Atlantic Treaty Organization. The strategic conception that underlies NATO is the assumption that the European members of the Atlantic Alliance are able to defend themselves through a co-operative effort against a military attack by the Soviet Union. But NATO has never developed a convincing philosophy of its concrete military purpose. All members of NATO are agreed upon one objective: to defend their independence without having to fight for it—that is, to deter aggression. But how is this purpose to be achieved? Is primary reliance to be placed upon atomic retaliation with the local forces of NATO performing the function of the "plate glass" or "trip wire," or is a prospective aggressor to be deterred by the inherent military strength of local forces? The members of NATO have not seen eye to eye on this fundamental question, and NATO itself, in its official proclamations and policies, has not seemed to be of one mind either.

More particularly, the declared purposes of NATO have been consistently at variance with the measures requested of its members for implementation of these purposes, and the measures requested, in turn, have been invariably at variance with the measures actually taken. If the strategic purpose of NATO is the ground defense of Western Europe against an attack by the Red Army, none of the different forces successively requested by NATO have appeared to be sufficient for that purpose, nor have the forces actually provided by the members of NATO ever even come close to fulfilling the requests. Furthermore, declared purposes, requested measures, and the measures actually taken have been subjected to a number of drastic and confusing changes that cannot be explained exclusively by the revolutionary transformations that military technology has been undergoing.

This confusion in policy, in itself conducive to political disunity and friction in day-by-day operations, has been magnified by the elaborate organizational superstructure that is intended to put the policies of NATO into practice. This superstructure, encompassing a plethora of committees in charge of co-ordinating a variety of political, military, and economic policies of the member states, must, even under the best of circumstances, make for friction and inefficiency. It magnifies these defects because it is much too ambitious in purpose and elaborate in operation for the agreed purpose of NATO to support it. In the absence of agreement on philosophy and basic policy, the elaborate organizational superstructure has been, as Generals de Gaulle and Montgomery pointed out in the fall of 1958, a source of weakness for the Atlantic Alliance.

An alliance, in its day-by-day operations, rests in good measure upon the mutual confidence in the willingness and ability of its members to co-operate effectively in achieving the common purpose. That confidence, in turn, rests upon the quality of the over-all policies pursued by the members of the alliance and upon the character and ability of its leading statesmen. In both respects, the Atlantic Alliance has shown itself to be deficient.

There can be no doubt that in both respects the prestige of the United States as the leader and backbone of the Atlantic Alliance has drastically declined. It is irrelevant for the purposes of this analysis whether this decline is rooted in objective facts or whether it is but the result of subjective pre-conceptions and emotions. Rightly or wrongly, the United States is no longer looked upon by its allies, as it was during the period immediately following World War II, as the leader whose strength and resolution, if not wisdom, can be relied upon to keep the Atlantic Alliance on an even course. Several factors are responsible for the crisis of confidence.

The main purpose of the Atlantic Alliance being the mutual defense of its members and the United States being its military backbone, the European members of the Atlantic Alliance have a natural interest in the military policies of the United States. They are not reassured by them. For the American emphasis upon the atomic deterrent and the concomitant neglect of con-ventional forces, operating within the new distribution of military power dis-cussed above, spells for them, if the deterrent should fail, either total destruc-tion or virtually total lack of defense. In either case, the alliance fails in its purpose.

However, it is not only effective power that allies expect from the strong-est member of the alliance. They also expect a reliable foreign policy that takes the interests of the allies into account. In the lack of political confi-dence between the United States and its European allies the Atlantic Alliance is weakened at still another point. In foreign policy it is sometimes, but by no means always, useful to keep the enemy guessing. But to keep your allies guessing, most of the time and on matters vital to them, about what you in-tend to do is bound to erode the foundations of confidence upon which the alliance in its day-by-day operations must rest. The allies of the United States have noted discrepancies between the policy pronouncements of our leaders and the actual policies pursued, which appear to them to have evolved into a consistent pattern of unreliability. Liberation, the unleashing of Chiang Kai-shek, agonizing reappraisal, the "new look," intervention in Indochina, the internationalization of the Suez Canal, the protection of the rights of Israel have been proclaimed as objectives of American foreign policy. Yet, in most instances, the foreign policy of the United States appears to our allies to have been at variance with these pronouncements or, at the very least, their implementation remains in doubt.

This slow accumulation of loss of confidence reached a critical stage in the Suez Canal crisis; for here unreliability in policy appeared to be joined by indifference, if not hostility, to the vital interests of America's principal allies. For the vital interests of the United States and its allies to coincide in Europe and diverge elsewhere is one thing; for the vital interests of its principal allies elsewhere to be opposed and destroyed by the United States is quite another. To the former, the allies of the United States could reconcile themselves with relative equanimity; the latter could not help but raise for our allies the crucial question as to whether the Atlantic Alliance was worth so high a price. That they answered the question in the affirmative testifies to the vitality of the alliance. Their resentment was kindled by the actual demonstration of their inability to pursue active foreign policies of their own without the support and against the opposition of one or the other of the superpowers. Thus under the dramatic impact of the experience that saw their interests and power destroyed in a region vital to themselves, with the approval and active participation of the United States, the Atlantic Alliance tended to transform itself for our allies from an association of like-minded nations into a burden grudgingly borne.

That like-mindedness has in the past been the result not only of a community of interests, but also of a common dedication to the ideals of freedom. When in the aftermath of World War II Communist totalitarianism threatened to engulf Western Europe, the United States was looked upon by its European allies as the symbol and the incarnation of that dedication. That image of the United States was tarnished by the temporary decline of freedom within its borders during the McCarthy period. Yet, while American prestige has been largely restored under the impact of the revival of the traditions of American freedom, there has remained a latent skepticism and general malaise, which cast their shadow over the Atlantic Alliance.

As far as long-range policies are concerned, the relations among nations must indeed be conceived in terms of interests. As concerns their day-by-day relations, we must also think in terms of personalities. We say that the United States and Great Britain have agreed on a certain policy, but tend to forget that Great Britain and the United States are abstractions and that in actuality the President and Secretary of State of the United States and the Prime Minister and Secretary for Foreign Affairs of Great Britain, speaking in the name of their respective nations, have agreed with each other. The smooth and effective operation of an alliance, then, depends in good measure upon the relations of trust and respect among its principal statesmen. There is no gainsaying the fact that the decline in such relations has become a great handicap in the day-by-day operations of the Atlantic Alliance. Regardless of the objective merits of the case, there can be no doubt that the leaders of our European allies no longer have the same confidence in the judgment and the authority of our leaders that they had in times past. These reactions have increased the strains under which the Atlantic Alliance operates at present.

The traditional political rhetoric on both sides of the Atlantic has tended to gloss over all these stresses and strains and has made it appear as though the Atlantic Alliance were something broader and smoother and also something more diffuse than it actually is. It is indeed built upon a rock of common interests, but the rock is of limited dimensions and its surfaces are sometimes rough. In spite of the great damage that the crisis of November 1956 has done to the Atlantic Alliance, it has been useful in circumscribing more closely its limits and demonstrating, for all to see, its still considerable strength.

III

While the Atlantic Alliance reposes upon the firm foundation of identical interests, no such general and reassuring statement can be made about the Western alliances with nations outside Europe. Considering Asia and the Middle East, it can be said only of the American alliances with Formosa, South Korea, South Viet Nam, and Japan that they are based upon identical interests. These nations, with the exception of Japan, owe their very existence as nations to the interests and power of the United States. Their survival as nations is inextricably tied to the interests and power of the United States. Yet only their complete dependence upon the United States has prevented some, if not all, of these nations from pursuing policies at variance with those of the United States. Thus the stability of these alliances rests upon both identical interests and extreme discrepancy of power.

Our alliance with Japan, like that with Germany, was during the first decade following World War II based upon the dual foundation of identical interests and overwhelming American power. Yet neither foundation can any longer be taken for granted. Three factors have combined to restore Japan's freedom of choice. First, Japan has again become a strong power. If the wartime memories of Japan's imperialism were not still alive in the rest of Asia, Japan would be a natural candidate for taking over the economic and political leadership of non-Communist Asia. Second, the atomic stalemate has had the same psychological effect on Japan as it had on Western Europe; the American alliance has become for Japan a mixed blessing if not a liability. Finally, to the degree that the aggressiveness of Stalinist and Chinese Korean war policies is replaced by a new flexibility that stresses the complementary character of Russian, Chinese, and Japanese interests, Japan may find a practical alternative to its identification with the United States.

The other Asian alliances, of which SEATO and the Baghdad Pact provide the outstanding examples, are of an entirely different type. They have three characteristics in common: complementary interests tending toward transformation into incompatible ones, a radically unequal distribution of benefits, and ideological emphasis.

These alliances, on the face of them, were conceived in terms of common action on behalf of common interests. However, in view of the remoteness of the apparent *casus foederis,* that is, Communist attack upon a member, and of the virtual impossibility, in case of such an attack, for most members to act in common, commitment to common action has receded into the background and been distilled into an anti-Communist ideological commitment. Of the Asian members, this commitment requires nothing more than membership in the alliance; it requires no common objective, policy, and action—beyond anticommunism at home and abroad. Yet of the Western members, especially the United States, it requires specific policies and actions on behalf of the Asian members.

The Asian members are interested in these alliances primarily because of the economic, military, and political support they receive from the United States. Many of them consider their membership in the alliance to constitute a special claim upon the American Treasury, American weapons, and American political support for their special national aspirations. In other words, this support is the price the United States pays for having the receiving nations as allies. However valuable it judges this membership to be, in terms of actual policies and measures, the United States bears a unilateral burden. The United States is under continuous pressure to act as an ally while the Asian allies, once they have signed the treaty of alliance, preserve virtually complete freedom of action. Their foreign policies, for instance *vis-à-vis* China, could hardly be different if they were not members of the alliance. In order to show the irrelevance of the alliance in terms of common objectives, policies, and actions, the Prime Minister of an Asian nation has indeed gone so far as to equate his country's membership in SEATO with membership in the United Nations.

In so far as all that the West wants is the maximum number of Asian allies and all that the Asian allies want is the maximum amount of Western support for their own specific national objectives, the two interests can be said to complement each other, provided these objectives are compatible with those of the other allies. In view of the Western emphasis upon the ideological character of the alliance and the concomitant neglect of concrete interests and policies, this compatibility will exist only by accident and not by design and, in view of the nature of the interests involved, is bound to be precarious. It is bound to disintegrate whenever a latent conflict of interests between two allies or an ally and another nation becomes acute. The conflicts between Pakistan and India over Kashmir, between Great Britain and Greece, and Turkey and Greece, over Cyprus, and between Iraq and Israel are cases in point. It is only because these alliances limit a commitment to common action to the very unlikely event of Communist aggression that they have survived such incompatibilities. The United States, in particular, is frequently forced into the uncomfortable position of having either to straddle the fence, as between Great Britain and Greece, or else to sacrifice its interests to its alliance, as between India and Pakistan.

Thus, by virtue of its alliance, the United States increases the armed strength of Pakistan and thereby forces India to increase its expenditures for armaments from thirty million pounds in 1955 to ninety million pounds in 1957. This diversion of scarce funds from economic development to armaments threatens India with an economic and political disaster, which the United States has a vital interest in staving off through financial aid. In consequence, the United States engages, as it were, in an armaments race with itself by proxy, its left hand supporting Pakistan by virtue of the alliance, its right hand aiding India by virtue of its vital interests.

As concerns the alliances among the nations of the Western Hemisphere, appearances are deceptive. As long as the supremacy of the United States within the Western Hemisphere provided unchallengeable protection for the independence of the American nations, these alliances could indeed be taken for granted. For the United States, these alliances provided complete safety, since, in view of its unchallengeable supremacy within the hemisphere and of the protection of two oceans, its security could be endangered only by a non-American nation acting in concert with an American one. For the other American nations, these alliances provided complete security from great-power domination, since the United States would use its superior power only for the protection and not for the subversion of their national independence.

This identity of interests and the ability of the United States to implement it has from the proclamation of the Monroe Doctrine to this day provided the rationale and lifeblood of the American state system. The intercontinental guided missile confronts this system with a challenge never before experienced. For the supremacy of the United States within the Western Hemisphere, as unchallengeable as ever from within, is of no avail as protection against these novel weapons of tomorrow. The United States can no more protect its American allies against these weapons than it can protect itself. The American allies of the United States will then view the alliance with the same misgivings with which the European allies and Japan view it already. They may no longer regard their interests to be identical with those of the United States and may conclude that safety lies not in closeness to, but rather in distance from, the United States.

IV

The Communist alliances present three different types, which must be sharply distinguished: the alliances of the Soviet Union and China with North Korea and North Viet Nam, the alliances between the Soviet Union and the nations of Eastern Europe, and the alliances of the Soviet Union with China and the United Arab Republic.

The position of North Korea and North Viet Nam within the Communist alliances is identical in the particulars that interest us here with the position of South Korea and South Viet Nam within their alliances with the United States. It is marked by complete identity of interests and extreme disparity of power.

The alliances between the Soviet Union and the nations of Eastern Europe, codified in the Warsaw Pact of 1955, are in a class by themselves. They are not true alliances in that they do not transform a pre-existing community of interests into legal obligations. It is their distinctive quality that a community of interests is irrelevant for their existence and operation and that they are founded on nothing but unchallengeable superiority of power. Power is here not superimposed upon common interests, as in a genuine alliance, but becomes a substitute for them. Thus the nation possessing such unchallengeable power makes the other contracting party subservient to its interests, regardless, and in spite of the divergence, of the latter's interests. Such so-called treaties of alliance are in truth in the nature of treaties establishing, in the legal form of alliances, relationships that are a modern version of protectorates or suzerainty, and the nations subjected to them are correctly called satellites rather than allies.

The nature of this relationship has not been affected, although it might well be in the future, by the development of a community of interests between the Soviet Union and certain satellites, such as Poland and Czechoslovakia. That community of interests results from the emergence of Germany as the predominant power in Europe. Poland and Czechoslovakia, situated as they are between two nations of superior strength, have had to seek protection either from one neighbor against the other or from Western Europe against both. Their present relationship to the Soviet Union provides this protection. Given a change in both Russian and German policies, this protective function might well form the basis for a future genuine alliance.

While this development is purely speculative, the relations between the Soviet Union and the satellites have undergone in recent years an actual transformation similar to that which has affected the Atlantic Alliance, and for similar reasons. The emergence of an atomic stalemate between the United States and the Soviet Union has loosened the ties of the satellite rela-tionship. As long as the military contest between East and West pitted Amer-ican atomic bombs against the Red Army, the latter could be regarded as the indispensable guardian of the Russian empire within and without. With the growth of Russian atomic power, the importance of the Red Army declined. The threat of mutual atomic destruction has stimulated both the desire for self-preservation in the form of neutralism and the aspirations for national independence that had lain dormant under the yoke of the Red Army.

These latent tendencies were brought to the fore by the "new look" of Russian policy following the death of Stalin. In response to it, the spirit of national independence started to push against the lid of Russian oppression, and the Russian proconsuls yielded to the pressure. They rehabilitated most of the national leaders who had tried to combine communism and at least a measure of national independence and relaxed the authoritarian controls over the economic and intellectual life of the satellites. Yet popular reaction went beyond domestic reforms to embrace national independence, that is, the end of the satellite relationship itself. At this point, the Soviet Union called a halt, reasserting the paramountcy of its interests supported by the supremacy of its power.

The events that occurred in the fall of 1956 in Hungary and Poland have clearly demonstrated in different ways the nature of the satellite relationship in contrast to a genuine alliance. Both countries, through their revolts against Russian rule, sought essentially to reassert their distinct national interests against those of the Soviet Union. In the process they were bound to put into question, and Hungary did openly challenge, the satellite status from which derived, in terms of law and power, their subservience to the Soviet Union. Yet while the Soviet Union could afford to make political, economic, and even military concessions, it could not risk the disintegration of its predominance over Eastern Europe by allowing the satellite system itself to be challenged. It was at this point that it brought its superior power to bear upon Hungary and forestalled, through this pointed example, a similarly open challenge on the part of Poland and other satellites.

In contrast, the alliances of the Soviet Union with China and the United Arab Republic are genuine alliances, based as they are upon a community of interests upon which the preponderant power of the Soviet Union is merely superimposed. The exact nature of the community of interests between the Soviet Union and China is a matter for speculation. Russian and Chinese interests appear to be identical in so far as their common objective is the strengthening and expansion of the Communist, and the weakening and retraction of the anti-Communist, camp. They appear to be complementary in so far as the alliance serves the Chinese interest in economic and military development and the Russian interest in keeping the United States militarily engaged and politically handicapped in the Far East.

Yet it cannot serve the interests of the Soviet Union to promote the development of Chinese power to the point where it threatens to jeopardize the present predominance of Russian power. On the other hand, China has a vital interest in reaching that point and thus making itself independent from Russian good will. For the governments of both nations know that if and when modern technology has been added to Chinese superiority in man power under strong political direction, China will have become the most powerful nation on earth. It is this eventuality that the Soviet Union must dread and try to forestall and that China must welcome and try to realize. This potential conflict of vital interests overshadows the alliance between China and the Soviet Union. It allows the Soviet Union for the time being to restrain Chinese policies, and it gives China the opportunity of exploiting for its advantage the actual and potential conflicts between the Soviet Union and its satellites and among the different groups competing for power within the Soviet Union.

The alliance between the Soviet Union and the United Arab Republic serves clearly complementary interests. The United Arab Republic is enabled by the military support it receives from the Soviet Union to pursue actively its specific interests in the Middle East and North Africa. The Soviet Union, on the other hand, has no stake in these specific interests except in so far as their active pursuit serves to maintain a state of tension that keeps the Western nations engaged and handicapped in still another region and threatens them with economic distress.

V

Considering the over-all picture of the alliances as it emerges from this analysis, one is impressed by the similarity of the changes that have occurred in the structure of the European alliances on both sides of the Iron Curtain. The seemingly irreversible trend toward a two-bloc system that marked the immediate postwar era has been arrested, if not reversed. The uncommitted nations not only want to remain uncommitted but have, with a few exceptions, also shown the ability to do so. On the other hand, many of the European nations that are committed as allies of one or the other of the superpowers would like to join the ranks of the uncommitted nations but have, with the exception of Yugoslavia, been unable to do so. They have at best been able to move to the outer confines of the blocs to which they belong, but have had to stop there. In consequence, the two-bloc system is in the process of loosening but not of breaking up.

The satellites may become even more unwilling and unreliable partners of the Soviet Union than they are already. Short of outside intervention, they cannot move out of the Soviet orbit as long as Russian interest backed by Russian power keeps them there. However, the interest of Russia in the domination of Eastern Europe has been perennial, regardless of drastic changes in the personnel, philosophy, and structure of government. The weakening of that interest cannot be foreseen short of a revolution in military technology that would make the control of outlying territory irrelevant. The power of the Soviet Union to keep the satellites under control cannot be challenged from within and is not likely to be challenged from without. Yet the alliance between the Soviet Union and China is a marriage of temporary convenience, which contains in the very terms of its existence the seeds of trouble.

The fate that may be in store for the Atlantic Alliance is similarly not its formal dissolution but rather its slow erosion to the point of becoming inoperative. The common fear of communism, either as subversion from within or aggression from without, and the common dedication to the values of Western civilization are likely to remain stronger than the disruptive tendencies of divergent and incompatible interests and thus to keep the common framework of the Atlantic Alliance intact. The demonstrated inability of even Great Britain and France to pursue positive foreign policies against the opposition of the United States adds to this outward stability of the Atlantic Alliance. The real danger lies in this common framework becoming an empty shell, drained of its vitality. History abounds with legal compacts, constitutional devices, and institutional forms that have survived, sometimes—as in the case of the Holy Roman Empire—for centuries, as ritualistic observances, or in the words of Chief Justice Marshall "a solemn mockery," without any longer being capable of directing the interests of men into the channels of common policies and actions. The Atlantic Alliance is indeed in danger of becoming just such a ritual to which nations continue to pay lip service, whose procedures they still observe, and whose institutional forms they maintain, while they plan and act as though it did not exist.

The danger that threatens the Atlantic Alliance from the unsettled German problem is, however, more serious than that. The tension between the German commitment to the Atlantic Alliance and the national goal of unification, to be achieved only with Russian consent, inevitably raises in German minds the question of whether that commitment and this objective are truly compatible and whether the former must not be sacrificed in order to achieve the latter. The logic of the argument implicit in this question can be prevented from becoming the rationale of the actual policy of Germany only by the intransigence of Russian, and the wisdom of American, policies. The danger of German defection from the Atlantic Alliance, then, raises in specific terms the general issue of the merits of our alliance policy and of our response to the structural changes that our alliances have undergone in recent times.

Our alliance policy partakes of the doctrinaire, legalistic, and mechanical character of much of American foreign policy. These perennial vices reappear here in a new setting. Instead of recognizing that there are useful, harmful, and superfluous alliances according to circumstances and discriminating among them in view of the interests to be served and the policies to be pursued, we have followed what might be called the collector's approach to alliances: the more alliances, the better. Or to put it more elaborately: the more nations sign a legal document declaring their support for our policies, the better. While once we were, on principle, against all "entangling alliances," now we are, again on principle, in favor of all alliances.

This emphasis upon the quantity of alliances and, more particularly, upon their military advantages—actual or illusory—has tended to jeopardize our political interests. Frequently, our allies have turned our interest in the alliance per se to their political advantage, without any corresponding political advantage accruing to us or, at worst, at the expense of our political interests. In consequence, the weak members of the alliance, knowing what they want to get out of it, have tended to convert the alliance into an instrument of their policies with the United States paying the political, military, and economic cost.

This tendency to see intrinsic merit in any alliance, regardless of the interests to be served, the benefits to be expected, and the liabilities to be met, has been most pronounced in Asia. SEATO, originating in an indiscriminate invitation by the United States to join, is indeed the classic example of such a misconceived alliance. Its membership was determined not by the United States in view of its interests but by the other members in view of theirs. Nor has the issue of the mutuality of benefits and liabilities been ever squarely faced. More particularly, the alliance has never been correlated to our over-all Asian interests, which—except for Formosa, South Korea, and South Viet Nam—are political rather than military.

SEATO is for the United States a useless alliance from the military point of view and a harmful one politically and economically in that it alienates the broad masses of Asians and imposes economic burdens without benefits. NATO, on the other hand, especially in view of its elaborate organizational superstructure but also in its very existence, may well prove to be a superfluous alliance—a view held by a minority within and outside the government when NATO was created in 1949. It may well be asked again, as it was then, whether the obvious identity of interests between the United States and the nations of Western Europe could not have been adequately served by a unilateral guarantee on the part of the United States, fashioned after the model of the Monroe Doctrine. While the very existence of NATO has made this question obviously academic, the rationale underlying it could still be put into practice by dismantling what is useless and harmful in NATO and strengthening what is useful, essential, and lasting. If the United States fails to reduce in time the structure of the alliances in Europe and Asia to the dimensions required by the interests that it has in common with its allies, it must be prepared to face sometime in the future a real crisis of its alliances, born of disappointment and divergent interests. While it now oscillates between unilateral action oblivious of the interests and sensibilities of its allies and excessive concern for the quantity of legal commitments, it will then have no choice but to go it alone.

These observations culminate in the conclusion that the problem of alliances must be considered in the context of the over-all character of world politics. If the task facing a nation is primarily military, not to be mastered by its isolated strength alone, a policy of alliances is the answer; and this answer is still the correct one in Europe and in certain exposed regions of Asia. In so far as the task is political, requiring a variety of means applied with subtlety, discrimination, and imagination, a policy of alliances will be useless, if not harmful; and this is indeed the situation that confronts the United States in most of the world where the issue is political allegiance and not military defense. A policy of alliances, in its doctrinaire insistence upon joining the club, in its legalistic concern with signatures and stipulations, in its mechanical counting of heads, then, serves as a substitute for political creativeness, the lack of which it may temporarily conceal. What it can neither conceal nor stave off is failure, which attends upon wrong policies as punishment follows the crime.

►STRESSES AND STRAINS IN "GOING IT WITH OTHERS"

ARNOLD WOLFERS

The success of American collective defense policies depends to a large extent on the United States' ability to maintain solidarity between nations composing the free world.

This problem is examined in the following penetrating analysis written by the Director of the Washington Center of Foreign Policy Research of Johns Hopkins University and Sterling Professor Emeritus of International Relations at Yale University.

Even before World War II came to an end, there were unmistakable indications that a radical shift was going to take place in American peacetime foreign policy. The traditional policy of "going it alone" was to be replaced by a policy of "going it with others." This change did not reflect any expectation that a new threat to American security would follow upon the defeat of the Axis coalition and make the United States dependent on the military support of others. It was assumed, on the contrary, that after the war the United States could look forward to a period of friendly relations with all of the remaining major powers. However, considerations of national security did

From *Alliance Policy in the Cold War,* ed. Arnold Wolfers (Baltimore: The Johns Hopkins Press, 1959), pp. 1-13.

affect American thinking and were a dominant motive behind the break with tradition. Isolationist sentiments vanished as a result of the bitter experiences of two world wars, which, it was believed, could have been avoided if the United States had collaborated with others prior to the outbreak of hostilities. What appeared to be needed, then, was American participation in an international organization devoted to the preservation of peace and the punishment of aggression. Only later, when the Soviet threat to American security materialized, did the new policy take on the form of an alliance policy directed against a specific country or group of countries.

The American response to the threat of Soviet or Sino-Soviet expansion is too narrowly described by "alliance policy" if the term "alliance" is used in the customary sense of a pact of mutual military assistance. For brevity's sake, however, "alliance policy" is employed . . . to cover all efforts to prevent other countries from siding with the camp of the Soviet opponent. As used here, the term suggests an American Cold War policy directed toward the development of an extensive system of alignments in which actual military alliances form the iron core.

The scope of American foreign policy is not, of course, exhausted by efforts to defend the non-Communist world against the economic, political, or ideological expansion of Soviet control. There continue to be other objectives of American policy, purely economic and humanitarian objectives, as well as the original purpose of preventing aggression from any quarter. These have not been wholly sacrificed to the necessities of the Cold War. However, as Sino-Soviet power has grown and as the threats to the United States and other non-Communist nations have become more fully appreciated, alliance or alignment policy for purposes of defense has come to dominate the scene and must do so as long as the East-West struggle continues unabated.

That the relations between the United States and its mighty Communist opponents should have become the focus of interest and attention both to policymakers and to students of international relations is not surprising. By comparison, the relationships within the non-Communist world seemed much less important and received, therefore, much less attention. Moreover, interallied relationships in view of their great diversity appear to elude treatment as a phenomenon with characteristics of its own. On closer examination, however, one can detect—apart from some more positive aspects—a series of disruptive or erosive forces operating within the entire American alignment system, forces that make their imprint on the relationships between the non-Communist countries and especially on the relations between the United States, the leader of the coalition, and the rest of its members. The present study seeks to throw light on these relations.

Because analysts are likely to concentrate on defects rather than on achievements, a distorted picture of the alliance system might be created if no mention were made here of the evidence of solidarity within the non-Communist world and of common resistance to Soviet blandishments and threats.

Again and again, conflicts either between the United States and other free countries (as in the Suez case) or between friends of the United States (as in the case of Cyprus) have threatened to defeat attempts at building up a comprehensive network of alignments. On other occasions, the attitudes of uncommitted countries have become a cause of alarm. At one moment, it looked as if Nasser were ready to cross over to the Soviet camp and to take other Arab countries with him; at another, Tito's defection to the East was confidently predicted. Yet, in spite of all the crises, rifts, and erosive forces besetting the Free World, none of its members—the "uncommitted" countries included—have so far voluntarily joined the Soviet bloc, and none of the countries allied with the United States in postwar collective defense arrangements have allowed resentment, fear, or a change of government to lead them into a policy of neutrality, although Iraq deserted its alliance with Great Britain. Quite generally, whenever the danger signals have been unmistakable, there has been a tendency to rally around the United States rather than to defect. Therefore, while complacency might well prove disastrous in view of the many centrifugal pulls to which the non-Communist world is exposed, it would be misleading to suggest that the future offers only the prospect of continuous and irreparable disintegration.

With these qualifications in mind, it would seem proper, however, to focus attention on the sources of serious tension between nations and groups of nations on whose solidarity the future independence and security of all of the non-Communist countries may depend. Only if the stresses and strains are carefully identified and understood is there hope of discovering appropriate ways of overcoming or reducing their harmful impact.

It might be argued that solidarity, even among close allies, has usually proved a perishable asset. Wartime coalitions have rarely long survived the termination of the war for which they were formed. However, the present danger is not the dissolution of a wartime coalition, but the dissolution of an alignment intended to prevent a war that has not yet occurred. Therefore, if the present coalition were to start breaking up before the threat that brought it into being had disappeared, it would fall far short of its original purpose. The return of the United States to a policy of "going it alone" would then become a desperate but inescapable alternative. Should the Cold War come to an end or fade into the background, conceivably the United States could afford to withdraw from military alliances while continuing its policy of "going it with others" in nonmilitary areas of co-operation and within the United Nations.

An inquiry into the chief causes of the many irritating conflicts that characterize relations with and among our friends and allies must take into consideration the numerous psychological features and motivations of the human actors in whose hands the conduct of alliance policy lies. The personalities and idiosyncrasies of leading statesmen, the preconceptions and biases of influential groups, and the emotions, resentments, fixed ideas, or peculiar anxieties of whole peoples can all become divisive forces. Since the success of a policy of alignment depends on the creation and maintenance of a sense of common interest, of mutual confidence among governments, and of solidarity among entire nations, these psychological factors can exert a decisive influence on the course of events. This is particularly true in an era in which leaders of unusual authority . . . carry so much responsibility that their personal approaches to problems or to one another may make or break alliances. Moreover, where so many peoples of widely divergent cultural backgrounds and ideologies are simultaneously involved in the process of hammering out common policies, national peculiarities like Indian pacifism or American moralism may become serious psychological handicaps, while such typical national attitudes as Arab fanaticism or the complaceny of democracies may create almost insuperable obstacles to concerted action.

While the human factors go far in determining the way in which alignments consolidate or dissolve, many of the psychological elements of stress and strain that make themselves so painfully felt in the case of the present American alignments with others can best be understood as reactions to particular aspects of the environment in which the coalition operates. In fact, one does injustice to the responsible governments if one fails to recognize the vexing external conditions—some of them unique—that tend to render collaboration among the non-Communist countries an extraordinarily delicate problem.

The geopolitical approach to international relations is not popular today, perhaps because of excessive claims made by its enthusiastic exponents. It makes sense, however, in this instance to stress the very marked geographical hurdles that lie in the path of American collective defense efforts. They represent such serious handicaps to the common pursuit of security *vis-à-vis* the Sino-Soviet bloc that they could prove fatal to the alignment system if nothing were done to counter their effects.

Soon after the fall of the Axis coalition, it became evident to those responsible for American foreign policy that the Soviet Union, occupying the area Mackinder called the "heartland" of Eurasia, had emerged from the war as an expansionist power of great military and industrial potential and extraordinary dynamism. Already it had extended its control far beyond the old borders of its predecessor, the Czarist Empire. More ominous was the fact that the rising giant was surrounded by a virtual power vacuum along its entire periphery, from Scandinavia and the British Isles, along the rimlands of Eurasia, to Japan and Korea.

It was also clear that the non-Communist countries on the Eurasian mainland and adjoining islands would not be able to generate enough strength or unity within the foreseeable future to contain the Communist bloc, should it attempt to take advantage of the weakness of its neighbors as was to be expected. If there was to be established and maintained any reasonable balance of power that would give assurance of continued freedom from Soviet control to countries interested in maintaining their independence, only one nation was strong enough to provide that balance, and this nation was located on the other side of the globe. Perhaps more by instinct than by premeditated design, the United States took upon itself the task of building an alliance system that would wield the necessary counterpower.

As the potential strength of the Sino-Soviet bloc matured, the United States gradually began to realize how ambitious was its project of spanning the oceans with a defensive coalition whose holdings on the shore of the

Eurasian land mass were, for the most part, easily accessible from the heartland but thousands of miles from insular America.

Under these circumstances, promises of United States assistance to countries across the oceans were not credible without additional evidence of American intentions. The only hope of effective deterrence and defense lay—and still lies today—in a projection of American power across the water barriers: the establishment and maintenance of a substantial American military presence in or close to the chief Eurasian danger areas.

Although it was an unavoidable consequence of geographical circumstances, the need for the projection of American power far beyond the confines of the United States almost inevitably places a heavy psychological mortgage on the alliance system. This deployment of forces is an easy target for hostile Soviet propaganda, which plays on such themes as "American occupation of sovereign countries" and "provocative American encirclement" of the Russian homeland. In the non-Communist countries that permitted or invited American forces to be stationed within their territories, those who for whatever reason are opposed to the alignment of their country with the United States condemn the American presence as an abnormal situation and as a threat to national independence. In fact, in the light of historical experience, it would have been more abnormal for the United States to have allowed a power vacuum to persist in areas adjoining a state whose leaders had frequently proclaimed it their duty to exploit the weaknesses of the "capitalist" enemy. Moreover, at the same time that it projected its own power across the oceans, the United States, at great financial sacrifice though with only moderate success, has sought to fill the vacuum with indigenous military and economic power, which, it was hoped, would eventually render superfluous American overseas deployment.

Whether normal or abnormal, the presence of American forces on the territory of its friends and allies places strains on their relations with the United States of a kind that was absent in former peacetime coalitions. Demands for "disengagement" or that the *Amis* go home" voiced strongly in some quarters abroad, are symptomatic of a psychological reaction that can weaken allied solidarity. One may wonder, in fact, that this reaction has not been more widespread and why it has not evoked from Americans a response of "bring the boys home," considering that, until very recently, the United States has been so strongly isolationist.

These problems of distance between members of the alliance are compounded by yet another geographical handicap. If one visualizes the alliance system in the form of a wheel, one could say that the friends and allies of the United States are spread out along its rim, each occupying the end of a spoke, while the United States is located at the hub of the wheel. Danger to any allied country—to the end of a spoke representing the Formosa Straits, or territories south of Soviet Turkestan, or on the Iron Curtain in Central Europe—is communicated to the United States at the hub as a threat to the entire wheel and elicits a correspondingly strong defensive reaction. No similar reaction, however, can be expected from countries located on opposite spokes or on remote sections of the rim. Instead, any American military action or exercise of "brinkmanship" in behalf of an ally in immediate danger tends to strike other more remote allies not only as a diversion of American attention and strength to tasks of minor importance, but as a risky maneuver that may involve them all in conflicts incapable of being localized. This attitude may appear parochial, but it is not dissimilar to the reactions of military theater commanders who would like all support channeled to their particular section of the front, despite the necessities of an over-all strategy that is hard for them to comprehend since they have not shared in its formulation.

Illustrations of this attitude are numerous. Just after West German newspapers had deplored American inflexibility in defense of Quemoy, the Berlin crisis turned the Adenauer government into the chief exponent of Western policies of unwavering firmness. On this occasion, in turn, some Asian allies of the West may well have feared threats to their security from excessive American concentration on the problems of Western Europe. Inevitably, then, the coalition leader whose strategy must be guided by global considerations will find it difficult to satisfy both the ally who, in a particular case, is on the firing line and those allies who happen to be remote from it.

The image of the wheel helps also to explain another and seemingly paradoxical aspect of the difficulties encountered by the leader of the coalition. In contrast to normal expectations, many of the nations, especially in Europe, that are directly exposed to Soviet encroachment have consistently shown less apprehension at Soviet intentions than the United States, which, until recently, was relatively safe from foreign attack. Often, Americans have been chided for their hysteria or suspected of exaggerating the Soviet menace in order to push their allies into more vigorous armament efforts. However, if one thinks in terms of the position of the "hub power"—sensitive to threats against any point on the wheel's rim—such a power must necessarily be particularly aware of the constant pressures exerted by the Soviets, first in one area, then in another. In a sense, Turkey is closer to the United States than to Denmark, Taiwan closer to the United States than to Pakistan.

Another hindrance to allied solidarity lies in the fact that the American alignment system is plagued by an unusually drastic discrepancy between the strength and prosperity of the United States and its allies. This is a source of tension, whether the issue is the distribution of collective defense burdens, the relative influence on policy open to members of the alignment system, or American interference—however subtle—in the internal affairs of allied countries. This situation is especially delicate because, among the friends and allies of the United States in need of assistance and protection, there happen today to be many who are exceptionally sensitive to foreign encroachments on their national independence. In the case of the new states, recently emancipated from Western colonial rule, this sensitivity is a natural result of their pride in an independence won after long and bitter struggles. Some of them refuse even to accept economic aid, generously offered with no strings attached, because they regard it as a new form of "economic imperialism." Some of the larger countries that not long ago enjoyed the prestige and benefits of empire and of world-wide influence are sensitive because dependence on another power is hard for them to accept. On the whole, the graceful adjustment of the former great powers to the *capitis diminutio* that has been their fate is worthy of admiration. But the United States itself must be given credit, too, for the relative lack of serious tensions within an alignment system where inequalities are so great. Rather than showing much disregard for the sovereignty, self-respect, and wishes of its allies, the United States has perhaps erred more in allowing itself to be blackmailed by some of even its weakest friends. Certainly, Soviet allegations that the allies of the United States have been turned into satellites and used as unwilling tools of egotistical imperial ambition are not borne out by the facts. Nevertheless, whenever any of America's allies feel that they are not sufficiently consulted on policy or not given sufficient support for their views, resentments are provoked that constitute another source of stress and strain.

Aggravating this source of tension within the alignment system is the new dimension to the power discrepancy that has been added by the nuclear age. There exists today within the coalition a sharp division between the nuclear "haves" and the nuclear "have-nots." With the exception of Britain [and France since February 1960] all of America's friends and allies currently belong to the second category, and even Britain [and France] must remain so far behind the United States in independent strategic nuclear striking power that a more than quantitative gulf will separate them from the United States for the foreseeable future.

In its early phase, the introduction of nuclear weapons did not place strains upon relations between the United States and its European allies; on the contrary, it helped tighten the bonds between them. During its short-lived monopoly of atomic power, the United States was able—or was believed able —to spread a protective nuclear umbrella over what was to become the NATO area and to offer Western Europe a reliable guarantee against Soviet attack. In fact, reliance on SAC became so deeply ingrained in the minds of those people in Western Europe who gave any thought to the Soviet danger or to the possibility of future war that it outlasted for years the period of the American nuclear monopoly.

Only after the successful launching of the first Soviet sputnik in 1957 did Europeans in growing numbers awaken to the disturbing fact of United States vulnerability to nuclear attack and thus to the possibility—or probability— that Soviet and American strategic nuclear power might neutralize each other. For the Europeans, this would mean the alliance with the United States had been deprived of what they considered its major value. Gone was the assurance that the grand deterrent of American nuclear power made Europe safe from any major attack or that a minor attack on Europe, if it occurred nonetheless, would automatically trigger an American blow at the Soviet homeland.

American nuclear capabilities have also placed a peculiar strain on United States relations with Asian countries. Despite the fact that race had nothing to do with the 1945 choice of atomic targets, Asians have not forgotten that the only atomic bombs ever used in war were dropped on a non-Caucasian people. As a result, there is some fear in Asia that the United

States might be less inhibited in employing nuclear weapons on battlefields outside the North Atlantic area. Whether such considerations strengthen Asian neutralism is difficult to estimate, since another factor, which we must examine, explains why so many countries today are pursuing policies of neutrality.

An American policy seeking to embrace most of the non-Communist world in a network of military alliances was almost certain to run up against the insuperable obstacle of neutrality. After opposing "entangling alliances" and insisting on a policy of neutrality for their own country for more than a century, Americans should hardly be surprised by this particular obstacle, unless they assume that *quod licet Jovi non licet bovi*. At all times, weak and vulnerable countries have sought refuge in neutrality and found it a source of protection, provided that their stronger neighbors held each other in check. For the non-Communist countries today, many of whom are weak and vulnerable, neutrality again appears as the most prudent policy. The more American and Soviet power have come to balance each other, the greater the premium on neutrality. Moreover, under conditions of a reasonably stable world balance of power, a policy of neutrality or of noncommitment to either of the opposing blocs offers advantages transcending mere immunity from attack. If free from ideological or moral inhibitions, a noncommitted country can swing toward one camp or toward the other as it sees fit and can hope thereby to elicit concessions from both. Leaders of relatively minor countries—a Mossadegh or a Nasser—are well aware of the influence they can exert by taking advantage of the opportunities open to noncommitted countries.

The United States has endeavored to make the best of a world in which neutrality has so many attractions. Realizing the impossibility of convincing even a bare majority of the non-Communist countries that their best interests would be served by joining with America in pacts of mutual military assistance, the United States has come to accept genuine neutrality as the maximum degree of "collaboration" that is possible with many of the non-Communist nations of the world. Certainly, neutrality is a far lesser evil than a swing of the uncommitted countries toward the Soviet camp. The more this has been recognized in the United States, the easier it has become for Americans to accept as valuable supplements to the Western alliance system such open or tacit assurance of friendship by the uncommitted states as may be attainable. . . . Relations with the uncommitted "third force" represent a particularly delicate aspect of American alignment policy.

A further source of interallied tension deserves attention: the discrepancy between the United States and other non-Communist countries in the variety of external conflicts with which they are faced. Whereas the security of the United States is directly endangered today only by the Sino-Soviet bloc, many of its friends and allies are absorbed by other dangers as well, threats to their national interests from non-Soviet quarters that often seem to them more immediate and real than the Communist threat. The Algerian rebellion strikes more deeply into the hearts of Frenchmen than any hypothetical threat to France's security emanating from beyond the Iron Curtain; Pakistanis are more inclined to turn their guns in the direction of eastern Kashmir than toward the Khyber Pass.

For American policymakers, meanwhile, who are able to concentrate American efforts exclusively on counterbalancing the Sino-Soviet bloc, it is a source of concern and often irritation that the same primary focus on the Sino-Soviet danger does not prevail among all non-Communist nations. Clearly, disputes between members of the alignment system are disruptive of over-all non-Communist solidarity and run counter to American interests.

As a consequence, the preservation and, when necessary, the restoration of peace within the Free World has become almost as much of a concern to American policymakers as the conduct of the Cold War itself. While there is bound to be pressure on the United States to take sides against the "aggressor" in any dispute between its friends and allies that erupts into armed conflict, it is also clear that American partisanship endangers the likelihood that the accused "aggressor" country would later participate willingly as an active member of the alignment system. Therefore, the general tendency has been for the leader of the coalition to serve as a neutral mediator who seeks to mend the fences of the alignment system by promoting a peaceful settlement between the disputants. However, even if successful, such mediation usually becomes a source of dissatisfaction with American behavior. While the compromises of a peaceful settlement will leave fewer wounds than collective security measures against a friendly country, both sides are inclined to feel that greater American backing of their positions would have resulted in a settlement more favorable to their interests. Neither the colonial nor anticolonial powers, for instance, and neither the Israelis nor the Arab states have spared the United States from harsh criticism for not giving them full support. The damage to the American alliance policy is obvious, though inescapable.

While the nuclear age has raised the strains of power inequalities to a new level of seriousness, the "revolutionary age" in turn has aggravated and increased the possibilities of internecine strife within the non-Communist world. Two forces are operating concurrently to keep the Free World in turmoil. One is the Communist ideological and propagandist onslaught on the tenets and institutions of the West; the other is the nationalist struggle against Western colonial rule and against any remnants of that rule that keep alive the bitter memories of colonialism. Both Communists and the vanguards of colonial emancipation—who are no less fanatically dedicated to their goal— make life difficult for any government seeking to co-operate with a United States, depicted as the mainstay of the hated *status quo*. Because American policy has been forced by the circumstances of the Cold War to place more emphasis than is popular on military defense and the preservation of order, the United States is falsely identified in many quarters with social reaction and militarism, a fact not conducive to the smooth operation of collaborative policies that depend on broad public support. Under such circumstances, an effort to create a favorable image of the United States in the minds of other peoples is not a negligible part of a policy of "going it with others."

►THE UNITED NATIONS CHARTER AND ALLIANCES

Collective self-defense and regional cooperation among member-nations is authorized and encouraged by the United Nations Charter. Articles referring to these problems are reproduced below. A commentary follows.

Article 51. Nothing in the present Charter shall impair the inherent right of individual or collective self-defense if an armed attack occurs against a Member of the United Nations, until the Security Council has taken the measures necessary to maintain international peace and security. Measures taken by Members in the exercise of this right of self-defense shall be immediately reported to the Security Council and shall not in any way affect the authority and responsibility of the Security Council under the present Charter to take at any time such action as it deems necessary in order to maintain or restore international peace and security.

CHAPTER VIII. REGIONAL ARRANGEMENTS

Article 52. 1. Nothing in the present Charter precludes the existence of regional arrangements or agencies for dealing with such matters relating to the maintenance of international peace and security as are appropriate for regional action, provided that such arrangements or agencies and their activities are consistent with the Purposes and Principles of the United Nations.

2. The Members of the United Nations entering into such arrangements or constituting such agencies shall make every effort to achieve pacific settlement of local disputes through such regional arrangements or by such regional agencies before referring them to the Security Council.

3. The Security Council shall encourage the development of pacific settlement of local disputes through such regional arrangements or by such regional agencies either on the initiative of the states concerned or by reference from the Security Council.

4. This Article in no way impairs the application of Articles 34 and 35.

Article 53. 1. The Security Council shall, where appropriate, utilize such regional arrangements or agencies for enforcement action under its authority. But no enforcement action shall be taken under regional arrangements or by regional agencies without the authorization of the Security Council, with the exception of measures against any enemy state, as defined in paragraph 2 of this Article, provided for pursuant to Article 107 or in regional arrangements directed against renewal of aggressive policy on the part of any such state, until such time as the Organization may, on request of the Governments concerned, be charged with the responsibility for preventing further aggression by such a state.

2. The term enemy state as used in paragraph 1 of this Article applies to any state which during the Second World War has been an enemy of any signatory of the present Charter.

Article 54. The Security Council shall at all times be kept fully informed of activities undertaken or in contemplation under regional arrangements or by regional agencies for the maintenance of international peace and security. . . .

CHAPTER XVII. TRANSITIONAL SECURITY ARRANGEMENTS

Article 106. Pending the coming into force of such special agreements referred to in Article 43 as in the opinion of the Security Council enable it to begin the exercise of its responsibilities under Article 42, the parties to the Four-Nation Declaration, signed at Moscow, October 30, 1943, and France, shall, in accordance with the provisions of paragraph 5 of that Declaration, consult with one another and as occasion requires with other Members of the United Nations with a view to such joint action on behalf of the Organization as may be necessary for the purpose of maintaining international peace and security.

Article 107. Nothing in the present Charter shall invalidate or preclude action, in relation to any state which during the Second World War has been an enemy of any signatory to the present Charter, taken or authorized as a result of that war by the Governments having responsibility for such action.

Commentary

Soviet-bloc alliances are presented by Moscow as being authorized by articles 53 and 107 of the Charter. "Until such time as the Organization may be charged with the responsibility for preventing further aggression" by former enemy states, these two articles seem to authorize collective action against Germany and Japan, enemy states which, on the day of the signature of the Charter, were still at war with members of the wartime coalition, called the United Nations. Thus, unlike Western alliances which are directed against any danger coming from without, Soviet alliances mention either Germany or Japan by name. The Soviet-Czechoslovak Alliance Treaty, signed in Moscow on December 12, 1943, mentions, for example, not only Germany but refers, using German terms, to the traditional German pressure toward the East *(Drang nach Osten)*. The Soviet-Bulgarian Treaty, signed on March 18, 1948, contains a formula which, with some variations, we find in most Soviet alliance treaties:

> In the event of one of the High Contracting Parties being drawn into military action against a Germany trying to resume her aggressive policy, or with any other State which directly or in any other form would be united with Germany in a policy of aggression, the other High Contracting Party will at once give military and any other aid, in accordance with the means at her disposal, to the High Contracting Party involved in military action.

In the Sino-Soviet Alliance Treaty Japan instead of Germany is mentioned. Communist China itself concluded an alliance treaty with East Germany on December 25, 1955 as did Russia and some other Eastern European Communist countries before; clearly, Communist Germany is not to be considered "a Germany trying to resume her aggressive policy." In the Communist interpretation, however, Western Germany and her ally, the United States, qualify as enemies under the terms of the treaty.

While Germany and Japan are mentioned, Soviet treaties are now, in practice, directed against all American alliances in Europe and Asia whether they include Germany and Japan or not.

The Soviet Union has bilateral defense treaties with China and all Eastern European Communist states. Most of them are linked together by inter-satellite bilateral treaties; thus Poland has not only a treaty with Russia but also with Czechoslovakia, Hungary, etc. It is an intricate web of bilateral treaties to which the Warsaw Pact of 1955 added a common command and political direction, imitating thus the structure of NATO. In reality the Warsaw Pact only publicly formalized the fact of the Soviet command and direction of the network of bilateral treaties as it had existed since 1945.

Western alliances are presented as authorized by Article 51 of the Charter; they either mention article 51 as their basis or quote its provisions verbatim, especially the pledge to report to the Security Council on the exercise of the right of collective self-defense and continue its exercise only "until the Security Council has taken measures necessary to maintain international peace and security."

The United Nations Charter has amplified the traditional and evident right of national self-defense by authorizing member nations to assist another state which, in their opinion, has become a victim of aggression. Aggression, however, has never been defined. And any action under the authority of the Security Council—which could stop collective self-defense measures—depends on the unanimity of its five permanent members, especially the Soviet Union and the United States. No wonder that article 51 has often been referred to as an elastic "free-for-all" clause. Together with the veto provision, it largely nullifies the seemingly centralized enforcement mechanism of Chapter VII. Thus, the dependence of Western alliances on article 51 is more verbal than real.

The Soviet Union has often questioned the relationship of Western alliances to article 51 as this article authorizes action only if and when an armed attack occurs. The West has answered by pointing to the fact that alliances are only preparation for, and not an act of, collective self-defense. Under modern conditions of warfare, collective self-defense cannot be improvised.

Western alliances usually determine the geographic area to which they apply. In case of conflicts in other than treaty area, they provide only for consultation. Unlike Soviet alliances, Western alliances do not mention the enemy by name. They merely pledge to meet a common danger "in accordance with their constitutional processes." This formula has been adopted in all treaties to which the United States is a party; it *may* mean that congressional approval would be required prior to military involvement. The only exception is the North Atlantic Treaty, which seems to provide for an automatic involvement of the United States forces in case of an armed attack. Article 5—the most important of the Treaty—says:

The Parties agree that an armed attack against one or more of them in Europe or North America shall be considered an attack against them all; and consequently they agree that, if such an armed attack occurs, each of them, in exercise of the right of individual or collective self-defense recognized by Article 51 of the Charter of the United Nations, will assist the Party or Parties so attacked by taking forthwith, individually and in concert with the other Parties, such action as it deems necessary, including the use of armed force, to restore and maintain the security of the North Atlantic area.

Any such armed attack and all measures taken as a result thereof shall immediately be reported to the Security Council. Such measures shall be terminated when the Security Council has taken the measures necessary to restore and maintain international peace and security.

Maps illustrating the United States commitments in the world, and main provisions of American defensive alliances will be found on front and back endpapers.

Article 52 refers to regional arrangements. It is therefore often understood as applying to those regional and semiconfederal arrangements which provide either for peace and order within the region (sometimes in addition to defense against external dangers) or for economic and social cooperation —as in the case of the Colombo Plan for Cooperative Economic Development in South and Southeast Asia.[1]

An example of a regional arrangement which combines defense against external dangers with the maintenance of peace and economic cooperation within the region is Organization of American States. Another example is, at least potentially, the Arab League which at present, however, seems preoccupied almost wholly with the problem of Israel.

Western European "Communities" represent the most advanced form of regional arrangements, motivated mostly by economic considerations and partly by political ones.

A brief description of three major European Communities follows:

European Community for Coal and Steel (1951) The Community was established by treaty April 18, 1951. Signatories were Belgium, France, the German Federal Republic, Italy, Luxembourg and the Netherlands. The Community exercises sovereignty over the six nations in all matters pertaining to coal and steel.

The Community pools the coal and steel resources of member states and eliminates trade barriers (such as customs duties) in these commodities, thereby creating a common, or free, market for coal and steel. The Community also stimulates joint research and enforces the first major anti-cartel law in European history.

The Community is Europe's first semi-federalized structure. It includes

---

[1] It has 18 members: Australia, Burma, Cambodia, Canada, Ceylon, India, Indonesia, Japan, Laos, Malaya, Nepal, New Zealand, Pakistan, the Philippines, Thailand, the United Kingdom (together with Singapore and British Borneo), the United States, and (Southern) Viet-nam. The idea for the Colombo Plan was born at a meeting of British Commonwealth Foreign Ministers, held at Colombo, Ceylon, in January, 1950.

a Council of Ministers, one from each government, to decide on policy; an Assembly elected by the parliaments of member states to serve in an advisory capacity; a Court of Justice to settle disputes and rule on treaty violations; and an administrative High Authority.

European Economic Community (1957). Euromarket established a common or free market for the same six-nation bloc and its overseas territories. Euromarket entails the gradual elimination of all tariff barriers among member states over a seventeen-year period and the creation of a uniform tariff system on imports from outside the region. Ultimately labor and capital as well as goods will have freedom of movement within Little Europe; member social security systems and wage rates will be standardized; trusts and cartels will be abolished. Euromarket is operated through the Council and Assembly of the Coal and Steel Community.

European Atomic Energy Community (1957). Euratom created a supranational atomic agency to spur atomic energy development in the six-nation community. While actual reactor construction will be left to individual members, Euratom will create a common or free market for nuclear raw materials and equipment, stimulate joint research and establish a reservoir of nuclear technicians to serve the membership.

TOPIC **20**

The Uses of Military Power

Advanced technology has brought about great changes in weapons, but the fundamental purpose of the use of military power has not changed since prehistoric times.

The purpose is to induce the rival to comply with our will; or to eliminate him completely as an independent entity; or to prevent him from imposing his will on others or destroying them.

Whether direct or indirect, warfare is a tool of policy. Under modern conditions preparation for and participation in warfare include the employment of political, economic and ideological forms of warfare in addition to the use of weapons in the narrower sense of the word.

►WHAT IS WAR?

KARL VON CLAUSEWITZ

Following is a short excerpt from a classic work, On War, *which has had an important influence on the theory of war and its relations to politics.*

The author was a Prussian general and writer on military strategy, born in 1780, who died at the age of 51.

From the book *On War,* by Karl von Clausewitz. Published by E. P. Dutton & Co., Inc. and reprinted with their permission.

War is nothing but a duel on an expensive scale. . . . War . . . is an act of violence intended to compel our opponent to fulfill our will. . . . Physical force . . . is therefore the means; the compulsory submission of our enemy to our will is the ultimate object. . . . Two motives lead men to War: instinctive hostility and hostile intention. . . . Even the most civilized nations may burn with passionate hatred of each other. . . . The disarming or the overthrow of the enemy, whichever we call it, must always be the aim of the Warfare. . . . If we desire to defeat the enemy, we must proportion our efforts to his powers of resistance. . . . The political object, as the original motive of the War, will be the standard for determining both the aim of the military force and also the amount of effort to be made. . . . War is no pastime; no mere passion for venturing and winning; no work of a free enthusiasm; it is a serious means for a serious object. The War of a community—of whole Nations and particularly of civilized Nations—always starts from a political condition and is called forth by a political motive. It is, therefore, a political act. . . . if we reflect that War has its root in a political object, then naturally this original motive which called it into existence should also continue the first and highest consideration in its conduct. Still, the political object is no despotic lawgiver on that account; it must accommodate itself to the nature of the means, and though changes in these means may involve modification in the political objective, the latter always retains the prior right to consideration. Policy, therefore, is interwoven with the whole action of War, and must exercise a continuous influence upon it as far as the nature of the forces liberated by it will permit; we see, therefore, that war is not merely a political act, but also a real political instrument, a continuation of political commerce, a carrying out of the same by other means. The political view is the object, War is the means, and the means must always include the object in our conception. . . . *War is only a continuation of state policy by other means.*[1]

* * *

War is only a part of political intercourse, therefore, by no means an independent thing itself. We know, certainly, that war is only called forth through the political intercourse of Governments and Nations; but in general, it is supposed that such intercourse is broken off by War, and that a totally different state of things ensues, subject to no laws but its own.

We maintain, on the contrary, that War is nothing but a continuation of political intercourse, with a mixture of other means. We say mixed with other means in order thereby to maintain at the same time that this political intercourse does not cease by the war itself, is not changed into something quite different, but that, in its essence, it continues to exist whatever may be the form or means which it uses and that the chief lines on which the events of the War progress, and to which they are attached, are only the general features of policy which run all through the War until peace takes place. And how can we conceive it to be otherwise? Does cessation of the diplomatic notes stop the political relations between different Nations and governments? Is not War merely another kind of writing and language for political thoughts?

[1] *On War,* Vol. I, pp. 1-23, *passim,* and p. xxiii.

It has certainly a glamour of its own, but its logic is not peculiar to itself. Accordingly, War can never be separated from political intercourse, and if, in the consideration of the matter, this is done in any way all the threats of different relations, are, to a certain extent, broken, and we have before us a senseless thing without an object. . . . That the political point of view should end completely when War begins is only conceivable in contests which are Wars of life and death from pure hatred: As Wars are in reality, they are, as we before said only the expressions or manifestations of policy itself. The subordination of the political point of view to the military would be contrary to common sense, for policy has declared the War; it is the intelligent faculty, War only the instrument, and not the reverse. The subordination of the military point of view to the political is, therefore, the only thing which is possible. . . . In one word, the Art of War, in its highest point of view is policy, but, no doubt, a policy which fights battles instead of writing notes.

According to this view, to leave a great military enterprise, or the plan for one, to *a purely military judgment and decision* is a distinction which cannot be allowed and is even prejudicial; indeed, it is an irrational proceeding to consult professional soldiers on a plan of a War, that they may give a *purely military opinion* upon what Cabinet ought to do. . . . Experience in general . . . teaches us that notwithstanding the . . . scientific character of military art in the present day, still the leading outlines of a War, are always determined by the Cabinet, that is, if we would use technical language, by a political, not a military, organ.

This is perfectly natural, none of the principal plans which are required for a War can be made without an insight into the political relations; and, in reality, when people speak, as they often do, of the prejudicial influence of policy on the conduct of a War, they say in reality something very different from what they intend. It is not this influence but the policy itself which should be found fault with. If policy is right, that is, if it succeeds in hitting the object, then it can only act with advantage on the War. If this influence of policy causes a divergence from the object, the cause is only to be looked for in a mistaken policy.

It is only when policy promises itself a wrong effect from certain military means and measures, an effect opposed to their nature, that it can exercise a prejudicial effect on War by the course it prescribes. Just as a person in a language with which he is not conversant, sometimes says what he does not intend, so policy, when intending right may often order things which do not tally with its own views.

This has happened times without end and it shows that a certain knowledge of the nature of War is essential to the management of political intercourse.

Once more: War is an instrument of policy; it must necessarily bear its character, it must measure with its scale: the conduct of War, in its great features, is therefore, policy itself, which takes up the sword in place of the pen, but does not on that account cease to think according to its own laws.[2]

[2] *On War,* Vol. 3, pp. 121-130, *passim.*

►THE MAIN CHARACTERISTICS OF WAR

QUINCY WRIGHT

Violence should be contrasted with the concept of war; propaganda, economic, and political fronts must be distinguished from the military.

Professor Emeritus of International Law at the University of Chicago, the author of A Study of War *defines war and discusses its four main characteristics.*

The historical events which have been called wars have been characterized by (1) military activity, (2) high tension level, (3) abnormal law, and (4) intense political integration.

I. MILITARY ACTIVITY

The most obvious manifestation of war is the accelerated movement and activity of armies and navies. While modern states are at all times engaged in moving naval and military forces around, in constructing battleships, guns, and munitions, in organizing and training armies and in making military appropriations, war is marked by a great acceleration in the speed of such activities. Such phenomena as mobilization, conscription, blockade, siege, organized fighting, invasion, and occupation may all occur without war; but they occur more frequently and on a larger scale during war. Each of the terms "battle," "campaign," "war," "arm's race," and "normal military activity" designates a certain intensity of military activity. . . .

II. HIGH TENSION LEVEL

Another manifestation of war is the high tension level of public opinion within the belligerent states. Attention is concentrated upon symbols of the nation and of the enemy. Only favorable attitudes toward the former and unfavorable attitudes toward the latter are expressed. . . .

III. ABNORMAL LAW

A third manifestation of war is the entry into force of new rules of law, domestic and international. Contracts with alien enemies are suspended. Resident alien enemies are interned or placed under supervision. Trading with the enemy is prohibited. Many treaties with the enemy are terminated or suspended. Military forces are free to invade the enemy territory and to attack its armed forces, limited only by the rules of war. Neutrals are obliged to prevent the use of their territory or vessels for military purposes by belligerents. Neutral vessels at sea are liable to visit and search and to capture if they assist the enemy. In the case of war, recognized as such in the legal sense, all these rules come into force. . . .

From *A Study of War* (Chicago: University of Chicago Press, 1942), chap. vii, pp. 685-700, *passim*. Reprinted by permission of The University of Chicago Press. Copyright 1942 by the University of Chicago.

Civil war, imperial war, and international war, if recognized as such, imply that both sides are to be treated as equals by other states designated neutrals. Both are entitled to the rights and powers of belligerents as long as the war lasts. . . .

Insurrection, colonial revolt, and aggression not recognized as legal war do not imply a duty of third states to treat the two parties as equals. In the case of insurrection or native uprising the recognized government has usually been favored by third states. The treatment of the Spanish Loyalists on a parity with the insurgents under the non-intervention agreement of 1936 was an exception in this respect. . . .

IV. INTENSE POLITICAL INTEGRATION

A further manifestation of war consists in legal, social, and political changes within the belligerent community, tending toward more intensive integration. Legislation regulates industry and directs it toward war production. Censorship comes into effect, and important instruments of communication are taken over by the government. Consumption may be rationed in many directions. Loyalties to church, party, or profession are subordinated to loyalty to the state.

The normal degree of government control of the activities of individuals varies greatly among states; but, however intense or loose the normal control, it becomes more intense in time of war. . . .

V. A DEFINITION OF WAR

War is a legal condition which equally permits two or more hostile groups to carry on a conflict by armed force. . . . To say that war implies a legal condition means that law or custom recognizes that when war exists particular types of behavior or attitudes are appropriate. War doesn't imply a sporadic or capricious or accidental situation but a recognized condition. . . .

To say that this condition pertains to hostile groups implies that the attitudes involved are social rather than individual and at the same time hostile rather than friendly. . . .

To say that the groups are carrying on a conflict means that the pattern of behavior is the instance of the type of group interrelationship which sociologists have termed "conflict." This pattern includes competitive games, forensic litigation, political elections, family brawls, feuds, sectarian strife, and other situations in which opposing but similar entities aware of and in contact with each other, are dominated by sentiments of rivalry and expectation of victory through the use of mutually recognized procedures. The pattern therefore involves a combination of separation and unity: separation in the fact of antagonism and hostility between entities, union in the fact of recognition by all entities concerned of a common objective (victory) and the procedure by which it is to be obtained (armed force). War does not, therefore, exist where the participants are so self-centered that each fails to recognize the other as a participant but treats it merely as an environmental obstacle to policy, as men treat wild animals or geographical barriers. War is, therefore, distinguished from armed activities such as the chase among primitive peoples or colonial development among modern nations. . . .

To say that the conflict is by armed force excludes forms of contentious procedure which permits only persuasive argument, intellectual skill, or friendly physical encounter, as in judicial trials, parliamentary debates and athletic games. The technique of arms implies the use of weapons to kill, wound, or capture individuals of the opposing side. War is thus a type of violence. The word "violence," however, includes also activities which are not war, such as assassination or robbery, riot and lynching, police action and execution, reprisals and interventions.

War, on the other hand, may involve activities other than violence. In modern war the propaganda, economic, and diplomatic fronts may be more important than the military front; but, if the technique of armed violence is not used or threatened, the situation is not war.

►NUCLEAR WEAPONS:
FOUR CRUCIAL QUESTIONS

KENNETH W. THOMPSON

Military strength today requires both conventional and nuclear capacities. The West especially, confronting a numerically superior rival, has been forced to turn its major efforts to the development of nuclear weapons. In so doing, its leaders face four crucial questions that weigh heavily on the minds of the citizenry: (1) What are the short- and long-range hazards of nuclear-weapons testing? (2) What are the prospects of a limited atomic war and its effects on the human race? (3) What are the chances of survival in all-out nuclear conflict? and (4) Is survival the only goal of foreign policy?

The Hazards of Nuclear-Weapons Testing

Military and scientific advisers disagree at some point on all four questions but within the debate there are areas of agreement that can be identified. Public opinion at home and abroad is deeply troubled by the hazards of atomic tests. The perils of modern weapons lie not only in war but also in weapons tests before the outbreak of conflict. For the first time in history, armaments imperil civilization even before warfare has broken out. Partly in recognition of this peril, both the United States and Great Britain on October 31, 1958, suspended nuclear tests for one year. The United States had earlier offered (on August 22, 1958) to take such a step to facilitate negotiations on the controlled cessation of tests. British and American leaders gave assurances that our test ban would be strictly observed unless the Soviet Union continued its testing. Evidence points to the fact that from late September to early November, the Soviet Union exploded at least 14 atomic devices at its Arctic test site. As far as can be determined the Soviets have conducted no tests since November 3, 1958. Since then the United States has extended its ban for an additional two-month period running through the end of 1959.

Various panels and commissions have dealt with the problem of nuclear fallout, the most recent being the Special Subcommittee on Radiation of the Joint Committee on Atomic Energy. Through public hearings held in May of 1959, the Subcommittee undertook to bring up to date the scientific information developed in 1957. It is on the basis of inquiries such as these that an estimate can be made of the dangers of fallout: offering no clearcut general conclusions but serving to sketch in at least the boundaries of the problem.

Some of the findings to date are reassuring. For example, radiation from fallout is still but a small fraction of radiation from natural background radiation in the earth and atmosphere. Authorities estimate that the amount of radioactive material blasted into the atmosphere and stratosphere by the nuclear powers results from a total of ninety to ninety-two megatons of fission explosions. Nearly half this material was produced by Soviet and American tests in 1957 and 1958 before the test moratorium. If tests are not resumed, the concentrations of strontium 90 in human bones from past weapons tests will reach a maximum in the period 1962-1965. For the world's population, the average concentration then is estimated at 7 strontium units. This amount is relatively small compared to the natural background radiation levels or to the maximum permissible concentration of 67 units cited by such groups as the International Commission on Radiological Protection and the National Committee on Radiation Protection. If cycles of testing continued over the next two generations, however, in the pattern of tests of the five years preceding the moratorium, the predicted average concentration of strontium 90 would be 48 strontium units.

Scientific opinion is divided on how fallout material enters the food chain and the degree of damage fallout can cause when it comes in contact with the human body. If there is no definitive answer to the central question of the amount of biological damage to present and future generations through increasing levels of fallout, there are nonetheless important areas in which dangers and warning signs can be discerned. Experts call attention to a series of newly observed potential problems and hazards. They urge an increasing emphasis on the so-called "hot-spot" problem. They note that since 1957 the fallout levels in certain areas may be unusually high. "Hot spots" covering several square miles are created when rain washes radioactive material out of an air mass containing a fairly high concentration of radioactive particles, as in a cloud from a recent test. Beyond this, the distribution of world-wide fallout is not uniform. About two-thirds of the stratospheric material is found in the Northern Hemisphere and about one-third in the Southern Hemisphere. The heaviest concentration is located in the Northern Hemisphere from 20 to 60 degrees north reflecting the fact that most of the tests have been conducted north of the equator. This also suggests that important areas in the United States fall within the zone of greatest exposure.

New problems also arise in connection with the so-called short-lived fission products such as strontium 89, barium 140, and iodine 131. Because these isotopes undergo a more rapid decay, observers had assumed that longer-lived isotopes like strontium 90 and cesium 137 constituted the only threat. However, experiments establish that radioactive substances do not remain in the stratosphere five to ten years, as the 1957 studies suggested, but rather from one to five years. Strontium 90 (which is chemically similar to calcium, concentrating in the bones and capable of producing bone cancer and leukemia) and cesium 137 (which concentrates in the muscles and flesh and is capable of causing genetic damage to the hereditary cells) are still considered the greatest peril in nuclear fallout. They take from twenty-eight to thirty years to lose half their radioactivity through decay. Nevertheless, the fact that fallout from the stratosphere is more rapid than was assumed has undermined the belief that short-lived isotopes would lose their radioactivity before falling to earth. Furthermore, some of these isotopes achieve selective concentration in a particular organ of the body, as does radioactive iodine in the thyroid. If the present test ban is maintained, the hazards from short-lived isotopes should be negligible, as they can be expected to decay and disappear. A more long-term danger arises from carbon 14, which according to recent findings has a radioactive half-life of 5,600 years. Surveys reveal that carbon 14 is produced by the bombardment of nitrogen in the atmosphere by the great flux of neutrons produced both by atomic and thermonuclear explosions. It is capable of producing damage equal to or exceeding that from other fallout materials, but spread over 1,000 years. However, over so extended a period, the continuous irradiation from natural sources will have even greater biological consequences than carbon 14.

In the face of the hazards, potential and real, of continued testing the case for maintaining the moratorium seems self-evident. Nevertheless, a government considering such a policy is confronted by at least three problems. The first is the fact that disarmament is not the prelude, but the consequence, of relaxed international tensions. The second stems from the persistent Soviet opposition to unlimited on-site inspection and Soviet demand for virtual self-inspection coupled with the protection of the veto in any enforcement system. The third results from new technical problems, such as the fact a United States nuclear explosion in the upper atmosphere is known to have gone undetected and a further United States report that underground tests can be conducted without detection. History may record that both of these problems were met through technical and political developments but despite some advances in arms negotiations between East and West at Geneva they remain obstacles to an agreement.

Prospects of a Limited Nuclear War

A second broad problem has its roots in the trend of modern states to modernize and streamline their limited-war capacities through substitution of small nuclear weapons for conventional military hardware. Military experts in the United States and Western Europe argue that parity with the Russians is impossible in conventional land armies where the Soviet Union enjoys a substantial comparative advantage in population and in ground forces in being.

They insist that small, highly mobile task forces equipped with limited nuclear weapons are more efficient and less costly to support.

Apparently Western Europe would be the principal theater of operations in which limited nuclear forces could be effective. Vast areas in Asia and Africa are relatively immune to these weapons not only because land masses and population factors restrict their use but because of the far-reaching moral and political consequences. The response of newly emergent peoples to the nation that used them first could be a decisive factor in the struggle. Europe, however, is an area in which small nuclear weapons are considered by some to be practical. It is argued that should war break out, both the Soviet Union and the United States would have a stake in keeping the outbreak of nuclear hostilities limited. At the point that the conflict deteriorated beyond this stage, Soviet and American soil, particularly in the era of intercontinental missiles, would come under fire. Moreover, Europeans, whose twenty-odd NATO divisions face several hundred Soviet divisions, likewise have an interest in counteracting numbers with highly efficient, self-contained nuclear units capable of keeping the enemy constantly off balance by never allowing any consolidation of territorial gains and by wiping out heavy concentrations of forces.

Proponents of a limited-nuclear-war strategy argue further that their policies need not result in unusually heavy casualties in human lives. In both conventional war and all-out nuclear war, cities and industrial centers become appropriate military targets. In limited war, by contrast, armies with high mobility and self-sufficiency replace cities as prime targets. Missiles and vertical-takeoff aircraft can be widely dispersed and concealed so that the elimination of a few important airfields is no longer essential. Opposing military forces are more important than communication systems or industrial centers for each unit is the depository of its own crucial weapons. This trend of thought foresees built-in restrictions to widespread destruction. It envisages sanctuaries, including cities and strategic nuclear forces (e.g. the Strategic Air Command), that will be relatively immune to nuclear strikes by the enemy. It questions whether limited nuclear war would be as destructive as conventional warfare, given this prospect of self-limitation. Finally, it urges that military experts not be defeatist about limited nuclear war at a time when the entire planning and development of our military establishment is built around nuclear weapons. The West, because of its superior industrial potential and its broader, more diversified technology, stands to gain more than the antagonist from the development of limited-nuclear-war capacities. Our very qualities of personal initiative and mechanical aptitude favor the West.

On the other hand, an equally responsible body of opinion has grave and serious doubts that a limited-nuclear-war strategy is possible. It asks whether the terms themselves are not in contradiction of one another. It points to the fact that modern war with a given technology has not been limited in the past. Witness the bombing of civilian centers and merchant ships in World War II. It argues that tactical nuclear weapons are now available that exceed in destructiveness the bombs used at Hiroshima and Nagasaki. The use of limited nuclear weapons will start a cycle of increasing military commitments that will eventuate in all-out nuclear warfare. A conventional war has a clearly defined cut-off point but a war fought with low-yield nuclear weapons would tempt the losing side to redress the balance by introducing weapons of greater and greater power. For the region that comprised the battlefield, a limited nuclear conflict would cause destruction approximating that from an all-out thermonuclear war. Europe would scarcely applaud limited as against total war if it were laid waste by tactical no less than strategic nuclear weapons, however preferable this result might be for the peoples within Soviet or American territory. If the aim of American policy is to preserve the people and civilization of Western Europe, limited nuclear warfare is not the way to do it. Nor can our allies be expected to see such a policy as in their self-interest.

A limited-nuclear-war strategy is questioned on other grounds as well. Its critics point out that it would require more, not fewer forces. Supporting strength for highly modernized forces must be increased and more widely dispersed. Greater reserves in proportion to front-line troops must be available to provide for the higher ratio of casualties anticipated. Thus limited nuclear warfare is not cheaper in cost or manpower than limited conventional warfare at any level of effort. For these reasons the United States and its NATO allies cannot overcome its relative weaknesses in manpower by this expedient.

The issue between the proponents and the foe of a limited-nuclear-war strategy can be resolved only if we clarify the purpose such capacities are intended to serve. There is at least reasonable doubt that such a strategy provides a short-cut to less painful military victory. However, agreement is possible on another level. For example, NATO's capacity for limited nuclear warfare may serve to deter the Russians from using their nuclear weapons in a limited attack. Without such a deterrent, NATO countries might more readily be exposed to Soviet aggression. The Russians, weighing the costs of introducing tactical nuclear weapons in a limited European war in which we lacked this capacity, might conclude that the risks were negligible. They might determine that they could quickly overrun European land armies. If our sole deterrent rested in strategic all-out retaliation they could conclude they would escape retaliation in kind. It is on this basis that a limited nuclear establishment probably has a rational basis as a deterrent even though it cannot be defended as the means of an easy victory in war.

The Chances of Survival in All-Out Nuclear War

Confronted with the specter of all-out war, President Dwight D. Eisenhower has summed up the dilemma in the phrase "there is no alternative to peace." The bombs dropped over Hiroshima and Nagasaki had an explosive equivalent of 20,000 tons of TNT (20 kilotons). Thermonuclear devices are presently available with an explosive equivalent of 20,000,000 tons of TNT (20 megatons) and there is apparently no upper limit. A 20-megaton weapon possesses a lethal radius of 8 miles and its area of total destruction is 48 square miles. Within such an area, 75 per cent of the population would be killed and the remainder critically injured. The radioactive effects of such a device would spread over an area larger than the state of New Jersey. If the enemy launched a successful attack on fifty of our metropolitan centers, at least 40 percent of the population, 50 percent of key facilities, and 60 percent of industry would be critically damaged.

In the face of these appalling figures, many are tempted to throw up their hands in despair. It should be remembered, however, that even if as many as 90 million Americans were killed in the first strike of a pre-emptive attack, this would still leave 90 million people alive. Agencies like the Rand Corporation and the present Administration of the State of New York urge consideration of measures that might increase the number of survivors to 120 or 150 million people. Some evidence exists that nonmilitary measures or programs of civil defense could appreciably increase our capacity to survive an initial nuclear attack and restore the national economy and democratic institutions. Nonmilitary defense measures would of course depend on the effectiveness of both strategic-offense and active-defense capabilities. The latter would involve the hardening and dispersal of United States nuclear resources. It would also involve the strengthening of Polaris and intercontinental-guided-missile capabilities and the development of more effective antimissile devices. Any responsible United States government is required to weigh and evaluate the costs and possible effectiveness of its nonmilitary defenses in relation to the costs and effectiveness of its strategic-offensive, air-defense, and local-war forces.

Nevertheless, within these limits, nonmilitary defense is theoretically possible. Radiation meters within improvised fallout shelters can guide decontamination work and indicate when it is safe to come out of shelters. A Rand study indicates that: "With no nonmilitary defense measures, a completely effective 150-city attack could result in 160 million deaths in the United States. . . . With a system of fallout shelters, and given several hours' warning . . . casualties might be reduced to 60 million. With a complete system of blast and fallout shelters, and even with only 30 to 60 minutes of warning, casualties might be held to 25 million." (Rand Report on a Study of Non-Military Defense, July 1, 1958, p. 12). Less warning might increase the casualties while prior strategic evacuation could reduce casualties still further. Moreover, costs would probably not be prohibitive. Suitably located mines might be adapted for both blast and fallout protection at an estimated cost for emergency 7-day occupancy of $25-35 per person. Light shelters for 90-day occupancy (food, bedrolls, cold rations, latrines, etc.) might cost $150 per person and corrugated steel shelters buried deep in the earth might be built with bunkroom accommodations for 90-day occupancy for from $300-400 per person. One engineering firm estimates that a system of deep rock shelters under Manhattan Island for 4 million people could be provided at a cost of $500-700 per person. While more research is needed before definitive answers are possible, prospects are sufficiently promising to warrant further thought and attention.

In other fields, prior planning and organized efforts might serve at least to ease the catastrophe. Agricultural products in storage as a result of price-support operations would be sufficient to supply a diet of 2000 calories per day to 180 million people for more than a year. These stocks are sufficiently dispersed to make them largely invulnerable to a city attack and after appropriate milling any grain, including crops close to harvesting, could be made suitable as emergency rations. The cost of 90 days' shelter rations for 180 million people would be $6-7 billion, plus storage and deterioration costs. Adjustment of crop patterns and land use after a 50-city attack should permit a safe recuperation of agricultural production.

Industry would be more vulnerable than agriculture. The 50 largest American cities contain only a third the total population but more than half the manufacturing capital. What could be produced outside the 50 destroyed cities in the first year after reorganization? One study suggests that surviving capital would permit a Gross National Product of 50-60 percent the pre-attack GNP. On a per capita basis, if 85 per cent of the population survived, this would mean a level comparable to that of 1929 or 1940. A further estimate suggests that the pre-attack GNP could be achieved in a decade. Industrial recovery would of course depend on such things as stockpiling in peace of construction materials for patching up partially damaged capital, sheltering normal inventories of metals, building materials and machinery, and sheltering complete plants or standby components of plants in the durable goods sector.

We have no intention of minimizing the disaster of a thermonuclear war by suggesting that perhaps there exist more promising means of alleviating the tragedy than has been generally recognized. Nevertheless the areas we have mentioned are but a few of the important spheres within which a broad research, development, and planning program would be necessary before authoritative estimates could be made more dependable than the hypothetical estimates cited above. In addition, the means are at hand for limiting the long-term biological damage to the population from total radiation and for enforcing countermeasures to contain the strontium-90 problem even after very large attacks. If we assume disaster could never strike or fatalistically rule out well-laid responses to catastrophe, the alleviation of the tragedy will be impossible.

Is Survival the Only Goal of Contemporary Foreign Policy?

A Rand Corporation study published in the summer of 1958 set forth some of the conditions under which surrender might be called for in the cold war. It analyzed the courses of action open to policymakers when faced with a prospective thermonuclear strike carrying the prospect of total destruction. Reaction from the Congress, the Executive, and the public was immediate and emphatic. Especially the more militant sectors of American opinion refused to countenance even hypothetical discussion of surrender. Nevertheless, responsible leaders privately ask the question: "What is the rational response to an ultimatum from the adversary threatening the destruction of 150 American cities?" Should the policymaker "press the button" or are there circumstances when surrender is the more defensible policy? If ours is the second

strike should we initiate it when we know it will come too late to prevent annihilation of more than half the population?

The present situation of a thermonuclear balance of terror presents an
unprecedented challenge to one well-established American doctrine. Americans have tended to affirm that we pursue fundamental values like freedom
and justice for which Americans would fight even if survival were jeopardized
thereby. Moreover, we believe that nations who put survival above all else
have frequently fallen victim to a tyranny that extinguished their national
existence. Short of the type of thermonuclear conflict where national existence
is imperiled, present-day leaders continue to hold to the view that survival
is not the only goal of our foreign policy. This is not to deny that in the final
resort a decision to surrender might be our only recourse. Yet a policy of
avoiding all risks of atomic war by unilateral disarmament or surrender would
quite probably bring the dread consequences it was calculated to prevent.

►LIMITED WARS IN THE ATOMIC AGE

In 1959, at a hearing before the Senate Armed Services Committee, Wilber
M. Brucker, Secretary of the Army, warned against the current overemphasis
on nuclear weapons to the detriment of conventional armaments. "While all
of us recognize the primacy of nuclear retaliation as the major deterrent to
general war," he said, "we must not in our zeal to provide this capability,
neglect to meet the force requirements for limited war." (The Soviet Union
possesses 175 combat divisions which he described as "modern, mobile, and
menacing.")

Since 1945 there have been eighteen limited wars. The chart of wars,
presented by the Secretary of the Army to the committee, is reproduced here
below (abbreviations: CHINATS for Chinese Nationalists; CHICOMS for
Chinese Communists; UK for United Kingdom and UNK for unknown).

[In addition to nuclear and conventional weapons, chemical warfare,
although not resorted to by either side during World War II, should not be
left out of the range of future possibilities of warfare. On June 16, 1959,
Major General William B. Creasy, former head of the U.S. Army Chemical
Corps, told the House of Representatives Science and Aeronautics Committee
that chemical warfare would be more "humane" than nuclear or conventional
warfare because chemicals could be used to "merely harass, make sick, or
kill." No destruction to industrial targets would be the result, an aspect which
a nation aiming at victory and hegemony would not overlook. General Creasy
told the representatives that gases had been developed that one "couldn't see,
smell, or feel" and that could set the congressmen dancing on the desk or
shouting Communist speeches, "or else kill almost instantly."]

WARS SINCE 1945

Date	War	●	■	Forces Involved, Thousands			
				Total		Land Forces	
				●	■	●	■
1. 1945-47	Indonesian War	Netherlands	Indonesia	140	140	130	140
2. 1945-49	Chinese Civil War	CHINATS	CHICOMS	1655	1622	1500	1622
3. 1945-54	Malayan War	UK	Communists	175	10	160	10
4. 1946-49	Greek Guerrilla War	Greece	Rebels	211	25	191	25
5. 1947-49	Kashmir Dispute	India	Pakistan	97	56	97	56
6. 1945-54	Indochina War	France	Viet Minh	500	335	450	335
7. 1948-49	Arab-Israel War	Israel	Arab League	UNK	UNK	98	105
8. 1950-53	Korean War	UN	Communists	970	1179	884	1153
9. 1954	Guatemalan Revolt	Government	Rebels	9	5	8.8	5
10. 1955	Argentine Revolt	Government	Rebels	16	40	15	5
11. 1956-58	Algerian Insurrection	France	Rebels	490	30	450	30
12. 1956	Sinai Campaign	Israel	Egypt	60	35	60	35
13. 1956	UK, French Seizure of Suez	UK, France	Egypt	99.5	35	60	35
14. 1957	Muscat and Oman	UK	Rebels	2.4	0.3	1.6	0
15. 1956	Hungarian Suppression	Hungarian Rebels	USSR	40	80	40	70
16. 1958	Lebanon-Jordan	US-UK	Rebels	UNK	UNK	18	11
17. 1958	Taiwan Strait	US-CHINATS	CHICOMS	200	195	88	135
18. 1958-59	Cuba	Batista	Castro	43	6-8	35	6-8

Presented to the Armed Services Committee of the U.S. Senate on January 22, 1959.

TOPIC 21

Moral Dilemmas in Politics

The subject of the following selections is the relationship between ends and means in politics.

Does the end justify any means, only some, or none? This dilemma is known to individuals as well as nations. If the choice is between one's death at the hand of an assailant or the assailant's death, most legal and ethical systems approve of killing in self-defense. If the end of foreign policy is proclaimed to be the preservation of a nation's prosperity, ideology, or life, and if this end can be achieved only by depriving other nations of their prosperity, ideology, or life, does the end justify the means of violence?

▶IN WHAT WAY PRINCES MUST KEEP FAITH

NICCOLÒ MACHIAVELLI

For over four hundred years, The Prince, *written by Florentine nobleman Machiavelli (1469-1527), has been considered a fascinating though controversial handbook of politics. It reflects the Florentine concept of the art of politics but contains many insights into the rules of successful politics in general. The following selection is one of twenty-six essays which make up Machiavelli's book.*

How laudable it is for a prince to keep good faith and live with integrity, and not with astuteness, every one knows. Still the experience of our times shows those princes to have done great things who have had little regard for good faith, and have been able by astuteness to confuse men's brains, and who have ultimately overcome those who have made loyalty their foundation.

You must know, then, that there are two methods of fighting, the one by law, the other by force: the first method is that of men, the second of beasts; but as the first method is often insufficient, one must have recourse to the second. It is therefore necessary for a prince to know well how to use both the beast and the man. This was covertly taught to rulers by ancient writers, who relate how Achilles and many others of those ancient princes were given to Chiron the centaur to be brought up and educated under his discipline. The parable of this semi-animal, semi-human teacher is meant to indicate that a prince must know how to use both natures, and that the one without the other is not durable.

A prince being thus obliged to know well how to act as a beast must imitate the fox and the lion, for the lion cannot protect himself from traps,

From *The Prince,* World's Classics series, Oxford University Press. Translation by Luigi Ricci, revised by E. R. P. Vincent.

and the fox cannot defend himself from wolves. One must therefore be a fox to recognize traps, and a lion to frighten wolves. Those that wish to be only lions do not understand this. Therefore, a prudent ruler ought not to keep faith when by so doing it would be against his interest, and when the reasons which made him bind himself no longer exist. If men were all good, this precept would not be a good one; but as they are bad, and would not observe their faith with you, so you are not bound to keep faith with them. Nor have legitimate grounds ever failed a prince who wished to show colourable excuse for the non-fulfilment of his promise. Of this one could furnish an infinite number of modern examples, and show how many times peace has been broken, and how many promises rendered worthless, by the faithlessness of princes, and those that have been best able to imitate the fox have succeeded best. But it is necessary to be able to disguise this character well, and to be a great feigner and dissembler; and men are so simple and so ready to obey present necessities, that one who deceives will always find those who allow themselves to be deceived.

I will only mention one modern instance. Alexander VI did nothing else but deceive men, he thought of nothing else, and found the occasion for it; no man was ever more able to give assurances, or affirmed things with stronger oaths, and no man observed them less; however, he always succeeded in his deceptions, as he well knew this aspect of things.

It is not, therefore, necessary for a prince to have all the above-named qualities, but it is very necessary to seem to have them. I would even be bold to say that to possess them and always to observe them is dangerous, but to appear to possess them is useful. Thus it is well to seem merciful, faithful, humane, sincere, religious, and also to be so; but you must have the mind so disposed that when it is needful to be otherwise you may be able to change to the opposite qualities. And it must be understood that a prince, and especially a new prince, cannot observe all those things which are considered good in men, being often obliged, in order to maintain the state, to act against faith, against charity, against humanity, and against religion. And, therefore, he must have a mind disposed to adapt itself according to the wind, and as the variations of fortune dictate, and, as I said before, not deviate from what is good, if possible, but be able to do evil if constrained.

A prince must take great care that nothing goes out of his mouth which is not full of the above-named five qualities, and, to see and hear him, he should seem to be all mercy, faith, integrity, humanity, and religion. And nothing is more necessary than to seem to have this last quality, for men in general judge more by the eyes than by the hands for every one can see, but very few have to feel. Everybody sees what you appear to be, few feel what you are, and those few will not dare to oppose themselves to the many, who have the majesty of the state to defend them; and in the actions of men, and especially of princes, from which there is no appeal, the end justifies the means. Let a prince therefore aim at conquering and maintaining the state, and the means will always be judged honorable and praised by every one, for the vulgar is always taken by appearances and the issue of the event; and the world consists only of the vulgar, and the few who are not vulgar are isolated when the many have a rallying point in the prince. A certain prince of the present time, whom it is well not to name, never does anything but preach peace and good faith, but he is really a great enemy to both, and either of them, had he observed them, would have lost him state or reputation on many occasions.

►STATESMANSHIP AND MORAL CHOICE

ARNOLD WOLFERS

Politics among nations is not necessarily more immoral than average private behavior. The chief difference pertains to unhappy circumstances which the statesman has to face without being able to change them. Often his choice is that of saving the life of his national community by the sacrifice of moral values; or exposing the community to mortal danger by adhering to principle. This is the theme of the following essay, written by a famous authority on international politics.

Throughout the ages moralists have expressed horror at the way princes and sovereign states behave toward each other. Behavior which would be considered immoral by any standard can obviously be detected in all realms of life; but nowhere does the contradiction between professed ethical principles and actual behavior appear so patent and universal as in the conduct of foreign relations. Governments spy on each other and lie to each other; they violate pledges and conduct wars, often at the cost of millions of lives and untold misery. . . .

. . . Do we not condemn and punish citizens for committing the very acts of violence, treaty violation or untruthfulness which we condone in international politics? Are we not constantly struck by the gulf that separates the relatively peaceful and humane life within the national borders of states from the events occurring on the international scene? It is this contrast—more apparent than true, as we shall see—that has led some to demand that statesmen be made to give up their sinful ways and to conform to the rules of behavior expected from individuals in an orderly community. Unfortunately, advice of this kind often proves so patently impractical that instead of inducing statesmen to mend their ways it provokes in them a sense of moral cynicism. What is the use of listening to moral advice, they ask, if statesmanship, capable of mastering the problems which present themselves in practice, is apparently incompatible with morality?

The fundamental discrepancy which seems to exist between the morality of "state" and private behavior would disappear only if it could be shown that politics conducted in a multistate system is not necessarily any more immoral than average private behavior, or that the chief difference pertains not to the degree of immorality prevailing in the two spheres of human action but to the

This selection is part of an article in *World Politics,* Vol. I, No. 2 (January, 1949).

circumstances under which men are required to act. Much of what strikes people as immoral practices of governments may prove to be morally justified by the peculiar and unhappy circumstances which the statesman has to face and which, moreover, he may often be unable to change.

Any ethical perfectionist will be shocked at such a suggestion. He will deny that any action that would be evil under one set of conditions could be morally justified under another. If men are held to be morally bound to act in accordance with an absolute ethic of love such as the Sermon on the Mount, obviously no set of circumstances, even circumstances in which the survival of a nation were at stake, could justify acts such as a resort to violence, untruthfulness, or treaty violation. The concern for self-preservation and power in itself would have to be condemned as evil. This being the case, the ethical perfectionist can offer no advice to statesmen other than that they give up public office and turn their backs on politics. As a matter of fact, in order to be consistent, the perfectionist, as some have pointed out, must give the same advice to private citizens, requiring of them that they abandon their concern for their own welfare, for family or business. If, as Hans Morgenthau holds, "the very act of acting destroys our moral integrity," only a life of saintliness could come close to satisfying perfectionist moral commands.

We must address ourselves exclusively then to the non-perfectionist who demands of man, not that he follow an absolute code of ethical rules—what Max Weber calls the "natural law of absolute imperatives"—but that he make the best moral choice which the circumstances permit.

But surely, it will be objected, no moralist, at least in our culture, could deviate so far from perfectionist standards as to condone even in wartime such inhuman practices as the torture of enemy soldiers or the shooting of hostages. One would wish that this objection would always be valid, but the fact is that the non-perfectionist cannot escape the conclusion that circumstances may justify what superficially appear to be the most despicable kinds of human conduct. Or would he condemn without careful prior investigation all the members of the French Resistance movement who, in the face of brutal Nazi tactics, are said to have answered their enemy in kind? What if they were unable to discover any other alternatives but either to stop in this repulsive fashion the horrors committed by the Nazis or else to leave their friends and their cause unprotected? This does not imply that circumstances morally justify every act of power politics from the violation of the pledged word to aggression and concentration camps; the chances are that in most instances they will not, whether because the cause is unworthy of such extreme sacrifices or because other means are available which will assure morally preferable over-all results. Nor does it mean that where circumstances do justify such acts men may not be guilty of having brought about these circumstances or of having failed to remove them.

There is nothing peculiar to international politics in this impact of circumstance. Our conscience revolts at the idea of men putting other men to death. Yet non-perfectionist moralists throughout the western world agree in condoning the acts of those who kill in self-defense, in obedience to an order to execute a criminal, in war, or possibly in the case of tyrannicide. In other cultures it has been considered morally proper, if not a moral duty, to put the first born, aging parents, or widows to death. One and the same act, then, will be judged differently depending on the context within which it is performed and depending also, of course, on the ethical standards by which behavior in general is judged.

This is not the place to enter upon the age-old discussion of what the standards of a non-perfectionist ethic should be, nor is such a discussion necessary for our purpose. However much non-perfectionists may disagree on ethical standards and thus on the nature and hierarchy of values, they hold in common the process by which they reach their moral judgments. They start with the conviction that there can be no escape from sacrifices of value whether, as theologians maintain, because of man's original sin and essential corruption, or because of the dilemmas of a world in which man is faced with incompatible moral claims. With this as a basis they hold that men, statesmen and private individuals alike, are morally required to choose among the roads open to them the one which under the circumstances promises to produce the least over-all destruction of value or, positively speaking, points toward the maximization of value.

Moral condemnation, according to non-perfectionist ethics, rests not on the fact that values have been destroyed, however deplorable or downright evil such destruction may be judged. Instead it is based on the conviction either that the action in question rested on false ethical standards or that in terms of agreed ethical standards a less destructive choice could and should have been made.

Thus a private citizen who breaks family ties in order to serve what he considers a higher cause may find himself condemned because his cause is not considered worth the sacrifice or because there were other less costly ways of attaining his end. Similarly a statesman who decides to break off diplomatic negotiations rather than to accept the terms of the opposing side may be judged wrong because he placed undue value on an increment of national prestige which was at stake or because he failed to appreciate properly the dangers involved in his choice of action. There is no difference either in the method of evaluation or in the ethical standards, whether the case be one of political or private behavior. In that sense the ethic of politics is but a part of general ethics. The question which remains to be answered, however, is why the sacrifices of value in international politics should be as widespread, continuous, and shocking in extent as they so obviously are. Is it because the circumstances under which foreign policy is conducted are so different and so unalterably different from those under which private citizens make their choices? . . .

The relations between sovereign states no less than the relations between other groups or individuals run the whole gamut from almost complete amity—take Canadian-American or Anglo-Canadian relations—to almost unmitigated enmity, as in the days of war. Amity and enmity appear as the two extreme poles of a wide scale of human relationships. It remains true, however, and a matter of great political and moral consequence, that the multistate system, for reasons which cannot be analyzed here, has a tendency to push relations between at least some states in the direction of enmity—and, for that matter, more so in our century than in the last. . . .

The concepts of amity and enmity can be usefully employed to shed light on the context within which statesmen are forced to make their choices. They stand for the two opposite and marginal extremes of human relationships. Behavior changes as the relationship approximates one or the other of these poles. The causes of enmity in inter-state relations are significant to the moral problem only to the extent to which statesmen may be responsible for bringing about or for not eliminating enmity, and thus become responsible for the consequences of such enmity.

One can imagine a condition of complete enmity between states. There would be no trace of community between them, no sense of commonly held values or of common interest. Each individual state would have to be looked upon as an entirely separate entity operating in the social vacuum of absolute anarchy. There would exist a state of latent if not actual war all the time, turning diplomacy into warfare with other means. With good reason nations could consider themselves in a constant state of emergency with all the things gravely endangered to which they attached value. It would be a situation, as we know it from the experience of total war, in which the sheer quest for survival would justify almost any course of action. "Out-group morality" of the most extreme type would prevail.

Take the other extreme, that of amity or the "friend-to-friend" relationship. While there would be no complete identification, a sense of community would exist sufficient to eliminate mutual fear and suspicion. There would be no expectation of violence and therefore no need for preparations with which to meet the dangers of conflict. Despite the fact that each state would be sovereign, or rather because each state would be free to handle its own affairs, such friendly nations could behave toward each other according to the codes of "in-group morality" and live in peace with each other.

The more relations between states degenerate toward enmity the more nations are justified in fearing for the things they cherish and the more reason they have to make and require sacrifices by which inimical claims can be defeated. Greater enmity therefore increases the likelihood that Machiavellian practices will become necessary and morally justified. The degree of amity or enmity thus appears as a morally portentous circumstance. While in a state of amity statesmen are likely to be able to choose between different avenues toward cooperation, compromise and conciliation. Enmity, however, may preclude such choices and place before the statesman a different set of alternatives. He may be able to take steps which will promise to mitigate if not to eliminate existing enmity. Often, however, he will have to choose between efforts to deter his opponent, thereby neutralizing the effects of enmity, and efforts to defeat him.

This cannot be said to be a peculiarity of international politics or of the multi-state system. The same phenomenon can be found in the relationship between father and son, employer and employee, white and colored man. There may be complete amity between them with no trace of distrust, no shadow of fear, no concern for self-protection, no awareness of conflicting demands or expectations. But here, too, relations may degenerate into fierce hostility for reasons too numerous to detail. Behavior then may change beyond recognition.

Two friends may live in almost perfect harmony. But let suspicion arise that one is seeking to exploit their hitherto harmonious relationship in some treacherous fashion. The other will feel justified in spying on his onetime friend. He may start laying traps. The case may end with one man killing the other. What is important to remember in this connection is that the killer may be judged to have been neither legally nor morally guilty, provided the treachery was flagrant enough. Not only our courts but public opinion in our country recognize the excuses of self-defense and unbearable provocation. . . .

It will be objected, and rightly so, that intra-state relations are less likely than inter-state relations to reach a degree of hostility that would call for the use of violence and other Machiavellian devices. The state protects many of the values to which people are attached. The state can also prohibit the use of means to which society is opposed and can enforce its prohibition—though only by the very means which the components of that society have renounced for themselves. . . .

Some governments are strong and ruthless enough to suppress the hostilities that would otherwise break out between warring factions, ethnic, social, or religious, but they do so by means of suppression, often tyrannical or terroristic. Rather than eliminate Machiavellian practices, such governments merely monopolize them. . . . Other governments are too weak to control the forces of internal enmity; then there are bloody revolts or civil wars. When that happens enmity often reaches a degree of fierceness which relations between states rarely approximate. Machiavellian practices of the most extreme kind become the order of the day.

Government or statehood, whether national or world-wide, is therefore no panacea against those aspects of power politics which are morally deplorable. The real evil is enmity and its threat to values to which people are devoted.

However, the moralist needs to be reminded of the fact that there is not only no sure way to eliminate the fateful circumstance of enmity but that at a given time there may be no way at all. Certainly the elimination of the multi-state system itself, whether within a region such as Europe or on a world-wide scale is not one of the objectives statesmen are free to choose and therefore morally obliged to choose under all circumstances. Even if a radical change in the existing order were morally desirable because there was reason to suppose that a regional federation or a world government would create circumstances of greater amity than exist today, the psychological prerequisites for a concerted move of major nations toward such a goal are beyond the control of governments.

If it be true that statesmen cannot at all times choose to work for conditions of world-wide amity under world government, is it not their moral duty at least to promote amity at all times and at all costs? Once it is conceded that enmity requires and justifies sacrifices of value often of the most shocking kind, it would seem as if no price paid for amity could be considered too high. Yet statesmen would be rendered incapable of maximizing value if, without respect for the context in which they were forced to operate in a given instance, the quest for amity were taken as the sole measure of their actions. Amity is a condition passionately to be desired; but there are times when efforts to bring it about will lead to disaster. It takes two to make friends. An attempt to establish bonds of friendship may be interpreted as a sign of weakness; the result may be aggression. Again the demands of the opponent may call for sacrifices of value greater than those connected with continued enmity. Firmness and even resort to force may under certain circumstances require less loss of life, less human suffering, less destruction of faith and principle than the most sincere attempt to eliminate the causes of hostility by concessions.

This is not the same as saying that power politics generally preclude the opportunity for persistent and active pursuit of amity—or of justice for that matter. There are many ocasions when disputes can be settled peacefully and when enmity can be eliminated or avoided, provided one side at least has enough courage, imagination and initiative. Sometimes a spirit of conciliation or even of generosity can do wonders in evoking a ready and sincere response. Whenever the lines of enmity are not irreparably drawn, there may remain room for moderation and self-restraint, for better understanding of each other's true designs and for fair compromise. While it is true that in the end it needs two to make friends, it is not always the other side which must take the first step. . . .

Whether moderation is politically practical or suicidal depends on the circumstances. Those who feel called upon to give moral advice to statesmen must be ready, if they are to be true to the tenets of non-perfectionist ethics, to demand restraint of power, charity and forgiveness in one situation, as when feelings of revenge and war passions run high, but to insist on a break with an opponent, if not on the use of violence, when weakness or procrastination threaten to bring on greater evils. If world government were not only practical but would, if established, temper enmities and help nations protect or attain what they rightly value most highly, it would be the moral duty of statesmen to seek to bring it about. As things stand today, however, lack of consensus among the major nations about the desirability of world government as well as about the kind of world government they would accept is so obvious that any attempt to establish such a government today would be more likely to lead to war than to reduce enmity.

To the extent that enmity exists and cannot be eliminated at a given moment it would appear to dictate to the statesman a course of action that will often run counter to his moral preferences. Does this not mean that those exponents of *Realpolitik* are right who claim that the statesman, instead of being able to make moral choices, is left with virtually no leeway, having to bow to the dictates of the "necessity of state"?

It confuses the moral issue to state the case in this way. The "necessities" in international politics and for that matter in all spheres of life do not push decision and action beyond the realm of moral judgment; they rest on moral choice themselves. If a statesman decides that the dangers to the security of his country are so great that a course of action which may lead to war is necessary, he has placed an exceedingly high value on an increment of national security.

Necessities of a similar kind are known to private citizens. Parents may decide that in order to save the family business they must try to get their son to enter the family firm. Although they know that they are asking him to choose a career he abhors, they are ready to sacrifice his happiness to the "necessity of family." A trade union leader who calls a strike which he knows to be ruinous to patrons to whom he is devoted makes and requires a painful sacrifice for the "necessities" of the labor movement. In every such case conflicting values, interests and loyalties call for choices in which what is deemed to be the higher cause or value calls for submission to its necessities.

It is no play on words to say that the necessity or reasons of state is but another of these necessities of life which become compelling only as a particular pattern of values is accepted. If the position of the statesman differs from that of private citizens it is because he must take upon himself the responsibility for sacrifices of value in order that others, as a nation, may protect or attain the things which they treasure. He may feel in duty bound to do so even though in a given instance he may disagree with the moral judgment of those to whom he is responsible. In that sense if in no other it may be justifiable to speak of the peculiar "demonic" quality of politics and public office, as Max Weber and other writers frequently do.

There is good reason why the controversy about the relationship between necessity of state and ethical standards should be rife in our culture. It points to a clash between two sets of ethical standards, one Christian or humanistic, the other nationalistic. Nationalistic ethics place what are called vital national interests—and not national survival only—at the very pinnacle of the hierarchy of values. The preservation or attainment of these values—territorial integrity, colonial possessions, *Lebensraum,* treaty rights or economic interests—are therefore assumed to justify the sacrifice of almost every other value whether it be life, generosity, humane treatment of others, truthfulness or obedience to the law. Especially, the interests of other nations count for little, if anything, on a nationalistic scale of values. . . .

As a matter of fact, the controversy between exponents of nationalistic and non-nationalistic ethical standards in our culture is not over the moral right to pay the price of survival. None but the perfectionists or absolute pacifists deny a nation which is engaged in a life and death struggle the right to make and demand every sacrifice necessary for victory.

But . . . nations engaged in international politics are faced with the problem of survival only on rare occasions. How otherwise could it be explained that most of the nations which have attained independence in recent centuries have survived when surely most of them most of the time have been devoted to anything but an unrestrained quest for power? . . .

As a rule, not survival but other "national interests" are at stake, such as the preservation of outlying bases and possessions, the protection of treaty rights, the restoration of national honor, or the maintenance of economic advantages. While it is a prerequisite of the system that nations attach a high if not the highest value to their survival, the same cannot be said of these other national interests. As a matter of fact, the moral dilemmas with which statesmen and their critics are constantly faced revolve around the question of whether in a given instance the defense or satisfaction of interests other than survival justify the costs in other values. Does the expropriation of American investments abroad, for instance, justify the choice of military intervention rather than of unpromising negotiation? Is it morally preferable to risk a loss of prestige with its possible dangerous consequences for the safety of the country rather than to insist on maintaining a position which threatens to provoke hostilities? In every case the interpretation of what constitutes a vital national interest and how much value should be attached to it is a moral question. It cannot be answered by reference to alleged amoral necessities inherent in international politics; it rests on value judgments.

Even national survival itself, it should be added, is a morally compelling necessity only as long as people attach supreme value to it. In that sense the multi-state system itself depends on a value pattern in which there is an element of nationalism. If at any time those who have the power to decide over the foreign policies of the major countries should come to attach higher value to the attainment of world government than to the preservation of independence, the psychological, though not necessarily all other practical, obstacles to world government would be removed. Until that happens nations are likely to consent to all kinds of Machiavellian practices, however much they may abhor them, whenever they are convinced that their independence can be saved in no other way.

International politics offer some opportunities and temptations for immoral action on a vast and destructive scale; they tend to present themselves in the guise of "necessity of state." Statesmen in command of the machinery by which public opinion can be manipulated may make it appear as if they were acting for the sake of objectives to which the people attach high value when in fact they are out to serve material personal interests or to satisfy personal ambitions for power. Where men wield as much power as they do in international politics there is room for an infinite variety of abuses for which the "necessity of state" can serve as a convenient cloak. Then again, statesmen may sincerely believe that a particular course of action is dictated by vital national interests; but judged by non-nationalistic standards of ethics they may be placing undue value on certain interests of their people or underestimating the value of things not pertaining to their nation which their policy would sacrifice.

While this makes moral criticism and self-criticism imperative, the difficulties which stand in the way of their proper use in international politics need to be emphasized. If it is hard for statesmen to make proper moral choices, it is not any easier for others to do justice to their conduct of foreign policy.

It is a baffling task, almost exceeding human capacity, to compare the value of an increment of national security with the value of human lives, or the value of a continued period of peace with the risks of a more destructive war in the future. Yet the statesman is faced with even more exacting and truly terrifying problems. Forced to make his choices whenever a decision is called for, he may have to compare the value of an uncertain chance of greater security with only roughly predictable risks of conflict and destruction. It may be easy with hindsight, and years after the event, to condemn a statesman for having failed to maximize value; but it also becomes increasingly difficult as time goes on to do justice to the inevitable lack of knowledge and foresight under which the decision-maker labored at the time. Yalta is a good example to illustrate this moral problem.

The trouble about much of the moral condemnation of foreign policies and with much of the moral advice tendered to statesmen goes back to a lack of appreciation of the kind of knowledge required for proper and useful moral criticism in international affairs. From a non-perfectionist point of view the circumstances, however technical, have to be taken into consideration; moral conviction and high ideals, much as they are needed to guide moral judgment, cannot by themselves offer an answer. Nor is this true in international politics only. It needs some knowledge of economics to judge whether an industrialist is exploiting his workers; he may be paying the highest wages the traffic will bear. It needs psychological understanding to decide whether in a particular situation divorce represents morally the least evil choice.

Similarly, in international politics where the circumstances are no less involved and technical, moral convictions cannot tell what roads are open to a statesman under the specific conditions under which he is forced to act, nor can they reveal what the political consequences and therefore the relative costs in terms of value of any one of several courses of action are likely to be. Will an alliance provoke war or will the failure to make a commitment tempt an aggressor? Will an appeal to the United Nations in a given case help bring about a peaceful settlement or instead create graver tension, perhaps even going so far as to destroy the organization? Disarmament may be morally the best choice under one set of circumstances; it may be downright evil in another in which it would place a nation—and small nations dependent upon it for their security—at the mercy of an ambitious conqueror. The same holds true for all the other panaceas or devices so dear to the heart of those who are most quickly ready to give moral advice to policy-makers or to condemn them for their actions. In one context it may be right to offer concessions whereas in another it may constitute "appeasement" with all of its evil consequences.

There might seem to be one exception to the rule that no general principle can guide non-perfectionist moral judgment on all occasions. It might seem proper to assume that the "defensive" side is always right and that every action is justified and justified only if necessary for the protection and preservation of values already possessed. Unfortunately, while individuals can disprove their guilt if they can rightly claim to have acted in self-defense, the case of nations is far more complex. Neither the nation's self nor its possessions are clearly circumscribed. May a nation defend as its self and its possessions only its territorial integrity and independence, or does the right of self-defense cover a way of life, national honor, living space, prestige, colonial possessions and economic rights abroad? *Status quo* powers whose main concern is the preservation of the values they possess and therefore the defense of the established order are prone to blame all Machiavellianism on those nations that seek to bring about change, whether it be revision of treaties, revolution of the social order or liberation from foreign domination. Yet, the "offensive" side may have a valid case for insisting that it has a vital need for things withheld from it and may rightly value them to a point where any means of attaining them become morally justified. Those who refuse to make the sacrifices of change or who, having brought about an unjust distribution of possessions and power are unwilling to correct it, may be guilty of provoking enmity and aggression. If the Moslems in India or the Zionists in Palestine resorted to violence, they were not defending an existing order but were seeking to establish new and independent national homes through changes in the existing order. They were not necessarily at fault merely because they wanted these changes so urgently or because they despaired of any means short of violence. The *beati possidentes* may be more peaceful and less inclined to initiate open hostility, but their guilt may lie in their self-righteous and blind devotion to the *status quo* or in the resentment which they evoke in others.

. . . Where there is so much room for moral choices as there is in international politics and where the destiny of entire nations depends on these choices, attempts to evade, silence or ignore moral judgment merely play into the hands of those who relish the uncriticized use or abuse of their power. . . .

The world will not fail to suffer from the immoral acts of statesmen as of other men in the future as it has in the past, nor does it look as though nations would soon be freed from the bitter consequences of international enmity, or from the appalling sacrifices inflicted and justified in the name of national interest and survival. . . .

Yet international politics are not beyond the pale of non-nationalistic, non-perfectionist morality. Statesmen need not be fooling either themselves or others if they contend, as they frequently do, that in specific instances they have restrained their nation's quest for power; nor need they apologize if, on occasion, they choose a conciliatory or even a generous course of action, though a more egotistical policy would promise more tangible national benefits. Despite the continued strength of nationalist sentiment in all parts of the world, there is no reason to assume that people value national benefits only. . . .

Under the circumstances usually prevailing in a multi-state system painful limitations are set on policies of self-negation, generosity or restraint of power. It would be utopian to expect drastic changes in this respect. But to say that the field of international politics is reserved for selfishness, brutality, self-righteousness or unrestrained ambition for power is not only cynical but manifestly unrealistic.

TOPIC 22

Statesmen Must Decide

The tension between morality and international politics has been analyzed in the preceding topic. The problem permeates the whole fabric of contacts and actions among nations. Several illustrations of this problem were
presented earlier (e.g., the Munich agreement between Hitler and the Western
Democracies, in Topic 15.) Two other illustrations of similar conflicts are
reproduced below: One concerns a U.S. compromise with a pro-Nazi French
official. The other pertains to the use of the atomic bomb.

►CRUSADE IN EUROPE

DWIGHT D. EISENHOWER

The following excerpt from Eisenhower's book, Crusade in Europe, *demonstrates how a crusade against nazism required a compromise with an ally of
nazism, who happened to be in North Africa on the eve of the American
invasion of Morocco, Algeria, and Tunisia.*

In mid-July 1942, General Marshall and Admiral King came to London
to meet with the British Chiefs of Staff. They were to discuss problems arising
out of realization that a very considerable period must elapse before a full-
blooded, decisive operation could be undertaken against the coasts of northwest Europe. They had to reckon with these factors:

The agreed-upon major strategical operation to be carried out jointly by
Great Britain and the United States could not be put into effect, because of
lack of forces and equipment, before late 1943 at the earliest, and, since the
fall of the year would be a most unpropitious time to begin such a campaign,
the prospective D-day, in the absence of some unforeseen, radical change in
the situation, might be postponed until the spring of 1944.

Russia was insistently demanding an offensive move by Great Britain
and the United States during 1942; and there was a lively fear that unless
such a move was undertaken the gravest consequences might ensue on the
Russian front.

The psychological reaction in the United States and Great Britain and
in all the occupied countries of Europe might be little short of disastrous if
positive action of some kind were not undertaken during 1942.

Whatever was attempted in 1942 would necessarily be on a much
smaller scale than the contemplated invasion of Europe and, so far as pos-

From *Crusade in Europe* by Dwight D. Eisenhower. Copyright 1948 by Doubleday &
Company, Inc. Reprinted by permission of the publisher.

sible, it should not seriously cut into the production and preparatory program then getting under way to make possible the final major operation.

The President had specifically ordered the United States Chiefs of Staff to launch some kind of offensive ground action in the European zone in 1942.

In view of these circumstances there seemed to be three lines of action deserving of earnest study.

The first was the direct reinforcement of the British armies in the Middle East via the Cape of Good Hope route, in an effort to destroy Rommel and his army and, by capturing Tripolitania, to gain secure control of the central Mediterranean.

The second was to prepare amphibious forces to seize northwest Africa with the idea of undertaking later operations to the eastward to catch Rommel in a giant vise and eventually open the entire Mediterranean for use by the United Nations.

The third was to undertake a limited operation on the northwest coast of France with a relatively small force but with objectives limited to the capture of an area that could be held against German attack and which would later form a bridgehead for use in the large-scale invasion agreed upon as the ultimate objective. The places indicated were the Cotentin Peninsula or the Brittany Peninsula. This proposed operation was called Sledgehammer.

No other course of action seemed feasible at the moment. . . .

On July 24 it was determined to proceed with the planning for the invasion of northwest Africa with an Allied force of all arms, to be carried out under an American commander. The operation received the name Torch. Its execution was approved by the President on July 25. Both governments agreed that the whole venture should have, initially at least, a completely American complexion. The hope was that French North Africa would receive the invading troops with no more than a nominal show of resistance, and the chances of this favorable development were considered to be much brighter if the operation was advertised as purely American. British standing in France was at a low ebb because of the Oran, Dakar, and Syrian incidents, in which British forces had come into open conflict with the French.

In his headquarters in the Claridge Hotel on July 26, General Marshall informed me that I was to be the Allied commander in chief of the expedition. . . .

From the inception of the invasion project, our governments carefully considered the possibility of including General de Gaulle, then in London, in Torch planning. Units under his command had taken part in the ill-fated Dakar expedition, where the attacking forces had to retire in confusion in the face of local French resistance. The British always believed that this fiasco resulted from leaks in De Gaulle's London headquarters. Our instructions from the two governments, possibly colored by this unfortunate early experience, were to the effect that under no circumstances was any information concerning the proposed expedition to be communicated to General de Gaulle.

There was confirmation of the assumption that General de Gaulle's presence in the initial assaulting forces would incite determined opposition on the part of the French garrisons. During the course of our planning in London a constant stream of information came to us from consuls and other officials whom our State Department maintained in Africa throughout the war. All of this information was to the effect that in the regular officer corps of the French Army De Gaulle was, at that time, considered a disloyal soldier. His standing with the resistance elements of the civil population was vastly different. But at that moment resistance elements, particularly in Africa, were inarticulate and ineffective—and we had to win over the armed services as a first objective.

It is possible to understand why De Gaulle was disliked within the ranks of the French Army. At the time of France's surrender in 1940 the officers who remained in the Army had accepted the position and orders of their government and had given up the fight. From their viewpoint, if the course chosen by De Gaulle was correct, then every French officer who obeyed the orders of his government was a poltroon. If De Gaulle was a loyal Frenchman they had to regard themselves as cowards. Naturally the officers did not choose to think of themselves in this light; rather they considered themselves as loyal Frenchmen carrying out the orders of constituted civilian authority, and it followed that they officially and personally regarded De Gaulle as a deserter.

Nevertheless, it was known that there was a strong anti-German and anti-Vichy sentiment in North Africa, even among some of the Army officers. It was believed possible that if a sufficient show of force could be made in the initial attack all these officers might find that their honor had been satisfied by token resistance and, bowing to the inevitable, would join in the fight against the traditional foe that had humiliated them in 1940. . . .

After some six weeks of intensive planning we were notified that Mr. Robert D. Murphy, the senior American State Department officer in North Africa, would pay us a secret visit to discuss with us the political implications and possibilities in that region. These factors remained among the great question marks of the entire operation. Vichy France was a neutral country and during the entire period of the war the United States had maintained diplomatic connection with the French Government. Never, in all its history, had the United States been a party to an unprovoked attack upon a neutral country and even though Vichy was avowedly collaborating with Hitler, there is no doubt that American political leaders regarded the projected operation, from this viewpoint, with considerable distaste.

Both the British and American governments believed that North African public opinion favored the Allies, and naturally desired to make the invasion appear as an operation undertaken in response to a popular desire for liberation from the Vichy yoke. Not only did we definitely want to avoid adding France to our already formidable list of enemies; we wanted, if possible, to make it appear that we had come into Africa on invitation rather than by force.

It was realized that, officially, some opposition would have to be made to the landing because within Europe itself the French dwelt constantly under the German heel. But if we could show that popular opinion was definitely in opposition to the Vichy rulers, any political antagonism to the invasion in Great Britain or America would be mollified.

Mr. Murphy, who had long been stationed in Africa, was early taken into the confidence of the President of the United States and informed of the possibility of military action in that region. With his staff of assistants he not only conducted a continuing survey of public opinion, but he did his best to discover among the military and political leaders those individuals who were definitely hostile to the Axis and occupying their posts merely out of a sense of duty to France. Affable, friendly, exceedingly shrewd, and speaking French capably, he was admirably suited for his task. Unquestionably his missionary work between 1940 and late 1942 had much to do with eventual success.

His trip to my headquarters in London, in the fall of 1942, was conducted in the greatest secrecy. In Washington, where he went first, he was placed in uniform, given a fictional commission as lieutenant colonel, and came to see me under the name of McGowan. I met him at a rendezvous outside the city and within a matter of twenty-four hours he was again on the way to Washington.

From Mr. Murphy we learned the names of those officers who had pro-Allied sympathies and those who were ready to aid us actively. We learned much about the temper of the Army itself and about feeling among the civil population. He told us very accurately that our greatest resistance would be met in French Morocco, where General August Paul Noguès was Foreign Minister to the Sultan. He gave us a number of details of French military strength in Africa, including information concerning equipment and training in their ground, air, and sea forces. From his calculations it was plain that if we were bitterly opposed by the French a bloody fight would ensue; if the French should promptly decide to join us we could expect to get along quickly with our main business of seizing Tunisia and attacking Rommel from the rear. It was Mr. Murphy's belief that we would actually encounter a mean between these two extremes. Events proved him to be correct.

On another point, however, he was, through no fault of his own, completely mistaken. He had been convinced by the French Generals Charles Emmanuel Mast, chief of staff of the French XIX Corps in Algeria, Marie Emile Bethouart, commander of the Casablanca Division, and others who were risking their lives to assist us, that if General Henri Giraud could be brought into North Africa, ostensibly to aid in an uprising against the Vichy government, the response would be immediate and enthusiastic and all North Africa would flame into revolt, unified under a leader who was represented as being intensely popular throughout the region. Weeks later, during a crisis in our affairs, we were to learn that this hope was a futile one. . . .

[By the beginning of November, all preparations for Torch were completed. On November 5, General Eisenhower left London to establish his headquarters inside the Rock of Gibraltar.]

During the course of the night and in the early morning hours of November 8 operational reports began to come in that were encouraging in tone. As anticipated, the landings at Algiers met almost no opposition and the area was quickly occupied. . . .

At Oran we got ashore, but the French forces in that region, particularly the naval elements, resisted bitterly. . . .

We knew that the attack on the west coast was launched, but there was no news of its progress. Actually at certain points, notably Port Lyautey, fierce fighting developed. The treacherous sea had given us the one quiet day in the month necessary to make the landing feasible, but the period of calm lasted only a short time and later reinforcing was most difficult. . . .

On the morning of November 9, General Clark and General Giraud went by air to Algiers in an effort to make some kind of agreement with the highest French authorities. Their mission was to end the fighting and to secure French assistance in projected operations against the Germans. . . .

Because of the earnest conviction held in both London and Washington that General Giraud could lead the French of North Africa into the Allied camp, we had started negotiations in October, through Mr. Murphy, to rescue the general from virtual imprisonment in southern France. An elaborate plan was devised by some of our French friends and Mr. Murphy, who had returned to Africa after his visit to London. General Giraud was kept informed of developments through trusted intermediaries and at the appointed time reached the coast line in spite of the watchfulness of the Germans and the Vichyites. There he embarked in a small boat, in the dark of night, to keep a rendezvous with one of our submarines, lying just offshore. A British submarine, commanded for this one trip by Captain Jerauld Wright of the United States Navy, made a most difficult contact with General Giraud and put out to sea. At another appointed place the submarine met one of our flying boats, and the general, with but three personal aides and staff officers, flew to my headquarters during the afternoon of November 7. The incident, related thus briefly, was an exciting story of extraordinary daring and resolution.

General Giraud . . . was well over six feet, erect, almost stiff in carriage, and abrupt in speech and mannerisms. He was a gallant if bedraggled figure, and his experiences of the war, including a long term of imprisonment and a dramatic escape, had not daunted his fighting spirit. . . .

General Giraud's cold reception by the French in Africa was a terrific blow to our expectations. He was completely ignored. He made a broadcast, announcing assumption of leadership of French North Africa and directing French forces to cease fighting against the Allies, but his speech had no effect whatsoever. I was doubtful that it was even heard by significant numbers. Radio communications with Algiers were very difficult but eventually a message came through that confirmed an earlier report: Admiral Darlan was in Algiers!

We discounted at once the possibility that he had come into the area with a prior knowledge of our intentions or in order to assist us in our purpose. Already we had evidence, gathered in Oran and Algiers, that our invasion was a complete and astonishing surprise to every soldier and every inhabitant of North Africa, except for those very few who were actively assisting us. Even these had not been told the actual date of the attack until the last minute. There was no question that Darlan's presence was entirely accidental, occasioned by the critical illness of his son, to whom he was extremely devoted.

In Darlan we had the commander in chief of the French fighting forces! A simple and easy answer would have been to jail him. But with Darlan in a position to give the necessary orders to the very considerable French fleet, then in Toulon and Dakar, there was hope of reducing at once the potential naval threat in the Mediterranean and of gaining welcome additions to our own surface craft. Just before I left England, Mr. Churchill had earnestly remarked, "If I could meet Darlan, much as I hate him, I would cheerfully crawl on my hands and knees for a mile if by doing so I could get him to bring that fleet of his into the circle of Allied forces."

But we had another and more pressing reason for attempting to utilize Darlan's position. In dealing with French soldiers and officials General Clark quickly ran afoul of the traditional French demand for a cloak of legality over any action they might take. This was a fetish with the military; their surrender in 1940, they asserted, had been merely the act of loyal soldiers obeying the legal orders of their civil superiors.

Without exception every French commander with whom General Clark held exhaustive conversation declined to make any move toward bringing his forces to the side of the Allies unless he could get a legal order to do so. Each of them had sworn an oath of personal fealty to Marshal Pétain, a name that at that moment was more profound in its influence on North African thinking and acting than any other factor. None of these men felt that he could be absolved from that oath or could give any order to cease firing unless the necessary instructions were given by Darlan as their legal commander, to whom they looked as the direct and personal representative of Marshal Pétain.

It was useless then, and for many days thereafter, to talk to a Frenchman, civilian or soldier, unless one first recognized the Marshal's overriding influence. His picture appeared prominently in every private dwelling, while in public buildings his likeness was frequently displayed in company with extracts from his speeches and statements. Any proposal was acceptable only if "the Marshal would wish it."

General Clark radioed that without Darlan no conciliation was possible, and in this view he was supported by General Giraud, who was then in hiding in Algiers. Clark kept me informed of developments as much as he possibly could but it was obvious that he was having a difficult time in his attempt to persuade the French to stop fighting our troops. . . .

On November 12, General Clark reported that apparently Darlan was the only Frenchman who could achieve co-operation for us in North Africa. I realized that the matter was one that had to be handled expeditiously and locally. To have referred it back to Washington and London would have meant inevitable delays in prolonged discussions. So much time would have been consumed as to have cost much blood and bitterness and left no chance of an amicable arrangement for absorbing the French forces into our own expedition.

Already we had our written orders from our governments to cooperate with any French government we should find existing at the moment of our entry into Africa. Moreover, the matter at the moment was completely military. If resulting political repercussions became so serious as to call for a sacrifice, logic and tradition demanded that the man in the field should take complete responsibility for the matter, with his later relief from command becoming the symbol of correction. I might be fired, but only by making a quick decision could the essential unity of effort throughout both nations be preserved and the immediate military requirements met.

We discussed these possibilities very soberly and earnestly, always remembering that our basic orders required us to go into Africa in the attempt to win an ally—not to kill Frenchmen.

I well knew that any dealing with a Vichyite would create great revulsion among those in England and America who did not know the harsh realities of war; therefore I determined to confine my judgment in the matter to the local military aspects. Taking Admiral Cunningham with me, I flew to Algiers on November 13, and upon reaching there went into conference with General Clark and Mr. Murphy, the American consul general in the area. This was the first time I had seen Murphy since his visit to London some weeks before.

They first gave me a full account of events to date. On November 10, Darlan had sent orders to all French commanders to cease fighting. Pétain, in Vichy, immediately disavowed the act and declared Darlan dismissed. Darlan then tried to rescind the order, but this Clark would not allow. Next the news was received in Algiers that the Germans were invading southern France, and now Darlan said that because the Germans had violated the 1940 armistice he was ready to co-operate freely with the Americans. In the meantime General Giraud, at first shocked to discover that the local French would not follow him, had become convinced that Darlan was the only French official in the region who could lead North Africa to the side of the Allies. When the Germans entered southern France Giraud went to Darlan to offer co-operation. The fighting at Casablanca had ceased because of Darlan's order; at other places the fighting was over before the order was received. The French officers who had openly assisted us, including Generals Bethouart and Mast, were in temporary disgrace; they were helpless to do anything.

After exhaustive review of the whole situation Mr. Murphy said, "The whole matter has now become a military one. You will have to give the answer."

While we were reaching a final decision he stepped entirely aside except to act upon occasion as interpreter. It was squarely up to me to decide whether or not the procurement of an armistice, the saving of time and lives, and the early development of workable arrangements with the French were worth more to the Allied forces than the arbitrary arrest of Darlan, an action certain to be accompanied by continued fighting and cumulative bitterness. Local French officials were still officially members of a neutral country, and unless our governments were ready formally to declare war against France we had no legal or other right arbitrarily to establish, in the Nazi style, a puppet government of our own choosing.

The arrangement reached was set forth in a document that outlined the methods by which the French authorities engaged to assist the Allied forces. It accorded to the Allied commander in chief, in a friendly, not an occupied, territory, all the necessary legal rights and privileges that were required in the administration of his forces and in the conduct of military operations. We were guaranteed the use of ports, railways, and other facilities.

The Allies merely stated that, provided the French forces and the civil population would obey Darlan's orders to co-operate militarily with us, we would not disturb the French administrative control of North Africa. On the contrary, we affirmed our intention of co-operating with them in preserving order. There was no commitment to engage our governments in any political recognition of any kind and Darlan was simply authorized, by the voluntary action of the local officials, and with our consent, to take charge of the French affairs of North Africa while we were clearing the Germans out of that continent. He agreed also to place our friend General Giraud in command of all French military forces in northwest Africa.

An important point was that we could not afford a military occupation, unless we chose to halt all action against the Axis. The Arab population was then sympathetic to the Vichy French regime, which had effectively eliminated Jewish rights in the region, and an Arab uprising against us, which the Germans were definitely trying to foment, would have been disastrous. It was our intention to win North Africa only for use as a base from which to carry on the war against Hitler. . . . Theoretically we were in the country of an ally. The actual effect of Darlan's commitment was to recognize and give effect to our position of dominating influence—but we would have to use this position skillfully if we were to avoid trouble.

Darlan's orders to the French Army were obeyed, in contrast to the disdain with which the earlier Giraud pronouncement had been received. Darlan stopped the fighting on the western coast, where the United States forces had just been concentrated against the defenses of Casablanca and were preparing to deliver a general assault. General Patton's earlier experiences in Morocco indicated that this would have been a bloody affair.

Final agreement with the French Army, Navy, and Air officials, headed by Darlan, was reached at Algiers on November 13. . . .

Official reports of all political problems had of course been periodically submitted to our two governments. Nevertheless, the instant criticism in the press of the two countries became so strong as to impel both the President and the Prime Minister to ask for fuller explanation. They got it in the form of a long telegram, which was given wide circulation among government officials in Washington and London. Even after long retrospective study of the situation I can think of little to add to the telegraphic explanation. I quote it here, paraphrased to comply with regulations designed to preserve the security of codes:

"November 14

"Completely understand the bewilderment in London and Washington because of the turn that negotiations with French North Africans have taken. Existing French sentiment here does not remotely agree with prior calculations. The following facts are pertinent and it is important that no precipitate action at home upset the equilibrium we have been able to establish.

"The name of Marshal Pétain is something to conjure with here. Everyone attempts to create the impression that he lives and acts under the shadow of the Marshal's figure. Civil governors, military leaders, and naval commanders agree that only one man has an obvious right to assume the Marshal's mantle in North Africa. He is Darlan. Even Giraud, who has been our trusted adviser and staunch friend since early conferences succeeded in bringing him down to earth, recognizes this overriding consideration and has modified his own intentions accordingly.

"The resistance we first met was offered because all ranks believed this to be the Marshal's wish. For this reason Giraud is deemed to have been guilty of at least a touch of insubordination in urging non-resistance to our landing. General Giraud understands and appears to have some sympathy for this universal attitude. All concerned say they are ready to help us provided Darlan tells them to do so, but they are not willing to follow anyone else. Admiral Esteva in Tunis says he will take orders from Darlan. Noguès stopped fighting in Morocco by Darlan's order. Recognition of Darlan's position in this regard cannot be escaped.

"The gist of the agreement is that the French will do what they can to assist us in taking Tunisia. The group will organize for effective co-operation and will begin, under Giraud, reorganization of selected military forces for participation in the war. The group will exhaust every expedient in an effort to get the Toulon fleet. We will support the group in controlling and pacifying country and in equipping selected units. Details still under discussion.

"Our hope of quick conquest of Tunisia and of gaining here a supporting population cannot be realized unless there is accepted a general agreement along the lines which we have just made with Darlan and the other officials who control the administrative machinery of the region and the tribes in Morocco. Giraud is now aware of his inability to do anything by himself, even with Allied support. He has cheerfully accepted the post of military chief in the Darlan group. He agrees that his own name should not be mentioned until a period of several days has elapsed. Without a strong French government we would be forced to undertake military occupation. The cost in time and resources would be tremendous. In Morocco alone General Patton believes that it would require 60,000 Allied troops to keep the tribes pacified. In view of the effect that tribal disturbance would have on Spain, you see what a problem we have." . . .

This arrangement was of course wholly different from that we had anticipated, back in London. But it was not only with respect to personalities and their influence in North Africa that our governments had miscalculated. They had believed that the French population in the region was bitterly resentful of Vichy-Nazi domination and would eagerly embrace as deliverers any Allied force that succeeded in establishing itself in the country. The first German bombing of Algiers—and there were many—proved the fallacy of this assumption. Of course there were many patriots, and after the Tunisian victory was assured their number increased, but in the early days of touch and go and nightly bombing the undercurrent of sentiment constantly transmitted to me was, "Why did you bring this war to us? We were satisfied before you came to get us all killed." In his final dispatch, written after the completion of the campaign, General Anderson had this to say about the early attitude of the inhabitants:

> . . . Many mayors, station- and post-masters and other key officials with whom we had dealings as we advanced (for instance, the civil telephone was, at first, my chief means of communicating with my forward units and with Allied Force Headquarters) were lukewarm in their sympathies and hesitant to commit themselves openly, while a few were hostile. I can safely generalize by saying that at first, in the Army, the senior officers were hesitant and afraid to commit themselves, the junior officers were mainly in favor of aiding the Allies, the men would obey orders; amongst the people, the Arabs were indifferent or inclined to be hostile, the French were in our favor but apathetic, the civil authorities were antagonistic as a whole. The resulting impression on my mind was not one of much confidence as to the safety of my small isolated force should I suffer a severe setback.

This was a far cry from the governmental hope that the people of North Africa would, upon our entry, blaze into spontaneous revolt against control by Nazi-dominated Vichy!

► "PASSION RAN HIGH IN ENGLAND ABOUT THE DARLAN DEAL"

WINSTON CHURCHILL

In his war memoirs the former British Prime Minister relates the violent reaction of the British public and press to the Eisenhower-Darlan agreement in North Africa.

The following excerpt refers to Churchill's decision to inform the House of Commons about the reasons for the deal in secret session.

. . . Passion ran high in England about the Darlan deal. It affected poignantly some of my friends who had been most affronted by Munich, with whose impulses I had moved at crucial moments before the war. "Is this then what we are fighting for?" they asked. Many of those with whom I was in closest mental and moral harmony were in extreme distress. . . . The press

Winston S. Churchill, *The Hinge of Fate* (Boston: Houghton Mifflin Co., 1950), pp. 638-643, *passim*.

gave full expression to this mood. Certainly there was a real and vivid case to be made and to be met. Not only Parliament but the nation found it hard to swallow "De Gaulle banned; Darlan uplifted." At the same time the facts could not be stated nor the arguments deployed in public. While in my mind, rightly or wrongly, I never had the slightest doubt that it was my duty to support General Eisenhower and to save the lives of the soldiers committed to the enterprise, I was acutely sensitive to the opposite argument, and understood, if only to override, the discarded alternative conviction. . . .

[On] December 10, a month after the landing, the mounting pressures in the circles of which I was conscious led me to seek refuge in Secret Session of the House of Commons. The speech which I then made was conceived with the sole purpose of changing the prevailing opinion, and I chose with the greatest care the points to make. I began with some severe understatements.

> The question which we must ask ourselves is not whether we like or do not like what is going on, but what are we going to do about it. In war it is not always possible to have everything go exactly as one likes. In working with allies it sometimes happens that they develop opinions of their own. Since 1776 we have not been in the position of being able to decide the policy of the United States. . . .
>
> The United States regards this as an American expedition under the ultimate command of the President of the United States, and they regard Northwest Africa as a war sphere which is in their keeping, just as we regard the Eastern Mediterranean as a theatre for which we are responsible. We have accepted this position from the outset and are serving under their command. That does not mean we have not got a great power of representation, and I am of course in the closest touch with the President. It does mean however that neither militarily nor politically are we directly controlling the course of events. It is because it would be highly detrimental to have a debate upon American policy or Anglo-American relations in public that His Majesty's Government have invited the House to come into Secret Session. In Secret Session alone can the matter be discussed without the risk of giving offense to our great Ally, and also of complicating the relationships of Frenchmen, who, whatever their past, are now firing upon the Germans.
>
> I hold no brief for Admiral Darlan. Like myself, he is the object of the animosities of Herr Hitler and of Monsieur Laval. Otherwise I have nothing in common with him. But it is necessary for the House to realize that the Government and to a large extent the people of the United States do not feel the same way about Darlan as we do. He has not betrayed them. He has not broken any treaty with them. He has not vilified them. He has not maltreated any of their citizens. They do not think much of him, but they do not hate him and despise him as we do over here. Many of them think more of the lives of their own soldiers than they do about the past records of French political figures. Moreover, the Americans have cultivated up to the last moment relations with Vichy which were of a fairly intimate character and which in my opinion have conduced to our general advantage. . . .
>
> I now turn to examine a peculiar form of French mentality, or rather of the mentality of a large proportion of Frenchmen in the terrible defeat

and ruin which has overtaken their country. I am not at all defending, still less eulogizing, this French mentality. But it would be very foolish not to try to understand what is passing in other people's minds, and what are the secret springs of action to which they respond. The Almighty in His infinite wisdom did not see fit to create Frenchmen in the image of Englishmen. In a State like France, which has experienced so many convulsions—Monarchy, Convention, Directory, Consulate, Empire, Monarchy, Empire, and finally Republic—there has grown up a . . . highly legalistic habit of mind. . . . Much therefore turns in the minds of French officers upon whether there is a direct, unbroken chain of lawful command, and this is held by many Frenchmen to be more important than moral, national, or international considerations. From this point of view many Frenchmen who admire General de Gaulle and envy him in his rôle nevertheless regard him as a man who has rebelled against the authority of the French State, which in their prostration they conceive to be vested in the person of the antique defeatist who to them is the illustrious and venerable Marshal Pétain, the hero of Verdun and the sole hope of France.

Now all this may seem very absurd to our minds. But there is one point about it which is important to us. It is in accordance with orders and authority transmitted or declared to be transmitted by Marshal Pétain that the French troops in Northwest Africa have pointed and fired their rifles against the Germans and Italians instead of continuing to point and fire their rifles against the British and Americans. I am sorry to have to mention a point like that, but it makes a lot of difference to a soldier whether a man fires his gun at him or at his enemy; and even the soldier's wife or father might have a feeling about it too. . . .

All this is done in the sacred name of the Marshal, and when the Marshal bleats over the telephone orders to the contrary and deprives Darlan of his nationality the Admiral rests comfortably upon the fact or fiction—it does not much matter which—that the Marshal is acting under the duress of the invading Hun, and that he, Darlan, is still carrying out his true wishes. In fact, if Admiral Darlan had to shoot Marshal Pétain he would no doubt do it in Marshal Pétain's name. . . .

I must however say that personally I consider that in the circumstances prevailing, General Eisenhower was right; and even if he was not quite right I should have been very reluctant to hamper or impede his action when so many lives and such vitally important issues hung in the balance. I do not want to shelter myself in any way behind the Americans or anyone else. . . .

I do not remember any speech out of hundreds which I made where I felt opinion change so palpably and decisively. This was no case for applause, but only for results. The Commons were convinced, and the fact that all further Parliamentary opposition stopped after the Secret Session quenched the hostile press and reassured the country. There was also the growing exhilaration of victory after so many hard months of disappointment or defeat. . . .

On the afternoon of December 24 Darlan drove down from his villa to his offices in the Palais d'Eté. At the door of his bureau he was shot down by a young man of twenty named Bonnier de la Chapelle. The Admiral died within the hour on the operating table of a near-by hospital. The youthful assassin . . . had worked himself into an exalted state of mind as the saviour of France from wicked leadership. . . .

He was tried by court-martial under Giraud's orders, and, much to his surprise, was executed by a firing squad shortly after dawn on December 26.

On receiving the news of Darlan's assassination General Eisenhower hurried back from the Tunisian front. In the circumstances the only thing to do was to nominate Giraud to fill the vacant place. . . .

Darlan's murder, however criminal, relieved the Allies of their embarrassment at working with him, and at the same time left them with all the advantages he had been able to bestow during the vital hours of the Allied landings. His authority had passed smoothly to the organization created in agreement with the American authorities during the months of November and December. Giraud filled the gap.

▶THE DECISION TO USE THE ATOMIC BOMB

LOUIS MORTON

The justification for using the atomic bomb was that it ended the war in the Pacific earlier. It had thus saved countless American and Japanese lives. As the nature of the force unleashed became apparent, many voices rose in protest against the decision, which—as it was expressed by J. P. Baxter— "blasted the web of history and, like the discovery of fire, severed past from present." [1] *Some protested in the name of humanity. Others attacked the decision as militarily unjustified. The problem is treated in the subsequent study of the reasons and arguments preceding the first use of an atomic weapon in history. The author is Deputy Chief Historian, Department of the Army.*

It is interesting to note that the following thorough study, while it is based on all relevant and available documentary material, cannot fully answer the question of what were the decisive reasons which induced the United States leaders to use the atomic bomb at that particular period of history; neither can it clarify with finality whether the Japanese surrender was brought about by the previous air bombardment and naval warfare, or the Soviet entry into the war which followed the first bomb on Hiroshima, or the second bomb on Nagasaki, or finally by the unprecedented personal interference of the Emperor in the military and political decision-making process of Japan.

The epic story of the development of the atomic bomb is by now well known. It began in 1939 when a small group of eminent scientists in this country called to the attention of the United States Government the vast

Excerpted by special permission from "The Decision to Use the Atomic Bomb," *Foreign Affairs*, January, 1957. Copyright by Council on Foreign Relations, Inc., New York.

[1] James Phinney Baxter, 3rd, *Scientists Against Time* (Boston: Little, Brown, 1946), p. 419.

potentialities of atomic energy for military purposes and warned that the Germans were already carrying on experiments in this field. The program initiated in October of that year with a very modest appropriation and later expanded into the two-billion-dollar Manhattan Project had only one purpose —to harness the energy of the atom in a chain reaction to produce a bomb that could be carried by aircraft if possible, and to produce it before the Germans could. That such a bomb, if produced, would be used, no responsible official even questioned. "At no time from 1941 to 1945," declared Mr. Stimson, "did I ever hear it suggested by the President, or by another responsible member of the Government, that atomic energy should not be used in the war." And Dr. J. Robert Oppenheimer recalled in 1954 that "we always assumed if they [atomic bombs] were needed, they would be used."

So long as the success of the project remained in doubt there seems to have been little or no discussion of the effects of an atomic weapon or the circumstances under which it would be used. "During the early days of the project," one scientist recalled, "we spent little time thinking about the possible effects of the bomb we were trying to make." It was a "neck-and-neck race with the Germans," the outcome of which might well determine who would be the victor in World War II. But as Germany approached defeat and as the effort to produce an atomic bomb offered increasing promise of success, those few men who knew what was being done and who appreciated the enormous implications of atomic energy became more and more concerned. Most of this concern came from the scientists in the Metallurgical Laboratory at Chicago, where by early 1945 small groups began to question the advisability of using the weapon they were trying so hard to build. It was almost as if they hoped the bomb would not work after it was completed.

On the military side, the realization that a bomb would probably be ready for testing in the summer of 1945 led to concrete planning for the use of the new weapon, on the assumption that the bomb when completed would work. By the end of 1944 a list of possible targets in Japan had been selected, and a B-29 squadron was trained for the specific job of delivering the bomb. It was also necessary to inform certain commanders in the Pacific about the project, and on December 30, 1944, Major-General Leslie R. Groves, head of the Manhattan District, recommended that this be done.

Even at this stage of development no one could estimate accurately when the bomb would be ready or guarantee that, when ready, it would work. It is perhaps for this reason—and because of the complete secrecy surrounding the project—that the possibility of an atomic weapon never entered into the deliberations of the strategic planners. It was, said Admiral William Leahy, "the best kept secret of the entire war" and only a handful of the top civilian and military officials in Washington knew about the bomb. As a matter of fact, one bright brigadier-general who innocently suggested that the Army might do well to look into the possibilities of atomic energy suddenly found himself the object of the most intensive investigation. So secret was the project, says John J. McCloy, that when he raised the subject at a White House meeting of the Joint Chiefs of Staff in June 1945 it "caused a sense of shock, even among that select group."

It was not until March 1945 that it became possible to predict with certainty that the bomb would be completed in time for testing in July. On March 15, Mr. Stimson discussed the project for the last time with President Roosevelt, but their conversation dealt mainly with the effects of the use of the bomb, not with the question of whether it ought to be used. Even at this late date, there does not seem to have been any doubt at the highest levels that the bomb would be used against Japan if it would help bring the war to an early end. But on lower levels, and especially among the scientists at the Chicago laboratory, there was considerable reservation about the advisability of using the bomb.

After President Roosevelt's death, it fell to Stimson to brief the new President about the atomic weapon. At a White House meeting on April 25, he outlined the history and status of the program and predicted that "within four months we shall in all probability have completed the most terrible weapon ever known in human history." This meeting, like Stimson's last meeting with Roosevelt, dealt largely with the political and diplomatic consequences of the use of such a weapon rather than with the timing and manner of employment, the circumstances under which it would be used, or whether it would be used at all. The answers to these questions depended on factors not yet known. But Stimson recommended, and the President approved, the appointment of a special committee to consider them.

This special committee, known as the Interim Committee, played a vital rôle in the decision to use the bomb. Secretary Stimson was chairman, and George L. Harrison, President of the New York Life Insurance Company and special consultant in the Secretary's office, took the chair when he was absent. James F. Byrnes, who held no official position at the time, was President Truman's personal representative. Other members were Ralph A. Bard, Under Secretary of the Navy, William L. Clayton, Assistant Secretary of State, and Drs. Vannevar Bush, Karl T. Compton and James B. Conant. Generals Marshall and Groves attended at least one and possibly more of the meetings of the committee.

The work of the Interim Committee, in Stimson's words, "ranged over the whole field of atomic energy, in its political, military, and scientific aspects." During the first meeting the scientific members reviewed for their colleagues the development of the Manhattan Project and described vividly the destructive power of the atomic bomb. They made it clear also that there was no known defense against this kind of attack. Another day was spent with the engineers and industrialists who had designed and built the huge plants at Oak Ridge and Hanford. Of particular concern to the committee was the question of how long it would take another country, particularly the Soviet Union, to produce an atomic bomb. "Much of the discussion," recalled Dr. Oppenheimer who attended the meeting of June 1 as a member of a scientific panel, "revolved around the question raised by Secretary Stimson as to whether there was any hope at all of using this development to get less barbarous [sic] relations with the Russians."

The work of the Interim Committee was completed June 1, 1945, when it submitted its report to the President, recommending unanimously that:

1. The bomb should be used against Japan as soon as possible.

2. It should be used against a military target surrounded by other buildings.

3. It should be used without prior warning of the nature of the weapon. (One member, Ralph A. Bard, later dissented from this portion of the committee's recommendation.)

"The conclusions of the Committee," wrote Stimson, "were similar to my own, although I reached mine independently. I felt that to extract a genuine surrender from the Emperor and his military advisers, they must be administered a tremendous shock which would carry convincing proof of our power to destroy the empire. Such an effective shock would save many times the number of lives, both American and Japanese, that it would cost."

Among the scientists working on the Manhattan Project were many who did not agree. To them, the "wave of horror and repulsion" that might follow the sudden use of an atomic bomb would more than outweigh its military advantages. "It may be very difficult," they declared, "to persuade the world that a nation which was capable of secretly preparing and suddenly releasing a new weapon, as indiscriminate as the rocket bomb and a thousand times more destructive, is to be trusted in its proclaimed desire of having such weapons abolished by international agreement." The procedure these scientists recommended was, first, to demonstrate the new weapon "before the eyes of representatives of all the United Nations on the desert or a barren island," and then to issue "a preliminary ultimatum" to Japan. If this ultimatum was rejected, and "if the sanction of the United Nations (and of public opinion at home) were obtained," then and only then, said the scientists, should the United States consider using the bomb. "This may sound fantastic," they said, "but in nuclear weapons we have something entirely new in order of magnitude of destructive power, and if we want to capitalize fully on the advantage their possession gives us, we must use new and imaginative methods."

These views, which were forwarded to the Secretary of War on June 11, 1945, were strongly supported by 64 of the scientists in the Chicago Metallurgical Laboratory in a petition sent directly to the President. At about the same time, at the request of Dr. Arthur H. Compton, a poll was taken of the views of more than 150 scientists at the Chicago Laboratory. Five alternatives ranging from all-out use of the bomb to "keeping the existence of the bomb a secret" were presented. Of those polled, about two-thirds voted for a preliminary demonstration, either on a military objective or an uninhabited locality; the rest were split on all-out use and no use at all.

These views, and presumably others, were referred by Secretary Stimson to a distinguished Scientific Panel consisting of Drs. Arthur H. Compton, Enrico Fermi, E. O. Lawrence and J. Robert Oppenheimer, all nuclear physicists of the first rank. "We didn't know beans about the military situation," Oppenheimer later said. "We didn't know whether they [the Japanese] could be caused to surrender by other means or whether the invasion [of Japan] was really inevitable. . . . We thought the two overriding considerations were the saving of lives in the war and the effect of our actions on the stability of the postwar world." On June 16 the panel reported that it had studied carefully the proposals made by the scientists but could see no practical way of ending the war by a technical demonstration. Almost regretfully, it seemed, the four members of the panel concluded that there was "no acceptable alternative to direct military use." "Nothing would have been more damaging to our effort," wrote Stimson, " . . . than a warning or demonstration followed by a dud—and this was a real possibility." With this went the fear, expressed by Byrnes, that if the Japanese were warned that an atomic bomb would be exploded over a military target in Japan as a demonstration, "they might bring our boys who were prisoners of war to that area." Furthermore, only two bombs would be available by August, the number General Groves estimated would be needed to end the war; these two would have to obtain the desired effect quickly. And no one yet knew, nor would the scheduled ground test in New Mexico prove, whether a bomb dropped from an airplane would explode.

Nor, for that matter, were all those concerned certain that the bomb would work at all, on the ground or in the air. Of these doubters, the greatest was Admiral Leahy, who until the end remained unconvinced. "This is the biggest fool thing we have ever done," he told Truman after Vannevar Bush had explained to the President how the bomb worked. "The bomb will never go off, and I speak as an expert in explosives."

Thus, by mid-June 1945, there was virtual unanimity among the President's civilian advisers on the use of the bomb. The arguments of the opponents had been considered and rejected. So far as is known, the President did not solicit the views of the military or naval staffs, nor were they offered.

Military Considerations

The military situation on June 1, 1945, when the Interim Committee submitted its recommendations on the use of the atomic bomb, was distinctly favorable to the Allied cause. Germany had surrendered in May and troops from Europe would soon be available for redeployment in the Pacific. Manila had fallen in February; Iwo Jima was in American hands; and the success of the Okinawa invasion was assured. Air and submarine attacks had virtually cut off Japan from the resources of the Indies, and B-29s from the Marianas were pulverizing Japan's cities and factories. The Pacific Fleet had virtually driven the Imperial Navy from the ocean, and planes of the fast carrier forces were striking Japanese naval bases in the Inland Sea. Clearly, Japan was a defeated nation.

Though defeated in a military sense, Japan showed no disposition to surrender unconditionally. And Japanese troops had demonstrated time and again that they could fight hard and inflict heavy casualties even when the outlook was hopeless. Allied plans in the spring of 1945 took these facts into account and proceeded on the assumption that an invasion of the home islands would be required to achieve at the earliest possible date the unconditional surrender of Japan—the announced objective of the war and the basic assumption of all strategic planning. . . .

Though the Joint Chiefs had accepted the invasion concept as the basis for preparations, and had issued a directive for the Kyushu assault on May 25, it was well understood that the final decision was yet to be made. By mid-June the time had come for such a decision and during that period the Joint Chiefs reviewed the whole problem of Japanese strategy. Finally, on June 18, at a meeting in the White House, they presented the alternatives to President Truman. Also present (according to the minutes) were Secretaries Stimson and Forrestal and Assistant Secretary of War John J. McCloy.

General Marshall presented the case for invasion and carried his colleagues with him, although both Admirals Leahy and King later declared they did not favor the plan. After considerable discussion of casualties and of the difficulties ahead, President Truman made his decision. Kyushu would be invaded as planned and preparations for the landing were to be pushed through to completion. Preparations for the Honshu assault would continue, but no final decision would be made until preparations had reached the point "beyond which there would not be opportunity for a free choice." The program thus approved by Truman called for:

1. Air bombardment and blockade of Japan from bases in Okinawa, Iwo Jima, the Marianas and the Philippines.

2. Assault of Kyushu on November 1, 1945, and intensification of blockade and air bombardment.

3. Invasion of the industrial heart of Japan through the Tokyo Plain in central Honshu, tentative target date March 1, 1946.

During the White House meeting of June 18, there was discussion of the possibility of ending the war by political means. The President displayed a deep interest in the subject and both Stimson and McCloy emphasized the importance of the "large submerged class in Japan who do not favor the present war and whose full opinion and influence had never yet been felt." There was discussion also of the atomic bomb, since everyone present knew about the bomb and the recommendations of the Interim Committee. The suggestion was made that before the bomb was dropped, the Japanese should be warned that the United States had such a weapon. "Not one of the Chiefs nor the Secretary," recalled Mr. McCloy, "thought well of a bomb warning, an effective argument being that no one could be certain, in spite of the assurances of the scientists, that the 'thing would go off.'"

Though the defeat of the enemy's armed forces in the Japanese homeland was considered a prerequisite to Japan's surrender, it did not follow that Japanese forces elsewhere, especially those on the Asiatic mainland, would surrender also. It was to provide for just this contingency, as well as to pin down those forces during the invasion of the home islands, that the Joint Chiefs had recommended Soviet entry into the war against Japan.

Soviet participation was a goal long pursued by the Americans. Both political and military authorities seem to have been convinced from the start that Soviet assistance, conceived in various ways, would shorten the war and lessen the cost. In October 1943, Marshal Stalin had told Cordell Hull, then in Moscow for a conference, that the Soviet Union would eventually declare war on Japan. At the Tehran Conference in November of that year, Stalin had given the Allies formal notice of this intention and reaffirmed it in October

1944. In February 1945, at the Yalta Conference, Roosevelt and Stalin had agreed on the terms of Soviet participation in the Far Eastern war. Thus, by June 1945, the Americans could look forward to Soviet intervention at a date estimated as three months after the defeat of Germany.

But by the summer of 1945 the Americans had undergone a change of heart. Though the official position of the War Department still held that "Russian entry will have a profound military effect in that almost certainly it will materially shorten the war and thus save American lives," few responsible American officials were eager for Soviet intervention or as willing to make concessions as they had been at an earlier period. What had once appeared extremely desirable appeared less so now that the war in Europe was over and Japan was virtually defeated. President Truman, one official recalled, stated during a meeting devoted to the question of Soviet policy that agreements with Stalin had up to that time been "a one-way street" and that "he intended thereafter to be firm in his dealings with the Russians." And at the June 18 meeting of the Joint Chiefs of Staff with the President, Admiral King had declared that "regardless of the desirability of the Russians entering the war, they were not indispensable and he did not think we should go so far as to beg them to come in." Though the cost would be greater, he had no doubt "we could handle it alone."

The failure of the Soviets to abide by agreements made at Yalta had also done much to discourage the American desire for further coöperation with them. But after urging Stalin for three years to declare war on Japan, the United States Government could hardly ask him now to remain neutral. Moreover, there was no way of keeping the Russians out even if there had been a will to do so. In Harriman's view, "Russia would come into the war regardless of what we might do."

A further difficulty was that Allied intelligence still indicated that Soviet intervention would be desirable, if not necessary, for the success of the invasion strategy. In Allied intelligence, Japan was portrayed as a defeated nation whose military leaders were blind to defeat. Though her industries had been seriously crippled by air bombardment and naval blockade and her armed forces were critically deficient in many of the resources of war, Japan was still far from surrender. She had ample reserves of weapons and ammunition and an army of 5,000,000 troops, 2,000,000 of them in the home islands. The latter could be expected to put up a strong resistance to invasion. In the opinion of the intelligence experts, neither blockade nor bombing alone would produce unconditional surrender before the date set for invasion. And the invasion itself, they believed, would be costly and possibly prolonged.

According to these intelligence reports, the Japanese leaders were fully aware of their desperate situation but would continue to fight in the hope of avoiding complete defeat by securing a better bargaining position. Allied war-weariness and disunity, or some miracle, they hoped, would offer them a way out. "The Japanese believe," declared an intelligence estimate of June 30, " . . . that unconditional surrender would be the equivalent of national extinction, and there are as yet no indications that they are ready to accept such terms." It appeared also to the intelligence experts that Japan might surrender at any time "depending upon the conditions of surrender" the Allies might offer. Clearly these conditions, to have any chance of acceptance, would have to include retention of the imperial system.

How accurate were these estimates? Judging from postwar accounts of Japan, they were very close to the truth. Since the defeat at Saipan, when Tojo had been forced to resign, the strength of the "peace party" had been increasing. In September 1944 the Swedish Minister in Tokyo had been approached unofficially, presumably in the name of Prince Konoye, to sound out the Allies on terms for peace. This overture came to naught, as did another the following March. But the Swedish Minister did learn that those who advocated peace in Japan regarded the Allied demand for unconditional surrender as their greatest obstacle.

The Suzuki Cabinet that came into power in April 1945 had an unspoken mandate from the Emperor to end the war as quickly as possible. But it was faced immediately with another problem when the Soviet Government announced it would not renew the neutrality pact after April 1946. The German surrender in May produced another crisis in the Japanese Government and led, after considerable discussion, to a decision to seek Soviet mediation. But the first approach, made on June 3 to Jacob Malik, the Soviet Ambassador, produced no results. Malik was noncommittal and merely said the problem needed further study. Another overture to Malik later in the month also came to naught.

At the end of June, the Japanese finally approached the Soviet Government directly through Ambassador Sato in Moscow, asking that it mediate with the Allies to bring the Far Eastern war to an end. In a series of messages between Tokyo and Moscow, which the Americans intercepted and decoded, the Japanese Foreign Office outlined the position of the government and instructed Ambassador Sato to make arrangements for a special envoy from the Emperor who would be empowered to make terms for Soviet mediation. Unconditional surrender, he was told, was completely unacceptable, and time was of the essence. But the Russians, on one pretext and another, delayed their answer until mid-July when Stalin and Molotov left for Potsdam. Thus, the Japanese Government had by then accepted defeat and was seeking desperately for a way out; but it was not willing even at this late date to surrender unconditionally, and would accept no terms that did not include the preservation of the imperial system.

Allied intelligence thus had estimated the situation in Japan correctly. Allied invasion strategy had been reëxamined and confirmed in mid-June, and the date for the invasion fixed. The desirability of Soviet assistance had been confirmed also and plans for her entry into the war during August could now be made. No decision had been reached on the use of the atomic bomb, but the President's advisers had recommended it. The decision was the President's and he faced it squarely. But before he could make it he would want to know whether the measures already concerted would produce unconditional surrender at the earliest moment and at the lowest cost. If they could not, then he would have to decide whether circumstances warranted employment of a bomb that Stimson had already labeled as "the most terrible weapon ever known in human history."

The Decision

Though responsibility for the decision to use the atomic bomb was the President's, he exercised it only after careful study of the recommendations of his senior advisers. Chief among these was the Secretary of War, under whose broad supervision the Manhattan Project had been placed. Already deeply concerned over the cost of the projected invasion, the political effects of Soviet intervention and the potential consequences of the use of the atomic bomb, Stimson sought a course that would avoid all these evils. The difficulty, as he saw it, lay in the requirement for unconditional surrender. It was a phrase that might make the Japanese desperate and lead to a long and unnecessary campaign of attrition that would be extremely costly to both sides. But there was no way of getting around the term; it was firmly rooted in Allied war aims and its renunciation was certain to lead to charges of appeasement.

But if this difficulty could be overcome, would the Japanese respond if terms were offered? The intelligence experts thought so, and the radio intercepts from Tokyo to Moscow bore them out. So far as the Army was concerned there was much to be gained by such a course. Not only might it reduce the enormous cost of the war, but it would also make possible a settlement in the Western Pacific "before too many of our allies are committed there and have made substantial contributions towards the defeat of Japan." In the view of the War Department these aims justified "any concessions which might be attractive to the Japanese, so long as our realistic aims for peace in the Pacific are not adversely affected."

The problem was to formulate terms that would meet these conditions. There was considerable discussion of this problem in Washington in the spring of 1945 by officials in the Department of State and in the War and Navy Departments. Joseph C. Grew, Acting Secretary of State, proposed to the President late in May that he issue a proclamation urging the Japanese to surrender and assuring them that they could keep the Emperor. Though Truman did not act on the suggestion, he thought it "a sound idea" and told Grew to discuss it with his cabinet colleagues and the Joint Chiefs. On June 18, Grew was back with the report that these groups favored the idea, but that there were differences on the timing.

Grew's ideas, as well as those of others concerned, were summarized by Stimson in a long and carefully considered memorandum to the President on July 2. Representing the most informed military and political estimate of the situation at this time, this memorandum constitutes a state paper of the first importance. If any one document can be said to provide the basis for the President's warning to Japan and his final decision to use the atomic bomb, this is it.

The gist of Stimson's argument was that the most promising alternative to the long and costly struggle certain to follow invasion was to warn the Japanese "of what is to come" and to give them an opportunity to surrender. There was, he thought, enough of a chance that such a course would work to make the effort worthwhile. Japan no longer had any allies, her navy was virtually destroyed and she was increasingly vulnerable to air attack and naval blockade. Against her were arrayed the increasingly powerful forces of the Allies, with their "inexhaustible and untouched industrial resources." In these circumstances, Stimson believed the Japanese people would be susceptible to reason if properly approached. "Japan," he pointed out, "is not a nation composed of mad fanatics of an entirely different mentality from ours. On the contrary, she has within the past century shown herself to possess extremely intelligent people. . . . " But any attempt, Stimson added, "to exterminate her armies and her population by gunfire or other means will tend to produce a fusion of race solidity and antipathy. . . . "

A warning to Japan, Stimson contended, should be carefully timed. It should come before the actual invasion, before destruction had reduced the Japanese "to fanatical despair" and, if the Soviet Union had already entered the war, before the Russian attack had progressed too far. It should also emphasize, Stimson believed, the inevitability and completeness of the destruction ahead and the determination of the Allies to strip Japan of her conquests and to destroy the influence of the military clique. It should be a strong warning and should leave no doubt in Japanese minds that they would have to surrender unconditionally and submit to Allied occupation.

The warning, as Stimson envisaged it, had a double character. While promising destruction and devastation, it was also to hold out hope to the Japanese if they heeded its message. In his memorandum, therefore, Stimson stressed the positive features of the warning and recommended that it include a disavowal of any intention to destroy the Japanese nation or to occupy the country permanently. Once Japan's military clique had been removed from power and her capacity to wage war destroyed, it was Stimson's belief that the Allies should withdraw and resume normal trade relations with the new and peaceful Japanese Government. "I personally think," he declared, "that if in saying this we should add that we do not exclude a constitutional monarchy under her present dynasty, it would substantially add to the chance of acceptance."

Not once in the course of this lengthy memorandum was mention made of the atomic bomb. There was no need to do so. Everyone concerned understood clearly that the bomb was the instrument that would destroy Japan and impress on the Japanese Government the hopelessness of any course but surrender. As Stimson expressed it, the atomic bomb was "the best possible sanction," the single weapon that would convince the Japanese "of our power to destroy the empire."

Though Stimson considered a warning combined with an offer of terms and backed up by the sanction of the atomic bomb as the most promising means of inducing surrender at any early date, there were other courses that some thought might produce the same result. One was the continuation and intensification of air bombardment coupled with surface and underwater blockade. This course had already been considered and rejected as insufficient to produce surrender, though its advocates were by no means convinced that this decision was a wise one. And Stimson himself later justified the use of the bomb on the ground that by November 1 conventional bombardment would have caused greater destruction than the bomb. This apparent contradiction is explained by the fact that the atomic bomb was considered to have a psychological effect entirely apart from the damage wrought.

Nor did Stimson, in his memorandum, consider the effect of the Soviet Union's entry into the war. By itself, this action could not be counted on to force Japan to capitulate, but combined with bombardment and blockade it might do so. At least that was the view of Brigadier-General George A. Lincoln, one of the Army's top planners, who wrote in June that "probably it will take Russian entry into the war, coupled with a landing, or imminent threat of landing on Japan proper by us, to convince them [the Japanese] of the hopelessness of their position." Why, therefore, was it not possible to issue the warning prior to a Soviet declaration of war against Japan and rely on that event, together with an intensified air bombardment, to produce the desired result? If together they could not secure Japan's surrender, would there not still be time to use the bomb before the scheduled invasion of Kyushu in November?

No final answer to this question is possible with the evidence at hand. But one cannot ignore the fact that some responsible officials feared the political consequences of Soviet intervention and hoped that ultimately it would prove unnecessary. This feeling may unconsciously have made the atom bomb solution more attractive than it might otherwise have been. Some officials may have believed, too, that the bomb could be used as a powerful deterrent to Soviet expansion in Europe, where the Red tide had successively engulfed Rumania, Bulgaria, Jugoslavia, Czechoslovakia and Hungary. In an interview with three of the top scientists in the Manhattan Project early in June, Mr. Byrnes did not, according to Leo Szilard, argue that the bomb was needed to defeat Japan, but rather that it should be dropped to "make Russia more manageable in Europe."

It has been asserted also that the desire to justify the expenditure of the two billion dollars spent on the Manhattan Project may have disposed some favorably toward the use of the bomb. Already questions had been asked in Congress, and the end of the war would almost certainly bring on a full-scale investigation. What more striking justification of the Manhattan Project than a new weapon that had ended the war in one sudden blow and saved countless American lives? "It was my reaction," wrote Admiral Leahy, "that the scientists and others wanted to make this test because of the vast sums that had been spent on the project. Truman knew that, and so did other people involved."

This explanation hardly does credit to those involved in the Manhattan Project and not even P. M. S. Blackett, one of the severest critics of the decision to use the bomb, accepted it. "The wit of man," he declared, "could hardly devise a theory of the dropping of the bomb, both more insulting to the American people, or more likely to lead to an energetically pursued Soviet defense policy."

But even if the need to justify these huge expenditures is discounted— and certainly by itself it could not have produced the decision—the question still remains whether those who held in their hands a weapon thought capable of ending the war in one stroke could justify withholding that weapon. Would they not be open to criticism for failing to use every means at their disposal to defeat the enemy as quickly as possible, thereby saving many American lives?

And even at that time there were some who believed that the new weapon would ultimately prove the most effective deterrent to war yet produced. How better to outlaw war forever than to demonstrate the tremendous destructive power of this weapon by using it against an actual target?

By early July 1945 the stage had been set for the final decision. Stimson's memorandum had been approved in principle and on July 4 the British had given their consent to the use of the bomb against Japan. It remained only to decide on the terms and timing of the warning. This was the situation when the Potsdam Conference opened on July 17, one day after the bomb had been successfully exploded in a spectacular demonstration at Alamogordo, New Mexico. The atomic bomb was a reality and when the news reached Potsdam there was great excitement among those who were let in on the secret. Instead of the prospect of long and bitter months of fighting the Japanese, there was now a vision, "fair and bright indeed it seemed" to Churchill, "of the end of the whole war in one or two violent shocks."

President Truman's first action was to call together his chief advisers— Byrnes, Stimson, Leahy, Marshall, King and Arnold. "I asked for their opinion whether the bomb should be used," he later wrote. The consensus was that it should. Here at last was the miracle to end the war and solve all the perplexing problems posed by the necessity for invasion. But because no one could tell what effect the bomb might have "physically or psychologically," it was decided to proceed with the military plans for the invasion.

No one at this time, or later in the conference, raised the question of whether the Japanese should be informed of the existence of the bomb. That question, it will be recalled, had been discussed by the Scientific Panel on June 16 and at the White House meeting with the JCS, the service Secretaries and Mr. McCloy on June 18. For a variety of reasons, including uncertainty as to whether the bomb would work, it had then been decided that the Japanese should not be warned of the existence of the new weapon. The successful explosion of the first bomb on July 17 did not apparently outweigh the reasons advanced earlier for keeping the bomb a secret, and evidently none of the men involved thought the question needed to be reviewed. The Japanese would learn of the atomic bomb only when it was dropped on them.

The secrecy that had shrouded the development of the atomic bomb was torn aside briefly at Potsdam, but with no visible effect. On July 24, on the advice of his chief advisers, Truman informed Marshal Stalin "casually" that the Americans had "a new weapon of unusual destructive force." "The

Russian Premier," he recalled, "showed no special interest. All he said was that he was glad to hear it and hoped we would make 'good use of it against the Japanese.' " One cannot but wonder whether the Marshal was preoccupied at the moment or simulating a lack of interest.

On the military side, the Potsdam Conference developed nothing new. The plans already made were noted and approved. Even at this late stage the question of the bomb was divorced entirely from military plans and the final report of the conference accepted as the main effort the invasion of the Japanese home islands. November 15, 1946, was accepted as the planning date for the end of the war against Japan.

During the conference, Stalin told Truman about the Japanese overtures —information that the Americans already had. The Marshal spoke of the matter also to Churchill, who discussed it with Truman, suggesting cautiously that some offer be made to Japan. "Mr. Stimson, General Marshall, and the President," he later wrote, "were evidently searching their hearts, and we had no need to press them. We knew of course that the Japanese were ready to give up all conquests made in the war." That same night, after dining with Stalin and Truman, the Prime Minister wrote that the Russians intended to attack Japan soon after August 8—perhaps within two weeks of that date. Truman presumably received the same information, confirming Harry Hopkins' report of his conversation with Stalin in Moscow in May.

All that remained now was to warn Japan and give her an opportunity to surrender. In this matter Stimson's and Grew's views, as outlined in the memorandum of July 2, were accepted, but apparently on the advice of the former Secretary of State Cordell Hull it was decided to omit any reference to the Emperor. Hull's view, solicited by Byrnes before his departure for Potsdam, was that the proposal smacked of appeasement and "seemed to guarantee continuance not only of the Emperor but also of the feudal privileges of a ruling caste." And should the Japanese reject the warning, the proposal to retain the imperial system might well encourage resistance and have "terrible political repercussions" in the United States. For these reasons he recommended that no statement about the Emperor be made until "the climax of Allied bombing and Russia's entry into the war." Thus, the final terms offered to the Japanese in the Potsdam Declaration on July 26 made no mention of the Emperor or of the imperial system. Neither did the declaration contain any reference to the atom bomb but simply warned the Japanese of the consequences of continued resistance. Only those already familiar with the weapon could have read the references to inevitable and complete destruction as a warning of atomic warfare.

The receipt of the Potsdam Declaration in Japan led to frantic meetings to decide what should be done. It was finally decided not to reject the note but to await the results of the Soviet overture. At this point, the military insisted that the government make some statement to the people, and on July 28 Premier Suzuki declared to the press that Japan would ignore the declaration, a statement that was interpreted by the Allies as a rejection.

To the Americans the rejection of the Potsdam Declaration confirmed the view that the military was still in control of Japan and that only a decisive act of violence could remove them. The instrument for such action lay at hand in the atomic bomb; events now seemed to justify its use. But in the hope that the Japanese might still change their minds, Truman held off orders on the use of the bomb for a few days. Only silence came from Tokyo, for the Japanese were waiting for a reply from the Soviet Government, which would not come until the return of Stalin and Molotov from Potsdam on August 6. Prophetically, Foreign Minister Tojo wrote Sato on August 2, the day the Potsdam Conference ended, that he could not afford to lose a single day in his efforts to conclude arrangements with the Russians "if we were to end the war before the assault on our mainland." By that time, President Truman had already decided on the use of the bomb.

Preparations for dropping the two atomic bombs produced thus far had been under way for some time. The components of the bombs had been sent by cruiser to Tinian in May and the fissionable material was flown out in mid-July. The B-29s and crews were ready and trained, standing by for orders, which would come through the Commanding General, U. S. Army Strategic Air Forces in the Pacific, General Spaatz. Detailed arrangements and schedules were completed and all that was necessary was to issue orders.

At General Arnold's insistence, the responsibility for selecting the particular target and fixing the exact date and hour of the attack was assigned to the field commander, General Spaatz. In orders issued on July 25 and approved by Stimson and Marshall, Spaatz was ordered to drop the "first special bomb as soon as weather will permit visual bombing after about 3 August 1945 on one of the targets: Hiroshima, Kokura, Niigata, and Nagasaki." He was instructed also to deliver a copy of this order personally to MacArthur and Nimitz. Weather was the critical factor because the bomb had to be dropped by visual means, and Spaatz delegated to his chief of staff, Major-General Curtis E. LeMay, the job of deciding when the weather was right for this most important mission.

From the dating of the order to General Spaatz it has been argued that President Truman was certain the warning would be rejected and had fixed the date for the bombing of Hiroshima even before the issuance of the Potsdam Declaration. But such an argument ignores the military necessities. For operational reasons, the orders had to be issued in sufficient time "to set the military wheels in motion." In a sense, therefore, the decision was made on July 25. It would stand unless the President changed his mind. "I had made the decision," wrote Truman in 1955. "I also instructed Stimson that the order would stand unless I notified him that the Japanese reply to our ultimatum was acceptable." The rejection by the Japanese of the Potsdam Declaration confirmed the orders Spaatz had already received.

The Japanese Surrender

On Tinian and Guam, preparations for dropping the bomb had been completed by August 3. The original plan was to carry out the operation on August 4, but General LeMay deferred the attack because of bad weather over the target. On August 5 the forecasts were favorable and he gave the word to proceed with the mission the following day. At 0245 on August 6, the bomb-carrying plane was airborne. Six and a half hours later the bomb was released over Hiroshima, Japan's eighth largest city, to explode 50 seconds later at a height of about 2,000 feet. The age of atomic warfare had opened.

Aboard the cruiser *Augusta* on his way back to the United States, President Truman received the news by radio. That same day a previously prepared release from Washington announced to the world that an atomic bomb had been dropped on Hiroshima and warned the Japanese that if they did not surrender they could expect "a rain of ruin from the air, the like of which has never been seen on this earth."

On August 7, Ambassador Sato in Moscow received word at last that Molotov would see him the next afternoon. At the appointed hour he arrived at the Kremlin, full of hope that he would receive a favorable reply to the Japanese proposal for Soviet mediation with the Allies to end the war. Instead, he was handed the Soviet declaration of war, effective on August 9. Thus, three months to the day after Germany's surrender, Marshal Stalin had lived up to his promise to the Allies.

Meanwhile, President Truman had authorized the use of the second bomb—the last then available. The objective was Kokura, the date August 9. But the plane carrying the bomb failed to make its run over the primary target and hit the secondary target, Nagasaki, instead. The next day Japan sued for peace.

The close sequence of events between August 6 and 10, combined with the fact that the bomb was dropped almost three months before the scheduled invasion of Kyushu and while the Japanese were trying desperately to get out of the war, has suggested to some that the bombing of Hiroshima had a deeper purpose than the desire to end the war quickly. This purpose, it is claimed, was nothing less than a desire to forestall Soviet intervention into the Far Eastern war. Else why this necessity for speed? Certainly nothing in the military situation seemed to call for such hasty action. But if the purpose was to forestall Soviet intervention, then there was every reason for speed. And even if the Russians could not be kept out of the war, at least they would be prevented from making more than a token contribution to victory over Japan. In this sense it may be argued that the bomb proved a success, for the war ended with the United States in full control of Japan.

This theory leaves several matters unexplained. In the first place, the Americans did not know the exact date on which the Soviet Union would declare war but believed it would be within a week or two of August 8. If they had wished to forestall a Soviet declaration of war, then they could reasonably have been expected to act sooner than they did. Such close timing left little if any margin for error. Secondly, had the United States desired above everything else to keep the Russians out, it could have responded to one of the several unofficial Japanese overtures, or made the Potsdam Declaration more attractive to Japan. Certainly the failure to put a time limit on the declaration suggests that speed was not of the essence in American calculations. Finally, the date and time of the bombing were left to Generals

Spaatz and LeMay, who certainly had no way of knowing Soviet intentions. Bad weather or any other untoward incident could have delayed the attack a week or more.

There is reason to believe that the Russians at the last moved more quickly than they had intended. In his conversations with Harry Hopkins in May 1945 and at Potsdam, Marshal Stalin had linked Soviet entry with negotiations then in progress with Chinese representatives in Moscow. When these were completed, he had said, he would act. On August 8 these negotiations were still in progress.

Did the atomic bomb accomplish its purpose? Was it, in fact, as Stimson said, "the best possible sanction" after Japan rejected the Potsdam Declaration? The sequence of events argues strongly that it was, for bombs were dropped on the 6th and 9th, and on the 10th Japan surrendered. But in the excitement over the announcement of the first use of an atomic bomb and then of Japan's surrender, many overlooked the significance of the Soviet Union's entry into the war on the 9th. The first bomb had produced consternation and confusion among the leaders of Japan, but no disposition to surrender. The Soviet declaration of war, though not entirely unexpected, was a devastating blow and, by removing all hope of Soviet mediation, gave the advocates of peace their first opportunity to come boldly out into the open. When Premier Suzuki arrived at the palace on the morning of the 9th, he was told that the Emperor believed Japan's only course now was to accept the Potsdam Declaration. The militarists could and did minimize the effects of the bomb, but they could not evade the obvious consequences of Soviet intervention, which ended all hope of dividing their enemies and securing softer peace terms.

In this atmosphere, the leaders of Japan held a series of meetings on August 9, but were unable to come to agreement. In the morning came word of the fate of Nagasaki. This additional disaster failed to resolve the issues between the military and those who advocated surrender. Finally the Emperor took the unprecedented step of calling an Imperial Conference, which lasted until 3 o'clock the next morning. When it, too, failed to produce agreement the Emperor told his ministers that he wished the war brought to an end. The constitutional significance of this action is difficult for Westerners to comprehend, but it resolved the crisis and produced in the cabinet a formal decision to accept the Potsdam Declaration, provided it did not prejudice the position of the Emperor.

What finally forced the Japanese to surrender? Was it air bombardment, naval power, the atomic bomb or Soviet entry? The United States Strategic Bombing Survey concluded that Japan would have surrendered by the end of the year, without invasion and without the atomic bomb. Other equally informed opinion maintained that it was the atomic bomb that forced Japan to surrender. "Without its use," Dr. Karl T. Compton asserted, "the war would have continued for many months." Admiral Nimitz believed firmly that the decisive factor was "the complete impunity with which the Pacific Fleet pounded Japan," and General Arnold claimed it was air bombardment that had brought Japan to the verge of collapse. But Major-General Claire Chennault, wartime air commander in China, maintained that Soviet entry into the Far Eastern war brought about the surrender of Japan and would have done so "even if no atomic bombs had been dropped."

It would be a fruitless task to weigh accurately the relative importance of all the factors leading to the Japanese surrender. There is no doubt that Japan had been defeated by the summer of 1945, if not earlier. But defeat did not mean that the military clique had given up; the Army intended to fight on and had made elaborate preparations for the defense of the homeland. Whether air bombardment and naval blockade or the threat of invasion would have produced an early surrender and averted the heavy losses almost certain to accompany the actual landings in Japan is a moot question. Certainly they had a profound effect on the Japanese position. It is equally impossible to assert categorically that the atomic bomb alone or Soviet intervention alone was the decisive factor in bringing the war to an end. All that can be said on the available evidence is that Japan was defeated in the military sense by August 1945 and that the bombing of Hiroshima, followed by the Soviet Union's declaration of war and then the bombing of Nagasaki and the threat of still further bombing, acted as catalytic agents to produce the Japanese decision to surrender. Together they created so extreme a crisis that the Emperor himself, in an unprecedented move, took matters into his own hands and ordered his ministers to surrender. Whether any other set of circumstances would have resolved the crisis and produced the final decision to surrender is a question history cannot yet answer.

Part V

NEGOTIATIONS

When nations are confronted with a challenge to their interests, they have the choice of three possible courses of action, depending on circumstances and the seriousness of the threat. They may try:

1. To *eliminate* the source of the challenge or the threat. This may be done by a legitimate use of force (for instance, by a police action which removes the assailant). Or, in the absence of police enforcement, nations, like individuals, may protect their interests by self-help. An individual may kill in self-defense. A nation may wage war for the same reason.

2. To *oppose* the threat by adequate power, to prevent the threat from being realized. Through a balancing process, or a policy of deterrence, the challenge may be kept in bounds and its effectiveness minimized.

3. To *neutralize* the threat by a compromise, which may be reached through negotiations.

Methods under 1 and 2 were analyzed in Part IV. In this section we are concerned with the third method, negotiations. Negotiations are defined as contacts between individuals or nations, established "with the view to coming to terms."[1]

For this purpose individuals often enter into direct contact with each other; or they may use intermediaries, such as attorneys-at-law or other representatives. The result of such negotiations may be a contract, lease, exchange of goods or services, definition of limits of one's estate, etc.

When nations negotiate and reach an agreement, it may be expressed in the form of:

(a) a communiqué or common declaration, stating the broad lines of the agreement. It may be a declaration of common principles or a general profession of common faith. One example is the Atlantic Charter, agreed on by President Roosevelt and Prime Minister Churchill in 1941.

(b) an alliance or a legally binding treaty or convention;

(c) a temporary or permanent organization which is to implement, interpret or enforce what has been previously agreed upon. On the basis of

[1] *Webster's New Collegiate Dictionary.*

preceding negotiations many such agencies have been established: the Commission for the Suppression of Slave Trade; the Permanent Court of Arbitration; the Coal and Steel Community in Western Europe; The League of Nations; the United Nations; and many others.

International treaties (their sum forming what is called the law of nations) and international organizations should be viewed not only as an end product of negotiations—which they always are—but also as a framework to encourage and facilitate negotiations and settlements of future issues.

The law of nations as well as some forms of international organization will be analyzed in Part VI.

Nations, being abstract entities, cannot enter into direct contact with each other, as individuals do. Nations establish contact with a view to coming to terms through the mediation of heads of government (summit meetings); foreign secretaries (foreign ministers' or their deputies' conferences or councils), specially appointed emissaries (Harry Hopkins under Roosevelt); or, most frequently, the diplomatic service.

Diplomatic missions and consular offices link all nations of the world in a network that permits communication and negotiation between nations, usually on a bilateral basis. These channels of communication are severed when a war breaks out or when a situation arises where one nation decides that diplomatic contacts with another are undesirable or not useful. This is so, for instance, in the case of the United States' nonrecognition of Communist China or in cases when an ambassador is recalled, downgrading our representation to that of a chargé d'affaires. Yet even in such a situation, or in the case of war, some aspects of negotiations between unfriendly or belligerent nations may still be carried on through the intermediary of the diplomatic missions of third parties. Even during fighting, belligerents negotiate through the intermediary of neutral nations (such as Switzerland) in order to reach agreement on exchange of prisoners of war or preparation for armistice or peace.

Diplomatic Negotiations

Diplomacy is usually defined as the practice of carrying out a nation's foreign policy by negotiations with other nations. This definition correctly stresses that diplomacy is an *instrument* of policy—not policy itself; the procedures of foreign policy and not the substance. "The formulation of policy is the responsibility of the statesmen," notes Sir Ivone Kirkpatrick, former Permanent Secretary of State of the British Foreign Office, and adds: "Execution is generally the task of the diplomats, who in every country except the United States are professionals." Sir Ivone refers here to the American practice of having successful businessmen or generous contributors to party election funds preside over the staff of professional foreign service officers as heads of U.S. embassies in Western Europe and other attractive countries of the world.

The professional foreign service was discussed in Part III, with emphasis on the duty of the professionals to be the "eyes and ears" of their country abroad. In this section the stress is on the second aspect of their duties and responsibilities: to be successful mouthpieces of their nation abroad. A diplomat not only evaluates the objectives and power of other nations, but interprets his own nation's policy and methods to others. One of his main tasks is to negotiate with foreign governments.

The fundamental characteristic of any negotiation is the desire of the participants to try to come to agreement. The term "agreement" generally involves participants only. An agreement reached by others may mean a serious threat to the interests of nonparticipants. Nations, like individuals, sometimes agree on a common plan of blackmail or attack against a third party, or a common defense against its threats. This is the usual purpose of negotiations for an aggressive or defensive alliance.

The duration and solidity of such agreement made *against* a third party depends on the duration and seriousness of the threat. Harmony and cooperation between allies is often only a reflection of the threat from the outside. While the danger persists, all other issues appear unimportant and are quite easily subordinated to the common effort of collective defense. When Stalin's rigidity was replaced by Khrushchev's flexibility, negotiations within NATO proved more difficult than they had been while Stalin was alive.

In their common opposition to nazism, America, Russia, and England were often able to negotiate successfully and agree on issues. This was so during the wartime summit meetings at Teheran, Yalta, and Potsdam. After the Nazi threat had been removed, new attempts at negotiations between western democracies and the Soviet Union usually ended in failure. The summit conference at Geneva, followed by a foreign ministers' meeting in 1955 and the foreign ministers' conference at Geneva in 1959 are examples.

On a different level, the fact that a common struggle *against* a third party is one of the best guarantees of successful negotiations and harmony was demonstrated by the modern history of India. Moslem-Hindu unity, achieved and maintained during their common struggle against the British rule, did not survive the successful elimination of the common enemy. After liberation, with accompanying blood-letting, India split into its Moslem (Pakistan) and Hindu parts.

Negotiations (derived from the Latin "negotium"—business) should be distinguished from contacts and meetings between nations which, in spite of appearances suggesting negotiations, have purposes other than "coming to terms."

Individuals, for instance, often meet for the sheer pleasure of seeing each other, or in order to exchange goods, services, viewpoints, information, jokes, or kisses. Previous "negotiations" may have prepared the ground for such exchanges.

At other times, individuals may meet to conduct what may appear as efforts to come to terms but in reality are meetings to exchange pointed remarks, insults, or threats; to denounce or ridicule one participant in front of others; or, to give challenge or even engage in a fight.

Similarly, only some meetings between statesmen and diplomats aim at, or have as a result, solutions of conflicts and settlement of issues.

The purpose of many an international conference is merely to multiply political as well as nonpolitical contacts and, thus, augment points of common interest; to tune down the polemical tone of public utterances; to examine rivals' proposals; or, generally speaking, to prepare the ground for possible settlement at a later date. Agreement to try to agree in the future is obviously preferable to disagreement.

In our era such a patient, long-term, and *gradual* approach to world conflicts is perhaps the only alternative to the present critical tension between blocs of nations.

Other diplomatic meetings may be organized for other purposes than negotiations. An unwary observer may be deceived by the polished language, smooth procedures, and diplomatic qualifications of the participants. He may thus mistake a nation's willingness to attend a conference for its desire to negotiate a settlement, whereas that nation's objective is to blackmail or dictate to the other participants; the public may confuse a meeting organized by all participants for propaganda purposes with a meeting for negotiation. Professional negotiators, the diplomats, are sometimes asked by their government not to negotiate but, on the contrary, to break off negotiations and diplomatic relations in a spectacular manner, or to deliver an ultimatum or declaration of war. Their role as diplomats, appointed to that government and country, is thus temporarily ended.

Or, finally, diplomats may be asked by their government to insult, threaten, or denounce a nation in front of the others. If threats do not reach a limit of unbearability, they may be often viewed as justifiable methods of pressure. A participant to negotiation who obstinately refuses to meet a concession with a counter-concession may be induced to more reasonable behavior by various threats or ultimatums. The threat to suspend negotiations is one of them. At other times diplomats, whose main role is to negotiate, engage in exchanging insults and threats only to show their muscle or rub in their own righteousness. In such a case the role of diplomats may be said to have been corrupted.

This often happens in the public phases of international conferences. Many statements are then made to prove to the audience that one is right and that the other side is wrong, or to make political capital in one's own country.

Both foreign ministers' conferences in Geneva (1955 and 1959) were full of examples of this. The purpose was to insult or threaten the opposite side. Similar procedures, contrary to the real meaning of diplomacy, may be observed during debate at the U.N. General Assembly.

The majority votes, which in the U.N. General Assembly conclude the preceding debates, are never legally binding (see p. 541) and cannot therefore settle anything by themselves. The real aim of many a debate in the United Nations is only to obtain as impressive a voting lineup of nations as possible. Thus, one nation and its policy may be publicly condemned, but the issue itself remains unsolved and international tension may be increased. This is not diplomacy in the real sense of the word, but propaganda. Instead of using radio, pamphlets, or film to denigrate a nation, it uses a different technique: a majority vote in the United Nations General Assembly.

Negotiations between Friends and between Enemies

A state of great amity does not make negotiations unnecessary. Nor does a state of great enmity exclude them.

Wherever men live and work in groups, conflicts of interest are bound to arise. Even in the most harmonious of families minor irritants appear and must be adjusted lest they become major ones. Experience shows that in an atmosphere of trust a concrete point of difference, however serious it may be in itself, often proves soluble through negotiations. Even when, for example, some serious clashes of economic interests disturb good neighborly relations between the United States and its two neighbors, Canada or Mexico, the hemispheric "family spirit" permits usually friendly and speedy solution.

On the other hand, where an atmosphere of enmity prevails, even a minor issue, however technical and nonpolitical it may be, often proves inseparable from the whole fabric of mutual fears. Every clash of interest is colored by the adverse political framework, and an effort to negotiate the issue usually proves futile.

The foregoing does not mean that negotiations among enemy nations are excluded because they are enemies. But such negotiations have to overcome difficult barriers. We have already mentioned a case where belligerents started negotiations to end a shooting war (the extreme form of enmity and suspicion). Enemies are sometimes willing to negotiate either because of utter exhaustion from the war or because they realize that their original objectives in the war cannot be achieved, despite tremendous losses in human lives and property. A compromise may seem better than continuation of war. Nations sometimes reach a reasonable compromise because they are equally frustrated.

If it is possible to *end* wars by negotiations, why should it be more difficult to *prevent* them by the same method? The answer is that the reality of war brings home some arguments with greater persuasiveness than the prospect of war. In its planning stage, war does not exclude the theoretical possibility of complete destruction of the rival, and therefore full satisfaction of one's goals.

This is one reason negotiations between rival nations fail in times of peace while the same rivals may successfully negotiate over the same issues toward the end of a war.

There is another difficulty which has often frustrated negotiations among rivals in times of peace. It has already been mentioned: it is the practical inseparability of any single dispute from the whole array of mutual fears and suspicions.

Nations often try to concentrate on what appears to be the most dangerous or immediate cause of conflict. Some believe that the armament race is such a single cause. Others may be convinced that too close a contact between the military forces of two rival nations, facing each other across inherently explosive territory (e.g., Germany) should be removed. They propose "disengagement." Still others consider human misery, poverty, and underdevelopment to be causes of unrest which, in turn, may produce international conflicts.

Statesmen and diplomats hope that in concentrating on disarmament, disengagement, or economic development, and separating these issues from other sources of enmity, they may creep up on the whole political conflict, step by step, progressing from one problem to another. Somewhat disparagingly, this indirect approach to peace is often called "peace by pieces." Its basic assumption is that cooperation among rivals in one field—disarmament or control of atomic energy, or in clearly nonpolitical fields such as trade, aid to underdeveloped areas, cooperation in cultural, educational, scientific and hygienic fields—may lead to cooperation in all fields. One of the promoters of such an indirect approach to peace (called *functionalism*) notes that a peaceful world society is "more likely to grow through doing things together in workshop and market place than by signing pacts in chancelleries." [2]

We shall have more to say about the possibilities and limitations of an indirect and nonpolitical approach to political conflicts in Part VI (Inis L. Claude's article on "The Theory of Functionalism," p. 608). At this point we may usefully examine one particularly popular and favored partial approach to the problem of international tension: disarmament.

Problems of Disarmament

The armaments race is often believed to be the single most important cause of fear and suspicion between nations, and consequently the major cause of many wars. We often hear that arms produce wars. But is this necessarily so?

Nations arm because they either fear or plan a war. The intention or fear comes first; military measures, advancing strategic lines, building bases abroad, etc., come second. Arms are not feared because they are composed of deadly explosives and metal but because behind them we suspect *intent* to use them. When such suspicion is absent, military might does not cause any fears. A small nation living in the shadow of an overwhelming military power may not be afraid of its neighbor. That depends on the real or assumed intentions of that power. Mexico does not fear the military might of the United States. Iran does fear the might of Russia.

This cause-and-effect relation has been also well illustrated by the Arab opposition to Israel's plan for regional disarmament in the Middle East. This proposal followed the Soviet plan for total disarmament, made in 1959. "The United Nations should not be bothered about any disarmament scheme with respect to the Middle East," said Mr. Ahmad Shukairy (Oct. 29, 1959), representing Saudi Arabia at the United Nations General Assembly. "The Middle East is ready to disarm without a plan, regional or otherwise, only when the reasons for the trouble are removed. Israel and disarmament in the Middle East are incompatible, and there is no room for both. . . . [For the Arab nations to disarm] at a time when a military aggression is rooted in the area is a national suicide which no nation represented here . . . would accept."

[2] David Mitrany, *A Working Peace System* (London and New York: The Royal Institute of International Affairs, 1946), p. 5.

It could hardly be put more bluntly: the existence of Israel has been the cause for Arab armaments; disarmament would then be possible only when Israel ceases to exist.

It should be recognized, of course, that the very existence of increased armament produces, in turn, additional suspicion, especially the fear that what has been produced might be used. Increased armaments are taken as an indication of increased ambition.

Many sincere efforts have been made to end the armament race through negotiations; their history is long. Long also is the list of failures, while the list of partial successes is extremely short. Confusion between cause and effect, that is, distrust and weapons, has often swirled nations into a vicious circle.

As armaments are the result of fear and suspicion, they cannot be substantially limited unless the original causes of fear and suspicion are eliminated. If the causes were really eliminated, then no disarmament conferences would be necessary since no nation would consider it useful to spend money on arms. But suspicion and fear can hardly be eliminated at conferences where nations disregard causes of the arms race and concentrate on quality and quantity of weapons. In such atmosphere of general mistrust, the only guarantee of successful disarmament agreement seems to be watertight mutual control.

Yet, here another vicious circle begins. If nations do not trust each other, they cannot allow other nations the unlimited access to their territory which would allow really efficient control. Unlimited inspection by a nation which cannot be trusted could be used for the purpose of spying.

Premier Khrushchev expressed this idea quite bluntly when he said the Soviet Union was not prepared to "open all its doors and its secret places to outsiders or to anyone except closest friends." According to Khrushchev, Western proposals for elaborate methods of supervision were designed to "prepare aggression." He added that "truly effective control over all aspects of arms reduction have to await the growth of more trust between the East and the West" than then existed.[3]

Khrushchev treated Eisenhower's proposal for mutual air inspection (the "Open Sky" proposal of 1956) in the same way. He called it a thinly disguised American plan to spy and to select targets for future American atomic bombardment.

The Soviet thesis apparently is: free inspection of all countries does not guarantee complete disarmament. It would only guarantee the success of capitalist intelligence. In Khrushchev's words: "We are in favor of general disarmament under control but we are against control without disarmament."[4]

The Western thesis seems to be: the Soviet concept of control, subject to Soviet veto, is inadequate. Disarmament without effective control would

---

[3] *New York Times,* July 13, 1958. N. S. Khrushchev's speech at the Soviet-Czechoslovak rally at Moscow's Lozhniki stadium, July 12, 1958.
[4] Speech to the U.N. General Assembly, Sept. 18, 1959, reprinted in the *New York Times,* September 19, 1959.

be suicide. In the words of a *New York Times* editorial: "The Soviets still seek a one-sided Western disarmament based on paper pacts the scraps of which litter their path to empire."

It may seem that the West almost stubbornly insists on effective control while the Soviet Union appears to have more trust in the West's implementation of disarmament agreements. One of the West's main reasons for its insistence lies in the nature of democratic society. If the Soviet Union does not adhere to a disarmament agreement, its system of highly centralized and uncontrolled power practically guarantees the secrecy of such transgressions. Democratic society, with all major decisions exposed to the consent or disapproval of the nation, can hardly conceal any deviations from original disarmament rules.

The clash between both theses crystallized once more during Premier Khrushchev's visit to the United States in the fall of 1959. In the somewhat improved international atmosphere of that time, Premier Khrushchev addressed the General Assembly of the United Nations in New York (September 18, 1959) and proposed that "over a period of four years all states should effect complete disarmament." All nuclear arms and missiles would be destroyed, all military bases dismantled, "armies, navies, and air forces would cease to exist, general staffs and war ministries would be abolished, and military institutions closed." At the end of this period nations would be left only with police forces to keep internal order. And then, and only then, free access to all countries for inspection could be established.

No wonder the reaction of the West to such a plan was cool, although cautiously so. The propagandistic plan for complete and general disarmament, however unrealistic it might be, appealed to tired and anxious men-in-the-street everywhere in the world.

"The Soviet plan puts the cart before the horse," commented a *New York Times* editorial. "In their [Soviet] program disarmament comes first and control later, and they bluntly state that in the present world situation 'there are no necessary prerequisites for establishing comprehensive control.' Should the West ever accept the Soviet disarmament plan, it might well wake up some morning to find uncontrolled Soviet armies marching to engulf it." [5]

Mutual trust and confidence, which both the West and the Soviet bloc consider a precondition for disarmament, obviously had not yet been established. But could they be established? To trust or not to trust, this was the question. To refuse peace could be as disastrous as to believe in the peaceful intentions of an aggressor.

In addition to the basic hurdle to disarmament—that arms are the effect and not the cause of world tensions—six other problems reappeared. These problems had not been solved during previous, more modest, attempts at partial or specifically atomic disarmament, and had caused their failure.

The six major problems connected with Soviet disarmament proposals are:

[5] *New York Times,* September 22, 1959.

1. So far, the Soviet Union has always made its assent to any partial inspection dependent on voting procedures: either numerical equality of Communist and non-Communist votes or the veto principle of the U.N. Security Council. This means that no inspection teams could be sent to the Soviet Union without specific assent of the Soviet government. The West could hardly rely on an inspection system which would be dependent on the assent of the potential or suspected violator. The only partial departure from the Soviet insistence on the veto was recorded during the 1958-1960 Geneva Conference on banning nuclear tests. The Soviet Union seemed to agree to a veto-free, on-site inspection provided that the number of such inspections would be limited to ten. The United States advocated one hundred on-site inspections a year.

2. A 100 percent foolproof control system is really impossible. Even if the Soviet Union were ready to accept some form of relatively effective inspection, such relative control could not replace mutual trust. In the 1930's the French argued that to have a reliable system of inspection-control of Germany's adherence to the formula of disarmament, a large group of inspectors would have to poke their bayonets into every haystack in Germany every day of every month of every year. Effective control of modern atomic weapons is further complicated by the fact that nuclear byproducts of peaceful projects can be easily used for military purposes.

3. Premier Khrushchev proposed that states should finally be left only with police forces to keep internal order. Yet, experience has shown that disorder in society usually occurs, not within nations, but between them. There is no indication of a change in this respect. Another problem concerning the police force is its size. A dictatorial state needs a more extensive police system than a democracy. A larger country's police establishment may represent an army to a small neighbor state. Communist China's police force could easily occupy Laos. Soviet police forces might suppress any attempts at revolution in Hungary, Poland, Czechoslovakia, or any other smaller Communist satellite.

4. Khrushchev's proposal clearly favors nations with vast populations. In complete disarmament, Southeast Asia, the Middle East, and Western Europe (unprotected by the barriers of oceans) would feel the full impact of Russia's and China's tremendous populations. The security of smaller countries and peace in general could not be maintained if these populous states were still to insist, as Secretary Herter suggested, "on going to war . . . with knives." We have already pointed out that a war which might start with knives and stones could degenerate into an atomic one. The destruction of existing atomic arsenals would not eliminate the knowledge necessary to produce atomic weapons.

5. According to Communist doctrine, capitalism may delay its inevitable doom by defense spending and wars. Military expenditures are said to prevent the United States and other non-Communist countries from falling into total economic crisis. Peace would destroy capitalism. This is why capitalism, by its nature, is warmongering.

In light of this theory Stalin would actually appear as the savior of capitalism. By constant threats, he induced the West to arm and thus save itself.

Has this theory been abandoned or is it being reasserted and another of Stalin's errors corrected? As the West would not dare to attack the Soviet bloc in the atomic era, Khrushchev may be trying to prove Lenin's thesis and bury capitalism in peace.

During his visit to the United States Premier Khrushchev inquired several times whether the American economy, contrary to Leninist thesis, could be converted into a peace economy without major disturbances. "They say it is possible," said Khrushchev, referring to his meeting with New York industrialists at Averell Harriman's house. But "I should add," later wrote Adlai Stevenson, "that Mr. K. concluded the subject with a twinkle in his darting eyes, 'at least that's what your industrialists all tell me; and what else could they say?' " [6]

We do not know what Khrushchev's real conclusion is.

6. Finally, there is a disturbing parallel in the Khrushchev plan with another Soviet proposal for equally general and complete disarmament. Soviet Foreign Minister Maxim A. Litvinov offered such a plan to a disarmament commission at Geneva in 1927. Litvinov's plan also suggested to the West the abolition of all armies, navies, general staffs, war ministries, and military academies.

One year later, in November, 1928, at the Sixth World Congress of the Communist International, one of its resolutions defined the Communist attitude toward disarmament in a partly Communist and partly capitalist world as follows:

> It goes without saying that not a single Communist thought for a moment that the imperialists would accept the Soviet total disarmament proposal. . . . The disarmament policy of the Soviet government must be utilized for the purpose of agitation . . . [these proposals] must be utilized as a means . . . to eradicate all pacifist illusion and carry on propaganda among the masses in support of the only way toward disarmament and abolition of war, *viz.,* arming of the proletariat, overthrowing the bourgeoisie and establishing the proletarian dictatorship.

Five years later, at the World Disarmament Conference at Geneva (February, 1932), Spain's delegate, the famous historian and writer, Salvador de Madariaga, used the following fable (attributed to W. S. Churchill) to illustrate his reservations on the Soviet proposal:

> Does Mr. Litvinov remember the fable about the animals' disarmament conference? When the animals had gathered, the lion looked at the eagle and said gravely, "We must abolish talons." The tiger looked at the elephant and said, "we must abolish tusks." The elephant looked back at the tiger and said, "we must abolish claws and jaws." Thus each animal in turn proposed the abolition of the weapons he did not have, until at last the bear rose up

[6] *New York Times,* September 29, 1959.

and said in tones of sweet reasonableness: "Comrades, let us abolish every-thing—everything but the great universal embrace."

Following the 1959 Soviet disarmament proposal the question was whether the theses of the Sixth World Congress of the Communist International and Señor Madariaga's fable should be viewed as things of the past or as still possessing relevance for the present.

In contrast to the failures in disarmament efforts when they are attempted by rival nations fearing one another, one may quote the unique phenomenon of total disarmament along the Canada-United States border. The absence of mutual suspicion makes any detailed disarmament treaties or controls unnecessary. The only exception was the Rush-Bagot agreement of 1817 which limited the naval armaments of Canada and the United States on the Great Lakes to three vessels each, of equal tonnage. This agreement has been faithfully adhered to and when, during World War II, due to Canada's ship-building the need to revise terms of the agreement arose, it was temporarily altered without any elaborate schemes of control and inspection.

Forms of Negotiations

A great variety of frameworks and procedures facilitates negotiations among nations. The description of some of them follows:

1. *Negotiation through permanent diplomatic channels.* This is the most usual form. Ambassadors and their staffs appointed to a foreign government approach its different departments (such as the ministries of foreign affairs, commerce, finance, defense) to negotiate literally thousands of minor and major issues each year.

2. *Negotiations through special meetings.* When a dispute or an issue proves to be particularly dangerous or difficult, it may be taken out of the routine diplomatic channels and transferred to some special meeting, usually distinguished by the authority of the participants.

Yet even special or summit conferences have to be prepared in detail through established permanent diplomatic channels.

Diplomatic negotiations conducted by the highest authorities are usually referred to as "personal diplomacy." Some of them—like the Geneva Conferences—have been prepared by means of the established permanent diplomatic channels. Others are marked by a high degree of informality and unpreparedness. Their purpose is not to negotiate agreement but rather to talk things over. During and after the Soviet Premier's visit to the United States in 1959 a new touch was added to this form of personal diplomacy: wife, children and other relatives were added to a travelling statesman's entourage to augment the appeal to the man-in-the-street as well as to the opposite numbers. It could be, perhaps, described as a new variation of personal diplomacy—"just us folks" diplomacy.

Negotiations may be conducted either on a *bilateral* or *multilateral* basis. Today, in contrast to previous centuries, the *multilateral* form of diplomacy, of both the parliamentary and the old-fashioned type, is the rule rather than the exception.

The United Nations headquarters in New York is a particularly fitting ground for the multilateral form of diplomacy. Some may value the informal aspect of U.N. diplomacy more than the public and parliamentary one. Many a thorny issue has been settled in the whispering quiet of the delegates' cocktail lounge rather than in the great U.N. halls which register, translate, and broadcast every single syllable. The United Nations' quiet diplomacy may be a more useful and important instrument than the formal machinery anchored in the charter.

3. *Parliamentary negotiations.* A special variety of multilateral diplomacy is the parliamentary form which emerged after World War I in the League of Nations and re-emerged after World War II in the United Nations.

This relatively novel form of negotiation among nations has certain features which the old-fashioned, mostly bilateral diplomacy did not have:

(a) The parliamentary form of multilateral diplomacy imitates some procedures and techniques customarily used by national legislative bodies, such as public debate, voting, reporting out of committees, etc. However, when these techniques are used in diplomatic negotiation, they do not produce legally binding decisions. While national assemblies accept majority rule as binding, this is not the case of the United Nations. The majority decisions of its General Assembly cannot be enforced.

Thus the seemingly "legislative process in the United Nations," as Secretary General Dag Hammarskjold rightly remarked, "serves its purpose only when it helps diplomacy to arrive at agreements between the national states concerned. It is diplomacy, not speeches and votes, that continues to have the last word in the process of peace-making."

It does not mean that a majority vote in the United Nations cannot have at least some limited effect on some countries. Such a vote may strengthen the opposition's argument against the government in a country responsive to a majority vote in its domestic affairs. For example, the UN condemnation affected British, French, and Israeli actions in the Suez area. Yet, even in this case the effect of the vote should not be overrated. A more important and determining factor was that both the Soviet Union and the United States, with their power to *implement* a policy, were part of the majority.

Dictatorial governments, on the other hand, are particularly insensitive to a majority vote because their domestic policies are based on the concept of one-party rule, that is, a rule without any opposition or any device for majority *vs.* minority decisions. There is no danger that any foreign opposition to the government's policies might become an instrument of domestic pressure. This is the case of the Soviet Union which (from the internal point of view) does not need to fear, or pay attention to, a negative vote in the United Nations. Of course, even a dictatorial state such as the U.S.S.R. tries to avoid any decrease in international prestige by being, for instance, continuously condemned by the U.N. General Assembly. In this indirect and limited sense, diplomacy by parliamentary procedures may then have some effect.

(b) The second aspect of the modern multilateral parliamentary form of diplomacy is the participation of nations other than those directly concerned. In contrast to nineteenth century diplomacy, we observe nations expressing views and casting their votes on issues which are dominantly local or regional and which, therefore, distant and less concerned nations cannot fully appreciate. These may sometimes vote as their great ally does or, worse, as their mood may command.

On the other hand, it may be said that in our interconnected and interdependent world any major issue does affect the world at large. It is therefore natural that Asians vote on matters affecting the security and developments of the Western Hemisphere, just as U.S. congressmen, elected by industrial districts in the East, often vote on purely agricultural measures affecting the West primarily. This may be taken as an indication of a growing awareness of interdependence in our world.

Open vs. Secret Diplomacy

When aristocrats were in charge of negotiations between nations, when their dealings were secret and national destinies were often mortgaged or exposed to hazardous enterprises without the knowledge and consent of the population, and when many wars ensued, people tended to identify the aristocratic forms of secret diplomacy with wars.

Democracy, it was argued, should act differently. In the pre-democratic era practically all aspects of government policies had been decided upon by aristocratic elites without the consent of the people. Foreign policy was no exception. Under democracy, on the other hand, the people are expected to control all aspects of government, including foreign policy. It would certainly be strange if the people were to participate in such trivial decisions as, say, sales of liquor, and if at the same time they were excluded from such a vital matter as foreign policy.

Woodrow Wilson expressed the demand for democratic control of foreign policy and *open* diplomacy by his famous sentence that under democracy "covenants among nations should not only be open but openly arrived at."

Even in his time it was realized that such a demand asks international society to do better than an integrated and relatively harmonious *national* community is able to do.

Even within a homogeneous democratic society many a delicate negotiation does not expose itself to the eyes and comments of the public. While a marriage or a divorce is finally proclaimed in public, negotiations are usually quite confidential and limited only to the directly interested parties. Similarly, running for public office or taking a public vote is usually preceded by a number of nonpublic negotiations. Woodrow Wilson himself did not consider it useful to invite the public to witness his preparatory discussions with Lloyd George or Clemenceau at the Peace Conference in Paris, nor did he abandon the secret code which he himself used to send messages to and from Washington, D. C.

"Open agreements represent the response to a sound demand," said Dag Hammarskjold in his interpretation of Woodrow Wilson's slogan, speaking on diplomacy at Ohio State University. "How and to what extent they should be 'openly arrived at,' on the other hand, is a principle which requires serious consideration in the light of the very aims which the public procedures intend to serve." [7]

"It is of course essential that all free peoples should know and understand the great issues of policy which may mean life and death for them," said the recipient of the Nobel Prize for Peace, Canada's former Secretary of State for External Affairs, Lester B. Pearson. [8] "But it is not essential, indeed it is often harmful for the negotiation of policy always to be conducted in glass houses which are often too tempting a target for brickbats. Open diplomacy now tends to become frozen diplomacy."

A similar fear that open diplomacy tends to become a propaganda duel was expressed by the former President of West Germany, Theodor Heuss. Criticizing the over-publicized summit meetings in his New Year's (1958) message to the German people, Theodor Heuss declared:

> International politics . . . has of late been accustomed to almost improvised meetings with flashlights, loudspeakers and press conferences. Politics should change its style. At this point I come to the statement of the cautious and brilliant George F. Kennan—his warning against publicity that considers itself democratic and that always tends to be interpreted as propaganda by each side. As regards this, I do not hesitate to take the liberty of being old-fashioned.

Thus, the Secretary General of the United Nations, the President of Germany, George F. Kennan, Lester B. Pearson, Harold Nicolson (Topic 23), and many other experienced diplomats or statesmen recommend that diplomacy by loudspeakers and diplomacy by insults (a contradiction in terms) be abandoned and the "old-fashioned" form of diplomacy be re-adopted. The term "old-fashioned" is misleading: what is actually meant is that nations should use diplomacy in its real and full sense. To do so means to learn and excel in the art of negotiations, which uses the techniques of persuasion, pressure, concession and counterconcession, and is able in this way to accommodate conflicting interests. Every negotiation is composed of (a) stages, many of which are and should be confidential; and (b) result, which in a democracy should be public in order to be discussed and approved or disapproved by appropriate parliamentary bodies. "If the *stages* become matters of public controversy before the *result* has been achieved," warns Harold Nicolson, "the negotiations will almost certainly founder."

Diplomacy and Peace

Negotiations may result in a more or less final settlement of an issue; or, more modestly, they may be provisionally concluded by an agreement not to settle the issue by the use of violent means and try to solve the conflict of interests at a later date. In both cases they represent important alternatives

---

[7] *New York Times,* February 6, 1958.
[8] Speech to the United Nations General Assembly, September 23, 1953.

to fatal slipping downhill toward an armed conflict. Among nations, negotiations appear to be the only alternative to tension and violence.

It should be recalled that negotiation—that is, a gradual, often unspectacular, accommodation of conflicting interests—has been the foundation of peaceful and well-integrated national communities. Informal adjustments of conflicting interests had led to political and moral consensus, the basis of effective government and law. The process of informal adjustments then continued under government and law which, in turn, came to represent additional and powerful inducement to peaceful solution of conflicts.

In the search for peace among individuals the agreement to agree at a later date has often been the first concrete step to peace and order. It well may be the like in the case of nations. The will to agree is dominant; the form by which such an agreement is reached is secondary. This point should be stressed. Establishment of some better forms of international intercourse and more adequate machinery would not mean that we could dispense with negotiation—that is, with a constant and patient search for common ground and harmony of interests. "Peaceful settlement involves less the adequacy of international institutions and more the will and national interests of states," noted Kenneth W. Thompson in his study on *The Problems of Nuclear Weapons* (excerpt reproduced in Topic 20). "The substance, not the form, of negotiations is important and the existing channels for discussion (within and outside the United Nations, in Geneva, and elsewhere) are more than sufficient. Indeed, the twentieth century may suffer from the illusion that international institutions of themselves assure peace. On the contrary, institutions are merely the forum within which conflicting foreign-policy goals may be harmonized—a task in the final analysis for diplomacy and statecraft."

Summary

Negotiations are contacts between nations which desire to come to terms.

They are carried on through (a) regular diplomatic channels, involving professionally trained negotiators such as ambassadors and foreign service officers; and (b) by means of special meetings of persons of the highest authority, or experts.

Negotiations may involve two or more nations; they may be carried out openly (by means of parliamentary procedures as in the U.N.) or confidentially.

The final result of negotiations is either a communiqué registering agreement or disagreement; or a proclamation of principles; or a legally binding treaty or convention; or, finally, an international agency or organization which is to serve as a framework for new negotiations and treaty-making.

The success of diplomatic negotiations largely depends on two conditions:

1. The subject should be suited for negotiation and eventual compromise. If both sides want everything, no compromise is possible.

2. Both sides should desire to remove not only the symptoms but also the cause of conflict. If enmity has produced armaments, these cannot be

eliminated, lowered, or controlled unless their cause—mutual distrust—is also alleviated. Amity permits even the most delicate problems to be handled successfully. Enmity and mistrust prevent even technical details from being solved.

If the intention to reach agreement is lacking, contacts among nations occur but are not negotiations in spite of their appearance. Their purpose is not coming to terms but publicly recording mutual accusations and disagreement for propaganda purposes.

TOPIC 23

Principles and Methods of Negotiations among Nations

In a world which remains divided by nationalism and ideology and lacks either political and moral consensus, negotiations aiming at compromise between different interests are the fundamental tool of statecraft.

By negotiations nations often succeed in removing dangerous points of friction; and, by negotiations, step by step, they may perhaps reach a greater degree of political and moral unity of the world.

There does not seem to be any other alternative.

What Demosthenes said about diplomacy in ancient Athens applies to the atomic age too:

> Ambassadors have no battleships at their disposal, or heavy infantry, or fortresses; their weapons are words and opportunities. In important transactions opportunities are fleeting; once they are missed they cannot be recovered. It is a greater offense to deprive a democracy of an opportunity than it would be thus to deprive an oligarchy or an autocracy. Under their systems, action can be taken instantly and on the word of command; but with us, first the Council has to be notified and adopt a provisional resolution, and even then only when the heralds and the Ambassadors have sent in a note in writing. Then the Council has to convene the Assembly, but then only on a statutory date. Then the debater has to prove his case in face of an ignorant and often corrupt opposition; and even when this endless procedure has been completed, and a decision has been come to, even more time is wasted before the necessary financial resolution can be passed. Thus an ambassador who, in a constitution such as ours, acts in a dilatory manner and causes us to miss our opportunities, is not missing opportunities only, but robbing us of the control of events. . . .

►THE EVOLUTION OF DIPLOMATIC METHOD

HAROLD NICOLSON

In the following selection a British historian and professional diplomat of world fame sketches the advance and decline in the growth of diplomatic method. Condemning diplomacy by loudspeaker or diplomacy by insult as contradictions in terms, he favors the traditional French method of diplomacy, courteous and dignified, continuous and gradual, and based on knowledge and experience.

By the French method I mean the theory and practice of international negotiation originated by Richelieu, analyzed by Callières [François de Callières, 1645-1717, wrote a classic manual on diplomatic method, *On the Manner of Negotiating with Princes*], and adopted by all European countries during the three centuries that preceded the change of 1919. I regard this method as that best adapted to the conduct of relations between civilized States. It was courteous and dignified; it was continuous and gradual; it attached importance to knowledge and experience; it took account of the realities of existing power; and it defined good faith, lucidity and precision as the qualities essential to any sound negotiation. The mistakes, the follies and the crimes that during those three hundred years accumulated to the discredit of the old diplomacy can, when examined at their sources, be traced to evil foreign policy rather than to faulty methods of negotiation. It is regrettable that the bad things they did should have dishonored the excellent manner in which they did them.

In drawing attention to the virtues of the French method I am not of course proposing to scrap all existing machinery and to return to the system of the eighteenth or nineteenth centuries. The conditions on which the old diplomacy was based no longer exist. Yet there seems no reason why we, in recognizing the faults of the old system, should ignore the many merits that it possessed. I am not, I repeat, suggesting that the old diplomacy should be reintroduced or even imitated: I am suggesting only that we should consider it objectively and with some realization that, as a method of negotiation, it was infinitely more efficient than that which we employ today.

Let me therefore consider five of the chief characteristics of the old diplomacy.

In the first place Europe was regarded as the most important of all the continents. Asia and Africa were viewed as areas for imperial, commercial or missionary expansion; Japan, when she arose, appeared an exceptional phenomenon; America, until 1897, remained isolated behind her oceans and her Doctrine. No war, it was felt, could become a major war unless one of the five Great European Powers became involved. It was thus in the chancel-

From *The Evolution of Diplomatic Method* (London: Constable & Co., Ltd., 1954), pp. 72-91.

leries of Europe alone that the final issue of general peace or war would be decided.

In the second place it was assumed that the Great Powers were greater than the Small Powers, since they possessed a more extended range of interests, wider responsibilities, and, above all, more money and more guns. The Small Powers were graded in importance according to their military resources, their strategic position, their value as markets or sources of raw material, and their relation to the Balance of Power. There was nothing stable about such categories. Places such as Tobago or Santa Lucia, at one date strategically valuable, lost all significance with the invention of steam. At one moment Egypt, at another Afghanistan, at another Albania, would acquire prominence as points of Anglo-French, Anglo-Russian, or Slav-Teuton rivalry: at one moment the Baltic, at another the Balkans, would become the focus of diplomatic concern. Throughout this period the Small Powers were assessed according to their effect upon the relations between the Great Powers: there was seldom any idea that their interests, their opinions, still less their votes, could affect a policy agreed upon by the Concert of Europe.

This axiom implied a third principle, namely that the Great Powers possessed a common responsibility for the conduct of the Small Powers and the preservation of peace between them. The principle of intervention, as in Crete or China, was a generally accepted principle. The classic example of joint intervention by the Concert of Europe in a dispute between the Small Powers was the Ambassadors Conference held in London in 1913 at the time of the Balkan Wars. That Conference, which provides the last, as well as the best, example of the old diplomacy in action, prevented a Small-Power crisis from developing into a Great-Power crisis. . . .

The fourth characteristic bequeathed by the French system was the establishment in every European country of a professional diplomatic service on a more or less identical model. These officials representing their Governments in foreign capitals possessed similar standards of education, similar experience, and a similar aim. They desired the same sort of world. As de Callières had already noticed in 1716, they tended to develop a corporate identity independent of their national identity. They had often known each other for years, having served in some post together in their early youth; and they all believed, whatever their governments might believe, that the purpose of diplomacy was the preservation of peace. This professional freemasonry proved of great value in negotiation.

The Ambassadors, for instance, of France, Russia, Germany, Austria and Italy, who, under Sir Edward Grey's chairmanship, managed to settle the Balkan crisis of 1913, each represented national rivalries that were dangerous and acute. Yet they possessed complete confidence in each other's probity and discretion, had a common standard of professional conduct, and desired above all else to prevent a general conflagration.

It was not the fault of the old diplomacy, by which I mean the professional diplomatists of the pre-war period, that the supremacy of Europe was shattered by the First World War. The misfortune was that the advice of these wise men was disregarded at Vienna and Berlin, that their services were not employed, and that other non-diplomatic influences and interests assumed control of affairs.

The fifth main characteristic of the old diplomacy was the rule that sound negotiation must be continuous and confidential. It was a principle essentially different from that governing the itinerant public conferences with which we have become familiar since 1919. The Ambassador in a foreign capital who was instructed to negotiate a treaty with the Government to which he was accredited was already in possession of certain assets. He was acquainted with the people with whom he had to negotiate; he could in advance assess their strength or weakness, their reliability or the reverse. He was fully informed of local interests, prejudices or ambitions, of the local reefs and sandbanks, among which he would have to navigate. His repeated interviews with the Foreign Minister attracted no special public attention, since they were taken for granted as visits of routine. In that his conversations were private, they could remain both rational and courteous; in that they were confidential, there was no danger of public expectation being aroused while they were still in progress. Every negotiation consists of stages and a result; if the stages become matters of public controversy before the result has been achieved, the negotiation will almost certainly founder. A negotiation is the subject of concession and counter-concession: if the concession offered is divulged before the public are aware of the corresponding concession to be received, extreme agitation may follow and the negotiation may have to be abandoned. The necessity of negotiation remaining confidential has never been more forcibly expressed than by M. Jules Cambon, perhaps the best professional diplomatist of this century. 'The day secrecy is abolished,' writes M. Cambon, 'negotiation of any kind will become impossible.'

An ambassador negotiating a treaty according to the methods of the old diplomacy was not pressed for time. Both his own Government and the Government with whom he was negotiating had ample opportunity for reflection. A negotiation that had reached a dead-lock could be dropped for a few months without hopes being dashed or speculation aroused. The agreements that in the end resulted were no hasty improvisations or empty formulas, but documents considered and drafted with exact care. We might cite as an example the Anglo-Russian Convention of 1907, the negotiation of which between the Russian Foreign Minister and our Ambassador in St. Petersburg occupied a period of one year and three months. At no stage during those protracted transactions was an indiscretion committed or a confidence betrayed.

Such, therefore, were some of the distinctive characteristics of the old diplomacy—the conception of Europe as a centre of international gravity; the idea that the Great Powers, constituting the Concert of Europe, were more important and more responsible than the Small Powers; the existence in every country of a trained diplomatic service possessing common standards of professional conduct; and the assumption that negotiation must always be a process rather than an episode, and that at every stage it must remain confidential.

I trust that my preference for professional to amateur methods of negotiation will not be ascribed solely to the chance that I was myself born and nurtured in the old diplomacy. I am fully conscious of the many faults that the system encouraged. The axiom that all negotiation must be confidential did certainly create the habit of secretiveness, and did induce men of the highest respectability to enter into commitments which they did not divulge. We must not forget that as late as 1914 the French Assembly was unaware of the secret clauses of the Franco-Russian Alliance or that Sir Edward Grey (a man of scrupulous integrity) did not regard it as wrong to conceal from the Cabinet the exact nature of the military arrangements reached between the French and British General Staffs. Confidential negotiations that lead to secret pledges are worse even than the televised diplomacy that we enjoy today.

Nor am I unaware of the functional defects which the professional diplomatist tends to develop. He has seen human folly or egoism operating in so many different circumstances that he may identify serious passions with transitory feelings and thus underestimate the profound emotion by which whole nations can be swayed. He is so inured to the contrast between those who know the facts and those who do not know the facts, that he forgets that the latter constitute the vast majority and that it is with them that the last decision rests. He may have deduced from experience that time alone is the conciliator, that unimportant things do not matter and that important things settle themselves, that mistakes are the only things that are really effective, and he may thus incline to the fallacy that on the whole it is wiser, in all circumstances, to do nothing at all. He may be a stupid man or complacent; . . . He may be of weak character, inclined to report what is agreeable rather than what is true. He may be vain, a defect resulting in disaster to all concerned. And he often becomes denationalized, internationalized, and therefore dehydrated, an elegant empty husk. A profession should not, however, be judged by its failures. . . .

The speeding up of communications has certainly done much to alter the old methods of negotiation. In former days it took many months before a dispatch could be received and answered and ambassadors abroad were expected to use their own initiative and judgment in carrying out the policy outlined in the instructions they had received on leaving home. Some ambassadors profited by this latitude to pursue a personal policy. 'I never,' wrote Lord Malmesbury, 'received an instruction that was worth reading.' . . . Yet . . . most ambassadors during the period of slow communications were so terrified of exceeding their instructions or of assuming an initiative that might embarrass their home government, that they adopted a purely passive attitude, missed opportunity after opportunity, and spent their time writing brilliant reports on situations that had entirely altered by the time their dispatches arrived.

Today a Foreign Secretary from his desk in Downing Street can telephone to six ambassadors in the course of one morning or can even descend upon them quite suddenly from the sky. Does this mean that a diplomatist today is no more than a clerk at the end of a line? Such an assumption would be much exaggerated. An Ambassador in a foreign capital must always be the main source of information, above all the interpreter, regarding political conditions, trends and opinions in the country in which he resides. In every democracy, in every cabinet or trade union, power at any given moment rests with three or four individuals only. Nobody but a resident ambassador can get to know these individuals intimately or be able to assess the increase or decrease of their influence. It must always be on his reports that the Government base their decision upon what policy is at the moment practicable and what is not. That in itself is a most important function and responsibility. But the ambassador also remains the chief channel of communication between his own government and that to which he is accredited. He alone can decide at what moment and in what terms his instructions can best be executed. It is he who, as Demosthenes remarked, is in control of occasions and therefore, to a large extent, of events. Moreover he remains the intermediary who alone can explain the purposes and motives of one government to another. If he be foolish, ignorant, vain or intemperate great misunderstandings may arise and damaging indiscretions be perpetrated. Important results may depend upon the relations that during his residence he has been able to cultivate and maintain, upon the degree of confidence with which he is regarded, upon his skill and tact even in the most incidental negotiation. Nor is this all. An ambassador should possess sufficient authority with his home government to be able to dissuade them from a course of action which, given the local circumstances, he knows will prove disastrous. Governments who, in spite of the telephone and the aeroplane, allow themselves to be represented in foreign capitals by ambassadors to whose judgment and advice they pay no attention are wasting their own time and public money. No newspaper, no banking firm, would consider for one instant being represented abroad by a man in whose opinion they placed no confidence. I do not agree, therefore, that improvements in means of communication have essentially diminished the responsibility of an ambassador, or to any important extent altered the nature of his functions. Let me once again quote the words of M. Jules Cambon:

> 'Expressions,' he writes, 'such as "old diplomacy" and "new diplomacy" bear no relation to reality. It is the outward form,—if you like, the "adornments"—of diplomacy that are undergoing a change. The substance must remain the same, since human nature is unalterable; since there exists no other method of regulating international differences; and since the best instrument at the disposal of a Government wishing to persuade another Government will always remain the spoken words of a decent man (*la parole d'un honnête homme*).'

II

No, it was not the telephone that, from 1919 onwards, brought about the transition from the old diplomacy to the new. It was the belief that it was possible to apply to the conduct of *external* affairs, the ideas and practices which, in the conduct of *internal* affairs, had for generations been regarded as the essentials of liberal democracy.

It was inevitable, after the first World War, that some such experiment should be made. On the one hand, the ordinary citizen, being convinced that the masses in every country shared his own detestation of war, attributed the breach of the peace to the vice or folly of a small minority, which must in future be placed under democratic control. On the other hand, when the Americans arrived as the dominant partners in the coalition, they brought with them their dislike of European institutions, their distrust of diplomacy, and their missionary faith in the equality of man.

President Wilson was an idealist and, what was perhaps more dangerous, a consummate master of English prose. He shared with Robespierre the hallucination that there existed some mystic bond between himself and 'The People,'—by which he meant not only the American people but the British, French, Italian, Rumanian, Jugo-Slav, Armenian, and even German peoples. If only he could penetrate the fog-barrier of governments, politicians and officials and convey the sweetness and light of his revelation to the ordinary peasant in the Banat, to the shepherds of Albania, or the dock-hands of Fiume, then reason, concord and amity would spread in ever widening circles across the earth. He possessed, moreover, the gift of giving to commonplace ideas the resonance and authority of biblical sentences, and, like all phraseologists, he became mesmerised by the strength and neatness of the phrases that he devised. During the long months of the Paris Peace Conference, I observed him with interest, admiration and anxiety, and became convinced that he regarded himself, not as a world statesman, but as a prophet designated to bring light to a dark world. It may have been for this reason that he forgot all about the American Constitution and Senator Lodge.

I have no desire at all to denigrate President Wilson, who was in many ways inspiring and inspired. He assumed a weight of responsibility greater than any single human being is constituted to support, and he was tragically crushed. Yet if we read again the tremendous sermons that he delivered during 1918 we shall find in them the seeds of the jungle of chaos that today impedes and almost obliterates the processes of rational negotiation. Let me, therefore, remind you, for a moment, of some of the Fourteen Points, the Four Principles, the Four Ends, and the Five Particulars.

The first of the Fourteen Points of January 8, 1918 provided that in future there should be nothing but 'open covenants of peace openly arrived at,' and that 'diplomacy should proceed always frankly and in the public view.' On reaching Paris, President Wilson quickly decided that by 'diplomacy' he had not meant 'negotiation,' but only the results of that negotiation, namely treaties. He also decided that the phrases 'openly arrived at' and 'in the public view' were relative only and contained nothing that need deter him from conducting prolonged secret negotiations with Lloyd George and Clemenceau, while one American marine stood with fixed bayonet at the study door, and another patrolled the short strip of garden outside. I can well recall how startled I was, on first being admitted to the secret chamber, to discover how original was the President's interpretation of his own first rule. Today, being much older, I realize that the method he adopted was the only possible method which, in the circumstances, could have led to any result.

The general public, however, were not similarly constrained to test the validity of the President's pronouncements against the hard facts of international intercourse. They continued to assume that by 'diplomacy' was meant both policy and negotiation, and to conclude that, since secret treaties were demonstrably evil things, negotiation also must never be secret but conducted always 'in the public view.' This is perhaps the most confusing of all the fallacies that we owe to President Wilson.

In the second of the Four Principles of a month later, the President announced that the system of the Balance of Power was now for ever discredited and that subject populations must be granted their independence, irrespective of the wishes of other States. In the Four Ends of the following July he foreshadowed the creation of a League of Nations which would establish, to quote his words, 'the reign of law, based upon the consent of the governed and sustained by the organized opinion of mankind.' He failed to realize that the public is bored by foreign affairs until a crisis arises; and that then it is guided by feelings rather than by thoughts. Nor did he foresee that it would be impossible to organize the same opinion in every country simultaneously, or that the conscience of mankind, as a means of sustenance, might prove inadequate when faced by a dictator controlling all means of information. In the Five Particulars on September 27 he pronounced that the rule of justice which America must achieve would be one that 'plays no favorites and knows no standards but the equal rights of the several peoples concerned.' This commandment was subsequently misinterpreted to signify that not the rights merely, but also the opinions and the votes of even the tiniest country were of a validity equal to that of a Great Power. Egalitarianism was thus for the first time extended to imply equality among nations, an idea which does not correspond to reality and which creates mixed ideas.

If read as a whole, the successive pronouncements made by President Wilson during those months of 1918, constitute a magnificent gospel. They embody conceptions which no man should either ignore or disdain. The misfortune was that the public imagined that what was intended as a doctrine of perfectability was in fact a statement of American intentions. Thus when America repudiated her own prophet, a regrettable dichotomy was created between the realists and the idealists in every country. The former concluded that the whole of the Wilson doctrine was sentimental nonsense, and the latter floated off into vague imaginings that what they wanted to happen was likely to occur. As the latter were in the majority, the practical politician found himself in an invidious position. It was the endeavor to reconcile the hopes of the many with the doubts of the few that brought such seeming falsity to foreign policy in the twenty years between 1919 and 1939.

The Covenant of the League of Nations was none the less a very sensible document which, had it been applied with consistent strength, might well have established something like the rule of law among nations. The Secretariat created at Geneva by Lord Perth was a truly remarkable innovation, which, had general confidence been maintained, might have provided the world with a machine far preferable to that of the old diplomacy. The trouble was that this fine experiment was based upon a view of human nature which, had it been a correct view, would have rendered any League unnecessary. The ordinary peaceful citizen came to suppose that violence could be restrained by reason: it was not until it was too late that he understood that it could only be restrained by force. The old systems of authority, such as the Balance of Power, the Concert of Europe, and the discipline of the Great Powers, had been discredited; the new theory of reason proved incapable of controlling the unreasonable; in place of the old methods of stability, a new method of the utmost instability was introduced.

You may be thinking that in devoting so much space to the new ideas of 1919, I am transgressing my own principle and confusing policy with negotiation, theory with practice. You may argue that, even after President Wilson had sought to apply to international relations the principles of American democracy, the diplomatists continued undismayed to weave the old tapestry of alliances and combinations, of big or little *ententes,* of pacts and conventions. Yet you will agree, I think, that two important changes were in fact introduced into diplomatic method in the period that followed the war of 1914-1918. The first was the refusal of the American legislature to ratify a treaty negotiated and signed by their own chief executive in person. That assuredly was an innovation of the utmost significance and one that dealt a heavy blow to the sanctity of contract and the reliability of negotiation. The second was the increasing practice of indulging in the method of diplomacy by conference. By that I do not mean merely the several *ad hoc* conferences, such as Spa, Cannes, Genoa, Lausanne, Stresa and so on: some of these were necessary and some were not. I am referring rather to the permanent state of conference introduced by the League system and later by United Nations. These conferences do little to satisfy the vague desire for what is called 'open diplomacy'; but they do much to diminish the utility of professional diplomatists and, in that they entail much publicity, many rumors, and wide speculation,—in that they tempt politicians to achieve quick, spectacular and often fictitious results,—they tend to promote rather than allay suspicion, and to create those very states of uncertainty which it is the purpose of good diplomatic method to prevent.

The defects, or perhaps I should say the misfortunes, of the new diplomacy are today magnified for us as if on some gigantic screen. The theory that all States are equal, even as all men are equal, has led to lobbies being formed among the smaller countries (as for instance between the Asians and the Latin-Americans), the sole unifying principle of which is to offer opposition even to the reasonable suggestions of the Great Powers. The theory that 'diplomacy should proceed always frankly and in the public view' has led to negotiation being broadcast and televised, and to all rational discussion being abandoned in favor of interminable propaganda speeches addressed, not to those with whom the delegate is supposed to be negotiating, but to his own public at home. . . .

It would, in my view, be an error to take as an example of modern diplomatic method the discussions that are conducted in the Security Council and the Assembly of United Nations. We may resent the wastage of time, energy and money: we may regret that, in transferring to external affairs the system of parliamentary argument, a more efficient type of parliament should not have been chosen as a model: we may deplore that the invectives there exchanged should add to the sum of human tension and bewilderment. Yet it would be incorrect to suppose that these meetings are intended to serve the purpose of negotiation: they are exercises in forensic propaganda and do not even purport to be experiments in diplomatic method. Such negotiation as may occur in New York is not conducted within the walls of the tall building by the East River: it is carried out elsewhere, in accordance with those principles of courtesy, confidence and discretion which must for ever remain the only principles conducive to the peaceful settlement of disputes.

It is not therefore either diplomacy by loud-speaker or diplomacy by insult, that we need consider, since these contain a contradiction in terms. It is whether the changes inspired, rather than introduced, by President Wilson in 1919 do not repeat and emphasize the defects of previous systems and render more difficult what must always remain the chief aim of diplomacy, namely international stability. Woodrow Wilson, with his academic intelligence and missionary spirit, did not realize that foreign affairs are *foreign* affairs, or that a civilization is not a linotype machine but an organic growth. He believed that the misfortunes of mankind were due to the faults of statesmen and experts and that 'the people' were always right: he did not realize that, although it may be difficult to fool all the people all the time, it is easy to fool them for a sufficient period of time to compass their destruction.

TOPIC 24

What Nations Can and Cannot Negotiate

The possibility of settling an issue depends on two factors:
1. Negotiators must have the will and the skill to reach an agreement.
2. The subject must be susceptible to settlement through compromise.

If aims and interests are mutually exclusive, as for instance, if one side wants what the other cannot concede even in part, as Hans J. Morgenthau noted, "no amount of talk will make either party yield." He then illustrated the problem by the following parallel:

"The two women who came before King Solomon, each claiming the baby as her own, raised an issue which in its very nature could not be settled through negotiations. The issue itself called for all or nothing, and the wise King, by giving the appearance of treating it as though it could be settled by a compromise, demonstrated that it could not."

In Morgenthau's opinion the Soviet hope and actions aiming at inheriting the world after communism has buried us, and our refusal to be buried or to concede the inheritance cannot be negotiated into a compromise. The Soviet belief "will not yield to a negotiated settlement, but only to the inescapable logic of facts." [1]

►THE PROBLEM OF INCOMPATIBLE PURPOSES

CHARLES BURTON MARSHALL

A former member of the United States Policy Planning Staff warns in this essay against the current tendency to view negotiations with the Russians as if they were an intercollegiate debate, a Quaker meeting, or haggling between Yankee traders.

In international affairs, as in other fields, simple terms are used to communicate about hugely complex, shifting, multifarious situations and relationships. There never would be time enough to think, to remember, or to discuss if one had always to describe fully the phenomena concerned. So to keep tabs on ideas, we put tabs on them. The tabs then tend themselves to become legal tender in the exchange places of ideas as if they had independent meaning and validity. This leads to a great deal of fallacy, and it becomes necessary from time to time to refresh comprehension of the processes for which the tabs are only symbols—in a shift of metaphor, to restore the edges of words dulled by ill usage.

A number of words and phrases in the common lexicon of international affairs come to mind as illustrations—*the cold war, balance of power, the rule of law, the battle for men's minds, containment, liberation, the free world, aggression, peace with justice, alliance,* and so on and on. Anyone can make his own list of the poster words which publicists, professors and practitioners use often with careless regard for the complex actualities.

Just now an overworked tab is *negotiation,* closely attended by *disengagement* and *relaxation of tensions.* It is to negotiation that I wish to give academic attention.

A catalogue of the vapid, inapposite things said with high solemnity during the last few months' debate on negotiations on both sides of the Atlantic would be as long as your arm. I can deal here with only a few of them.

"What harm would there be in our talking to the Russians?" is a question put by a Midwestern newspaper. The same issue contained two long news items demonstrating that in fact our Government was doing just that already, and being talked to voluminously in turn. The idea that negotiation is necessary to cure Washington or Moscow of being tongue-tied is obviously

---

[1] Hans J. Morgenthau, "What the Big Two Can, and Can't, Negotiate." *New York Times Magazine,* September 20, 1959.

The selection is from the article, "The Problem of Incompatible Purposes," *East-West Negotiations* (2nd ed., Washington Center of Foreign Policy Research, 1959).

specious. Has there even been a time of fuller communication between adversaries than the present?

"Negotiation at least might lead to better understanding even if it did not produce agreements," a professor said at a dinner meeting. One hears this idea repeatedly. It is as if a reservoir of reconciliation were secreted in the rock waiting only to be smitten by negotiation, whereupon it would gush forth in abundant streams. The nub, I suspect, is that in fact our Government and the one in Moscow actually understand each other quite well.

One current notion about negotiation attributes to it qualities of an intercollegiate debate—an exercise in histrionics and logic, with the decision going to the side scoring best in presentation. It is as if at a certain point in the argument across the table Khrushchev might say to Mr. Dulles, "All right, you've got me! I can't answer that one. So what are your terms?"

Another notion attributes to negotiation the characteristics of a one-shot business deal. Let us call this the haggling theory of negotiation—or the Yankee trader theory. One can imagine the American and the Russian arguing about prices and the quality of the goods—Mr. Dulles making for the door in feigned scorn with Mr. Khrushchev turning around with a shrug to put the fabrics on the shelf and then each turning back to renew the bargaining until at last the price is right.

A third notion conceives of negotiation in terms of a Quaker meeting—as if the spirit of togetherness descends upon a gathering, bringing new insights, new efficacy, and a new spirit of reconciliation through the interaction of souls in propinquity. This view of negotiation let us label as the inspirational theory.

In searching for illustrations of these views of negotiation, I happened to come across all three in one context. It is an item in a recent issue of *Saturday Review*. It refers to a speech by Alf Landon to a teachers' meeting in Kansas and characterizes him as sounding "more like a yeasty young liberal than a former Republican candidate for President." The article then quotes him as urging "that we should use our Yankee ingenuity in a summit meeting," continuing, "Instead of saying no-no-no to the Soviets' proposal for a summit conference, why don't we sit down and start arguing?" The quotation then goes on: "The Secretary of State says we can't trust them. Who wants to? Americans were famous once as Yankee traders who always got their money's worth. They didn't bother about the religion, the political philosophy, or sincerity of the other party, just so the deal suited them." The *Saturday Review's* writer endorses all that and adds on his own: "The time seems ripe for a fresh, imaginative, and inspired approach to international relations."

There we have the three—sit down and start arguing, get your money's worth and don't worry about sincerity, and finally get inspired.

According to my dictionary *negotiate* means "1. To treat for, obtain, or arrange by bargain, conference, or agreement. 2. To transfer for a value received, as a note, bond, or other written obligation. 3. To accomplish or cope with successfully, as to *negotiate* an obstacle. 4. To treat or bargain with others." Negotiation embraces then the process of talking about terms, the achievement of terms, and the terms.

Clearly we are already in the midst of negotiations, and long have been, if we mean only the process of talking about terms—at least about the terms for talking about terms. The Russians have been busily propounding the conditions for a spider's feast. Mr. Eisenhower and Mr. Dulles have been assiduously—and properly—rejecting these. In this Mr. Dulles has been accused of inflexibility—which is the pejorative word for firmness.

The reason why negotiations have not progressed to the achievement of terms (in this case even the achievement of terms for trying to achieve terms) is not a lack of inspiration or yeastiness. It is not even a lack of understanding.

We do understand the Russians.

Basically, and quite clearly, the Russians do seek world domination. A great many experts on Russia may deny this. They will point to the remoteness and theoretical character—and hence the supposed irrelevancy—of the ultimate aspirations of the Marxist ideology and contend that there is no active desire whatsoever in the Kremlin rulers really to subjugate Western Europe, etc. This is really not the point. The point is that the Russian rulers do set as their goal and actively pursue the condition that all problems exterior to Russia deemed important to them are to be settled their way. This does not mean that the Russian rulers aspire to see the Red flag over the Quai d'Orsay or Whitehall. It merely means paramountcy for Russian purposes when the issues are drawn.

On the other hand the Russians understand us quite well. I can state this only as a supposition. I cannot give personal assurance about it. Our own purposes and interests make unacceptable to us the condition of world relations coveted by the Russians.

This mutuality of understanding is what impinges upon negotiation in the sense of achievement of terms.

In a negotiation which advances to terms, each side seeks ends and brings means. Each side conceives its ends in terms of means to be tendered by the other. In a one-shot deal—the Yankee trading sort of negotiation—means and ends settle out in an exchange if the price is right, and the seller awaits other customers while the buyer takes home the goods or goes to other markets. This has no bearing on the sort of negotiation which the U.S. is being exhorted to undertake. The point at issue is the conditions for a continuing relationship. Whether at the summit or elsewhere the basic bargaining must be on how in broadest terms the entities concerned are to relate themselves to each other. If we wish to draw a metaphoric parallel, the most apt would be the sort of negotiation which took place between the U. A. W. and General Motors in 1937. Here the issue was whether the company and the union would thenceforth relate themselves to each other in a continuing bargaining relationship. That issue settled, the other elements in contention fell into place more or less readily.

The conditions of successful collective bargaining shed some light on the problem of negotiating with the Russians. In collective bargaining that works, the adversariness of the parties is limited by their recognized need of each other. Their ends are not the same. They may even be opposite, but they are compatible. Each side seeks satisfaction of its own ends at a minimum practicable expenditure of means to satisfy the ends sought by the other, but neither hates nor fears *per se* the ends which the other seeks, and so neither feels compelled to suspect or distrust the use which the other might make of a success.

Between the Russians and us such conditions do not exist. Debate is not likely to convince either party to the contrary. A basis for Yankee trading is lacking. The inspiration of tete-a-tete is not likely to cause either side to forget the facts.

In this perspective the argument about locus—whether to negotiate at a mysterious summit or along even more mysterious corridors of professional diplomacy—becomes as derivative and arid as a question whether Neville Chamberlain or Nevile Henderson was the best man for doing business with Hitler. If a universe of discourse making for compatible ends were shared, negotiations at whatever level might be productive of the longed-for solutions. If this were so, moreover, the problems and dangers which men of good will wish to abate would not exist.

This brings us to the vaunted relaxation of tensions. One hears that the Russians harbor thoughts of bringing this about and need to be met only halfway. If by the phrase one means a sag along our side of the confrontation— a disengagement, an abatement of the challenge which we carry to Russian purposes—then the answer is that, of course, the Russians are ready for it and want it the worst way. If it means that the Russians are in a mood for modifying the intensity and constancy of their own desires, one can only answer that the mood is deeply concealed, and its existence a matter of guesswork.

This does not mean an endlessly static situation. The material relevancy of certain means may alter from one stage to another, and problems may move up or down in the scale of negotiability; particular impasses may become unblocked, as occurred, for instance, in the case of the Austrian Peace Treaty. The time when it will become possible to transform the situation by putting means of high importance into the bargain and to reconcile ends seems remote, however.

If there is to be relaxation of tensions otherwise than on terms of capitulation, it will be only in the inward sense: a reassertion of captaincy over our own spirits and resolving to live calmly in danger for a long time to come. I am not hopeful that this will be done easily. I can almost hear the yeasty throngs chanting:

> One-two-three-four
> Terminate the cold war!
> Five-six-seven-eight
> Hurry and negotiate!

The problem is how to restore balance to our side, how to dispel the beguiling notion that negotiation of itself is a means of redressing dangers and achieving harmony of interest, rather than merely an avenue along which one may proceed to success, impasse, or catastrophe, depending on the ratios of will and resources between the adversary parties. To counter the surge of demand for negotiation under conditions of high disadvantage to our side it will be necessary to abandon the secondary and unattractive propositions that clutter up the American case and to concentrate on a few basic and sound propositions: a proper insistence on the baleful character of the adversary, the necessity of American interposition, in fact and not merely in promise, on the continent; and the indispensability of NATO. Above all, it will be necessary to correct our imprudent strategic reliance on a thermonuclear weapon that frightens our friends more than it cows our putative enemies.

► NEGOTIATION WITH THE SOVIETS:
LESSONS OF THE PAST

JOHN C. CAMPBELL

Negotiations with the Soviets cannot yield satisfactory results unless three errors of the past are avoided, namely: (1) failure to assess Soviet policy correctly; (2) failure to define our own objectives clearly and pursue them consistently; (3) failure to relate military power to political objectives. The author, former member of the United States Policy Planning Staff, is now Director of Political Studies, Council on Foreign Relations.

The tensions of the Cold War have produced a great longing for surcease among the peoples of the world, and especially the peoples of Europe. The new Soviet leaders, more flexible in their tactics than the aging Stalin, have been able to capitalize on that longing and to exploit the elements of disunity and weakness in the West. They have adopted policies, including some unexpected concessions such as the turnabout on the Austrian treaty, which virtually compel the United States to unhinge its own policies from former rigid positions and to negotiate seriously if it is to hold its own in Europe and keep the Western alliance together. Another factor of overwhelming importance is the growth of nuclear power on both sides to the point where a general war must be regarded, by governments and by peoples, as "unthinkable." Not only does this development put greater pressure on both sides to seek a real agreement on disarmament. It also tends to transfer the struggle to other levels, though without resolving unsettled problems, removing sources of conflict or reducing the dangers of military action short of general war.

The United States will thus have to meet the challenge of a many-faceted competition. It may also have unexpected opportunities, since the Communist bloc as well as the free world will be subject to new influences and new pressures. It would be unwise, therefore, to proclaim any one issue or meeting to be the "acid test." If agreements are not reached, the problems will still be

Excerpted by special permission from *Foreign Affairs,* January, 1956. Copyright by Council on Foreign Relations, Inc., New York.

there and we shall have to negotiate on them again. This is a prospect which justifies a search for some guiding principles in the experience of that earlier period ten to twelve years ago which was also one of fluidity, of opportunities (most of them lost) and of frequent negotiation: the closing years of World War II and the first months of "peace." The circumstances of today, obviously, differ widely from those of 1944 or 1945. But the main problem is the same: How to establish a basis for relations with the Soviet Union that will give the world some promise of real peace while safeguarding our own security?

The tragedy of that earlier period, all the more poignant because of the high hopes of the American and other peoples after the great sacrifices of the war, lay in the failure to reach a fair and stable settlement in Europe. As a consequence, one hundred million Europeans merely exchanged the Nazi yoke for that of the Soviets, while the free countries of Western Europe were forced into a position where they had to take desperate measures to safeguard their own independence and prevent the balance of power being tipped even more heavily against them. For that tragedy two developments were mainly responsible: 1, the presence of the Soviet armies in Eastern Europe and a large part of Germany, and 2, the decision of the Soviet leadership to push its power and control as far as conditions would permit.

These two developments were beyond the capacity of American policy and diplomacy to change except in a marginal sense. Geography, military decisions and the magnitude of their victories determined the location of the Soviet armies in the closing stages of the war. Their own concepts of national interest and of Marxist doctrine determined the course chosen by the Soviet leaders. To exaggerate what the United States could have done is as little justified as to maintain that its record is beyond criticism. Moreover, the principal objective of American policy toward the Soviet Union had to be to keep the Russians fighting as effectively as possible until Hitler's defeat was assured. Such an objective carried the inevitable risk that the postwar Soviet Union might present a threat to world security. What we have to ask ourselves is not why we "lost the peace" after winning the war, but to what degree American statesmanship was remiss in not perceiving the meaning of what was going on and in not using all its opportunities, in dealing with the Russians, to influence the course of those developments and mitigate their harmful effects.

II

Our mistakes of omission and commission at that time fall into three general categories: failure to assess Soviet policies correctly; failure to define our own objectives clearly and pursue them consistently; and failure to relate military power and military decisions to political objectives.

The miscalculations as to Soviet purposes were partly the product of naïve hopes of the President and some of his close advisers. But in many respects they were peculiarly the product of the psychological atmosphere of the time. The American people were fighting a global war. To them and to their leaders it had to be a war with some promise of a just and lasting peace to follow victory. Obviously, this would require that the major Allied Powers coöperate in establishing it. It was an easy transition from the knowledge that Russian coöperation was essential to the assumption that it would be forthcoming. President Roosevelt, after all, had some knowledge of Soviet history and only a year or so before had himself been shocked and incensed by the Soviet pact with Hitler and the attack on Finland. But his "grand design for peace" could be realized only with Soviet coöperation and he was not going to give it up without a thorough test.

The real cause for criticism is not that the test was made—it had to be made—but that it was allowed to last so long, and that hopes, unwarranted though understandable, were allowed to color official thinking on what the Soviet leaders said and what they did. For example, Stalin's soft-pedalling of Communism and his appeals to Russian nationalism and to religion were interpreted more as fundamental changes in the nature of the Soviet system than as temporary concessions and tactics necessary to get popular support for the war. Many in Washington were sure that the Soviet Government, in its own interest, would turn all its energies to domestic reconstruction after the war and that for this it would need contented neighbors and help from the West. This opinion had logic, but it did not represent Stalin's view of Soviet interests. It was a favorite theory that the association of Russia in the war effort of a world coalition would somehow "civilize" the Soviet Union so that it would conform to the general rules of international society. The President is said to have regarded the Soviet Union as a large and uninhibited St. Bernard puppy which would in due course be trained and "housebroken." Unfortunately he underestimated the puppy's innate unconcern with the rules of the house as well as his own capacities as a trainer.

Some of the analyses of today bear an ominous resemblance to those of the war period. Thus it is said that the Soviet régime is undergoing basic change favorable to the prospects of genuine coöperation in the West; that it may face economic collapse; that, beset by fear of nuclear war and by internal problems, it must retreat on the international front. To found policies on such theories, without further evidence, could be disastrous. On the other hand, to assume that no change has taken or will take place, that nothing can be negotiated and that conflict is inevitable, could be equally disastrous. The recent "soft line" may be a transient tactical shift to confuse and divide the West. It may be an attempt to stabilize the situation in Europe in order to concentrate on Asia. It may be something more fundamental, reflecting a desire for long-term relief from the burdens and dangers of the Cold War, perhaps for some real accord on disarmament. These theories must be tested by the facts as they develop before any one of them is made the basis for demands or for concessions and before we proceed on a course that may be wrong. . . .

The second major failure of the war period was the inability of the United States to develop a clear concept of the extent of its own interest in Europe and to pursue that interest with purpose and consistency. America's "peace aims," stated in the Atlantic Charter and later declarations, were an equitable and stable settlement of territorial questions, economic recovery and future unhampered trade, and a new world security organization to safeguard the peace. These general purposes did not provide an adequate basis for taking concrete decisions related to the shifting balance of power in Europe. Even though the outlines of that problem could be clearly foreseen, American leaders deliberately chose not to approach it in those terms. Secretary Hull, in his own words, was "grounded to the taproots in the iniquitous consequences of the system of spheres of influence and balance of power." Unfortunately, the Soviet decision to participate in a world security organization, on which he and the President counted so heavily, did not mean the advent of the rule of law and the end of power relationships among nations.

Early in the war the President and Mr. Hull made the decision that all territorial issues and specific details of the postwar settlement should be left to the peace table. They had several good reasons for such a decision, not the least of which was the danger to the common war effort of any squabbling over the spoils of a victory not yet won. As Sumner Welles has cogently argued, however, this decision prevented American diplomacy from even attempting, in the early stages of the war when Russia was in no strong bargaining position, to press for agreement on concrete territorial and political issues as the basis for an acceptable European settlement. Stalin may not have agreed. At no time, even in the dark days of 1941, did he modify his claim to the territory gained in 1939-40 through collusion with Hitler. And even if he had agreed, would he in victory have kept a promise extracted from him in time of peril? Such an attempt, nevertheless, might have exposed at a much earlier date the real aims of the Soviet leaders and enabled the United States to react more rapidly and effectively in the crucial months of 1944 and 1945.

In any event, once the Soviet armies were on the march westward, it was apparent that decisions could not be postponed to some hypothetical peace conference. The Russians would make them by the technique of the accomplished fact. Yet when the time came to talk and bargain with the Kremlin, we took no position at all. At the Moscow conference of 1943, when Poland and Jugoslavia came up for discussion, Secretary Hull gave the impression that the United States had no real interest in Eastern Europe. President Roosevelt at Teheran left the burden of the discussion on this subject to Mr. Churchill. The papers prepared for the American delegation at Yalta presented a fairly detailed picture of the dangers both to our principles and to our power position that would flow from the continuance of what was going on in Eastern Europe. The tragedy of Yalta was not that American interests or free nations were "sold out" but that the clear issues that had arisen were not argued in forceful and concrete terms, and that the American negotiators were content with appearances of agreement that had no basis in political reality.

The Yalta Declaration on Liberated Europe was admirable in its proclaimed purpose of assisting in the establishment of broadly representative provisional régimes in the liberated and former enemy states, and then in the holding of free and unfettered elections. As Professor Sontag has said in these pages, America has no need to apologize for championing such principles.

But the fact that Stalin accepted the American draft with only one insignificant verbal change, almost without discussion, should have provided more cause for second thoughts than apparently was the case. The ink on it was scarcely dry when Moscow imposed a puppet government on Rumania. Throughout all Eastern Europe the consolidation of Communist power went right ahead.

Stalin undoubtedly read the meaning of the declaration in the light of all that had gone before and especially of his agreement with Churchill the previous October, the famous deal which disposed of the fate of the Balkan countries in terms of percentages of Soviet and Western influence. Stalin probably regarded it as a harmless or even useful device behind the fine words of which the two Powers could proceed as they had already agreed; his restraint in the Greek affair would seem to confirm that supposition. The United States, he had some right to assume, was following the British lead in this part of the world. The vigor of the American reaction to his later moves in Rumania, Bulgaria and Poland must therefore have surprised him, though it certainly did not divert him from his course.

[The author refers here to Winston Churchill's visit to Moscow on October 9, 1944. In his war memoirs (Volume VI, *Triumph and Tragedy*) Winston Churchill gives the following account of the "famous" deal:

At ten o'clock that night we held our first important meeting in the Kremlin. There were only Stalin, Molotov, Eden, and I, with Major Birse and Pavlov as interpreters. . . .

The moment was apt for business, so I said, "Let us settle about our affairs in the Balkans. Your armies are in Roumania and Bulgaria. We have interests, missions, and agents there. Don't let us get at cross-purposes in small ways. So far as Britain and Russia are concerned, how would it do for you to have ninety per cent predominance in Roumania, for us to have ninety per cent of the say in Greece, and go fifty-fifty about Yugoslavia?" While this was being translated I wrote out on a half-sheet of paper:

Roumania
    Russia   90%
    The others   10%
Greece
    Great Britain   90%
      (in accord with U.S.A.)
    Russia   10%
Yugoslavia   50-50%
Hungary   50-50%
Bulgaria
    Russia   75%
    The others   25%

I pushed this across to Stalin, who had by then heard the translation. There was a slight pause. Then he took his blue pencil and made a large tick upon it, and passed it back to us. It was all settled in no more time than it takes to set down.

Of course we had long and anxiously considered our point, and were only dealing with immediate war-time arrangements. All larger questions were reserved on both sides for what we then hoped would be a peace table when the war was won.

After this there was a long silence. The pencilled paper lay in the center of the table. At length I said, "Might it not be thought rather cynical if it seemed we had disposed of these issues, so fateful to millions of people, in such an offhand manner? Let us burn the paper." "No, you keep it," said Stalin.[1]]

President Roosevelt at Yalta did not impress on Stalin that he had any real concern with what the Russians had already done in the Balkans. The State Department indeed, while well informed on the mass executions of "Fascists," deportations, persecution of non-Communist groups and studied humiliation of official Western representatives that marked Soviet and Communist conduct in those countries, had deliberately refrained from telling this story to the American people in order not to "rock the boat." Moscow could draw its own conclusions from that. . . .

The United States had fluctuated in a state of hazy uncertainty between a strong stand on principle for self-determination and free elections in Eastern Europe on the one hand, and on the other a "realism" which recognized that this area was remote from the centers of American power and a matter primarily for settlement by Britain and Russia. On the latter theory, the vital interests of America nowhere clashed with those of Russia, and thus we were in a position to play a sort of mediator rôle. Neither line was followed steadily and consistently. The principles remained general and unrealizable in areas of Soviet occupation, and at the same time they brought about a negative or at best distrustful American attitude toward Mr. Churchill's rather desperate attempts in 1944 to save something from the wreckage by the methods of direct and specific deals with Stalin and by military action in Greece. As for the rôle of mediator, this idea served only to annoy the British; Stalin never regarded his two allies as anything but an "Anglo-Saxon front" despite studied American efforts to avoid offending the Russians by any appearance of "ganging up" on them with previously agreed Anglo-American proposals.

In a review of this record it is only fair to recall the circumstances of the time and the limitations on American policy. The United States had abandoned isolation only when forced to do so by the war. The Administration was guardedly approaching the question of postwar commitments in preparing Congress and the public for participation in a new world organization to replace the League. No consideration was given to possible American guarantees to the nations of Western Europe, much less to those of Eastern Europe which seemed more remote and less vital to United States security, as in fact they were. The principles of free elections and national independence were in accord with our traditions. They also constituted a sound formula for a policy of *cordon sanitaire,* if this had been our policy, but to make them stick we would have had to risk a break with Russia; it was fatuous to expect to put such principles into effect with Stalin's coöperation and goodwill. . . .

[In the future], we should avoid the pitfalls of negotiation in generalities.

[1] Winston S. Churchill, *Triumph and Tragedy* (Boston: Houghton Mifflin Co., Copyright 1957), pp. 227-228.

Let us proclaim our own principles to the world but not rely for their fulfillment on Soviet adherence to new "Yalta declaration." . . . To be worthwhile,
any settlements will have to be specific and in such terms as not to trade
concrete advantages for promises and to permit equivalent compensatory redress in case of Soviet violation. . . .

The record of our wartime decisions is punctuated by a number of occasions when a clearer conception of political objectives and of the rôle of
military power in attaining them might have left the West in a much more
favorable position than was its lot at the close of the final wartime conference
at Potsdam. Such a conclusion is necessarily based on speculation. Most of
the cases, moreover, involved decisions in which great weight necessarily had
to be given to military strategy or prior commitments regardless of the political factors. But it is worth considering what would have happened "if."

The decision against a 1944 campaign through Trieste to Vienna or
Budapest, based on unconvincing military grounds and on loyalty to the
grand strategy agreed upon with Stalin at Teheran, killed the only hope of
forestalling Soviet occupation of the middle Danube area; the President actually proposed that he and Churchill submit their differences on the point to
Stalin for decision.The failure in 1944 to conclude an armistice with Bulgaria,
which was not at war with the U.S.S.R., before the arrival of Soviet troops at
the frontier delivered the country into Soviet hands, deprived the Western
Powers of a chance to draw the line at the Danube instead of at the northern
border of Greece. A decision in 1945 to push on and liberate Prague, instead
of pointedly leaving this honor to the Russians, would have had immense
symbolic and political value even though it might not have changed the fate
of Czechoslovakia. The decision to withdraw American forces which at the
end of the fighting held a sizable part of the Soviet zone of Germany deprived
the West of its best bargaining counter to compel the Russians to fulfill their
obligations with respect to Germany and Eastern Europe; although the zones
had already been agreed on, it was quixotic to be in such a hurry to apply
this past agreement against ourselves at a time when the Russians had torn
up the recently concluded Yalta agreements and taken full advantage of their
own military advances. Moreover, this handing over to Soviet rule of people
who had thought they were under our protection, like the forcible repatriation
of Soviet citizens, did irreparable damage to America's prestige and good
name. Finally, there was the catastrophic demobilization of American forces
in Europe; once that process began our paper protests could only be taken
for just that.

The lesson of the relationship of policy and diplomacy to power seems
to have been learned, though it must be learned by the Congress and the
public as well as by the Executive. The power situation is now no longer that
of 1944-45, with armies on the march and filling the vacuums left in the
wake of Axis defeat. It is more fixed and rigid as both parties, tacitly accepting the line of the Iron Curtain as their military frontier, have built up their
armed strength on both sides of it. But it is not static or unaffected by politics
both national and international. The United States must maintain the power,
both over-all and on the spot in Europe, to deter resort to force and to sup-

port its diplomacy. At the same time, in its diplomacy it must carefully calculate the effect of various proposals—such as for reduction or withdrawal of Soviet and Western forces in Germany or for arms limitation on both sides of the Iron Curtain—on its relative power position. We can perhaps accept a deal which affects both sides about equally, provided the political consequences are acceptable. . . .

Another useful lesson has to do with the nature and timing of the positions we take in negotiations. The danger of being pressed into a bad agreement because of unwillingness to face the public reaction to non-agreement is self-evident. Furthermore, having seen the folly of failing to take a firm position on a point until it was hopelessly lost, we should be aware of the dangers of remaining on the defensive, of letting negotiations be confined to areas where Western vulnerabilities can be exploited. Thus, in negotiating on Europe, we should talk about all Europe, about Russia's satellites as well as about Germany and NATO. The most fruitful approach, however, does not lie in flat demands for free elections in Eastern Europe, which can only result in unproductive deadlock, but rather in exploring such matters as increased East-West contacts, mutual withdrawal of forces and regional arms limitation on both sides of the Iron Curtain, which could open the door to more far-reaching developments.

Finally, there is the indefinable matter of public attitudes and "atmosphere." It is somewhat ominous that Soviet spokesmen are so insistent on proclaiming the end of the Cold War, even while they yield nothing at Geneva and extend the war to new areas. We can expect periodic shifts in the Soviet line as they seek to win advantage by one means or another. American opinion is bound to be influenced by such phenomena as the smiles and camaraderie of the "summit" meeting, the loudly announced reductions of armed forces, and the friendly farm experts eating their way through church suppers in Iowa, just as it is influenced by the stony obstinacy of Mr. Molotov. The best answer to the risks involved in such reactions is an increased effort to inform the public and a policy which does not fluctuate with each Soviet maneuver. During the last war the American government and people developed an unreasoningly hopeful attitude which actually was more helpful to Soviet than to American interests in its effect on the negotiations of that time. Both as a government and as a people we shall have to look more than superficially at the smiling spirit of Geneva lest, as it fades from view and reappears like the Cheshire cat, we miss its resemblance to the grinning spectre of Yalta.

Part VI

INTERNATIONAL LAW
AND ORGANIZATION

Law and government represent practical responses to man's need to define and regulate his contacts with fellow men within a given territory. Evolution of domestic law and government has reflected man's awareness as well as acceptance of the simple yet dominant fact that he was not meant to be alone in this world.

Contacts with other men proved inevitable but also (and often) mutually advantageous. Defense against nature or an external enemy was more effective when based on an organized collective effort. With the evolution of civilization, many tasks could be handled better by division of work, specialization, or delegation of authority. Thus, men have learned not only to live and defend themselves together, but also effectively to work and create in a community. The community of life has become the community of interests and endeavors.

This applies to nations, too; but only partly. No matter when and how the first national unit emerged, it was soon made to realize that a similar process of organization was taking place in other areas, some of them not too distant. Tribes and nations, too, were not to be alone in this world.

Commercial invasion and military aggression forced the most undesirable, yet very frequent form of contact upon nations or empires, regardless of their illusions about their isolation or uniqueness. Europe was forced into contacts with Mongols, Tatars, Turks, and other invaders from Asia. Western Europeans, in turn, forced their contacts upon Asians, Africans, and American Indians. Other contacts followed a more peaceful pattern.

However, all nations were finally made to realize that contacts with other nations are inevitable and sometimes also desirable. A nation might have desired complete isolation from the rest of the world; but it had to enter into contact at least with its immediate neighbors with the aim of determining where its isolated sovereign territory ended and its neighbors' territory began. Such contacts were the beginning of international legal rules based on mutual consent. Other agreements and rules flow from this basic agreement.

The inevitability of contacts and the necessity of defining or regulating them may be described as the parent source of all legal systems and administrative organs among both individuals and nations. The difference is that nations' awareness and acceptance of this inevitability and desirability of mutual contacts and cooperation have been slow in developing. The process has not fully matured yet. Nations still tend to glorify and practice the concept of "going it alone" and create common rules and organs only when there is really no other choice.

Many centuries ago, when there were still many unpopulated or very thinly populated areas in the world, it was perhaps conceivable that a territorial unit (a tribal territory, city state, or empire) could organize itself and expand without ever coming into immediate contact with similarly organized territorial units. Expansion without collision is inconceivable in our overcrowded world. All the habitable surface of our planet has been fully divided among territorial states and their dependencies. No political vacuum has been left, with the exception of the open sea and parts of the arctic and antarctic regions. Contacts among nations are constant and intensive.

The increase in contacts among nations has corresponded to the growth of international legal rules and agencies. Having agreed on delineations of their territories, nations could not stop at that. Movements of persons (e.g., rights and duties of diplomatic envoys or merchants), vessels, goods, later traffic of mail, currencies, patents, books (copyright), aircraft, and radio signals necessitated additional agreements.

Some interests were so patently common to several nations that their mutual observation did not require a precise formulation and a formal treaty. Thus nations' usual behavior hardened into custom and has acquired the validity of legal rule, observed by all.

Other interests required negotiations and a compromise solution. Compromise was then incorporated into a formal treaty binding upon those (and only upon those) who had consented to it. This was the beginning of law among nations, based on explicit consent. The custom law was based on an implicit consent.

Other problems—such as, for instance, navigation on a river dividing two sovereign territories—required not only an agreement on mutual rights and duties but also an agency with the authority to implement the common agreement. This was the beginning of international organization and government.

Simultaneously, nations found it possible to agree on techniques by which their agreements could be interpreted by an impartial arbiter. Techniques of arbitration binding upon those (and only those) who have consented to them were a beginning of the international judiciary system.

Subjects of International Agreements

Below is a partial list of subjects covered by documents legally binding upon nation states: political and military cooperation; modes of acquiring state territory (cession, occupation, accretion, and subjugation); commerce, agriculture, finance, transport, and communication; registration, publication, expiration, voidance, cancellation, renewal, reconfirmation, and interpretation of international treaties; diplomatic and consular intercourse and immunities; international labor standards; international protection of minorities; regulation of statelessness; extradition of criminals; legal provisions for the open sea (navigation and ceremonials on the open sea); navigation on international rivers; navigation, fishery, and jurisdiction on territorial gulfs and bays; navigation on straits; international regulation of fisheries and whaling; wireless communication; civil aviation.

The preceding subjects are considered to be part of that branch of international law called the *law of peace*. It regulates the rights and obligations of nations in the periods of peace.

The second branch of international law is called the *law of war*. It regulates the rights and obligations of belligerents and nonbelligerents in war. Traditionally it includes legal arrangements concerning the following partial list of subjects: distinction between regular and irregular armed forces; declaration of war; rupture of diplomatic intercourse and consular activity; treatment of wounded, prisoners of war, and shipwrecked; punishment of war crimes by international organs; rights and duties of nonbelligerents; blockade; contraband; visitation, capture, and trial of neutral vessels; etc.

The difference between the law of war and the law of peace was originally formulated by Hugo Grotius (1583-1645), whose book, *On the Law of War and Peace,* represents the first attempt to study, interpret, and codify existing customs in the intercourse among nations. These customs had gradually hardened into a set of legal obligations and duties. A present-day standard book on international law written by L. F. L. Oppenheim, Professor of International Law at Cambridge University, and edited by his successor, Sir Hersch Lauterpacht, is divided into two volumes: the first entitled "Peace," and the second, "Disputes, War and Neutrality." (Excerpts from the first volume are reproduced in Topic 25.)

This traditional difference between the law of war and the law of peace is not as meaningful today as it used to be. In many cases the two branches of law overlap. International organizations, such as the League of Nations and the United Nations, are clearly based on combination of both branches of law: their aim is not only to prevent war or punish an aggressor by military collective action but also to promote negotiations, peaceful contacts, lawmaking among nations, as well as their economic cooperation, human welfare and progress of underdeveloped areas.

In this connection it should be stressed that international organization is always based on a formal international treaty determining the purpose and techniques of such common agency. Both the international treaty and the international organization are therefore the end product of preceding successful negotiations. But at the same time they both represent a basis for creating additional rules and establishment of additional agencies and organs. Thus many international legal documents have a function similar to that of a national constitution: while they are the record of past agreements, they are also a framework for future ones. The machinery they establish is meant to produce additional agencies to meet new needs as they arise.

The Nature of International Law

If law is defined as a body of rules for human conduct, set and enforced by a sovereign political authority, international law cannot be called law. There is no sovereign political authority which could give and enforce law for the whole community. There is also no central judicial authority which would hand down interpretations of law binding upon all.

If, on the other hand, law is defined as a body of rules for human conduct within a community, which by common consent of this community shall be enforced by any external power (not necessarily sovereign) then international law is law—provided that the existence of community and consensus can be proved.[1]

Although we are not able to determine the final validity of one of many definitions of law, we may however note the following observable fact: nations often consider (or say they consider) some rules as legally binding and act accordingly.

In this way international law, as a body of rules considered legally binding upon sovereign nations, assists them in peaceful regulation of their contacts. By defining their mutual rights and obligations, nations are able to eliminate at least those conflicts which could result from uncertainty or misunderstanding as to what these rights and obligations are. As one of the greatest authorities on international law noted: "International law is a means of enabling the day-to-day business of states to be conducted in normal times along orderly and predictable lines, and that is no small service.

. . . The truth is that (international law) is neither a myth on the one hand, nor a panacea on the other, but just one institution among others we can use for the building of a better international order." [2]

Different and conflicting interpretations of the term "international law" and its theory and practice are partly due to one difficulty which we have already encountered in previous chapters: when an institution which has proved effective on the domestic scene moves to the international one, the different surroundings, especially the lack of consensus, change its features as well as effectiveness. We are familiar with the performance of government, law, courts, legislative organs, administration, and police enforcement on the domestic scene; this familiarity with their function and effectiveness often hinders our understanding of the limited performance of their international counterparts. International law, government, courts, and enforcement often resemble the domestic institutions in name only.

In analyzing any legal system as to its completeness and effectiveness one is bound to inquire into the following six fundamentals:

1. Does a given legal order express a more or less general consensus of the community? Is there a community?

---

[1] The term "external" as used in the preceding definition (it is that of Professor L. F. L. Oppenheim, whose essay on the subject is reproduced in Topic 25) represents the contrast to enforcement by an "internal" power, which resides within an individual, such as conscience, religious conviction, ethical or ideological creed, morality, etc.

[2] J. L. Brierly, "The Outlook for International Law," p. 17, and "Preface to Fifth Edition," *The Law of Nations* (Oxford: Clarendon Press, 1954), p. v.

2. How and by whom are legal rules created? That is: what is the nature of the legislative process?

3. Are the rules clear and accessible to all members of the community? This is partly the problem of codification.

4. How and by whom are legal rules interpreted and conflicts resolved? That is: what is the nature of the judicial process?

5. How and by whom are the rules enforced in the case of noncompliance? That is: what is the nature and effectiveness of the machinery of enforcement?

6. How can law be adjusted and completely altered to correspond to new social and economic conditions as well as to the change in mores, ethical rules, ideological dogmas, and religious commandments? That is: what are the procedures of peaceful change?

Is There a Community?

International society is divided into two or three major ideological blocs; it is also divided into eighty to ninety nation-states which claim to be (a) sovereign; (b) independent; and (c) equal to each other.

These divisions and concepts symbolizing them already answer the question as to the existence of a community and its general consensus. If it exists at all, it is a weak one. Matters on which sovereign nations agree are equal or lesser in number and importance than those on which they disagree. This is the opposite of the definition of political and moral consensus which dominates the national scene.

Terms such as sovereignty, independence, and equality require further clarification.

Sovereignty is usually defined as the supreme legal authority of the state to give and enforce the law within a certain territory.

This definition is also that of *independence:* the legal authority of a state within its territory means independence from the legal authority of any other state or combination of states. This principle is recognized by the United Nations charter: "Nothing contained in the present Charter shall authorize the United Nations to intervene in matters which are essentially within the domestic jurisdiction of any state" (Article 2, par. 7).

The terms "sovereignty" and "independence," therefore, mean that nations do not recognize any authority above them except the one which they consent to create and submit to on the basis of their sovereign and independent will.

The English term "sovereignty" has been adopted and adapted from the French word *"souverain,"* which, at the end of the Middle Ages, described the authority of a king who did not have any superior authority above himself. It was introduced into political and legal science by Jean Bodin in his book *De Republica,* which appeared in 1577. His book tried to justify the centralization of royal power initiated by Louis XI (1461-1483) against the opposition of former feudal lords and barons (former *souverains*) and continued under Henry III (1551-1589). To Bodin "the essence of statehood, the quality that makes an association of human beings a state, is the unity of its government; a state without a *summa potestas* (that is, supreme sovereign power) would be like a ship without a keel." He defined a state as "a multitude of families and the possessions that they have in common ruled by a supreme power and by reason." Bodin was convinced that a confusion of uncoordinated independent authorities must be fatal to a state, and that there must be one final source and not more than one from which its laws proceed. The essential manifestation of sovereignty, he thought, is the power to make the laws, and since the sovereign makes the laws, he clearly cannot be bound by the laws that he makes. (The relations between the concept of the law of nature and early international law are analyzed by Oppenheim in Topic 25.)

Such power would appear as supreme without any restriction whatsoever. Yet, according to Bodin, there are some laws that do bind the sovereign: "the divine law, the law of nature or reason, that law that is common to all nations, and also certain laws which he calls the *leges imperii,* the laws of government," or, as we would say today, the laws of the constitution. "Sovereignty for [Bodin] was an essential principle of internal political order, and he would certainly have been surprised if he could have foreseen that later writers would distort it into a principle of international disorder, and use it to prove that by their very nature states are above the law." [3]

Western scholars differ in their estimates of sovereignty according to their views on its compatibility with an international legal order. Whatever their interpretation of the original intentions of Jean Bodin may be, they observe a curious metamorphosis which has transformed the doctrine of sovereignty from a principle of internal order into a key element in the fragmentation of society and in the development of international, that is, intersovereign law.

Some authors consider sovereignty and international law to be compatible even though the emphasis on sovereignty and national independence is bound to produce a very weak legal system.

Professor Brierly comments thus on their efforts to reconcile the doctrine of the *absolute* sovereignty of states with the concept of binding international law:

> One formula, for example, is to say that international law is a law of *co-ordination* but not of *subordination,* and even Oppenheim, though he was no believer in absolute sovereignty, yet felt obliged to attribute to international law a specific character not shared by law in general, and tells us that it is usually regarded as a law *between,* but not *above,* the several states. Yet if states are the subjects of international law, as Oppenheim admits that they are, the law must surely be above them, and they must be subordinate to it. [4]

Professor Georg Schwarzenberger notes, on the other hand, that "sovereignty means that in all matters which are not of international concern by

---

[3] J. L. Brierly, *Law of Nations* (Oxford: Clarendon Press, 1954), pp. 8, 9, 10, *passim.*
[4] *Ibid.,* p. 47.

reason of international treaties and customary law, states are free from out-side interference." [5]

Professor Hans Kelsen opposes the use of the term "sovereignty" be-cause of its ambiguity: "There is in the English language no specific term to express the idea that the state as the national legal order is subordinated only to the international legal order . . . and not another national legal order. . . . (The German term '*Völkerrechtsunmittelbarkeit*' is not translatable)." [6]

Professor Philip C. Jessup, on the other hand, states that "sovereignty is the archfiction of international law. . . . Sovereignty is essentially a concept of completeness. It is also a legal creation and, as such, is a paradox, if not an absolute impossibility, for if a state is sovereign in the complete, it knows no law." [7]

Soviet leaders and lawyers seem to adhere to the traditional concept of state sovereignty as expressed by Jean Bodin in 1577. The Great Soviet Encyclopedia defines sovereignty as "the supremacy of state power, its inde-pendence from any other power and self-determination in deciding all ques-tions of a state's internal and foreign policy." [8]

The Soviet expert on international law and former foreign minister, late A. Y. Vyshinsky, supported this definition by asserting that "sovereignty means the independence of a given state authority of any other authority, either within or without the frontiers of its state." [9]

While adhering to the conventional theory of sovereignty, Soviet spokes-men qualify the concept by politically interesting conditions. So, for instance, they make a distinction between *formal* and *real* sovereignty. One of the Soviet textbooks on international law states that "not all formally sovereign states are actually independent. Many sovereign states direct their foreign policy completely in accord with the counsel of other powers. . . . The sover-eignty of a bourgeois state may in actuality be only a paper sovereignty and cover over a very real dependence of the given state." [10]

Soviet authors also emphasize the difference between the concept of *popular* sovereignty on one hand and *state* sovereignty on the other, which may or may not be merged into one. In accordance with Lenin's theory on the state, the Soviet theorists argue that in capitalist societies the state, being an instrument of the capitalist oligarchy, represents a separation of "state sovereignty" and "popular sovereignty." It follows then, that if the Soviet Union intervenes in support of "popular sovereignty," it does not act against the real right of sovereignty but only against the false sovereignty of the state. With reference to the Soviet Union, it is, of course, asserted that there the

---

[5] Georg Schwarzenberger, *A Manual of International Law* (London: Stevens, 1950), p. 127.
[6] Hans Kelsen, *Principles of International Law* (New York: Rinehart & Co., 1952), pp. 112-114. (Other portions of his work are reproduced in Topic 26.)
[7] "International Law in the Post-War World," *American Society of International Law Proceedings,* 1942.
[8] *Bolshaya Sovietskaya Entsiklopedia,* article "Suverenitet," Vol. LIII, col. 95 (Moscow, 1946).
[9] *Literaturnaya Gazeta,* No. 45, June, 1948.
[10] *Mezhdunarodnoye Pravo (International Law),* eds. V. N. Durdeneveskii and S. B. Krylov (Moscow, 1947), p. 117.

sovereignty of the people and the sovereignty of the state have become one and the same thing.

The meaning of sovereignty, as we have seen, is a matter of controversy, not only among Western scholars, but also between the Communist and non-Communist portions of the world. The discrepancy between the legal concept of right and authority and the practical possibility of asserting them under concrete political and economic conditions is, of course, real. It should be noted that this is not an exceptional phenomenon, applying only to the right of sovereignty. For example, our legal right to reign supremely over our money is not altered from the legal point of view by the impossibility of exercising our authority after the money has been stolen from us. We still possess it legally.

A similar discrepancy between sovereignty and the impossibility of asserting it has induced many observers to conclude that the term "sovereignty" is so meaningless that it should be eliminated from our vocabulary altogether. "We propose to waste no time in chasing shadows and will therefore discard the word entirely." [11]

Notwithstanding this and other similar propositions, "sovereignty" remains a generally recognized attribute of nation-states. In the past it was used solely with reference to them. We now note the tendency to use it also with reference to blocs of nations. One ideological bloc is deemed sovereign vis-à-vis another bloc, although both recognize that they are simultaneously composed of smaller sovereign units.

In August, 1958, the former candidate for the United States presidency, Adlai E. Stevenson, discussed the alleged Soviet principle of noninterference in the domestic matters of sovereign states with Soviet Premier N. S. Khrushchev.[12] Stevenson mentioned the Soviet armed intervention in Hungary and the new Soviet denunciation of Tito. Adlai Stevenson described the discussion as follows:

> He let me have it. . . . "The trouble is [said Khrushchev] that Americans poke their noses where they should not. . . . I am sure that neither Tito nor Kadar authorized Mr. Stevenson to raise this question. If I wrote Comrade Tito (and he emphasized the word Comrade), he would undoubtedly be deeply shocked and all the more so would Comrade Kadar, for these are internal matters. . . . It would be better not to raise questions that relate solely to us and foreign Communist parties. We and Tito are Communists, and somehow we will settle this affair. It is an internal affair."

In a subsequent article Stevenson summarized the Soviet concept of bloc-sovereignty as follows:

> When I cited Hungary and Yugoslavia as examples of flagrant Soviet interference, [Khrushchev] sharply informed me that what went on in the Communist part of the world was none of the United States' business. . . .

[11] Roland R. Foulke, *A Treatise on International Law* (Philadelphia: John C. Winston Co., 1920), p. 69.
[12] *New York Times*, August 27, 1958. By permission of North American Newspaper Alliance, the distributor of Stevenson's article.

However, he evidently considers everything that happens in the non-Communist part a legitimate concern of the Soviet Union.

A similar concept of a broader sovereignty which may contain other sovereignties within its framework was voiced almost simultaneously at the U.N. General Assembly. It was during a debate over the United States support of Lebanon's and Jordan's sovereignty and independence against the Syrian attempts at overthrow and subversion.

The spokesman of Saudi Arabia, Ahmad Shukairy, condemned what he termed the United States' intervention in the internal affairs of the Arab world as follows:

> If the Arabs are treated as peoples or nations, a set of political considerations come into play. If they are treated as one single people, one single nation, then all those considerations will have to be reversed and reversed without mercy. . . . Arab imperialism [the spokesman had in mind the Western accusations against one Arab state attempting to subvert and annex another one] is inconceivable. It is unthinkable for one to enslave himself, to capture his own land, to subdue his own people, and to conquer his own fatherland. One can conceivably conquer others, dominate others, infiltrate in the territory of others. But no Arab is an alien to any Arab, and no Arab country is foreign to another Arab country. This is the main premise upon which we call the United Nations to act.[13]

This statement was not couched in legal but in political terms; but with regard to our subject matter it would mean that the United Nations was asked to treat different Arab nations, which had become individual members of the United Nations Organization after having met the necessary qualification of sovereign nation states, as if they were only one sovereign entity in their collective relations with the non-Arab world.

Equality is another term with a double meaning. As all nations refer to their equal status, the term requires clarification.

Equality may mean absolute equality in power, wealth, and intellectual capacities. Obviously such equality exists nowhere in the world. Within a nation individuals are rich or poor, clever or stupid, privileged or underprivileged. Some have influence, others have none. A labor union leader, a chairman of a congressional committee, a financier, an eloquent orator, chief of the secret police, the secretary of a totalitarian party—they all are more powerful than others and therefore unequal in their capacity to act or not to act.

The same is true of nations. Terms such as "great powers," "medium powers," "small powers," "would-be powers" refer to their different capacities to act or resist the actions of others.

If they were equal, their equality could—perhaps—lead to a general consensus, community, and unity. We say perhaps, as even in a society of ideally equal units there would be nothing to prevent some of them from combining their equal powers in order to isolate and oppress one of them.

[13] *New York Times*, August 16, 1958.

Equality may also mean equality before the law. Law may impose identical duties or confer identical rights upon individuals or groups of unequal capacities and thus make them equal before the law. It should be noted, however, that equality before the law does not necessarily mean equality of rights and duties.

Within a nation individuals are deprived of some rights in spite of the recognized principle of equality before the law: minors, feeble-minded persons, or criminals have lesser rights than others. Women, as a general rule, are not required to perform combatant duties. In England, the original source of the concept of human and civil rights, some Englishmen do not possess the right to stand for election in the House of Commons: lunatics, lords, bankrupts, and not so long ago, Roman Catholics.

In international law, littoral states obviously have other rights and duties than inland states. As we shall see, nations which otherwise insist on their sovereignty and equality may be induced to accept voting patterns which depart from the concept "one vote per one nation."

Professor Hans Kelsen defines the concept of equality in the law and before the law as follows:

> Legal inequality of states is not incompatible with a legal regulation of interstate relations. As a matter of fact, there are treaties by which privileges are conferred upon some of the contracting states, and are not conferred upon the others, which do not lose their quality as states by such treatment. The Charter of the United Nations confers upon five great powers the privilege of the so-called veto right, without violating the principle of equality allegedly established by general international law. And in spite of the legal inequality of the states under the Charter, the latter proclaims in its Article 2, paragraph 1: "The Organization is based on the principle of the sovereign equality of all its Members." It is evidently not equality in the law, but equality before the law, by which is meant the right of equality attributed by jurisprudence to individuals as well as to states, in spite of the fact that men as well as states are actually not equal. But there are differences which the law does and differences which the law does not recognize as relevant. Equality before the law means that the law-applying organs, in applying the law, must not make a difference which is not recognized by the law, that the law shall be applied as the law intends to be applied. Equality before the law means application of the law in conformity with the law, lawfulness, legality. It is a postulate directed at the law-applying organs, not a "right" of the subjects.[14]

The concept of equality—in combination with the concepts of sovereignty, independence, and self-determination—leads logically to the following principles and practices in international organizations:

Every state has a right to one vote only. Such a vote, when cast by the weakest state, is equal to the vote of the largest and most powerful one. A vote cast by India is in principle equal to that of Yemen.

No international decision is considered *legally* binding (although it may

[14] *Principles of International Law,* p. 155. Copyright 1952 by Hans Kelsen. Reprinted by permission of Rinehart & Company, Inc., New York, publishers.

have some moral significance) unless sovereign nations sovereignly agree to it. The acceptance of the principle of unanimity, which is the basis of most international political organizations, is an example of such agreement. It seems to be also the principle guiding the great powers' summit conferences.

There have been several departures from both the principle of "one vote per one nation" and that of "unanimity." Under what circumstances may nations depart from the principle of sovereign equality in voting procedures?

(1) When matters to be determined by a vote are unimportant, nations often agree to a majority rule or a weighted-vote system. This plan is accepted in some international administrative agencies such as the Universal Postal Union. Its decisions are not expected to affect the vital national interests of member states. In the U.N. Security Council majority determines *procedural* matters.

(2) Nations depart from the principle of unanimity and agree to majority votes when these do not result in binding orders but merely permissions to adopt some measures. Such international permissions are not decisions in the real sense of the word. They are usually described as resolutions or recommendations; they leave it to the sovereign decision of the addressees to determine whether to follow or not to follow the recommendation. Recommendations may carry with them a considerable moral or psychological weight. Yet they are not legally binding upon those who have not voted for the recommendation. They are not even binding upon those who did vote for them. This is why nations accepted the principle of majority votes in the United Nations General Assembly, Economic and Social Council, and Trusteeship Council. They often seem to submit their cases to them; actually they do not submit anything at all, as decisions of these organs are neither binding nor enforceable.

The only exception of a majority decision which is legally binding is that of the International Court of Justice. In reality, however, it does not mean very much in view of the fact that the jurisdiction of the Court itself has to be first established by the consent of the parties to a dispute. If a nation feels that in a given dispute it would be difficult for it to comply with an objective finding of the Court, it chooses not to accept its jurisdiction. This is psychologically preferable to a situation in which a nation would voluntarily accept the jurisdiction of the Court and then not comply with its verdict if it turns out to be contrary to that nation's vital interests.

Professor Oppenheim notes, in this connection:

> The general principle of International Law [is] that no State can be compelled to litigate against its will. We must, therefore, seek as the basis of the jurisdiction of the Court the consent of the litigants, given either generally and in advance, or *ad hoc* and upon the occurrence of the dispute. International society has not yet reached, as national societies have, the point at which any creditor or party injured can summon his debtor before a court without the latter's consent to go there.[15]

[15] L. Oppenheim, *International Law,* New York: Longmans, Green & Co., copyright 1955. Vol. II, p. 57.

(3) Finally, nations may depart from the principle of unanimity or equal vote when they have no other choice.

They have done so in international financial institutions in which the contributions to the common fund differ greatly from nation to nation. Contributing nations often refused to accept the proposition that the "beggar nations" were to tax and administer the financial resources of the rich nations. It is a sort of a modernized revolt against "taxation without adequate voting power." When confronted with the choice between an international financial institution in which all would be equal but without any funds, and an institution with sufficient funds yet dominated by the contributors, nations have often accepted a weighted vote. In the International Monetary Fund and International Bank for Development and Reconstruction, the United States has more than a hundred times as many votes as the member-state with the lowest contribution. In the International Institute of Agriculture, England has twenty-two, the United States twenty-one, France nineteen, and other nations lesser numbers of votes.

In the United Nations Security Council, procedural matters are determined by the majority of any seven votes out of the total eleven. Substantive matters are decided by a majority of seven, which must include the concurring votes of the five permanent members of the Council. For the decision as to whether a matter is procedural or substantive, the concurring vote of the five great powers is again required. If the great powers were unanimous, they could, with the help of two nations, rule the world and make decisions which would be binding upon all. Theoretically seven powers could impose their decision on the other seventy-five or eighty.

Has the principle of equality been seriously impaired by the veto arrangement of the United Nations charter? Professor Hans Kelsen, as we have seen, believes that inequality of rights and duties is compatible with the principle of equality before the law.

Professor Oppenheim, on the other hand, writes as follows:

> While in the General Assembly the principle of equality of representation and of voting power is, in general, the guiding rule . . . the principle of equality of voting power in the Security Council is substantially impaired as the result of the requirement, as a rule, of the concurrence of all the permanent members of the Security Council in decisions other than those relating to matters of procedure. One of the consequences of that inequality of voting power is that the ascertainment and enforcement, by an overriding decision of the Council, of obligations of pacific settlement and of International Law generally is legally possible only as against those members of the United Nations which are not permanent members of the Security Council. To that extent the relevant provisions of the Charter must be deemed to be contrary to the principle, which is of a fundamental character, that, regardless of any other aspect of equality, all members of a political community ought to be equal before the law.[17]

In San Francisco, at the time of the creation of the world organization, medium and small powers viewed the prospect of the five great powers'

[17] L. F. L. Oppenheim, op. cit., Vol. I, pp. 279, 280.

directorium with apprehension. Their opposition was, however, quieted when they were confronted with the prospect of having the United Nations without great powers. Neither the Soviet Union nor the United States would have joined an organization in which they could be outvoted by any three powers on any vital issue. It would be unrealistic to imagine that these two super-powers could accept as a legally binding decision what, let us say, Albania, Honduras, and Yemen would agree on.

The reluctance of sovereign nations to submit their vital interests to the judgment of other sovereign nations (even if their collective judgment repre-sented an overwhelming majority of all less one) is the main reason for the limited practice of rule by international majority. Only in a community based on political and moral consensus can majority decisions be accepted as a device of peaceful change, "a sublimated war which replaces bullets with ballots" as it was expressed once by Walter Lippmann.

There are, however, additional reasons which induce nations to resolve their conflicts by other methods than majority votes:

(a) The majority, as we all know is not always right; often it is wrong. It would be a fallacy to equate majority with wisdom or justice. While in domestic societies unwisdom or unjustice may be often repaired at the next election, on the world scene an error on the part of international majority may be fatal.

(b) An international majority when manipulated in some great power's interest may prove tyrannical.

One should recall here the wise words written by a French statesman and critic more than a century ago. Alexis de Tocqueville wrote on the sub-ject of the majority rule as follows:

> A majority taken collectively may be regarded as a being whose opinions, and most frequently whose interests, are opposed to those of another being, which is styled a minority. If it be admitted that a man, pos-sessing absolute power, may misuse that power by wronging his adversaries, why should a majority not be liable to the same reproach? Men are not apt to change their characters by agglomeration. . . . No one will assert that a people cannot forcibly wrong another people; but parties may be looked upon as lesser nations within a great one, and they are aliens to each other. If, therefore, one admits that a nation can act tyranically towards another nation, can it be denied that a party may do the same towards another party? . . . The power to do everything, which I should refuse to one of my equals, I will never grant to any number of them.[16]

(c) Of a national majority composed of more or less equal citizens it may be said that, at least, it is superior in numbers if not always in wisdom. On the world scene, however, even such assumption of numerical superiority of a majority is debatable. Do five votes cast by Guinea, Honduras, Yemen, Luxembourg, and Jordan represent a majority when they are opposed by a minority of four composed of Communist China, India, the Soviet Union, and

[16] Alexis de Tocqueville, *Democracy in America* (Henry Reeve translation as revised by Francis Bowen, and further corrected by Phillips Bradley), vol. I, pp. 269-270, footnote included (New York: Alfred A. Knopf and Vintage Books, 1954).

the United States (representing about 1½ billion human beings)? In terms of the number of their inhabitants—and other ingredients of national power—nations forming an impressive majority of votes may often in fact represent but an insignificant fragment of mankind.

The United Nations General Assembly system "gives every nation or pseudo-nation an equal vote," noted Viscount Cherwell, addressing the British House of Lords (April 1957—significantly a few months after the British-French adventure in Suez and its condemnation by the General Assembly). "And this is, of course, ridiculous. . . . The most civilized nations are equated with tiny states, many of whose inhabitants are fetichists who cannot even read or write. Nations containing 5 percent of the world's inhabitants can get a majority in the Assembly; with 10 percent a two-thirds majority could be achieved. [If a population weighting system were adopted, Nehru and Chou En-lai could claim] nearly two-fifths of the weight of the whole world for their personal views."

Sir Winston Churchill addressing American and English lawyers in London's Guildhall (August 1957), expressed a similar opinion of the U.N. majorities: "It is anomalous that the vote or prejudice of any small country should affect events involving populations many times exceeding their number, and affect them as momentary self-advantage may direct."

Karl Lowenstein, William Nelson Cromwell Professor of Jurisprudence and Political Science at Amherst College, in a letter to the *New York Times* (March 3, 1957), made the following proposal with reference to the extreme inequality of nations and their equal votes in the Assembly: Five votes should be assigned to a great, three votes to a middle, and one vote to a small power. This proposal, however, has a poor chance of being adopted. As there is no reasonable yardstick of national power—population, income per capita, productive capacity, literacy and others proved inadequate or inacceptable—Professor Lowenstein added:

> To escape this dilemma it is suggested . . . that each nation determine for itself to which category it wishes to belong. . . . There is no danger that every small nation will aspire to the rank of a great power. . . . No stampede for the front row in the U.N. is likely to occur . . . because great powers—and this is the core of the proposal—. . . will have to bear the sacrifices in manpower and money for the effective enforcement of justice and peace.

It should be noted that in 1957, having lost their influence over the anti-colonial majority in the United Nations General Assembly, Western statesmen and writers began to re-evaluate and tone down their former praise of the collective wisdom of the Assembly. V. V. Aspaturian discusses this change in Topic 27.

(d) In international conferences governments, not their people, cast the votes. In many cases, however, Communist governments or military and fascist cliques do not express the will of their people. What is then the value of their vote in the U.N. General Assembly? When either the Western or the Soviet Union nations claim that the majority of the Assembly supports their particular line of policy, they conveniently disregard what in another context, they had been previously saying about the lack of representativeness of either the Communist or capitalist governments.

(e) Although a majority decision on important matters is almost never accepted as legally binding, it is claimed that a majority decision has, at least, the value of moral pressure or represents an expression of approval and disapproval by world public opinion. If a two-thirds majority of the United Nations General Assembly is capable of exercising some psychological and moral pressure, it should be noted that some nations are particularly sensitive, and others quite unresponsive to such pressure. Only nations which also on the domestic scene yield to the pressures of public opinion can be expected to be sensitive to its international counterpart.

Noting the lack of responsiveness to the expression of the United Nations opinion on the part of dictatorships, Sir Winston Churchill (in the above-quoted speech) issued the following warning: "There are many cases where the U.N. have failed. Hungary does creep across my mind. We cannot be content with an arrangement where our new system of international law applies only to those who show themselves willing to keep [to it]."

Returning now to the question whether there is a community and consensus to form a basis for an effective legal system we may conclude: The principle of sovereign equality and the ensuing reluctance to abide by majority decisions are not the causes but the symptoms and effects of the lack of international consensus and absence of a community in a real sense of the word. To say this does not mean that some legal rules cannot be agreed on and be observed. Where there is a clear evidence of mutual benefits resulting from the observance of legal rules, they are most scrupulously adhered to and do not need enforcement. This is so in the case of many international treaties dealing with nonpolitical matters such as trade, finance, tariffs, communications, diplomatic immunities and some customs which are not even incorporated into treaties.

Wherever interests of sovereign states are identical, complementary, or at least not too contradictory, there is community and consensus and there emerges a set of rules which function as well as any national legal system. Such community exists in cases of regional arrangements but it is rather rare on a world scale.

If there is no community of interests, the balance of power may provide a secondary basis for international law. "Where there is neither community of interest nor balance of power," states Morgenthau, "there is no international law." [18]

In support of his statement Morgenthau quotes the foremost modern teacher of international law, Professor Oppenheim, who in his original version of his major work (1912 edition) called the balance of power "an indispensable condition of the very existence of international law." Professor Oppenheim then added:

[18] Hans J. Morgenthau, *Politics Among Nations* (New York: Alfred A. Knopf, 1954), p. 252. The author also notes that Professor Lauterpacht, the editor of subsequent editions of Oppenheim's standard work, has eliminated the statement concerning the balance of power.

. . . a Law of Nations can exist only if there be an equilibrium, a balance of power, between the members of the Family of Nations. If the Powers cannot keep one another in check, no rules of law will have any force, since an overpowerful State will naturally try to act according to discretion and disobey the law. As there is not and never can be a central political authority above the Sovereign States that could enforce the rules of the Law of Nations, a balance of power must prevent any member of the Family of Nations from becoming omnipotent.

How Is Law Created?

Legal rights and obligations may flow from two major sources:

a) The first one is a specific consent to rights and obligations by all parties concerned. Thus rights and duties are defined and created for those, and only for those, who have indicated their agreement. The result is a highly decentralized legal order containing a great variety of arrangements and leaving some areas completely unregulated or undefined. This is the method by which nations create mutual rights and duties.

The consent may be recorded in a formal treaty. Or consent may be implicit. The lack of objection to a situation or behavior may be construed as agreement.

An implicit agreement constitutes custom. An explicit agreement is incorporated in a treaty, pact, covenant, contract, or convention. In international law "convention" usually describes a multilateral treaty, not the meeting which has led to it.

Not only among nations, but also within nations, individuals regulate their contacts by treaty or custom. A tenant limits his power over his financial resources by pledging regular payments of rent; a landlord limits his power over the house by permitting the tenant to occupy and use part of the house. Individuals thus limit or expand their rights by contracts beyond what these rights would be in the absence of a treaty. A great majority of such treaties based on mutual consent are usually scrupulously observed. A minor portion of them is violated and has then to be enforced.

b) The second source of legal rights and obligations may be a central agency which enacts laws binding upon all members of the community without asking them specifically and individually to consent to them. A legislative authority (a parliament in a democracy; an office of legal experts who translate the ruling party's will into legal formulas in an authoritarian state) enacts laws on the basis of delegation of legislative authority. This delegation may be real, imagined, or usurped.

The result of such creation of legal rules is a legal system which is uniformly and automatically binding upon all.

In some societies there may be more than one legislative assembly. This is so in the case of federations. There, either the constitution, people's vote, or a supreme court has the power to delimit each legislature's domain and determine the hierarchy in the case of local legislation clashing with the national law. As we shall see, there is no constitution nor possibility of holding a world plebiscite in the case of a conflict of laws. And the International Court of Justice is neither supreme nor really a Court, in the real sense of the word.

Legal rules among nations are, therefore, based on either explicit or implicit consent, that is, on treaties or customs. When there is no such explicit or tacit agreement, there is no law; there is only a chaos of unilateral claims as to what the rights and obligations are or ought to be.

Where there is agreement, no detailed law-making is necessary. This can be well illustrated by the case of the law of the sea. All nations agree that "the high seas being open to all nations, no State may validly purport to subject any part of them to its sovereignty." This is a quote from Article 2 of the Geneva Convention on the High Seas, of April 27, 1958.

The principle was expressed for the first time by Hugo Grotius in his book, *Mare Liberum (Freedom of the Seas)*, published in 1609. In it, Grotius defended the right of the Dutch and everybody else to navigate around the Cape of Good Hope and to trade with the Indies against the Portuguese claim to exclusive rights of navigation and commerce on the sea.

Since the freedom of navigation for ships of all nations is in harmony with the interests of all nations, this principle has not been seriously contested since the seventeenth century. Thus, when in 1958 a conference on the law of the sea was held in Geneva, the principle was reaffirmed in a new convention.

Nations, however, failed again to agree on the question where the high seas begin and where they end. Several attempts to find a compromise in view of contradictory claims were made. One conference was held at the Hague in 1930. In February, 1958, at Geneva, eighty-six nations sought to agree on the problem of the so-called territorial sea, contiguous zone, and the continental shelf. They have only partly succeeded.

Problems touching upon the extension of territorial sovereignty into the sea, exemplify the difficulty of creating a common concept of law when national interests and concepts are in sharp conflict. The Geneva conference of 1958 was unable to reach an agreement as to the depth of the territorial sea. The great maritime nations (France, Japan, the United Kingdom, and the United States) keep on adhering to the traditional three-mile rule, which set a zone on the basis of the firing power of a primitive coastal gun. Some other nations claim four miles (Sweden, Norway, and Finland), other nations claim six miles (Yugoslavia, Uruguay, Spain, Greece, Israel, Italy). Twelve miles of territorial waters are claimed by Indonesia, Libya, Ecuador, Venezuela, the United Arab Republic, Saudi Arabia and Communist Bulgaria, Rumania and the Soviet Union. West Germany considers the territorial seas to be determined "in accordance with international law" which probably means that in the absence of international law the territorial waters of West Germany are undetermined. Burma, Turkey, and Portugal reserve the right to fix a limit for their territorial sea in the future. India, together with Mexico, proposed at Geneva that every state be entitled to fix the breadth of its territorial sea up to a limit of twelve miles from the coast or other base line applicable. In view of this multitude of unilateral claims, it is not the law but the naval strength of a nation which determines whether its concept of territorial waters will be respected by others.

In addition to the problem of the territorial sea there exists the concept of the so-called *contiguous zone*. According to the customary international law, a state may exercise preventive and protective control over a belt of the high seas contiguous to its territorial sea. The zone, in which the exercise of such control is authorized, may not extend beyond twelve miles from the base line from which the breadth of the territorial sea is measured. The purpose for which control can be exercised beyond the territorial sea proper is limited by Article 24 of the Convention to the prevention and punishment of infringements of customs, fiscal, immigration, or sanitary regulations of the coastal state.

Finally, the development of techniques for drilling on the sea-bed and from floating derricks gave rise to claims by the coastal states for extensive rights over the sea-bed not only below the territorial sea and the contiguous zone, but also beyond their limits. This is the so-called continental shelf. The Fourth Geneva Convention that deals with the *continental shelf,* defined it in its article 1, as follows:

> The sea-bed and subsoil of the submarine areas adjacent to the coast but outside the area of the territorial sea to a depth of 200 meters or, beyond that limit, to where the depth of the superjacent waters admits the exploitation of the natural resources of these said areas.

The coastal state exercises sovereign rights over the continental shelf, but only for the purpose of exploring the sea-bed and subsoil and exploiting its natural resources. This particularly concerns offshore oil deposits.

An expert on international law and a direct participant at the Geneva conference on the law of the sea, Max Sorensen, expressed his opinion on the work of this law-creating international gathering as follows:

> The law of the sea as it stands today is in many respects more certain and definite than it was before the Geneva conference. . . . Nobody who studies the four [Geneva] conventions with an unprejudiced mind can fail to be favorably impressed by the wide range of subjects regulated. . . . The negative side of the account cannot be overlooked, however. . . . The breadth of the territorial sea is more controversial than ever. The codification [of the law of the sea] . . . will remain a half measure . . . unless supplemented by the recognition . . . of compulsory jurisdiction for the settlement of legal disputes between states. It is a discouraging fact that . . . the conventions adopted at the Geneva conference contain no single provision recognizing the duty to have recourse to arbitration or judicial proceedings for settlement of the disputes that will inevitably arise out of the application of the conventions.[19]

[19] Max Sorensen is Professor of Public Law at the University of Aarhus. He was the head of the Danish delegation at the Geneva Conference. The preceding paragraphs referring to the Geneva conference are based on his lucid analysis, published in November 1958, as No. 520 of *International Conciliation* (The Carnegie Endowment for International Peace), pp. 253-255, from which the above quote was taken. *By permission.*

How Clear Is International Law?

Clarity and precision add to law's effectiveness. They also help eliminate some conflicts based on misunderstanding of the law. Its clarity may also add to the willingness of nation-states to submit disputes to judicial settlement.

Article 15 of the Statute of the International Law Commission defines codification as "the more precise formulation and systematization of international law in fields where there has been extensive State practice, precedent, and doctrine."

This may mean one of two distinct processes: (a) custom law and the decisions of tribunals may be translated into formal treaties or codes with little or no alteration of law; or (b) custom or existing treaties may be modified so as to reconcile different practices and concepts.

The difference between making a completely new law or substantially modifying an old one may disappear in actual practice. The United Nations charter (art. 13) distinguishes, however, between the two: "The General Assembly shall initiate studies and make recommendations for the purpose . . . of encouraging the progressive development of international law and its codification."

The preceding discussion on the law of the sea has shown that one and the same conference can be engaged in both codifying existing rules and customs and developing also new ones. Such a conference tried to reconcile conflicting views and practices, modified them, and thus, in practice created new rules.

The process of codification reduces the confusing multitude of conflicting claims and practices. But in order to secure ratifications of a new international treaty by as many nations as possible, international law-makers often sacrifice the demand for precision and clarity for the sake of uniformity. Resulting rules are then easily accepted because they are vague and ambiguous and lend themselves to different national interpretations.

The codification of international law must, therefore, avoid two dangers: imprecision on one side and rigidity on the other. Too specific rules would either prevent ratification by national governments, or such ratifications would remain on paper because the ratifier would be reluctant to comply with such new rules.

Under the auspices of the League of Nations, the first Conference on the Progressive Codification of International Law was held at the Hague in 1930.

Professor Oppenheim, commenting on its works, voiced the following reservation:

> The Hague Conference of 1930 revealed clearly the difference between codification conceived as a systematization and unification of agreed principles and codification regarded as agreement of hitherto divergent use and practices. Its progress and result showed that . . . in particular, the securing of agreement on existing differences is primarily a method of policy and cannot well be settled by conferences of legal experts. In view of the fact that international conferences are governed by the rule of unanimity, there is a danger that attempts to reach agreement may result in reducing the volume

of the rules eventually agreed upon, for the reason that the issues may be unduly determined by the most persistent or least progressive State or States. The product of codification may thus retard instead of advancing the progress of International Law. . . . In so far as codification implies uniform regulation, its scope must necessarily be limited for the reason that in many cases the diversity of interest and conditions render uniformity difficult or undesirable. . . . The Conference shows that even with regard to generally non-controversial matters, the work of codification requires lengthy preparation and discussion which cannot always usefully take place in the hurried atmosphere of an international conference. Thus, the programme of the Conference in 1930 was probably too ambitious inasmuch as it attempted within the space of one month to codify three important branches of International Law.

Samples of codification which have proved at least partially successful and binding upon nations which have ratified them are, for instance:

(a) The final act of the Congress of Vienna (1815) which codified international law in the field of navigation on international rivers (arts. 108, 117), and the classification of diplomatic agents—ambassadors, ministers plenipotentiary, and consuls (art. 118);

(b) Several conventions in the field of communication, inland and maritime navigation, civil aviation (such as the General Telegraphic Convention of 1865, the General Postal Convention of 1874, the Convention on international civil aviation of 1944, four Geneva Conventions on the Law of the Sea of 1958, etc.);

(c) Many conventions of a scientific, economic or humanitarian character, such as the imposing series of conventions concluded under the aegis of the International Labor Organization, or the Geneva Conventions of 1949, which codified all the international instruments developed since 1864 for the protection of victims of war; namely, the convention on the Amelioration of the Condition of the Wounded and Sick in the Armed Forces in the Field, Amelioration of the Condition of the Wounded and Sick and Shipwrecked at Sea, Treatment of Prisoners of War, Protection of Civilians in Time of War, The International Opium Convention of 1931, the Slavery Convention of 1926, etc.

If through codification international law becomes more precise, more uniform, and more generally known, this justifies all the efforts which codification necessitates. It should be, however, borne in mind that a greater compliance with legal rules may not necessarily ensue. Nations which are resolved and have the necessary strength to break the law will do so whether it is codified or not.

In order to facilitate development of international law and codification of existing rules, practice, doctrine and precedent, the United Nations General Assembly established (on November 21, 1947) an International Law Commission. In November, 1948, it elected its first fifteen members. They were experts who were to serve in their private capacity rather than under instruction from their government.

The quality of this expert body's work has been high. Its recommendations have formed the basis of many international treaties. The 1958 Geneva Conference, which succeeded in codifying large portions of the law of the sea, "could never have accomplished its task without the International Law Commission's carefully prepared draft," notes Max Sorensen. "Whatever happens, the International Law Commission has proved its worth."

Unfortunately, it is not the quality of the International Law Commission's work which will determine the acceptability of its recommendations by national governments. "Experts might agree upon principles which would contribute to the well-being of the international community," said a recent book on International Organization,[20] "but governments would weigh these principles in terms of national interest."

Arbitration and Judicial Settlement

The difference between arbitration and judicial settlement is a major one within nation-states.

Arbitration denotes the process by which two parties to a dispute agree on the personality of an umpire and further agree that they will abide by his award. Instead of duels, individuals often have used this "third-party" technique to solve their differences. Nations have also used this technique instead of war. This process was already known to ancient civilizations and to Europe in the Middle Ages.

Judicial settlement means a process by which parties to a dispute or an individual violating a public law may be *compelled* to appear before a court. The judge then hands down an *enforceable* decision.

However, in relations among nations the judiciary settlement lacks its compulsory and enforceable character. Nations have no duty to submit to a court. And a court's decision is rarely enforceable by means other than war. Here, again, the similarity between domestic and international institutions is more in the name and external forms than in the content.

The difference between international arbitration and international adjudication is a relatively minor one; it refers mostly to the structure, principles, and permanency of the court in contrast to arbitrators.

> "It is well established in international law," noted the Permanent Court of International Justice in one of its advisory opinions, "that no state can, without its consent, be compelled to submit its disputes with other states either to mediation or arbitration, or to any other kind of pacific settlement. Such consent can be given once and for all in the form of an obligation freely undertaken, but it can, on the contrary, also be given in a special case apart from any existing obligation." [21]

This is the same principle as the one which applies to arbitration. A treaty of arbitration usually stipulates the nature of the arbitrating body and

[20] L. Larry Leonard, *International Organization* (New York: McGraw-Hill Book Co., Inc., 1951), p. 273.
[21] Permanent Court of International Justice, "Eastern Carelia Advisory Opinion," *Series B,* No. 5, p. 27.

also the principles according to which the arbitrators are to give their award. In this sense, the arbitration differs from the judicial settlement of the International Court of Justice, whose principles for decision have been established by its Statute and cannot be changed by the parties to a dispute.

Two similarities between arbitration and judicial settlement among nations are, however, essential: (1) no state can, as a general rule, summon another to appear either before an arbiter or a judge for the purpose of settling a dispute; (2) states, however, can establish the jurisdiction of a court or an arbiter either by a general agreement with regard to all or some of their future disputes or by a special agreement with reference to one particular dispute only.

The development of arbitration among nations has extended over many centuries. But real progress was made in the development of its techniques at the first conference at the Hague in 1899 and at the second conference at the Hague in 1907.

The second Hague conference agreed on the convention for the pacific settlement of international disputes. Out of its ninety-seven articles more than half deal with arbitration. Under article 55 of that convention (1907) states may either select one or more arbitrators as they please, or they may use the Permanent Court of Arbitration which had been organized on the basis of a previous convention agreed to in the first Hague conference. The term "Court of Arbitration" is to some extent a misnomer, as the Court of Arbitration does not decide the cases as a body. A tribunal is established for each special case by selecting a number of arbitrators from the list of the members of the Court. Those lists are appointed by nation-states which are supposed to choose and then appoint not more than four individuals "of recognized competence in questions of international law, enjoying the highest moral reputation." (Article 44 of the Convention.) The arbitration court is really only a list of names out of which the parties in each case select, and thus constitute the court.

A new step forward was made after World War I, when in addition to the Permanent Court of Arbitration, but not quite superseding it, a Permanent Court of International Justice was established under the Covenant of the League of Nations. This court, again created at the Hague, was supposed to resemble a domestic court of justice by its permanency and constant availability to the parties in a dispute. Its jurisdiction could be established only on the basis of agreement of parties to a dispute.

There is no central authority to execute an arbitration or judicial award against a state which refuses to comply with it although it had originally accepted the jurisdiction and the binding character of the Court's award. There are practically no cases, however, of simple refusal to abide by the award. Instead of appearing as violators of international law or of an award whose binding character they had recognized in advance, the states prefer not to appear at the court; or they may claim (after the award) that the arbitrator or the court had exceeded his jurisdiction. When, for instance, on December 15, 1949, the International Court of Justice ruled that in the dispute between Great Britain and Albania, concerning the naval incidents in the Corfu

Channel, Albania was to pay damages to England whose destroyers were sunk after having hit Communist mines, Albania refused to pay. She argued that she had accepted the jurisdiction of the Court as to the question whether the duty to pay damages existed but that she had never consented to the jurisdiction of the court to fix the amount to be paid.

The award given in 1831 by the King of Holland in the North-Eastern boundary dispute between Great Britain and the United States was not considered binding by the parties on the ground that the arbitrator had exceeded his powers.

After World War II the Permanent Court of International Justice was dissolved (April, 1946) and in its place the International Court of Justice was established. According to the charter, the International Court of Justice at the Hague counts among the six principal organs of the United Nations. Article 93 of the charter declares that all members of the United Nations are *ipso facto* parties to the statute of the International Court of Justice. The Court has a new name. In reality it is a continuation of the old world court. The statute of the International Court of Justice is practically identical with that of the Permanent Court of the League of Nations. Relevant aspects of the Court and its Statute are analyzed by Professor Oppenheim in Topic 25.

The reader is advised to acquaint himself with the Statute of the International Court of Justice, in particular with articles 1-13, 34, 36 (Optional Clause), 38 (Sources of Law), 55, 59, 60, and 65.

(a) *Optional Clause.* As was said before, the jurisdiction of this Court can be established only on the basis of express consent of the parties concerned and with regard to one or all their disputes in the future. The Statute contains the so-called *Optional Clause* (art. 36) which creates the possibility (hence the term "optional") of establishing compulsory jurisdiction of the court, *ipso facto* and without special agreement, in relation to any other member or state accepting the same obligation, the jurisdiction of the court in all *legal* disputes.

The term *legal,* occurring in article 36 of the Statute, points to the fundamental distinction between legal and political disputes (or "justiciable" and "non-justiciable" disputes). Also in domestic law, only some disputes may be settled on the basis of law. No domestic court will accept, for instance, the role of an arbiter in a controversy concerning the merits of lyrical poetry as opposed to an epos; or a claim that an existing law is bad and should be changed.

A court cannot change a law. This is the role of legislators. A court can only interpret law as it is. If a court has the power of judicial review, it also can annul a law. But it cannot proclaim a new one.

If the plaintiff and the defendant do not accept a given law as their common ground, their conflict is then political and not justiciable. It cannot be solved by an arbiter or a court. The most serious disputes which divide one nation from another are precisely of this kind. They may be a mixture of political and legal issues. They may be believed to be legal. Or they may be dressed up as legal ones.

A few samples suffice to illustrate this point.

When, in 1935, Hitler challenged the post-Versailles legal order in Europe (especially the demilitarization of the Rhineland; disarmament clauses; the independence of Austria; inclusion of the German minority in Czechoslovakia; and the existence of the Polish state) his aim was to change the *status quo*. No interpretation of this order by a court could satisfy his demand for a complete change.

Since the 1950's Algerian rebels and the French Government have been engaged in a political, nonlegal conflict. The French Government invokes the law, as would any party which tries to maintain the *status quo*. According to the French Constitution, northern Algeria is part of metropolitan France. A court, if asked to interpret the law, could not find otherwise on the basis of legal documents. The Algerian rebels, however, challenge this law and want to create another legal order, the result of which would be the separation of Algeria from France.

When, in 1958, the Soviet premier presented the Western powers with an ultimatum to abandon their positions in Western Berlin, he did not even challenge their original legal right to be in Berlin. He demanded a change, using a very simple and blunt argument: it was impossible, he said, "to prolong the situation any longer."

These three examples of political conflict in which one side invokes the law, and the opposite side claims the revolutionary or political right to change it, sufficiently demonstrate that courts cannot help in disputes of a nonlegal nature. Conflicting parties have no common legal ground. The demand for change and the opposition to it constitute a conflict which can be solved either by force or by negotiations. A new order, one either imposed or agreed to, would then be the result.

In 1903 Great Britain and France concluded a treaty in which they agreed to settle by arbitration all differences of a legal nature, which did not affect their vital interests, their independence, their honor, or the interests of third states. This formula does not only represent a distinction between legal and political disputes but excludes from international adjudication such legal disputes as would be connected with the political ones by affecting the vital interests, independence, and honor of the states.

The determination of what is legal and what is political has been traditionally left to the discretion of sovereign nations. A nation may prevent the submission of its dispute to an objective nonpartial judicial body by claiming that a dispute which appears to the opposing party as being legal is really political in nature. Once an attempt was made by the United States and England and France to permit a third party to decide whether a dispute was legal or political. This sensational departure from the traditional principle that sovereign nations sovereignly decide whether their conflicts are to be submitted to international adjudication, was embodied in the arbitration treaties signed on August 3, 1911, between the above nations. Article 3 provided that, in cases where the parties disagreed as to whether or not a dispute was subject to arbitration, the question should be submitted to a third party (Joint High Commission of Inquiry); and that if all (or all but one) of the members of that commission decided the question in the affirmative, the case should be settled by arbitration. It should be noted that such a departure from the principle of sovereignty was possible only among these three Western democracies which in 1911 represented a very close association, very similar to a real community. Yet, this article was struck out by the American Senate and the treaties were never ratified.

Nations are so anxious to preserve their freedom to submit or not to submit to international adjudication that even when they accept the compulsory jurisdiction of the World Court according to article 36 of the Statute (see above), they attach several reservations to their signatures on the Optional Clause. Only thirty governments out of eighty-two subscribed to the Optional Clause. With minor exceptions, all of them had attached rather wide reservations. The nations of the Communist world have never subscribed to the Optional Clause. The British declaration of acceptance (September, 1929) excluded from international jurisdiction "disputes with regard to questions which by international law fall exclusively within the jurisdiction of the United Kingdom." The United States, which in 1946 for the first time in history found it possible to accept the Optional Clause, went even further in limiting the acceptance of the Clause. The United States excluded "disputes with regard to matters which are essentially within the domestic jurisdiction of the United States, as determined by the United States." There are other reservations by the United States, especially with regard to disputes arising under multilateral treaties, but the exception quoted above means that the United States is practically free from any obligation to submit even a legal dispute if it chooses to claim that the matter is essentially within the domestic jurisdiction, as determined either by the President or the Congress. The exact meaning of the term "essentially" is debatable; it is certainly broader than that of the term "exclusively," which might have been used.

By a declaration dated February 18, 1947, recognizing as compulsory the jurisdiction of the International Court of Justice, the Government of France also had made a reservation concerning "disputes relating to matters which are essentially within the national jurisdiction as understood by the Government of France." This declaration was canceled by a declaration dated July 9, 1959.

By a further declaration dated July 10, the Government of France has reserved "disputes relating to matters which, by international law, fall exclusively within the national jurisdiction."

It should be further noted that the obligation of the compulsory jurisdiction may only be operative as against an opponent who has accepted the same obligation.

In 1959 the United States suggested a departure from this practice in a speech by Vice-President Richard M. Nixon. Addressing the Academy of Political Science at New York (April 13, 1959), Vice-President Nixon proposed that all future American-Soviet treaties should contain a clause in which both world powers were to pledge themselves to submit disputes concerning the interpretation of these treaties to the World Court. Past agreements and treaties between the Soviet Union and the United States have often led to opposing interpretation as to their meaning. The American interpretation of

the Yalta accords is in direct conflict with the Soviet one. The Soviet interpretation of the agreement concerning the reunification of Germany, reached
at the first summit conference at Geneva, is in conflict with the American
one. "The summit conference has since been characterized by some as failure," noted Vice-President Nixon, "but in terms of agreements, as such, it
was a success." He added then a concrete proposal:

> The crucial question remained—how was the agreement to be effective
> when the parties disagreed as to what it meant? This is typical of a problem
> that can arise wherever any agreement is entered into between nations.
>
> In looking to the future what practical steps can we take to meet this
> problem? I will not even suggest to you that there is any simple answer to
> this question. But I do believe there is a significant step we can take toward
> finding an answer.
>
> We should take the initiative in urging that in future agreements pro-
> visions be included to the effect: (1) that disputes which may arise as to the
> interpretation of the agreement should be submitted to the International
> Court of Justice at the Hague; and (2) that the nations signing the agree-
> ment should be bound by the decision of the court in such cases.

(b) *Record of Arbitration and Adjudication.*[22] The record of arbitration
and international adjudication confirms the preceding analysis that only very
few serious disputes dividing nations have been settled through these
procedures.

Between 1902 and 1914 the Permanent Court of Arbitration issued
fourteen arbitral awards. Eleven were quite marginal and relatively unimportant (such as the status of ship captains, the status of French nationals in
Muscat, etc.). Only three concerned disputes of political importance, such as
a boundary question between Holland and Portugal on the Island of Timor in
1914, and a dispute between the United States and Britain concerning fishing
in the Bering Sea and North Atlantic. After World War I some additional
arbitrary awards were granted by other arbiters than the Permanent Court of
Arbitration. Again, out of the total of sixty-two arbitrary awards, only three
or four would be considered politically important and interesting. One of
these was the 1938 arbitration rendered by presidents of six American republics on the issues of the Chaco War between Bolivia and Paraguay, a procedure that had been agreed to in the peace treaty of the same year. This
arbitration drew the final boundary line between Paraguay and Bolivia.
Another boundary dispute of political import was settled by arbitration between Chile and Peru in 1925.

The record of the Permanent Court of International Justice (1920-
1946) shows sixty-five cases and twenty-seven advisory opinions. Again, the
overwhelming majority of these cases concerned claims for payment of compensation or minor territorial matters.

---

[22] This section is a digest of the study "Law, Politics, and International Disputes," by
Lincoln Bloomfield, senior staff member of the Center for International Studies, Massa-
chusetts Institute of Technology. His study was published as No. 516 of *International
Conciliation* (New York, Carnegie Endowment for International Peace, January 1958).
He is also the author of *Evolution or Revolution, The United Nations and the Problem
of Peaceful Territorial Change.*

All disputes which made the headlines of those days were either handled as nonlegal political disputes by the League of Nations or were not handled at all. In the first category, that is, disputes handled by the political body rather than the Court, were the disputes concerning the Saar, Danzig, the Greek-Turkish war, the Japanese attack against Manchuria, the Chaco war, the Hungarian-Yugoslav crisis of 1934, the Polish-Lithuanian dispute, and the Italian aggression against Abyssinia. And the most important and explosive issues were not handled even by the League, such as Germany's challenge to the whole order of Europe beginning in 1933, with Hitler's seizure of power in Germany, the Spanish Civil War, the Japanese attack against China in 1937, the dismemberment and then occupation of Czechoslovakia, and finally the crisis of the summer of 1939, leading to World War II.

The record of the International Court of Justice has remained as unimpressive as that of its predecessors. Technical and marginal issues are the rule; a mildly explosive issue is an exception. There seems scant probability that the most serious disputes dividing the Communist and the Western world (Germany, China, Middle East, Eastern Europe, etc.) could ever find their way to the World Court. They are not legal but political. One side proposes a solution totally inacceptable to the other. There is no common ground, legal or other.

Enforcement of Law

It has already been noted that many international rules or obligations do not need any enforcement to be complied with. It is in the interest of the parties concerned to abide by them. This is so, for instance, in the case of trade and tariff treaties.

In the case of a violation of a rule or obligation, the general rule is that nations have to take the defense of their interest into their own hands. Only in the case of aggression or serious threat to peace, international organizations, such as the League of Nations or the United Nations, provide membernations with some machinery of collective enforcement. (Its limitations were subject to a detailed analysis by Kenneth W. Thompson in Topic 8.)

There is no provision for international enforcement in less serious cases.

In domestic law self-help is an exception to the rule; generally speaking, citizens rely on law enforcement as determined by executive organs and performed by the police establishment.

In international law, enforcement other than through self-help is exceptional and difficult to set in motion. (Analyses of collective actions under the United Nations will be found in Topic 27.)

It should be noted that self-help does not necessarily mean the use of violence and war. In answer to a violation of a political or economic obligation nations have often seized other nations' assets, vessels, goods, or citizens. It is a very frequent and often effective form of enforcement through self-help.

The U.N. charter has introduced a novel form of self-help through collective action. In article 51 of the charter, nations are authorized to assist a nation in the exercise of self-help. (Topic 19 contains an analysis of collective self-help.) Collective self-defense according to the U. N. Charter applies only to the case of aggressive war. It does not apply to other violations of international law and order.

Peaceful Change and International Organization

No society is static. Circumstances change. New problems arise. "No peace system can be expected to work for any length of time unless it contains adequate provision for bringing about changes in the *status quo* as required by changing conditions," Frederick S. Dunn rightly pointed out in his often quoted book *Peaceful Change*.[23]

We have noted that courts or arbitrators can interpret the law but cannot change it. In Part I we have analyzed the combination of factors—free press, public opinion, parliament, courts and administration—which produce the possibility of peaceful change on the domestic scene.

How can international society adjust its rules and life to changing conditions and concepts?

Negotiations are one possibility (they were discussed in Part V). The combination of negotiations and international organization is another possibility, or rather, a variety of the first one.

International conferences (or intertribal meetings) called in the past for the purpose of ending violence and introducing a period of peace and cooperation, have always contained some elements which (today) we usually associate with the concept of a modern international organization. Any conference or organization, for instance, needs some physical area where it may conduct its business (negotiations, or dictating to the defeated enemy). It also needs some machinery for the purpose of recording terms of agreement. Sometimes, in addition, a conference establishes an agency with authority to supervise, or report on, national implementation of international agreements.

Any international conference, even if very temporary, is potentially a permanent one. Or it may engender one. As we see, the difference between an international conference and international organization is rather fluid. Their aims are often identical: if conferring nations agree that they have some common purposes they may agree also to establish a permanent organization and give it the task of attempting the realization of these common purposes.

At present, the term "international organization" is usually reserved to those international bodies which are more or less permanent and whose aim it is to prevent future fighting rather than only terminate a war. When we say, "international organization" we do not mean a supranational one. We mean an organization based on agreement as expressed by sovereign nations. In his book *International Organization,* L. Larry Leonard defines international organization as a fairly permanent agency, "to which the member states have assigned responsibility and authority and through which each government may advocate policies and objectives in furtherance of its national interest.

[23] Frederick S. Dunn, *Peaceful Change* (New York: Council on Foreign Relations, 1937), p. 2.

This definition places great emphasis on international organizations as instruments of nation-states and recognizes limitations on these organizations."[24]

The history of international organization is as long as that of conferences and negotiations. The degree of success for either has always been related to the will of the participants to cooperate.

Many of the earlier efforts to establish permanent international organizations with the aim of preventing the use of violence in relations between cities, empires or nations rightly assumed that one of the preconditions for success of a collective action was the common concept of the things to fight against or fight for.

> In the year 1000 a council at Poitiers . . . passed a resolution which obligated the princes of the Church to oppose war by forceful means. . . . Under the energetic Archbishop Aimon of Bourges several punitive expeditions were carried out against rebellious knights; the Archbishop may, in fact, be considered as the earliest predecessor of the commander of a modern international armed force. Priests in large numbers fought in his peace enforcement army to safeguard the inherent justice and the disinterested nature of the intervention.[25]

When the temporal power of the Catholic Church declined in Europe and the power of sovereign princes and sovereign states reasserted itself, philosophers, thinkers, and poets thought of cooperative arrangements among those sovereign units resembling either the modern form of federalism or the modern form of international organization. Dante Alighieri (1265-1321) suggested that a new empire ruled by a monarch should be superimposed over the princes and the cities continuously fighting each other.

In the early seventeenth century the French King Henry IV was credited with the idea that Europe should end its fratricidal religious wars and establish a kind of federation composed of fifteen more or less equal and religiously homogeneous units. Smaller states were to be included in those basic fifteen units. As the Russian and the Turkish Empires represented much greater and more powerful units, they were supposed to be excluded from the continental European federation. The federation was to be directed by a federal council which was to "clear up and determine all the civil, political, and religious affairs of Europe, whether within itself or with its neighbors."[26]

In 1623 a French monk, Emeric Crucé, proposed the establishment of a world assembly and a world court to promote peace by negotiation and arbitration. International law was to be enforced through collective military sanctions. Not only Christian States but also Turkey, China, and Persia were to be members.

Similar plans followed: in 1693 William Penn suggested a parliament of

[24] Leonard, *op. cit.*, p. 5.

[25] Stefan T. Bossony, "Peace Enforcement," *Yale Law Journal*, Vol. 55, No. 5 (August, 1946), p. 910.

[26] These suggestions were first proposed by the Duke of Sully, apparently on the basis of ideas of his king Henry IV. The full description is contained in Sir John A. R. Marriott, *Commonwealth or Anarchy, A Survey of Projects of Peace.* (New York: Columbia University Press, 1939), p. 48.

Europe; in 1712 Abbé Saint Pierre proposed a permanent senate of Christian states in Europe which would make its decisions by a simple majority. In some cases a two-thirds majority was to be required.

Similar ideas were advocated by Sir Thomas More (1516), Jean Jacques Rousseau (1761), Immanuel Kant (1795), Claude de Saint-Simon (1814), and many others.

The number of different plans increased with the increasing violence of wars. Some were based on federal ideas; some anticipated the League of Nations; some pivoted on common ideology, as did the league of Christian states proposed to resist the Turkish invasions, suggested in 1461 by a Czech king, George of Podebrady.

The nineteenth century witnessed the beginning of international coopera-tion in nonpolitical fields. The beginning of what we today call functional or specialized international agencies is connected with the great-power confer-ence concluding the Napoleonic wars, that is, the Congress of Vienna, held in 1814 and 1815. Among other things, the great powers agreed then that sev-eral problems, theretofore usually considered to be within the sovereign domain of each nation, were the concern of more than the directly involved nation. Thus they agreed on a limited degree of cooperation with regard to such problems as the navigation on rivers crossing or forming the boundary of more than one state—the so-called international rivers. An international commission which was to regulate navigation on the Rhine was established in 1804. The international commission for the Danube was created in 1856.

The Congress of Vienna also began to deal with nonpolitical human-itarian problems. The abolition of the slave trade thus became a matter for international concern and action. This was the first milestone. The Universal Declaration of Human Rights is another, and certainly not the last one.

A modern international organization should therefore be viewed not only as a permanent one (in contrast to the temporary ones of the past) but also as an agency concerned with both political and nonpolitical problems such as economic, social, and humanitarian cooperation. A modern international organization, whether it is global (as is the United Nations) or regional (as are the Organization of American States or the European Communities), tries to handle all questions, political, economic, social, legal, and humanitarian— as part of one function and in connection with one another.

When we use the term "global," we are aware of the fact that so far no international organization has succeeded in including all mankind. The United Nations organization is called universal although the largest Asian nation, Communist China, and the largest European nation, Germany, are not mem-bers. Together with Viet-nam, Korea, and some African territories, about one billion people are thus not represented in the United Nations.

A modern international organization is more than a sheer framework for multilateral diplomacy; but it is also much less than international government with an authority to rule.

Modern international organization reflects the fundamental need of na-tions to have their frequent, intensive, and varied contacts regulated and possible clashes peacefully solved. It also reflects the conviction that peaceful settlement cannot be the result of some specific settlement on one isolated, however important, issue. Modern international organization proposes to use all available methods to achieve cooperation and peace: diplomatic negotiations, law-making and law-interpreting, economic and social cooperation, and concern for human rights.

In the United Nations we can distinguish four main methods of approach to conflict and tension among nations:

(a) *Political*—this includes negotiation and all methods of peaceful change, including the so-called "third-party" techniques. Chapter VI of the charter contains provisions relating to this aspect.

(b) *Functional*—this includes all the activities, the aim of which is to promote economic, social, and humanitarian cooperation among nations, and the well-being of underdeveloped or non-self-governing peoples.

(c) *Military Security*—Chapter VII of the charter defines and provides for measures, the aim of which is to prevent the use of violence or punish those who would use it.

(d) *Legal*—this includes not only promotion of international treaties and their codification but also the establishment of the International Court of Justice, which the charter considers one of the six main organs of the United Nations. Their description follows.

The main organs of the United Nations charter are described below:

Security Council. 11 members: 5 permanent (U.S., Britain, France, U.S.S.R., China); 6 nonpermanent, elected for 2-year term by General Assembly. Meets any time it is necessary. Has primary responsibility for maintaining peace. May investigate any dispute and recommend a basis for settlement. Determines the existence of a threat to the peace, or an act of aggression, and decides what measures shall be taken to restore peace. All nonprocedural decisions require 7 votes, including the 5 permanent members (veto provision). Decisions are binding on all U.N. members.

General Assembly. Includes all U.N. members. Meets annually. Sessions last 3 to 4 months. May discuss any matter within scope of Charter. May make recommendations on any matter within scope of Charter unless item is on Security Council agenda. ⅔ vote required on all important matters. Elects nonpermanent members of Security Council, some members of the Trusteeship Council, and all members of Economic and Social Council. Together with the Security Council elects 15 judges of the International Court of Justice and the Secretary General for a 5-year term. It admits new members to U.N. upon recommendation of Security Council. Approves U.N. budget. Supervises work of Economic and Social Council and Trusteeship Council. Receives annual reports from Security Council and all other U.N. organs. Has created several committees dealing with procedural matters and six standing (main) committees (First Committee—Political and Security; Second Committee—Economic and Financial; Third Committee—Social Humanitarian, and Cultural; Fourth Committee—Trusteeship; Fifth Committee—Administrative and Budgetary; Sixth Committee—Legal.) Has created many special commissions and bodies to carry on its work, such as: Disarmament Commission, Committee on Information from Non-Self-Governing Territories, International Atomic Energy Agency.

Economic and Social Council. 18 members, elected by General Assembly for 3-year terms. Makes studies and reports regarding international economic, social, cultural, educational, health, and related matters, including human rights. May make recommendations on above matters to General Assembly, to members of the U.N., and to the specialized agencies. Meets usually twice a year for periods of 4 to 6 weeks each. Majority vote required for its decisions. Much of its work is done through special commissions. It co-ordinates work of *U.N. Specialized Agencies.* See Topic 28.

Trusteeship Council. Variable number of members, half of whom are administrators of trust territories, and half of whom are not. Five Great Powers are members *ipso facto* in their respective categories of either trust administering or nonadministering nations. The remaining members are elected by General Assembly for 3-year terms. Considers the reports of states administering trust areas. Examines petitions from inhabitants or groups in trust areas. Sends visiting missions periodically to the various trust territories. Submits an annual report on each trust territory to General Assembly. Meets twice a year. Majority vote required for its decisions.

Secretariat. Headed by the Secretary-General who is chief administrative officer of U.N. Secretary-General makes annual report to General Assembly on work of U.N. He may also bring to the attention of the Security Council any matter he thinks endangers peace and security. Staff of Secretariat numbers between 3,000 and 4,000. They are international civil servants, not delegates from national governments. They provide services and assistance for all U.N. organs. Main Secretariat Headquarters is in New York.

International Court of Justice. Located at the Hague, Netherlands. 15 judges, elected by General Assembly and Security Council for 9-year terms. May arbitrate any dispute states are willing to submit to it. Has no compulsory jurisdiction, except over narrowly defined legal disputes which states may have agreed in advance to submit to compulsory adjudication.

Chapters XII and XIII of the Charter, which deal with the trusteeship system, were reproduced in Topic 2.

Summary

There is no central legislative agency which would have the power to enact law binding on all nations. International law is therefore a web of either formal or tacit agreements binding sovereign nations, and only those who have specifically consented to them.

International courts resemble domestic courts but no nation can be compelled to appear before them against its will. Awards of international courts are rarely enforceable. Submission of disputes to international courts is usually voluntary.

International conferences, such as the U.N. General Assembly, resemble parliaments in their attempts to formulate policies for all and enact general rules. Their enactments, however, have no validity of law. They are either permissions to act if nations so desire; or recommendations to sovereign nations to accept some international standard as a guide for their domestic legislation.

International executive agencies have only a limited authority to enforce what has been agreed on previously. Specialized economic, social, or humanitarian agencies, as a rule, can recommend measures and supply information, send technicians, and initiate measures only upon request of sovereign nations.

International law and organization are the end products of diplomatic negotiations. International organization is also the framework for additional negotiations with the possible aim of expanding or improving the framework.

International law and organization are more complex and often more effective than they used to be. Yet, they are still rudimentary.

In the present era their evolution in the right direction seems more vital than ever before in history.

At this point the reader should familiarize himself with the main provisions of the United Nations Charter, in particular with Chapter IV (The General Assembly), V (The Security Council), VI (Pacific Settlement of Disputes), and VII (Action with respect to Threats to the Peace, Breaches of the Peace, and Acts of Aggression).

TOPIC 25

The Law of Nations

Normal functioning and full development of any law presuppose a community of political, juridical, and ethical outlook. Do these prerequisites of law and government exist on the international scene?

In the past, the law of the "civilized" Christian nations excluded a major part of the world on the basis that it was uncivilized because un-Christian. Similarly, the Communist and the non-Communist halves of the present world tend to view each other as uncivilized in matters of ideology and governmental system, or at least as forming two opposite and irreconcilable poles.

It may be recalled that according to Marxism-Leninism, which is the dominant creed of governments ruling over one billion people, law and government are the expression of class interests. Lenin said that the state and its law are the organs of "class domination, the organ of oppression of one class by another. Its aim is the creation of order which legalizes and perpetuates this oppression by moderating the collision between classes."

Lenin's definition seems to exclude the possibility of a common legal ground between opposing classes and their instruments, that is, their states and legal systems. Can a state dominated by the proletariat and a state dominated by its enemies, the capitalists, form a community?

"So long as the U.S.S.R. is compelled to remain an island encircled by capitalism," wrote E. A. Korovin, a Russian writer, "any restriction of Soviet sovereignty (in favor of international law) must needs entail concessions of a more or less serious character to the political and economic principles opposed to her own. . . . Any restrictions of her sovereignty . . . would delay the advent of socialist revolutions."

Similarly, in the 1930's Nazi writers excluded the possibility of a community with enemy races. Some Nazi writers stressed then the idea of "intercorporative international law . . . . built on the principle of racial consanguinity."

►COMMUNITY AND LAW

L. F. L. OPPENHEIM

The following selection demonstrates a great belief in and hope for further development of the system of international law. Soviet and Nazi intrusions into the sphere of international law are considered by the author as essentially transient. L. F. L. Oppenheim was Professor of International Law at the University of Cambridge and a foremost authority on international law. His two-volume work, International Law, *edited by Professor Lauterpacht, is generally considered* the *authoritative book on the law of nations.*

Law of Nations or International Law is the name for the body of customary and conventional rules which are considered legally binding by civilized states in their intercourse with each other. This is in contradistinction to mere usages or to morality, which cannot be considered legally binding. Such part of these rules as is binding upon all the civilized states without exceptions, as, for instance, the law connected with legation and treaties, is called *universal* International Law, in contradistinction to *particular* International Law which is binding on two or a few states only. . . .

The Law of Nations is a law regulating primarily the intercourse of states with one another, not that of individuals. As, apart from International Law, there is as yet no superior authority above sovereign states, the Law of Nations is usually regarded as a law *between,* not above the several states, and is, therefore, since the time of Bentham, also called International Law. Only the so-called Public International Law, which is identical with the Law of Nations, is International Law, whereas the so-called Private International Law is not, at any rate, not as a rule. The latter concerns such matters as fall at the same time under the jurisdiction of two or more different states. And as the Municipal Laws[1] of different states are frequently in conflict with each other respecting such matters, there has evolved a body of principles for avoiding or limiting such conflicts. What is now termed Private International Law may, however, at the same time become International Law in proportion as States agree by law-making treaties upon rules the application of which would solve such conflicts.

From *International Law* (New York: Longmans, Green & Co., copyright 1955), pp. 4-35, *passim.*

Almost from the beginning of the science of the Law of Nations the question has been discussed whether the rules of International Law are *legally* binding. [Some] defined Law as a body of rules for human conduct set and enforced by a sovereign political authority. If indeed this definition of Law be correct, the Law of Nations cannot be called Law, for International Law is a body of rules governing the relations of sovereign states between one another. There is not a sovereign political authority above the sovereign States which could enforce such rules. However, this definition of Law is not correct. It covers only the written or Statute Law within a State, that part of the Municipal Law which is expressly made by Statutes of Parliament in a Constitutional State or by some other sovereign authority in a non-Constitutional State. It does not cover that part of Municipal Law which is termed unwritten or customary Law. There is, in fact, no community and no State in the world which could exist with written Law only. Everywhere there is customary Law in existence besides the written Law. This customary Law was never expressly enacted by any law-giving body, or it would not be merely customary Law. Those who define Law as rules set and enforced by a sovereign political authority do not deny the existence of customary Law. But they maintain that the customary Law has the character of Law only through that indirect recognition on the part of the State which is to be found in the fact that courts of Justice apply the customary Law in the same way as the written Law, and that the State does not prevent them from doing so. This is, however, nothing else than a fiction. Courts of Justice having no law-giving power could not recognize unwritten rules as Law if these rules were not Law before that recognition, and States recognize unwritten rules as Law only because Courts of Justice do so.

For the purpose of finding a correct definition of Law it is indispensable to compare morality and Law with each other for both lay down rules, and to a great extent the same rules, for human conduct. Now the characteristic of rules of morality is that they apply to conscience, and to conscience only. An act loses all value before the tribunal of morality, if it was not done out of free will and conscientiousness, but was enforced by some external power or was done from some consideration which lies outside the boundaries of conscience. On the other hand, the characteristic of rules of Law is that they shall, if necessary, be enforced by external power. Rules of Law apply, of course, to conscience quite as much as rules of morality. But the latter required to be enforced by the eternal power of conscience only, while the former required to be enforced by some external power.

If these are the characteristic signs of morality and of Law, we are justified in stating the principle: a rule is a rule of morality, if by common consent of the community it applies to conscience and to conscience only; whereas, on the other hand, a rule is a rule of Law, if by common consent of

[1] "Municipal law" as used by Professor Oppenheim and other experts in international law does not refer to the law of a municipality or city, but to a *national* law which controls relations between individuals and groups within a state and between individuals and the state. "Municipal law" is used, therefore, in contradistinction to the term "international law" which is primarily concerned with legal relations between states.

the community it will eventually be enforced by external power. Without some kind of both morality and Law, no community has ever existed, or could possibly exist. . . . We may say that Law is a body of rules for human conduct within a community which by common consent of this community shall be enforced by external power, that is, external to the person against whom they are enforced.

The essential conditions of the existence of Law are, therefore, threefold. There must, first, be a community. There must, secondly, be a body of rules for human conduct within that community. And there must, thirdly, be a common consent of that community that these rules shall be enforced by external power. It is not an essential condition, either, that such rules of conduct should be written rules, or that there should be a law-making authority or a law-administering court within the community concerned. If we find this definition of Law correct, and accept these three essential conditions of Law, the existence of Law is not limited to the State community only, but is to be found everywhere where there is a community.

As the first condition is the existence of a community, the question arises, whether an international community exists whose Law could be the Law of Nations. Before this question can be answered, the conception of a community must be defined. A community may be said to be the body of a number of individuals, more or less bound together through such common interests as create a constant and manifold intercourse between the single individuals. This definition of a community covers not only a community of individual men, but also a community of individual communities, such as individual states. But is there in existence a universal, international community of all individual states? This question had already, before the First World War, been decided in the affirmative, as far as the states of the civilized world were concerned. Science and art, which are by their nature to a great extent international, created a constant exchange of ideas and opinions between the subjects of the several states. Of the greatest importance were, however, agriculture, industry, and in particular, trade. It is international trade which has created navigation on the high seas and on the rivers flowing through different states. It is, again, international, commercial, and other interests which have called into existence the nets of railways which cover the continents, and the international postal, telegraphic, radiotelegraphic and radiotelephonic arrangements.[2]

Cultural, scientific and humanitarian interest, have called for international co-ordination and organization. In addition to various permanent organs and institutions of the League of Nations, of the United Nations, and of the International Labour Organisation, a number of international offices and international commissions have been established for the administration of international business, and a permanent Court of Arbitration, and, later, an International Court of Justice have been set up at the Hague. Though the individual States are sovereign and independent of each other, though there is

[2] Introductions to Parts I and VI, as well as the subsequent selections, challenge this optimistic estimate of international community.

no international government above them, there exists a powerful unifying factor, namely their common interests. The influence of that unifying factor is liable to suffer a set-back whenever economic nationalism, political intolerance, and the pursuit of self-sufficiency on the part of sovereign states tend to create artificial barriers among the people composing them. Whenever that happens, the authority and reality of International Law are likely to weaken. But such retrogression, being contrary to the natural tendencies of development and to the realities of national intercourse between States, must be regarded as temporary and as leaving essentially intact the existence of an international community. Neither do differences in culture, in the economic structure, or in the political system, affect as such the existence of the international community as one of the basic factors of International Law. The object and resulting scope of the rules of International Law being limited, its existence is not conditioned by a uniformity of outlook and tradition which plays an important, although not indispensable, part in securing the rule of law within the State.

Thus the first essential condition for the existence of law is, at least in the long run, a reality. But the second condition cannot be denied either. For hundreds of years more and more rules have grown up for the conduct of the States between each other. These rules are to a great extent customary rules. But side by side with these customary and unwritten rules more and more written rules are daily created by international agreements, . . . and the vast number of general conventions often referred to as law-making or legislative treaties.

Equally an affirmative answer must be given to the question whether there exists a common consent of the community of States that the rules of international conduct shall be enforced by external power? Governments of States, and the public opinion of the whole of civilized humanity, agree and consent that the body of rules for international conduct which is called the Law of Nations shall, if necessary, be enforced by external power, in contradistinction to rules of international morality and courtesy, which are left to the consideration of the conscience of nations. In the absence of a central authority for the enforcement of the rules of the Law of Nations, States have on occasions to take the law into their own hands. Self-help, and intervention on the part of other States which sympathize with the wronged one, are the means by which the rules of the Law of Nations can be and actually are enforced. And, subject to the obligations of the Charter of the United Nations and of the General Treaty for the Renunciation of War,[3] war is the ultimate

[3] This Treaty, signed on August 27, 1928, is usually referred to as the Briand-Kellogg Pact or Pact of Paris. It came about largely owing to the initiative of France, represented by Aristide Briand, and the United States, represented by Frank B. Kellogg. More than sixty nations, including all the great powers, adhered to the Pact. Its Article I said: "The High Contracting Parties solemnly declare, in the name of their respective peoples, that they condemn the recourse to war for the solution of the international controversies and renounce it as an instrument of national policy in their relations with one another." The effect of the Pact is not to abolish the institution of war as such. War still remains lawful as a means of legally permissible self-defense or as a measure of collective action, for instance as authorized or ordered by the United Nations.

instrument for defending violated legal rights vital to the existence of States. Moreover, the Covenant of the League and the Charter, by providing for a system of sanctions for repressing the violation of its principal obligation, have elevated enforcement of the law to the authority of a recognized principle of conventional law.

The term "conventional rule" is used throughout this work to indicate a rule created by express agreement. It is true that there is at present no central Government above the Governments of the several States, which could in every case secure the enforcement of the rules of International Law. For this reason, compared with Municipal Law and the means available for its enforcement, the Law of Nations is certainly the weaker of the two. A law is the stronger, the more guarantees are given that it can and will be enforced. It is, in the present circumstances, inevitable that the Law of Nations must be a weaker law than Municipal Law, as there is no international Government above the national ones which could enforce the rules of International Law in the same way as a national Government enforces the rules of its Municipal Law. This weakness becomes particularly conspicuous in time of war, for belligerents who fight for their existence will always be apt to brush aside such rules of the Law of Nations concerning warfare as are supposed to hinder them in the conduct of their military operations. But a weak law is nevertheless still law.

In practice International Law is constantly recognized as law. The Governments of the different States are of opinion that they are legally, as well as morally, bound by the Law of Nations. Likewise, the public opinion of all civilized States considers every State legally bound to comply with the rules of the Law of Nations. States not only recognize the rules of International Law as legally binding in innumerable treaties, but emphasize constantly the fact that there is a law between themselves. They moreover recognize this law by their Municipal Law ordering their officials, their civil and criminal courts, and their subjects to observe such conduct as is in conformity with the duties imposed upon their sovereign by the Law of Nations. If a violation of the Law of Nations occurs on the part of an individual State, the public opinion of the civilized world, as well as the Governments of other States, stigmatizes such violation as a violation of law pure and simple. On the other hand, the inadequacy of public opinion as a compelling and motivating force is in itself an expression of the weakness of International Law as a body of legal rules.

Violations of International Law are certainly frequent, especially during war. But the offenders always try to prove that their acts do not constitute a violation, and that they have a right to act as they do according to the Law of Nations, or at least that no rule of the Law of Nations is against their acts. The fact is that States, in breaking the Law of Nations, never deny its existence, but recognize its existence through the endeavor to interpret the Law of Nations as justifying their conduct. And although the frequency of the violations of International Law may strain its legal force to the breaking point, the formal, though often cynical, affirmation of its binding nature is not without significance.

Basis of the Law of Nations

If law is . . . a body of rules for human conduct within a community which by common consent of this community shall be enforced through external power, common consent is the basis of all law. It will be noted that 'common consent' is a sociological rather than a legal explanation of the validity of the law. What, now, does the term 'common consent' mean? If it meant that all the individuals who are members of a community must at every moment of their existence expressly consent to every point of law, such common consent could never be proved. The individuals, who are the members of a community, are successively born into it, grow into it together with the growth of their intellect during adolescence, and die away successively to make room for others. The community remains unaltered, although a constant change takes place in its members. 'Common consent' can therefore only mean the express or tacit consent of such an overwhelming majority of the members that those who dissent are of no importance whatever, and disappear totally from the view of one who looks for the will of the community as an entity in contradistinction to the wills of its single members. . . . Those legal rules which come down from ancestors to their descendants remain law so long as they are supported by the common consent of those descendants. New rules can only become law if they find common consent on the part of those who constitute the community at the time. It is for that reason that custom is at the background of all law, whether written or unwritten.

The customary rules of International Law have grown up by common consent of the States—that is, the different States have acted in such a manner as to imply their tacit consent to these rules. As far as the process of the growth of a usage and its turning into a custom can be traced back, customary rules of the Law of Nations came into existence in the following way. The intercourse of States with each other necessitated some rules of international conduct. Single usages, therefore, gradually grew up, the different States acting in the same or in a similar way when occasion arose. As some rules of international conduct were from the end of the Middle Ages urgently wanted, the writers on the Law of Nature prepared the ground for their growth by constructing certain rules on the basis of religious, moral, rational, and historical reflections. Hugo Grotius' work, *De Jure Belli ac Pacis, libri iii.* (1625), offered a systematized body of rules which recommended themselves so much to the needs and wants of the time that they became the basis of the subsequent development. When afterwards, especially in the nineteenth century, it became apparent that customs and usages alone were not sufficient, or not sufficiently clear, new rules were created through law-making treaties being concluded which laid down rules for future international conduct. Thus conventional rules gradually grew up side by side with customary rules. . . .

Since the Law of Nations is based on the common consent of individual States, States are the principal subjects of International Law. This means that the Law of Nations is primarily a law for the international conduct of States, and not of their citizens. As a rule, the subjects of the rights and duties arising from the Law of Nations are States solely and exclusively. An individual human being, such as a king or an ambassador for example, is not directly a subject of International Law. Therefore, all rights which might necessarily have to be granted to an individual human being according to the Law of Nations are not, as a rule, international rights, but rights granted by Municipal Law in accordance with a duty imposed upon the State concerned by International Law. Likewise, all duties which might necessarily have to be imposed upon individual human beings according to the Law of Nations are, on this view, not international duties, but duties imposed by Municipal Law in accordance with a right granted to, or a duty imposed upon, the State concerned by International Law. Thus, for instance, the privileges of an ambassador are granted to him by the Municipal Law of the State to which he is accredited, but that State has the duty to grant these privileges according to International Law.

While it is of importance to bear in mind that primarily States are subjects of International Law, it is essential to recognize the limitations of that principle. Its correct meaning is that States only create International Law; that International Law is primarily concerned with the rights and duties of States and not with those of other persons; and that States only possess full procedural capacity before international tribunals. Further than this that principle does not go. In particular, when we say that International Law regulates the conduct of States we must not forget that the conduct actually regulated is the conduct of human beings acting as the organ of the State. . . . Also, although States are the normal subjects of International Law they may treat individuals and other persons as endowed directly with international rights and duties and constitute them to that extent subjects of International Law. Persons engaging in piracy are subject to duties imposed, in the first instance, not by the municipal law of various States but by International Law. . . . Although individuals cannot appear as parties before the International Court of Justice,[4] States may confer upon them the right of direct access to international tribunals. . . .

Since the Law of Nations is based on the common consent of States as sovereign communities, the member-States of the Family of Nations are equal to each other as subjects of International Law. States are by their nature certainly not equal as regards power, territory and the like. But as members of the community of nations they are, in principle, equal, whatever differences between them may otherwise exist. This is a consequence of their sovereignty in the international sphere. As such the abstract principle of State equality, while still forming part of International Law, is open to objections of the kind levelled against other extreme manifestations of State sovereignty. The Charter of the United Nations, although professedly based on the principle of 'sovereign equality' of States, embodies far-reaching derogations from the conception of equality of States in the accepted sense.

[4] Article 34 of the Statute of the International Court of Justice provides as follows: 'Only States may be parties in cases before the Court.'

Sources of the Law of Nations

The different writers on the Law of Nations disagree widely with regard to the kinds and numbers of sources of this law. The fact is that the term 'source of law' is used in different meanings by the different writers on International Law, as on law in general. It seems that most writers confuse the conception of 'source' with that of 'cause,' and through this mistake come to a standpoint from which certain factors which influence the growth of International Law appear as sources of rules of the Law of Nations. This mistake can be avoided by going back to the meaning of the term 'source' in general. Source means a spring or well, and has to be defined as the rising from the ground of a stream of water. When we see a stream of water and want to know whence it comes, we follow the stream upwards until we come to the spot where it rises naturally from the ground. On that spot, we say, is the source of the stream of water. We know very well that this source is not the cause of the existence of the stream of water. Source signifies only the natural rising of water from a certain spot on the ground, whatever natural causes there may be for that rising. If we apply the conception of source in this meaning to the term 'source of law,' the confusion of source with cause cannot arise. Just as we see streams of water running over the surface of the earth, so we see, as it were, streams of rules running over the area of law. And if we want to know whence these rules come, we have to follow these streams upwards until we come to their beginning. Where we find that such rules rise into existence, there is the source of them. Of course, rules of law do not rise from a spot on the ground as water does; they rise from facts in the historical development of a community. Thus in Great Britain a good many rules of law rise every year from Acts of Parliament. 'Source of law' is therefore the name for an historical fact out of which rules of conduct rise into existence and legal force.

As the basis of the Law of Nations is the common consent of the member-States of the Family of Nations, it is evident that there must exist as many sources of International Law as there are facts through which such common consent can possibly come into existence. A State, just as an individual, may give its consent either directly by an express declaration, or tacitly by conduct which it would not follow in case it did not consent. The sources of International Law are therefore twofold—namely: (1) *express* consent, which is given when States conclude a treaty stipulating certain rules for the future international conduct of the parties; (2) *tacit* consent, that is, implied consent or consent by conduct, which is given through States having adopted the custom of submitting to certain rules of international conduct. Subject, therefore, to what has been said above . . . about the meaning of 'common consent' and below about the binding force of general principles of law, treaties and custom must be regarded as the exclusive sources of the Law of Nations.

Custom is the older and the original source of International Law in particular as well as of law in general. For this reason, although an international court is bound in the first instance to consider any available treaty provisions binding upon the parties, it is by reference to international custom that these treaties are interpreted in case of doubt. This explains why the Permanent Court of International Justice, whose jurisdiction has been almost universally invoked for the purpose of interpreting treaties, has largely relied upon and, in turn, made a substantial contribution to the development of customary International Law.

Treaties are the second source of International Law, and a source which has of late become of the greatest importance. As treaties may be concluded for innumerable purposes, usually such treaties only are regarded as a source of International Law as stipulate new general rules for future international conduct or confirm, define, or abolish existing customary or conventional rules of a general character. Such treaties may conveniently be called *law-making treaties*. Since the Family of Nations is not at present a State-like community, there is no central authority which could make law for it in the way that Parliaments make law by statutes within the States. The only way in which International Law can be made by a deliberate act, in contradistinction to custom, is by the members of the Family of Nations concluding treaties in which certain rules for their future conduct are stipulated. Of course, such law-making treaties create law for the contracting parties solely. *Universal* International Law is created only when all or practically all the members of the Family of Nations are parties to these treaties. . . . Many law-making treaties are concluded by a few States only, so that the law which they create is *particular* International Law. On the other hand, many law-making treaties have been concluded which contain *general* International Law, because the majority of States, including the leading Powers, are parties to them. General International Law has a tendency to become universal because such States as hitherto did not consent to it will in future either expressly give their consent or recognize the rules concerned tacitly through custom. . . .

Thus custom and treaties are the two principal sources of International Law. The Statute of the International Court of Justice recognizes this expressly in laying down that the Court shall apply: '(*a*) international conventions, whether general or particular, establishing rules expressly recognized by the contesting States; (*b*) international custom, as evidence of a general practice accepted as law.' But although these are the principal sources of the Law of Nations, they cannot be regarded as its only sources.

. . . The Statute of the International Court of Justice authorizes it to apply, in addition to treaties and custom: '(3) The general principles of law recognized by civilized nations.' The meaning of that phrase has been the subject of much discussion. The intention is to authorize the Court to apply the general principles of municipal jurisprudence, in particular of private law, in so far as they are applicable to relations of States. The Court has seldom found occasion to apply 'general principles of law.' . . . But paragraph 3 of Article 38 nevertheless constitutes an important landmark in the history of International Law inasmuch as the States parties to the Statute did expressly recognize the existence of a third source of International Law independent of, although merely supplementary to, custom or treaty. . . .

The formal incorporation of that practice in the Statute of the Court marks the explicit abandonment of the positivist view according to which treaties and custom are the only sources of International Law, with the result that in their absence international tribunals are powerless to render decisions. It equally signifies the rejection of the naturalist attitude according to which the law of nature is the primary source of the Law of Nations. It amounts to an acceptance of what has been called the Grotian view which, while giving due—and, on the whole, decisive—weight to the will of States as the authors of International Law, does not divorce it from the legal experience and practice of mankind generally.

Decisions of courts and tribunals are a subsidiary and indirect source of International Law. Article 38 of the Statute of the International Court of Justice provides that, subject to certain limitations, the Court shall apply judicial decisions as a subsidiary means for the determination of rules of law. In the absence of anything approaching the common law doctrine of judicial precedent, decisions of international tribunals are not a direct source of law in international adjudications. In fact, however, they exercise considerable influence as an impartial and well-considered statement of the law by jurists of authority made in the light of actual problems which arise before them. They are often relied upon in argument and decision.

The International Court, while prevented from treating its previous decisions as binding (see article 59 of the Statute), has referred to them with increasing frequency. It is probable that in view of the difficulties surrounding the codification of the International Law, international tribunals will in the future fulfill, inconspicuously but efficiently, a large part of the task of developing International Law.

The Statute of the International Court of Justice enumerates as a subsidiary source of International Law 'the teachings of the most highly qualified publicists of the various nations.' It is indicative of the present potentialities of that particular source that the Court has so far found no occasion to rely on it. In pleadings before international tribunals the disputants still fortify their arguments by reference to writings of international jurists, but with the growth of international judicial activity and of the practice of States evidenced by widely accessible records and reports, it is natural that reliance on the authority of writers as evidence of International Law should tend to diminish. . . .

A factor of a special kind which also influences the growth of International Law is the so-called Comity *(Comitas Gentium, Convenance et Courtoisie Internationale, Staatengunst).* In their intercourse with one another, States observe not only legally binding rules and such rules as have the character of usages, but also rules of politeness, convenience, and goodwill. Such rules of international conduct are not rules of law, but of Comity. Thus, for instance, it is as the result of a rule of Comity and not of International Law that States grant to diplomatic envoys exemption from customs duties. . . .

Some Observations on the History and
Development of International Law

International law in the meaning of the term as used in modern time did not exist during antiquity and the first part of the Middle Ages. . . .

International Law . . . owes its existence as a systematized body of rules to the Dutch jurist and statesman Hugo Grotius, whose work, *De iure belli ac pacis (On the Law of War and Peace),* appeared in 1625, and became the foundation of all later development. . . . Grotius . . . bears by right the title of "Father of the Law of Nations." Hugo Grotius was born at Delft in Holland in 1583. He began to study law at Leyden when only 11 years old, and at the age of 15 he took the degree of Doctor of Laws, at Orleans in France. Even before he had the intention of writing a book on the Law of Nations, Grotius took an interest in matters international. For in 1609, when only 24 years old, he published . . . a short treatise under the title *Mare Liberum (The Open Sea),* in which he contended that the open sea could not be the property of any State, whereas the contrary opinion was generally prevalent. But it was not until fourteen years later that Grotius began . . . to write his *De iure belli ac pacis,* Libri III., and of which it has rightly been maintained that no other book, with the single exception of the Bible, has ever exercised a similar influence upon human minds and matters.

Grotius as a child of his time, could not help starting from the Law of Nature, since his intention was to find such rules of a Law of Nations as were eternal, unchangeable, and independent of the special consent of the single State. Long before Grotius, the opinion was generally prevalent that above the positive law, which had grown up by custom or by legislation of a State, there was in existence another law which had its roots in human reason, and which would therefore be discovered without any knowledge of positive law. This law of reason was called Law of Nature or Natural Law.

[Grotius] did not deny that there already existed in his time a good many customary rules for the international conduct of the States, but he expressly kept them apart from those rules which he considered the outcome of the Law of Nature. He distinguishes therefore between . . . the customary law of nations—he calls it . . . *voluntary* law—and the [Law of Nature], concerning the international relations of the States, afterwards called the *natural* Law of Nations. The bulk of Grotius's interest is concentrated upon the natural Law of Nations, since he considered the voluntary of minor importance. . . . Although he mainly and chiefly lays down the rule of the natural Law of Nations, he always mentions also voluntary rules concerning the different matters.

But the modern Law of Nations has another, though minor, founder, besides Grotius, and this is an Englishman, Richard Zouche (1590-1660), professor of civil law at Oxford and a judge of the Admiralty Court. . . . The book through which he acquired the title of "second founder of the Law of Nations," appeared in 1650 . . . [it] has rightly been called the first manual of the *positive* Law of Nations. The standpoint of Zouche is totally different from that of Grotius in so far as, according to him, the customary Law of

Nations is the most important part of that law, although as a child of his time, he does not at all deny the existence of a natural Law of Nations. It must be specially mentioned that Zouche was the first to use the term *ius inter gentes* (law between nations) for that new branch of law. Grotius knew very well and says, that the Law of Nations is a law *between* the States, but he called it *ius gentium* (law of nations), and it is due to his influence that until Bentham (a century and half later) nobody called the Law of Nations *inter*-national law.

The distinction between the natural Law of Nations, chiefly treated by Grotius, and the customary or voluntary Law of Nations, chiefly treated by Zouche, gave rise in the seventeenth and eighteenth centuries to three different schools of writers of the Law of Nations—namely the "naturalists," the "positivists," and the "grotians."

"Naturalists" . . . is the appellation of those writers who deny that there is any positive Law of Nations whatever, as the outcome of custom or treaties, and who maintain that all Law of Nations is only a part of the Law of Nature. . . .

The "positivists" are the antipodes of the naturalists. They . . . not only defend the existence of a positive Law of Nations, as the outcome of custom or the international treaties, but consider it more important than the natural Law of Nations, the very existence of which some of the positivists deny, thus going beyond Zouche. . . .

The "grotians" stand midway between the naturalists and the positivists. They keep up Grotius's distinction between the natural and the voluntary Law of Nations, but, in contradistinction to Grotius, they consider the positive or voluntary of equal importance to the natural, and they devote therefore their interest to both alike.

►THE ABSENCE OF COMMON STANDARDS

KENNETH W. THOMPSON

The following selection raises some doubts as to the assumption that—as Oppenheim puts it—"there exists an international community embracing all independent States and constituting a legally organized society.".

The essence of the philosophy of Charles de Visscher of Belgium, former member of the International Court of Justice, is briefly presented by Kenneth W. Thompson.

The setting in which we face the problems of international life bears little resemblance to the late medieval or early modern period. Religiously, we enjoy not the benefits of one ecclesiastical union but the fruits of separatism and diversity. Legally, the sufficiency of contemporary international law

From *Christian Ethics and the Dilemmas of Foreign Policy* (Durham: Duke University Press, 1959), pp. 12-16, *passim*.

is questioned even by its protagonists. The context in which relations between ethics and international politics work themselves out is illustrated by the philosophy of . . . an international jurist, perhaps the wisest of our day. . . .

Judge Charles de Visscher of Belgium, Catholic philosopher and former member of the International Court of Justice, has been more widely known in Europe than on the American continent. An English translation of his classic work, *Theory and Reality in Public International Law,* has brought him closer to American writers and recently the American Society of International Law singled out his treatise as the most important publication of the year. Some go so far as to compare its importance to the writings of Grotius and Vattel. If students of international law and morality were to distill from de Visscher the essence of his philosophy, they would probably include the following elements:

First, the world hopes for but does not possess genuine world community. Despite modern communications and the unifying compulsion of western technology, there are pitifully few basic solidarities in the present international order. Ironically, the mass media have the effect of making national communities more autonomous, homogeneous and exclusive than at any time in history. The collective societies around the globe that feed on the products of a nation-wide press, radio and television networks run the inevitable risk of thinking the same thoughts, despising the same enemies, and falling victim to the same unifying slogans. They do not necessarily become, in spite of greater literacy or travel, more tolerant, understanding, or compassionate toward foreign peoples, although for parts of the population this advance is palpably realizable. The modern nation-state in contact with the harsh realities of the external world tends to become more cohesive, more conscious of itself and its problems, and more resistant to unifying forces from outside its boundaries. The imperatives of national survival demand greater unity for a single people huddling together within national boundaries that protect it against extinction. Even the Soviet threat, for example, is a spur to better American science, education, and production, not for greater world-wide achievements in these fields. International society, lacking in dominant incentives to greater solidarity, substitutes for them a call for sacrifice and the appeal to a common supranational good, but this attainment seems not open to the great majority of mankind. For most of the newer nations, the margin of their resources even broadly conceived, is barely sufficient for national survival. The pursuit of a common good is a luxury they cannot indulge themselves. To mention three examples, the struggling North African states in the Maghreb (Tunisia, Morocco, and eventually Algeria) dream of not one but three national universities. No first-class training center for diplomats or central bankers can be found in all of Latin-America, perhaps because nearly every "Republic" aspires to have one of its own. And in the supposedly more developed states, the "fourth country" drive for thermonuclear weapons has already become a burning issue in France, Switzerland, and Sweden. In the nation-state, it is the most highly political experiences and the claims of vital interest that evoke supreme solidarities. In the international realm, the opposite is true, for minor solidarities of an economic or technical order are often found. The nearer the approach to vital questions like the preservation of peace and the prevention of war, the less influence the community has on its members. "If the international community, or more accurately the sense of such a community, finds so little echo in individual consciences, this is less because power obstructs it than because the immense majority of men are still infinitely less accessible to the doubtless real but certainly remote solidarities that it evokes than to the immediate and tangible solidarities that impose themselves upon them in the framework of national life."

Secondly, Judge de Visscher firmly believes that "neither politics nor law will ensure equilibrium and peace in the world without the 'moral infrastructure.' " Neither positive law walled off from its philosophical or moral roots nor a highly abstract natural law which in any case the contemporary western world has largely abandoned seem capable of filling this need. The infrastructure of the present order is essential to understanding contemporary world politics. At present, in matters political, men are disposed to transfer their most important moral impulses to the state. "The morality that peoples practice in their mutual relations is in large measure the product of their historical partitioning. They are refractory to a higher morality only because their sentiments like their interests continue to gravitate exclusively about the units which are today the Nation-States. These, though theoretically subordinate to the higher unity, are in fact real and almost absolute centers of moral cohesion. . . . 'Sacred egoism,' the fascist formula, was only the blustering expression of a certain collective morality which makes the national good the supreme good and civil duty the absolute duty.' " "Merely to invoke the idea of an international communiy, as is the habit, is immediately to move into a vicious circle, for it is to postulate in men, shut in their national compartments, something they still largely lack, namely the community spirit, the deliberate adherence to supranational values." The criticism Judge de Visscher levels against much of twentieth-century international law is that "it exaggerated the specificity of international law, separating it off from the moral, social and political data which form its sphere of application and condition its effectiveness." No social or legal reform that would succeed can ignore the moral infrastructure. The failure of collective security, the outlawry of war, and the sweeping appeals to world-wide public opinion are all examples of thinking that suffers from the illusion that moral foundations are unimportant.

Third, Judge de Visscher calls for a transvaluation of the present structure in terms of a drastic change in the modern conception of the state and its power. Whether his positive solution will suffer the shipwreck to which others have fallen prey remains to be seen. He maintains that the ends of the state must be subordinated to those of the human person. The human end of politics from a purely formal point of view "may be defined as the pursuit of the common good, understood as that which in a community should ensure the good of each in the good of the collectivity." Whenever the notion of the common good is no longer harnessed to human ends, there sets in a fatal deterioration in the ends of power. These human ends have been dealt with somewhat naively and impatiently in declarations by the United Nations in the proposed Covenant of Human Rights. But de Visscher concludes:

> It is the fate of any idea of a highly spiritual character to be exposed to some distortion when it is introduced into a new environment . . . [Yet] the bond that is being established beyond any shadow of doubt between the rights of man on the one hand, and the maintenance of peace and respect for law on the other, constitutes the first assertion by the international organization of a great moral and civilizing principle. A . . . functional conception of power here joins hands with Christian doctrine, making human values— the only values that can command universal acceptance—the ultimate point of convergence of peace and law. We must neither count upon its immediate efficacy, nor reject the hopes that it awakens.

TOPIC 26

International Enforcement

When nations agree on some common rules or establish a common agency, there is no guarantee that they will abide by the rules or cooperate with the agency in the future. Can their compliance be enforced? We have seen that there is no central authority with the power to enact, interpret, or enforce the rights and obligations of nations.

A government may discover that its obligations, based on a previous voluntary consent, unfavorably affect the nation's vital interests. In such a case the statesmen will compare and weigh the advantages of their adherence to, or violation of, the agreed rules. And they will break the rules of agreement if they come to the conclusion that it is in the interest of their country to do so.

Several methods have been devised and used to prevent such unilateral breach of an agreement. Here are six:

1. *Solemn Oath.* The present-day ceremonial signings of treaties are supposed to underline their validity. They are probably the remnants of the ancient method of solemn oath.

2. *Taking Hostages.* In the eighteenth century two English lords were sent to France as hostages in order to guarantee English adherence to the treaty of Aix-La Chapelle (1748), according to which Cape Breton Island was to be restored by England to France.

3. *Blocking of National Assets Abroad.* This is another method of enforcing compliance with international treaties.

4. *Occupation* of a portion of national territory. The Peace Treaty with Germany in 1919 stipulated for instance that "the German territory situated

to the west of the Rhine, together with its bridgeheads, will be occupied by Allied and Associated troops for a period of fifteen years . . . as a guarantee for the execution of the present treaty by Germany."

5. *Treaty of Guarantee.* This term refers to a great number of treaties which may have also other purposes than guaranteeing the fulfillment of a treaty, such as a guarantee of other nations' neutrality or independence. In a narrower sense—and in the present context—we refer to those guarantee treaties which obligate one or more nations to uphold the terms of a treaty against its violator. The guarantor thus accepts the duty to act as a policeman and do what is in his power to secure the fulfillment of the treaty.

Minority treaties, mentioned in Part I, belonged to this category. The League of Nations was supposed to do all in its power to insure the rights of national minorities in the new states.

Automatic enforcement through guarantee treaties is severely limited by the following factors:

(a) The guaranteed party must request the assistance of the guarantor. In some extreme cases this may not be possible. An occupied state, imprisoned leaders, or national minority may not be able to ask for support.

(b) The guarantor must be willing to render the assistance. His original interest in the situation as created by the treaty may change, however, and he may be now sympathetic to the cause of the violator of the treaty.

(c) The guarantor must also be available to perform his police duties. If a costly war or internal situation ties his hands, the state's appeal for enforcement will go unheeded.

(d) Finally, it is an accepted rule that a guarantor is not obliged to render assistance if his previous advice to the party now claiming assistance was disregarded.

6. *Collective Security.* It is the enforcement of law and prevention of violence by all law-abiding nations united against the actual or potential violator. Kenneth W. Thompson discusses the theory and practice of collective security in Topic 8.

It should be noted at this point that the United Nations and other international instruments provide for military and police enforcement of obligations and duties only in cases where the violation of contract threatens international peace and security. For other kinds of breaches of contract there is usually no other provision than individual or collective self-help.

►CENTRALIZED ENFORCEMENT AND SELF-HELP

HANS KELSEN

The author of the following selection defines and discusses some of the basic concepts of law enforcement: delict, sanction, centralized execution of sanctions, and the principle and evolution of self-help.

From *Principles of International Law,* copyright, 1952, by Hans Kelsen. Reprinted by permission of Rinehart & Company, Inc., New York, Publishers.

Hans Kelsen was for many years Professor of Political Science at the University of California. He is the author of numerous books on the theory of law and international law.

As a coercive order the law is that specific social technique which consists in the attempt to bring about the desired social conduct of men through the threat of a measure of coercion which is to be taken in case of contrary, i.e., legally wrong, conduct. This conduct, which is the specific condition of the sanction, is called "illegal act," "crime," "tort," "delict." The last-mentioned term covers all possible kinds of legally wrong conduct.

If the behavior which constitutes the condition of the sanction is called "delict," this term has no moral connotation. It means only a definite behavior against which a sanction is provided for by the law. . . . In order to induce individuals to a certain conduct an authority may threaten them with an evil to be forcibly inflicted upon them in case they act contrarily. . . . The threatened evil we call a sanction. . . . Sanctions have the character of acts of coercion; for they are to be carried out against the will of those subject to the order, by the employment of physical force if necessary. . . .

In early law the execution of the sanction was decentralized, that is to say it was left to the individual whose interest was violated by the behavior of another individual which constituted the delict. This primitive legal technique is called the principle of self-help. It prevails in primitive law, which in case of murder authorizes the relatives of the murdered man to kill the murderer and his relatives. This is so-called blood revenge; and blood revenge is a sanction provided by primitive law. If a man did not pay his debt or did not repair a damage caused by him, the law authorized the creditor or injured party to take away, by force if necessary, some property of the debtor or the one responsible for the damage. This is the sanction provided by primitive law for a violation of the obligation to pay a debt or to repair a damage. Under such primitive law to have a right (in the specific sense of the term) means to be authorized by the law to execute a sanction. It is a characteristic of a technically more developed legal order that the execution of the sanction is centralized. This centralization consists in the establishment of a special organ, a tribunal, competent to ascertain in a definite procedure the fact that a delict has been committed, and to order the sanction provided for by the law; and in the establishment of a special executive organ competent to carry out the sanction ordered by the tribunal. . . .

If peace is conceived as a state of absence of force, the law then provides only for relative, not for absolute, peace. The peace guaranteed by the law is not a state of complete absence of force, a state of anarchy. It is the state of a force monopoly, namely, the force monopoly of the legal community. . . .

The force monopoly of the community may be centralized or decentralized. It is centralized if the social order institutes, according to the principle of division of labor, special organs for the execution of the sanctions provided for by the order. This, as has been pointed out, is the case when a legal order institutes tribunals competent to ascertain in a procedure, determined by the law, whether a delict has been committed and who is responsible for it, and when the legal order institutes special organs to execute the sanctions ordered by the tribunals. The force monopoly of the community is decentralized if the principle of self-help prevails, that is to say, if the legal order leaves these functions to the individuals injured by the delict, as in the case of blood revenge. Although in this case the individuals appear to "take the law in their own hands," they may nevertheless be considered as acting as organs of the community. Even if the principle of self-help prevails, legal and illegal employment of force are to be distinguished. The relative of a murdered individual who takes revenge by killing the murderer or his relatives is not a murderer. The avenger does not violate the law; he executes the law and hence may be considered as an organ of the legal community constituted by the legal order. But he is not a special organ instituted according to the principle of division of labor, as a court or a sheriff is. . . .

Where the principle of self-help prevails, the legal order may authorize or even obligate subjects who are not the immediate victims of the delict to assist the victim in his lawful reaction against the delict, in his execution of the sanction. But the principle of self-help is eliminated if the legal order reserves the execution of the sanction to a special organ, that is, if the force monopoly of the community is centralized. If the members of the legal community are obliged—and not only authorized—to assist the victim of a delict in his legitimate reaction against the delict, that is to say, in the execution of the sanction, or if the execution of the sanction is reserved to a special organ of the community, we speak of collective security. Hence there are two stages in the development of collective security: the first is characterized by the fact that the principle of self-help still prevails, but the members of the community are legally obliged to assist the victim of a delict, especially the victim of an illegal employment of force, in his legal reaction against this delict, namely, in the execution of the sanction; the second is characterized by the fact that the execution of the sanction is reserved to a central organ of the community, and that means that a centralized force monopoly of the community is established.

It stands to reason that collective security is more effective if the force monopoly of the community is centralized than if it is decentralized. The most obvious defect of a decentralized force monopoly consists in the fact that there is no authority, different from and independent of the parties concerned, competent to ascertain in a concrete case that a delict has been committed. . . .

It is characteristic of national law that it determines the conditions under which force may lawfully be employed. If employed under these conditions the employment of force is legal; it has, as a rule, the character of sanction. If employed under other conditions it is illegal; it has a character of a delict. It is a characteristic feature of national law that the employment of force is, as a rule, either a sanction, or a delict.

International law is law in the same sense as national law, provided that it is, in principle, possible to interpret the employment of force directed by one state against another either as sanction or as delict. . . . Legally, conduct of a state can be considered a delict only if international law attaches to this conduct a sanction directed against a state responsible for this conduct.

►THE UNITED NATIONS SECURITY COUNCIL

LELAND M. GOODRICH

The assumptions concerning the role and activities of the main United Nations organ of international enforcement and prevention of violence are critically examined by Dr. Goodrich, who is Professor of International Organization and Administration at Columbia University. The author is one of the editors of International Organization, *the leading quarterly journal concerned with matters pertaining to international law and government.*

I

The peace and security provisions of the Charter appear to have been based in part on conclusions that were drawn by their authors with respect to the causes of the failure of the League system. First of all, it was rightly believed that a major cause of the failure of the League system was its lack of universality, and particularly the absence of the United States. Consequently, the first concern of the Charter-makers was to have as members all the major powers in the Organization, and above all the Soviet Union and the United States. Secondly, it was believed that a weakness of the League system was its provision that sanctions should be applied against every aggressor, irrespective of whether or not it was a major power, and whether or not all the major powers joined in applying them. Consequently the authors of the Charter stressed the need of agreement among the permanent members of the Security Council as a condition of enforcement action, thus returning to the principle underlying the European Concert in the nineteenth century. Thirdly, it was believed that an important reason for the failure of the League system was the absence of any effective provision for the use of military force and the unwillingness of states under a voluntary system to take such extreme measures for defeating aggression. Therefore, the authors of the Charter were concerned with placing effective military force at the disposal of the Organization and making certain that it would be used when necessary. Finally, it was apparently believed, by some at least, that the League system was weakened by the failure of the Covenant clearly to delimit the respective responsibilities of Council and Assembly. Therefore the Charter-makers sought to define the limits of the responsibilities of the UN counterparts of these two organs.

As written at San Francisco, after a lengthy process of elaboration in which the United States government played a leading role, the Charter set the

From *International Organization,* Vol. XII, No. 3 (Summer, 1958), pp. 274-287. Footnotes partly omitted.

maintenance of international peace and security as the first purpose of the Organization. It prescribed two principal approaches to the achievement of this purpose: collective measures for preventing or removing threats to the peace and suppressing acts of aggression or breaches of the peace, and adjustment or settlement of international disputes or situations by peaceful means. The regulation of armaments was made a subsidiary approach with emphasis upon agreements to make armed forces and facilities available to the Security Council and upon achieving "the least diversion for armaments of the world's human and economic resources" consistent with the assured maintenance of international peace and security.

The primary responsibility for doing these things was placed on the Security Council, an organ so constructed and with voting procedures so defined that no decision other than a procedural one could be taken except with the concurrence of the five permanent members. This gave assurance that no action could be taken against a permanent member or without its consent. The powers given to the Security Council were such as to give assurance that once the permanent members were in agreement and had the support of two other members—which would in all likelihood not be difficult to achieve—effective action could be taken to maintain peace and security. The requirement of unanimity, moreover, was regarded as assurance that the coercive power vested in the Council would not be abused. Thus, in effect, the maintenance of international peace and security was to be made the responsibility of a "concert of the permanent members."

It was assumed that the members of this concert would each have an interest in the maintenance of peace and security, following a war which had imperilled them all. Furthermore, the members of the Council were required to act in accordance with the Purposes and Principles of the Organization, as set forth in Chapter I, in discharging their responsibilities. But it was also recognized that the concert might not always materialize in fact.

> The underlying theory, however, was that if one of the major powers were to prove recalcitrant, or were to refuse to abide by the rules of international behavior that were being inscribed in the Charter, a situation would be created in which the recalcitrant nation might have to be coerced; and it was apparent that no major nation could be coerced except by the combined forces of the other major nations. This would be the equivalent of a world war, and a decision to embark upon such a war would necessarily have to be made by each of the other major nations for itself and not by any international organization.[1]

There was no disagreement among the major powers at San Francisco or in previous discussions on the principle that unanimity of the major powers should be required. There was disagreement as to how far the principle should be applied in disputes involving one or more of the major powers. The view of the United Kingdom was that no one, even a permanent member of the Council, should be allowed to vote in its own case. The Soviet view was that

[1] Leo Pasvolsky, "The United Nations in Action," *Edmund J. James Lectures on Government,* Fifth Series, Urbana, University of Illinois Press, 1951, p. 80-81.

the unity of the major powers was the important consideration and no provision should be included in the Charter which would tend to encourage disagreement. At Yalta, however, Stalin accepted President Roosevelt's proposal that a member of the Council, party to a dispute, even though a permanent member, should not be allowed to veto a decision which the Council might take in the performance of its function of peaceful settlement or adjustment. The agreement reached at Yalta did not fully hold at San Francisco, however, when it became evident that it was not interpreted in like manner by all the parties to it. Extensive further discussions among the four sponsoring governments were necessary before final agreement was reached on the scope of the unanimity requirement. By the San Francisco agreement, accepted by France, it was made clear that the requirement of unanimity of the permanent members did not apply to Council decisions to consider and discuss matters brought to its attention, or to decisions inviting parties to disputes to be heard. On the other hand, the "chain of events"[2] theory as elaborated in the Statement was interpreted as preventing the Security Council from deciding to conduct an investigation or take any subsequent non-procedural decisions save with the concurrence of the permanent members, the one exception to the rule being that above indicated. Furthermore, the Statement asserted that the question whether or not a particular matter was procedural was itself nonprocedural. While the Statement contained no commitment not to use the right of veto excessively or unreasonably, it did contain the statement that it was

> not to be assumed . . . that the permanent members, any more than the nonpermanent members, would use their "veto" power wilfully to obstruct the operation of the Council,

and representatives of the permanent members reaffirmed their sense of responsibility in Conference discussions.

With respect to the division of powers between the Security Council and the General Assembly, there was even less disagreement among the permanent members up to the time of the San Francisco Conference. The Tentative Proposals of July 18, 1944, which the United States submitted to the other participants in the Dumbarton Oaks Conversations gave the executive council

[2] ["Chain of events" is a term which was used by great powers in their reply to questions and objections raised by lesser powers with regard to Yalta agreement on the voting procedure in the Security Council. In San Francisco small and medium powers submitted about two dozen questions concerning the interpretation of the voting procedure in specific situations. In their replies great powers agreed that the veto did not apply to procedural questions; the veto also could not prevent a *discussion* of a dispute under the pacific settlements provisions of Chapter VI. The veto, could, however, block *"decisions or actions"* under Chapter VI or Chapter VII.

[Great powers argued that decisions and actions, even if undertaken with the aim to promote pacific settlement of an issue, "may well have major political consequences and may even initiate a *chain of events* which might, in the end, require the Council . . . to invoke measures of enforcement." The great powers' interpretive reply further stated that "this chain of events begins when the Council decides to make an investigation, or determines that the time has come to call upon states to settle their differences, or makes recommendations to the parties."—I.D.]

(Security Council) the "primary responsibility for the peaceful settlement of international disputes, for the prevention of threats to the peace and breaches of the peace, and for such other activities as may be necessary for the maintenance of international peace and security." They empowered the General Assembly "to take action in matters of concern to the international organization which are not allocated to other organs by the basic instrument," and specifically

a. to make on its own initiative or on request of a member state, reports on and recommendations for the peaceful adjustment of any situation or controversy, the continuance of which it deems likely to impair the general welfare;

b. to assist the executive council, upon its request, in enlisting the cooperation of all states toward giving effect to action under consideration in or decided upon by the council with respect to:

1) the settlement of a dispute the continuance of which is likely to endanger security or to lead to a breach of the peace;

2) the maintenance or restoration of peace; and

3) any other matters within the jurisdiction of the Council.

This proposed delimitation of the respective responsibilities of the two organs was substantially accepted at Dumbarton Oaks and incorporated into the Dumbarton Oaks Proposals. This not only represented Department of State thinking, but it was in line with Soviet reluctance to permit extensive participation by the lesser powers in the activities of the Organization in the maintenance of international peace and security.

At San Francisco, a variety of pressures—the insistence of the lesser powers on a larger measure of participation, growing skepticism regarding the likelihood of cooperation among the major powers, and the insistence of Republican leaders and Congressional members of the United States delegation—led to the broadening of the powers of the General Assembly, particularly by the inclusion of Articles 10 and 14,[3] and the consequent blurring of the line dividing Security Council and General Assembly responsibilities and powers. Thus the Charter foundation was laid for the subsequent development of the role of the General Assembly in the field of action originally reserved to the Security Council. The primary role of the Security Council was further jeopardized by the inclusion of Article 51 recognizing explicitly "the inherent right of individual or collective self-defense" in case of an armed attack upon a Member, until such time as the Security Council has taken measures necessary to the maintenance of international peace and security.

II

The most striking trend in the practice of the UN since its establishment has been the increasing inability of the Security Council to serve the purposes for which it was intended and the growing preference of Members to make use of the General Assembly. This trend has been accompanied by the

---

[3] While Article 10 authorizes the General Assembly to *discuss* any question, Article 14 authorizes the Assembly to make *recommendations* with regard to the peaceful adjustment of any situation impairing the general welfare or friendly relations among nations.

gradual breakdown of the lines of functional separation between the Security Council and the General Assembly, drawn up at Dumbarton Oaks and preserved, though with important modifications, at San Francisco, and by the gradual assumption by the General Assembly of an active role in the maintenance of international peace and security.

A quantitative measurement of the trend, though obviously inadequate, provides us with an indication of the changing role of the Security Council within the UN machinery. The declining frequency of the meetings of the Security Council in a world beset with conflicts, together with the increasing number of political questions considered by the General Assembly in comparison with the number considered by the Council, underscores the diminishing role of the Council. The figures are extremely illuminating:

Period	Meetings of the SC	Substantive Political Questions[4] Considered by the	
		SC	GA
Jan. 17, 1946-July 15, 1946	50	5	2
July 16, 1946-July 15, 1947	108	8	4
1947-1948	180	8	5
1948-1949	92	8	11
1949-1950	46	6	10
1950-1951	72	7	19
1951-1952	43	6	12
1952-1953	26	1	14
1953-1954	59	4	11
1954-1955	22	3	15
1955-1956	32	1	11
1956-1957	52	6	13

Since the peak reached in the period from July 1947 to July 1948, there has been a general decline in the number of meetings. Even in the period comprising the crises which simultaneously arose in the Middle East and Hungary in the fall of 1956, the frequency of Council meetings registered merely a moderate reversal of the trend. The provision of Rule I of the Provisional Rules of Procedure of the Security Council that "the interval between meetings shall not exceed fourteen days" was fairly well observed during the first three years, when there were only three instances in which the interval between meetings exceeded fourteen days. The situation began to deteriorate in 1949, and has not been remedied since.

Although the decline in the number of meetings of the Security Council and the number of new questions submitted to it would appear to be indicative of a decline in the importance attached to the work of the organ, one would not be justified in drawing conclusions regarding the effectiveness of the Council from these figures alone. Before passing final judgment upon the degree to which the Council has been effective in reforming its Charter responsibilities it is necessary to examine in some detail the Council's actual record of performance in the principal fields of its activity. These can be

[4] Substantive political questions are those designated "Political and Security Questions" in the Annual Reports of the Secretary-General on the Work of the Organization and which do not relate to constitutional, organizational or procedural matters, including the admission of new Members or the representation of Members.

roughly defined as four in number: 1) the taking of collective measures to keep or restore international peace and security in case of threat or actual violation; 2) the peaceful settlement or adjustment of disputes and situations; 3) the regulation of armaments; and 4) the performance of certain organizational functions, including the recommendation of new members and the recommendation of a Secretary-General.

In the performance of the first function, the Council has achieved a considerable measure of success in dealing with those situations where its permanent members, for whatever reasons, have had a sufficient interest in the maintenance of restoration of international peace and security to agree on a common course of action. Thus in dealing with the situation in Indonesia created by Dutch "police" action to re-establish the authority of the Netherlands in Indonesia, the Security Council was able eventually to get the parties to agree to the cessation of hostilities leading to an acceptable political settlement. It must be recognized, however, that Security Council action alone might not have been effective without strong supporting action of an economic nature by the United States and certain Asian states. The major powers were unwilling, however, to use military force to achieve their purpose.

In dealing with the Palestine question during the initial period of crisis, the Security Council achieved considerable success. Although it was not willing to undertake the enforcement of the partition plan recommended by the General Assembly in its resolution of November 29, 1947, it did exercise steady and increasing pressure on the parties to the hostilities which broke out after the Israeli declaration of independence of May 14, 1948, to cease fighting and agree to permanent armistice arrangements. Largely as a result of this pressure, the armistice agreements were concluded, and a system of international supervision under the general oversight of the Council was established. Until the Israeli attack of late October 1956, this system was effective in preventing a resumption of general hostilities, notwithstanding the failure of the UN to achieve a peaceful settlement of outstanding issues, occasional incidents of violence, and the deterioration of relations between the Soviet Union and the western powers.

The Security Council also achieved a considerable measure of success in dealing with hostilities involving India and Pakistan over Kashmir. The parties acceded to the proposal made by the Council's commission that a ceasefire be concluded under a system of international observation established with the consent of the parties, and a condition of non-fighting has since been maintained, even though efforts to settle the dispute have failed.

Only under exceptional conditions, has the Council been at all effective in dealing with threats to or breaches of the peace where the vital interests of permanent members have been directly in conflict. When, following the Communist *coup* in Czechoslovakia in February 1948, the complaint of Soviet intervention in that country was brought before the Council, any action, even the appointment of a committee to study the situation, was prevented by Soviet vetoes. It is difficult to see how any effective action could have been taken in any case, even if the right of veto had not existed, unless the western powers were willing to risk the unleashing of a general war.

In September 1948, the Council was asked to consider the situation resulting from the Soviet blockade of Berlin. The Soviet Union, by its veto, prevented any action from being taken. Again it is difficult to see what the Council could have done, even without the veto, without risking a general war, other than provide, as it did, the occasion for representatives of the interested parties to meet and negotiate.

When north Korean forces attacked the Republic of Korea on June 25, 1950, the Security Council was presented with a unique opportunity to take action in a situation involving the conflicting vital interests of permanent members, since the Soviet representative was absent in protest against the seating of the Chinese representative appointed by the Nationalist government. This condition of affairs proved to be temporary, and when the Soviet representative returned to the Council at the beginning of August, the possibility of making further use of the Council to guide and determine UN action ceased.

It was this situation which led to the adoption by the Assembly of the "Uniting for Peace" resolution of November 3, 1950, by which the Assembly asserted for itself, under a liberal interpretation of Charter provisions, the right to consider any threat to the peace, breach of the peace, or act of aggression, if the Council, because of lack of unanimity of its permanent members, had failed to discharge its primary responsibility, and to make appropriate recommendations, "including in the case of a breach of the peace or act of aggression the use of armed force when necessary." While the General Assembly was to exercise this "residual responsibility" only after the Council had failed to take action and had removed the item from its agenda, the fact that this could be done by a procedural vote made it impossible for a permanent member by its veto to prevent Assembly consideration. Thus, the relationship between Council and Assembly which had been spelled out in the Department of State proposal of July 18, 1944, and in the Dumbarton Oaks Proposals and maintained in principle in the Charter was explicitly redefined to permit a majority of seven in the Council, in the face of opposition by as many as four of the permanent members, to transfer the consideration of an alleged threat to or breach of the peace to the General Assembly. Thus the way was prepared for making the Council's "primary responsibility" largely nominal, unless the permanent members were in full accord, and for making the Assembly's "residual responsibility"—based on extremely liberal Charter interpretation—major in fact, at least for as long as the cold war continued.

The Hungarian and Middle East crises in October 1956 again demonstrated that the Council was incapable of acting in a situation involving the conflicting vital interests of the major powers, though in the latter case it was not the cold war that was mainly responsible. In both cases, action was taken by the General Assembly, in the first case with no visible effect on the actual course of events and in the second case effectively. This experience tended to show that even when the General Assembly acts, the chances of successful action are small unless the United States and the Soviet Union are on the same side.

In discharging its second function, the peaceful settlement or adjustment of international disputes and situations, the Security Council has had very limited effectiveness. The disputes and situations that have been brought to its attention have, almost without exception, fallen into one or the other of two main categories: 1) disputes and situations resulting from the cold war— the ideological-power conflict between the communist powers and the western powers; and 2) disputes and situations resulting from the conflict of interests between the more advanced western powers, including particularly the colonial powers, and the states, mainly of Asia and Africa, which had recently emerged from colonial domination or have strong attachments to the cause of Asian-African nationalism.

In dealing with disputes and situations in the first category, the Council has only exceptionally had some measure of success. Pressure brought to bear through the Council appears to have influenced the Soviet Union to withdraw its military forces from Iran in 1946 after that country had complained of their illegal presence. Following a Council recommendation, the dispute between the United Kingdom and Albania over damage to United Kingdom ships in the Corfu Channel was submitted to the International Court of Justice for decision. However, Albania did not accept the award of damages. The Council was not able to agree on the appointment of a governor of the Free Territory of Trieste. It was unable by its own action to bring about a settlement of the dispute leading to the Berlin blockade. It was unable to take decision on various complaints submitted to it at the time of the Korean conflict. For the most part, the parties initiating UN consideration of cold war questions have considered the General Assembly better suited to their purposes.

In handling disputes and situations in the second category, the Council has not been much more effective. Only in the Indonesian case did it play a major part in bringing about an agreed settlement. The fact that the Soviet Union has generally aligned itself with the Asian and African states in their differences with the West and that some of the other permanent members have taken a rigid stand in opposition has largely eliminated the possibility of agreement among the permanent members of the Council on any course of action. Even the major western powers themselves have often been in disagreement, largely due to the unwillingness of the United States to go as far as the United Kingdom and France in opposing Asian and African claims. Generally speaking, the Asian and African Members have preferred to bring the questions involving claims against the West before the General Assembly where their voting strength is proportionately greater. When the western powers find it in their interest to bring a question before the Security Council, as in the case of the Anglo-Iranian oil dispute or the Suez Canal dispute, any effective Council action is likely to be prevented by a Soviet opposition or by disagreement among the western powers themselves.

The disputes between the Arab states and Israel and between India and Pakistan over Kashmir do not completely fit into either of the above categories. Here, too, the Council has failed as an organ of peaceful settlement. And one of the decisive factors in these cases, as in the ones previously considered, has been the failure of the permanent members to agree, as the result of their conflicting interests in the cold war. Without this agreement, not only may the Council be prevented from taking a decision, but even if it is able to take a decision as the result of one or more abstentions by a permanent member, the authority of the Council is greatly weakened.

In the performance of its third function, the achievement of agreement on the regulation of armaments, the Council has a record of complete failure. In the first place, it has been unable to conclude any agreement with Members by which they would undertake to place military forces and facilities at the disposal of the Council. This has been due to the inability of the permanent members, the members of the Military Staff Committee, to agree on the principles to be applied in the conclusion of these agreements. As a result, the Council has not had available to it the military forces essential to the full discharge of its responsibility for the maintenance of peace. Without these forces it can only recommend military measures, as it did in the Korean case. Secondly, all efforts that the Security Council has made to prepare proposals for the regulation of national armaments, whether atomic or conventional, have ended in complete deadlock due to the inability of the major powers to agree. Nor has the Assembly, which has taken the leading initiative in disarmament discussions, been more successful.

In discharging its functions relating to membership and the internal organization of the UN, the Security Council has had a mixed record. Because of vetoes cast by the Soviet Union, a deadlock developed over the admission of new members with the result that from 1950 to 1955 not a single new member was admitted. Indicative of the seriousness of the situation was the fact that in 1953 21 applications for membership were listed by the UN as not having been favorably acted upon by the Council. Down to December 14, 1955, the UN admitted only nine new members. The log-jam was broken in December 1955 when, under the terms of a "package deal," sixteen new members were admitted and since that time, six other new members have been taken in. At the present time, only the Republic of Korea, the Mongolian People's Republic, the Democratic People's Republic of Korea, the Democratic People's Republic of Vietnam and Vietminh stand outside because of refusal of the Council to act favorably on their applications, and of these only two are outside solely because of the use of the veto in the Council. It would be highly subjective to attempt any evaluation of how well the Security Council has performed its membership function. Probably the UN is nearer universality of membership at the present time as the result of the deadlock in the Security Council and the resulting necessity of a "package deal" than it would have been if the Assembly alone had controlled admissions. On the other hand, many qualified states were kept out for years, when the Assembly stood ready to admit them, solely because the use of the veto prevented favorable Council action.

In performing its recommending function in connection with the appointment of a Secretary-General, the Council has probably contributed to strengthening the role of that official in the work of the Organization. The requirement of agreement of the major powers increases the likelihood that the Secretary-General will have their confidence, which in turn is helpful, if not essential, to the full and most effective use of his powers. While the Council, due to the Soviet veto, did prevent the reappointment of Trygve Lie in 1950, the use of the General Assembly to break the deadlock did not produce very satisfactory results. In 1953, the Council recommended, and the Assembly appointed, Dag Hammarskjöld as Lie's successor. Experience since then has demonstrated the advantage of having a Secretary-General who commands the confidence of the major powers.

III

Clearly the Security Council has failed to discharge its Charter responsibilities in the manner and with the degree of effectiveness which the authors of the Charter envisaged. Furthermore, there can be little doubt that the Council has declined greatly in prestige and has seemed to most Members of the UN less useful than in the beginning. This decline has been accompanied by a corresponding increase in the prestige and use of the General Assembly. What have been the reasons for the Council's decline?

The one reason upon which most people would seem to agree is the "veto." It is common to cite the number of vetoes cast and to draw the conclusion that the excessive use of the veto has been the cause of the Council's failure. Eighty-nine vetoes were cast in the Security Council up to May 2, 1958. The number of vetoes cast, however, does not tell the whole story regarding the influence of the veto on the work of the Council. It is necessary, first of all, to consider the nature of the proposals that have been vetoed. Of the total number, 48 vetoes were cast on proposals to admit new members, and in some instances the same country was "vetoed" four times. Thirty-nine were used to defeat proposals made in connection with the discharge by the Council of its responsibility for the maintenance of international peace and security. Two vetoes have been cast in connection with the appointment of the Secretary-General.

If we consider only the vetoes that fall into this second category, we find a number of cases where the majority of the Council's members appear to have maneuvered to force the minority permanent member to repeat its veto on substantially the same issue for the record. For example, during the consideration of the Greek complaint against its northern neighbors in August 1947, the Soviet Union cast two vetoes consecutively, first on the Australian draft resolution and then on the United States draft resolution. The second veto must have been anticipated since the United States resolution was stronger than the Australian and therefore more objectionable to the Soviet Union.

The veto of a proposal has not necessarily prevented its substance from being put into effect. In the Syrian and Lebanese case, for example, the United States draft resolution expressing the confidence of the Security Council that the United Kingdom and French troops would be withdrawn "as soon as practicable" was not adopted due to the negative vote of the Soviet Union, which wanted a stronger resolution urging the immediate withdrawal of foreign forces. Nevertheless, the representatives of France and the United Kingdom declared that their governments were willing to give effect to the majority opinion, and the withdrawal of forces was carried out to the satisfaction of all concerned.

On the other hand, in those situations where the cooperation of the vetoing power is necessary to the carrying out of the proposal, the veto simply registers a factual situation. Even if the right of veto did not exist and the proposal were adopted by the required majority, there would be little likelihood that the dissenting major power would back down, if a vital interest was at stake, except under compulsion that might risk general war. Thus, if the Security Council had been able to take a decision in the Czechoslovak and Hungarian cases notwithstanding Soviet opposition, there is little reason to believe that the results would have been different since the majority members were not prepared to take those measures of coercion which alone had any chance of influencing Soviet action.

Concentration of attention upon the voting procedure of the Council as an explanation of Council weakness seems somewhat misplaced, since the real cause lies deeper than a mere organizational or procedural defect. The veto, when used, reflects the schism in the relations among the permanent members of the Council. It is a symptom, rather than the cause, of a disunited world.

The primary cause of the decline of the Security Council and especially of its role in relation to the General Assembly must be sought in the breakdown since 1945 of the wartime alliance of the Soviet Union, the United Kingdom, and the United States—the alliance whose continuation was the assumption upon which the idea of the Security Council as the guarantor of peace was constructed. The rivalry among the major powers induced them in many cases to use the Security Council as a tool for propaganda purposes to advance their divergent political objectives rather than to harmonize the action of nations in the attainment of common purposes, as intended by the authors of the Charter. Furthermore, these same powers discovered that for purposes of appealing to world opinion, and gaining support for their respective policies and programs in the cold war the General Assembly provided a more effective forum than the Security Council.

The work of the Security Council has been hampered by the conflicts among former Allied powers over the peace settlements. The authors of the Charter had remembered the onus attached to the Covenant of the League because of its close association with the settlements after the First World War. Accordingly, they provided a separate machinery for the making of the peace treaties with the Axis powers after the Second World War. Contrary to their hopes, however, the Allied unity broke down soon after the disappearance of the common enemies, and from the outset the Security Council had to carry burdens beyond its capacity, to deal with questions arising from the differences among the major powers concerning the peace settlements, such as the question of Greece, Iran, and Czechoslovakia, the status of the Free Territory of Trieste, and the Berlin and the Korean questions. Deadlocks over the terms of the major peace settlements, moreover, were bound to make agreement on other issues more difficult to achieve.

Another cause contributing to the diminishing role of the Security Council has been the post-war emergence of numerous new nations in Asia and

Africa, their crucial role in the world's balance of power, and their general preference for the Assembly rather than the Council for bringing their influence to bear in connection with the issues of colonialism, human rights, and disarmament. The anxiety of the major powers to win resounding political victories by the support of these newly independent states has helped the Assembly to gain further importance.

In addition, the advance in the use of mass media of communications and the increasing role of public opinion in the governmental process have tended to revolutionize traditional views on the relative merits of public discussion and participation in foreign policy making on the one hand, and quiet diplomacy and private negotiations on the other. The result has been that the attention of the strategists of national policy has turned to the manipulation and exploitation of the General Assembly as a world forum. Doubtless the Assembly provides a more spectacular arena to wage the "war of ideas" than a small body like the Council.

IV

It would seem likely that any amelioration of the relations among the major powers would bring about an improvement in the effectiveness of the Security Council; it would also reduce the desire of the major powers to turn to the General Assembly for political propaganda reasons. Amelioration of the major power relations does not, however, appear to be a sufficient condition to bring about the complete revival of the Security Council as the predominant organ for the maintenance of international peace and security as envisaged by the authors of the Charter, because the newly independent, non-western nations would be most reluctant to relinquish their power of effectively influencing political developments in the world through the General Assembly rather than through the Security Council, unless the composition of the Security Council is revised to meet their objections to its west-slanted membership. With the world situation as it is, it seems probable that the major questions of political adjustment, of the cold war as well as of the liquidation of colonialism, will remain the primary concern of the General Assembly rather than of the Council. The Security Council is more likely to confine itself to dealing with specific disputes or situations related to the maintenance of peace and security, which require swiftness of action and continuity of study and surveillance by the international organization, and about which the permanent members are able to achieve some measure of agreement.

The inclination of the western states to clarify and bring to the fore the residual responsibility of the Assembly in matters related to peace and security, as exemplified by their support for the "Uniting for Peace" resolution, appears to have been checked as a result of their realization of the new situation brought about by the increase in the voting power of the Asian and African states, often unsympathetic to the West. In fact, the Asian and African states have come to possess a potential veto over Assembly decisions. In consequence, the passage of west-sponsored resolutions through the Assembly can no longer be taken for granted. It was noteworthy that when the Syrian-Turkish question (1957) was brought before the Assembly, the representatives of Australia, France, the Netherlands, the United Kingdom, and the United States raised the constitutional issue that the proper place to deal with a threat to the peace under the Charter was the Security Council, not the Assembly. This was in marked contrast to the Soviet silence regarding the competence of the Assembly in connection with the question. The seeming reversal of the positions of the western and communist states on the respective roles of the Security Council and the General Assembly on questions of peace and security is indicative of the fluidity of Members' preferences for one organ over another, stemming from the changing political configuration of these organs, caused partly by the addition to the Asian and African group of recently admitted states and partly by the trend of some members of this group of nations towards neutralism.

Setting aside broad political considerations which would ultimately determine the relative roles for peacemaking of the Security Council and the General Assembly, several advantages which the Council possesses over the Assembly, from an organizational point of view, are worth noting. The Security Council is an executive committee of a small size in a state of constant alertness. Its members, even non-permanent members chosen for two-year periods, can accumulate considerable knowledge and skill with respect to disputes and situations brought to its attention. It is able to act at a moment's notice, continue its supervisory functions without intermission, and serve as an effective negotiating body. In comparison, the size and lack of continuity of the General Assembly, together with the publicity attendant on its consideration of questions and the deficiency of experience of some of the delegates to the Assembly, suggest that it is primarily a forum of the nations for the discussion of questions of a general character, rather than an organ suited to perform intricate diplomatic functions of negotiation and conciliation. The establishment of subsidiary organs like the Interim Committee, the United Nations Commission on Korea, and the Advisory Committee on the United Nations Emergency Force, may overcome some of the organizational deficiencies of the Assembly. But an effective use of the Security Council would have several advantages not possessed by the subsidiary organs of the Assembly. It would also avoid an unnecessary duplication of functions.

Proposals have been made for the strengthening of the Security Council to enable it to perform more effectively the functions assigned to it by the Charter. These may be divided into two categories: those calling for revision of the powers and voting procedures of the Council, and those involving some change of the Council's composition.

The frustration resulting from the frequent use of the veto has led to the following suggestions: 1) abolish the veto completely and accord equality in voting to all members of the Security Council; 2) substitute for the requirement of the absolute unanimity of all permanent members that of a qualified unanimity by which the favorable votes of three or four of the permanent members would be necessary for a decision; 3) restrict the use of the veto to clearly defined areas and eliminate it from the pacific settlement of disputes and the admission of new members; 4) alter the fundamental nature of the Security Council by substituting powers of recommendation for its present enforcement powers; and 5) strengthen further the role of the General Assembly by giving it enforcement powers. Suggestions 1) and 2) seem unacceptable at the present to any of the permanent members. Suggestion 3) has been espoused by the United States since the Vandenberg Resolution of June 1948. This was confirmed by President Eisenhower in his letter to Premier Bulganin dated January 12, 1958. Formal adoption of suggestion 4) would mean a retrogression of international organization, although it is not more than an acknowledgment of the existing state of affairs in the Security Council arising from the failure to implement provisions of Article 43. It is also unlikely that the major powers would agree to the expansion of the powers of the Assembly, unless they have a share in the voting commensurate with the responsibility which they have to assume. A prerequisite to such agreement would be solution of the complicated question of weighted voting in the General Assembly. In short, suggestion 3) appears to be the only proposal which has some hope of acceptance by the powers constituting the permanent members, although there is no indication that the Soviet Union has changed its view on the "chain of events" theory by which it justified extension of the veto to the peaceful settlement of disputes. Thus, even the adoption of suggestion 3) would have to await substantial relaxation of tensions between the western powers and the communist bloc, and this relaxation would make it largely unnecessary.

The question of change of composition of the Security Council has two facets, namely, the increase in the number of the non-permanent members of the Council, and additions to or elimination of the permanent members. The former question has already arisen in the Assembly and is probably easier to solve than the latter. Though an informal "gentleman's agreement" was reached among the major powers in London in 1946 on the allocation of non-permanent seats, the increase in the number of Member States, in particular from Asia and Africa, has brought about intensified pressures for a reconsideration of the original allocation. It has also given rise to contests for non-permanent seats, as evidenced in the Yugoslav-Philippine rivalry of 1955 and the Japanese-Czechoslovakian competition of 1957.[5] In its eleventh and twelfth sessions the General Assembly had before it a proposal by Latin American states and Spain to increase the number of non-permanent members of the Security Council, but decided to postpone consideration until the following session. The Latin American proposal for an increase of two non-permanent seats in the Council was favored by the western powers, but was opposed by many Asian and African nations who felt that the allocation of merely one of the two proposed seats to their region and the other to Europe was not proportionate to their increased number.

The question of the expansion of membership of the Council must be carefully weighed in the light of the aspirations of various regions of the world to be justly represented on the Council and the requirement to preserve the advantages inherent in a small, compact Council. The rise of India as a spokesman of the neutral nations and the recovery of west Germany, Italy,

[5] And the Polish-Turkish struggle for votes in 1959.

and Japan as influential powers, though west Germany is not yet a Member of the UN, may give rise to the question of their permanent—or semi-permanent—membership in the Council. There is no doubt that the question of the representation of China also has a crucial importance for the revitalization of the Council as an organ reflective of the reality of the power in the world.

Of more importance than formal changes for the immediate future of the Security Council would be the improvement of the Council proceedings by the use of informal techniques not requiring revision of voting procedure or composition. Among such techniques, mention might be made of the following: an effective use of private, as against public, meetings of the Council, depending on the nature of the problem, as illustrated by the three private Council meetings held in connection with the question of the nationalization of the Suez Canal in October 1956; the vitalization of the provisions of Article 28 (2), which have remained dormant, regarding periodic meetings of the Council attended by foreign ministers or heads or other members of government; the appointment of a rapporteur or conciliator for a situation or dispute brought to the Council, who would make efforts at conciliation before the Council enters into the consideration of the substance of the question, along the lines of the Assembly resolution 268 B (III); and other measures of private diplomacy within the framework of the Security Council, making use of the good offices of the Secretary-General, as exemplified by his repeated trips to the Middle East since the spring of 1956 at the request of the Security Council.

The Security Council may indeed have an increasingly important role to play in the task of keeping the peace, provided that a discriminating choice is made by its members of the various instruments and techniques of diplomacy at its disposal. As part of the "evolution of emphasis and practice" of the over-all United Nations machinery, it may yet become an active and vigorous guardian of the peace, though it is not likely to achieve the stature envisioned by the architects of the Charter.

TOPIC 27

Peaceful Settlements of International Disputes

To solve their conflicts, individuals and nations have often used one of the following methods:

1. *Violence,* which determines the validity of the claim by the victory of one and the defeat of the opposing party.

2. *Direct negotiations,* in which two or more opposing parties reach a compromise solution, equally satisfactory or equally unsatisfactory to both. (This was the subject of Part V.)

3. The so-called *"third-party" techniques.* The opposing parties agree that a third party might assist in finding terms of settlement.

Regional and universal international organizations have been established whose primary aim is to eliminate the first method—violence—altogether. They are to facilitate direct negotiations or to make other techniques available to the parties in dispute.

The United Nations charter (Chapter VI, Article 33), which enumerates various methods of pacific settlement of disputes, places negotiations at the top of the list in contrast to the League of Nations Covenant. Thus it stresses that the United Nations organization was meant to supplement, but not supplant, direct negotiations among nations, which are still the best and most effective method of solving disputes.

"Parties to a dispute the continuance of which is likely to endanger the maintenance of international peace and security," states Chapter VI, article 33, of the U.N. charter, "shall, first of all, seek a solution by negotiation, enquiry, mediation, conciliation, arbitration, judicial settlement, resort to regional agencies or arrangements, or other peaceful methods of their choice." Working definitions of "third-party" techniques follow:

Enquiry consists in the service which a third party or a commission may offer by ascertaining the precise facts which have given rise to a dispute. This already may help a peaceful settlement of the dispute as often the excitement and emotional involvement obscure the facts which have caused the dispute.

Mediation and good offices generally refer to the offer of a third party to help bring about negotiations between two states in conflict. Some writers distinguish between mediation and good offices. Good offices are described as various kinds of action tending to bring about a new contact between the conflicting states, while mediation consists of offering a direct channel for negotiations between the conflicting parties. In practice, however, the terms "good offices" and "mediation" often merge.

Conciliation represents an effort to settle a dispute by referring it to a conciliator or a commission of persons who, after having clarified the facts, suggest a settlement of the dispute. It is this proposal of settlement which differentiates conciliation from the previous method of mediation. Writers and journalists referring to this process often use the terms "mediator" and "conciliator" interchangeably, in spite of the above difference.

Arbitration represents a settlement of a dispute among nations through a legally binding decision rendered either by an umpire or a commission or a tribunal other than the International Court of Justice on the basis of previous agreement of the conflicting parties to abide by it. Here lies the difference between conciliation and arbitration: the proposal of settlement offered by a conciliator is not considered to be legally binding.

Judicial settlement refers actually to an arbitration award which is issued by the International Court of Justice. The difference between arbitration and judicial settlement in international law is not fundamental. Both awards are based on law and are legally binding on the basis of previous agreement of the parties to a dispute. The main difference is in the character of the adjudicating body.

►THE UNITED NATIONS:
AN ADDED INSTRUMENT TO DIPLOMACY

DAG HAMMARSKJÖLD

The United Nations has not been intended as a substitute for diplomatic negotiations but rather as an added instrument. This opinion is expressed by the Secretary General of the United Nations, in his introduction to the annual report on the work of the world organization, submitted to its General Assembly in September, 1959.

Secretary General Hammarskjöld notes that a number of major diplomatic conferences recently took place, mainly outside the United Nations: the nuclear powers' conference on controlled cessation of tests, at Geneva (1958-1960), the Berlin issue (Geneva, 1959) and several regional issues, handled by regional conferences of Arab, Latin American, Asian, or African states, outside the framework of the U.N. The series of summit conferences, begun in Paris in May 1960, was to take the world leaders successively to London, Moscow, and Paris, but not to New York, the U.N. Headquarters.

He raises two questions: do these negotiations outside the organization represent a danger of lapsing into bilateralism in an era which requires a universal approach to peace? And do these diplomatic negotiations outside the U.N. indicate that the organization had failed to meet the demands of its members?

Hammarskjöld further stresses the new, unexpected and useful function of permanent delegations with the U.N. and the evolution of the role of the Secretary General.

This intense diplomatic and political activity has a dual significance. On the one hand, it indicates that various international problems have been brought to a point where they call for renewed and urgent efforts to find a solution. On the other hand, the broadening and deepening of personal contacts on different levels, to which this situation has given rise, has introduced a new constructive element which may strengthen the hope that ways to reconciliation and to a reduction of tensions may be found.

In both respects, these are the virtually unanimous evaluations voiced by Governments, and they are naturally also those of the United Nations. However, from the point of view of the United Nations, the development requires also special consideration for the light it may throw on its role and on the way in which the Organization should serve its purposes.

The Charter is quite clear about such diplomatic efforts. It states in

Selected passages from the *Report of the Secretary-General for 1958-1959* (New York: United Nations, 1959).

Article 33 that "the parties to any dispute, the continuance of which is likely to endanger the maintenance of international peace and security, shall, first of all, seek a solution by negotiation, inquiry, mediation, conciliation, arbitration, judicial settlement, resort to regional agencies or arrangements, or other peaceful means of their own choice."

Further, it states in Article 36, regarding the Security Council, that the Council should take into consideration any procedures for the settlement of a dispute which have already been adopted by the parties. This rule has been understood to have reference especially to efforts on a regional basis or through regional organizations like the Organization of American States.

Thus, while the Charter establishes for its main organs the primary responsibility for the achievement of the purposes of the Organization, and gives access to its procedures to any State which appeals for its assistance for these purposes, the United Nations is not intended to be a substitute for normal procedures of reconciliation and mediation but rather an added instrument providing, within the limits of its competence, a further or ultimate support for the maintenance of peace and security. Viewed in this light, the various diplomatic and political activities in the course of the past year are in full harmony with the intentions expressed in the Charter. They may even be said to reflect obligations which Member nations have assumed in the Charter. Also, irrespective of this formal aspect of the matter, those who support the work of the Organization must welcome all such serious efforts to further the purposes for which it was set up, whatever the specific form such efforts may take.

Nevertheless, recent diplomatic developments call for attention in so far as they might reflect a situation which in other respects should be of concern to the Governments which co-operate in the Organization and are interested in developing it to its full capacity. This would be the case if the extended use of diplomatic negotiations and political contacts outside the Organization reflected a neglect of the possibilities which the Organization offers, because of a lapse into bilateralism, disregarding legitimate third party interests. Likewise, the situation would be a reason for concern if it reflected a view that the Organization is not able to meet the demands which Member nations are entitled to put on it.

There is no reason to give to the developments which have taken place an interpretation along either of the lines to which I have just referred. These developments are not only in keeping with the principles of the Charter but are also free, I believe, from implications which impair the position of the Organization in principle. They do, however, give a natural reason for a renewed consideration of the ways in which the United Nations functions and fulfills its purposes. . . .

It has so often been said that the world of today is one which requires organized international co-operation on a basis of universality that one repeats it with hesitation. However, there are reasons to do so. It still seems sometimes to be forgotten that—whatever views may be held about the United Nations as an institution—the principle of organized international co-operation on a basis of universality which is at present reflected in this Organization is one which has emerged from bitter experiences and should now be considered as firmly established. No international policy for the future can be envisaged which does not recognize this principle and is not willing to give it adequate implementation in practice.

The United Nations is the means to an end, not an end in itself. While the principle of co-operation on a basis of universality is now a definite part of international politics aiming at peace and security, this does not necessarily apply to the Organization as the practical instrument for such a policy, and especially not to its specific working methods. Were it to be felt that the Organization with its present procedures failed to provide the best means by which this basic principle could now be implemented, we would be facing a situation where the choice would be one between revolution and evolution. We should have to choose between the creation of a new international organization, based on the principle of universality like the United Nations although different in other respects, and an evolution of procedures of the present Organization which would make it a more adequate instrument for implementation of the principle.

Certainly, nobody would feel that there are reasons for even a hypothetical consideration of the first alternative. In fact, were unforeseeable developments to threaten the Organization with disintegration, there would undoubtedly be a rallying of Members in its support which would carry it on fundamentally as at present conceived. Therefore, the only practical question is, whether an evolution of procedures should be envisaged in order to adapt the United Nations more adequately to the needs as experienced and, if so, what the development should be.

This leads, in turn, to two questions. What, in *constitutional* terms, is the degree of adaptability of the procedures of the Organization; and what, in *practical* terms, are their capacity for adaptation and the directions in which such adaptations might be indicated

As regards the first question, it should be noted that the Charter as an international treaty establishes certain common goals for international co-operation and creates certain organs which the Member States may use in their co-operation towards these goals. The statement of objectives in the Charter is binding and so are the rules concerning the various organs and their competence, but it is not necessary to regard the working methods indicated in the Charter as limitative in purpose. Thus, they may be supplemented by others under the pressure of circumstances and in the light of experience if these additional procedures are not in conflict with what is prescribed. As is well known, such an evolution has in fact taken place, and it has thus been recognized that such new procedures may be developed when they prove productive in practice for efforts towards the objectives of the Charter. In this respect, the United Nations, as a living organism, has the necessary scope for a continuous adaptation of its constitutional life to the needs. How fully the opportunities thus offered have been utilized so far and how they might usefully be explored further are questions which need more study and evaluation before a complete reply can be given. Such studies must, in the first place, be undertaken by the Member Governments themselves in support of, and in the course of, deliberations in the various organs of the United Nations. The subject is very wide and it is possible here to make only a few observations.

A development of special significance is the establishment of permanent delegations at United Nations Headquarters with standing senior representation there for all Members of the Organization. While in one sense reducing the practical importance of the public sessions of the various organs, this development has, basically, tended to give these organs greater real weight in present-day diplomacy. The public debate, and the decisions reached, gain added significance when the attitudes presented in public result from practically uninterrupted informal contacts and negotiations. Thus, it does not belittle the importance of the formal proceedings in the General Assembly, the Councils and other United Nations organs if it is understood that, to an increasing extent, their role has come to provide for a public confrontation of views which have developed in negotiations under other forms, and for the registration of a resulting consensus, or, when this has not been achieved, of a difference of opinion with the relative support apparent from the votes.

The importance this evolution has given to the experienced work of the permanent delegations is obvious. They are today to a decisive extent pioneers in the development of international co-operation within the United Nations, giving to the work of the major organs a perspective which is not less valuable for being less publicized. The permanent representation at Headquarters of all Member nations, and the growing diplomatic contribution of the permanent delegations outside the public meetings—often in close contact also with the Secretariat—may well come to be regarded as the most important "common law" development which has taken place so far within the constitutional framework of the Charter. It is to be hoped that it will continue and increase in strength.

The observations just made have a bearing on the evaluation of the work of the principal United Nations organs and on the way their work may be furthered.

In a previous annual report I made some comments on the significance of voting in the United Nations. There is no reason to repeat here what was said then beyond observing that later experiences have confirmed the view then expressed that, whatever legal standing the Charter may provide for the results of the votes, the significance of these results requires further analysis before a political evaluation is possible. This observation applies to the composition of majorities and minorities as well as to the substance of resolutions. These resolutions often reflect only part of what has, in fact, emerged from the deliberations and what, therefore, is likely to remain as an active element in future developments. In these circumstances, it is natural for those who are not close to the United Nations sometimes to underestimate the results of the work of the General Assembly and other organs, and equally to overestimate the significance of a formal voting victory or a voting defeat.

Well known factors have in recent years tended to reduce the public role of the Security Council. However, what has been said above applies with equal force to the Council. Constant talks and negotiations among, and with, members of the Security Council have given the Council a continuing life and importance and enabled it to exert its influence during the intervals when it does not meet in public. It may be asked if the time is not now ripe to give formal expression to this fact by the organization of regular meetings of the Council in executive session. Such meetings would not as a rule be devoted to particular issues brought to its attention, but to any aspect of the international situation which may prove of concern to the Council because of its responsibilities under the Charter. Sufficient experience seems now to have been gained in the Council of the value of the kind of deliberation for which such meetings might give an opportunity to warrant that the suggestion be given serious consideration by Member nations. . . .

In considering the evolution of procedures of the principal United Nations organs, attention may also be given to the developing functions of the Secretariat. There have been, in the first place, various decisions taken in recent years by the General Assembly or the Security Council under which the Secretary-General has been entrusted with special diplomatic and operational functions, which he is responsible for carrying out within the wide framework of general terms of reference laid down in the resolutions and, naturally, in the Charter itself. This, also, represents an evolution of the procedures of the United Nations for which no explicit basis is to be found in the Charter—although it may be said to fall within the scope of the intentions reflected in Article 99[1]—and to which neither the League of Nations, nor the United Nations during its earlier years, presented a significant counterpart. These decisions should not, of course, be considered as setting precedents changing the constitutional balance among the various organs of the United Nations. However, they have pointed to the possibility of developing new methods of approach of great practical significance, which, after the thorough testing needed, may become part of a common law of organized international cooperation.

It should also be noted that in some recent cases of international conflict or other difficulties involving Member States the Secretary-General has dispatched personal representatives with the task of assisting the Governments in their efforts. This may be regarded as a further development of actions of a "good offices" nature, with which the Secretary-General is now frequently charged. The steps to which I refer here have been taken with the consent or at the invitation of Governments concerned, but without formal decisions of other organs of the United Nations. As a matter of course, the members of the appropriate organ of the United Nations have been informed about the action planned by the Secretary-General and were given an opportunity to express views on it. . . .

The main significance of the evolution of the Office of the Secretary-General in the manner referred to above lies in the fact that it has provided means for smooth and fast action, which might otherwise not have been open to the Organization. This is of special value in situations in which prior public debate on a proposed course of action might increase the difficulties that such

---

[1] In Chapter XV (The Secretariat) Article 99 authorizes the Secretary-General to "bring to the attention of the Security Council any matter which in his opinion may threaten the maintenance of international peace and security."

an action would encounter, or in which a vacuum might be feared because Members may prove hesitant, without fuller knowledge of the facts or for other reasons, to give explicit prior support in detail to an action which, however, they approve in general terms or are willing should be tried without formal commitment.

It goes without saying that none of the developments to which I have referred has changed the basic character of the Office of the Secretary-General, or its place in the Organization in relation to the General Assembly, the Security Council or other main organs. . . .

The wider functions which in specific cases have been exercised by the Secretary-General fully maintain the character of the United Nations as an organization whose activities are wholly dependent on decisions of the Governments. . . .

►WORLD ORGANIZATION'S THREE PHASES

VERNON V. ASPATURIAN

Three phases have characterized the evolution of the United Nations since 1945:

1. The first phase (1945-1948) was marked by the dominant position of the Security Council, in accordance with the charter. Its dominant position was based on the assumption of harmony of the five great powers, their collective wisdom and peacefulness. No threat was expected to emanate from one of the five "policemen" of the world. The charter which described the five great powers by name also seemed to assume that they were to remain the same: once a great power, always a great power. Like any amendment to the charter, inclusion of an additional great power, were it to emerge (e.g., India) would be possible only if none of the existing five were to object to it and cast a veto.

2. The second phase (1948-1957) was marked by the decline in authority and work of the Security Council; correspondingly the importance of the General Assembly increased, not exactly in accordance with the text and the spirit of the charter. This period was marked by the United States' ability to command a majority vote in the United Nations, composed of Western European and Latin American allies and friends of the United States. This majority permitted the collective action in Korea and passing the "Uniting for Peace" Resolution in 1950 which, in the sixties, might be used by the anti-colonial majority to the detriment of those who had drafted the Resolution in 1950.

3. The third phase has been marked by the ever-growing voting power of Asian and African nations, following their mass admission (1955-1957).

The third phase is subject to a searching analysis by Vernon V. Aspaturian, Professor of Political Science at Pennsylvania State University.

This is an excerpt from V. V. Aspaturian's article, published in *The Yale Review,* Vol. XLVI (Summer, 1957), p. 551. Copyright Yale University Press.

The anti-colonial majority is likely to expand further before it diminishes in influence. Aside from divided Germany and neutral Switzerland, all prospective members of the United Nations will be drawn from Asia and Africa. . . . The United Nations is no longer, as it was in the years right after the Second World War, an exclusive club reserved for "peace-loving" states and dedicated to preserving the existing political order against the revival of fascism, nor is it any longer the anti-Soviet coalition of the Korean War; instead, it now threatens to become an organization whose main obsession is to purge the world of the real and imagined inequities of Western colonialism.

The present anti-colonial majority in the Assembly is a curious and unstable amalgam of Communist, neutralist, and anti-Communist states, divided by ideological incompatibilities, personal animosities, conflicting ambitions and aspirations, and political rivalries; yet it is sufficiently cemented together by a common passion against colonialism to consign the former dominant anti-Soviet majority to an ill-deserved oblivion from which it was only temporarily retrieved as a result of the Soviet intervention in the Hungarian uprising. The solid nucleus of this ascendant constellation is the Asian-African bloc of 27 states (including Japan but not Turkey), only recently intoxicated by a heady elixir of moral self-rectitude brewed at Bandung, preponderantly neutralist in sentiment, but embracing pro-Western countries like the Philippines and Pakistan as well as implacable regional rivals like Egypt and Iraq, yet excluding, for purposes of transparent expediency, the two pariah states of Israel and Nationalist China. The Asian-African bloc, which was augmented by fully one-half of the twenty-one new members, is the largest single regional grouping in the Assembly and, although not united on all issues, by itself constitutes one-third of the total membership. Without a single additional vote, this bloc can veto any important Assembly resolution as effectively as any Great Power can frustrate the work of the Security Council.

To this doctrinaire core of anti-colonial sentiment must be added the nine votes of the Soviet bloc, which enthusiastically supports the dismemberment of the Western colonial empires as the quickest way to subvert the power of the Atlantic alliance, and the vote of Communist Yugoslavia. Thus the core of the current anti-colonial majority is an irreducible minimum of 37 votes which will unwaveringly support a straight anti-colonial ticket—more than enough to stop any important resolution obnoxious to this group.

To pass a resolution it favors, the anti-colonial bloc needs to pick up only seventeen additional votes, and they are easy enough to find among the large and sprawling Latin-American contingent, the four Scandinavian states, and assorted members like Finland, Austria, and Greece, all of which are anti-colonial in sentiment, although they reserve for their own judgment the definition of a "colonial" issue. . . .

Originally conceived during an anti-fascist crusade and fortified by the prestige of a great military victory, the UN was brought into being to preserve the postwar peace through a system of collective security, resting, not upon the slender reed of "world public opinion," but upon a foundation of power, with the Great Powers its cornerstones. Yet, however flawless its theoretical conception, collective security under the Charter was doomed to remain a formula shrouded in ambiguity as long as it was impossible or inexpedient to agree upon a definition of the peace to be preserved or an objective identification of the culprit who threatens it. The founders purposely avoided defining aggression, leaving this onerous task to their successors, who only [in 1956] disbanded a special committee which, after more than two years of inconclusive wrangling, confessed an inability to arrive at a common definition of the most serious international crime under the Charter.

When the ghost of fascism failed to materialize after the war, the UN directed its energies into quixotic sorties against the only avowed fascist state in existence, Franco Spain. But as it became apparent that the real threat to the peace emanated from within the organization itself, the United Nations tried to wiggle out of the contradictions of the Charter and was gradually, if at first imperceptibly, transformed from an abortive anti-fascist organization, vainly scouring the world for new Hitlers, into a coalition prepared to deal with aggression inspired by one of its own police captains. Then it became evident that just as "world public opinion" failed to deter Japan, Hitler, Mussolini, and Stalin in the days of the League, so the massive numerical anti-Soviet majorities in the General Assembly failed to subdue the ambitions of a dictatorial regime whose interests conflicted with those of a majority in the Assembly.

This should have come as no surprise since Stalin told both Roosevelt and Churchill at Yalta that he "would never agree to having any action of the Great Powers submitted to the judgment of the smaller powers."

Conceived as an expedient weapon of the moment to halt Communist aggression, the American-invented "Uniting for Peace" resolution permanently shifted the center of gravity of the UN from the Security Council to the General Assembly. This meant that as long as the United States commanded automatic majorities in the Assembly, conflicts between American policy and that of the United Nations could be kept to a minimum, but with the recent influx of new members that era is over. The United Nations was released from the predictable whims of a few powerful lions on the Security Council only to be at the mercy of the machinations of a menagerie of lesser beasts in the General Assembly, furtively maneuvering to contrive a numerical majority purporting to be the custodian of the "conscience of mankind."

Ever since Cicero expressed the opinion that "the consensus of opinion among all nations, on whatever matter, may be taken for the law of nature," statesmen in the Western World, and particularly in Britain and the United States, have been searching for an institutionalized expression of "world public opinion" which would embody not only universal moral truth but in its transcendent omnipotence would be, in the words of Woodrow Wilson, "the mistress of the world."

Although the triple assumption that a "world public opinion" exists, that it invariably reflects moral wisdom, and that its power is irresistible is unsupported by logic and disproved by experience, this persisting illusion has been sedulously nurtured and propagated by American statesmen, whose diplomatic wisdom is often exceeded by their good intentions. Although both

Moscow and Peking successfully defied the resolutions of the Assembly during the Korean War, an intrepid Dulles, unembarrassed by this dismal record or the even more wretched experience of the League, told a Senate group on January 18, 1954, that the UN "has become a place where world opinion can register and exert a moral authority which no nation, however powerful or despotic, publicly disdains or wholly disregards."

Although Secretary Dulles has expressed a good deal of nonsense about "majority will" and "world public opinion," he once correctly observed that "the United States and no doubt others would be reluctant to subject itself to the will of the majority who might not represent world-wide opinion . . . but are free to act in accordance with their own views of policy and expediency." Nevertheless, American policy has placed the "conscience of mankind" in the hands of the small powers, most of which are weak, newly independent, internally unstable, not highly developed, and reflecting not a corporate conscience or wisdom but merely a spectrum of all the passions, interests, and prejudices that bless and curse mankind. Small states, no less than large, are actuated by their own national interests, not necessarily by abstract virtue, and in a world without a universally accepted code of morality or conception of truth, each state tends to identify its own interests, aspirations, and ideology with that of humanity. The true moral quality of this conglomeration of contradictory and conflicting hopes and interests can never rise above the political motives and moral judgments of the Ibn Sauds and Nassers, who are apt to confuse vengeance with justice, or the Khrushchevs and Titos, who equate eternal truth with Communism, or the Nehrus and Sukarnos, who tend to confuse their own shortcomings with exploitation, and others who happen to determine the policies of their own individual countries. In an association embracing despotisms, democracies, and every cunning and subtle variation in between, it is a cruel deception to pretend that its parliamentary procedures can have any real resemblance to those in a democracy organized within a pre-accepted moral and constitutional order governed by the rule of law.

In the United Nations, where majorities do not correspond to the actual distribution of population, wealth, power, or enlightenment, "majority will" is a synthetic contrivance expressing the lowest common denominator of interests and passions which temporarily and adventitiously shape it, while "majority rule," under these conditions, is an unmitigated vice. . . .

As long as midget states like Luxembourg and San Salvador enjoy parity with Russia and the United States, juridical absurdities like Jordan and Nepal have the same vote as China and India, and outrageous fabrications like the Ukraine and Byelo-Russia have equal voice with bona fide states with legitimate interests, universality, instead of mirroring world reality and the "moral conscience of mankind," merely substitutes one illusion for another. Until the one state-one vote formula in the General Assembly is replaced with one more clearly in focus with the power and demographic realities of the world, it is better for the United Nations to function as an international forum and clearing house for disputes and discords than to be burdened with the fiction that it is an effective security organization entrusted with the wisdom of mankind. . . .

At this juncture, the Assembly of the United Nations appears doomed to the same paralysis as exists in the Security Council, with various blocs sufficiently powerful to thwart two-thirds majorities but unable to produce them.

TOPIC 28

Economic, Social, and Humanitarian Cooperation

Modern scientific and industrial progress has greatly increased the frequency and intensity of contacts among nations. It has also created new problems which, as nations were soon bound to recognize, could no longer be dealt with on a national basis.

New solutions and new agencies were required to deal with such problems as: (a) movement of finished products and raw materials; (b) international transportation, communication, and exchange of information; (c) problems of currency, credits, and tariffs; (d) problems of sanitation and epidemic diseases; (e) criminal or inhuman activities transcending national boundaries (such as slave trade, traffic in women and children for immoral purposes, traffic in narcotic drugs, etc.)

It was first in the economic, social, and humanitarian fields that the concept of *permanent* international organization was to replace the traditional concept of occasional negotiations through diplomatic channels or conferences. Thus, in 1804 the Rhine River Commission was established on a permanent basis. In 1856 it was agreed to add a similar commission in reference to international navigation on the Danube. In 1874 the General Postal Union was established; it was reorganized in 1878 as the Universal Postal Union. It is now one of the Specialized Agencies of the United Nations.

Similar developments took place in the field of *commerce* and *finance*;[1] of *science* and exchange of *information*;[2] and of *health* and *sanitation*.[3]

Today, ten main agencies that deal with economic and social problems are affiliated with the U.N. Economic and Social Council. They are called Specialized Agencies; their names, alphabetical designation, date of formation, and geographic location of headquarters follow:

1. Universal Postal Union (UPU, 1875, Bern)
2. International Labor Organization (ILO, 1919, Geneva)

---

[1] International Union for the Publication of Customs Tariffs (1890); International Union for the Protection of Industrial Property.
[2] International Bureau of Weights and Measures (1875); International Council for the Exploration of the Sea (1902); International Institute of Agriculture (1905).
[3] Sanitary Councils of Constantinople and Tangiers (1838 and 1840); International Office of Public Health.

3. International Bank for Reconstruction and Development (The Bank, 1944, Washington)
4. International Monetary Fund (IMF, 1944, Washington)
5. International Civil Aviation Organization (ICAO, 1944, Montreal)
6. Food and Agriculture Organization (FAO, 1945, Rome)
7. United Nations Educational, Scientific and Cultural Organization (UNESCO, 1945, Paris)
8. World Health Organization (WHO, 1946, Geneva)
9. International Telecommunication Union (ITU, 1934, Geneva)[4]
10. World Meteorological Organization (WMO, 1947, Lausanne)

The Economic and Social Council has created additional agencies and commissions which supplement and sometimes duplicate the work of the Specialized Agencies. The commissions and agencies of the Economic and Social Council are divided into two main categories: functional and territorial. Among the *functional* commissions we find the following: (1) Transport and Communications; (2) Statistical; (3) Fiscal; (4) Population; (5) Social (with a connection with the International Children's Emergency Fund); (6) Human Rights (and its subcommittee on Prevention of Discrimination and Protection of Minorities; (7) Status of Women; (8) Narcotic Drugs.

There are four *regional* Economic Commissions concerned with Europe, the Far East, the Middle East, and Latin America. In addition, some U.N. programs combine the work of Specialized Agencies and Commissions into larger wholes. This is the case of the U.N. Technical Assistance programs.

Many more international organizations dealing with economic or social matters are only loosely connected or have no connection whatsoever with the United Nations, such as the Coal and Steel Community of Europe; mutual assistance and economic planning projects of the Sino-Soviet bloc; the Colombo Plan in Asia; Inter-American Agencies; etc.

Their mushroom growth does not reflect any sudden vogue or unrealistic "pactomania." Largely, they represent more or less adequate responses to urgent needs for regulation and cooperation in our interdependent world.

In addition to the following study by Professor Claude, the reader should consult the text of the United Nations Charter, Chapter IX (International Economic and Social Co-operation).

►THE THEORY OF FUNCTIONALISM

INIS L. CLAUDE, JR.

In contrast to political activities, whose primary concern is the prevention of war and elimination of national insecurity, functional activities refer to economic, social, technical, and humanitarian matters. They may be described

---

[4] Successor to International Telegraphic Union (1865).

From *Swords into Plowshares*, by Inis L. Claude, Jr., © Copyright 1956, 1959 by Inis L. Claude, Jr. Reprinted by permission of Random House, Inc.

as nonpolitical. Successful achievement in these nonpolitical aims is useful in itself. Some observers expect that in addition to this, economic and social cooperation may lead to cooperation in the political field. The theory of functionalism is essentially an assertion and defense of the proposition that international cooperation in nonpolitical fields is a major prerequisite for the ultimate solution of political conflicts and the elimination of war. In the following selection Professor Inis L. Claude, Jr. of Harvard University critically examines the theory of functionalism.

[The theory of functionalism] has been most elaborately developed and persuasively stated by David Mitrany, particularly in his book, *A Working Peace System.*[1]

In Mitrany's terms, "the problem of our time is not how to keep the nations peacefully apart but how to bring them actively together." He would not approach the problem of peace directly, by organizing around the points of national conflict, but indirectly, by seeking out the areas of mutuality, and "binding together those interests which are common, where they are common, and to the extent to which they are common." Mitrany abjures the effort to devise a comprehensive blueprint for the organization of international relations, preferring instead to rely upon the pragmatic development of special-purpose organizations, which he thinks will tend to evolve their own distinctive structural patterns, procedural systems, and areas of competence in accordance with the inherent requirements of their functional missions. This method is recommended as one which "seeks, by linking authority to a specific activity, to break away from the traditional link between authority and a definite territory. . . . " It is a *horizontal* approach, shifting attention away from the vertical divisions of human society which are symbolized by the sovereignty of states, toward the various strata of social need which cut across national dividing lines. It stresses the question of what contributions are essential to the creative work of solving common problems rather than that of what sacrifices are required for the negative task of reconciling conflicting interests.

Mitrany explicitly links functionalism to the ultimate prevention of war and development of authoritative world political institutions. He sees the ideal of peace in terms of national coactivity rather than national coexistence; he puts his faith "not in a protected peace but in a working peace," and believes that a peaceful world society is "more likely to grow through doing things together in workshop and market place rather than by signing pacts in chancelleries." He states his thesis as follows:

> Sovereignty cannot in fact be transferred effectively through a formula, only through a function. By entrusting an authority with a certain task, carrying with it command over the requisite powers and means, a slice of sovereignty is transferred from the old authority to the new; and the accumulation of such partial transfers in time brings about a translation of the true seat of authority.

[1] David Mitrany, *A Working Peace System* (London and New York: The Royal Institute of International Affairs, 1946).

> [Functionalism is a method] which would . . . overlay political divisions with a spreading web of international activities and agencies, in which and through which the interests and life of all the nations would be gradually integrated.

Mitrany hypothesizes the development of successive layers of functional collaboration, creating "increasingly deep and wide strata of peace—not the stand-offish peace of an alliance, but one that would suffuse the world with a fertile mingling of common endeavor and achievement." This gradual evolution constitutes what Mitrany calls a process of "federation by instalments," or, in Frederick L. Schuman's felicitous phrase, "peace by pieces."

The functional theory rests upon a very complex conception of the nature and causes of war, and promises a correspondingly elaborate set of results bearing upon the establishment and maintenance of peace. The basic assumptions and prescriptions of functionalism in regard to the problem of peace may be divided into three broad segments.

In the first place, war is regarded as the product of the objective conditions of human society. It is the result neither of man's native instinct nor of his acquired sinfulness, neither of the state's inherent nature nor of its irrational policy; war is a disease of global society, caused by grave deficiencies in the economic and social circumstances of mankind. Poverty, misery, ill-health, illiteracy, economic insecurity, social injustice, exploitation, discrimination—these are the factors which create the desperation, apathy, frustration, fear, cupidity, and hatred which make the world susceptible to war. This diagnosis owes much to the Marxian insistence upon the significance of material determinants for political conditions, but its popularity has not been confined to representatives of any particular school of thought. The notion that war is traceable to deep-seated causes in the economic and social realm has become part of the standard intellectual currency of the twentieth century.

Given this assumption, functionalism sets out to treat the basic ailments of mankind. It proposes to elevate living standards in backward areas, reduce the interference of national frontiers with the working of the complex global economy, minimize the factors that make for economic instability, and promote the attainment of higher levels of health, literacy, culture, and social justice. This is not merely a program for aiding the poor by enlisting the altruistic, or the enlightened selfish, assistance of the rich; much of the business of functionalism relates to the solution of problems which affect the most highly developed sector of the world, precisely because it is highly developed. Functionalism undertakes to grapple with the effects of both the excessive primitiveness of underdeveloped regions and the excessive intricacy of economic and social relationships in the intensely industrialized parts of the world. Thus, it hopes to extirpate the roots of war.

In the second place, functionalism attributes the phenomenon of war to the institutional inadequacy of the national state system. The state is at fault, not because it is intrinsically a fighting organism, as the power politician would have it, but because it is increasingly an inappropriate and ineffectual agency for doing what has to be done in order to promote the economic and social health of the human family. The state system imposes an arbitrary and rigid pattern of vertical divisions upon global society, disrupting the organic unity of the whole, and carving the world into segments whose separateness is jealously guarded by sovereignties which are neither able to solve the fundamental problems nor willing to permit them to be solved by other authorities. Peace requires solutions of economic and social problems which can be achieved only by problem-solving agencies coterminous in territorial competence with the problem areas. The appropriate administrative unit varies with the nature of the problem, but it only accidentally corresponds to the boundaries established by the state system; more and more, the problems which are crucial to the fitness of human society for sustaining a peaceful regime are becoming bigger in scope than national states. Hence, the mission of functionalism is to make peace possible by organizing particular layers of human social life in accordance with their particular requirements, breaking down the artificialities of the zoning arrangements associated with the principle of sovereignty.

Beyond this, functional theory purports to provide an indispensable laboratory for the experimental development of organizational patterns and techniques which may serve as models for the ultimately necessary machinery of internationalism on the highest political levels. In the long run, the world requires a replacement for the state system. The essential process of institutional invention can be expected to gain momentum by being put into operation first in the areas of recognized common interest.

Finally, functionalism envisages its task in terms of the alteration of the subjective conditions of mankind. War is caused by the attitudes, habits of thought and feeling, and allegiances which are fostered by the state system. Functional organizations may, by focusing attention upon areas of common interest, build habits of cooperation which will equip human beings for the conduct of a system of international relations in which the expectation of constructive collaboration will replace that of sterile conflict as the dominant motif. Working international agencies will create a system of mutual advantages which will assume too great a value in the eyes of its beneficiaries for them to contemplate disrupting it by permitting resort to war. Men will recognize international organization as the giver of good gifts which their states are no longer able to provide; they will cease to regard the derogation of sovereignty as a dubiously permissible national sacrifice, and come to think of it as a transfer of authority which is essential to the attainment of desirable results, a profitable investment in the good life. Thus, fundamental loyalties will be increasingly shared by the state and the agencies of the world community, the sentiment of human solidarity will be deepened, and the subjective basis will be prepared for progressively broader and more effective cooperation among the peoples of the world.

This concept involves not only the notion of transforming the international outlook of particular human beings, but also that of transferring competence from one set of human beings to another. So far as the traditional ruling classes of international affairs, the diplomats and the military men, are concerned, functionalism is perhaps a project for *evasion* as much as for *conversion*.

For all its emphasis upon the underlying economic and social roots of war, it does not altogether avoid the concoction of a devil theory; its villains are those gentlemen—perhaps more properly described as inveterate sinners in the national interest than as genuine devils—who have long held something approaching a monopolistic control of the conduct of relations among states. Functionalism comes very close to regarding these officials as incorrigible. Long habituated to the treatment of international affairs as an area of conflict and competition, they are unlikely to be swayed by the new mode of thought. Hence, functionalism envisages a process of circumvention, described hopefully by H. G. Wells as the evolution of "a comprehensive world control in the presence of which Foreign Offices would fade out, since, by reason of the conditions of their development, they are themselves incapable of establishing peace," and sarcastically by Georg Schwarzenberger as a project by which the "vicious dragons" who are presumed to inhabit Foreign Offices are to be "cleverly outwitted by gallant reforming knights."

More seriously, the expectation of functionalism is in line with the concept of multilevel interpenetration of governments which was brilliantly formulated by J. A. Salter after World War I. The development of specialized international agencies dealing with problems outside the scope of traditional diplomacy will result in making virtually every department of government a kind of Foreign Office, and bring into the active conduct of international relations a host of national officials whose professional training and interests give them a predisposition to concentrate upon the pragmatic issues of how to solve common problems for the common advantage, rather than to focus upon questions of national prestige and sovereign authority. Internationalism will well up from the collaborative international contacts of officials in labor, health, agriculture, commerce, and related departments, eventually endangering the citadels in which diplomatic and military officials sit peering competitively and combatively at the world outside the state.

In summary, functionalism proposes to promote peace by eliminating objective conditions which are deemed conducive to war, introducing new patterns of organization which may transform the global institutional system, and initiating the development of subjective trends which may cause the "erosion" of sovereignty, thereby assisting "states to work together and so gradually develop a sense of community which will make it psychologically more difficult to press the claims of sovereignty in ways that are anti-social." [2]

The analysis of the theoretical structure of functionalism may be approached in yet another way, this time giving emphasis not to the general propositions concerning the nature of the causes of war and the conditions of peace, but rather to the sequential steps in the logic according to which functional theory envisages the ultimate production of a world capable of sustaining peaceful relationships.

[2] Brierly, "The Covenant and the Charter," *British Yearbook of International Law,* 1946, p. 93.

The first of these is what I should call the "separability-priority" thesis. It involves the assumption that human affairs can be sliced into layers, that the concerns of man are so stratified that economic and social problems can, in a preliminary fashion, be separated from political problems and from each other. Having adopted this assumption, functionalism then proceeds on the theory that the treatment of economic and social matters should take priority.

The next step in the logic of functionalism is the assertion of a thesis which may be variously described as a doctrine of transferability, expansibility, ramification, or accumulation. Some have argued that men, having learned the arts of fruitful international cooperation at the level of technical or economic problems, will transfer their new skills and habits of mind to the development of collaborative solutions at the highest political levels. Writing before the First World War, Paul S. Reinsch adumbrated a "concentric circles" concept of international organization, according to which the idea of multilateral attack upon world problems will function like a pebble dropped into the international pond, giving rise to a series of circles of cooperation which will expand from the limited area of technical agencies to the vast circumference of a global political and security organization. Paul G. Hoffman has suggested that "The good thing about the spirit of unity is that it ramifies out; when you cultivate habits of unity in the economic sphere, they naturally spread over to the political sphere and even to the military sphere when the need arises."[3] Others have intimated, rather vaguely, that the accumulated agenda of constructive work under functional organizations will produce such a preoccupation that men will abandon war in a fit of absent-mindedness; they will forget to fight because they will be "too busy with things that matter."

In all these cases, the point is the same, however it may be expressed: the separability of economic and social problems from political problems is only provisional, and they are ultimately inseparable. International action at one level affects the other level, and leads to comparable action at the other level. This assumption of the effective connecting link lies at the heart of functional theory.

It should be noted that the functionalist promise to transform the political mentality and allegiance of human beings rests upon a logic which emphasizes both the irrational and the rational aspects of human nature. On the one hand, functionalism assumes that political unity must be built, pearl-wise, around a central irritant; it offers a new type of common enemy—such as poverty, pestilence, or ignorance—to serve as the focal point around which men may unite. It similarly stresses the irrational side of human behavior when it suggests that men are such creatures of habit that they will forget to clash in political matters once they have become accustomed to cooperating in other areas. Finally, however, functionalism postulates a transfer of loyalties to the international community in response to the growing usefulness of functional agencies. This notion that men can be expected to distribute their allegiances on the basis of a utilitarian calculation implies a significant con-

[3] *Peace Can Be Won* (New York: Doubleday, 1951), p. 62. Copyright, 1951, by the Great Books Foundation.

cept of the rationality of the human loyalty structure. At bottom, the logic which expects a sense of world community to derive from the operation of functional agencies is rigorously rationalistic.

Evaluation of Functional Theory

The concept of functionalism as an approach to peace is an extraordinarily attractive doctrine in many ways and for many reasons. It may appear to be an easy way out of the dilemma which confronts modern civilization. Men who have come to regard the directly political approaches as nothing better than prescriptions for humanity's beating its bloody head against the stone wall which guards national sovereignty may be heartened by the notion that there are poorly watched backdoors through which access may be gained. Functionalism may be regarded as a device for sneaking up on sovereignty, full of hopeful possibilities for establishing the groundwork of international community.

It has the great merit of appealing both to humanitarian idealism and to national self-interest. Pacifists may see functionalism as an admirably non-military approach to peace and security, and they may be joined by other men of exceptional good will and moral sensitivity in noting with approval the contrast between its positive, constructive aspects and the negative, restrictive, preventive character of other approaches to peace. There is a widespread urge to agree with Salvador de Madariaga that "Peace is no policy.... The only way to secure peace is to stop bothering about it and begin to work together to carry out together the business of the world." There is much to be done to convert the world into a good society, and it is reassuring to be told that the doing of it is a major contribution to peace—not to mention that it is convenient to have governments persuaded that it is a legitimate and necessary part of their business to support and subsidize the doing of it.

Here the element of national self-interest begins to obtrude, and a major strength of the appeal of functionalism begins to emerge. Functionalism proposes not to squelch but to utilize national selfishness; it asks governments not to give up the sovereignty which belongs to their peoples but to acquire benefits for their peoples which were hitherto unavailable, not to reduce their power to defend their citizens but to expand their competence to serve them. The realist who repudiates the expectation that altruism can become a major factor in international politics may find much to hope for in a system of organization which invites states to the common pursuit of common interests.

Moreover, functionalism is capable of striking a responsive chord in both conservative and liberal hearts. To the conservative, it may appear as an organic, naturalistic, evolutionary approach to world organization. Mitrany's formulation of the theory is empirically oriented in the best tradition of British conservatism. Functionalism eschews the rigidity of a formula and the neatness of a blueprint; it projects the growth of international organization as needed and in accordance with needs. It is flexible and opportunist; it makes an appeal to common sense for the discovery of practicable solutions to definite problems, rather than to the radical urge of doctrinaires to devise an ingenious scheme for the comprehensive reform of international arrangements. At the same time, the liberal may regard functionalism as a distinctively modern, progressive concept. Mitrany writes like a social democrat, and he finds his great inspiration in the New Deal's notable invention, the TVA. Functionalism represents the application of the welfare state philosophy to the international sphere, emphasizing the responsibility of international agencies for rendering services rather than merely enforcing controls, and for extending their concern into areas hitherto falling within the private entrepreneurial domain of the national state.

Lastly, functionalism has all the earmarks of a profound and sophisticated approach to the problem of war. To those who are weary of superficial approaches, it justifies itself by burrowing deep under the surface of reality to find the roots of the problem. To those whose skepticism is excited by panaceas, it offers the appeal of a system which prescribes specific treatment for the primary ills from which war derives, instead of a cheap patent remedy for the secondary symptoms of human society's malaise. Functionalism seems to emerge from the diagnostic clinic, not the drug counter, of the internationalist movement.

On the other hand, the student of international organization will do well to keep his critical wits about him when he is confronted with the functional answer to the problem of world order. The impressiveness of the theory and attractiveness of the program of functionalism are not in themselves evidence of either the theoretical validity or the practical adequacy of this approach to peace. The testing of functionalism may well begin with the posing of some fundamental questions in regard to its basic assumptions.

The central thesis that war is a product of unsatisfactory economic and social conditions in the global community should arouse a bit of skeptical eyebrow-arching. Charles Malik of Lebanon has stated the challenge to the cliché: "The poor, the sick, the dispossessed, must certainly be done justice to. But to suppose that there will be peace when everybody is materially happy and comfortable, is absolute nonsense." Hans Kelsen has insisted upon reversing the functionalist proposition: "It is not true that war is the consequence of unsatisfactory economic conditions; on the contrary, the unsatisfactory situation of world economy is the consequence of war." The recent history of the world clearly fails to confirm the existence of a direct correlation between national economic backwardness and aggressiveness; it was advanced Germans, not primitive Africans, who shattered world peace in 1939. The debate concerning the role of economic factors and motivations in world politics is an involved and quite possibly an interminable one, certainly not one to be settled here. The point is that the analysis of the causes of war and the conditions of peace falls into the category of unfinished business, and that the assumptions which underpin the functional approach should be regarded as hypotheses, not established verities.

The logical apparatus of functionalism, involving the concepts of the preliminary separability of the economic and social strata from the political, the essential priority of action in nonpolitical layers, and the ultimate impact of results achieved there upon the problems of the political stratum, requires cautious evaluation. Is it in fact possible to segregate a group of problems and subject them to treatment in an international workshop where the nations shed their conflicts at the door and busy themselves only with the coopera-tive use of the tools of mutual interest? Does not this assumption fly in the face of the evidence that a trend toward the politicization of all issues is operative in the twentieth century? Considering only the problems which may most appropriately be styled economic and social, it is possible that the hori-zontal slicing in which functionalism engages may be quite as unfavorable for their proper administrative treatment as the vertical segmentation imposed by the national state pattern; excessive stratification is no more helpful than excessive compartmentalization. As Gerhard Bebr has warned, "the artificial dissection of organic economic ties into separate economic organizations under independent authorities endangers their viability."

Assuming the feasibility of marking off a distinctively nonpolitical sector of human affairs, it is not self-evident that work in this area should or can be assigned first place on the international schedule. In objective terms, it may be that "the elements of order are the prerequisite of economic and social progress," and that "to forward the world's material welfare and human rights the peoples must first be freed from the scourge of modern war." Re-verting to the subjective sphere, we may ask whether states can in fact be induced to join hands in functional endeavor before they have settled the outstanding political and security issues which divide them. Functionalism's insistence upon putting first things first does not settle the matter of what things are first.

If it be granted that the assumptions and prescriptions of functionalism are valid up to this point, it remains necessary to raise questions concerning the efficacy of the functional process as preparation for a solution of the ultimate problems of world order. If economic and social organization is in-deed the horse, can it in fact pull the political cart? This is again an area of legitimate doubt.

The concentric circle theory is subject to the criticism that it begs some very big questions in assuming that the dropping of the functional pebble pro-duces a steady progression of ever-widening circles of cooperation, reaching out without limit to encompass finally the whole area of the international pond. This metaphorical concept makes sense only if it can be assumed that the global waters offer a placid surface for the rippling-out process; in fact, the lashing winds and roaring waves of world politics are always likely to play havoc with the developing pattern of functional circles. The problem of the recurrent setback, the interruption and disruption by war of the projects of functionalism for the eventual elimination of war, poses a critical dilemma. Moreover, it is not lightly to be assumed that the expansibility of the con-centric circle pattern is unlimited. There may be barriers to the encirclement of vital political areas which the momentum of functional development can-not cross. Functionalism cannot guarantee that one thing leads inexorably and interminably to another in international relations.

The assumption of the rational transference of human loyalties is also a fit subject for skeptical scrutiny. How malleable is human allegiance? Do men actually shift their emotional bonds so as always to keep them connected with the entities from which their real blessings flow? Can functional agencies do enough, fast enough, conspicuously enough, to capture the imagination of peoples and elicit from them the rational recognition of, and, consequent emotional dedication to, the values of an organized international community? Functional activities are likely to be helpful, but unlikely to be stirring and sensational; international agencies are likely to find themselves stimulating and facilitating the provision of services and solution of problems by national states, with the credit redounding to the states rather than being entered to the account of internationalism. If this were not so, governments could be expected to arrange that it should become so, since the responsible agents of national states are not likely to wax enthusiastic about the sponsorship and subsidization of projects for undermining the normative foundations of the state system. There is room for doubt that functionalists have found the key which infallibly opens the doors that keep human loyalties piled up in sovereign warehouses, thereby permitting those loyalties to spill out into the receptacles of internationalism.

Finally, it must be noted that functionalism is not in a hurry, and its claim to offer hope to the world is implicitly based upon the supposition that a long period is both necessary and available for working out solutions to the problems of the world. How much time does man have at his disposal for building the foundations of peace? The honest answer probably is that no one can say, and the urgent insistence of doctrinaires that the sand is running out and that quick solutions are certainly possible because they are obviously necessary is no more worthy of uncritical acceptance than the smug assumption of functionalists that there is a long run and their stodgy insistence that there is no satisfactory substitute for the methods of gradualism. Nevertheless, there is ample justification in the atomic age for giving serious thought to the question of time limits; as Carlos Romulo suggested at the tenth anniversary meeting of the United Nations,

> Our clients are the next generation . . . but there may be no next generation unless we do today what has to be done for the two billion clients who are now alive.
>
> What makes our age unique, I suppose, is that the immediate questions and the ultimate questions are locked together.

The Practice of Functionalism

Functionalism is not merely a recipe to be studied, but also a pudding to be tasted; the twentieth century has seen the transfer of functionalism from the cookbooks and experimental kitchens to the serving tables of international organization. Hence, the major business of evaluation must be related to an examination of the actual dish. . . .

The designers of the world's new organizational system after World War II assigned major importance to the creation of machinery for international collaboration in economic and social fields. Pre-existing special-purpose agencies were retained, remodeled, or replaced, and new ones were instituted to round out the battery of functional institutions. These organizations, which soon numbered ten, were affiliated with the United Nations as Specialized Agencies. The central organization was equipped with an Economic and Social Council, subordinate to the General Assembly, which in turn created an elaborate apparatus and set itself to the task of supplementing and coordinating the functional activities of the Specialized Agencies. Unlike the League, the United Nations system was, in its original conception, a full-fledged experiment in the application of the functional theory to international affairs. The ambitiousness of its scope and the decentralized character of its administrative pattern were both largely the products of American initiative and insistence.

The first decade since the drafting of the Charter has seen the steady enlargement of the functional program of the United Nations system. This development has doubtless been in some measure a compensatory reaction, like that of the League, to the frustration of organizational endeavors in the most sensitive political fields. It has been stimulated by the conversion of the first Secretary-General, and of many other international officials and national leaders, to the view that "poverty remains mankind's chief enemy," when confronted with the reality that misery, disease, and ignorance are the chief facts of life for more than half of the world's population. It has been facilitated by the fortuitous circumstance that the American conception of how best to combat the spread of Communism has largely coincided with the functionalist conception of how best to build the foundations of a peaceful world society; as a result of this contingency, the critical portion of the financial support for the developing program has been provided by a government which is much more deeply committed to anti-Communism than to functionalism. Its political dynamics have been supplied primarily by the newly emergent peoples of the non-European world, whose conception of what is needed to achieve the goals of national advance has tended to coincide with functionalism's doctrine of what is needed to achieve the purpose of international order; thus, the effective political demand for expansion of the program has emanated mainly from states which are more deeply committed to specific national interests than to the general propositions of functional theory.

The special motivations of the United States and the governments of underdeveloped countries have combined with the broader incentives of men like Trygve Lie to produce the Expanded Technical Assistance Program, a coordinated project of the United Nations and several Specialized Agencies, which is the most significant expression of the enlarged concern of contemporary international organization with the application of functionalism.

The functional experiment of the United Nations is full-scale in terms of the number of international agencies and the diversity of the technical, economic, social, and humanitarian problems which are placed within their range. But to say that the agencies are competent to *deal* with problems is not to say that they are equipped to *solve* them. The experiment is decidedly less than full-scale in terms of the conferment upon functional agencies of authority to make decisions, to order compliance, to command resources, and to initiate and conduct activities.

To a limited extent, organs of the United Nations system have acquired powers of a legislative and executive nature in regard to their special substantive areas, including the responsibility for framing technical regulations and the right of following up the passage of resolutions by methods considerably more meaningful than the mere expression of hope for faithful implementation by states. Some advance has also been made toward development of actual operational competence by international agencies; the temporary International Refugee Organization, set up to deal with the massive human displacement of the immediate postwar period, and the participating agencies of the technical assistance program are striking examples of international bodies which have directly administered and managed field programs, doing jobs through their own personnel and with their own budgetary resources.

However, the primary functions of United Nations machinery have been of a more modest nature. They have included fact-finding, research into the nature and magnitude of problems, idea-sharing, sponsorship of consultation among experts and responsible officials of national governments, and encouragement of the standardization and harmonization of national programs and policies. In short, international agencies have been largely confined to the work of helping governments to help themselves and encouraging governments to help each other. What the former Director-General of the World Health Organization wrote concerning his organization applies generally to the whole system:

> WHO is not a supra-national health administration. It cannot act in place of and for the national health authorities in any area of public health. Its only role is to use all possible means of international co-operation in order to provide certain essential elements which those authorities need to promote the health of their peoples. The rest is up to each individual nation itself.

Evaluation of Functional Practice

The evaluation of functionalism in operation may well begin with an examination of the problem of coordinating the instruments of international collaboration. Since World War II, there has been such a proliferation of multilateral mechanism that it has seemed that the world was in danger of being overwhelmed by the sheer complexity of its apparatus. The difficulty of creating and maintaining order in the United Nations workshop, so as to avoid wasteful duplication of effort and loss of efficiency through the friction of agencies working at cross-purposes, is compounded by the fact that the Specialized Agencies have an autonomous status based upon their own constitutional documents, nonidentical membership lists, and widely scattered headquarters.

The problem of coordination has been further complicated by the tendency of the Economic and Social Council to generate its own quota of institutional offspring, new units requiring controls to prevent their overlapping and conflicting with each other as well as with established agencies outside the United Nations proper. This has posed the question of who is to coordinate the coordinators. Moreover, the member states of the United Nations have given free rein to their instinct of institutional procreativity, siring regional and other limited-membership agencies with something approaching abandon. The result of all this activity is that the world is so filled with a chaotic jumble of specialized instrumentalities of multilateral cooperation, within the United Nations, attached to the United Nations, and divorced from the United Nations, that governmental chiefs can hardly be expected to remember to what organizations their states belong, much less to develop consistent national policies toward and within those organizations. If conflict is the major problem of international political organization, confusion is an equally serious problem in the functional sphere.

The record of the United Nations is not entirely unimpressive in dealing with this problem. One of the earliest tasks of the Economic and Social Council was to serve as a kind of "Hoover Commission" for the international community, and it achieved a considerable rationalization of the world's haphazard institutional pattern, even though it has not subsequently been able to curb tendencies to re-create confusion and duplication. . . .

In the final analysis, the profusion of international agencies may be evidence of the vitality of the idea of international community, and the confusion may simply prove that multilateral institutions, like national ones, are owned and operated by human beings; after all, the tangle is no worse in the global system than in Washington or other national capitals. In an era of big government and big international organization, a certain amount of confusion and inefficiency is inevitable, and it may even be salutary. The problem of coordination in the United Nations system will never be solved, and ought never to be abolished, but it seems likely that it can be managed.

A closely related problem of functionalism in operation is that of maintaining a reasonably clear and restricted focus of international activities and a keen sense of discrimination in determining the allocation of limited resources. The tendency toward excessive proliferation is matched by the tendency toward undisciplined scattering of organizational efforts. Functionalism is dedicated to the proposition that there are many roads to peace, but it does not envisage the exploration of every back street and country lane that any member of the party finds fascinating.

Postwar functional agencies have experienced difficulty in concentrating on important matters, rejecting trivial proposals, and abjuring interesting diversions. They stand in constant peril of being treated as hobbyhorses to be ridden off in all directions at once. . . .

The most basic questions to be faced in evaluating the working experiment in functionalism which is being conducted under the auspices of the United Nations are political questions. Functional theory invites this kind of examination, since its emphasis upon economic and social matters is explicitly justified in terms of ultimate political impact; functional experience demands it, since the intrusion of political factors is almost invariably one of the earliest facts of life brought to bear upon a fledgling agency for international cooperation in any field whatever.

The clearest lesson of United Nations experience is that functionalism's assumption of the preliminary separability of political and nonpolitical matters does not hold true—not in this generation, at any rate. We are not vouchsafed the privilege of warming up the motors of international collaboration in a sheltered area of concordant interests, getting off to an easy start and building up momentum for crashing the barriers of conflicting interests that interpose between us and the ideal of world order. The dilemma of functionalism is that its ultimate impact upon politics may never be tested because of the immediate impact of politics upon functionalism. . . .

This point has been increasingly recognized. In 1950, the leading professional officials of the Specialized Agencies were torn between asserting the doctrine, enshrined in the constitutional documents of the agencies, that functional activities would bring an end to political conflict, and warning that political conflict would put an end to functional activities; they ended up by stressing the latter point. The Director-General of the World Health Organization, for instance, expressed the view that peace was a prerequisite for the successful working of the Specialized Agencies, thus implicitly adopting the position that the preamble to the constitution of his own agency should be altered to read, not "The health of all peoples is fundamental to the attainment of peace and security," but rather "The health of all peoples is dependent upon the attainment of peace and security." The actual order of priorities, as distinguished from the order assumed by functionalism, dictates the preliminary analysis of the influence of politics upon organized economic and social cooperation.

The two great political struggles which have developed in the United Nations, the cold war between the Soviet Communist bloc and the anti-Communist bloc led by the United States, and the separate but closely intertwined conflict between the non-European attackers of colonialism and the heirs of the colonial system, have both impinged sharply upon functional operations. Separately and in combination, they have decisively affected the answers to basic questions of national participation, of the uses to which the machinery of collaboration can and should be put, and of the scope and distribution of the functional effort. . . .

The political animosity between the opponents in the cold war has thus far denied functionalism the opportunity to test its capacity for weaving pacifying webs between them. The major antagonists have either refrained from joint participation in functional agencies, thereby eliminating the possibility that they might be joined by the subtle threads of functional activity, or they have made their common membership an occasion for the raucous proclamation of conflicting political interests rather than the coperative pursuit of common economic and social interests. In terms of functional theory, the knitting of economic and social bonds between the United States and the Soviet Union is the critical peace-building task of our time; yet, this is precisely the job that functionalism cannot even begin to perform until *after* some sort of political peace has been established between the two great powers. The politics of the cold war shows no susceptibility to being transformed by functional programs; rather, it shows every indication of being able to transform functional workshops into political arenas. . . .

The failure of functionalism under United Nations auspices to demonstrate its validity as a means of achieving the immediate or even of initiating the ultimate reduction of political tension between the United States and the Soviet Union does not mean that the functional approach to international organization has been entirely discredited. The agencies of international economic and social cooperation have displayed a notable gift of institutional inventiveness; such of their creations as the international expert, the comprehensive survey mission, and the special-purpose international working team may prove to be major contributions to the future development of human civilization. In substantive terms, they have hardly been able to keep up with the job of making the world a livable place; the gap between the living standards of developed and underdeveloped countries is steadily widening, and many of the latter countries are swimming against a demographic current which forces them to push forward with great speed in order simply to remain in the same place. Nevertheless, the situation of mankind is less unsatisfactory than it would have been without the strenuous international efforts of the last decade.

The functional experiment of the United Nations represents the laying of the groundwork for the first systematic global attack upon basic economic and social problems, the beginning of the definition of the assignment which devolves upon the organized international community, and the initiation of the process of learning how to tackle the job. The actual achievements thus far are substantial and significant, even though not spectacular, world-shaking, or world-saving. Above all, the record to date indicates that functional activity is, at least in the short run, more dependent upon the political weather than determinative of the political weather. In the long run, however, it may be that the economic and social work of international organization will prove to be one of the means of developing a system whereby man can control his political climate.

Three Challenges for
American Foreign Policy

It is sobering to remind ourselves that fifty years from now Americans looking back upon our foreign relations will judge us as at present we judge our forebears. It may not be completely idle to speculate for a moment on the possible character of their judgment. What will their estimate be? Will they say that we lived in an age of greatness which flourished as America slowly, hesitatingly, but unflinchingly assumed a position of world leadership? Will they say that as we grew stronger, our wisdom, responsibility and justice deepened, or will it be true of us as of the great powers of the past, whether Roman Empire, Greek Republic or French State, that we were corrupted by power, enfeebled by perplexities, internal dissension, and uncertainty, and destroyed by our loss of the capacity to act within the limits of our power? What will they say about the intellectual climate, about the spirit in which we approached our problems, about the philosophy of foreign relations of the people and our intellectual and political leaders? How will they judge the courage of those in authority and the responsiveness of what historians call the goodhearted but often half-informed ordinary people? What will they think of our devotion to moral principles or our qualities in that realm the ancients call practical wisdom? Will it be the judgment of history that our fateful position as an island of plenty and prosperity in a global sea of poverty and insecurity tempted us after numerous encounters with our hapless but ungrateful friends to withdraw to the safe haven of the American continent? Is it possible that the baffling pace and bewildering complexity of world problems will exceed the capacities of human resources to cope with them and keep them in check or solve them in at least a provisional way? Or will human resourcefulness and ingenuity find new ways of encompassing our difficulties? Can we discover the moral resources for acting when we cannot foresee the consequences of our actions, for choosing between practical alternatives weighed down with ambiguities and imperfections, and for guiding the people to accept the things they might do if they had the grasp and knowledge

Based on a speech delivered by Kenneth W. Thompson at the Army War College, September, 1959.

623

that their leaders possess? I am inclined to think that questions like these are the crucial issues and the standards by which we shall be judged, not our professions of high principle, repeated affirmations of devotion to institutions like the United Nations or the flaunting of appeals to the moral conscience of mankind.

The State of the American Mind

It would be reassuring to say that America in its time of challenge from the brutalities, complexities and uncertainties of the external world had put its own house in order and organized its thoughts and ideas. A democracy for more than a century-and-a-half with successes that outdistance the fondest hopes of the founding fathers, we are endlessly tempted to maintain that our free institutions are secure, our rights safeguarded and our conception of domestic and international politics clear and sure. Our accomplishments in every realm pay tribute to American inventiveness; we are a positive people with faith in the future and in man as the measure of things, including the God that is sometimes seen in the image of man. As a successful people we easily grow impatient with the failings, on the one hand, of nations whose greatness is presumed to lie in the past or, on the other, of newly emerging states painfully groping toward a better life. From the throne of the world, we look to Europe and Asia not as equals but as peoples to be understood, however compassionately, each in their own less fortunate terms. Sometimes we approach our problems not in the fresh curiosity and wonder of the young child but, ironically at the dawning of our leadership, with the fixed doctrines of the self-made, older man. We speak to Europeans in the condescending tone of greater morality. We see Europe as a civilization whose past greatness is beclouded by imperialism, colonialism and power politics, sins from which we assume we are free. Europe is like the aging father who has had his chance while we as the aspiring and buoyant youth seek with our virtues to crowd out all his ancient and unhappy failings. In much the same spirit, we expect the misery, poverty and exploitation of underdeveloped regions to yield to the command of our material resources, for we view the world's economic problems in the light of the relative social equality which has been attained in American economic life. In unguarded moments we see their economic and political development as more our goal than the will of the local peoples.

Now of course this brief commentary largely exaggerates the American outlook and singles out certain tendencies that are less than the whole of American thinking. I have deliberately overstated and not for a moment would I leave an impression that this viewpoint is dominant for all. Notably since World War II, American foreign policy has cut loose from the moorings of "splendid isolation" and consciously embraced the firm ties of partnership with peoples in Europe and Asia. We have mutual assistance arrangements with more than forty nations and our loyalty to the United Nations is beyond dispute. We can point to the Marshall Plan as an act of almost unparalleled generosity. Yet the tendency of seeing ourselves as morally and spiritually, if

not geographically, apart from the other nations of the world is always present, although hidden beneath the surface, ready to erupt or appear. It affects our approach to problems like diplomacy, foreign aid, or the use of force, and influences the trend toward a too sanguine point of view about prospects of charting the future. The brutalities, complexities and uncertainties of foreign relations escape us and we falter particularly in the realm of means where discriminate judgments, not higher instincts, are at stake.

Three Challenges to America

I fear more the unsettling effects of our way of viewing international problems than their substance, perplexing and bewildering as they may be. For one thing there is little we can do to change the outside world and the existence and recurrence of trouble. It promises to be with us always in much the way that irritations and frustrations are a part of our personal life. Most of us learn to take the good with the bad in daily life but are distressed when we find that international society is brimming over with ambition, greed, injustice and selfish interests. Not many of our personal problems can be solved unequivocally and most of us walk the thin knife's edge that separates certainty from uncertainty, security from insecurity, and hope from despair. The fabric of international life is at least as variegated and resistant to tidy answers and neat resolution. Moreover, sweeping and decisive solutions to problems on the world scene are almost always a subtle blending of some broad plan of action and our particular interests, passions and enthusiasms. They are propositions that doubtless would be valid if the world were cast in our image and if others had reason to be as fair-minded, progressive, satisfied and law-abiding as we seek to be. But there are still massive differences in wealth, power and national values and our standards are not those that others would embrace. This lends an air of pretentiousness to our claims that states should abide by the precepts that profit us more than them.

I see the challenge of American foreign policy especially in three corners of our national and international life. The first challenge is that of democratic diplomacy. It arises in part from problems inherent in marshalling domestic support for our programs while at the same time putting our best foot forward in the eyes of the rest of the world. In rallying a consensus in support of policies, we say things to ourselves that from the standpoint of other peoples might better be left unsaid. In this the United States is of course not unique, and we do well in reflecting on it to curb our impatience with other world leaders. . . . The American experience is, however, made especially poignant because we are a vast sprawling continent of great diversity of political and religious belief with a constitutional system in which power and responsibility are broadly diffused, although less in foreign affairs than for the conduct of national government. Thus we speak in many voices, some raucous and strident, as we seek to persuade one another of the right course to follow. No purpose would be served by minimizing the incredible complexity and difficulty of relating the national interest to the demands of national politics and reconciling them both with the legitimate aspirations of our allies and friends. We are bound to suffer and cause offense even with those states to whom we are bound most closely by geography, history and common traditions. An editorial in *The Economist* (London) on November 17, 1956 observed: "Between us and the Americans it is, in a sense, a tale of two inferiority complexes: ours because we harp upon prestige, without recognizing that prestige can only be earned by our success in managing our affairs and in gaining the respect of others and cannot be bolstered by words and gestures; theirs because by ill-timed criticism and an indifference to their allies' interests, they still work off the last traces of their long-gone colonial (and isolationist) status."

All these problems are magnified by the sharp acceleration of the pace at which decisions must be made and the sheer magnitude of international business. For several decades following the Civil War, American Secretaries of State were able to combine their duties with part-time legal practice. One recalls the comment of an earlier Secretary of State, Thomas Jefferson, that for over two years nothing had been heard from the Ambassador to Madrid. If another year brought no word, Jefferson proposed to write him. The state machinery for international affairs has also been greatly expanded. The American Foreign Service as late as 1929 numbered 3,000 officials while today more than 22,000 are on its rosters. Every day a dozen or more international conferences are in session with an American delegation present fortified by staff and instructions. Indeed it is no exaggeration to say that every few minutes of every day some American delegate is asked to express American policy at an international meeting at some point on the globe. Secretary Dulles during the first ten months of office met with a committee or subcommittee of Congress on no less than 70 occasions, averaging a little less than 2 meetings a week. Instantaneous systems of communication and rapid means of transportation literally make the modern diplomat a "minute man." One recalls that Secretary of State Dulles received word of the 1958 revolution in Iraq in the early morning hours of July 14 and almost immediately the world awaited a response from the leading free world power. Reactions that in earlier decades could be deliberate, measured and gradually worked out now must be formulated much as the orders of a Company Commander in World War II. Consider the speed with which President Eisenhower and Premier Khrushchev have fired successive salvos in their continuing war of words.

Public and Personal Diplomacy

How have we as a great democracy sought to conduct diplomacy? The first and most novel pattern of diplomacy to crystallize since 1945 found expression in the United Nations and in affiliated agencies of "public diplomacy." For the tortuous paths of traditional diplomacy it substituted international forums. Public diplomacy reflects an all-pervasive faith in parliamentary procedures, in the rule of the people and in straightforward, rational exchange among all nations. It translates into global terms the supreme political attainments of free people within the democratic state. It stands as the very antithesis of secret diplomacy by a concert of leaders or the pre-eminent countries.

However the resemblance to national parliaments of even the strongest and most universal world institution, the United Nations, can be misleading. For example, the General Assembly can listen and recommend but it cannot legislate. Its Councils and Secretariats and the International Court of Justice are executive and judicial organs only in the most limited and restricted sense. Secretary Dag Hammarskjöld has reasoned: "A voting victory in a national legislature leads to decisions which have the force of law. The legislative process in the United Nations, on the other hand, leads only to the passage of recommendations which do not have the force of law." He concludes: "Since the legislative processes of the United Nations do not lead to legislation . . . the value of public debate in the U.N. can be measured only by the degree to which it contributes to the winning of agreement by the processes of diplomacy. If public debate contributes to winning consent either immediately or in the long run, it serves the purpose of peace-making. If it does not so contribute, then it may be a useless, or even harmful exercise."

The problems of "diplomacy in a goldfish bowl," or, in Ernest Bevin's phrase, "the bear pit" frequently take on a stubbornly intractable quality that many United Nations architects scarcely anticipated. Publicity has been both a virtue and a vice. It has kept the spotlight of public opinion on world affairs, but it has also encouraged actors, in striking a pose for national publics, to take inflexible positions from which retreat or compromise proved impossible. Sometimes [Assembly votes] have allowed conflicts of interest to persist untouched or have actually contributed to the increase of tensions.

The tempering and limiting of the worst excesses of public diplomacy has not forestalled a counter-tendency. The Eisenhower administration has espoused "personal diplomacy" as a corrective to "diplomacy in the goldfish bowl." The first Geneva Conference, the United States-Canadian-Mexican Conference at White Sulphur Springs, and the meeting with India's Prime Minister Nehru and Britain's Prime Minister Macmillan illustrate a new and emerging pattern. It is a pattern ostensibly based upon the President's partiality "for talking things out rather than negotiating things out." It reflects the view that many of the abrasive causes of friction can be blunted and dissolved when leaders from other nations, sitting across a table from Mr. Eisenhower, become persuaded of his good intentions. The personal touch of a famous personality at his best in an atmosphere of genial informality is placed on the scales of world diplomacy.

Personal diplomacy is further a present-day household word because of the proclivities of recent American Secretaries of State, particularly Mr. John Foster Dulles. In one respect, diplomacy has come full circle since the days when prince addressed himself to prince without benefit of diplomatic intermediaries. Both the President and the late Secretary prided themselves on direct contacts with foreign leaders. In Mr. Dulles' words: "I fly because I go to meet heads of government, foreign ministers of other countries, and in a few minutes or at most few hours of personal consultation you can achieve a much better understanding than you can possibly achieve by going through the processes of communicating through notes and writing to each other." The belief is current that when two reasonable men sit down together, the difficulties that have loomed large in correspondence may suddenly evaporate.

In two important respects, personal diplomacy has changed the character of the diplomatic art. On one hand, the role of the professional diplomat or ambassador tends to be downgraded. In a crisis, the State Department may rush in the Secretary or a high ranking trouble-shooter. The Ambassador runs the risk of becoming a glorified handy man or messenger boy either whispering into the ear of his minister flying in and departing by jet stream or carrying the latest set of documents between the State Department and another country's foreign office. On the other hand, the independence and authority, judgment and maneuver historically open to professional diplomats have been sharply cut back. Lester B. Pearson sensing this has asked: "Where do all these developments leave the professional? . . . Are they now mere ciphers to give cocktail parties, to meet planes and to entertain Congressmen . . . ?" He notes: "Before the twentieth century, Ministers devoted their time and energy to working out policy on the advice of their experts. . . . Ambassadors executed these policies . . . and by their manner of doing so . . . often influenced them." Now the process has been drastically altered. For example, in the past, the groundwork was laid for every important settlement through patient and protracted efforts carried on through established diplomatic channels. The preliminary soundings and orderly exchanges by duly authorized representatives in embassies abroad frequently carried negotiations to the point where all that remained for executives and ministers was the ratification of agreements carefully prepared at the working diplomatic level. There is danger in a process which leads men to think that nothing of importance can be settled except personally by the highest officials at the summit. It robs diplomacy of subtlety of maneuver based on extensive informal contacts through ambassadors engaged oftentimes in pointless or hypothetical talk —"if we do this, will you do that, etc.?" But more important still if the chief minister is continuously on the wing from Karachi to Paris to Manila, a vacuum grows up at the center at the point where larger policies must be evolved. If no one remains in Washington continually in personal touch with the dozens of issues that call for decision, leadership and adaptation become the high-priced casualty of personal diplomacy. The price in fact may be a ship of state modern and marvellously appointed but without a captain at the helm.

If I may state as specifically and directly as I can the challenge of present-day diplomacy it is this: Neither public nor personal diplomacy are by themselves adequate to the task, yet both are probably a permanent part of the present international landscape. They are in fact at opposite ends of a spectrum. One emphasizes public speeches, mass assemblies, and resolutions emerging from open forums; the other stresses informality and man-to-man conferences free of protocol, agendas and advanced preparation. (At White

Sulphur Springs in 1957 the Canadians on the eve of a Canadian-American little summit Conference did not know the topics to be discussed.) Yet these novel patterns so divergent in conception and design share one thing in common. Both public and personal diplomacy constitute a revolt against traditional diplomacy. They are "the new diplomacy."

The doubts men have about personal diplomacy stem from a single source. The first rule of diplomacy has always been that negotiations were essential when national interests came into conflict. Since conflicts arise from causes more basic than personal hostility, personal amiability by itself can hardly resolve them. Sir Harold Nicolson has argued:

"Diplomacy is the art of negotiating documents in a ratifiable and dependable form. It is by no means the art of conversation. The affability inseparable from any conversation . . . produces illusiveness, compromises and high intentions. Diplomacy if it is ever to be effective, should be a disagreeable business, and one recorded in hard print."

Any agreement if it comes in the cold war will almost certainly be the product of long, tedious, even agonizing preparation by professional diplomats. The Austrian Peace Treaty will be a case study for years to come of a settlement based on a decade of long and arduous diplomatic preparation. Our contemporaries who see in personal diplomacy the key to world peace are correct but so are those who stress preparations at appropriate diplomatic levels. Somehow these two approaches must be blended in modern diplomacy if civilization is to survive.

Military Preparedness

The second challenge arises because of the central place that armaments and power continue to hold in world politics today. This is true despite the revolution in weapons with which we are confronted.

The military establishments of nations remain the most explicit element of foreign policy. Diplomacy and military strength appear to go hand in hand. In an earlier day, the great powers sent gunboats up the rivers of states they were seeking to influence. Today in the cold war the postwar distribution of power is closely related to the position of the Red Army at strategic points in the heart of Europe. Germany's demoniacally successful diplomacy in the inter-war period must be seen as the direct outgrowth of superior military preparedness. The explosion and testing of atomic weapons by the Soviet Union has been joined with periodic and deliberate strategic moves in the cold war.

Nevertheless, the difficulties inherent in maintaining military establishments that will not suffer defeat are increasingly complex. A nation may clearly recognize the need for military organs capable of supporting the foreign policies it pursues but be limited in the margin of its economic resources that can be turned to military use. Some countries exhaust their resources in attaining a viable economy; others like the United States have a surplus with which to meet its foreign military and political commitments. Belgium cannot afford to devote the same part of its gross national product to military ends as can the Soviet Union or the United States. Thus in both absolute and relative terms, the military establishment of smaller powers including the newer states must lag behind.

But the problem of military security is equally perplexing for the great powers. If the present crisis between east and west were a simple clash either of military systems or political ideologies, we would doubtless face the future with greater confidence and hope. However, honest men admit that most of us vacillate between a military and ideological view of the struggle. The problem of arriving at valid and acceptable policies is at root the problem of defining the nature of the crisis. The uncertainty we feel about policies is basically an uncertainty over the crisis. There is irony in this perplexity because most informed observers in the early days of the cold war were convinced that the Russian threat to western civilization was identical with the Nazi menace. As such, the recipe for dealing with it was assumed to be the same. It was said that if our leaders had occasion to learn anything from over two centuries of national experience, it was that foreign policy divorced from strength is likely to be impotent. Following two world wars, the U.S. dismantled its military establishment as an earnest of its peaceful intentions and goodwill. In both cases, aggressive forces bent on expansion seized on such acts to press forward into areas defenseless against their power. Both Germany and the Soviet Union imposed their will upon helpless nations that fell within their zone of control.

The lesson this taught Western leaders was that weakness could be no substitute for security, that policies harnessed to power were more likely to succeed than those drawing strength from high ideals and noble expectations alone. Belgium in World War I and the Baltic States in World War II succumbed not because they were lacking in morality, but because they found no means of securing their national frontiers.

The West has carried this discovery into the atomic and thermonuclear age. It is possible to argue that such peace as we have known since 1945 is the outcome of a "balance of terror." There are signs that the Soviet Union more than once marched up to the brink, threatening to engulf Greece and Turkey, Iran and Berlin, only to march down again when it met resistance. Conversely, where resistance proved ambiguous, uncertain or divided, as in Egypt, Syria and in the Far East, the spread of the Soviet sphere of influence flowed across boundaries that had long marked the limits of Russian power.

Seen from this approach, the immediate military threat is unquestionably the gravest danger. Those who hold to this view call for even greater urgency in the multiplication of more powerful weapons of destruction, for new strategic doctrines and for missile bases and a nuclear weapons pool.

At war with this first approach is a second that urges us to display equal vision and energy in seeking political and economic solutions as in launching expanded military programs. It points to the Soviet technical assistance program pledging $1.5 billion to the underdeveloped areas and to the evidence of successful Soviet penetration into the Middle East. The scene and tactics of Russian imperialism have shifted. Subversion, infiltration and indirect aggression (disguised as appeals to anti-colonialism, anti-interventionism and anti-Westernism) have put the West on the defensive on its weakest front.

Ultimate weapons in these areas are bound to have ambiguous effects, since their use against great numbers of agrarian peoples spread over vast areas seems doubtful at best. Crises that have passed without their deployment in Indo-China, Korea and Egypt serve to reinforce such doubts. Because they neither possessed nor saw the relevance of these terrible weapons, the newer nations have led the movement for their outlawry.

However, the contradictory reactions in the newer states to thermonuclear devices is best seen in the effects of the sputniks. In the same countries that urge us to disarm, American prestige and virtue suffered a grievous blow when the Soviet Union launched the first satellite. Despite continuous criticism of America throughout Asia and Africa for its materialism and preoccupation with purely technological and military advance, confidence in American policy was gauged by these very standards so deplored.

The issue between the two approaches is not one that can be measured and appraised by a barometer of the rise and fall of Stalinism in the Soviet Union. If Stalinism means a brutal and heedless sacrifice of every goal to the goals of the Communist society, Stalinism lives as much today as ever. However, the fact is that Stalin no less than his successors pursued Russian objectives along more than one front even though the accent on economic-political warfare seems recently to have increased. It is undeniably the case that the Russian military threat survives the death of Stalin; and if anyone has any doubt, he need only look to the sputniks, to the stress on force and to the hundreds of Russian divisions guarding Soviet frontiers. Or he can listen to the threats and counterthreats of the Russian tyrants brandishing the instruments of force at each emerging crisis, e.g., the Suez crisis, Hungary, Poland, the Turkish-Syrian and the Berlin disputes. But the countless moves and counter-moves on the political and economic front are equally real, and with Soviet tactics of advance and retreat, the contest shifts almost imperceptibly from one type of warfare to another or sometimes is joined simultaneously on all sides. The greatest risk an observer can run is to exclude one or the other dimension of the crisis in his zeal to describe reality in shades of black and white.

Assuming then that the present crisis is partly but not exclusively military in nature, there are other problems to be faced. Three errors are commonly made in appraising the military component of foreign policy. First, military power is often confused with national power, and a nation's capacity to impose its will is equated with its military establishment. By contrast, military power is like the fist whose force depends on the health and vitality of the body politic and the whole society. Troops in being are an important determinant of a successful foreign policy, but without other foundations they will not suffice. Second, the military element is often viewed in more static terms than is appropriate. The democracies in two world wars, while they have been the last to arm, have rallied their forces to gain victory in the end.

Third, it is difficult to analyze and foresee the most effective distribution of the components of military force. For example, what comprises a strong military force today? Is it large ground forces, hydrogen bombs or intensive research? Is a small highly specialized army more desirable than a large number of ground forces, or are both essential for a nation that seeks to be strong? The answers to these questions will probably be decisive in determining future influence in the world of states, yet it is sobering that estimates must be made on the basis of contingencies that cannot be foreseen. We know in a general way that an effective foreign policy must be supported by a military program that can safeguard national security. But this leaves those who make decisions with the painful task of distributing resources among alternative means of defense without any certainty of the kind of war they may have to fight.

Beyond this, the weapons of today may not be used in future wars because technology has rendered them obsolete. It is said that conventional weapons are fast being supplanted by new and more deadly weapons and therefore traditional armaments fail to provide an adequate basis for foreign policy. On the other hand, there are military experts who question whether atomic and hydrogen weapons will ever be used, given the prospect of mutual annihilation. Is it not fair then to ask whether the stockpiling of an unlimited supply of weapons that no nation would dare to use furnishes a state with the requisite military support? If so, a military establishment grounded in conventional weapons may fall short of providing an adequate defensive military posture, but so may a policy aimed at superior atomic capacities. This constitutes the challenge in the armaments field with which both defense specialists and disarmament negotiators must cope.

Foreign Aid

The third challenge for America relates to foreign aid. Even if there were no Russian threat, this country by virtue of its traditions and its interest in a stable world where civilized values can survive would carry an obligation to help the hungry and underprivileged of the world. No people can live any longer as "islands unto themselves" and both Christianity and Judaism teach that because men have a touch of God within them, they cannot rest so long as suffering, injustice and exploitation prevail. Americans especially have never even in periods of isolationism been willing to confine themselves to narrowly parochial interests. De Tocqueville with unrivaled penetration observed: "if an American were condemned to confine his activities to his own affairs he would be robbed of one half of his existence."

Yet if we are honest with ourselves we must confess that acts of national generosity are prompted by a subtle blending of altruism and self-interest. Support for the Marshall Plan particularly in the Congress drew strength from those who saw it as a means of holding back Russian expansionism. Our aid to the newer countries receives partial justification from the large-scale efforts of a tireless adversary to implant the communist alternative as a solution to problems of economic development around the world. There are signs that we do our cause more harm than good if we impute altogether sinister and selfish motives to the communists and unqualified generosity to ourselves.

Beyond this, technical assistance has passed the stage where noble intentions exhausted our responsibility. I say this in full recognition that moral impulses must remain the indispensable human ingredient of foreign aid. . . . There are two levels for thinking about foreign aid. The one is the level of man's relation to man, and the other the level of public policy—interconnected as they are. In the year 1960, a growing respect for human dignity is everywhere apparent even when but partly fulfilled. Thus who would not rather be healthy than sick, fed than hungry, housed than destitute, or capable of giving their children a fair chance in life. Obviously vast differences persist both in desire and ability to reach these goals, but whether we like it or not, the universal claims of all mankind for a better life place heavy burdens on us all. In this common task, man-to-man relations in the so-called fledgling nations present a severe moral test. When you are the grand benefactor and your friend is the humble supplicant the temptation to be less than Christian tests a living ethic to its roots. A good parent who sacrifices nobly for the good of his children runs a not inconsiderable risk of becoming obsessed with his own goodness. Among nations and their officials this risk is no less acutely aggravated by obsessions over superior wealth and national attainments. The American goal overseas is essentially one of translating the best in the missionary enterprise into secular terms, but this calls for discrimination between the best and the worst.

In foreign policy, however, the harsh imperatives of national self-interest come into play at the other level of technical aid. American resources are not unlimited and their allocation will be based on considerations of strategy and the potentialities for economic and political development of those we aid. If we are to succeed in combining wisdom with generosity, several hard questions will have to be answered. I refer to questions such as the following: Is effective technical assistance possible through short-run planning and annual appropriations? Is the real issue more aid or a streamlining of present programs? Is its function the bolstering of unpopular regimes with greater instruments of oppression or cooperation in the transition to a more tolerable political order? What about the heavy preponderance of military aid in countries whose first need is for economic development? Have we achieved a proper balance between public and private investment abroad? Is the machinery of government in the United States geared to wise decisions on foreign aid? Do we have at hand a hard core of trained officials capable of carrying on the tasks of utmost urgency? Have we conceived of economic development in other countries in terms of a model eminently suited to the American scene but alien to another's problems? Have we the language specialists, political and economic advisors, engineers and technicians appropriate to the task or are we doing enough to supply these needs? Is there a role for international civil servants in countries whose memories of a colonial past color and infect their response? Do we know the answer to the perennial question whether multilateral or bilateral aid is most promising in countries "x," "y" and "z"?

No serious person imagines that fixed answers are readily available to all these troubling and complicated issues. But history will never forgive the faithful citizen and his chosen representatives if they reflect on the broader issue and leave the details to chance. Success or failure on all great public questions hinges on the diligence with which the hard problems are attacked. Diplomacy, military policy and foreign aid at one stage at least have become everybody's business, for false answers will always be defended by the words "this is what the people want." Unless an informed electorate becomes as preoccupied with complex means as noble ends, the United States will go the way of Greece and Rome before us. At this point the three challenges for American foreign policy are in fact one challenge facing us all.

INDEX